International Law and Marine Areas beyond National Jurisdiction

# Publications on Ocean Development

A SERIES OF STUDIES ON THE INTERNATIONAL, LEGAL, INSTITUTIONAL AND POLICY ASPECTS OF OCEAN DEVELOPMENT



VOLUME 95

The titles published in this series are listed at *brill.com/pood*

# International Law and Marine Areas beyond National Jurisdiction

*Reflections on Justice, Space, Knowledge and Power*

*Edited by*

Vito De Lucia, Alex Oude Elferink and Lan Ngoc Nguyen

BRILL
NIJHOFF

LEIDEN | BOSTON

Library of Congress Cataloging-in-Publication Data

Names: De Lucia, Vito, editor. | Oude Elferink, Alex G., 1962- editor. | Ngoc Nguyen, Lan, editor.
Title: International law and marine areas beyond national jurisdiction : reflections on justice, space, knowledge and power / edited by Vito De Lucia, Alex Oude Elferink, and Lan Ngoc Nguyen.
Description: Leiden ; Boston : Brill/Nijhoff, 2022. | Series: Publications on ocean development, 0924-1922 ; vol. 95 | Includes index. | Summary: "The legal regime of marine areas beyond national jurisdiction (ABNJ) has received much attention in the last decades. The ongoing process in regards of an agreement on the conservation and sustainable use of marine biodiversity in ABNJ, initiated in the early 2000s (BBNJ process) is crucial evidence of this. However, this process reflects entrenched interests and political and legal structures, muting other voices and alternative approaches. International Law and Marine Areas beyond National Jurisdiction investigates competing constructions of ABNJ and their role in the creation and articulations of legal principles, which provides a broader perspective on the BBNJ process"– Provided by publisher.
Identifiers: LCCN 2021048921 | ISBN 9789004506350 (hardback) | ISBN 9789004506367 (ebook)
Subjects: LCSH: Marine resources conservation–Law and legislation. | Marine resources development–Law and legislation. | Marine biodiversity conservation–Law and legislation. | Law of the sea. | Environmental law, International.
Classification: LCC K3485 .I55 2022 | DDC 346.04/695616–dc23/eng/20211105
LC record available at https://lccn.loc.gov/2021048921

Typeface for the Latin, Greek, and Cyrillic scripts: "Brill". See and download: brill.com/brill-typeface.

ISSN 0924-1922
ISBN 978-90-04-50635-0 (hardback)
ISBN 978-90-04-50636-7 (e-book)



This book is printed on acid-free paper and produced in a sustainable manner.

Printed by Printforce, the Netherlands

# Contents

# Acknowledgments and Preface

This book has its origins in a Work Program on Area beyond National Jurisdiction (ABNJ) of the then K.G. Jebsen Centre for the Law of the Sea (currently the Norwegian Centre for the Law of the Sea) of UiT The Artic University of Norway, which was developed in 2016. As the Work Program indicated, the topic of ABNJ was selected because it provided a cross-cutting theme, which allowed integrating the research of staff at the Jebsen Centre and beyond. The focus of this Work Program, however, was mostly explained by the fact that the regime for ABNJ was and currently remains, so to speak, the last frontier in developing the governance framework for the ocean, of which the United Nations Convention on the Law of the Sea laid the basis in 1982. In that sense, it provides a testing ground for determining how the law of the sea is responding to the unprecedented challenges of climate change and a still increasing ecological footprint of humanity.

At the time the Work Program on ABNJ was developed by Vito De Lucia, the idea of the book project was present in embryonic form. Most other activities of the Work Program focussed on the ongoing consultations on the (future) regime for the conservation and sustainable use of biodiversity beyond national jurisdiction under the aegis of the United Nations General Assembly (BBNJ process). In that light, it was decided to use the book project to cast the net wider and also look beyond the BBNJ process and try to uncover the deeper currents that have shaped and continue to shape the regime of ABNJ.

In December of 2019 we convened a workshop at the School of Law of Utrecht University to discuss the initial draft chapters with our contributors. We take this opportunity to thank all of our contributors for the constructive and inspiring input for each other's chapters and our initial ideas for the concluding chapter during the workshop, as well as their patience in dealing with the numerous requests we made during their further work on their chapters. As the time that has elapsed since the workshop indicates, seeing this project through to fruition was not without challenges. The fact that one of the editors figures twice as an author of one of the substantive chapters was not a conscious choice, but a result of one of our contributors withdrawing at a relatively late stage. As editors, we felt that we could not do without a discussion of the issue of area-based management tools and marine protected areas, which is part and parcel of the BBNJ process and offers an interesting perspective on how the regime for ABNJ developed over the last couple of decades. More in general, the long gestation of this project in part is due to the Covid-19 pandemic, and to a larger extent probably reflects current academic practices, which force one to divide her/his attention between (too) many different activities.

As should be obvious, this project would not have been possible without our authors. We cannot thank them enough for bearing with us all this time. However, there are also a number of others we would like to thank for their contributions: The KG Jebsen Centre for the Law of the Sea, the Norwegian Centre for the Law of the Sea and the Utrecht Centre for Water, Ocean and Sustainability Law for making the funding for the 2019 Utrecht Workshop and editorial assistance available; Işik Girgiç for her assistance in preparing a report of that workshop, which provided important input for providing further guidance to our authors; Mana Tugend for her diligence and patience in taking care of the final editing and lay out of the manuscript and making it ready for submission to the publisher and Ruda van Ravenstein for preparing the index. Finally, our appreciation goes to Marie Sheldon and Kelley Baylis and other staff at Brill for getting this book ready for submission to its intended audience.

*Vito De Lucia, Lan Ngoc Nguyen and Alex Oude Elferink*
Tromsø, Utrecht and Amersfoort
30 July 2021

# Figures and Tables

## Figures



## Tables

# Table of Acronyms

| | |
|---|---|
| ABMT | Area-Based Management Tool |
| ABNJ | Areas Beyond National Jurisdiction |
| AC | Århus Convention |
| APEI | Areas of Particular Environmental Interest |
| AWNJ | Areas Within National Jurisdiction |
| BBNJ | Marine Biodiversity Beyond National Jurisdiction |
| CBD | Convention on Biological Diversity |
| CCAMLR | Commission for the Conservation of Antarctic Marine Living Resources |
| CCZ | Clarion-Clipperton Zone |
| CHM | Common Heritage of Mankind |
| CLCS | Commission on the Limits of the Continental Shelf |
| COP | Conference of the Parties |
| CPR | Common-Pool Resources |
| DAR | Derecho, Ambiente y Recursos Naturales |
| DOALOS | UN Division for Ocean Affairs and the Law of the Sea |
| DOC | China-ASEAN Declaration on the Conduct of Parties in the South China Sea |
| EA | Escazú Agreement |
| EBSA | Ecologically or Biologically Significant Area |
| ECLAC | Economic Commission for Latin America and the Caribbean |
| EEZ | Exclusive Economic Zone |
| EIA | Environmental Impact Assessment |
| FAO | Food and Agriculture Organization of the United Nations |
| FPIC | Free, Prior and Informed Consent |
| ICCPR | International Covenant on Civil and Political Rights |
| ICJ | International Court of Justice |
| IGC | Inter-Governmental Conference |
| ILBI | International Legally Binding Instrument |
| ILC | International Law Commission |
| IMO | International Maritime Organization |
| IOC | Intergovernmental Oceanographic Commission |
| ISA | International Seabed Authority |
| ITLOS | International Tribunal for the Law of the Sea |
| IUCN | International Union for Conservation of Nature |
| LHU | Lancaster House Undertakings |
| LOSC | United Nations Convention on the Law of the Sea |
| LTC | Legal and Technical Commission |
| MEA | Multilateral Environmental Agreement |

| | |
|---|---|
| MGRS | Marine Genetic Resources |
| MPA | Marine Protected Area |
| MSR | Marine Scientific Research |
| NAFO | Northwest Atlantic Fisheries Organisation |
| NCP | Non-Compliance Procedure |
| NEAFC | North East Atlantic Fisheries Commission |
| NIEO | New International Economic Order |
| NGRM | National Ganga Rights Movement |
| NGO | Non-Governmental Organisation |
| OSPAR | Oslo and Paris Convention for the Protection of the Marine Environment in the Northeast Atlantic |
| PrepCom | Preparatory Committee |
| PRfN | Participatory or Procedural Rights for Nature |
| PSMA | Agreement on Port State Measures to Prevent, Deter and Eliminate Illegal, Unreported and Unregulated Fishing |
| REMP | Regional Environmental Management Plan |
| RFMO | Regional Fisheries Management Organisation |
| RoN | Rights of Nature |
| RSP | Regional Sea Program |
| SBSTTA | Subsidiary Body on Scientific, Technical and Technological Advice |
| SDC | Seabed Dispute Chamber |
| SDG | Sustainable Development Goal |
| SEAFC | South East Atlantic Fisheries Commission |
| SUA | Convention for the Suppression of Unlawful Acts Against the Safety of Maritime Navigation |
| TK | Traditional Knowledge |
| UNCLOS | United Nations Conference on Law of the Sea |
| UNEP | United Nations Environmental Programme |
| UNESCO | United Nations Educational, Scientific and Cultural Organization |
| UNFSA | Agreement for the Implementation of the Provisions of the United Nations Convention on the Law of the Sea of 10 December 1982 relating to the Conservation and Management of Straddling Fish Stocks and Highly Migratory Fish Stocks |
| UNICPOLOS | United Nations Informal Consultative Process on the Law of the Sea |
| UNGA | United Nations General Assembly |
| UNSC | United Nations Security Council |
| WIPO | World Intellectual Property Organization |
| WSSD | World Summit on Sustainable Development |
| WTO | World Trade Organization |

# Notes on Contributors

*Nigel Bankes*
is Professor of law and holder of the chair of natural resources law at the University of Calgary where he has taught since 1984. Bankes held an adjunct appointment as professor of law with the KG Jebsen Centre for the Law of the Sea (now Norwegian Centre for the Law of the Sea), at UiT The Arctic University of Norway from 2012 to 2019.

*Richard Barnes*
holds a Chair in International Law at the University of Lincoln and is Adjunct Professor of Law at the Norwegian Centre for the Law of the Sea at UiT The Arctic University of Norway. He has published widely on international law of the sea, including *Property Rights and Natural Resources* (Hart 2009) and co-edited *The United Nations Convention on the Law of the Sea: A Living Instrument* (BIICL 2016), *Research Handbook on Climate Change, Oceans and Coasts* (Edward Elgar 2020) and *Frontiers in International Environmental Law: Oceans and Climate Challenges* (Brill 2021). Richard is Current Legal Developments Editor of the International Journal of Marine and Coastal Law. He has advised a range of public and private bodies, including the WWF, the European Parliament, and the UK Department for Environment, Food and Rural Affairs, and appeared on numerous occasions before Parliamentary committees to provide expert evidence on fisheries law.

*Kristine Elfrida Dalaker*
is a PhD Research Fellow at the Norwegian Centre for the Law of the Sea (NCLOS), UiT The Arctic University of Norway in Tromsø, Norway, where she focuses on ocean governance issues. The title of her PhD thesis is 'Robust Institutional Arrangements for the Conservation and Sustainable Use of Marine Biodiversity in Areas Beyond National Jurisdiction'. She was previously the Associate Director (Administration and Special Projects) at the Centre for International Law (CIL) at the National University of Singapore.

*Vito De Lucia*
is Professor of Law at the Norwegian Centre for the Law of the Sea (NCLOS) and faculty of Law, UiT The Arctic University of Norway. His most immediate research interests are located at the intersection of critical jurisprudence, international law and ecology. He is author of *The Ecosystem Approach in International Environmental law. Genealogy and Biopolitics* (Routledge 2019).

*Tore Henriksen*
is Professor and Director of Norwegian Centre for the Law of the Sea at UiT The Arctic University of Norway. His main research interests have been within international fisheries law and international environmental law. He teaches law of the sea, public international law and environmental law.

*Baine P Kerr*
is a PhD Candidate with the Netherlands Institute for the Law of the Sea and Utrecht Center for Water, Oceans, and Sustainability Law, Utrecht University School of Law, the Netherlands. He received a LL.M from Utrecht University in Public International Law, and a J.D. from UCLA School of Law. Before coming to Utrecht University, he was a Deputy Attorney General at the Los Angeles office of the California Department of Justice where he practiced coastal, environmental, and land use law.

*Elisa Morgera*
is Professor of Global Environmental Law at the University of Strathclyde Law School, Glasgow, UK, and member of the Strathclyde Centre for Environmental Law and Governance. She is the director of the One Ocean Hub, a global interdisciplinary research collaboration across the UK, Africa, South Pacific and the Caribbean, as well as UN agencies and other international partners. The One Ocean Hub is pioneering research on human rights and the marine environment with a view to better connecting marine and social sciences, law and the arts, to support fair and inclusive decision-making for a healthy ocean whereby people and planet flourish (Grant Ref: NE/S008950/1).

*Joanna Mossop*
is an Associate Professor in the Law Faculty, Victoria University of Wellington, New Zealand. Her research interests are in the law of the sea. She has published on a range of topics including marine biodiversity beyond national jurisdiction, dispute settlement, maritime security and areas under national jurisdiction. Her book *The Continental Shelf beyond 200 nautical miles: Rights and Responsibilities* (Oxford University Press 2016) was a co-winner of the JF Northey Memorial Book Award. In 2019 New Zealand nominated her to the list of concilators and arbitrators under Annexes V and VII of the United Nations Convention on the Law of the Sea.

*Lan Ngoc Nguyen*
is an Assistant Professor of Public International Law at Utrecht University School of Law, Department International and European Law and a Senior Research

Associate of the Netherlands Institute for the Law of the Sea, Utrecht Centre for Water, Oceans and Sustainability Law. Prior to joining Utrecht University, Lan worked at the Ministry of Foreign Affairs of Vietnam and served as an intern at the Legal Office of the International Tribunal for the Law of the Sea. Lan holds a B.A in International Relations (summa cum laude) from the Diplomatic Academy of Vietnam, an LL.M in International Law (First Class Honours) and a PhD from the University of Cambridge. Her research interests lie in law of the sea, settlement of international disputes and the management and resolution of maritime disputes in Asia Pacific.

*Alex Oude Elferink*
is the Director of the Netherlands Institute for the Law of the Sea (NILOS) and an associate of the Utrecht Centre for Oceans, Water and Sustainability Law (UCWOSL), School of Law, Utrecht University, the Netherlands. He is the author of *The Delimitation of the Continental Shelf between Denmark, Germany and the Netherlands; Arguing Law, Practicing Politics?* (Cambridge University Press 2013) and the co-editor of *The Oxford Handbook of the Law of the Sea* (Oxford University Press 2015) and *Maritime Boundary Delimitation: The Case Law; Is it Consistent and Predictable?* (Cambridge University Press 2018). He has advised governments om various law of the sea issues and has been acting as counsel for Nicaragua in a number of cases before the International Court of Justice.

*Margherita Paola Poto*
(Prof. Dr. in Administrative Law, University of Turin, Italy) is a mum, an ally of the Earth, and a researcher at the Faculty of Law, UiT The Arctic University of Norway (Romssa/Tromsø). She is currently working on food, health, and the environment within the matrix of the Agenda 2030, and exploring methodological approaches to law based on the ethics of empathy, compassion, and care.

*Henrik Ringbom*
is Head of Research at Åbo Akademi University in Turku, Finland, and holds part-time professorships at the Scandinavian Institute of Maritime Law (University of Oslo), and at the University of Turku in Finland. His previous work experience includes being Head of Unit for Marine Environment, Training and Statistics at the European Maritime Safety Agency (EMSA) in Lisbon (2007–2012) and Administrator at the Maritime Safety Unit of the European Commission in Brussels (1997–2003). He has published widely in the field of European and international shipping and environmental law and

is the author of the book *The EU Maritime Safety Policy and International Law* (Brill 2008) and editor of *Jurisdiction over Ships* (Brill 2015) and *Autonomous Ships and the Law* (Routledge 2021). He is currently a board member of the European Maritime Safety Agency and is the past President of the Finnish Maritime Law Association.

# Table of Cases

## Permanent Court of Arbitration

*Barbados v Trinidad and Tobago* (Award, 11 April 2006) PCA 2004–02.
*Guyana v Suriname* (Award, 17 September 2007) PCA 2004-04.
*Chagos Marine Protected Area Arbitration* (*Mauritius v United Kingdom*) (Award, 18 March 2015) PCA Case 2011–03.
*Arctic Sunrise Arbitration* (*Kingdom of the Netherlands v. Russian Federation*) (Award on the Merits, 14 August 2015) PCA 2014-2.
*South China Sea* (*Philippines v China*) (Award on Jurisdiction and Admissibility, 29 October 2015) PCA.
*South China Sea Arbitration* (*Philippines v China*) (Award, 12 July 2016) PCA Case 2013–19.
*Enrica Lexie* (*Italy v. India*) (2 July 2020) PCA 2015-28.

## International Tribunal for the Law of the Sea

*M/V 'Saiga'* (*Saint Vincent and the Grenadines v Guinea*) (Prompt Release, Judgment) ITLOS Reports 1997.
M/V *'Saiga'* (*No.2*) (*Saint Vincent and the Grenadines v. Guinea*) (1 July 1999) ITLOS 2.
*Southern Bluefin Tuna Cases* (*provisional measures*) (*New Zealand v. Japan; Australia v. Japan*) (27 August 1999) ITLOS 3 and 4.
*MOX Plant* (*Ireland v United Kingdom*) (Provisional Measures) ITLOS Reports 2001.
*The Grand Prince Case* (*Belize v France*) (Prompt Release, Judgment) ITLOS Reports 2001.
*Tominmaru* (*Japan v Russian Federation*) (Prompt Release, Judgment) ITLOS Reports 2005–07.
*Responsibilities and Obligations of States sponsoring persons and entities with respect to activities in the Area* (Advisory Opinion, 1 February 2011) ITLOS, Seabed Disputes Chamber.
*Delimitation of the Maritime Boundary between Bangladesh and Myanmar in the Bay of Bengal* (*Bangladesh v Myanmar*) (Judgment, 14 March 2012) ITLOS Reports 2012.
*The M/V 'Louisa' Case* (*Saint Vincent and the Grenadines v Kingdom of Spain*) (Merits Judgement, 28 May 2013) ITLOS.

*The 'Arctic Sunrise' (Kingdom of the Netherlands v Russian Federation)* (Provisional Measures, 22 November 2013) ITLOS.
*M/V 'Virginia G' (Panama v Guinea-Bissau)* (Judgment, 14 April 2014) ITLOS 4.
*Request for Advisory Opinion submitted by the Sub-Regional Fisheries Commission* (Advisory Opinion, 2 April 2015) ITLOS Reports 2015.
*M/V Norstar (Panama v Italy)* (Judgment, 10 April 2019) ITLOS.
*M/T 'San Padre Pio' (Switzerland v Nigeria)* (Provisional Measures, 2019) ITLOS.

## International Court of Justice

*SS 'Lotus'* [1927] PCIJ Series A No 1.
*Fisheries Case (UK v Norway)* [1951] ICJ Reports 1951.
*South West Africa (Liberia v. South Africa) (Ethiopia v. South Africa), Second Phase* (Judgment) [1966] ICJ Reports 47.
*Barcelona Traction, Light and Power Company, Limited (Belgium v Spain)* (Judgment) [1970] ICJ Reports 3.
*Fisheries Jurisdiction Case (UK v Iceland)* (Merits, Judgment) [1974] ICJ Rep 3.
*Fisheries Jurisdiction Case (Federal Republic of Germany v Iceland)* (Merits, Judgment) [1974] ICJ Rep 175.
*Delimitation of the Maritime Boundary in the Gulf of Maine Area (Canada v United States)* [1984] ICJ Reports 246.
*Legal Consequences of the Construction of a Wall in the Occupied Palestinian Territory* (Advisory Opinion) [2004] ICJ Reports 136.
*Questions relating to the Obligation to Prosecute or Extradite (Belgium v. Senegal)* (Judgment) [2012] ICJ Reports 422.
*Whaling in the Antarctic (Australia v. Japan: New Zealand intervening)* (Judgment) [2014] ICJ Reports 2014.
*Legal Consequences of the Separation of the Chagos Archipelago from Mauritius in 1965* (Advisory Opinion, 25 February 2019) ICJ.
*Application of the Convention on the Prevention and Punishment of the Crime of Genocide (The Gambia v Myanmar)* (Provisional Measures, 23 January 2020) ICJ.

## Inter-American Court of Human Rights

*Case of the Saramaka People v. Suriname*, Judgment (Preliminary Objections, Merits, Reparations and Costs) 28 November 2007.

*Case of the Kichwa Indigenous Communitiy of Sarayaku v Ecuador Judgement* (Merits and Reparations) 27 June 2012.
*Case of Kaliña and Lokono Peoples v Suriname*, Judgment (Merits, Reparations and Costs) 25 November 2015.

## Arbitral Tribunal

*Southern Bluefin Tuna* (*New Zealand v Japan; Australia v Japan*) Award on Jurisdiction and Admissibility (2000) XXIII RIAA 1.

## National Courts

*Vincent v Lake Erie* [1910] 109 Supreme Court of Minnesota 456, 124 NW 221.
*Le Louis* [1817] EWHC 165 (Admlty) 1464, 1475.

# Table of Treaties

## International Treaties

International Convention on the Regulation of Whaling (adopted 2 December 1946, entered into force 10 November 1948) 364 UNTS 1953.

Charter of the Organization of American States (opened for signature 30 April 1948, entered into force December 13, 1951) 119 UNTS 3.

Convention on the Prevention and Punishment of the Crime of Genocide (opened for signature 9 December 1948, entered into force 12 January 1951) 78 UNTS 277.

Declaration on the maritime zone (signed and entered into force 18 August 1952) 1006 UNTS 325.

Convention on the Territorial Sea and the Contiguous Zone (opened for signature 29 April 1958, entered into force on 10 September 1964) 516 UNTS 205.

Convention on the High Seas (opened for signature 29 April 1958, entered into force 30 September 1962) 450 UNTS 11.

Optional Protocol of Signature concerning the Compulsory Settlement of Disputes (opened for signature 29 April 1958, entered into force 30 September 1962).

Convention on the Continental Shelf (opened for signature 29 April 1958, entered into force 10 June 1964) 499 UNTS 311.

Convention on Fishing and Conservation of the Living Resources of the High Seas (opened for signature 29 April 1958, entered into force 20 March 1966) 559 UNTS 285.

Antarctic Treaty (adopted on 1 December 1959, entered into force 23 June 1961) 402 UNTS 71.

International Covenant on Economic, Social and Cultural Rights (opened for signature 16 December 1966, entered into force 3 January 1976) 6 ILM 360.

Convention for the Protection of the Marine Environment and the Coastal Region of the Mediterranean (adopted 16 February 1976 and amended 10 June 1995; entered into force 12 February 1978 and 9 July 2004, respectively) 1102 UNTS 45.

Convention on the Conservation of Migratory Species of Wild Animals (signed 23 June 1979, entered into force 11 January 1983) 1651 UNTS 333.

Convention on the Conservation of Antarctic Marine Living Resources (opened for signature 20 May 1980, entered into force 7 April 1982) 1329 UNTS 48.

United Nations Convention on the Law of the Sea (opened for signature 10 December 1982, entered into force 16 November 1994) 1833 UNTS 3.

Convention Against Torture and other Cruel, Inhuman or Degrading Treatment or Punishment (opened for signature 10 December 1984, entered into force 26 June 1987) 1465 UNTS 85.

Convention for the Suppression of Unlawful Acts Against the Safety of Maritime Navigation (adopted 10 March 1988; entered into force 1 March 1992).

Additional Protocol to the American Convention on Human Rights in the Area of Economic, Social and Cultural Rights (opened for signature 17 November 1988, entered into force 16 November 1999) 28 ILM 156.

Convention on Biological Diversity (signed 5 June 1992, entered in force 29 December 1993) 1760 UNTS 79.

Convention for the Conservation of Southern Bluefin Tuna (opened for signature 10 May 1993, entered into force 20 May 1994).

United Nations Agreement for the Implementation of the Provisions of the United Nations Convention on the Law of the Sea of 10 December 1982 relating to the Conservation and Management of Straddling Fish Stocks and Highly Migratory Fish Stocks (opened for signature 4 August 1995, entered into force 11 December 2001) 2167 UNTS 3.

Convention for the Protection of the Marine Environment of the North-East Atlantic (OSPAR Convention) (opened for signatures 22 September 1992, entered into force 25 March 1998) 23 LOSB 32.

Agreement to Promote Compliance with International Conservation and Management Measures by Fishing Vessels on the High Seas (opened for signature 29 November 1993, entered into force 24 April 2003) 2221 UNTS 91.

Agreement relating to the implementation of Part XI of the United Nations Convention on the Law of the Sea of 10 December 1982 (signed 18 July 1994, entered in force 16 November 1994) 1836 UNTS 3.

Protocol to the Convention on the Prevention of Marine Pollution by Dumping of Wastes and Other Matter (opened for signature 7 November 1996, entered into force 24 March 2006) 36 ILM 1.

Annex V on the Protection and Conservation of the Ecosystems and Biological Diversity of the Maritime Area (opened for signature 23 July 1998; entered into force 30 August 2000).

Convention on the Protection of Underwater Cultural Heritage (opened for signature 2 November 2001, entered into force 2 January 2009) 2562 UNTS 3.

Ilulissat Declaration (adopted 28 May 2008).

## National Treaties

American Declaration on the Rights and Duties of Man (adopted 2 May 1948) O.A.S. Res XXX.

Arab Charter on Human Rights (adopted 23 May 2004).

CHAPTER 1

# Areas beyond National Jurisdiction – Looking at and beyond the BBNJ Process

*Alex Oude Elferink, Vito De Lucia and Lan Ngoc Nguyen*

## 1 Introduction

Considering developments in the law of the sea in recent times, an edited volume on areas beyond national jurisdiction (ABNJ) might strike one as not being overly original. However, as editors of this volume we believe that the particular focus we have adopted, which is further addressed in section 3 of this chapter, distinguishes the current work from much of the academic literature on this topic. Before considering that point, we believe it however pertinent to provide the reader with some primers on the term 'areas beyond national jurisdiction' as employed in the modern law of the sea (section 2). After these two sections, we provide the reader with an overview of the individual chapters that make up this volume in section 4 of this chapter, which is followed by some brief concluding remarks in section 5.

## 2 Locating Areas beyond National Jurisdiction in the Law of the Sea

The term 'areas beyond national jurisdiction' has only recently made its appearance in the law of the sea. A search for the term in the WorldCat database,[1] which was accessed through the website of the Library of the Peace Palace,[2] gives no hits for the period 1950–2000, 89 hits for the period 2001–2010 and 351 hits for the current decade.[3] However, compelling as they may be, what do these figures actually tell us?

1 According to Wikipedia, WorldCat 'itemizes the collections of 17,900 libraries in 123 countries and territories ... The subscribing member libraries collectively maintain WorldCat's database, the world's largest bibliographic database' see <https://en.wikipedia.org/wiki/WorldCat> accessed 16 December 2020 (footnotes omitted).

2 *Peace Palace Library; The international law library* available at <www.peacepalacelibrary.nl/> accessed 16 December 2020.

3 Moreover, of the 89 hits for the period 2001–2010, 84 hits concern the period 2005–2010. A search for the acronym 'ABNJ' commonly used for the term 'areas beyond national

 | DOI:10.1163/9789004506367_002

The ocean beyond national jurisdiction of coastal States, in the modern law of the sea, with its inception in 17th century European colonial expansion, was first identified by the term 'high seas'. Traditionally, the high seas compromised most of ocean space, except for a narrow band of territorial sea, for which most States claimed a breadth of 3, 4 or 6 nautical miles. As detailed in chapters 2, 4 and 5 of this volume, the second half of the 20th century witnessed a gradual demise of the spatial extent of the high seas and a gradual curtailment of the freedom of the high seas. Coastal State jurisdiction over the water-column was extended to 200 nautical miles and, in the case of the continental shelf, beyond that distance, provided the relevant conditions of Article 76 of the United Nations Convention on the Law of the Sea (LOSC) are met. The freedom of the high seas has been restricted in two ways. First, by declaring the seabed and ocean floor and the subsoil beyond national jurisdiction (Area) to be the common heritage of mankind (CHM).[4] Secondly, as is discussed in further detail in a number of the chapters that are to follow, high seas freedoms are currently accompanied by increasingly stringent regulation to *inter alia* sustainably manage resources and protect and preserve the marine environment. Still, the high seas and the Area collectively remain a vast expanse. One study from 2011 indicates that the oceans cover 335 million square kilometers, of which 130 million square kilometers are part of the exclusive economic zone (EEZ) and continental shelf within 200 nautical miles from the baselines of coastal States. In addition, the continental shelf beyond 200 nautical miles from the baselines covers some 28 million square kilometers of ocean space.[5] This implies that the water column beyond national jurisdiction actually covers 205 million square kilometers and the Area 178 million square kilometers, or respectively about 61 and 53% of the surface area of the oceans. In addition, it should be realized that the volume of these areas, due to their greater average water depth than that of areas within national jurisdiction (AWNJ) covers an even greater part of the world's oceans.

---

jurisdiction' resulted in zero relevant hist for the period 1950–2000, 7 for the period 2001–2000 and 131 for the current decade.

4 UNGA Res 2749 (XXV) of 17 December 1970.

5 See Tina Schoolmeester and Elaine Baker (eds), *Continental Shelf; The Last Maritime Zone; Status in Sept. 2010* (UNEP/GRID-Arendal 2011) 16. It may be noted that the latter figure only concerns the continental shelf beyond 200 nautical miles in respect of which coastal States have submitted (preliminary) information in accordance with LOSC art 76. A number of States with significant continental shelf areas beyond 200 nautical miles, including Canada, Denmark and the United States had not submitted such information in 2011, indicating that the actual area of continental shelf beyond 200 nautical miles is more than 28 million square kilometers.

As the references to 'beyond the limits of national jurisdiction' included in resolution 2749 (XXV) and the LOSC indicate,[6] the bifurcation between areas within and beyond national jurisdiction obviously was already recognized by the law of the sea prior to the coining of the term 'areas beyond national jurisdiction'. The use of this term, however, is not without problems. First, the reference to 'national jurisdiction' in both terms is to coastal State jurisdiction. In that sense, the term 'areas within national jurisdiction' to a certain extent is a misnomer, as coastal States only have limited sovereign rights and jurisdiction in the EEZ and the continental shelf, while other States have primary jurisdiction over certain activities in these zones. The term 'areas beyond national jurisdiction', although expressing the absence of coastal State jurisdiction, otherwise could be said to be misguided. Control over activities in the high seas and the Area largely remains based on the exercise of jurisdiction by the flag State over vessels flying its flag.[7] Second, it may be noted that the Revised Draft Agreement provides that 'Areas beyond national jurisdiction means the high seas and the Area'.[8] Part VII of the Convention implies that high seas regime applies to the continental shelf beyond 200 nautical miles.[9]

Notwithstanding LOSC's reference to ABNJ as seemingly constituting a single ocean space, and although it contains some recognition of the ambition expressed in its Preamble 'that the problems of ocean space are closely interrelated and need to be considered as a whole',[10] the Convention mainly approaches the high seas and the Area as distinct areas, in which activities are mostly regulated on a sectoral basis.[11] In that sense, the current recourse

6 The LOSC uses the wording 'beyond the limits of national jurisdiction' in two instances, namely in the 6th preambular paragraph, which refers to resolution 2749 (XXV) and art 1(1)(1) which defines the Area as 'the seabed and ocean floor and subsoil thereof, beyond the limits of national jurisdiction'. In addition, art 142(1) and (2) of the LOSC respectively refer to mineral recourses 'across limits of national jurisdiction' and mineral resources 'lying within national jurisdiction'.

7 In practice the absence of effective control and exercise of jurisdiction remains one of the main challenges to the sustainable use and conservation of the high seas and the Area. See also Ringbom (ch 11) in this volume.

8 Revised draft text of an agreement under the United Nations Convention on the Law of the Sea on the conservation and sustainable use of marine biological diversity of areas beyond national jurisdiction (17 November 2019) (UN Doc a/conf.232/2020/3) (Revised Draft Agreement) available at <https://undocs.org/en/a/conf.232/2020/3> accessed 27 July 2021, art 1(4).

9 For a further discussion of how the law (of the sea) has grappled with the complexity of the ocean environment, and, as is argued, has failed to come up with a fully satisfactory answer, see De Lucia in ch 2 of this volume.

10 LOSC 3rd preambular paragraph.

11 In light of the drafting history of the LOSC, that approach in relation to the high seas and the Area could be said to represent a more than logical outcome. The ideological

to the term 'areas beyond national jurisdiction' could be said to be more than a convenient shorthand for referring to the high seas and the Area. Rather, it reflects a recognition of the need for a common approach to governing this part of ocean space. This reflection is borne out by the current negotiations on the agreement on the conservation and sustainable use of marine BBNJ. The four thematic elements addressed by the agreement (area-based management tools (AMBTs) including marine protected areas (MPAs); environmental assessments; marine genetic resources (MGRs); and capacity building and transfer of technology) all are equally relevant to the high seas and the Area. Obviously, a common approach to both areas in a future agreement on the conservation and sustainable use of marine BBNJ does not in itself achieve a coherent governance regime for the oceans. First, as regards ABNJ themselves, the agreement will be an add-on to the existing regime. This for instance implies maintaining the existing jurisdictional scheme, based on flag state jurisdiction, with its all too well-known limitations as regards effective control of activities taking place on the high seas.[12] Second, a future Agreement under the United Nations Convention on the Law of the Sea on the conservation and sustainable use of marine biological diversity of areas beyond national jurisdiction (BBNJ Agreement) will consolidate the existing division of the oceans in areas within and beyond national jurisdiction.[13] The current negotiations on that agreement demonstrate the tenacity with which coastal States defend their interests in relation to their maritime zones. This remains a major obstacle to achieving an integrated ecosystem-based approach to ocean governance.[14]

---

divide between developed and developing States, with the latter espousing the new international economic order and the common heritage regime in relation to the Area and its mineral resources, and the latter intent of safeguarding traditional high seas freedoms, made a common approach to both areas problematic.

12 See also Ringbom (ch 11) in this volume.

13 On the use of the term 'BBNJ Agreement' and related terms see below, section 3.

14 For an excellent discussion of the different aspects of the relationship between areas within and beyond national jurisdiction see Tullio Treves, 'Principles and objectives of the legal regime governing areas beyond national jurisdiction' in Alex Oude Elferink and Erik J Molenaar (eds), *The International Legal Regime of Areas beyond National Jurisdiction: Current and Future Developments* (Brill 2010) 7–25, 8–12. Treves among others observes:

> Why are States insisting to act on the basis of the 'high seas only' approach? The reasons are ideological and historical. State sovereignty is seen as the supreme value: any idea that could question recently obtained and hard fought extensions of it are considered with suspicion and rejected offhand by a substantial number of States. In the present situation of the world, the vast majority of States does not seem to be ready to consider rules – and, even more so, institution-based management – that could be perceived as taking away parcels of their newly-acquired sovereign rights and jurisdiction over adjacent seas. The very LOS Convention, notwithstanding the many nuances one can find in its provisions, is seen by most States as the consecration of the coastal State approach (ibid 12).

See also De Lucia (ch 2) in this volume.

## 3 A Brief Primer to Recent Developments in Relation to the Legal Regime for ABNJ

The legal regime of ABNJ has received much attention in the last decade. As noted above, the issue currently is primarily considered at the intergovernmental conference (IGC), which has been convened ty the United Nations General Assembly (UNGA) to negotiate the agreement on the conservation and sustainable use of marine biological diversity of ABNJ. This process was initiated under the aegis of the UNGA in the early 2000s, and is also referred to as the BBNJ process. The negotiating agenda is comprised of four main items: ABMTs, including through the establishment of MPAs; MGRs, including the sharing of benefits arising from their utilization; environmental impact assessments; and capacity building and technological transfer.[15]

15 As is also indicated by the discussion in the chapters included in this volume, developments in relation to the legal regime of ABNJ have also taken place and will continue to take place beyond the remit of the BBNJ process. A good point in case is ch 11 by Ringbom, discussing developments in relation to flag State jurisdiction, an issue that will likely not be developed upon in the BBNJ Agreement at all. For recent literature on the BBNJ process see eg. Robert Blasiak and others, 'The role of NGOs in negotiating the use of biodiversity in marine areas beyond national jurisdiction' (2017) 81 Marine Policy 1; Robin Warner, 'Strengthening Governance Frameworks for Conservation and Sustainable Use of Marine Biodiversity in Areas beyond National Jurisdiction: Southern Hemisphere Perspectives' (2017) 32 International Journal of Marine and Coastal Law 607; Kristina Gjerde and others, 'Conservation and sustainable use of marine biodiversity in Areas Beyond National Jurisdiction: Options for underpinning a strong global BBNJ Agreement through regional and sectoral governance' (2018) STRONG High Seas Project 17 available at <www.prog-ocean.org/wp-content/uploads/2018/08/STRONG-High-Seas-Policy-Brief_Options-for-underpinning-BBNJ-agreement.pdf> accessed 21 May 2021; Penelope Ridings, 'Redefining environmental stewardship to deliver governance frameworks for marine biodiversity beyond national jurisdiction' (2018) 75 ICES Journal of Marine Science 435; Margaret A Young and Andrew Friedman 'Biodiversity Beyond National Jurisdiction: Regimes and Their Inter-action' (2018) 112 AJIL Unbound 123; Vito De Lucia, 'The Ecosystem Approach and the negotiations towards a new Agreement on Marine Biodiversity in Areas beyond National Jurisdiction' (2019) 2 Nordisk miljörättslig tidskrift/Nordic Environmental Law Journal 7; David Freestone 'The UN Process to Develop an International Legally Binding Instrument under the 1982 Law of the Sea Convention: Issues and Challenges' in David Freestone (ed), Conserving Biodiversity in Areas beyond National Jurisdiction (Brill 2019); David Leary, 'Agreeing to disagree on what we have or have not agreed on: The current state of play of the BBNJ negotiations on the status of marine genetic resources in areas beyond national jurisdiction' (2019) 99 Marine Policy 21; Joanna Mossop, 'Dispute Settlement in the New Treaty on Marine Biodiversity in Areas beyond National Jurisdiction' (23 December 2019) NCLOS Blog available at <http://site.uit.no/jclos/files/2019/12/J-Mossop-Dispute-Settlement-in-the-BBNJ-Treaty-NCLOS.pdf> accessed 12 May 2021; Alex G Oude Elferink, 'Exploring the future of the institutional landscape of the

At the global level, the issue also has been on the agenda of the Conference of the Parties to the Convention on Biological Diversity (CBD).[16] Regional seas conventions and regional fisheries management organizations in a number of regions also have been paying increasing attention to the protection and preservation of the marine environment in ABNJ. However, most regional seas conventions remain focused on AWNJ and regional fisheries management organizations primarily remain focused on managing and conserving the fish stocks covered by their mandate and not the wider ecosystem.

These legal developments have been largely caused by advances in scientific knowledge and the development or expected future development or intensification of economic activities. The growing attention for ABNJ has raised the awareness that there are legal and regulatory gaps, which have been the main driver for the BBNJ process.[17] The controversies that emerged within the context of the ongoing BBNJ process offer a useful map of the divisions within the international community with respect to some of these issues,[18] which we have used in connection with the definition of the research focus of the project and the topics of its individual chapters.

At this point, we would like to provide the reader with a brief introduction to the use of the terms 'BBNJ process' and 'BBNJ Agreement' and related terms. The term 'BBNJ process' is used to loosely refer to the process that has its origins in the activities of the CBD and the UNGA in relation to BBNJ, and which culminated in the ongoing negotiations on a future BBNJ Agreement. Apart from the term 'BBNJ Agreement' much of existing literature instead refers to the Internationally Legally Binding Instrument under the United Convention on the Law of the Sea, using the acronym ILBI. For this volume, we have opted not to use this term, in light of the fact that there currently are two negotiating text of the BBNJ Agreement, prepared by the Ambassador Rena Lee, the

---

oceans beyond national jurisdiction' (2019) 28(3) Review of European, Comparative & International Environmental Law 236.

16 The relationship between the role of the UNGA and the CBD is further considered in ch 7 of this volume. Convention on Biological Diversity (signed 5 June 1992, entered in force 29 December 1993) 1760 UNTS 79 (CBD).

17 See eg, Report on the work of the United Nations Open-ended Informal Consultative Process on Oceans and the Law of the Sea at its fifth meeting Letter dated 29 June 2004 from the Co-Chairpersons of the Consultative Process addressed to the President of the General Assembly (UN Doc A/59/122 of 1 July 2004).

18 See for example, Report of the Preparatory Committee established by General Assembly resolution 69/292: Development of an international legally binding instrument under the United Nations Convention on the Law of the Sea on the conservation and sustainable use of marine biological diversity of areas beyond national jurisdiction (UN Doc A/AC.287/2017/PC.4/2).

president of the IGC on an international legally binding instrument under the United Nations Convention on the Law of the Sea on the conservation and sustainable use of marine biological diversity of areas beyond national jurisdiction.[19] Those text do not title the agreement as an 'ILBI', but use the terminology on which we based our choice for the acronym BBNJ Agreement. The current volume does employ the term 'ILBI', in case this is called for by the specific context. Where specific refence is made to the two negotiating texts prepared by Ambassador Lee, the current volume refers to them as respectively the Draft Agreement and the Revised Draft Agreement.

## 4 Research Focus of the Current Project

A legal research project on ABNJ at this point in time necessarily will have to devote considerable attention to the BBNJ process. However, the project casts a significantly wider net than the negotiating agenda of the IGC, reflecting on broader theoretical questions, and questions that are not explicitly on that agenda but are nonetheless important for understanding the challenges that the legal regime for ABNJ may pose to the law of the sea. These include, for example: questions of principle such as that related to the role of the CHM in the legal regime for ABNJ; governance[20] and management questions related to the role of ecosystem approaches in a future BBNJ Agreement; questions related to the role of coastal States in relation to ABMTs and MPAs in ABNJ; and questions related to the appropriate institutional architecture for the governance of ABNJ, including the role of existing bodies and institutions vis-à-vis a global body that may, or may not, be set up under future BBNJ Agreement.

19 Draft text of an agreement under the United Nations Convention on the Law of the Sea on the conservation and sustainable use of marine biological diversity of areas beyond national jurisdiction (17 May 2019) (UN Doc A/CONF.232/2019/6) (Draft Agreement) available at <https://digitallibrary.un.org/record/3811328?ln=en> accessed 27 July 2021.

20 Brian C Chaffin, Hannah Gosnell, and Barbara A Cosens, 'A decade of adaptive governance scholarship: synthesis and future directions' (2014) 19(3) Ecology and Society Art 56. To provide some guidance on the notion of governance, we refer to Chaffin, Gosnell and Cosens (at 1) who submit that 'environmental governance' refers to a 'set of regulatory processes, mechanisms and organizations through which political actors influence environmental actions and outcomes' and that 'environmental governance is the system of institutions including rules, laws, regulations, policies and social norms, and organizations involved in governing environmental resources use and/or protection'.

Importantly, different legal principles, regulatory perspectives, and institutional solutions are underpinned by different and at times conflicting social constructions of global ocean spaces and of ABNJ in particular. As Philip Steinberg observed in his book *The Social Construction of the Ocean*, the ocean is

> a space that simultaneously is constructed as a fecund (and/or endangered) space of nature, an empty space that facilitates movement, a frontier suitable for expropriation and territorialization, an arena for scientific research, a force-field for military adventures, and a laboratory wherein alternative futures are imagined and practiced.[21]

These different constructions in turn reflect and are used to justify particular legal visions and regimes: CHM, freedoms of the high seas, sovereignty, environmental stewardship, scientific cooperation. Some of these constructions may also co-exist and compete, as evident in the ongoing discussions regarding MGRs, located at the intersection of multiple and conflicting views about ocean space and its resources.[22]

Against this backdrop and in light of current developments in relation to the legal regime for ABNJ, the present book aims at offering an in-depth consideration of the following questions:

- competing constructions of the oceans, and of ABNJ in particular, and their role in the creation and articulations of legal principles;
- the legal principles underpinning the legal regimes of ABNJ and their role in the development of those regimes;
- the legal regimes applicable to ABNJ and the challenges they face;
- the spatial dimensions of the legal regimes applicable in ABNJ; and
- institutional architectures, interplays and conflicts in ABNJ governance.

On the basis of these issues, the editors in turn mapped a set of four themes that frame the project:

- *justice* – understood in terms of access to and utilization of marine resources, living and non-living, both in relation to the intra- and the inter-generational dimension;

21 Philip Steinberg, *The Social Construction of the Ocean* (Cambridge University Press 2001). This summarizing quotation is taken from Steinberg's own website, see <https://philsteinberg.wordpress.com/research/ocean-space/> accessed 30 July 2021.

22 See further chs 2, 4, 6 and 9 in this volume.

- *space* – broadly speaking with reference to the way space is understood and regulated in the law of the sea with regards to ABNJ. This theme also invites individual contributors to look at ABNJ from a series of non-doctrinal, socio-legal perspectives, such as eg law and geography;
- *knowledge* – this theme is intended to capture knowledge in its various dimensions, eg as expressed in the political epistemology embedded in law of the sea, marine scientific research and the right to science, the role knowledge, or its lack, plays in the construction of legal principles and regimes; and
- *power* – this theme centers on the ways power is distributed and how it affects decision-making in relation to ABNJ, the distribution of rights and obligations, jurisdiction over ocean areas as well as activities, and participation in the relevant legal and governance processes.

These themes were selected as each in a different yet complementary manner enables a contextual analysis of the law of the sea, its emergence, its biases, its impacts. Additionally, these themes allow assessing the environmental and socio-economic outcomes that the current and proposed law applicable to ABNJ (will) produce(s). What interests are served by the law, who and what is left out and how might different approaches lead to different outcomes?

From the outset, the editors acknowledged that these themes would traverse the chapters differently, not necessarily being equally relevant to all of them. What is to be underlined though is that by operating as a framing that traverses the entire book, these themes would ensure a coherent set of chapters that justifies their publication as part of an edited volume. Additionally, these themes will allow the chapters to be read together rather than as separate discussions of broadly related issues, and to extract some general trends, ideas and reflections related to the future of ABNJ governance, which provide the basis for a substantive concluding chapter.

## 5 Introduction of the Individual Chapters

Based on the key issues presented above, the editors identified a list of specific topics and invited contributing authors. We asked our authors to consider how the topic under consideration in their chapter related to questions and themes identified in section 4 above. As we explained in that connection, the current project was intended to cast a significantly wider net than the negotiating agenda of the IGC. At the same time, in light of the centrality of the BBNJ process to the development of the regime for ABNJ, we asked the authors to also reflect upon the question how the topic under consideration in their chapter related to the BBNJ process, and if so, how?

Vito De Lucia in chapter 2 explores the role of the circular relation between sovereign legality and 'territorial thinking' on the one hand, and a cartographic understanding of space on the other, in the construction of ocean commons as spaces that fall outside of the scope of sovereign power. The chapter offers a problematization of territorial thinking and the sovereign spatial ordering of the sea that it underpins, with the aim of opening a conversation on other ways to think the sea, law, space and, ultimately, about ocean commons.

Chapter 3 by Nigel Bankes explores the application of Hohfeld's idea of fundamental legal concepts to the LOSC and the Draft Agreement on the conservation and sustainable use of marine BBNJ. As Bankes concludes, the importance of a Hohfeldian approach to the BBNJ process is that it helps us focusing on how the law defines relationships and in this way helps us to look beyond 'superficially conclusory labels', of which the term 'areas beyond national jurisdiction' is yet another example, as should also be apparent from the discussion in section 2 above.

In chapter 4, Tore Henriksen maps key past and current debates on the regime of the part of the oceans beyond coastal State jurisdiction. As is also pointed out by Henriksen, this debate has received considerable attention in the law of the sea literature. However, this history remains an essential background to understanding the current debate on ABNJ, and the chapter is one of the first attempts to include the BBNJ process in a long view on the history of the law of the sea.

Lan Ngoc Nguyen in chapter 5 examines the development and application of the principles of freedom of the high seas and CHM in order to understand the balance to be struck between individual freedom and collective interests in ABNJ. Nguyen argues that given the narrowing gap in the application of the two principles, at least in terms of resources, they can no longer be viewed as opposing principles, but are now aligned along a gradient of fading differences. As a result, the governance regime for ABNJ need not be overly concerned with the issue of which guiding principle should prevail but should rather focus on the collective interests that need to be protected based on the consideration of equity.

In chapter 6, Margherita Paola Poto confronts the current State-centered vision of ocean governance based in the LOSC with an ocean rights perspective. Although the latter perspective might seem distant from the actual trajectory of the BBNJ process, which remains firmly grounded in the State-centered vision, it does provide an alternative frame to investigate the failure of the current law to achieve ocean sustainability.

Chapter 7 by Alex Oude Elferink and Baine Kerr considers how the BBNJ process came about and focusses on developments in the framework of the UNGA and the CBD, which both have addressed the four thematic issues covered by the BBNJ process. What explains the central role of the UNGA and might a process driven by the CBD have resulted in a different approach?

In chapter 8, Oude Elferink considers how the relationship between ABMTs and MPAs in ABNJ has developed in general terms in relevant global frameworks, starting from the LOSC up to the current negotiating text of a future BBNJ Agreement. The chapter next considers developments in a number of specific regimes, to see how they compare to the developments in the relevant global frameworks discussed previously. The chapter argues that the existing regime of ABMTs and MPAs is permeated by a sectoral approach and that ABMTs in legal terms are therefore 'favored' over MPAs, hindering a holistic approach to the protection and of the marine environment.

Science is essential to producing knowledge about the oceans and shaping decisions about its governance regime and the sustainable use and conservation of ocean space and its resources. Chapter 9 by Elisa Morgera considers the relationship between the regime for science in the law of the sea and the human right to science. The chapter argues that to achieve an equitable regime for ABNJ, it is essential to have a regime for marine science that is fully aligned with the right to science.

In chapter 10, Richard Barnes takes fisheries in ABNJ as an example of how the 'development of a legal regime for ABNJ is closely bound up with wider social, political and economic concerns'. Fisheries nowadays is by far the human activity in ABNJ that impacts most on the sustainable use and conservation of biodiversity in these areas. At first sight, there would seem to be every reason to bring fisheries under the purview of a future BBNJ Agreement. However, fisheries interests have largely succeeded in keeping this activity outside the BBNJ process, making the question how this exclusion is justified by legal and non-legal arguments of particular importance.

As was also observed above, a future BBNJ Agreement will be based on the existing jurisdictional framework contained in the law of the sea and public international law generally, implying the primacy of flag State jurisdiction in relation to activities in ABNJ. In that light, Henrik Ringbom in chapter 11 considers the nature and extent of flag State jurisdiction and how other forms of jurisdiction may complement flag State jurisdiction, where it fails to sufficiently protect the common concern of the international community in ABNJ. Another key feature of a future BBNJ Agreement will be its institutional architecture. The main issue is how the newly created architecture of a future BBNJ

Agreement will relate to existing institutions dealing with issues and activities in relation to BBNJ. This issue is addressed by Kristine Elfrida Dalaker in chapter 12, who, applying Elinor Ostrom's theory of polycentric governance, concludes that 'an [expanded regional seas program as defined in the chapter] ... would likely meet Ostrom's institutional design principles, resulting in a robust set of institutional arrangements for the conservation and sustainable use of marine biodiversity in ABNJ'.

The provisions on dispute settlement to be included in a future BBNJ Agreement until now have received limited attention at the IGC. As the analysis by Joanna Mossop in chapter 13 points out, although compulsory dispute settlement under the LOSC has shown to have a potential to clarify the law also as regards ABNJ, the nature of ABNJ and legal relationships pertaining to them also point to the limitations of compulsory dispute settlement in this respect. Mossop considers in particular how these problems might be overcome and *inter alia* considers the options of giving the Conference of the Parties to a future BBNJ Agreement the power to request advisory opinions and make use of non-compliance procedures, which are commonly used in multilateral environmental agreements.

In chapter 14, the editors look at the main commonalities and variations in relation to the themes that we identified in the preceding chapters. Apart from revisiting the four themes, chapter 14 also reflects on a number of other issues that we consider deserve separate mention in the concluding chapter of a book dealing with the legal regime of ABNJ, namely, firstly, the relationship between ABNJ and AWNJ, and, secondly, the future development of the regime for ABNJ, including the question what role a future BBNJ Agreement might play in this respect.

## 6 Concluding Remarks

With the draft of future BBNJ Agreement still under consideration at the IGC, a book on the regime of ABNJ might seem to be untimely. However, we are convinced that much of what is discussed in the present volume will remain current in the years to come. As is explained in the preceding sections, the focus of the volume is not solely on the negotiation of the future BBNJ Agreement, but rather seeks to (also) paint the broader picture of the legal and extra-legal considerations that have shaped the regime for ABNJ, as well as to open novel conversations. As should already be apparent from this introductory chapter, a future BBNJ Agreement, although it likely is the last major elaboration of the LOSC and will play a key role in the governance of ABNJ, will at the same time operate as part of the law of the sea and public international law generally, and hence has to be viewed in that broader context.

CHAPTER 2

# Ocean Commons and an 'Ethological' Nomos of the Sea

*Vito De Lucia*

## 1 Introduction

In recent times, one of the key questions under study and then under negotiations in relation to the oceans has been the question of the governance of ocean commons.[1] More specifically, after an initial mapping of fragilities and vulnerabilities of marine ecosystems of the deep sea and the identification of corresponding governance gaps, a process was initiated with the view of adopting a new global treaty on marine biodiversity in areas beyond national jurisdiction (BBNJ).[2] This process, however, has arguably reaffirmed a specifically 'cartographic' understanding of space, which made the notion of ocean commons equivalent to areas that are outside the scope of sovereign power or jurisdiction. In this respect, ocean commons are already well delineated by the UN Convention on the Law of the Sea (LOSC) and are comprised of the so-called Area (that is, the 'seabed and ocean floor and subsoil thereof, beyond the limits of national jurisdiction')[3] and the high seas.[4] The notion of a cartographic understanding of space reflects the role of maps and map-making in the construction of space in Europe from at least the 16th century onwards.[5] Cartography, as a science of map-making and as a technology of power, has

1 For further discussion see Oude Elferink and Kerr (ch 7) in this volume.

2 UN General Assembly (UNGA), 'International Legally Binding Instrument under the United Nations Convention on the Law of the Sea on the Conservation and Sustainable Use of Marine Biological Diversity of Areas Beyond National Jurisdiction' (24 December 2017) UN Doc A/RES/72/249.

3 United Nations Convention on the Law of the Sea (opened for signature 10 December 1982, entered into force 16 November 1994) 1833 UNTS 3 (LOSC) art 1(1).

4 The high seas are really a residual maritime zone, or one could say it is the 'default' condition of the sea, except there were sovereign legality has extended its reach. LOSC art 86 defines in fact the high seas as 'all parts of the sea that are not included in the exclusive economic zone, in the territorial sea or in the internal waters of a State, or in the archipelagic waters of an archipelagic State'.

5 John Pickles, *A History of Spaces Cartographic Reason, Mapping and the Geo-Coded World* (Routledge 2003); Doreen Massey, *For Space* (Sage 2005).

 | DOI:10.1163/9789004506367_003

two aspects which are crucial for how space is understood and constructed, and thus are crucial for the purposes of this chapter. Cartography presupposes an observer – the map maker –, which is outside the map and dominates it; and it represents space as a surface.[6] Cartographic space is thus flattened by a sovereign gaze. This cartographic spatiality has been 'foundational for territorial space'[7] and has played a pivotal role in the construction of the national and colonial State.[8] Moreover, a cartographic understanding of ocean commons, I suggest in this chapter, is both a reflection and an inverted refraction of a sovereign legality, which in this chapter will be interchangeably referred to as sovereign legality, sovereign *nomos* and sovereign spatiality. This sovereign *nomos* proceeds in turn from what can be described perhaps as 'territorial thinking', which is, circularly, underpinned by a cartographic understanding of space. It is this circular mechanism that facilitates the construction of ocean commons as those spaces that fall outside of the scope of sovereign power. This logic has had at least three consequences. First, it has organized ocean commons in proprietary terms through a 'trinary' appropriated/appropriable/non-appropriable. Second, it has articulated a crucial distinction between the spatially non-appropriable (ocean commons as space) and the substantively appropriable (resources available in such oceanic commons). Third, it has rendered the notion of ocean commons dependent on and vulnerable to the ebbs and flows of sovereignty, and to the oscillating relation between knowledge, technology and power that materializes, as I will show, in historically contingent but logically coherent, processes of territorialization. The sea, however, has also resisted the ability of sovereign power to encroach in a fully territorial manner on ocean commons due to the particular materialities of sea water and oceanic spaces, such as its mobility, fluidity, depth, or more generally what Peters and Steinberg have described as 'wet' and 'more-than-wet' ontology.[9] These particular materialities have led commentators to speak of terraqueous sovereignty[10] or liquid

---

6 ibid 107.

7 Jeppe Strandsbjerg, 'The Cartographic Production of Territorial Space: Mapping and State Formation in Early Modern Denmark' (2008) 13(2) Geopolitics 335, 335.

8 Pickles (n 5).

9 Respectively Philip Steinberg and Kimberley Peters, 'Wet Ontologies, Fluid Spaces: Giving Depth to Volume through Oceanic Thinking' (2015) 33(2) Environment and Planning D: Society and Space 247; Kimberley Peters and Philip Steinberg, 'The ocean in excess: Towards a more-than-wet ontology' (2019) 9(3) Dialogues in Human Geography 293.

10 Costas Constantinou and Maria Hadjimichael, 'Liquid Entitlement: Sea, Terra, Law, Commons' (2020) Global Society.

entitlements,[11] to signify variably the mobile, legally nuanced, flexible and limited purchase of sovereignty and of sovereign power over oceanic spaces.

This chapter shall problematize this territorial thinking and the sovereign spatial ordering of the sea that it underpins, notwithstanding terraqueous or liquid articulations thereof, and then offer reflections for an 'ethological'[12] approach to imagine the relation between sea, space and law, by drawing on richer, multidimensional, conceptions of space and by recuperating a semantic inflection of *nomos* that anchors it to a diffuse normativity that is immanent in the 'thing', rather than emanating from sovereign legality as a command. The goal of the chapter is to open a conversation on other ways to think about ocean commons. The chapter is structured as follows. Section 2 problematizes the notion of ocean commons that underpins the ongoing BBNJ negotiations. Sections 3 through 5 discuss the ebbs and flows of the sovereign *nomos* in its encounter with the sea and with oceanic spaces: the initial projections of territorial thinking onto coastal waters; the significant transformations of sovereign legality after its encounter with the large oceanic expanse that followed the discovery of the Americas; the crystallization of the *mare liberum* doctrine; and the new wave of territorialization that was inaugurated by the Truman Proclamations. Section 6 presents in some ways an inversed perspective, and posits the idea of a recalcitrant sea, resisting the projection of sovereign legality, which has in fact remained incomplete, unstable and liquid. The section thus discusses the graded intensity of the territorialization of the sea. Section 7 offers some initial thoughts for re-imagining ocean commons, before drawing some conclusions.

## 2 Ocean Commons and the BBNJ Process

Despite the multiple narratives and legal regimes associated with the notion of commons,[13] international law generally constructs and understands global commons as spatial domains, that is, geographically delimited areas. Global commons are, to a significant extent, *ocean* commons.[14] It is thus the law of the

11 Liam Campling and Alejandro Colás, 'Capitalism and the sea: Sovereignty, Territory and Appropriation in the Global Ocean' (2018) 36(4) Environment and Planning D: Society and Space 776.

12 Thanos Zartaloudis, *The Birth of Nomos* (Edinburgh University Press 2019).

13 Vito De Lucia, 'The Concept of Commons and Marine Genetic Resources in Areas beyond National Jurisdiction' (2018–2019) 5 Maritime Safety and Security Law Journal.

14 The other global commons traditionally is outer space, and then Antarctica is considered a *sui generis* global commons, given its special legal status; see De Lucia (ibid) 2ff.

sea that articulates in large part the spatial delineation of the global commons, and it does so through very precise zonal delimitations of marine areas. The key delineation contrasts areas *within* and areas *beyond* national jurisdiction (ABNJ). Sovereignty is thus the crucial determinant of what marine areas are to be considered, legally speaking, commons.

In the last decades, the question of the governance of ocean commons has been one of the key questions in relation to the oceans. These questions touched especially on a series of urgent topics such as the ability to adopt marine protected areas, the regulation of the utilization of marine genetic resources and a more comprehensive framework for undertaking environmental impact assessments, but also have inevitable and potentially important implications for the institutional architecture of ocean commons.[15] After initial mapping of fragilities and vulnerabilities of marine ecosystems of the deep sea and the identification of corresponding governance gaps,[16] a process was initiated under the aegis of the UN and in the context of the LOSC framework, with the view of adopting a new global treaty on BBNJ.[17]

This process, however, reflects arguably a cartographic understanding of the notion of ocean commons, and their spatiality is equivalent to areas that are outside the scope of sovereign power or jurisdiction. Ocean commons are thus the so-called Area (that is, the deep seabed and the ocean floor beyond the limits of national jurisdiction) and the high seas.

The idea of commons, to be sure, 'traverses international law in multiple ways'.[18] With respect to the law of the sea, however, global commons have a specific spatial character, as they are the result of sovereign delineations and boundary-making. Thus, ocean commons are those spaces that remain literally *outside* of sovereign legality. They are residual, are what remains unclaimed (or unclaimable), they exist only insofar as territorial sovereignty cannot or will not reach.[19]

---

15 See Oude Elferink (ch 8), Morgera (ch 9) and Dalaker (ch 12) in this volume.

16 UNGA, 'Report of the Open-ended Informal Consultative Process on Oceans and the Law of the Sea' (26 June 2003) UN Doc A/58/95 and UNGA, 'Resolution Adopted by the General Assembly on 17 November 2004' (4 February 2005) UN Doc A/RES/59/24, (17 November 2004). See Oude Elferink and Kerr (ch 7) in this volume, for early discussions of ABNJ in the context of the CBD.

17 UNGA, 'International Legally Binding Instrument under the United Nations Convention on the Law of the Sea on the Conservation and Sustainable Use of Marine Biological Diversity of Areas Beyond National Jurisdiction' (24 December 2017) UN Doc A/RES/72/249.

18 De Lucia, 'Commons and Marine Genetic Resources' (n 13) 4.

19 For extra-territorial jurisdiction at sea, eg flag state jurisdiction, see Ringbom (ch 11) in this volume.

These marine ABNJ – the high seas and the Area – have however in common only their being *outside*. They are otherwise *different*. The high seas are comprised of all oceanic waters *not* under national jurisdiction[20] and is subject to a regime a freedom. As such is a space 'open to all states'.[21] Additionally, and perhaps importantly, '[n]o State may validly purport to subject any part of the high seas to its sovereignty'.[22] The Area, which includes the deep seabed, the ocean floor and the subsoil beyond the limits of national jurisdiction,[23] is by contrast subject to a regime of *collective* ownership and international management, under the principle of common heritage of mankind (CHM)[24] and the combined framework constituted by Part XI of LOSC and the 1994 Implementation Agreement. Here the legal regime is opposed to that of the high seas, as it is not an unclaimable space open to all, but a regulated space under *collective* ownership, and thus claimed by humanity in its entirety.[25]

Ocean commons are also organized through a legal tripartition that juxtaposes areas already appropriated (ie, areas within national jurisdiction), areas that cannot be appropriated (the global commons proper, considered as *res communes omnium*), and discrete resources that, while located in oceanic spaces that, qua global commons, are not appropriable, can themselves be appropriated (as they are considered *res nullius*).[26] Thus, sovereign legality has articulated a crucial distinction between the spatially non-appropriable (ABNJ) and the substantively appropriable (resources available in such oceanic common spaces), disassembling thus ocean space in a cartographic flat

20 The high seas regime is however also, though only residually, applicable to the seabed and subsoil.

21 LOSC 87.

22 ibid art 89.

23 ibid art 1(1)(1) states in this respect that the Area 'means the seabed and ocean floor and subsoil thereof, beyond the limits of national jurisdiction'.

24 LOSC art 136 states that the Area, as well as its 'resources' (by which is intended 'all solid, liquid or gaseous mineral resources in situ in the Area at or beneath the seabed, including polymetallic nodules', as per LOSC art 133), are the CHM. This distinction between a spatial area and a resource will be picked up again late in the chapter.

25 Humanity, incidentally, is a problematic concept that is 'screaming' for a critical unpacking in ways similar to the 'Anthropos', on which see especially Anna Grear, 'Deconstructing Anthropos: A Critical Legal Reflection on "Anthropocentric" Law and Anthropocene "Humanity"' (2015) 26 Law Critique 225.

26 This is the logic that Milun, for example, understands as creating so-called 'political uncommons', whereby the rhetoric of the global commons is utilized to transform common resources located in the global commons into appropriable ones (ie *res nullius*), Kathryn Milun, *The Political Uncommons The Cross-Cultural Logic of the Global Commons* (Routledge 2011).

extension and in a *depth-less* yet *volumetric*[27] resource base. In the context of the BBNJ negotiations, this logic is particularly relevant for marine genetic resources (MGRs), one of the four topics under negotiation.[28] In this respect, even in the ocean commons, the sovereign conceptual framework remains operational, by delineating the *outside* of common spaces and by directly seizing upon discrete resources. These are in fact characterized as either *res nullius* that can be freely appropriated in open spaces (eg, the high seas) not subjected to any sovereign, or as CHM (in the Area), subject to a collective sovereign that still facilitates regimes of exploitation.

This is the spatio-legal and conceptual premise for the ongoing BBNJ negotiations, which should lead to the adoption of a global Treaty that shall give further implementation to the LOSC.[29] As the BBNJ negotiations draw on and near a possible conclusion, it is useful to reflect on the prevailing cartographic concept of ocean commons that underpins them, as well as on some questions that challenge this cartographic rendering of space. The latter in turn reflects the modern understanding of space, as well as nature, as extension, and its operationalization through past processes of territorialization that have delimited ocean commons to date. At the same time, there is a clear regulatory intent to further delineate and govern the ocean commons in the context of the BBNJ negotiations. In this respect, it is useful to note how the history of the law of the sea is in many ways the history of a territorial projection, which is often referred to as 'creeping coastal state jurisdiction'.[30] Indeed, as Molenaar observes, creeping coastal State jurisdiction 'has been one of the principal drivers in the development of the modern international law of the sea'.[31] This tendency towards the encroachment on common ocean spaces and the processes

27 Steinberg and Peters (n 9) observe how a vertical focus on volume, while correcting the horizontalism of cartographic spatial imagination, remains 'terrestrial' (at 254), 'abstract and dematerialized' (at 247) and fails to consider the depth, rapidity and mobility of the oceans (at 254).

28 The others being area-based management tools, including marine protected areas; environmental impact assessments; and capacity building and the transfer of marine technology, UNGA, 'International Legally Binding Instrument under the United Nations Convention on the Law of the Sea on the Conservation and Sustainable Use of Marine Biological Diversity of Areas Beyond National Jurisdiction' (24 December 2017) UN Doc A/RES/72/249.

29 ibid.

30 See eg, Barbara Kwiatkowska, 'Creeping Jurisdiction Beyond 200 Miles in the Light of the 1982 Law of the Sea Convention and State Practice' (1991) 22(2) Ocean Development and International Law 153.

31 Erik J Molenaar, 'Multilateral Creeping Coastal State Jurisdiction and the BBNJ Negotiations' (2021) 36(1) The International Journal of Marine and Coastal Law 5, 6.

of territorialization that underpinned such encroachment, has been fueled by the concept of adjacency. I will not address in any comprehensive manner this crucial concept, which has 'fundamental importance'[32] for the law of the sea, and rather remand the reader to existing literature.[33] However, some notations may be useful, in light of its renewed role in the context of the BBNJ negotiations that may further limit and delimit the high seas, to the extent that adjacency has been utilized as a potential legal basis for giving coastal States preferential rights or responsibility in ABNJ that are adjacent to their exclusive economic zone (EEZ).[34]

## 3 Adjacency and Territorial Projection: The Sovereign Nomos at Sea

Adjacency is considered to have been 'a key basis and rationale for State authority at sea since at least the era of classical antiquity',[35] and has arguably taken two forms: a unilateral one, which is the precise reflection of the sovereign legality that underpins international law and that, as we shall see, further reflects a land-based territorial thinking; and a multilateral one, which, as Molenaar suggests, indicates the specifically collective inflection of jurisdictional claims on relevant oceanic spaces, in turn reducing incrementally the ocean commons, compressing the formal regime of freedom that flows from the current legal regulation of the high seas. The expansion of jurisdiction seaward has indeed determined one of the greatest 'enclosures' or 'grabs' in history,[36] as estimates suggest that the zoning of the LOSC has 'shrunk' the commons by about 'forty percent or more of ocean space'.[37] Yet the will to project sovereign control seaward is not a modern phenomenon, as already suggested by Molenaar,[38] and reflects the processes of territorialization through

32 ibid 10.

33 Joanna Mossop and Clive Schofield, 'Adjacency and Due Regard: The Role of Coastal States in the BBNJ Treaty' (2020) 122 Marine Policy 103877; Jinyuan Su, 'The Adjacency Doctrine in the Negotiation of BBNJ: Creeping Jurisdiction or Legitimate Claim?' (2021) 52(1) Ocean Development and International Law 41; Molenaar (n 31).

34 Mossop and Schofield (ibid).

35 Molenaar (n 31) 9.

36 Constantinou and Hadjimichael (n 10) 13, citing in turn Pardo ('enclosures') and Ranganathan ('grabs'), see footnote ibid for full references.

37 ibid.

38 Which refers to ancient Rome, for example, Molenaar (n 31). However, see also Rolf Strootman, Floris van den Eijnde and Roy van Wijk, *Empires of the Sea. Maritime Power Networks in World History* (Brill 2020).

which sovereign legality has projected its territorial framework onto the sea. In this respect, adjacency has been a crucial concept to solve pressing legal questions related to safety, resource access and control, power and the ability to *jus dicere*, that is to declare applicable law. Empires have always encompassed, to different degrees and for different purposes, sea waters and 'sea appropriations',[39] although limitedly to coastal waters or closed seas.[40] Thus the ancient Republic of Rome considered the Mediterranean Sea as *mare nostrum* ('our sea'),[41] and exercised *imperium* and *jurisdictio* despite considering it a *res communis omnium* that could not be appropriated.[42] Security and fisheries were often the key interests at stake for claims of sovereign control over sea spaces and for the emergence of the *territorial* sea.[43] In the 13th century, for example, some forms of maritime sovereignty had begun developing, in particular within the northern Mediterranean,[44] and in the North of Europe.[45] Such sovereignty translated into the right to collect taxes and to restrict navigation, rights that were acquiesced to as sovereigns at sea rendered services to all by combating piracy,[46] and was the result of a complex set of arguments that would transfer a land-based territorial logic onto sea spaces. This was the case, for example, at the onset of modernity for example, when Italian marine Republics had to articulate powers, rights and duties that they might exercise in the sea spaces outside of the coastal areas under their jurisdiction.[47] Questions such as 'do land sovereigns have jurisdiction in marine areas adjacent to their territory, and up to which distance from the coast?' were discussed and eventually

---

39 Carl Schmitt, *The Nomos of the Earth in the International Law of the Jus Public Europeaum* (Telos Press Publishing 2006 German Original 1950).

40 See eg Thomas Fulton, *The Sovereignty of the Sea: An Historical Account of the Claims of England to the Dominion of the British Seas, and of the Evolution of the Territorial Waters* (The Lawbook Exchange 2010 Original 1911). See also Philip Steinberg, 'Lines of Division, Lines of Connection: Stewardship in the World Ocean' (1999) 89(2) The Geographical Review 254.

41 David J Bederman, 'The sea' in Bardo Fassbender and Anne Peters (eds), *The Oxford Handbook of the History of International Law* (Oxford University Press 2012) 363.

42 But also in ancient Greece and elsewhere in the world similar conditions applied, see eg Strootman, van den Eijnde and van Wijk (n 38) especially chs 2, 3 and 4.

43 See eg Fulton (n 40) especially ch 2 through 5 (fisheries) and ch 7 (security).

44 The so-called 'maritime republics' (Genoa, Pisa and most of all Venice) claimed *dominium* (often at first *de fact*, and only later becoming *de jure*) over significant portions of the seas. Venice for example exercised *dominium maris* in the entire Adriatic Sea, while Genoa attempted to do the same with regards to the Ligurian Sea, see Fulton (n 40) 1–24.

45 ibid 4.

46 ibid 338ff.

47 Prometeo Cerezo de Diego, 'Origenes de la Teoria del Mar Territorial en Bartolo de Sassoferrato' (1977) 30(2/3) Revista Española de Derecho Internacional 237.

answered in the positive, with arguments that, drawn from Roman law, found in the duties to maintain peace a legitimate basis to extend such duties to marine areas adjacent to land, including islands.[48] The projection of territorial thinking on marine spaces is quite evident, and even more so in relation to the question of the seaward extension of such jurisdiction. Drawing in this case on Canon law rather than on Roman law, the question would be resolved by recourse to the notion of vicinity (marine spaces that could be considered legitimately under jurisdiction had to be 'near'). Such vicinity would be calculated on the basis of walking distances (two days of walking representing the standard for what could be considered 'near'), which in turn would be translated into a spatial measurement equivalent to 100 nautical miles to which jurisdiction based on adjacency could extend.[49] This extensive jurisdictional projection on to marine spaces, while it did not seek to appropriate sea spaces, extended the operation of municipal law and the power to *jus dicere* to such spaces, on the basis of territorial proximity and adjacency. However, such claims would later unravel with the emergence of the principle and practice of *mare liberum*, which compressed significantly territorial jurisdiction and the maritime entitlements that could be legitimately claimed on the basis of adjacency to a thin strip of land that could be brought under national jurisdiction only as far as the reach of the *vis armorum* (that is, the capability of weapons and military power), which gave rise to the so-called cannon shot rule,[50] later standardized to 3 nautical miles.[51] This unravelling followed largely the trajectory impressed on the development of law of the sea by the discovery of the Americas, even if, still in the 17th century, many jurists would argue that property in the sea and its resources would belong 'to those to whom the nearest continent belonged',[52] thus reiterating medieval conceptions of sovereign

48 ibid 245.

49 ibid 246. See also Paolo Marchetti, 'Spazi, ordinamenti e confini tra tardo medioevo ed età moderna' in Luigi Lacchè (ed), *Ius gentium, ius communicationis, ius belli: Alberico Gentili e gli orizzonti della modernità* (Giuffrè 2009) 26.

50 'Cannon shot rule' in Jonathan Law and Elizabeth Martin (eds), *A Dictionary of Law* (7th edn, Oxford University Press 2014 (2009)).

51 Marchetti (n 49) 29.

52 D P O'Connell and I A Shearer (eds), *The International Law of the Sea: Volume I* (1st edn, Oxford University Press 1988) 4. See also Mónica Brito Vieira, 'Mare Liberum vs. Mare Clausum: Grotius, Freitas, and Selden's Debate on Dominion over the Seas' (2003) 64(3) Journal of the History of Ideas 361. Schmitt, *Nomos of the Earth* (n 39) 178, calls the debate 'the hundred-year book war' and he also underlines the many different goals of the participants to this war, from freedom of overseas evangelical missions, to freedom as a tool to break the Spanish and Portuguese monopoly of trade, to questions of fisheries and fishing rights in coastal seas (ibid 179).

jurisdiction extending at sea by way of adjacency and articulating an early idea of the notion that the land dominates the sea. The discovery indeed had a profound effect on sovereign legality as it had to confront large oceanic spaces.

## 4 From Scratches on the Soil to Global Lines

When thinking about international law and space (which is arguably something we 'need more' of, as Henry Jones observed)[53] an inevitable starting point is often German legal philosopher Carl Schmitt.[54] Schmitt has produced a comprehensive framework for thinking law and space, which he articulates especially in his book *Nomos of the Earth,*[55] though already in his earlier and more philosophical book *Land and Sea*[56] Schmitt argued that all law 'emanates from a land appropriation that orders space'.[57] This particular and foundational act of land appropriation, for Schmitt, constitutes at the same time the fundamental spatial ordering and organizing principle of each Epoch,[58] its *Nomos*.[59] *Nomos*, in Schmitt's view, thus *orders* and *orients* a community and the space it controls.[60] As this primordial line is drawn, space is delineated and marked,

53 Henry Jones, 'Lines in the Ocean: Thinking with the Sea about Territory and International Law' (2016) 4(2) London Review of International Law 307, 342.

54 See eg Stephen Legg (ed), *Spatiality, Sovereignty and Carl Schmitt* (Routledge 201) or Jones (ibid). It is important to note how Schmitt's personal politics, particularly his support of National Socialism in the 1930's, remain problematic today, and elicits important reflections, such as Joseph Weiler 'Cancelling Carl Schmitt?' EJIL Talk!, 13 August 2021, https://www.ejiltalk.org/cancelling-carl-schmitt/. However, his theoretical approach and his work on law and the political, on sovereignty and on the state of exception also remains an important site of engagement for critical (international) legal theory, legal geography and political philosophy, Stephen Legg, 'Introduction' in Legg (ibid). One major philosopher drawing on Schmitt's work is, of course, Giorgio Agamben. See otherwise references in this paper, in this footnote and throughout.

55 Schmitt, *Nomos of the Earth* (n 39).

56 Carl Schmitt, *Land and Sea. A World Historical Meditation* (Telos Press Publishing 2015 Original 1942). See also Eduardo Mendieta, 'Land and Sea' in Legg (n 54).

57 ibid 262.

58 Schmitt draws his periodization from Wilhelm Grewe, *The Epochs of International Law* (tr Michael Byers, Walter de Gruyter 2000).

59 Schmitt, *Nomos of the Earth* (n 39). For other lineages and for the complex linkages between *nomos,* land and law in ancient Greece see eg Zartaloudis (n 12). The latter seems to confirm, however, how the linkage between *nomos* and distribution and sharing, whether in ritual or pastoral contexts remain constantly strong across lineages.

60 Cornelia Vismann, 'Starting from Scratch: Concepts of Order in No Man's Land' in Bernd-Rüdiger Hippauf (ed), *War, Violence and the Modern Condition* (De Gruyter 1997) 46.

and law emerges as a particular spatial order.[61] This act of boundary-making, argues Schmitt, determines the birth of law. Recalling what has been called the 'obliging etymology' of *nomos*,[62] Schmitt observes how its primordial meaning is linked to the delimitation of pastures.[63] *Nomos*, suggests thus Schmitt, is 'the measure by which the land in a particular order is divided and situated'.[64] Law, in this sense, is the primeval act of appropriating, delimiting and allocating land (or a territory).[65] This primeval act establishes a spatial order that delineates simultaneously the internal order of a community – its mode of organization, its land distribution, its relationship with its territory – and its external relations, making manifest and actionable the community's boundary against *others*.[66] Indeed, even the concept of peace appears deeply linked with the concept of boundary.[67] Law is thus *telluric*,[68] that is, is fundamentally connected to the soil, to the land, and to its demarcation and its appropriation.

International law follows, arguably, the same logic.[69] Indeed, the key original mode of acquisition of property in land, as well as of territory, is occupation, that is, an occupation followed by the drawing of boundaries. Lack of clear and permanent delimitations, by contrast, provided precisely a crucial legitimation for the dispossession of lands inhabited by the native populations

61 ibid. See also Schmitt, *Nomos of the Earth* (n 39).

62 Peter Fitzpatrick, *Modernism and the Grounds of Law* (Cambridge University Press 2001) 91.

63 Schmitt, *Nomos of the Earth* (n 39) 70.

64 ibid.

65 From this point of view, *nomos* belongs to realm of natural law, is a crucial part of *quod natura omnia animalia docuit*, (that is, that which nature teaches to all animals), D. 1.1.1.3 (Ulpianus 1 inst.). This is specifically the understanding of natural law of Roman legal sensitivity, which is obviously altogether different than the modern natural law, all centered on human reason; for a discussion of the differences see eg, Passerin D'Entreves, *Natural Law. An Introduction to Legal Philosophy* (Transaction Publishers 2009); Micehl Villey, *Le Droit et les Droits de l'Homme* (Presses Universitaires de France 2008).

66 See in general Daniel-Erasmus Khan, 'Territory and Boundaries' in Bardo Fassbender and others (eds), *The Oxford Handbook of the History of International Law* (Oxford University Press 2013), for both a brief anthropological anchoring and an account of some 'early records of territory and boundary making', this latter being section 2, at 229ff.

67 ibid 229, where he refers of the German term '*um-frieden/Umfriedung*' which still maintains the 'etymological bridge' between the two concepts.

68 The adjective telluric derives from *Tellus*, which is the Latin name of the goddess of the earth: hence telluric indicates something earthly; see also 'Telluric' Merriam-Webster.com Dictionary available at <www.merriam-webster.com/dictionary/telluric> accessed 4 August 2020.

69 Schmitt, *Nomos of the Earth* (n 39) 80ff. See also Tayyab Mahmud, 'Geography and International Law: Towards a Postcolonial Mapping' (2007) 5(2) Santa Clara Journal of International Law 525.

in the newly discovered Americas. Physical markings, what Deleuze and Guattari call 'striation',[70] articulate a particular orientation to the land which takes one of the forms through which property can be both established and recognized. Indeed, only European forms of permanent settlement, farming practices and harvesting patterns – again rehearsing the primeval link of *nomos* with the delimitation of fields and pastures – could give rise to the necessary characteristics of continuity, exclusivity and intensity upon which property (and, relatedly, sovereignty) claims could (and to a large extent still) rest. Thus, modern law considers land that is not striated a monstrosity, a 'desert' (Tocqueville), a 'wasteland' (Locke), on account of the fact that the native of the Americas did not possess – in the sense of showing evidence of *dominium* and thus also of sovereignty[71] – the land they occupied.[72] And as the land did not bear native signs of striation, it could be considered legitimately as *terra nullius*, and lawfully occupied.[73]

This colonial and inherently parochial logic, inevitably, carried over to sea, where however, it could not unproblematically unfold in the same manner as on land. Early forms of *dominium maris*[74] remained indeed confined to mediterranean seas (with the exception perhaps of North Sea), that is, local seas never too far into the wide oceanic waters and encompassed by lands.[75]

The advent of the age of discovery broke this primordial link between law and land. The expansion of human activity across the vast world oceans led law to dematerialize and thus promoted what Carl Schmitt called 'global linear thinking'.[76] A new spatio-legality begun thus to emerge. Sovereignty was abstracted from physical geography and occupancy, to rest solely on measurements and mathematical abstractions. Nature ceased to be a wonder and the repository

---

70 Thom Kuehls, 'Between Sovereignty and Environment: an Exploration of the Discourse of Government' in Karen T Liftin (ed), *The Greening of Sovereignty in World Politics* (MIT Press 1998) 43.

71 As an 'absence of property signals absence of sovereignty' (ibid 43).

72 ibid 43–44.

73 And occupation, it is perhaps not necessary to note, is one of the modes of original (as opposed to derivative, say through contract) acquisition of property in the roman and European legal tradition.

74 It must be noted that, however, in such cases, sometimes sovereignty manifested primarily as *imperium*, rather than *dominium stricto sensu*. This is an argument that Philip Steinberg has developed to contest the view that links line drawing with sovereign division a la Schmitt, and rather reframe line drawing, and marine governance, as premised on the 'common norm of stewardship', Steinberg, 'Lines of Division' (n 40) 254.

75 See eg Filippo Ruschi, 'Leviathan e Behemoth. Modelli egemonici e spazi coloniali in Carl Schmitt' (2007) Jura Gentium.

76 Schmitt, *Nomos of the Earth* (n 39) 86–87.

of myth and became the object of scientific knowledge that must be measured, calculated and classified. Law had thus to dematerialize. A Schmitt observed, this momentous transformation of the apprehension of space qua space also promoted the 'hitertho unimaginable problem of the spatial ordering of the Earth by international law'.[77] At this juncture, however, two trajectories met and collided. The new global linear thinking determined the delineation of a space imagined only as a cartographic representation of the oceans; yet, lines were projected on to it, in various attempts to categorize the sea in accordance with a territorial logic and legal precision. In this respect, the Treaty of Tordesillas[78] of 1494 offers the key example. The treaty, whereby Spain and Portugal, having agreed on their respective zones of influence in the global oceans in accordance with several papal bulls,[79] marked, according to Schmitt, the first example of a legal regime de-linked from physical geography, and constructed following what he calls 'global lines'.[80]

The Tordesillas attempt failed. Yet, later new lines marked more prosaically how the rule of law ceased at sea, in ways that reflected the shifting power relations between European maritime powers at the time. More precisely, law ceased beyond the so-called 'lines of amity', a verbal agreement reached alongside the signing of the Peace of Cateau-Cambrésis of 1559.[81] These lines ran South and West, respectively, along the Tropic of Cancer and the Prime Meridian through Ferro, in the Canaries Islands.[82] Past these lines, '[t]erritorial conflicts, acts of piracy, and other forms of extraterritorial violence'[83] would be accepted and would not, importantly, threaten the stability of the rule of law and the integrity of interstate treaties on the European side of the lines. These lines served as devices to bracket off the violence of colonial and oceanic realms from the civility of European relations, regulated under the law

77 Schmitt, *Nomos of the Earth* (n 39) 86.

78 Treaty of Tordesillas between Portugal and Spain (7 June 1494), in Elihu Lauterpacht and others (eds), *International Law Reports: Consolidated Table of Treaties* (vols 1–125, Cambridge University Press).

79 On this see eg Henry Jones, 'Lines in the Ocean: Thinking with the Sea about Territory and International Law' (2016) 4(2) London Review of International Law 307.

80 Schmitt, *Nomos of the Earth* (n 39) 86ff.

81 Peace of Cateau-Cambrésis (3 April 1559).

82 For a detailed analysis and critique of the intricacies of the geographical and cartographic aspects of these 'lines', and especially with regards to the prime meridian, see Garrett Mattingly, 'No Peace beyond What Line?' (1963) 13 Transactions of the Royal Historical Society 145.

83 Mark Netzloff, 'Lines of Amity The Law of Nations in the Americas' in Tracy Sowerby and Joanna Craigwood (eds), *Cultures of Diplomacy and Literary Writing in the Early Modern World* (Oxford University Press 2019) 54.

of nations. And even though their actual existence has been called into question,[84] the symbolic and theoretical relevance of such lines remains useful for the purposes of this chapter, at least insofar as it reproduces a longstanding imaginary of thresholds between order and chaos and between state of nature and society[85] that at sea (though also on land) played an important role for the construction and reproduction of the self-image of European sovereign legality.[86]

After the Reformation however, with the rise of the Dutch Republic as a sea power, the modern regime of the seas began in fact to take shape, with its initial point perhaps to be found in the Treaty of Utrecht.[87] As Schmitt argues, that Treaty marks a fundamental shift that begins to anchor the idea of freedom of the sea not in an 'elemental' perspective characterized by the absence of law,[88] but in a juridically systematic one. The freedom of the sea begins thus to be contained within clear juridical lines, through the emergence of a significant role for the flag state and the elimination of so-called amity lines, which, as we have seen, delimited, during the elemental phase, areas altogether free from the rule of law, and rather open to the rule of power.[89]

The main architect of the modern regime of the seas is often considered to be the Dutch lawyer Hugo Grotius. The occasion was a dispute between the Dutch East Indies Company – which Grotius advised – and Portugal. Grotius defended the Dutch company interests and sought to establish a legitimate title for Dutch access to sea trade. Grotius outlined more concisely his theory in a 66 pages extract entitled: '*De Mare Liberum sive De Jure Quod Batavis Competit ad Indicana Commercia Dissertatio*' ('On the Free Sea, or on the Right Which Belongs to the Dutch to Take Part in the East Indian Trade').[90] The argument for the freedom of the seas, in other words, had always been aimed at defending the right of the Dutch to trade in the East Indies. *De Mare Liberum* was

84 ibid.

85 For a critical theoretical discussion of this threshold see eg Vito De Lucia, 'Semantics of Chaos: Modernity, Law and the Commons' (2018) 12(2) Pólemos Journal of Law, Literature and Culture.

86 More pragmatically, however, the lines of amity were a threshold that effectively denied political agency to any entity or community other than European Sovereign States, and thus facilitated land appropriations overseas, see Schmitt, *Nomos of the Earth* (n 39) 92ff.

87 ibid 181.

88 Which hinges on the idea that the sea is 'impervious to human law' and a test bed for strength (ibid).

89 ibid.

90 Hugo Grotius, *The Freedom of the Seas, Or, the Right Which Belongs to the Dutch to Take Part in the East Indian Trade* (Lawbook Exchange Ltd 2011) 7.

not a theoretical treatise, but rather a 'lawyer's argument'.[91] However, Grotius' argument, while opposed by the likes of Selden, that argued contrariwise in favor of the British Crown's claim that vast tract of seas south and east of the British isle were 'inseparable and perpetual appendant of the British Empire',[92] prevailed (albeit eventually there will be a disjunction between the freedom of navigation and the rights to jurisdictional control and resource extraction).

Despite the fact that eventually, as we shall see, Selden's position would be largely vindicated by recent developments in the law of the sea, Grotius further delineated the clear distinction between the traditional order of land and the emerging order of the oceans, in this sense anticipating Schmitt's view that land and sea are legally incommensurable. Property has its origin in occupancy, Grotius wrote in fact, and the sea could never be occupied or subject to servitude.[93] To describe acts of navigation as occupancy would be absurd since a 'ship sailing over the sea no more leaves behind itself a legal right than it leaves a permanent track'.[94] This argument was put forward by Grotius against the Portuguese claim that 'the acts of navigating at an earlier date than other peoples'[95] would amount to occupancy, and hence establish *dominium*. Grotius viewed by contrast the oceans are a '*res communis omnium*', that is, common to all mankind. Not even the Pope could legitimately dispose over areas which, as *res communis*, are beyond ownership and thus cannot be object of commercial transactions. Indeed, as Ruschi observes, '[a]s *res communis omnium* the sea was out of the jurisdiction of the *dominus mundi* and therefore legally immeasurable, foreign to any legal title'.[96] Schmitt in this respect underlined the lack of character of the ocean, where he understood the term character in the original sense of engraving, scratching.[97] At sea, observed Schmitt, 'there is nothing but waves'.[98]

---

91 James Brown Scott, 'Introductory Note' in Hugo Grotius (ed), *Freedom of the Seas or the Right Which Belongs to the Dutch to Take Part in the East Indian Trade* (Oxford University Press 1916) vii.

92 ibid ix.

93 For a fuller analysis of Grotius's argument, see eg Alex Oude Elferink, 'De Groot – A founding father of the law of the sea, not the Law of the sea convention' (2009) 30 Grotiana 153.

94 Hugo Grotius (ed), *Commentary on the Law of Prize and Booty*, with an Introduction by Martine Julia van Ittersum (Liberty Fund 2006) 334 available at <http://oll.libertyfund.org/titles/1718> accessed 6 February 2015.

95 Ibid.

96 Filippo Ruschi, 'Space, Law and Power in Carl Schmitt' (2008) IV(1) Jura Gentium Rivista di filosofia del diritto internazionale e della politica globale Section 1, para 6 (there is no page number, as it is an online journal) available at <www.juragentium.org/topics/thil/en/nomos.htm> accessed 30 July 2021.

97 Schmitt, *Nomos of the Earth* (n 39) 42–43.

98 ibid.

Grotius framework stretched the caesura between coastal waters and high seas and set the framework under which the law of the sea has operated since. However, the telluric logic of sovereignty, its territorial legality, has in recent times re-activated the power of adjacency and has rekindled processes of territorialization of ocean spaces that had been effectively unraveled by Grotius' argument for the freedom of seas. Yet Grotius had foreseen such processes of seaward creeping claims, as he mused that 'if the sea can be occupied up to one hundred miles', what can 'prevent it being occupied up to 150, thence to 200 and so on? If water is property up to the 100th mile, why can not the water which is immediately contiguous to the property be equally property?'[99]

## 5 From *Mare Liberum* to the Territorialization of Ocean Commons

A *nomos* premised on the sea as its elemental referent, articulates a new spatio-legality where sovereignty becomes the result of a cartographic calculation rather than a specific material impression on the soil. Schmitt emphasizes thus the conflict between the concrete spatial order of the soil and the 'abstract normativism of the legal code' that obtains, in his view, at sea.[100] The two *nomos*, Schmitt argues, are juxtaposed temporally, logically and legally.

By contrast, I wish to emphasize, the *continuity* between concrete and abstract legalities as two different modes of the sovereign embrace over territory, understood not as land (and thus juxtaposed to the sea), but as a political technology that may be equally deployed on land and at sea (and in the air and outer space).[101] This deployment, I suggest, is the result of processes of territorialization that expand, retract, oscillate and unfold as knowledge and technology evolve and political conflicts shift. The logic, however, remains the same, regardless of the site in which spatial relations, processes of territorialization and forms of legal orderings obtain. In fact, modern sovereignty is perhaps more fruitfully enabled by a cartographic, geometrical and abstract logic than its land-oriented articulation which severely limited its reach and scope to tangible and physically containable locales.

---

99 Grotius, *De Mare Liberum*, as quoted in Oude Elferink, 'De Groot' (n 93) 157.
100 Vismann (n 60) 48. See also Fitzpatrick (n 62) 92.
101 For an assessment of how legal regimes reflect the background of activities that need to be regulated, with particular focus on a contextualization of the role of Grotius in relation to both the law of the sea and the LOSC, see Oude Elferink, 'De Groot' (n 93).

In this chapter, the continuity of how law orders spatially land and sea, is captured, as anticipated in the introduction, by expressions such as sovereign legality, sovereign *nomos* or sovereign spatiality (expressions which I am using interchangeably). This sovereign spatiality is in turn animated by a territorial logic that reflects the modern obsession with thresholds, delimitations, appropriations, controls and exclusions.[102] It also reflects a particular manner in which law neutralizes space by, paradoxically, spatializing the world as geometric and calculable. Indeed, this sovereign spatiality reflects an understanding (or rather a construction) of space as a static set of coordinates represented in/by maps, or at best as 'the sphere ... of a discrete multiplicity of inert *things*'.[103] This cartographic space however, is crucial for sovereign legality, which needs and produces a spatial order that articulates claims of 'singularity, stability and closure',[104] as such simultaneously contributing to the constitution and enforcement of both cartographic space and the sovereign imaginary that sustains it and is sustained by it.

This territorial logic fueled in turn the territorialization of the sea. Territorialization is understood for the purposes of this chapter as a process of transforming places into space and then space into territory. So, in terms of process, there are two transformations involved. One from places, understood as a multiplicity of living and lived habitats, to a cartographic, singular, regularized, geometric space, and entails the transformation of the living into the measurable. The second transforms space into territory and entails the transformation of the measurable into the controllable.

Territorialization understood this way chimes with the notion of 'territoriality' as articulated by Campling and Colas, for whom it denotes the 'range of strategies aimed at producing and regulating space(s)'.[105] Territorialization as understood in this chapter also chimes with the notion of territory as articulated by Stuart Elden. Elden suggests that territory is a 'political technology' underpinned by techniques aimed at 'measuring' and 'controlling' physical space and its contents (people, resources, etc.).[106] These two operations, in turn, reflect the technical and the legal, or, in other words, knowledge and power.[107] Territorializing the sea means thus the transformation of seascapes

102 On the 'thresholds of modernity', and on the implications of these for *legal* modernity see De Lucia, 'Semantics of Chaos' (n 85) 393.

103 Massey (n 5) 107.

104 ibid 109.

105 ibid.

106 Stuart Elden, 'Land, Terrain, Territory' (2010) 34(6) Progress in Human Geography 799, 799.

107 ibid.

into measurable space, where the purpose of measurement is control. Territorialization is a process through which the sea is 'disciplined' and made 'predictable and comprehensible'.[108] Importantly, as Henry Jones observes, also following Elden, territory is 'an historical, geographical, and political concept, which is in constant need of being exercised and performed' and 'is the effect of practices … which makes it bounded and controlled'.[109]

Having now outlined the notion of territorialization, it is possible to turn towards the processes of its projection at sea. From the point of view of the first transformation, from place to space, the territorialization of the sea begun with the age of discovery, the onset of global trade by sea and the emergence of a new spatio-legality, whereby sovereignty is abstracted from its physical, material dimension, and rests solely on measurements and mathematical abstractions. Its second transformation, however, did not begin in any meaningful manner until the 1930s.

From the 1930s onwards in fact, legal expediency and technological development (that is, the encounter of power and knowledge)[110] fostered a new process of territorialization of the sea rationalized by the 'urgent necessity for international regulation of the exploitation of the biological wealth of the sea'.[111] This process initiated with the Conference on the Progressive Codification of International Law held at The Hague,[112] which was to develop international law on three main topics, one being territorial waters, including questions of 'the breadth of the territorial waters under the sovereignty of the coastal state'.[113] As Morel observes, 'following the collapse of the Conference … the rate of expansion of coastal-state jurisdiction increased markedly'.[114] Subsequently, the process was significantly accelerated by the 1945 Truman Proclamations.[115]

108 Jones (n 79) 307.

109 ibid (footnotes omitted).

110 For an account of how legal expediency and technological innovation reflect the nexus of power and knowledge in the law of the sea see eg Surabhi Ranganathan, 'Ocean Floor Grab: International Law and the Making of an Extractive Imaginary' (2019) 30(2) European Journal of International Law 573.

111 League of Nations Committee of Experts' 'Report on the Exploitation of the Products of the Sea' 232, cited in James B Morel, *The Law of the Sea. A Historical analysis of the 1982 Treaty and its Rejection by the United States*, (McFarland and Company 1992) 3.

112 Which was to develop international law on three main topics one being territorial waters, (ibid).

113 Hunter Miller, 'The Hague Codification Conference' (1930) 24 American Journal of International Law 674, 675.

114 Model (n 111) 3.

115 See eg Michael P Scharf, *Customary International Law in Times of Fundamental Change Recognizing Grotian Moments* (Cambridge University Press 2013) especially ch 5, 'The

President Truman issued his famous Proclamations to establish a) sovereign jurisdiction and control over 'the natural resources of the subsoil and sea bed of the continental shelf beneath the high seas but contiguous to the coasts of the United States as appertaining to the United States';[116] and b) 'conservation zones in those areas of the high seas contiguous to the coasts of the United States'.[117] While the goal of the first proclamation was to subject the continental shelf and its resources to exclusive sovereign control on the basis of it being a natural prolongation of the land territory, the goal of the conservation zone was more modestly to condition the right of entry to the participation of foreign vessels to any conservation program the United States would put in place for the conservation and protection of fisheries resources. This second Proclamation however, fueled further unilateral declarations aimed at ensuring more effective conservation of marine areas that until then fell under the regime of the high seas. Chile, Ecuador and Peru, proposed the so-called theory of biological unity to justify claims of sovereign jurisdiction over large areas of what was then high seas, and adopted a Declaration through which they claimed under their 'exclusive sovereignty and jurisdiction … the sea along the coasts of their respective countries to a minimum distance of 200 nautical miles from these coasts'.[118] These claims were explained on the basis that there exists a 'perfect unity and interdependence … between the communities that live in the sea, which supports their life, and the coastal population which requires both to survive'.[119]

---

Truman Proclamation on the Continental Shelf'. For a critical history of the scramble for the territorialization of the continental shelf and the appropriation of the resources therein, as well as the role of legal scholars and their legal arguments, see Ranganathan (n 110).

116 Proclamation No. 2667, 'Policy of the United States with Respect to the Natural Resources of the Subsoil and Sea Bed of the Continental Shelf' (28 September 1945) available at <www.trumanlibrary.gov/library/proclamations/2667/policy-united-states-respect-natural-resources-subsoil-and-sea-bed> accessed 30 July 2021.

117 Proclamation No. 2668, 'Policy of the United States with Respect to Coastal Fisheries in Certain Areas of the High Seas' (28 September 1945) available at <www.trumanlibrary.gov/library/proclamations/2668/policy-united-states-respect-coastal-fisheries-certain-areas-high-seas-1> accessed 30 July 2021.

118 Declaration on the maritime zone (signed and entered into force 18 August 1952) 1006 UNTS 325, para II.

119 C.E.P. memorandum, as quoted in US Department of States, *Santiago Negotiations on Fishery Conservation Problems* among Chile, Ecuador, Peru, and the United States, Santiago, Chile, 14 September–5 October 1955, US Doc 8, 36, 'Comments on the proposal of Chile, Ecuador and Peru' (26 September 1955) retrieved from <https://books.google.no/books?id=BJpOAAAAMAAJ&printsec=frontcover&hl=no#v=onepage&q&f=false> accessed 30 July 2021.

These attempts were eventually accepted and later cemented through the maritime zoning regime enshrined in LOSC.[120] And while not susceptible of visible physical markings and material incisions, LOSC effectively and legally delineated the seas as if it were land (albeit with some important modulations, as we shall see later). The sea is now largely fragmented and ordered both vertically and horizontally. The sovereign spatial ordering of the Earth has thus extended its reach to sea by way of territorial thinking and telluric decisions that reflect the sovereign logic that Schmitt saw as largely foreign to the oceanic domain. Law, as a sovereign command, acts as a material force that integrates and disintegrates both land and sea in its incessant compulsion to assert its fundamental spatial ordering, to establish perimeters, boundaries, delimitations, borders, thresholds. However, the second transformation in the process of territorialization of the sea – from space to territory – has remained incomplete, as the sea has resisted this compulsion to territorialize, has opposed its living and lived materialities to the abstracting effect of modern geometric legality, has been a recalcitrant place revolting against its transformation into territory. Thus, sovereignty at sea has remained incomplete, uncertain, ambiguous fragmented in practice despite its conceptual unity, so that we can perhaps only speak of *gradients* of sovereignty.[121]

## 6 Recalcitrant Sea, Gradients of Sovereignty

It is the very zonal architecture of the LOSC that immediately offers a snapshot of a graded intensity of the territorialization of the sea, both at the level of the water column, where we find internal waters, the territorial sea, the EEZ and the high seas and at the level of the underlying ocean floor and subsoil, where we find submerged territory, continental shelf, and the Area. Sovereignty moves through these maritime zones and as its distance increases from its telluric fulcrum, its force dissipates and its reach diminishes. Yet even where sovereignty does not reach, it operates through its absence, by defining *ocean* commons as those spaces that lies *outside* of national jurisdiction, that is, outside of the reach of sovereignty, in any of its positive forms: *dominium*,

120 See for example Henriksen (ch 4) in this volume.

121 On land, boundaries are arguably certain, and the key uncertainties reflect competing claims – though of course at the sociological level there are many areas where sovereignty is thin, not enforced in many respects etc. Maybe this distinction between land and sea boundaries could be further discussed, with the view of challenging the peculiar position of the sea, but such discussion exceeds the scope of this chapter.

*imperium, jurisdictio*. For example, while *dominium* has for large part of the history of the law of the sea been resisted, especially due to the Grotian argument that sea waves cannot be marked or bound, jurisdiction has progressed more easily, whether creeping or not, individually or collectively.[122]

The key necessary to unlock the logic at play is that sovereignty as a logic should be read as disjointed from its concrete manifestations. The latter may be only partial, incomplete or truncated, and only manifest one of its three central elements, *dominium, imperium* and *jurisdictio*, yet its conceptual logic remains operational.[123] Now, this fragmentation of sovereignty's characters however, also illustrates the plasticity of sovereignty to adapt and adjust as it unfolds on the material world and accommodates resistant and recalcitrant oceanic materialities, such as its mobility and its liquidity.[124]

Scholars have attempted to capture these *gradients* of sovereignty at sea through framings such as 'liquid entitlements' or 'terraqueous territory'. However, these are all different ways to capture the same phenomenon: how sovereign legality subsumes the sea and engulfs it under the general principle that 'land dominates the sea'.[125] This principle manifests precisely a telluric projection that remains fundamental for the territorialization of the sea and is the basis of each 'encroachment on maritime expanses'.[126] These framings try to capture variable inflections of the territorializing template, of the territorial thinking and of the telluric logic that project sovereign legality onto the sea. These framings offer, however, also ways to recognize and theoretically organize the instability of this subsumption, a subsumption always inevitably exhibiting an excess that could not be fully integrated in the paradigm of telluric sovereign control.[127] These framings, or ways to try and understand the

122 On multilateral creeping jurisdiction see for example Molenaar (n 31).

123 See in this respect Karen T Liftin, 'The Greening of Sovereignty. An Introduction' in Liftin (n 70), who unpacks sovereignty in its constitutive elements – control, autonomy, authority – and argues that in current international environmental context, some aspects may be reasserted while others are weakened.

124 On this see eg, Peters and Steinberg (n 9).

125 See eg, *Fisheries Case (UK v Norway)* [1951] ICJ Reports 1951, 116 (133): 'It is the land which confers upon the coastal State a right to the waters off its coasts'. This was later reiterated in the *North Sea Continental Shelf case* [1969] (Judgment) ICJ Reports 1969, 3, para 96: '… the land is the legal source of the power which a State may exercise over territorial extensions to seaward'.

126 ibid.

127 It must be however noted how this mobility, or liquidity, this volumetric perception of space obtains also on land, thus perhaps negating or at least reducing the specific 'difference' of the ocean – borders on land are not etched except there where human transport routes intersect them – but in jungles, forests, mountains there are markers, but not

articulation of sovereignty and ambiguous and incomplete processes of territorialization at sea exceed and move significantly past Schmitt's idea of sea appropriations, yet they also appear to miss the common sovereign, territorializing logic fueling these incomplete subsumption.

The first of these framings is the notion of *liquid entitlement* articulated by Constantinou and Hadjimichael.[128] Liquid entitlement reflect 'a less formal understanding and more graduated, flexible management of sovereignty',[129] which the authors in turn link to 'liquid authority' in international law. Here the authors considers this flexibility to be one element of 'informal governance structures and arrangements ... and regime complexity'.[130] Here the key consideration for the purposes of this chapter is probably that this liquid entitlement refracts at the level of law and governance the liquid materiality of the oceans. Yet this illustrates, in the view of the present author, the plasticity of sovereign legality rather than being a hinder to its full unfolding at sea. This consideration is indeed further corroborated by the historical unfolding of the processes of territorialization outlined briefly above, which show how sovereignty manifests concretely as a function of the interactions, combinations and shifts of knowledge and technology and how they can underpin and facilitate – or by contrast delay – the unfolding of power.

The second framing is that of *terraqueous territoriality*. This framing emphasizes the *continuity* (as opposed to the hierarchy) between land and sea from the perspective of capitalist accumulation. Terraqueous territoriality, importantly, refers to a 'distinctly capitalist articulation of sovereignty, territory and appropriation in the capture and coding of maritime space',[131] and reflects 'capital's attempt at transcending the land-sea distinction, working on the assumption that, while there are irreducible material properties attached to land and sea, these change in time and place'.[132] Indeed, Campling and Colás suggests that it is '[c]apital accumulation [that] seeks to territorialise the sea through forms of sovereignty and modes of appropriation drawn from experiences on land'. However, the authors observe how in so doing, sovereign legality 'encounters particular tensions thereby generating distinctive spatial effects',[133] which, in

continuous lines – except in key spatial intersections that intend to wall off intrusions, migrations and the common social porosity of lands.

128 Constantinou and Hadjimichael (n 10).

129 ibid 6.

130 ibid.

131 Campling, and Colás (n 11) 777.

132 ibid.

133 ibid 776.

turn, give rise to this terraqueous territoriality, a hybrid form of sovereign control that reflects and is resisted by the mobilities, liquidity and materialities of the ocean.[134]

LOSC is identified in this respect as a crucial step for the construction of this terraqueous territoriality, and for articulating a series of liquid entitlements through specialized spatial regimes such as the EEZ, the archipelagic State regime, the concept of islands, and the continental shelf,[135] each of which operates on the basis of adjacency to project territorial thinking and practice onto the sea.[136] The archipelagic regime in particular is illustrative of the transformational effects of sovereign legality on ocean spaces, whereby large tracts of sea are 'internalized' so that archipelagic waters come to constitute the largest share of the sovereign territory of such 'ocean states'.[137] The EEZ is similarly identified by Campling and Colás as 'emblematic' of a terraqueous territoriality reflecting a capitalist coding of the sea, 'in that it incorporates sovereignty (exclusive), appropriation (economic) and territory (zone) in its very title'.[138]

Each of these partial unfoldings of sovereignty, however, are projections of the same territorializing logic, and emanate from the fundamental notion of adjacency, thus further vindicating the general principle that land dominates the sea. The example of the archipelagic State regime, while peculiar in that land and water form a unitary territory, offers nonetheless (or perhaps precisely because of that peculiarity) a significant illustration of the argument proposed earlier that the concept of territory as a political technology is fully applicable with regards to both land and sea, and of how thus sovereign legality extends with the same ease to land and sea.

134 However, see also Paul Foley and Charles Mather, 'Ocean grabbing, terraqueous territoriality and social development' (2019) 7(3) Territory, Politics, Governance 297, in which they give the notion of terraqueous territoriality but given it distinct normative inflections, with the view in the first instance to articulate a normative argument to support the idea that people living on land contiguous to marine resources ought to have priority in developing these resources, claims that can be captured with the notion of adjacency rights.

135 Constantinou and Hadjimichael (n 10) 8ff.

136 Although the archipelagic State regime defines and archipelago as an 'group of islands, including parts of islands, interconnecting waters and other natural features which are so closely interrelated that such islands, waters and other natural features form', LOSC art 46.

137 Constantinou and Hadjimichael (n 10) 8, citing Mohamed Munavvar, *Ocean States: Archipelagic Regimes in the Law of the Sea* (Martinus Nijhoff 1995). See also John G Butcher and R E Elson, *Sovereignty and the Sea: How Indonesia Became an Archipelagic State* (NUS Press 2017).

138 Campling and Colás (n 11) 780.

## 7 Reimagining Ocean Commons: Towards an 'Ethological' Nomos?

This underlying logic of sovereign spatiality has always made it difficult for international law to engage with the materiality of the oceans, outside of the mere adaptation to the 'imperviousness'[139] of the sea to law. This territorial, sovereign *nomos* of the sea, however, is not ineluctable and inevitable. It may rather be only one trajectory among many possible. As Schmitt himself muses in his book Land and Sea, humans may not merely be land-dwellers; humans may also harbor a sea perspective that would inevitably lead to a different understanding of space, a different anthropological point of view, indeed a different 'historical consciousness'.[140] And with a different historical consciousness comes a different *nomos*, a legal ordering of space – and of oceanic space in particular – that need not proceed from a sovereign logic. Here perhaps an 'ethological' inflection of *nomos*, as alluded to by Zartaloudis in his recent and comprehensive genealogy of *nomos*[141] may be useful. But I will return to this after having articulated a different conception of space, which is crucial for being able to re-imagine ocean commons.

When exploring space, and how law and space co-constitute each other in processes that involve various co-producing combinations of power and knowledge, and that have multiple implications for justice, it is important to have a rich understanding of spatial concepts. Sovereign legality articulates a spatial ordering that is primarily concentrated on constructing space in a linear, calculable cartographic manner in order to slice it in its sovereign components across surfaces that can be delineated and divided into neatly separated zones.[142] As explained above, this sovereign legality transforms place into space and space into territory through processes of territorialization that are singular and are not able, or willing, to imagine space as plural and multidimensional, notwithstanding the gradients of sovereignty discussed above. These processes, and the sovereign legality that underpins them, only subject space to rationalizations across horizontal and vertical boundaries, in a zonal matrix that moves seaward from land and from surface water through the water column to the ocean floor. There are other, more fruitful ways to think about space, however.

139 Schmitt, *Nomos of the Earth* (n 39) 181.
140 Schmitt, *Land and Sea* (n 56) 47.
141 Zartaloudis (n 12).
142 Despite problems such as ambulatory baselines etc. which again point to the need for sovereign to be plastic and adapt to the mobility of the oceans.

Geographer Doreen Massey offers in this respect a rich understanding of space as dynamic, simultaneous and storied. Space, for Massey, is not, as indeed for sovereign spatiality, a static set of coordinates as represented in/by maps, nor 'the sphere … of a discrete multiplicity of inert *things*'.[143] Space is rather constituted by heterogenous practices and processes, is the 'sphere of a dynamic simultaneity'.[144] In this sense, space is not an already-interconnected whole', but is rather the result of ongoing, dynamic, mobile, changing interconnections.[145] Space is thus, for Massey, constantly incomplete, made and remade through new interconnections, new arrivals, new relations, and as such remains inevitably 'unfinished' and 'undetermined'.[146] Space is a mobile category made of 'loose ends and ongoing stories'.[147] Cartography, through its flat and static understanding of space, can never represent this mobile, incomplete, unfinished world. Yet, cartographic space is crucial for sovereign legality, which needs and produces a spatial order that articulates claims of 'singularity, stability and closure',[148] as such simultaneously reflecting a cartographic understanding of space *and* contributing to the constitution and enforcement of such cartographic space as well as of the imaginary that sustains it.

Massey emphasizes both how space is storied, and the plurality and temporal simultaneity of such stories, so that she characterizes space as a 'simultaneity of stories'.[149] This narrative, dynamic, plural and simultaneous nature of space, points then to an understanding of space that also underpins the notion of place, offering a conceptual counter-move that mirrors and resists the territorializing transformation of place into space and then into territory and may be mobilized for the re-imagination of ocean commons. If space is a simultaneity of stories, place, for Massey, is a '*spatio-temporal event*',[150] where stories are constantly actualized, produced and reproduced, entered into and into relations with. The notion of spatio-temporal event seeks to indicate how space and time cannot be delineated and must be understood *together*. It also indicates how space has histories and is thus not a temporally static or fixed object. Human activities as well as the law that regulates them, are thus elements of a multifaceted set of stories, processes and practices that constitute

143 Massey (n 5) 107.
144 ibid.
145 ibid.
146 ibid.
147 ibid.
148 ibid 109.
149 ibid 130.
150 ibid (emphasis in the original).

space. Space is, thus, 'deep'.[151] As such, each story, process and practice must be situated *within* such spatial simultaneities and the spatio-temporal events they contribute to constituting, rather than *outside* of them, as interventions that seek to impose a sovereign spatial ordering on a 'blank space'[152] so as to *fix* that which is mobile, so as to determine that which is undetermined, and so as to separate that which can only be understood together.

This richer understanding of space and place asks many questions of law and to law, as it opens opportunities for thinking other spatial imaginaries that, in turn, may underpin other constructions and other legal framing of ocean commons. Indeed, whose commons do we speak about, when we attempt to rearticulate commons as places, as spatio-temporal events and not a merely cartographic spatial domains falling within the various articulations of sovereign legality, or outside of it? Whose voices and stories become relevant? How many places can exist within the same spatial coordinates? Are the stories of marine life less relevant for law than the human stories that contribute to a specific human spatialization of the oceans?[153] And can or should law try to capture any or all of them? How many legalities can we imagine or discover in the ocean commons? What legalities or inter-legalities are possible to imagine and articulate in oceanic spaces that are no longer only *dimensional* and where their only content is surfaces to cross and resources to extract,[154] but places that are inhabited, storied, and alive?

While these are all difficult questions, they are all relevant in the context of the BBNJ negotiations, which are likely to have significant implications for the governance of ocean commons. It may be thus possible to open for a reconsideration of the meaning of space, trying to unravel the processes of transformation of place into territory, with the view of disarticulating the neat separation between geometric space and the matter contained within that space. This is a move to displace sovereign spatiality, which is linear, calculable, analytical and

151 Recognizing the depth of space is a move that Steinberg and Peters make to further problematize the cartographic space, even as attempts have been made to challenge its 'horizontalism' through 'opening up a vertical world of volume', Steinberg and Peters (n 9) 247.

152 Massey (n 5) 121–23, where she speaks of writing (referring to the 'scriptural economy' that emerged at the time of the discovery) as that activity that is able to construct on a *blank space* (the page) 'a text that has power over the exteriority from which it has been first been isolated' (at 122).

153 On this see, for example, Poto (ch 6) in this volume; Vito De Lucia, 'Ocean Commons, Law of the Sea and Rights *for* the Sea' (2019) 23(1) Canadian Journal of Law and Jurisprudence 45.

154 See eg Philip Steinberg, *The Social Construction of the Ocean* (Cambridge University Press 2011).

abstract. It also exceeds the understanding of space as merely interconnected (interfacing with air and land, and through ocean connectivity[155]), insofar as interconnections needs to be understood dynamically and as constantly produced and reproduced through stories. This dynamic, mobile, multidimensional, material, storied vision of space problematizes thus the cartographic legal production of ocean space which territorializes the seas through sovereign delineations and maritime zoning. Sovereign knowledge, as well, reflects this perspective, as even ecological knowledge will remain cartographic if all it contributes is a different spatial delineation: from political boundaries to ecosystem boundaries. A different spatial perspective that emphasizes the simultaneities and the plurality of stories that constitute space resists the terrestrial and territorial 'ontology of bounded zones and emplaced points of power and knowledge'.[156]

Here we can return to the idea of an 'ethological' *nomos*. Zartaloudis suggests that the spatial ordering articulated through the notion of *nomos* was often 'ethological'.[157] This ethological inflection of *nomos* indicates how spatial orderings reflect a practice that is a way of being or of doing things, one crucially chiming with an understanding of space as storied and with an understanding of place as a spatio-temporal event. Thus, the co-constitution of space and law, far from reflecting a uniform sovereign legality, is also multistoried and reflective of a multiplicity of practices, processes, agencies, materialities and stories. This is perhaps not far from Schmitt's critical analysis of the global linear thinking that underpinned the apprehension of the entire globe within sovereign spatiality with the discovery and the onset of modernity. *Nomos* is perhaps to be reimagined as plural and localized, as 'only valid in (and only because of) a particular situation or milieu'.[158] Sovereign legality perhaps has already encountered such material barriers and has had to adapt to them through liquid forms of entitlements or terraqueous articulations that could never fully enthrall oceanic spaces and places as territory. Yet its tendency, its aspiration remains underpinned and fueled by the constant tension towards such territorialization.

155 See on this eg Ekaterina Popova and others, 'Ecological connectivity between the areas beyond national jurisdiction and coastal waters: Safeguarding interests of coastal communities in developing countries' (2019) 104 Marine Policy 90.

156 Steinberg and Peters (n 9) 253.

157 Zartaloudis (n 12) xxxvii. On the role of ethos for the re-imagination of law see also Vito De Lucia, 'Thinking Law, Ecology, and the Commons' in Anna Grear, and David Bollier (eds), *The Great Awakening: New Modes of Life amidst Capitalist Ruins* (Punctum Book 2020).

158 Zartaloudis (n 12) xxxv.

One possibility to reimagine ocean commons perhaps rests on learning and listening to the oceans. As Zartaloudis observes, in fact, an ethological inflection of *nomos* does not align with volitional legality (which reflects and is expressed by the sovereign command), but rather with a diffuse legality that captures an 'objective' normativity (as Zartaloudis calls it, to distinguish it from the subjective normativity arising from the will), that is, a normativity *of* and *in* the thing.[159] As such, space, far from its flattened representation that sovereign legality offers and imposes on it, could be understood as an enabler of a legality that is commensurate with its voices, materialites and agencies.[160] The problematic spatial delineations that still underpin the BBNJ negotiations offer an opportunity for drawing out some implications that arise from such considerations. Hydrothermal vents offer a useful example. Hydrothermal vents are key yet problematic ecosystems in the context of the topic of MGRs, as they trespass maritime zones and elude neat delineations. Hydrothermal vents indeed inhabit multiple worlds: the water column, the seabed and the subsoil; the living and the non-living; the fluid and the solid. They occupy multiple spatialities, are constituted by a multiplicity of stories and traverse multiple temporalities. Their complexity is difficult to grasp for sovereign legality, whose focus remains on questions such as to which maritime zone they belong, to which domain (the living or the non-living) and thus, consequently, which legal regime is applicable.[161]

Another option would be though to consider them as one of the storied materialities that law needs to listen to in order to understand how their contribution to a particular, unique spatial order is co-constitutive of law, rather than being merely a recipient of sovereign legality that ignores their peculiar materiality.

This sensibility for a normativity that inhabits things and reflects their materialities undoubtedly recalls ancient philosophies of natural law[162] or

159 ibid.

160 See Poto (ch 6) in this volume, for some arguments in this direction.

161 See eg Joanna Mossop, 'Towards a Practical Approach to Regulating Marine Genetic Resources' (2019) 8(3) ESIL Reflections. It may be useful to note that some of the complex questions being discussed might to some extent be addressed with sufficient political will. However, and this is one of the central points raised here, there exist arguably some fundamental limitations that cannot be undone by political will, as some of these complexities arguably require a significant shift in the fundamental logic and spatio-legal imagination of the law of the sea.

162 By utilizing the adjective ancient I intend to refer specifically to the Roman theories of natural law, rather than the modern natural law theories that underpinned, for example Grotius' legal thinking. See on this difference De Lucia, 'Right *for* the Sea' (n 153) 45; Vito

indigenous cosmologies, and I have articulated elsewhere some ways in which such approaches to law may offer useful ways to alter the conversation on how law and oceans may co-constitute each other.[163] The legal categories that underpin and delineate the commons, such as *res communes omnium*, could be rethought, by way of re-activating some of their forgotten semantic field,[164] in ways that would also enlarge the scope of relevant stories, and would contribute towards an operationalization of such different spatial imagination. Ocean commons would then reflect different ways to imagine space, thus traversing existing jurisdictional boundaries and existing both *within* and *outside* current sovereign spaces. Their governance would require significantly different and more transversally cooperative mechanisms (such as those that have been discussed in terms of 'post-sovereign environmental governance')[165] that would also reflect the depth and the storied nature of space, as well as the multitude of voices and of perspectives for/from which oceans are commons.

This diffuse normativity further resonates with some of the voices that have raised similar questions in the context of the ongoing BBNJ negotiations. Oceanic ontologies such as those of Pacific islanders reflect in fact a world that is not telluric, but liquid, where the sea engulfs and dominates the sparse parcels of emerged land; and it connects, creates relationships.[166] Yet thinking a novel *nomos* of the sea entails imagining a different legality, one that embraces precisely those aspects of oceanic materialities that are *problematic* for sovereign legality. The goal is however not of delineating a space of freedom that, albeit with the many limitations of contemporary law of the sea, remains premised on the key dichotomies such as state of nature/sovereign legality that, still responding to the political and legal imaginary paradigmatically articulated by Thomas Hobbes, was radically implemented at the time of the amity lines. An ethological *nomos* of the sea must reflect a transient emergence of spatial assemblages which are mobile, unstable, the result of practices enacted by a multiplicity of agencies, that shift in time and space through ocean mobilities. These oceanic spaces are temporary, contingent sites that offer themselves as spaces and places only through the practices and processes

---

De Lucia, 'Rethinking the Encounter Between Law and Nature in the Anthropocene: From Biopolitical Sovereignty to Wonder' (2020) 31(3) Law and Critique 329.

163 De Lucia, 'Right *for* the Sea' (n 159).

164 ibid.

165 Bradley Karkkainen, 'Post-Sovereign Environmental Governance' (2004) 4(1) Global Environmental Politics 72.

166 Juniper Ellis and Epeli Hau'ofa, 'A New Oceania: An Interview with Epeli Hau'ofa' (June 2001) 15(1) Antipodes 22.

that inhabit them, through the stories that enliven them, and as such strain the capacity of sovereign legality to adapt to their continuous fluctuations.

This in turn may mean moving past the distinction between ocean commons and ocean spaces under national jurisdiction, as the notion of commons exceeds greatly the notion of delineated spaces that remain outside of sovereign control. All spaces are co-constituted, all are commons insofar as they are the result of a multiplicity of practices, processes, stories contributing to their co-constitution and offering emergent legalities.

## 8 Conclusions

This chapter has endeavored to problematize sovereign legality and its cartographic understanding and construction of space, with the view of re-imagining the idea of ocean commons. This cartographic understanding of ocean commons, I suggested, reflects and refracts a fundamental spatio-legal ordering, a *nomos*, that proceeds from what I have described as 'territorial thinking'. Law of the sea is permeated by such territorial thinking, and indeed has developed through increasing incursions and projections of territorial sovereignty into oceanic spaces. Thus, sovereignty has been all along the arbiter of the commons, it has been the crucial lens for deciding what the commons are (spaces outside of sovereignty) and where they are (beyond the limits of sovereign space). The sovereign *nomos* has in other words *always* negatively defined the commons through its absence: all those areas that fall outside of the scope of sovereign power are, thus, common. Sovereign legality has however also *always* moved to encroach on ocean commons, though what I have called processes of territorialization, which have been cemented with the adoption and entry into force of LOSC and its maritime zoning of the oceans.

Despite these effective processes of territorialization however, the sea has arguably *always* resisted the ability of sovereign power to encroach upon it in a fully territorial manner due to the particular materialities of sea water and oceanic spaces. These particular materialities have led commentators to speak of terraqueous sovereignty or liquid entitlements, to signify variably the mobile, legally nuanced, flexible and limited purchase of sovereignty and of sovereign power over oceanic spaces. This recalcitrance of the sea has opened up other ways to think space that might unsettle such telluric sovereign legality and the cartographic spatiality it rests on. The underlying logic of sovereign spaces has indeed always made it difficult for international law to engage with the materiality of the oceans. Yet sovereign legality is not ineluctable and inevitable. It may rather be only one trajectory among many possible. This chapter has offered initial reflections on alternative trajectories, with the view of opening the conversation at a time where a new global treaty is being negotiated that may further strengthen sovereign legality precisely in those ABNJ that, together, constitute today ocean commons. But if ocean space is connected, storied, multiple, layered and complex, if space is co-produced by a multiplicity of agencies, what do we speak about when we speak of ocean commons?

CHAPTER 3

# The Nature of Legal Relations between States and the Proposed BBNJ Agreement

*Nigel Bankes*

## 1 Introduction*

This chapter explores the application of Hohfeld's ideas of fundamental legal concepts to the Law of the Sea Convention (LOSC)[1] and to the proposed agreement under the United Nations Convention on the Law of the Sea on the conservation and sustainable use of marine biological diversity of areas beyond national jurisdiction (ABNJ) (hereafter revised draft Agreement).[2] The chapter first provides an outline of Hohfeld's ideas of fundamental legal concepts and the relationships between them. Second, it addresses the question of whether a theory that was principally developed to consider legal relations in the context of domestic private law, and in the context of judicial reasoning has, or should have, any purchase in the context of public international law. Third, the chapter provides some examples of how the application of Hohfeld's ideas of fundamental legal concepts and the relationships between them offers insights with respect to the interpretation and application of the LOSC. Finally, the chapter offers a Hohfeldian reading of some elements of the revised draft Agreement.

---

* I would like to thank Jonnette Watson Hamilton, Julia Gaunce, Erik J Molenaar and the editors of this volume for their comments on drafts of this chapter.

1 United Nations Convention on the Law of the Sea Law (signed 10 December 1982, entered into force 16 November 1994) 1833 UNTS 3 (LOSC).

2 Revised draft text of an agreement under the United Nations Convention on the Law of the Sea on the conservation and sustainable use of marine biological diversity of areas beyond national jurisdiction, 18 November 2019, UN Doc A/CONF.232/2020/3. The Intergovernmental Conference to consider the draft text was due to re-convene for its fourth session from 23 March 2020 to 3 April 2020 but it has been postponed in light of the COVID-19 pandemic. A programme of intersessional work continues available at <www.un.org/bbnj/sites/www.un.org.bbnj/files/bbnj_intersessional_programmeofwork_final.pdf> accessed 3 May 2021.

 | DOI:10.1163/9789004506367_004

## 2 Hohfeld's Ideas of Fundamental Legal Concepts and the Relationships between Them

Hohfeld wrote about fundamental legal concepts and the relationships between them at the beginning of the twentieth century.[3] He was part of a school of legal philosophy known as analytical jurisprudence which aimed 'to express clearly the formal concepts used by judges and lawyers in legal reasoning'.[4] 'Hohfeld's general strategy' as noted by Pierre Schlag 'was to describe these basic legal conceptions as relations of legal form – that is to say, stripped so far as possible of substantive content'.[5] Hohfeld gives us a methodological approach rather than a specific normative or doctrinal content; he tells us '*how* to think, not *what* to think',[6] but he also (and this may be particularly important when we are inventing or negotiating a new regime) helps reveal 'worlds of legal possibilities, of choices to be made in fashioning legal regimes, that we would otherwise pass by'.[7] His work emphasizes that law is fundamentally concerned with legal relationships and not with physical objects or geography. To offer an example from the law of the sea, the exclusive economic zone (EEZ) is a geographical zone that, if proclaimed, extends up to 200 nm from the baselines from which the breadth of the territorial sea is measured, but as lawyers we are interested in the legal relationships between the coastal State and other legal actors within that space, or more specifically the bundle of rights, duties, powers, liberties, liabilities and immunities that structure the relationship between the coastal State and those other actors.

Hohfeld's starting position was that the word 'right' is misused and overused and that it is a gross over-simplification to reduce legal relations between parties to the dichotomy of rights and duties (or obligations).[8] He suggested that it should be possible to obtain greater analytical clarity were we to adopt more precise descriptors of different entitlements and legal relationships. His focus was very practical.[9] In particular, he observed that the word right was often

3 His most famous article is Wesley Newcomb Hohfeld, 'Some Fundamental Conceptions as Applied in Judicial Reasoning' (1913) 23 Yale Law Journal 16.

4 Joseph Singer, 'The Legal Rights Debate in Analytical Jurisprudence from Bentham to Hohfeld' (1982) Wisconsin Law Review 975, 984.

5 Pierre Schlag, 'How to do things with Hohfeld' (2015) 78 Law and Contemporary Social Problems 185, 188.

6 ibid 189.

7 ibid 192.

8 Hohfeld (n 3) 28.

9 Andrew Halpin, 'Hohfeld and Rules' in Shyam Balganesh, Ted Sichelman and Henry Smith (eds), *The Legacy of Wesley Hohfeld: Edited Major Works, Select Personal Papers, And Original Commentaries* (Cambridge University Press 2018).

used to include three other types of legal entitlements, specifically a power, an immunity or a privilege, and that in each case it was possible to identify the opposite of such an entitlement: no-right, duty, disability and liability.[10]

Hohfeld would have us reserve the term 'right' for a claim, enforceable by the state, that another person has a duty to act in a certain way.[11] A power is the ability of a party to change a legal entitlement of another. A privilege (many subsequent commentators have substituted the term 'liberty' for privilege[12]) is the freedom to engage in a particular activity without committing a wrong, and an immunity is the security from having one's entitlement changed by another.[13] It is characteristic of both international law and domestic law that legal liberties are rarely codified or stated since they exist within the interstices of other more positive norms.[14]

Having identified these legal concepts, Hohfeld then expressed them in the form of two tables: one signalling jural opposites (or contradictories[15]) and the other a set of jural correlatives. The concept of jural opposites is designed to capture the idea that a legal actor must have one or other of the two opposites but cannot have both at the same time. For example, a person cannot have both a liberty to do something (or not) and a duty to do that thing. A correlative captures the nature of a legal relationship from the perspective of the two different parties to the relationship. For example, if A has a right, B has a duty. 'The expressions are equivalent'.[16] The two tables are as follows:

Most commentators have focused attention on the insights revealed by the concept of correlatives. It is easiest to explain the idea of correlatives with some examples. For each of the four sets of correlatives I provide three

---

10 Hohfeld (n 3) 30.

11 Some refer to this strong form of right as a claim-right insofar as the party with the right has a claim against the party owing the duty. See eg, Jeremy Waldron, 'Introduction' in Jeremy Waldron (ed), *Theories of Rights* (Oxford University Press 1984) 6. See also Henry Shue, *Basic Rights: Subsistence, Affluence and US Foreign Policy* (2nd edn, Princeton University Press 1996) 14–15.

12 See Glanville Williams, 'The Concept of a Legal Liberty' (1956) 56 Colorado Law Review 1129, 1131.

13 Singer (n 4) 986. This paragraph draws on Singer's admirable summary of the 'primary legal entitlements'.

14 Williams (n 12) 1130, '[m]ost legal liberties are not to be found stated in law books, because there is generally no point in making these negative statements … there is no entry of "breakfast, liberty to eat" in the index to the *Corpus Iuris*'. The classic international law statement of this proposition is the *SS 'Lotus'* [1927] PCIJ Series A No 1, 18.

15 See Williams (n 12) 1135, they 'can better be called contradictories, because taken together they exhaust the relevant field of discourse'.

16 Singer (n 4) 987.

TABLE 3.1 Jural opposites

| | | | |
|---|---|---|---|
| Right | Privilege (Liberty) | Power | Immunity |
| No-right | Duty | Disability | Liability |

TABLE 3.2 Jural correlatives

| | | | |
|---|---|---|---|
| Right | Privilege (Liberty) | Power | Immunity |
| Duty | No-right | Liability | Disability |

HOHFELD (N 3) 30.

examples: one example drawn from domestic law, one example drawn from the terms of a bilateral treaty (the Columbia River Treaty (CRT) between the United States and Canada),[17] and one example drawn from the LOSC.[18]

***Right/Duty***

A1. If Y owes X a sum of money, one can say that X has a right to payment and that Y has a duty to pay.

A2. Under the CRT, Canada has a duty to build and operate the treaty dams and the United States has a right to have those dams built and operated in accordance with the terms of flood control and operating plans.[19]

A3. Ships of all States have a right of innocent passage through the territorial sea of the coastal State.[20] The coastal State has a duty not to hamper that passage.[21]

17 Treaty between Canada and the United States of America relating to Cooperative Development of the Water Resources of The Columbia River Basin (signed 17 January 1961, entered into force 16 September 1964) 587 UNTS 19 (CRT).

18 I have chosen to provide these three types of examples both to illustrate the potentially broad application of Hohfeld's idea but also to move Hohfeld's ideas from the familiar territory of domestic law (principally private law), through to a bilateral, synallagmatic treaty relationship and then to a more complex multilateral treaty context, thus anticipating to some degree the discussion in part 3 of the relevance of Hohfeld for international law.

19 CRT arts II and IV.

20 LOSC art 17.

21 LOSC art 24(1).

***Liberty/No-right***

B1. If the domestic law of the State does not restrict the emission of carbon dioxide, then one can say that X Co has a liberty to emit carbon dioxide and that Y (and all other persons) has no right that X Co cease emitting carbon dioxide. Put another way, X Co commits no wrong in continuing to emit carbon dioxide. It is also the case that Y and all other persons equally enjoy the liberty to emit carbon dioxide.

B2. Under the CRT, each party is free to divert water for consumptive use from the Columbia River without requiring the consent of the other.[22] The other party to the treaty has a no-right to stop the diversion.

B3. The ships of all States enjoy, inter alia, freedom of fishing (subject to conditions) in the high seas.[23] Putting aside the matter of conditions that may have to be satisfied before the freedom may be exercised (and such conditions may be very extensive and create right/duty relationships[24]), it follows that every other State has a no-right to interfere with that freedom (and equally, all may exercise that same freedom).

Examples B1 and B3 both demonstrate that the liberty/no-right correlative relationship describes the typical structure of an open access commons and thus that a liberty exercised by one may cause harm to another with no avenue of recourse.[25] If Z1 and Z2 both have an equal freedom to harvest the resource and a no-right to prevent the other from engaging in that harvest – *unless there is some other relevant norm governing the relationship between those parties* – there is an open access commons. An open access commons ceases to be open access when duties (ie conditions or pre-conditions to access) erode or ultimately replace the original liberty or freedom.[26]

22 CRT art XIII.

23 LOSC art 87.

24 The Fish Stocks Agreement significantly qualifies this freedom with respect to straddling and highly migratory fish stocks, see Agreement for the Implementation of the Provisions of the United Nations Convention on the Law of the Sea of 10 December 1982 relating to the Conservation and Management of Straddling Fish Stocks and Highly Migratory Fish Stocks (UNFSA) (signed 4 August 1995, entered into force 11 December 2001) 2167 UNTS 3. See also Michaela Young, 'Then and Now: Reappraising Freedom of the Seas in Modern Law of the Sea' (2016) 47(2) Ocean Development & International Law 165; Nguyen (this volume).

25 Or *damnum absque injuria*. See Singer (n 4) 994; Williams (n 12) 1143–44; and see Martti Koskenniemi, 'The Politics of International Law' (1990) 1 European Journal of International Law 1, 18–19.

26 See *Fisheries Jurisdiction (UK v Iceland)* (Merits, Judgment) [1974] ICJ Rep 3 [72] and *Fisheries Jurisdiction (Federal Republic of Germany v Iceland)* (Merits, Judgment) [1974] ICJ Rep 175 [64].

*Power/Liability*

C1. A legal power is the ability of X to change the nature of the legal relationship between X and Y (for better or for worse).[27] For example, if Y offers to sell a particular property to X, X has the power to accept that offer and create a binding contract between X and Y. Y experiences the liability to have the nature of its legal relationship changed.[28] Equally, in a domestic public law context, consider a permit that contains the clause 'subject to such additional conditions as the regulator may prescribe'. The regulator holds a power while the permittee has a liability.

C2. Under the CRT the United States has the legal power to direct Canada to operate additional non-treaty storage within Canada for flood control purposes. Canada has a liability with respect to the operation of the dams affected by this power.[29]

C3. The coastal State has the power to take necessary measures with respect to foreign flagged vessels to ensure compliance with its laws pertaining to the living resources of the EEZ. Foreign flagged vessels have a corresponding liability to the exercise by the coastal State of such measures including boarding, inspection and arrest.[30]

*Immunity/Disability*

D1. An immunity in favour of Y arises when X cannot exercise a power (ie X has a disability or no power[31]) in relation to Y. For example, in a federal state the property of a sub-unit of the federation may be immune from taxes levied by the other order of government.[32]

---

> It is one of the advances in maritime international law, resulting from the intensification of fishing, that the former *laissez-faire* treatment of the living resources of the sea in the high seas has been replaced by a recognition of a duty to have due regard to the rights of other States and the needs of conservation for the benefit of all.

27 It is clear that Hohfeld uses the term liability in a special sense since liability carries a negative connotation in most contexts. See Andrew Halpin, 'Rights, Duties, Liabilities and Hohfeld' (2007) 13 Legal Theory 23, 26.

28 Once a contract is created there will ordinarily be mutual correlative rights and obligations eg X's duty to complete the transfer (and Y's right to the benefit of the transfer) and Y's duty to tender the purchase monies and X's right to demand payment.

29 CRT art IV(2)(b).

30 LOSC art 73(1); *M/V 'Virginia G' Case* (*Panama v Guinea-Bissau*) (Judgment, 14 April 2014) ITLOS [256].

31 A disability is the opposite of a power in Hohfeld's statement of jural opposites.

32 See for example (Canada) *Constitution Act, 1867*, s 125: 'No Lands or Property belonging to Canada or any Province shall be liable to Taxation'.

D2. Under the CRT each party has an immunity from responsibility to the other to the extent that a delay in commencing operations is not wilful or reasonably avoidable.[33]

D3. Warships on the high seas have complete immunity from the power (jurisdiction) of any State other than the flag State. States other than the flag State have a disability (the absence of power) in relation to warships.[34]

It bears emphasizing that a single set of facts may give rise to multiple Hohfeldian relations between the same parties[35] or, as Schlag puts it, the different conceptions 'can be aggregated in a variety of ways into some greater whole as jural composites'.[36] For example, flag States have a due diligence obligation to ensure that their vessels do not fish in the EEZ of the coastal State except in accordance with the laws and regulations of the coastal State.[37] That vessel also has (as already noted) a liability corresponding to the power of the coastal State to take the necessary measures to ensure compliance with its laws pertaining to the living resources of the EEZ. This layered complexity may limit the utility of this analytical approach.[38] Indeed, some have criticized Hohfeld as being unduly reductionist. In response, Halpin reminds us that Hohfeld also emphasized the

33 CRT art XVII(4).

34 LOSC art 95 and similarly for government ships on non-commercial service, art 96.

35 Halpin, 'Rights, Duties' (n 27) 28 (and following Peter Jaffey, 'Duties and Liabilities in Private Law' (2006) 12 Legal Theory 137) offers a useful example drawing on *Vincent v Lake Erie* [1910] 109 Supreme Court of Minnesota 456, 124 NW 221, a vessel owes a duty not to use a private wharf; the same vessel has a liberty to use the wharf in the event of storm but has a duty to pay for any damage caused to the wharf. See also Williams (n 12) 1143. Philip Allott, 'Power Sharing in the Law of the Sea' (1983) 77 American Journal of International Law 1, 10 refers to the 'layering of legal relations'.

36 Schlag (n 5) 189 gives the example of the estate in fee simple or a corporation. Hohfeld might give the example of ownership (see Antony M Honore, 'Ownership' in A G Guest (ed), *Oxford Essay in Jurisprudence* (Oxford University Press 1961) describing 11 elements of ownership) while for the purposes of this essay we might use the example of sovereignty, as to which see Judge Jesus' dissenting opinion in *The M/V 'Louisa' Case* (*Saint Vincent and the Grenadines v Kingdom of Spain*) (Merits Judgement, 28 May 2013) ITLOS [41] noting that 'as a matter of practice, the sovereignty of the coastal State over its territorial sea is translated into rights, jurisdictions and freedoms it exercises daily'.

37 LOSC, art 62(4). See also *Request for an Advisory Opinion Submitted by the Sub-Regional Fisheries Commission* (2 April 2015) ITLOS (*IUU Fishing*), [105] and [123]. A coastal State has a right to have the flag State exercise that duty. See also the somewhat different explanation in the *South China Sea Award* (*Philippines v China*) (Award, 12 July 2016) PCA Case No 2013–19 [740]–[741] to the effect that LOSC art 62(4) imposes an obligation directly on private parties whereas the obligation of the State arises as a result of the duty of due regard under LOSC art 58(3).

38 Nicolas Bamforth, 'Hohfeldian Rights and Public Law' in Matthew Kramer (ed), *Rights, Wrongs and Responsibilities* (Springer 2001) 5.

importance of 'an aggregate-level analysis' and thus the importance of general statements rather than simply the articulation of '(innumerable) individual legal relations'.[39] Others might suggest that Hohfeldian analysis lacks any practical significance insofar as States and other actors routinely fail to distinguish different uses of the term 'right' in their actual practice. This is hardly surprising; the rhetorical appeal of the language of rights is extremely powerful and it is thus tempting to invoke the language of rights even if there is no correlative duty.[40] But in concrete cases it is the task of the court and the legal analyst to eschew the rhetoric and unpack the resulting legal relationships.[41]

## 3 Does Hohfeld's Analytical Framework Have Any Purchase in Public (International) Law?

Hohfeld developed his scheme principally with private law relationships in mind. This suggests the need to deal head-on with the question of whether Hohfeld's framework has any application to public law generally and to public international law specifically.

Private law relationships are often bilateral, synallagmatic relationships and it is easier to apply Hohfeld in such a context. It is certainly more complicated in public law. For example, in a judicial review case there is typically no straightforward right/duty correlative such as one sees in private law.[42] Standard of review/margin of appreciation issues as well as the discretionary nature of administrative law remedies may further complicate the application of Hohfeld.[43] Furthermore, public law is principally about controlling power (in the sense of jurisdiction) rather than about rights, and begins from a different starting point. Private law begins with the proposition that the individual

---

39 Halpin, 'Hohfeld and Rules' (n 9) 11.

40 For example, we often see phrases such as 'right of free speech', right of way' or 'right of self-defence' whereas each is more correctly labelled a liberty. The term 'right' is perhaps used 'because it conjures up the idea of something that can be insisted on': Williams (n 13) 1142. For examples in LOSC see the many references in Part V to 'sovereign rights' where the 'rights' are more correctly labelled powers. See also LOSC art 194.

41 For a concrete example of unpacking in the law of the sea context see Separate Opinion of Judge Ad Hoc Murphy in *M/T 'San Padre Pio'* (*Switzerland v Nigeria*) (Provisional Measures, 2019) ITLOS [25] observing that while provisional measures might be awarded to protect the rights of a State (LOSC art 290) there could be no provisional measures award to protect the duties or obligations of a State, even if a State in its pleadings might characterize those interests as 'rights'.

42 Bamforth (n 38) 12.

43 ibid 18–19.

is free to act unless that action causes harm to others. Domestic public law begins with the proposition that a decision maker has only the authority or power conferred by law.[44] International law reflects both ideas. It acknowledges the freedom to act absent some positive law restricting that freedom,[45] but it also contemplates limitations on sovereign power, albeit arising by consent and frequently in a negotiated bilateral or multilateral context.[46]

It is also important to acknowledge that private and public law may use different terminology to describe legal relationships. For example, public law (including public international law) will frequently use the term jurisdiction to connote the exercise of a power, whereas the term jurisdiction is unknown within private law. But, so long as we are open to these differences in terminology, Hohfeld may still offer insights. Thus, whether we describe the power of A to make new rules as the exercise of a power or the exercise of jurisdiction, the key point is that it creates a correlative liability for another legal actor (B); a relationship that is quite different from a right/duty relationship between A and B.

It may be particularly difficult to apply Hohfeld to a negotiated multilateral text where the parties have embraced constructive ambiguity and may have been reluctant to be precise about the nature of the protection afforded to a particular claim.[47] But constructive ambiguity is perhaps more likely to attach to a standard of behaviour rather than the correct characterization of a legal relationship. For example, LOSC adopts the open-textured term 'due regard' to mediate the relationships between coastal States and others within the EEZ. But while there may be lots of different possible interpretations of what due regard may require, the relationship between the coastal State and others is a true right/duty relationship.[48] Much the same may be said of the many occasions in which the LOSC establishes due diligence obligations of conduct; the nature of the legal relationship is clear even though the content of the obligation may be open-textured.[49]

---

44 ibid 15.

45 See *SS Lotus* (n 14).

46 John R Morss, 'The Legal Relations of Collectives: Belated Insights from Hohfeld' (2009) 22 Leiden Journal of International Law 289; *Advisory Opinion on the Threat or Use of Nuclear Weapons* [1996] ICJ 226.

47 Not all consider this to be unsurmountable obstacle. Allott (n 35) 5–8 clearly finds Hohfeld useful notwithstanding the 'invisible hand' of the consensus approach to negotiations.

48 LOSC arts 56(2) and 58(3). This is explored in more detail below.

49 See *Advisory Opinion, Responsibilities and Obligations of States sponsoring persons and entities with respect to activities in the Area* (February 1, 2011) ITLOS, Seabed Disputes Chamber (*Certain Activities*); *IUU Fishing* (n 37) and *South China Sea Award* (n 37). One example of deliberate ambiguity in characterizing the nature of the legal relationship in

While some of these objections may lead us to be cautious in applying Hohfeld to the public international law sphere, none are fatal. Even though public law may frequently be concerned with the proper exercise of power rather than claim-rights, that may only serve to confirm the value of Hohfeld's approach by causing us to focus on the power/liability relationship rather than a right/duty relationship. John Morss, in an essay subtitled 'Belated Insights from Hohfeld' develops this theme further[50] and encourages us to think about the full range of correlatives in the context of international law (specifically in that case, the protection of the rights of minorities). For example, he suggests that the right of self-determination 'might be more usefully considered a liberty rather than a (claim-) right'.[51]

Bilateral treaties often exhibit a synallagmatic structure and the examples above from the Columbia River Treaty confirm that it is fairly easy to apply Hohfeld in such a context. But even in the context of multilateral treaties such as the LOSC, the draft Articles of the International Law Commission on State Responsibility make it clear that a State may invoke the responsibility of another State if an obligation is owed to that State individually or to 'a group of States including that State, or the international community as a whole'.[52] While this may give rise to difficult questions in individual cases as to whether a breach 'specially affects' a particular State or radically changes the position of all other States to whom the obligation is owed,[53] this alone does not make Hohfeld's approach to legal relations inapplicable.

In addition, we might note that while synallagmatic relationships in private law were Hohfeld's principal concern, Hohfeld did use some public law examples in his principal essay. For example, he too uses taxation exemptions as an example of an immunity claim – partly in order to dispel 'any lingering misgivings as to the "*practical*" importance of accuracy and discrimination in legal conceptions and legal terms ...'[54]

---

LOSC is the adoption of the term 'interest' at various points in the text. This is explored further in the next part.

50 ibid. See also John R Morss, 'Power and International Law: Hohfeld to the Rescue?' (2011) 2 The Western Australian Jurist 93.

51 Morss, 'Legal Relations of Collectives' (n 46) 299 and also 301 suggesting that adoption of 'Hohfeldian grammar' may lead to greater analytical precision and a more nuanced debate.

52 ILC, Draft Articles, Responsibility of States for Internationally Wrongful Acts (2001), art 42.

53 ibid and commentary [12] and [13].

54 Hohfeld (n 3) 55 (emphasis added).

## 4 Application of Hohfeld within the Context of the LOSC

Others have also concluded that Hohfeld offers insights in an international law context and specifically in the context of the LOSC. This part begins by examining Philip Allott's Hohfeld-influenced analysis of 'power-sharing' in the law of the sea and considers how such a 'power' analysis (rather than a 'rights' analysis) might inform judicial approaches to the scrutiny of coastal State powers. Section two offers a Hohfeldian analysis of the status of ABNJ under the LOSC. Section three applies Hohfeld's analytical approach to two law of the sea cases.

### 4.1 *Allott: 'Power Sharing in the Law of the Sea'*

In an influential article published at the time of the conclusion of the LOSC, Philip Allott reviewed the Convention's law-making process.[55] Allott acknowledged the 'invisible hand' of the consensus approach to law-making,[56] yet at the same time he both explicitly and implicitly adopts Hohfeld's language and classifications to describe the Convention. Thus, he acknowledges that 'the Convention makes constant use of the eight fundamental Hohfeldian forms of jural relations'[57] and Allott himself uses Hohfeldian vocabulary to describe and analyse the Convention. In referencing the comprehensiveness of the Convention, for example, Allott notes that '[i]t has a rule for everything. The rule may be a permissive rule. It may be an obligation. It may confer an explicit freedom or leave a residual liberty by not specifying a right or duty'.[58] Furthermore, the Convention makes its rules 'by the process of legal classification. … It establishes relationships between legal persons by applying jural relationships to them'.[59]

It is no coincidence that Allott's article is entitled 'Power Sharing in the Law of the Sea', and it is evident that he uses the word 'power' in its juridical sense, rather than in the realist's sense of political power.[60] The debt to Hohfeld is

55 Allott (n 35).
56 ibid 5–7.
57 ibid 9.
58 ibid 8.
59 ibid.
60 But the two are interconnected. See Philip Allott, 'Making the new international law: law of the sea as law of the future' (1985) 40 International Journal 442, 453 observing that 'law is the distributive mechanism par excellence because law distributes power; and power is the most actual and inescapable feature of human social experience. Actual power over actual persons is constituted by law into legal power over legal persons. Actual power is constituted into legal power by means of a conditioned delegation … society always retains the power of overseeing the exercise of the legal powers it delegates'.

even clearer when Allott describes two fundamental features of the legislative process of the Convention, namely 'the layering of legal relations' and the 'delegation of power'.[61] The Convention, he observes:

> … is a massive structure of powers. We tend to overlook the extent to which treaties confer powers *as opposed to more static forms of right*. It seems that treaties are more and more conferring powers but the LOS Convention is without parallel or precedent in the scale of its delegation of power. Powers obviously give rise to special problems for international law. Powers are a sort of delegated legislative function. The law allows me to choose at some later date to alter somebody else's legal position with impunity and to my advantage.[62]

Allott, informed by Hohfeld, offers two important insights here into the structure of the LOSC. First, by emphasizing power, Allott emphasizes not only the conferral of power but also control over the exercise of power through the introduction of 'power modifiers' in the text which can then serve as a standard against which to assess the exercise of that power in any particular case.[63] In domestic law we would denominate this process the process of judicial review. Second, and as the italicized language emphasizes, a power/liability relationship is more dynamic than a right/duty relationship insofar as it contemplates the exercise of power over time, whether by a particular category of State (eg coastal State or flag State) or by a standard setting organization.[64]

The conferral of powers by the Convention is obvious in Part XI (The Area), but also in Part V dealing with the powers of the coastal State in the EEZ. What is also apparent however is that the text of the LOSC rarely uses the term 'power' and does not do so at all in Part V of the Convention.[65] Instead, the Convention

61 Allott, 'Power Sharing' (n 35) 10.

62 ibid (emphasis added).

63 ibid 11. By power modifiers Allott has in mind examples such as art 73(1) and the phrase 'such measures … as may be necessary' in art 73(1) which qualifies the power of the coastal State to take measures for its EEZ to ensure compliance with its laws and regulations.

64 See W Van Reenen, 'Rules of Reference in the new Convention on the Law of the Sea in particular connection with pollution of the sea by oil from tankers' (1981) XII Netherlands Yearbook of International Law 3; Catherine Redgwell, 'Mind the Gap in the GAIRS: The Role of Other Instruments in LOSC Regime Implementation in the Offshore Energy Sector' (2014) 29 International Journal of Marine and Coastal Law 600.

65 'Power' is used in its more colloquial sense in several articles of the LOSC such as arts 22 and 23 (nuclear-*powered* ships) and art 13 (power cables). The most Hohfeldian uses of the term power are found in references to the right (or power) of visit (art 110) and in Part XI

prefers the language of 'sovereign rights' and 'jurisdiction'.[66] But the language of power is often more apt insofar as it offers a more accurate description of the ensuing juridical relationships between States,[67] but also because it highlights the potential for judicial review of the exercise of such a power.[68] The dissenting and separate opinions in *M/V 'Virginia G'*[69] offer an example of how to operationalize this approach. That decision, it will be recalled dealt, inter alia, with the question of whether the coastal State's (Guinea-Bissau) enforcement measures were 'necessary' to ensure compliance with its laws for the conservation and management of the living resources of the EEZ.

### 4.2 *The Status of ABNJ under the LOSC*

This section provides a Hohfeldian analysis of the legal status of ABNJ under the LOSC. While the legal status of these areas is principally a function of Part VII (High Seas), and Part XI (The Area),[70] other provisions of the Convention, such as elements of Part XII (Marine Environment)[71] and Part XIII (Marine Scientific Research),[72] also apply to ABNJ.

From a Hohfeldian perspective, the high seas are characterized by four sets of legal relationships. First, no State may exercise sovereignty over any part of the high seas. This represents a true right/duty relationship. Each State has a duty not to claim sovereignty and a right not to have another State make such a claim.[73] Second, the high seas are characterized by a set of liberties or

---

dealing with the powers of the Authority, the Assembly and the Council and then again in arts 224 and 225 dealing explicitly with powers of enforcement.

66 See in particular LOSC arts 56 and 73.

67 Consider for example art 193, which refers to the sovereign right of States to exploit their natural resources. Analytically this is a power and not a right because it does entail a correlative duty for any other actor.

68 See also Vaughan Lowe, 'The Politics of Law-Making and the Changing Character of Norm Creation' in Michael Byers (ed), *The Role of Law in International Politic* (Oxford Scholarship Online 2016) 218, 'Why should we not effect a paradigm shift and approach the regulation of State power on the basis of the public law model'.

69 *M/V 'Virginia G'* (n 30) Joint Dissenting Opinion of Vice-President Hoffmann and Judges Marotta Rangel, Chandrasekhara Rao, Kateka, Gao and Bouguetaia and see especially the Dissenting Opinion of Judge ad hoc Sérvulo Correiga who repeatedly characterizes the coastal State's authority under art 73 as a power at paras 16, 17 and 19.

70 The revised draft Agreement defines 'areas beyond national jurisdiction' to mean the high seas and the Area.

71 See in particular arts 192, 194 and 209.

72 See in particular arts 256 and 257, the right (freedom) to conduct marine scientific research in the Area and in the water column beyond the limits of the EEZ.

73 LOSC art 89; *M/V 'Norstar' (Panama v Italy)* (Judgment, 10 April 2019) ITLOS [215]. See also *Activities in the Area*, (n 49) [180] discussing obligations owed to the world

freedoms, supported by the correlative absence of a right of another State (a 'no-right') to interfere with those liberties. These liberties are at least partly enumerated in Article 87.[74]

Third, the exercise of the liberty or freedom may be circumscribed by additional duties. Such duties may be general or specific. For example, Article 87(2) imposes a general duty of due regard for the interests of other States with respect to all of the freedoms enumerated in Article 87(1).[75] More specific restrictions are imposed on the freedom of fishing through the conservation and management duties of Articles 116–119, 192 and 194 of the LOSC as well as duties under the UNFSA for those States that are party to that Agreement.[76] These duties are Hohfeldian right/duty obligations the performance of which is subject to a due diligence standard.[77]

Fourth, some of the enumerated liberties are further protected by the exclusive nature of the flag State's authority with respect to its vessels which affords those vessels a degree of immunity from the jurisdiction of other States.[78] While that immunity is far from complete, the best jural correlative descriptor of the relationship between flag States and other States is that of immunity/disability. The majority of ITLOS put it this way in its recent decision on the merits in *M/V 'Norstar'*:

> The Tribunal notes that another corollary of the open and free status of the high seas is that, save in exceptional cases, no State may exercise jurisdiction over a foreign ship on the high seas. Freedom of navigation

community as a whole and referencing art 48 of the ILC Articles on State Responsibility. It might also be possible to explain it as a universal disability (absence of power) to make such a claim.

74 LOSC art 87: (a) freedom of navigation; (b) freedom of overflight; (c) freedom to lay submarine cables and pipelines, subject to Part VI; (d) freedom to construct artificial islands and other installations permitted under international law, subject to Part VI; (e) freedom of fishing, subject to the conditions laid down in section 2; (f) freedom of scientific research, subject to Parts VI and XIII. See also *M/V 'Louisa'* (n 36) Separate Opinion, Judge Paik, [23], 'Article 87 of the Convention, which provides for the freedom of the high seas, imposes upon States an obligation not to impede that freedom'.

75 This formulation draws on the language of art 2 of the Geneva Convention on the High Seas with the substitution of due regard for reasonable regard. I examine this formulation and its use of the word 'interests' in more detail in the next section. It bears emphasizing that the word 'interest' does not readily fit within Hohfeld's conceptual framework and it is hard to identify what the correlative (or opposite) of an interest might be.

76 UNFSA (n 24).

77 *IUU Fishing* (n 37) and *South China Sea Award* (n 37).

78 *M/V 'Norstar'* (n 73) [225]; and see Joint Dissenting Opinion of Judges Cot, Pawlak, Yanai, Hoffmann, Kolodkin and Lijnzaad and Judge Ad Hoc Treves [17]–[20].

would be illusory if a ship – a principal means for the exercise of the freedom of navigation – could be subject to the jurisdiction of other States on the high seas. In its Judgment in *The Case of the S.S. 'Lotus'*, the Permanent Court of International Justice stated:

> It is certainly true that – apart from certain special cases which are defined by international law – vessels on the high seas are subject to no authority except that of the State whose flag they fly. *In virtue of the principle of the freedom of the sea, that is to say, the absence of any territorial sovereignty upon the high seas, no State may exercise any kind of jurisdiction over foreign vessels upon them.* [79]

While there is much in common between the legal status of the high seas and the legal status of the Area, there are also important differences. The key similarity is that no State may claim sovereignty with respect to either the high seas or the Area.[80] As above, this is a mutual right/duty relationship as between States. The principal difference is that while the resources of the high seas are subject to appropriation through the exercise of the freedom (or liberty) of fishing, the resources of the Area are the common heritage of (hu)mankind[81] and as such are not subject to appropriation – except in accordance with the terms of Part XI.[82] In Hohfeldian terms, this must mean that the right/duty relationship that precludes claims of sovereignty also applies to the resources of the Area.[83] A further difference is that whereas the LOSC does not itself fill the power vacuum that ensues with respect to the high seas (other than to confirm the exclusive authority of the flag State with respect to its vessels – along with associated obligations, as well as rules of general application),[84] LOSC does do

79 *M/V 'Norstar'* (n 73) [216] (emphasis in the quotation from *SS Lotus* added by ITLOS). See also [222] 'As no State may exercise jurisdiction over foreign ships on the high seas, in the view of the Tribunal, any act of interference with navigation of foreign ships or any exercise of jurisdiction over such ships on the high seas constitutes a breach of the freedom of navigation, unless justified by the Convention or other international treaties'.

80 LOSC arts 89 and 137.

81 LOSC art 136.

82 LOSC art 137.

83 Alternatively, we may say that all States are under a disability and as such cannot exercise a power with respect to such resources. Resources of the Area are defined as 'all solid, liquid or gaseous mineral resources *in situ* in the Area at or beneath the seabed, including polymetallic nodules'.

84 *Activities in the Area* (n 49) [97]. The power vacuum is in part filled by rules of reference developed by organizations such as IMO. See Van Reenen (n 64) and Redgwell (n 64) and for an example see *South China Sea Award* (n 37) [1081]–[1083] (incorporation by reference of the Convention on the International Regulations for Preventing Collisions at Sea (adopted 20 October 1972, entered into force 15 July 1977) 1050 UNTS 1976 (COLREGS).

so in the case of the Area and its resources, partly by articulating a complex set of primary norms and partly by creating an elaborate administrative law structure pursuant to which the global community delegates rule-making powers to bodies established by Part XI (as modified by the Part XI Implementation Agreement).[85] Contracting parties may assume duties directly to the extent they engage in seabed activities themselves[86] or indirectly through the vehicle of sponsorship.[87]

### 4.3 *Hohfeldian Analysis of Judicial Reasoning: Law of the Sea Examples*

This section of the chapter uses Hohfeld's ideas of legal relationship to unpack the reasoning in three decisions: the two *Fisheries Jurisdiction* cases and part of the decision in the *Chagos Award*. All of these decisions deal with the legal relationships between the coastal State and other States. The *Fisheries Jurisdiction* cases engage Article 2 of the 1958 Geneva Convention on the High Seas (now reflected in Article 87 of the LOSC); the part of the *Chagos Award* analysed here engages Article 56(2) of the LOSC.

In the *Fisheries Jurisdiction* cases the Court accepted that Article 2 of the Geneva Convention on the High Seas was generally declaratory of established principles of international law and emphasised that the Convention's articulation of the freedoms of the high seas was 'subject to the consideration that they shall be exercised by all States with reasonable regard to the interests of other States in their exercise of the freedom of the high seas'.[88] It followed from this that Iceland's unilateral action excluding the British and German trawler fleets from Iceland's newly established 50 nm exclusive fishing zone infringed the principle enshrined in this article.[89] While Iceland might have preferential fishing rights in this zone,[90] such a concept is 'not compatible with the exclusion of all fishing activities of other States'.[91] Neither did the idea of preferential

85 Agreement relating to the Implementation of Part XI … UN Doc A/RES/48/263, 17 August 1994.
86 *Activities in the Area* (n 49) [79] and [145].
87 ibid [74]–[78] and [108].
88 *Fisheries Jurisdiction* (n 26), UK [50], FRG [42].
89 ibid UK [67], FRG [59].
90 ibid UK [68], FRG [60]. And see also at UK [60], FRG [52] noting that the 'preferential rights of the coastal State come into play only at the moment when an intensification in the exploitation of fishery resources makes it imperative to introduce some system of catch-limitation and sharing of those resources, to preserve the fish stocks in the interests of their rational and economic exploitation'. The 'right' is perhaps better expressed as a power – a power to alter the legal position of other States that cannot claim an historic interest.
91 ibid UK [62], FRG [54].

rights require the phasing out of the 'traditional fishing rights' of other States since the 'reference to the interests of other States in the exploitation of the same stocks clearly indicates that the preferential rights of the coastal State and the established rights of other States were considered as, in principle, continuing to co-exist'.[92]

It is notable how easily in these paragraphs the Court moves from the language of interests to the language of rights,[93] but what the Court is really suggesting is that any *power* that Iceland might have to establish an exclusive zone to protect its special interests, was not opposable against Britain or Germany – the two fleets have an immunity, and Iceland a corresponding disability in the exercise of its power.[94] Given these competing legal entitlements, it followed for the Court that the *reciprocal* duty of 'reasonable regard' recognized in Article 2 of the Geneva Convention entailed 'an obligation to keep under review the fishery resources in the disputed waters and to examine together, in the light of scientific and other available information, the measures required for the conservation and development, and equitable exploitation, of those resources …'[95] It might also entail negotiations, the objective of which 'should be the delimitation of the rights and interests of the Parties, the preferential rights of the coastal State on the one hand and the rights of the Applicant on the other, to balance and regulate equitably questions such as those of catch-limitation. share allocations …'[96] Once again, the Court moves almost seamlessly (but misleadingly) from interests to rights and back. A stricter application of Hohfeld's ideas can serve to unpack and clarify these passages.

There are three sets of relationships operating here. First, and as noted above, the Court concludes that international law has moved to a position that recognizes that Iceland has a power to take measures within an adjacent zone to protect its special dependency.[97] This would ordinarily necessarily entail that other States would have a liability with respect to those measures. However, that power is not opposable against the UK, Germany and other historic fishing States and thus Iceland has a disability with respect to such States (which States can also be said to have a correlative immunity). The second

92 ibid UK [69], FRG [61].

93 There are many other paragraphs in the judgment referencing the 'rights' of both parties eg UK [71], [72], [76] and [78] as well as in the formal *dispositive* [3], [4] (b) and (d); FRG [63], [65] [68] and [70] and the *dispositif*.

94 ibid UK [71], FRG [63]. The liberty or freedom of the UK and Germany to fish is protected from unilateral abrogation.

95 ibid UK [72], FRG [64].

96 ibid UK [73], FRG [65].

97 ibid UK [58]–[60], FRG [50]–[52].

set of relationships is based on the parallel freedom of both Iceland and the UK and Germany to engage in the fishery and the correlative no-right of each in relation to the others' freedom.[98] The third and final set of relationships is based on a reciprocal duty of due regard to the freedoms of others. It is this duty (and not the existence of an 'interest') that triggers the mixture of procedural (duty to negotiate) and substantive (equitable allocation) obligations that the Court articulates. In Hohfeldian terms, each of Iceland, Germany and the UK has a right that the other observe its due or reasonable regard obligations in good faith; and each has a correlative duty to do so.

In sum, Iceland incurred international responsibility by treating the UK and Germany as if neither had an immunity. Furthermore, Iceland could not unilaterally abrogate the freedoms of the UK and Germany (just as neither the UK nor Germany could abrogate Iceland's) but, on a go-forward basis, each of Iceland, the UK and Germany have the rights and obligations associated with the duty of due regard.

Seen in this light, the concept of an 'interest' referred to in Article 2 serves to obfuscate rather than clarify. Indeed, it gives rise to the question what the word adds, if anything, to the clause. We can answer this by considering whether there is any difference in these two formulations:

> A. These freedoms ... shall be exercised by all States with reasonable regard to the interests of other States in their exercise of the freedom of the high seas.
>
> B. These freedoms ... shall be exercised by all States with reasonable regard to the exercise by other States of their freedom of the high seas.

The first formulation is that of Article 2 of the Geneva Convention (and, with the substitution of 'due' for 'reasonable', also the language of Article 87(2) of the LOSC). The second formulation drops the word 'interest' and draws attention to what is really at stake – the accommodation of parallel freedoms based on the duty of reasonable (or due) regard.

Although the obligation of due regard appears elsewhere in the LOSC, it is only in Article 87 that the duty is owed in relation to the identical and parallel freedoms of each State.[99] The duty of due regard in Article 142, for example, is a duty owed by a party responsible for activities within the Area that may affect

98 See the 'B' examples in Part 2 above (text to n 19–34).

99 Note as well that second part of para 2 of art 87 departs from this model insofar as it requires a State exercising its high seas freedom to have due regard 'for the rights under this Convention with respect to activities in the Area'.

straddling resource deposits, to have regard for the 'rights and legitimate interests of coastal States'.[100] Neither of the due regard formulations in Article 56(2) or 58(3) involve due regard obligations for parallel freedoms. Thus, in Article 56, the coastal State must have regard to 'the rights and duties of other States' but the rights and duties of those other States will be very different from those of the coastal State, and in many cases will be more accurately characterized as freedoms. Other States (Article 58(3)) must have due regard 'for the rights and duties of the coastal State' when 'exercising their rights and performing their duties' under the Convention within the EEZ of the coastal State. But here the conflict is far more likely to be a conflict between the freedoms of the other State (as paragraph 1 of Article 58 recognizes) and the powers or jurisdiction of the coastal State. In sum, from an Hohfeldian perspective there is considerable terminological confusion in Articles 56 and 58. The implications of that confusion become important when we try to understand what 'due regard' requires in each particular category of relationships. In other words, we should expect that 'due regard' might have a different content depending upon the nature of the entitlement for which due regard must be had. Due regard for a mutually shared freedom might look very different from due regard for a right. In fact, one might reasonably expect that due regard for the *rights* of a party would, at a minimum, entail observance and non-impairment of those rights.[101]

The leading decision on due regard is the *Chagos Arbitration*.[102] In that case (which engaged Article 56(2) of the LOSC) the rights in question derived from the so-called Lancaster House Undertakings (LHU) rather than the Convention itself. So far as relevant to the EEZ (where the duty of due regard applied[103]), the two rights in question were the reversionary right of Mauritius

100 Unlike art 87 which identifies the freedoms to which each State must have due regard, art 142 does not further specify the 'rights and legitimate interests of the coastal State' to which those engaged in activities in the Area must have due regard. Art 142 presumably means to reference all of the exclusive rights of the coastal State established under both Part V (EEZ) and Part VI (continental shelf) even though they may be more accurately described as powers. In addition, a coastal State also has rights under the applicable provisions of Part XII (Protection and Preservation of the Marine Environment) that speak to the obligations of all States and with respect to all marine areas. These provisions include arts 192, 194 and 206 which impose duties on all States and thus afford the coastal State a correlative right with respect to non-coastal States.

101 See *IUU Fishing* (n 37) [124] and [129] and *South China Sea Award* (n 37) [743–744], [753] and [756]–[757].

102 *Chagos Marine Protected Area Arbitration* (*Mauritius v United Kingdom*) (Award, 18 March 2015) PCA.

103 In addition to the obligation of due regard in art 56(2), the UK also owed Mauritius a duty of good faith with respect to the LHU within the territorial sea pursuant to art 2(3) of the LOSC and further obligations under art 194(4) of the LOSC. All three sets of obligations

to the archipelago should the Chagos Islands no longer be required for military purposes, and the right to the benefit of any minerals or oil discovered in or near the Archipelago.[104] These rights are true claim-rights. The UK had a correlative duty of due regard with respect to those rights and that duty extended to all the entitlements that Mauritius might assume as a coastal State when the Archipelago and surrounding waters reverted to it at some time in the future.[105]

The Tribunal took the view that the content of the duty of due regard would vary with the circumstances and the nature of the rights in question, and in most cases would 'involve at least some consultation with the rights-holding State'.[106] There was no 'uniform obligation to avoid any impairment of Mauritius' rights'.[107] The Tribunal gives no authority for such a dismissive view of the nature of rights, but this may simply be a lack of precision in the Tribunal's reasoning – grounded in its adoption of the loose terminology of the LOSC itself. Recall that the decision that was the subject of Mauritius' complaint in this case was the UK's unilateral decision to create a marine protected area (MPA) covering the entirety of the EEZ of the Chagos Archipelago. That was the exercise of a power. The LHU did not, in terms, prohibit the creation of an MPA. Rather, the question that the Tribunal had to answer was this: what did good faith performance of the contingent duty to return the archipelago require of the UK prior to the contingency being triggered? A clear understanding of the scope of that duty determines the correlative right of Mauritius to which the UK must accord due regard.

In the end the Tribunal does not give us a clear picture of how it interprets the right of return. Indeed, the Tribunal does not confine itself to the language of rights (the actual wording of Article 56(2)) but repeatedly uses the formulation 'rights and interests'.[108] What we do know however is that the Tribunal concluded that the UK had not discharged its obligation; and to some degree

according to the Tribunal have a similar content: ibid [520] and [540]. But note that while the majority of the Tribunal resists the conclusion that the rights derived from the LHU were directly incorporated in art 2(3) of the LOSC the Tribunal never expressly explains what is incorporated in arts 56(2) and 194(4). Is it the rights themselves or is it just the duty of good faith with respect to the observance of the undertakings?

104 *Chagos Award*, ibid [298] and [304]. The LHU also provided for fishing rights [297] but the Tribunal concluded that it had no jurisdiction over fishing rights in light of LOSC art 297(3)(a).

105 ibid [304].

106 ibid [519].

107 ibid.

108 ibid [534] and [535].

it offers the UK's dealings with the United States as a possible example of what due regard might have looked like.[109] But one has to be careful with that line of reasoning. The rights of the US had different origins. They were based on a series of bilateral agreements and the US was entitled to the benefit of a duty of good faith performance of those bilateral agreements.[110]

Hohfeld developed his ideas of fundamental legal concepts and the relationships between them as a means of examining judicial reasoning in a private law context. This last section demonstrates that this analytical method can be applied to international decisions and can be used to both clarify the issues and critique the resulting judicial reasoning. In particular, it demonstrates that careful identification of the nature of the juridical relationships between States may help calibrate the content of the duty of due (or reasonable) regard.

## 5 The Revised Draft Agreement

We can now turn to offer an Hohfeldian analysis of the revised draft Agreement.[111] The analysis necessarily builds upon the analysis in Part 4.2 of the legal status of ABNJ under the LOSC. The draft Agreement itself recognizes this, both in its Preamble[112] and in draft Article 4(1):[113]

> Nothing in this Agreement shall prejudice the rights, jurisdiction and duties of States under the Convention. This Agreement shall be interpreted and applied in the context of and in a manner consistent with the Convention.

---

109 ibid [528] and [535].

110 Vienna Convention on the Law of Treaties (signed 23 May 1969, entered into force 27 January 1980) 1155 UNTS 331, art 24.

111 The analysis is based on the draft text prepared for the fourth meeting of the Intergovernmental Conference (n 2). The text is still under negotiation and much of the text is bracketed. A compilation of textual proposals submitted by delegations for the fourth meetings runs to over 400 pages: 'Textual proposals submitted by delegations by 20 February 2020 …' available at <www.un.org/bbnj/sites/www.un.org.bbnj/files/textual_proposals_compilation_-_28_feb_2020.pdf> accessed 3 May 2021.

112 Preamble para 2: '*Stressing* the need to respect the balance of rights, obligations and interests set out in the Convention'.

113 While the inclusion of duties is curious (it is not clear to me how one might prejudice a 'duty') equally curious is the omission of freedoms and interests (especially with respect to the latter given the formulation adopted in the Preamble, ibid).

Before examining the details of the revised draft Agreement, it is useful to reflect at a general level on the differences between the LOSC, the UNFSA and this draft Agreement. A principal observation is that whereas LOSC was a power-conferring and power-sharing agreement,[114] the revised draft Agreement builds on existing jural relations that are premised in large part on the *absence* of geographically or territorially based authority (ie the power or jurisdiction of a coastal State) and the *presence* of flag State jurisdiction or power. Much as the UNFSA sought to superimpose additional duties on parties exercising high seas fishing freedoms, the revised draft Agreement is largely concerned to add to the obligations (duties) of flag States under Article 94 of the LOSC[115] as well as to establish new duties for States that have any jurisdiction or control over activities that are subject to the terms of the agreement. To the extent that the revised draft Agreement confers powers, it does not (for the most part[116]) confer powers on States individually, but instead on the institutions that the Agreement proposes to create, in particular, the Conference of the Parties.[117]

There are four principal substantive parts to the Agreement. Part II addresses marine genetic resources (MGRS) including benefit sharing; Part III deals with area-based management tools (ABMTS) including MPAS; Part IV deals with environmental impact assessment (EIAS); and Part V deals with capacity building and transfer of marine technology.[118] The only one of these four parts that expressly addresses the status of areas beyond national jurisdiction, or the resources of these areas, is Part II and in particular Article 9 of Part II. Given that, I begin with that article and its companion Article 10.

---

114 See discussion in part 4.1 above drawing on Allott, 'Power Sharing' (n 35).

115 See Ringbom (this volume) examining flag State jurisdiction.

116 In commenting on a draft of this chapter Oude Elferink observed that the draft Agreement does confer limited powers on individual States such as the power to initiate consideration of an MPA. It is also the case as noted above that many of the provisions of the draft Agreement are premised on the existing powers of the flag State to make rules for its vessels that may be engaged in the activities the agreement seeks to regulate.

117 Revised draft Agreement art 48 and Part VI generally; in addition, there are many references in the substantive provisions of the text conferring powers on the COP. I discuss some of these powers in the following section. On the status of the institutional elements of the draft Agreement, see eg Alex G Oude Elferink, 'Exploring the future of the institutional landscape of the oceans beyond national jurisdiction' (2019) 28 Review of European, Comparative & International Environmental Law 236.

118 Other parts are Part I, General Provisions; Part VI, Institutional Arrangements; Part VII, Financial Resources and Mechanism; Part VIII, Implementation and Compliance; Part IX, Settlement of Disputes; Part X, Non-Parties; Part XI Good Faith and Abuse of Rights; and Part XII, Final Provisions.

## 5.1 *Marine Genetic Resources*

As currently structured, Article 9, entitled 'Activities with respect to marine genetic resources of areas beyond national jurisdiction' comprises five paragraphs. Paragraph 1 establishes the liberty or freedom of all States to carry out activities with respect to marine genetic resources of areas beyond national jurisdiction[119] on the conditions laid down in the Agreement.[120] It follows from this that a State commits no wrong in engaging in (or authorizing other legal entities to engage in) these activities, provided that such activities comply with the conditions laid down in the Agreement. It further follows that no state has a right or a power to interfere with such activities. The paragraph is therefore structurally similar to Articles 87 and 90 of the LOSC (discussed above). Paragraph 2 is effectively a proviso to paragraph 1 and establishes a due regard obligation owed to 'the rights and legitimate interests of any coastal State' when 'marine genetic resources of ABNJ are also found in areas within national jurisdiction'.[121] The provision is evidently modelled on article 142(1) of the LOSC insofar as it serves only to protect the rights and interests of a coastal State and not (as with Article 87(2) of the LOSC) other States exercising their parallel freedom.[122] This 'gap' might be filled by an additional clause modelled on Article 87 of the LOSC.[123]

Paragraph 3 is modelled on Article 137 of the LOSC. It provides that:

> [3. No State shall claim or exercise sovereignty or sovereign rights over marine genetic resources of areas beyond national jurisdiction [, nor shall any State or natural or juridical person appropriate any part thereof]. No such claim or exercise of sovereignty or sovereign rights [nor such appropriation] shall be recognized.]

119 I maintain that this is analytically a liberty although the text does not use that label. The actual text of the first part of the clause adopts the passive voice and reads as follows: 'Activities with respect to marine genetic resources of ABNJ may be carried out by all States and their natural or juridical persons'.

120 An earlier reference to engaging in such activities 'with due regard for the rights, obligations and interests under the Convention' has now been struck.

121 It is not clear to me when this provision is triggered; must the MGRs be the 'same' MGRs? See also art 10(5).

122 See discussion above in Parts 4.2 and 4.3. It is true however that art 87(2) contains a second due regard obligation this time with respect to 'the *rights* under this Convention with respect to activities within the Area' (emphasis added).

123 Such a clause might be a free-standing clause or might be added to para 1 with text along the following lines: 'and with due regard to the activities carried out by other States Parties and their natural or juridical persons'.

If adopted in its entirety, the paragraph would appear, as is the case with Article 137 of the LOSC, to establish a set of Hohfeldian right/duty relationships, and as such would contradict the legal relationship established by paragraph 1 (or at the very least seriously limit the scope of the freedom recognized in paragraph 1). On the other hand, were the negotiators to adopt only the first part of the first sentence of the clause,[124] the resulting formulation would be more similar to Articles 87 and 90 of the LOSC. But there would still be significant differences. In the case of the LOSC high seas provisions, the prohibition on claiming sovereignty does not preclude freedom of fishing and, as part of that freedom, the exclusive ownership of fish as personal property as and when captured (ie reduced to possession). Should paragraph 3 be adopted with the two bracketed references prohibiting appropriation, then we would have to conclude that the freedom to carry out activities with respect to MGRs would be seriously attenuated. There would no longer be even a conditional open access regime.

In sum, paragraph 1 creates or recognizes a liberty, whereas paragraph 3 establishes a right/duty relationship that has the potential to radically limit the scope of the liberty conferred by paragraph 1 (depending on which version of the text is adopted). The unresolved tension here reflects the division of opinion between those supporting a regime based on high seas freedoms and those who support a common heritage model.[125]

Paragraph 4 suggests that the utilization of MGRs of ABNJ shall be for the benefit of (hu)mankind as a whole.[126] However, while the clause is framed in mandatory declaratory terms, it does not itself work through the legal implications of this status. Thus, while it may have some interpretive significance, it does not itself establish any new Hohfeldian legal relationships.[127]

---

124 ie '[n]o State shall claim or exercise sovereignty or sovereign rights over marine genetic resources of areas beyond national jurisdiction'.

125 See Vito De Lucia, 'The Question of the Common Heritage of Mankind and the Negotiations towards a Global Treaty on Marine Biodiversity in Areas Beyond National Jurisdiction: No End in Sight?' (2020) 16(2) McGill Journal of Sustainable Development Law 139, 140–41, 143–44 and 150–54.

126 Art 9(4): [The utilization of marine genetic resources of ABNJ shall be for the benefit of mankind as a whole, taking into consideration the interests and needs of developing States, in particular the least developed countries, landlocked developing countries, geographically disadvantaged States, small island developing States, coastal African States and developing middle-income countries.].

127 The clause is similar to LOSC art 136 which simply declares the Area and its resources to be the common heritage of (hu)mankind. But it is principally art 137 that works through the legal implications of that declaration. There are also important differences between LOSC art 136 and draft art 9(4) of the Agreement. In particular, the declaration in para 4

Paragraph 5, much like Article 141 of the LOSC, provides that activities with respect to the utilization of MGRs of ABNJ shall be carried out exclusively for peaceful purposes. This paragraph, if adopted as is stands, would establish an additional reciprocal set of right/duty relationships, whereas paragraph 4 (like Article 140 of the LOSC) articulates a goal, or a set of goals, but as noted above, lacks the specificity required to establish new legal relationships between the parties.

Article 10 of the draft Agreement deals with the regulation of access to MGRs of areas beyond national jurisdiction. The Article deals with both *in situ* access and *ex situ* access. Paragraphs 1 and 2 deal with *in situ* access. As currently structured, paragraph 1 offers two alternative regimes. Alternative 1 requires notification to the Secretariat – potentially prior to and/or post – any access or collection activities. Alternative 2 contemplates a permit regime, albeit one operating under domestic law rather than under international law.[128] Indeed, regardless of whether we are operating under a permit regime or a mere notification regime, paragraph 2 requires States Parties to take the necessary legislative, administrative or policy measures to ensure that *in situ* access is subject to the indication of the geographical coordinates of where MGRs 'were accessed',[129] capacity building, transfer of marine technology, deposit of samples in open source platforms, contributions to the special fund, EIAs and such other terms and conditions as determined by the Conference of the Parties. In either case therefore, the core of the access/collection regime is established under domestic law subject to the minimum conditions established by paragraph 2. These conditions serve to limit the liberty conferred by Article 9(1) by layering on to that liberty a set of duties and correlative rights, but they do not contradict that liberty, much as the conditions that the LOSC and the UNFSA impose on the exercise of the freedom of fishing do not convert the freedom to a right/duty relationship.[130]

Article 10(3) deals with *ex situ* access to MGRs and requires Contracting Parties to take the necessary legislative, administrative or policy measures to ensure that *ex situ* access to MGRs is 'free and open'. While the language of

is limited to the utilization of the MGRs and para 4 does not use the language of common heritage.

128 The unstated premise of this regime is, as noted above (n 116), the power of the flag State to make laws for its vessels engaged in activities in the areas subject to the proposed agreement.

129 The imperfect tense (rather than the future 'will be accessed') is an odd choice here if both the notification and permit regimes are intended to be *prospective* in nature.

130 See the discussion above in Parts 4.2 and 4.3.

'free and open' is perhaps suggestive of a liberty, in fact that language is simply descriptive of the type of regime that each State must put in place. Thus, much as with Article 10(2), the text imposes upon each Contracting Party a duty, and each Contracting Party would have a correlative right to require of another Party that such an access regime is put in place.

Article 10(5) adopts a harder version of the limited duty of due regard established in Article 9(2). It does this by requiring that State Parties shall take the necessary measures to *ensure* that activities under its jurisdiction or control with respect to MGRs shared with a coastal State are subject to notification and consultation 'with a view to avoiding infringement of the rights and legitimate interests' of such States.[131]

Finally, draft Article 13 confers a power on the Conference of the Parties (COP) to '[... adopt appropriate rules, guidelines or a code of conduct for the utilization of marine genetic resources of areas beyond national jurisdiction.]' States Parties have a correlative liability to the exercise of this power and such rules, guidelines or a code of conduct may create reciprocal duties/rights for States Parties, if and when adopted.

### 5.2 *Area-based Management Tools*

From an Hohfeldian perspective, the crucial elements of Part III dealing with ABMTs are likely those provisions dealing with decision making and thence the implementation of the resulting tools. Since the areas that we are concerned with are, by definition, beyond the jurisdiction of any State, decision-making under Part III is not concerned with the powers or jurisdiction of an individual State but with the circumstances under which the COP can adopt 'objectives, criteria, modalities and requirements', and even establish MPAs or other area-based management approaches, along with appropriate conservation and management measures.[132] In Hohfeldian terms, this is the exercise of a power which may serve to limit or constrain liberties that might otherwise exist under LOSC or under Article 9(1) of this Agreement.[133] Once validly

131 The language here is evidently based on LOSC art 142(2). Both provisions are predicated upon a clear understanding of the contours of the rights and legitimate interests of the coastal State. See discussion of the *Chagos Award* in section 4.3. It is far from clear what is entailed by avoiding an infringement of a legitimate interest, but logically it must require something less demanding than avoiding an infringement of a right.

132 Revised draft Agreement art 15 (1)(b)(ii) and Article 19(1)(a)[Alt. 1(d)].

133 It follows that these provisions of the draft Agreement are power conferring but on a much more limited scale than, say, the provisions of Part XI of the LOSC.

adopted, such measures may create Hohfeldian rights/duties for Contracting Parties.[134]

### 5.3 *Environmental Impact Assessments*

Part IV of the revised draft Agreement establishes a series of Hohfeldian duties/rights with respect to the conduct of EIAs. Thus, under Article 22, a State has a duty to assess 'the potential effects of planned activities under their jurisdiction or control'.[135] Other States have a correlative right to have that State conduct the assessment. Other articles, such as Article 24 (thresholds for EIAs), Article 30 (screening), and Article 31 (scoping), follow a similar structure. In addition, Part IV confers powers on various bodies. For example, Articles 27(2) and 35(3) contemplate that the COP may establish guidelines for the conduct of EIAs and preparation of EIA reports respectively, while Article 29 contemplates having the COP prepare an indicative list of activities that normally require preparation of an EIA based on recommendations of the Scientific and Technical Body. Bracketed alternative text in Article 38 would, if adopted, confer significant decision-making authority (power) on the COP with respect to determining whether or not proposed planned activities could proceed. Were such a power to be exercised the result would likely be new duty/right obligations for States.

### 5.4 *Capacity Building and Transfer of Marine Technology*

Part V of the revised draft Agreement comprises a statement of objectives (Article 42) and five operative articles. It draws inspiration, at least in part, from Part XIV of the LOSC dealing with the development and transfer of marine technology (but not capacity building), and affords special attention to the needs and interests of developing States Parties. While the articles make frequent use of the mandatory 'shall', closer inspection reveals that this only rarely results in an Hohfeldian right/duty relationship or indeed any other type of Hohfeldian claim.[136] Instead, many of the formulations offer descriptions or definitions and do not establish new duties. Article 44 on the modalities for capacity building and transfer of marine technology is a case in point. While the opening paragraph establishes some sort of duty to build capacity and transfer technology (much will depend upon the final choice of verb), other

134 Revised draft Agreement art 20(1) and (3).

135 ibid art 22(1).

136 It is somewhat ironic, but not surprising, given the commercial interests involved, that it is the provisions dealing with protection of intellectual property that most lend themselves to an Hohfeldian right/duty categorization. See revised draft Agreement art 45.

paragraphs are more descriptive. For example, paragraph 3 indicates that capacity building and transfer of marine technology shall not be duplicative, while paragraph 4 indicates that activities shall be responsive to the needs and priorities of developing States Parties. Article 46 is similar and largely describes types of capacity building and transfer of marine technology.

Part V also has the potential to invest the COP with important powers to develop detailed modalities, procedures and guidelines for capacity building and transfer of marine technology,[137] and to develop types of capacity building and transfer of marine technology[138] as well as provisions for monitoring and review,[139] but all of these provisions are bracketed. Once again, if these powers were to be confirmed in the final text and subsequently exercised, they have the potential to create new right/duty relationships for States.

## 6 Conclusions

Hohfeld's scheme offers a methodology for unpacking legal texts to reveal with greater precision and transparency the legal relationships between different parties. That methodology as the introduction notes is concerned to tell us *how* to think, not *what* to think.[140] In other words, Hohfeld does not provide normative advice as to what we ought to include in the proposed agreement, but he can help us think about the implications of the different legal relationships or entitlements that the agreement constructs.[141]

Hohfeld has not been widely and systematically used by scholars of international law, but this chapter has tried to demonstrate the potential value of Hohfeld's analytical method in the context of the law of the sea generally and more specifically in the context of BBNJ process and the revised draft Agreement. At the same time, it must be recognized that it is challenging to apply Hohfeld's method to a draft and bracketed text that is embedded in a tradition of other texts (most specifically the LOSC) that do not adopt Hohfeld's specific terminology.[142] As the chapter notes, the negotiators and drafters

137 ibid art 44(5).

138 ibid art 46(2) and (3).

139 ibid art 47(3).

140 See n 5 and referencing Schlag.

141 For another view noting the implications of the contingent choice of entitlement see Guido Calabresi and A Douglas Melamed, 'Property Rules, Liability Rules and Inalienability: One View of the Cathedral' (1972) 85 Harvard Law Review 1089.

142 The tradition of course starts earlier with the Geneva Conventions (1958) and one can trace important concepts and terminology through the various texts. For example, we

of the LOSC were frequently imprecise in the language that they adopted to describe the legal relationships they were endorsing or creating. While the language of freedoms is used appropriately in the text for Hohfeldian privileges or liberties, the same cannot be said for the text's overuse of rights and duties. While there are instances (eg the right of innocent passage) where there is a correlative duty to accompany the right, in many more cases there is no such duty, and the entitlement is more correctly described as a power. It is hard to quantify what is lost with the adoption of incorrect or misleading labels, but it can lead to a lack of precision, and in some cases may lead to inappropriate assumptions or generalizations. For example, I have suggested that in applying the obligation of due regard it will be important to understand the nature of the entitlement to which one must have due regard: is that entitlement a claim-right, a freedom enjoyed in common, or a legitimate interest or just an interest? One would expect the content of due regard to diminish as we move across this spectrum of entitlements. This should have been an important part of the Tribunal's inquiry in the *Chagos Award*, but it was not. The failure to make that inquiry in *Chagos* is perhaps particularly significant given that the rights in question in that case (the reversionary right and the right to the benefit of any mineral exploitation) were true claim-rights. It might follow from this that the UK actually has (contrary to what the Tribunal suggests) a duty not to impair those rights. While due regard for the interests of another State might only entail consultation, due regard for a claim-right should require more.

Drawing on the insights of Philip Allott, the discussion of the LOSC also emphasized the extent to which the LOSC is in fact a power-conferring instrument even though the text so rarely uses the word power, preferring instead the language of jurisdiction, rights and sovereign rights. These terms are less transparent than the word power and its correlative term liability, particularly when constructing a legal order of the oceans. Central to the existence of a legal order is the recognition that no power is unlimited, and it is an important task of courts and arbitral bodies (to the extent that they have jurisdiction) to review the exercise of power in light of the power modifiers stipulated by the LOSC, just as it is their task to interpret and apply the right/duty obligations that may be layered on top of an underlying freedom.

The revised draft Agreement inevitably builds upon the conceptual language of the LOSC, a language that is effectively baked into the negotiations;

---

can trace the word 'interests' through art 2 of the Convention on the High Seas and art 1 of the Convention on the Fishing and Conservation of the Living Resources of the High Seas through to art 87(2) of the LOSC and with the variant of 'legitimate interests' in art 142 and carried in to the draft Agreement in arts 9(2), 10(4) and 15(5) as 'legitimate interests'.

we are too far down the road to back away from that.[143] But Hohfeld's analytical framework is still helpful in unpacking the text and illuminating the legal relationships that it establishes. Hohfeld may also help us think about the implications of departing from the conceptual language of the LOSC. For example, I observed above that the LOSC's use of freedoms conformed with Hohfeld's analytical approach (using the language of privilege or liberty), and yet the word freedom does not appear in the draft Agreement. Instead, the negotiating parties to this point have adopted the passive formulation that appears in Article 9(1). That formulation may disguise the fact that freedoms exercised in common may lead to conflict, which conflict might be mediated by an appropriately drafted due regard obligation as explored in the *Fisheries Jurisdiction* cases. As explained above, those cases established that competing parallel freedoms entailed both procedural and substantive obligations for the States concerned. The due regard clause currently included in Article 9 does not speak to this point and instead only protects the rights and interests of the coastal State. I cannot say that this omission is a result of eschewing the conceptual language of freedoms but the failure to adopt the language of freedoms in the draft Agreement may make the point harder to see. While it is no doubt important to be specific about the legal relationships between the coastal State and other States and their natural and juridical persons engaged in MGRS activities in areas beyond national jurisdiction, it is also important to be specific about the legal relationships as between non-coastal States and as between the natural and juridical persons of those different non-coastal States exercising parallel and potentially competing freedoms.

Finally, Hohfeld's analytical framework helps illuminate the different ways in which legal relationships change over time. For example, the LOSC changed the relationship between coastal States and other States by enhancing the power or jurisdiction of coastal States at the expense of the liberties or freedoms of other States. Similarly, both the LOSC and the UNFSA curtail the exercise of historic freedoms by layering on top of them a dense network of duties (affording correlative rights to others). The proposed BBNJ Agreement adds to this transformative effect by establishing additional duties for States and other actors engaging in activities in areas beyond national jurisdiction. In some cases, these additional duties are sourced in the primary rules of the treaty, while in other cases the treaty delegates this function to others, whether that be an institution established by the treaty or to some other standard setting organization. Whatever the mechanism, the effect is to transform an open-access

143 See discussion of 'interest(s)' in n 74 and n 139.

resource regime into something else; something along a spectrum that moves from a regulated access regime to a common heritage regime where there is no freedom to appropriate the resource. Much of the debate with respect to the MGRs provisions of the draft Agreement relates to the question of where along this spectrum we should place the MGRs regime. What Hohfeld tells us is that the specific and detailed layering of duties is legally more significant than the use of superficially conclusory labels such as common heritage or common concern – while recognizing that such labels have significant rhetorical appeal.[144]

144 See De Lucia (n 126) exploring the tension between pragmatic approaches to the treatment of MGRs rather than approaches based upon common heritage considerations.

CHAPTER 4

# Mapping Key Past and Current Debate on Areas beyond National Jurisdiction

*Tore Henriksen*

> The history of the law of the sea is part and parcel of a wider vision for the law of nation's connection with globalization[1]

## 1 Introduction

The objective of the chapter is to give an overview of the debates on the status of areas beyond national jurisdiction (ABNJ) of the past and the present. The purpose is to inform and prepare the reader for the subsequent chapters. This includes mapping central themes of different periods and to assess how they have affected the development of the law of the sea and the current debate on the ABNJ.

The process towards adoption of a third Implementing Agreement under the United Nations Convention on the Law of the Sea on Conservation and Sustainable Use of Biodiversity in Areas beyond National Jurisdiction (BBNJ)[2] has touched upon at least two themes, which may be recognisable throughout the history of the law of the sea:

– the legal status of the natural resources of the deep-sea bed: The potential high commercial value of deep-sea minerals and, in later years, marine

1 David J Bederman, 'The Sea' in Bardo Fassbender and Anne Peters (eds), *The Oxford Handbook of the History of International Law* (Oxford University Press 2012) 359–80, 361.

2 The BBNJ process involves the Intergovernmental Conference (IGC) on an international legally binding instrument under the United Nations Convention on the Law of the Sea (LOSC) on the conservation and sustainable use of marine biological diversity of areas beyond national jurisdiction, established under UN General Assembly (UNGA) Res 72/249, its PrepCom and the Ad-hoc Open-ended Informal Working Group established under UNGA Res 68/20. Relevant documents are available at <www.un.org/bbnj/content/background> (accessed 29 December 2020).

 | DOI:10.1163/9789004506367_005

genetic resources (MGRS), have raised discussions on the right to access them and their governance.[3] Particularly developing States have feared and are fearing of losing out, that the access to these resources be reserved for States with economic and personnel resources.
– adjacency: Even if the jurisdiction of the coastal State gradually has been extended seawards, there have been debates on the role of the coastal State in the governance of the resources and/or areas adjacent to their zones of jurisdiction, such as preferential right and restrictions on activities in ABNJ that could undermine the sovereign rights of the coastal States.[4]

The two themes may be understood in the context of two important drivers in the development of the law of the sea: the quest for territory and globalization.[5] Territory, in the setting of oceans, has meant providing States access to the oceans for transport and for the utilisation of its resources. The law of the sea throughout the centuries has been dominated by the competition between the exercise of territorial authority in the form of exclusive rights over the sea and the idea of the freedoms of the seas.[6] These debates have been further driven by impacts of globalization such as technological developments and the subsequent entry of new participants including new industries and developing countries in the exploitation of marine natural resources. Globalization may be defined as '...the increasing worldwide integration of economic, cultural, political, religious, and social systems'.[7] Technological developments made the oceans and their resources gradually accessible in an economic manner. It led

3 Surabhi Ranganathan, 'Ocean Floor Grab: International Law and the Making of an Extractive Imaginary' (2019) 30 European Journal of International Law 573, 594–95; David Leary, 'Marine Genetic Resources in Areas beyond National Jurisdiction: Do We Need to Regulate Them in a New Agreement?' (2018–19) 5 Maritime Safety and Security Law Journal 22.

4 See the historical context to the present debate in Joanna Mossop and Clive Schofield, 'Adjacency and due regard: The role of coastal States in the BBNJ treaty' (2020) 122 Marine Policy 1, 2–3.

5 Daniel-Erasmus Khan, 'Territory and Boundaries' in Bardo Fassbender and Anne Peters (eds), *The Oxford Handbook of the History of International Law* (Oxford University Press 2012) 225–49, 225–26.

6 D P O'Connell, *The International Law of the Sea: Volume I* (1st edn) (Oxford University Press 1982) 1; E D Brown, 'Freedom of the High Seas Versus the Common Heritage of Mankind: Fundamental Principles in Conflict (1983) 20 San Diego Law Review 21; Tullio Treves, 'Historical Development of the Law of the Sea' in Donald Rothwell and others (eds) *The Oxford Handbook of the Law of the Sea* (Oxford University Press 2015) 1–23, 2.

7 John Black, Nigar Hashimzade and Gareth Myles, *A Dictionary of Economics 3rd Edition* (Oxford University Press 2009), available at <www.oxfordreference.com/view/10.1093/acref/9780199237043.001.0001/acref-9780199237043-e-1359?rskey=GfnrTk&result=1262> accessed 22 March 2021.

to intensified competition between States over the ocean resources and later over maritime spaces, challenging the traditional freedoms of the high seas. These technological developments did also result in the extended jurisdiction of coastal States. The entry of newly independent and mostly developing States led to questions on the fairness of the existing law of the sea, till then dominated by a few States.

The first debate in of the modern law of the sea in the 17th century is often described as the 'battle of the books'.[8] The debate centred on whether States were competent to exercise exclusive authority over ocean space. The proponents of the freedoms of the high seas such as Grotius argued that the oceans were limitless and not susceptible to appropriation. Their opponents – including Selden – referred to State practice arguing that States indeed were regulating ocean space, such as fisheries. The freedoms of the high seas prevailed as the dominating paradigm.[9] Even if States did not make territorial claims as such, the freedoms of the high seas provided them equivalently with an adequate space for maritime activities, access to marine resources and other economic activities.

From the 20th century the freedoms of the high seas regime have been challenged by a wider set of interests – typical of globalization – going beyond commercial interests and security issues. The high seas, its space and resources were not any longer reserved for a few maritime States. Their positions were challenged by other States, on access to the marine resources and later by the recognition of the need to conserve the marine living resources and to protect the marine environment following intensified use and pollution of the oceans and its resources.[10] The gradual conditioning of the freedoms of the high seas may be described as a second paradigm, applicable until the present. It implied rivalry between the commercial and military interests in maintaining the freedoms of the sea and the interests in restricting the freedoms in terms of ocean zones of coastal State control.[11] Again, this related to disputes over territorial or zonal authority, and the ability of States to control access to resources.

The chapter is organized temporally to map how the two themes identified above have been addressed throughout the history of the law of the sea. The purpose is also to explore how they relate to the ongoing BBNJ process: Are there differences and/or similarities with the previous debate?

---

8 Treves (n 6) 4; Bederman (n 1) 369.
9 Bederman (n 1) 369; Treves (n 6) 5.
10 ibid 22–23.
11 O'Connell (n 6) 13.

Section 2 covers the period 1945 till the late 1960s. In this period the law of the sea was for the first time codified in a multilateral process facilitated by the United Nations (UN) through the International Law Commission (ILC) and the first and second UN Conference on Law of the Sea (UNCLOS I and II). The UN has been instrumental in later developments of the law of the sea, including the on-going BBNJ process. The balancing between individual and collective interests has varied throughout the last 75 years. This first period witnessed the dominance of individual interests through the extension of coastal State jurisdiction. More recently, in the context of the BBNJ process for example, collective interests are central. However, it might be a challenge moving the law in that direction, as it is likely to conflict with strong or well-established interests and practices, as was witnessed in the process that resulted in the UN Convention on the Law of the Sea (LOSC).

Section 3 covers the period from the late 1960s till today. During the 1960s and early 1970s, colonies in Africa and Asia gained independence, thereby changing the world map and diversifying the interests and claims in relation to the governance of the oceans. This was manifested throughout the negotiations leading to adoption of the 1982 LOSC.[12] The developing States advocated justice by arguing for the 200 nautical mile exclusive economic zone (EEZ) and the common heritage of mankind (CHM) status of the deep-sea bed beyond national jurisdiction and its mineral resources. The BBNJ process is also about justice, including topics such as access to MGRs and benefit sharing advocated by developing States.

The extension of the fisheries jurisdiction through the EEZ did not provide the coastal State with exclusive control over the living marine resources. Some species have an area of distribution also covering ABNJ. Coastal States argued that they have some preferential rights in respect of these transboundary species. This was addressed through the 1995 Fish Stocks Agreement (UNFSA).[13] As the BBNJ treaty aims at the conservation and sustainable use of biodiversity in ABNJ, there are questions about the transboundary perspectives – similar to those of the marine living resources: Should the coastal State have a particular say in establishing area-based measures in ABNJ adjacent to their EEZs?

12 United Nations Convention on the Law of the Sea (opened for signature 10 December 1982, entered into force 16 November 1994) 1833 UNTS 3 (LOSC).

13 United Nations Agreement for the Implementation of the Provisions of the United Nations Convention on the Law of the Sea of 10 December 1982 relating to the Conservation and Management of Straddling Fish Stocks and Highly Migratory Fish Stocks (opened for signature 4 August 1995, entered into force 11 December 2001) 2167 UNTS 3 (UNFSA).

## 2 Balancing Freedoms and National Control: Between Unilateralism and Multilateralism

### 2.1 *General*

This section investigates the period from 1945 till the end of the 1960s, which involved the first successful multilateral attempts to legislate the law of the sea. 1945 marked a turning point in the history of the law of the sea. The period was initiated by unilateral State actions such as the 1945 Truman proclamations,[14] which expanded the areas within national jurisdiction (AWNJ) at the expense of the high seas regime. It is also marked by increased multilateralism facilitated by the United Nations (UN), which led to the codification of the law of the sea through the four 1958 Geneva Conventions.[15]

This section aims at providing perspectives for understanding the present debate on BBNJ. The codification of the law of the sea represented a stage or phase in the development of the law introducing concepts, principles, and rules of the Geneva conventions, such as the continental shelf, that continue to impact the law. The legal developments of this period were started by coastal States unilaterally extending their jurisdiction seawards and claiming preferential rights in adjacent waters of the high seas. This section also examines the prevailing interests and focuses on the codification process whether other interests than those of individual coastal States had an influence on the codification process. In the following, the unilateral actions leading to the development of the law of the sea (section 2.2) will be addressed first, before the codification process through the UN (section 2.3).

14 Presidential Proclamation No. 2667, 28 September 1945, 'Policy of the United States With Respect to the Natural Resources of the Subsoil and Sea Bed of the Continental Shelf' available at <www.trumanlibrary.gov/library/public-papers/150/proclamation-2667-policy-united-states-respect-natural-resources-subsoil> accessed 22 July 2021; Presidential Proclamation No. 2668, 28 September 1945, 'Policy of the United States with Respect to Coastal Fisheries in Certain Areas of the High Seas' available at <www.archives.gov/federal-register/codification/proclamations/02668.html> (accessed 22 July 2021).

15 The four Geneva Conventions are the Following: The Convention on the Territorial Sea and the Contiguous Zone (opened for signature 29 April 1958, entered into force on 10 September 1964) 516 UNTS 205 (CTS); the Convention on the High Seas (opened for signature 29 April 1958, entered into force 30 September 1962) 450 UNTS 11 (HSC); the Convention on Fishing and Conservation of the Living Resources of the High Seas (opened for signature 29 April 1958, entered into force 20 March 1966) 559 UNTS 285 (CFCLR); the Convention on the Continental Shelf (opened for signature 29 April 1958, entered into force 10 June 1964) 499 UNTS 311 (CSC); and the Optional Protocol of Signature concerning the Compulsory Settlement of Disputes (opened for signature 29 April 1958, entered into force 30 September 1962) UN Doc A/CONF.13/L.58.

### 2.2 *Nationalisation through Unilateral Action*

The Truman proclamations on the continental shelf[16] and on the conservation zones on the high seas[17] involved claims to exclusive rights over the natural resources of the seabed and subsoil adjacent to US coasts and jurisdiction to regulate fisheries in designated areas of the adjacent high seas.

The US arguments were primarily based on notions of justice, referring to 'reasonable and just' claims, and the fact that the petroleum and mineral resources are located in areas, which are an extension of the US land mass.[18] This argument resonated with the 'land dominates the sea' doctrine, which was confirmed a few years earlier by the ICJ in the *Fisheries Jurisdiction* case.[19] Interestingly, the US argument seemed to construct the idea that the continental shelf was an original concept, not infringing on the high seas regime. In fact, both Truman proclamations underlined that the character of high seas of the waters above the continental shelf was not affected.

Although the main rationale of the US for claiming preferential rights in adjacent parts of the high seas was the '… urgent need for protecting coastal fisheries resources from destructive exploitation …', the real motive was to secure preferential rights.[20] These resources were of special importance to its coastal communities. Under the proclamation, the US was competent to exercise jurisdiction over fishing vessels in designated areas of the high seas for these purposes. It recognised that other States were entitled to fish in these areas and signalled that it would collaborate on joint development and management of fisheries where nationals of several States were involved.[21]

The proclamations struck a chord of that time as they did not meet any objections.[22] The US initiative was followed *inter alia* by Latin American States arguing for a 200 nautical mile zone, distancing themselves from Grotian rules.[23] These coastal States used similar arguments as the US for nationalisation, the need to ensure subsistence for their population and to provide for

16 Presidential Proclamation No. 2667 (n 14).
17 Presidential Proclamation No. 2668 (n 14).
18 Ranganathan (n 3) 581.
19 See eg *Fisheries Case* (*UK v Norway*) [1951] ICJ Reports 1951, 116, 133: 'It is the land which confers upon the coastal State a right to the waters off its coasts'.
20 Presidential Proclamation No. 2668 (n 14).
21 ibid.
22 Ranganathan, 'Ocean Floor Grab' (n 3) 581.
23 Robert L Friedheim, *Negotiating the New Ocean Regime* (University of South Carolina University Press 1993) 19–20; Ann Hollick','The Origins of 200-Mile Offshore Zones' (1977) 71 American Journal of International Law 494, 500.

economic development.[24] Again, either camouflaging it as preferential rights or outright claiming territorial rights, these States aimed at controlling access to and exploitation of important marine resources.

### 2.3 *Multilateralism: Balancing between Freedoms and Sovereign Rights/ Preferential Rights*

With the adoption of the Geneva conventions, the legal order for the oceans was clarified providing for stability and predictability. This subsection will, as indicated above, look at the interests involved in the process and how they were balanced. It relates particularly to the collective interests of States in maintaining the freedoms of the high seas.

#### 2.3.1 Codification of the Law of the Sea

The International Law Commission (ILC) included in its first year of operation (1949) the high seas regime as one of its priority areas.[25] This was triggered by recent State practice such as continental shelf claims that had 'profound repercussions' for the regime.[26]

Its discussions and analyses of the high seas regime came to include the fisheries and the continental shelf regime. The ILC recognised that coastal States had legitimate interests in the conservation of high seas fisheries.[27] '… The "special" character of the interest of the coastal State was based on the geographical adjacency to the high seas area'.[28] However, this special interest did not involve precedence *per* se over the interests of States exercising the freedom of fishing.[29] Until 1953, its reports included a proposal to establish under the UN a body competent to adopt legally binding regulations in high seas fisheries in case States were not able to agree on regulations.[30] The body would serve the interests of the international community as a whole. In later reports, arbitration had replaced a UN body as the default mechanism.[31]

---

24 Declaration on the maritime zone (signed and entered into force 18 August 1952) 1006 UNTS 325.

25 Yearbook of the International Law Commission (1949) 43.

26 ibid 235; Treves (n 6) 11–13.

27 Articles concerning the Law of the Sea with commentaries, Yearbook of the International Law Commission (vol 2, 1956) 286–87.

28 ibid 288 (para 14).

29 ibid.

30 Yoshinobu Takei, *Filling regulatory gaps in high seas fisheries: Discrete high seas fish stocks, deep-sea fisheries and vulnerable marine ecosystems* (Martinus Nijhoff 2013) 22; Yearbook of the International Law Commission (vol 2, 1953) 218–19.

31 Yearbook of the International Law Commission (vol 2, 1955); Report of the International Law Commission to the General Assembly, UN Doc A/2934: Regime of the High Seas,

Similarly, as concerns the continental shelf regime, it had been argued that its resources should not be allocated to the coastal State, but entrusted to the international community.[32] However, it was concluded that such '... internationalization would meet with insurmountable practical difficulties, and would not ensure the effective exploitation of natural resources necessary to meet the needs of mankind'.[33] The littoral State was in a better position to provide for the effective exploitation of the natural resources of the continental shelf.[34]

The 1958 UN Conference on the Law of the Sea (UNCLOS I) resulted in the adoption of the four Geneva conventions. The Continental Shelf Convention (CSC) provided the coastal State with sovereign rights over the natural resources on the continental shelf.[35]

The High Seas Convention (HSC) defined the high seas as '... all parts of the sea not included in the territorial sea or internal waters of a State'.[36] The lack of reference to the continental shelf created uncertainty about the relationship between the two zones. The list of the freedoms of the high seas did not include the exploitation and exploration of the natural resources of its seabed and subsoil.[37] There was different readings of this omission.[38] ILC had considered that exploitation of the natural resources of the seabed of the high seas had not '...assumed sufficient practical importance to justify special regulation'.[39] The inadequate regulation of the high seas regime made it vulnerable to future challenges, which is recognizable from the debate of recent years on the status of MGRs in ABNJ.[40]

Under the 1958 Convention on Fishing and Conservation of the Living Resources of the High Seas (Fishing Convention), States were instructed to cooperate on necessary conservation measures.[41] The Fishing Convention

Article 31 30–31), Cf. Articles concerning the Law of the Sea with commentaries, Yearbook of the International Law Commission (vol 2, 1956) 286–87.

32 Yearbook of the International Law Commission (vol 2, 1950) 384, para 198; Yearbook of the International Law Commission 1956 (n 31) 296.

33 ibid.

34 Yearbook of the International Law Commission 1950 (n 32) 384, para 198.

35 CSC (n 15) art 2.

36 HSC (n 15) art 1.

37 ibid art 2.

38 Bernard H Oxman, 'The High Seas and the International Seabed Area' (1989) 10 Michigan Journal of International Law 526, 530.

39 ibid.

40 Lyle Glowka, 'The Deepest of Ironies: Genetic Resources, Marine Scientific Research, and the Area' (1996) 12 Ocean Yearbook 154, 155.

41 CFCLR (n 15).

recognised that the coastal State had a 'special interest' in the conservation of living marine resources in high seas areas adjacent to its territorial sea.[42]

### 2.3.2 International Legislation: Adapting to Practice Rather than Developing New Law

The codification process was to a large degree driven by and responsive to State practice. The lawyers involved – practitioners and academics – adopted a pragmatic approach.[43] They did not aim at dramatic changes to the law, rather sought to address pressing needs. Friedheim described the period as focusing on solving problems rather than considering principles.[44] The US had started a worldwide movement that could not be stopped or reversed, giving coastal States exclusive rights to marine natural resources. The function of international law was understood as adapting the law to this development rather than the opposite. Right or wrong, scholars argued that international law indeed could be developed through an international conference under the auspices of the UN and not be left to the practice of the powerful States.[45]

The drawback of such a pragmatic approach was that no investigations were undertaken of the needs for regulations and/or of alternative models of governance. Proposals or ideas to establish international institutions charged with managing fisheries and petroleum resources of the high seas that could even strengthen the high seas regime were not seriously considered. Even if large parts of the oceans remained high seas, the obligations of States remained bilateral.[46] It was still the interests of the individual States to control space and resources, and not that of the international community, that prevailed.

Anand offered a sober analysis of the codification process: '… In sum, after the two UN Conferences, the law of the sea remained essentially the traditional law …'[47] The lesson from this period seems to be that the international conferences do not provide for quick and radical changes but aim at consolidating the law driven by State practice.

---

42 ibid arts 6(1) and 8.

43 Ranganathan, 'Ocean Floor Grab' (n 3) 592–93.

44 Friedheim (n 23) 19.

45 Euripides L Evriviades, 'Third World's Approach to the Deep Seabed' (1982) 11 Ocean Development and International Law 201, 207.

46 Surabhi Ranganathan, 'The Law of the Sea and Natural Resources' in Eyal Benvenisti and Georg Nolte (eds), *Community Interests Across International Law* (Oxford University Press 2018) 121, 124.

47 R P Anand, 'Winds of change in the law of the sea' in R P Anand (ed), *Law of the Sea: Caracas and beyond*, (Brill 1980) 36, 41.

## 3 Progressive Development: Consolidating the ABNJ Regimes and Further Nationalisation

### 3.1 *General*

This section investigates the period from the late 1960s until today, including the on-going BBNJ process. After the adoption of the 1958 Geneva conventions, new States gained their independence and changed the composition of the world community, with respect to both the number of States and the range of interests that found a voice. They were mostly developing States located in the Global South, often having other priorities for the development of the law of the sea than the traditional (developed) maritime States.[48] According to Anand, the newly independent developing States in Africa and Asia broke '… open the exclusive and powerful club of western Christian powers and Japan, forming the active community of States'.[49] What started in the late 1960s as a concern among developing States about the legal regime for the exploitation of the minerals of the seabed led to a process that culminated with the adoption of the 1982 LOSC. They sought to change the '… imbalance in the international legal and economic order …'[50] However, as pointed out by Ranganathan, the developing States did not fully accept the proposals to subject vast areas of the seabed to the status of the CHM: They represented a diverse set of interests and together with developed States, they argued for extending their zones under national jurisdiction, including the continental shelf.[51] As coastal States, they were concerned about the control over the exploitation of natural resources in their coastal waters.[52] These claims resonated with the adoption of the UNGA resolution on permanent sovereignty over natural resources.[53] The purpose was partly to correct historical injustice and to have a recognition that an equal right to a full control and free use of natural resources is a crucial condition for the political autonomy and the economic development of a State.[54]

48 Christopher C Joyner and Elizabeth A Martell, 'Looking Back to See Ahead: UNCLOS III and Lessons for Global Commons Law' (1996) 27 Ocean Development and International Law 73, 76.

49 Anand, 'Winds of change' (n 47) 42.

50 Evriviades (n 45) 208.

51 Ranganathan, 'Natural Resources' (n 46) 128.

52 Anand, 'Winds of change' (n 47) 39–40.

53 UNGA resolution 1803 (XVII) of 14 December 1962, 'Permanent sovereignty over natural resources'.

54 Petra Gümplová, 'Sovereignty over natural resources – A normative reinterpretation' (2020) 9 Global Constitutionalism 7, 16.

The following two subsections investigates the rights of developing States to access and to participate in the governance of deep-sea resources and the preferential rights of coastal States, consistent with the two themes, identified in section 1, which were particularly debated in the years leading up to and following the adoption of the LOSC. Section 3.2 explores the latter-mentioned theme. First, it includes debates on the status of ABNJ as CHM (section 3.2.1) from the initial proposals in the late 1960s during the third UN Conference on the Law of the Sea (UNCLOS III) to its incorporation in the LOSC and the later amendments of the 1994 Implementation Agreement.[55] This is aimed at providing insight into the conflicting interests and how they were overcome and resolved, which is of relevance to the on-going BBNJ process. The subsection further investigates the more recent debate on the status of MGRs in ABNJ (section 3.2.2), having parallels to the discussions of the 1970s. It is in recent years that the deep-sea regime of the LOSC and consequently the CHM is being put into operation, *inter alia* through regulations on exploration and exploitation developed through the International Seabed Authority (ISA). Protection of the marine environment is one of the components of CHM and the so-called sponsoring States have an important role in ensuring that the environmental regulations adopted by ISA are complied with. Section 3.2.3 investigates what this role entails and whether the CHM implies that developing States have different roles or responsibilities as sponsoring States.

The second theme is explored in section 3.3. Even if coastal States had their jurisdiction significantly expanded through the 200 nautical mile EEZ, there was still a debate on whether they enjoyed preferential rights in regard of straddling and highly migratory fish stocks in adjacent areas of the high seas (section 3.3.1). This debate was addressed through the 1995 UNFSA and the requirement of compatibility (section 3.3.2). The debate in regard of transboundary fish stocks resonates with the debate in the BBNJ process where arguments have been made that coastal States should enjoy preferential rights in adjacent areas of the ABNJ (section 3.3.3).

55 Agreement relating to the implementation of Part XI of the United Nations Convention on the Law of the Sea of 10 December 1982 (signed 18 July 1994, entered in force 16 November 1994) 1836 UNTS 3.

### 3.2 *The Seabed beyond the Continental Shelf/National Jurisdiction as Common Heritage of Mankind*

#### 3.2.1 The Incorporation of the Common Heritage of Mankind into the Law of the Sea

In the mid-1960s, many States, including Malta, were concerned that the seabed and its resources would either be part of the continental shelf of coastal States or subjected to occupation, both options favouring developed States.[56] During a UNGA debate in 1967 over the status of the seabed, Malta's ambassador, Arvid Pardo, proposed that the seabed and ocean floor 'underlying the seas beyond the limits of present national jurisdiction' be designated 'the common heritage of mankind'.[57] The concept of CHM had already been explored by UN agencies as possible means to regulate seabed mining.[58] Pardo argued that the consequences of the appropriation of the seabed may be incalculable and that States should consider some form of international jurisdiction and control over the seabed beyond the limits of present national jurisdiction, 'before events take an irreversible course'.[59] He later described the application of the traditional principles of the high seas as creating 'intolerable injustice of reserving the plurality of the world's resources for the exclusive benefit of a few States'.[60] His intervention was part of a broader movement both to stop the tendency of creeping national jurisdiction into ABNJ and to redefine its *res communis* character which benefited only a few States.[61] With this initiative a new dimension was introduced to law of the sea – equity – and more value driven approaches.

Following Pardo's speech, the UNGA established the Ad-Hoc Seabed Committee, charged with examining the use of the seabed outside national jurisdiction in the interest of mankind.[62] In its 1969 report, the Committee concluded that parts of the seabed lay beyond national jurisdiction.[63] As

56 Ranganathan, 'Natural Resources' (n 46) 127.

57 Arvid Pardo, UNGA, First Committee, 15th Meeting 1 November 1967, UN Doc A/C.1/PV.L515, paras 10(a) and 13.

58 Ranganathan, 'Natural Resources' (n 46) 127.

59 Pardo, UNGA Meeting (n 57) para. 7.

60 Arvid Pardo, 'An International Regime for the Deep Seabed: Developing Law or Developing Anarchy' (1969) 5 Texas International Law Forum 204, 207.

61 John E Noyes, 'The Common Heritage of Mankind: Past, Present, and Future' (2011–2012) 40 Denver Journal of International Law and Policy 447, 457; Helmut Tuerk, *Reflections on the Contemporary Law of the Sea* (Brill 2012) 33; Rüdiger Wolfrum, 'The Principle of the Common Heritage of Mankind' (1983) 43 Zeitschrift für ausländisches öffentliches Recht und Völkerrecht 312, 315.

62 UNGA Res 2340 (XXII).

63 O'Connell (n 6) 460.

the work of the Committee progressed, the conflicting values became evident: individual interests by States arguing the freedoms of the seas on the one hand versus community interests by States advocating some sort of stewardship on the other hand.[64] The majority of States agreed on establishing some sort of shared ownership regime between all States.[65] Even the US accepted such idea, realising the need for providing its industry with predictability and stability.[66] Subsequently, the UNGA declared the seabed beyond national jurisdiction as CHM.[67]

#### 3.2.1.1 *UNCLOS III: Clash of Values*

UNCLOS III (1973–82), was charged with establishing 'an equitable international regime' for the oceans.[68] An important component was the deep-sea bed regime. Both during UNCLOS III and after the adoption of the LOSC the concept or principle of CHM was criticised for its ambiguity.[69] This was not surprising, given the different views of developing and developed States on the legal regime pertaining to the resources of the deep seabed.[70] The introduction of the New International Economic Order (NIEO) added to these controversies, challenging the Western ideology of economic liberalism.[71] Morgera has described the NIEO as an attempt by the developing countries to 'radically restructuring the global economic system by prioritizing the objective of development …'[72] The NIEO was grounded in UNGA resolutions.[73] Its goal was

64 Joyner and Martell (n 48) 76.

65 Lea Brilmayer and Natalie Klein, 'Land and Sea: Two Sovereignty Regimes In search of A Common Denominator' (2001) 33 New York University Journal of International Law and Politics 703, 727.

66 Ranganathan, 'Natural Resources' (n 46) 128.

67 UNGA Res 2749 (XXV).

68 UNGA Res 2750 V (XXV) para 2; UNGA Res 3067 (XXVIII). Reservation exclusively for peaceful purposes of the seabed and the ocean floor, and the subsoil thereof, underlying the high seas beyond the limits of present national jurisdiction and use of their resources in the interests of mankind, and convening of the Third United Nations Conference on the Law of the Sea, para. 3.

69 Noyes (n 61) 447.

70 Lawrence Juda, 'UNCLOS III and the New International Economic Order' (1979) 7 Ocean Development and International Law Journal 221, 226.

71 ibid; Boleslaw Adam Boczek, 'Ideology and the Law of the Sea: The Challenge of the New International Economic Order' (1984) 7 Boston College and International Comparative Law Review 1, 2; Ranganathan, 'Ocean Floor Grab' (n 3) 595.

72 Elisa Morgera, 'The Need for an International Legal Concept of Fair and Equitable Benefit Sharing' (2016) 27 European Journal of International Law 353, 358.

73 Declaration on the Establishment of a New International Economic Order, UNGA Res 3201 (S-VI); Program of Action on the Establishment of a New International Economic

to change the existing international economic world order that hampered the development of the newly independent States: 70% of the world population, and only 30% of the income. The basic principles for the NIEO required more just and equitable conditions by promoting broader cooperation between States, just and equitable relationship between the prices of raw materials exported and imported by developing States and preferential non-reciprocal treatment of developing States.[74]

There were disagreements between States on several of the components of CHM. Some opponents of the CHM saw the regime as 'the greatest land grab of all, which threatened commercial enterprise by vesting control of the seabed in a kind of supergovernment answerable to no one'.[75] In between the two extremes, some developed States from Scandinavia and Western Europe took a pragmatic approach.[76] They recognised that they were not able to prevent the adoption of the CHM and sought compromises.[77]

#### 3.2.1.2 *CHM in the LOSC*

Article 140 paragraph 1 of the LOSC stipulates that the activities of the deep seabed area are to be carried out for 'the benefit of mankind as a whole', implying distributional justice as an important purpose.[78] The CHM, described as a fundamental legal principle, was elaborated through a regime of principles and obligations including:[79]

- non-appropriation;[80]
- the resources of the deep seabed belong to the humankind as a whole;[81]
- governance through common management;
- use for peaceful purposes;[82]

---

Order, UNGA Res 3202 (S-VI); Charter of Economic Rights and Duties of States, UNGA Res 3281 (XXIX).

74 Declaration on the Establishment of a New International Economic Order, UNGA Res 3201 (S-VI), para 4.

75 Ranganathan, 'Ocean Floor Grab' (n 3) 577 with reference to Ely, 'One OPEC Is Enough!' (1981) 5 Regulation 19.

76 Friedheim (n 23) 290.

77 ibid.

78 Rüdiger Wolfrum, 'Common Heritage of Mankind' (2009) Max Planck Encyclopedia of International Law para 19.

79 Dire Tladi, 'The Common Heritage of Mankind and the Proposed Treaty on Biodiversity in Areas beyond National Jurisdiction: The choice between Pragmatism and Sustainability' (2015) 25 YIEL 113, 124–27; Noyes (n 61) 450–54; Ranganathan, 'Natural Resources' (n 46) 125.

80 LOSC art 89 (high seas) and art 137 (1) (Area).

81 ibid art 137(2).

82 ibid arts 88 and 141.

- sharing of benefits; and
- protection and preservation of the marine environment.

The controversies or differences surrounding the concept of CHM have particularly concerned the governance, access to the resources and sharing of benefits. The fact that *the resources belong to humankind as a whole*, implies that the rights of individuals or States to access the resources are dependent on some sort of concession or licence adopted under the provisions of Part XI of the LOSC.[83] Developed States argued that the CHM should be limited to improvements in the distribution of benefits derived from the exploitation of the resources.[84] However, the developing States rejected that the freedom of access should be a component of CHM, arguing that the concept provided humankind with property rights similar to ownership.[85]

The Nixon administration had recognised the need for an international trusteeship zone to prevent further nationalisation.[86] This policy was reversed with the Reagan administration, which built on a more liberal approach to property rights.[87] It was based on the Lockean notion that ownership is acquired by those who find the natural resources, invest labour and capital in extracting them, take the risks, and consequently those with the greatest connection to the resource.[88]

Restricting the right to access to the mineral resources presupposes the existence of a *common management* regime. The regime involved a global, institutionalized mechanism competent to regulate all activities and to distribute the benefits equitably.[89] CHM presumes the establishment of an international institution – the ISA (or Authority) – competent to manage the resource on behalf of mankind.[90] All the States parties to the LOSC are members of the ISA. The US, the proponent of free access to the mineral resources was critical of the establishment of the ISA, and in particular its competence to restrict

83 LOSC art 137(2).
84 See for an overview Tuerk (n 61) 36–37.
85 ibid.
86 Ranganathan, 'Ocean Floor Grab' (n 3) 583.
87 R P Anand, *Studies in International Law and History* (Springer 2004) 182.
88 Doug Bandow, 'UNCLOS III: A Flawed Treaty' (1982) 19 San Diego Law Review 475, 478–79; Louis B Sohn, 'The Law of the Sea Crisis' (1984) 58 St. John's Law Review 237, 258–60.
89 Ranganathan, 'Ocean Floor Grab' (n 3) 592.
90 Tladi (n 79) 126; LOSC art 137(2). The Authority is set up under LOSC Part XI section 4 whereas its areas of competence are regulated in same part, section 3 (as amended by the 1994 Implementation Agreement).

entry into the market, set production limitations, and mandate the transfer of technology, which violated 'rights of economic liberty'.[91]

*Sharing of benefits* is an essential element of CHM and may include both monetary and non-monetary benefits.[92] There is a close link between benefit sharing and the NIEO movement, which aimed at accommodating the needs of developing States.[93] Tladi argues that the implementation of the CHM hinges on the benefit-sharing element.[94]

The CHM principle included both preferential treatment to ensure economic development and provided for a *de facto* equal participation.[95] Preferential treatment was facilitated through provisions ensuring the transfer of technology, establishment of production policy and the role of the Enterprise.[96] Examples of *de facto* equal participation included States receiving revenues equivalent to direct participation in deep seabed activities and restricting the activities of the deep seabed mining States and supporting activities of other States.[97]

Under the leadership of the Group of 77, third world States joined against prospective deep seabed mining States, particularly the US.[98] However, although the developing States were successful in adopting a Part XI in accordance with their positions and interests, their triumph was short-lived. On 30 April 1982, in the vote on the LOSC, 130 States were in favour, 4 opposed, and 17 abstained.[99]

#### 3.2.1.3 *The 1994 Implementation Agreement: Watering down the CHM?*

As the LOSC was to enter into force, initiatives were taken to ensure its universal application by attracting the ratification and accession of developed States.[100] This led to the negotiation and adoption of the 1994 Implementation Agreement, which in reality amended Part XI of the LOSC.[101] According to

91 Bandow (n 88) 480.
92 LOSC art 140(2).
93 Noyes (n 61) 470.
94 Tladi (n 79) 126–27.
95 Wolfrum, 'The Principle' (n 61) 321–22.
96 See eg LOSC arts 144, 150–151, 153 and Annex III.
97 ibid.
98 Joyner and Martell (n 48) 78–79.
99 Summary Record of 182nd plenary meeting; Official Records, Volume XVI, UN Doc A/CONF.62/SR.182, 154–55 (paras 27–28).
100 Louis B Sohn, 'International Law Implications of the 1994 Agreement' (1994) 88 The American Journal of International Law 696.
101 See n 55 for full title.

Oxman, the amendments responded to the criticism of the US.[102] It provided the US and other industrial States with increased influence on decision-making and incorporated marked-based principles.[103]

The Implementation Agreement strengthened the role of the 36 member-Council, one of the principal organs of ISA at the expense of its plenary organ, the Assembly.[104] Its decisions are to be based on the recommendations of the Council.[105] The procedures for the elections to the Council were amended, securing the US a permanent seat, if it were to accede to the Convention. The decision-making procedures of the Council provide the US and developed States with *de facto* veto power.[106]

Furthermore, ISA is no longer competent to set a ceiling on production, to limit production, to require licenses for participation and production or to require transfer of technology.[107] The Enterprise, an organ under the ISA, was competent to carry out exploration and exploitation activities in the Area.[108] The US and other States were critical to such role arguing that it would discriminate private actors, by forcing them to cooperate through joint ventures with the Enterprise or developing countries. Under the Implementation Agreement, the Enterprise had lost its privileged status and is subject to the same conditions as any private contractor.[109] Private contractors are neither required to fund one mining site of the Enterprise.[110]

The LOSC provides few details on how the benefits from the activities of the Area shall be shared. The Assembly shall adopt rules and procedures for the equitable sharing of financial and other economic benefits, '... taking into particular consideration the interests and needs of developing States and peoples that have no attained full independence or other self-governing status'.[111] As noted above, under the revised decision-making procedures, providing the Council with extended power, the developed/industrialized States have extensive influence in designing and practicing the equitable sharing regime.

102 Bernard Oxman, 'Law of the Sea Forum: The 1994 Agreement on Implementation of the Seabed Provisions of the Convention on the Law of the Sea. The 1994 Agreement and the Convention' (1994) 88 American Journal of International Law 687.
103 ibid 695.
104 LOSC art 159 (1).
105 Implementation Agreement, Annex, section 3, para 4.
106 ibid annex, section 3, paras 15(a) and (b).
107 ibid annex, section 6, para 7 and section 5, para 2.
108 LOSC art 170.
109 Implementation Agreement, annex, section 2, para 4.
110 ibid annex, section 2, para 3.
111 LOSC art 160(2)(f).

#### 3.2.1.3 *Present Status of* CHM

The Implementation Agreement has been subjected to different and even conflicting assessments. Stevenson and Oxman were concerned that the political controversy over deep seabed mining had dominated the debate for too long and creating misconceptions of the LOSC.[112] Their hope was obviously that the Implementation Agreement could attract a more positive and constructive attention to the LOSC. Noyes argued that the traditional elements of CHM were still in place: The basic features banning sovereign claims, ensuring equitable sharing of benefits, the peaceful purposes and environmental protection. On the opposite end, Anand argued that the US got 'all it wanted' through the Implementation Agreement and the practice of the ISA.[113] The international community had backtracked to satisfy Washington. The CHM principle had lost its original meaning, as advocated by Pardo, argued Anand.[114] He concluded: 'The deep seabed will now be exploited on commercial terms, irrespective of the needs and interests of the weaker members of the international community'.[115]

The Implementation Agreement reflects a pragmatic approach. It was pragmatic in the sense that the objective of ensuring universal application of the CHM regime – and indeed of the LOSC as a whole – was viewed as more important than insisting on a principled stance. The consequence was that the ideas of economic liberalism again prevailed over the ideas of community interests and justice. The developed States, capable of exploring and exploiting the resources of the deep-sea had the decisive say. The alternative would have been a fragmented international legal order, where developed States could have developed a parallel regime for the exploration and exploitation of the minerals of the deep sea based on traditional freedoms of the high seas in competition with the deep seabed regime of the LOSC.

Similar situations may occur in the BBNJ process. Although constituting the majority of the world community, the developing States and their call for community-based solutions that promote equity and justice may clash with proponents of economic liberalism. Again, to ensure universal application of a legally binding instrument on BBNJ, demands for more fundamental changes to the law may be left for non-principled compromises.

112 John R Stevenson and Bernard H Oxman, 'The Future of the United Nations Convention on the Law of the Sea' (1994) 88 The American Journal of International Law 488.

113 Anand, *International Law and History* (n 87) 195.

114 ibid 196; Noyes (n 61) 464.

115 ibid.

### 3.2.2 The Legal Status of MGRS: CHM or Part of the Freedoms of the High Seas?

The debate of recent years has not only been concerned with the implementation of the CHM regime and its potential inadequacies. It has been extended to whether it includes other resources than minerals, such as MGRS.

#### 3.2.2.1 *Introducing Marine Genetic Resources to the Law of the Sea*

The Convention on Biological Diversity (CBD) introduced genetic resources as a new legal concept, also relevant in the law of the sea.[116] The CBD aims at the conservation of biodiversity, sustainable use of its components and the fair and equitable sharing of the benefits of the utilization of the genetic resources.[117] In the ABNJ, the CBD is applicable to processes and activities under the jurisdiction or control of Contracting Parties.[118] They are required to cooperate with the aim of conservation and sustainable use of biological diversity.[119] There are no clear answers as how to apply the obligations under the CBD to the ABNJ, consistently with the rights and obligations of States under the law of the sea.[120]

A concern is the status of MGRS in the ABNJ, as the adoption of the CBD revealed gaps in the international regulatory framework for MGRS.[121] The debate on the status of MGRS raised questions as to the ability of the LOSC to adapt to new knowledge and technological developments. One of the 'deepest of ironies' of the LOSC, it was argued, was that the MGRS, probably the 'most immediately exploitable and lucrative resource' of the Area, are not referred to in the Convention.[122]

---

116 Convention on Biological Diversity (signed 5 June 1992, entered in force 29 December 1993) 1760 UNTS 79 (CBD) art 2 (definition) and art 15 (access to genetic resources).

117 ibid art 1.

118 ibid art 4.

119 ibid art 5.

120 Louise Angelique de La Fayette, 'A New Regime for the Conservation and Sustainable Use of Marine Biodiversity and Genetic Resources Beyond the Limits of National Jurisdiction' (2009) 24 The International Journal of Marine and Coastal Law 221, 276; CBD art 22.

121 Robin Warner, 'Developing New Regulatory Paradigms for the Conservation and Sustainable Use of Marine Biodiversity in Areas Beyond National Jurisdiction' in Robin Warner and Stuart Kaye (eds), *Routledge Handbook of Maritime Regulation and Enforcement* (Routledge 2016) 397.

122 Glowka, 'Deepest of Ironies' (n 40) 155.

#### 3.2.2.2 *Four Approaches to the Status of MGRs in ABNJ*

The application or non-application of the CHM to MGRs have been widely debated in the literature.[123] There have been four broad approaches to the relevance of CHM to MGRs.[124] They have been introduced at different times, some even before the BBNJ process started and some may have been subject to subsequent modifications or changes.

The arguments of the *first* approach that MGRs are part of the CHM, are based on the interpretation of the LOSC and in particular its Part XI, where it is stated that the both the resources of the Area *and* the Area itself are the CHM.[125] This entails that MGRs are naturally encompassed by the CHM regime.

Others argue that MGRs are part of the freedoms of the high seas and freely accessible to all States.[126] The status of MGRs is arguably the same as mineral resources in ABNJ before the adoption of the LOSC.[127] Therefore, according to the *second approach* there is an urgent need for a debate on the future status of MGRs: whether it should be retained as a freedom, be included by CHM regime or regulated through a new legal regime.[128] Freely accessible MGRs would only benefit a handful of States.[129]

Proponents of the *third* approach, recognizing that MGRs are part of the freedoms of the high seas, acknowledge the need to fill the gaps evident in the present regime.[130] However, this could be undertaken within the existing framework of Part VII of the LOSC under which there is an obligation of States to cooperate.

The *fourth* approach involves analyses that are not preoccupied on whether MGRs belong to either of the two regimes. They were more concerned with

---

123 See eg Penelope Ridings, 'Redefining environmental stewardship to deliver governance frameworks for marine biodiversity beyond national jurisdiction' (2018) 75 ICES Journal of Marine Science 435.

124 David Leary, 'Moving the Marine Genetic Resources Debate Forward: Some Reflections' (2012) 27 International Journal of Marine & Coastal Law 435, 439.

125 Alex G Oude Elferink, 'The Regime of the Area: Delineating the Scope of Application of the Common Heritage Principle and Freedom of the High Seas' (2007) 22 International Journal of Marine & Coastal Law 143, 147ff.

126 Glowka, 'Deepest of Ironies' (n 40) 168.

127 Lyle Glowka, 'Genetic Resources, Marine Scientific Research and the International Seabed Area' (1999) 8 Review of European Community & International Environmental Law 56, 58–59.

128 ibid.

129 Glowka, 'Deepest of Ironies' (n 40) 155.

130 Craig Allen, 'Protecting the Oceanic Gardens of Eden: International Law Issues in Deep Sea Vent Resources Conservation and Management' (2001) 13 Georgetown International Environmental Law Review 563.

finding pragmatic – non principled – solutions and less with defining the legal status of MGRs.[131] One commentator described the promotion by developing States of the 'common heritage solution' as a 'fundamentalist' approach.[132] Another argued that it was unlikely that the status of MGRs would '… reflect the CHM principle in any "pure", Pardo-esque form, if at all'.[133] The consequence was that the proponents of CHM status ignored the possibility of finding solutions that are more practical.

The (fourth) pragmatic approach was criticised by proponents of the CHM status.[134] Their concern was that important elements of CHM are lost without any real consideration. It was '… the [CHM] principle [that] is the thread that binds the proposed elements of a new treaty together – that is, conservation and sustainable use, including benefit sharing, area-based management tools (ABMTs) including marine protected areas (MPAs), environmental impact assessments (EIAs) and capacity building, and technology transfer'.[135]

Parallel to the academic debate, the Ad Hoc Open-ended Informal Working Group[136] was established in a recognition of the need for a more systematic approach to addressing the gaps regarding conservation of marine biodiversity in ABNJ.[137] The debate in the Working Group (2006–15) included the status of MGRs, which was one of the most controversial issues discussed.[138] Its outcome document did not conclude on the status of the MGRs other than including marine genetic resources, and benefit sharing as one of the recommended topics for negotiations at an intergovernmental conference.[139] The status of

131 Seemingly also Louise Angelique de La Fayette (n 120) 221–80.

132 David Leary, 'Moving the Marine Genetic Resources Debate Forward: Some Reflections' (2012) 27 International Journal of Marine & Coastal Law 435, 438.

133 Noyes (n 61) 469.

134 Tladi (n 79) 114; Vito De Lucia, 'The Question of the Common Heritage of Mankind and the Negotiations towards a Global Treaty on Marine Biodiversity in Areas beyond National Jurisdiction: No End in Sight?' (2020) 16(2) McGill Journal of Sustainable Development Law 140; Alice B M Vadrot, Arne Langlet and Ina Tessnow-von Wysocki, 'Who owns marine biodiversity? Contesting the world order through the "common heritage of humankind" principle' (2021) Environmental Politics available at <https://doi.org/10.1080/09644016.2021.1911442> accessed 22 July 2021.

135 Tladi (n 79) 131.

136 Full title: Ad Hoc Open-ended Informal Working Group to study issues relating to the conservation and sustainable use of marine biological diversity beyond areas of national jurisdiction, established by UNGA Res/59/24, para 73.

137 Warner (n 121) 401; UNGA Res/59/24 (n 136) Oceans and the law of the sea, para 73.

138 ibid.

139 Outcome of the Ad Hoc Open-ended Informal Working Group to study issues relating to the conservation and sustainable use of marine biological diversity beyond areas of national jurisdiction and Co-Chairs' summary of discussions, in Annex to Letter dated 13

MGRs is still unresolved in the ongoing intergovernmental conference. A principle that the utilisation of MGRs shall be '… for the benefit of mankind as a whole …' is placed in brackets in the revised draft text of an agreement on the conservation and sustainable use of BBNJ (Revised Draft Agreement) prepared by the President of the conference.[140]

#### 3.2.2.2 *The Debate on the Status of MGRs: Between CHM and Part of the Freedoms of the High Seas*

The positions taken in the debate on status of MGRs have clear parallels to the debate during UNCLOS III on the status of minerals of the deep-sea bed, particularly between those arguing for CHM status and those arguing for the freedoms of the high seas. In between, there are voices arguing for compromise solutions, probably reflective of the development in recent years of the deep-sea regime as evidenced by the Implementation Agreement.

Still, the CHM principle and its implications in respect of MGRs are fraught with ambiguities.[141] Similar to the regime for deep seabed minerals, the principle needs to be transformed into concrete rules, standards, and practices. Furthermore, the question is what remains of the original CHM principle following the amendments made through the Implementation Agreement. The question is most relevant for the BBNJ process. It is natural to assume that the CHM principle would have the same application to MGRs as to minerals under the LOSC. Consequently, the core element (in addition to common management) would include procedures for benefit sharing, unless the other elements of CHM, such as preferential treatment are reintroduced into a new legal instrument. The latter does not seem very likely given the positions of States. It may explain the attempts to find a middle ground by highlighting benefit-sharing. The benefit-sharing element has become a central element of the debate, but will there be any benefits to redistribute?[142] The question is whether the debate on the status of MGRs as CHM is more of a symbolic than a substantive character.

---

February 2015 from the Co-Chairs of the Ad Hoc Open-ended Informal Working Group to the President of the General Assembly.

140 Revised draft text of an agreement under the United Nations Convention on the Law of the Sea on the conservation and sustainable use of marine biological diversity of areas beyond national jurisdiction (Revised Draft Agreement). Note by the President (18 November 2019) art 9(4), cf art 5(c), UN Doc A/Conf.232/2020/3.

141 Common Heritage of Mankind is listed as one of possible general principles of the Revised Draft Agreement, art 5.

142 Ranganathan, 'Ocean Floor Grab' (n 3) 597.

### 3.2.3 Implementing the CHM: The Role of Developing States in Protecting the Marine Environment

The protection and preservation of the marine environment is one of the components of the CHM. The common management component of the CHM principle included a regulatory framework for the protection of the marine environment.[143] As the exploration and exploitation of mineral resources of the Area became more feasible, the debate on the implications of the CHM moved from theoretical to 'practical' approaches. The ISA started to develop the Mining Code, which includes a comprehensive set of rules, regulations and procedures to regulate prospecting, exploration and exploitation of marine minerals.[144] Several regulations for exploration of minerals such as polymetallic nodules have been adopted.[145] The ISA is currently developing regulations for the exploitation of minerals of the deep-sea.[146]

The focus of the debate in relation to mining within academia subsequently moved to questions on the implementation of the CHM principle, including the protection of the marine environment.[147] There were critical reviews of the adequacy of the regulations in addressing the potential negative effects of mining operations on the environment.[148] There were calls for a comprehensive review of the regulatory regime. This included calls for more scientific knowledge, providing for public participation in the decision-making processes, revising the licensing schemes, assessing the need to start seabed mining, and setting environmental targets.[149]

---

143 ibid 596.

144 International Seabed Authority: Mining Code available at <www.isa.org.jm/mining-code> accessed 22 July 2021.

145 Regulations on Prospecting and Exploration for Polymetallic Nodules in the Area, Annex of Decision of the Council of the International Seabed Authority relating to amendments to the Regulations on Prospecting and Exploration for Polymetallic Nodules in the Area and related matters, ISBA/19/C/17, available at <www.isa.org.jm/mining-code/regulations> accessed 22 July 2021.

146 Draft Exploitation Regulations, available at <www.isa.org.jm/mining-code/ongoing-development-regulations-exploitation-mineral-resources-area> accessed 22 July 2021.

147 Ranganathan, 'Natural Resources' (n 46) 133.

148 Aline Jaeckel, Jeff A Ardron and Kristina M Gjerde, 'Sharing benefits of the common heritage of mankind – Is the deep seabed mining regime ready?' (2016) 70 Marine Policy 198; Aline Jaeckel, Kristina M Gjerde and Jeff A Ardron, 'Conserving the common heritage of humankind – Options for the deep-seabed mining regime' (2017) 78 Marine Policy 150; Erik van Doorn', Environmental aspects of the Mining code: Preserving humankind's common heritage while opening Pardo's box?' (2016) 70 Marine Policy 192.

149 Jaeckel, Gjerde and Ardron, 'Conserving' (n 148).

#### 3.2.3.1 *Due Regard Obligation of Sponsoring States: Preferential Treatment of Developing States?*

The 2011 Advisory Opinion of the ITLOS Seabed Dispute Chamber (SDC) on Responsibilities and obligations of States with respect to activities in the Area (hereafter sponsoring States)[150] included statements on the environmental protection obligations of States, as *inter alia* entailing an obligation of due diligence to protect the marine environment, which is supplemented by the precautionary approach.[151] This provides a framework for constraining the activities of private enterprises, which have become the dominant players after the Implementation Agreement.[152]

In the context of the themes of this chapter, it is the elaboration of the SDC on the responsibilities of developing States when participating in deep-sea bed mining activities that is relevant.[153]

The ISA asked SDC to give an advisory opinion on *inter alia* the legal responsibilities and obligations of States Parties to the LOSC in respect of their sponsorship activities in the Area.[154] The background was that two small Pacific island developing States (Nauru and Tonga) were involved in planned projects in the Area as sponsoring States to private companies.[155] Sponsorship by a State Party is required for private companies to engage in mining activities on the deep-sea bed.[156] The sponsoring State Party is required to ensure that activities undertaken by companies under its jurisdiction are in conformity with the Part XI of the LOSC.[157] If these two small developing States risked

150 *Responsibilities and obligations of States with respect to activities in the Area* (Advisory Opinion, 1 February 2011) ITLOS Reports 2011 (*Sponsoring States*), 10 available at <www.itlos.org/en/main/cases/list-of-cases/case-no-17/> accessed 22 July 2021.

151 Donald K Anton, Robert A Makgill and Cymie R Payne, 'Seabed Mining – Advisory Opinion on Responsibility and Liability' (2011) 41 Environmental Policy and Law 60, 65; Rosemary Rayfuse, 'Differentiating the Common: The Responsibilities and Obligations of States Sponsoring Deep Seabed Mining Activities in the Area' (2011) 54 German Yearbook of International Law 459, 487–88.

152 Duncan French, 'From the Depths: Rich Pickings of Principles of Sustainable Development and General International Law on the Ocean Floor – the Seabed Disputes Chamber's 2011 Advisory Opinion' (2011) 26 International Journal of Marine & Coastal Law 525, 566.

153 *Sponsoring States* (n 150) paras 4 and 151ff.

154 ibid para 1.

155 David Freestone, 'Responsibilities and Obligations of States Sponsoring Persons and Entities with Respect to Activities in the Area' (2011) 105 The American Journal of International Law 755, 760.

156 LOSC art 153(2)(b).

157 ibid art 139.

significant responsibility as sponsoring States, it would in effect mean they were excluded from taking part in seabed activities.[158]

The outcome of the Advisory Opinion, it is argued, is an important step for the development of the deep-sea regime.[159] This does not only relate to the clarification of the due diligence obligations of sponsoring States in regard of the environment, but also whether developing States enjoy preferential treatment compared with that granted to developed States. The point of departure of the SDC was the fifth paragraph of the preamble of LOSC that it will '... contribute to the realization of a just and equitable international economic order which takes into account the interests and needs of mankind as a whole and, in particular, the special interests and needs of developing countries ...'[160] This objective prompted SDC to investigate whether developing sponsoring States enjoyed some sort of preferential treatment under Part XI/the Implementation Agreement, specifically in respect of the duty of State Parties under Article 139 of the LOSC to ensure that activities undertaken under its control or jurisdiction are carried out in conformity with its Part XI.[161] It did identify certain provisions aimed at 'enabling [them] to participate in deep seabed mining on an equal footing with developed States'.[162] However, SDC noted that none of the provisions setting out the responsibilities of States specifically provides for preferential treatment of developing sponsoring States in respect of their due diligence obligation. The provisions on responsibility apply equally to all sponsoring States.[163] The alternative would promote sponsoring States 'of convenience' that according to the Chamber would '... jeopardize uniform application of the highest standards of protection of the marine environment, the safe development of activities in the Area and protection of the common heritage of mankind'.[164]

The Advisory Opinion provides insight into the role of States and in particular developing States in the activities of the Area, which is relevant for the debate in the BBNJ process, on questions on equity and justice and in particularly in regard of possible CHM status for MGRs. The primary take-home is that sponsoring States – irrespective of status as developed or developing – are

158 Freestone (n 155) 756.

159 Yoshifumi Tanaka, 'Obligations and Liability of Sponsoring States Concerning Activities in the Area: Reflections on the ITLOS Advisory Opinion of 1 February 2011' (2013) LX Netherlands International Law Review 205, 230.

160 *Sponsoring States* (n 150) para 151.

161 ibid paras 152ff.

162 ibid para 163.

163 ibid para 158.

164 ibid para 159.

equally required to take the necessary measures to ensure that the entities under their jurisdiction comply with the legislation adopted to fulfil their international obligations. Consequently, it may be demanding for developing States – also others than Nauru and Tonga – to comply with the standard of due diligence and force them to refrain from becoming sponsoring States.

#### 3.2.3.2 *What Remains of Preferential Treatment?*

The SDC also investigated provisions that provide for preferential treatment of developing States, *inter alia* Article 148 of the LOSC.[165] The latter provides for the promotion of '... the effective participation of developing States in activities of the Area ...', having due regard for their special needs and interests. This signals that developing States should be granted preferential treatment and provided *de facto* equal participation, elements of CHM as referred to above. However, the SDC establishes that there is no general clause on preferential treatment and that such requirements must be derived from specific provisions.[166] SDC reviewed such provisions, which include the promotion of marine scientific research in the Area for the benefit of developing States, of transfer of technology to developing States and for training opportunities.[167] These provisions are mostly formulated in general terms suggesting that they do not entail any 'hard' obligations. Similarly formulated obligations may be found in Part VII of the UNFSA as well as Part V of the Revised Draft Agreement.[168] Given the obligations of the sponsoring State, which seems to be formulated similarly in the Revised Draft Agreement, questions on the effective participation of developing States in ABNJ activities may still be raised.[169]

## 3.3 *Status of Coastal States in High Seas Fisheries Governance*

### 3.3.1 The EEZ as a Means for a More Equitable Distribution of Marine Resources

In the negotiations preceding UNCLOS III, there were proposals to establish an international authority competent to regulate fisheries on the high seas, similar to those contemplated by the ILC some decades earlier.[170] Again, such proposals were considered impossible given the strong resistance by States to

165 *Sponsoring States* (n 150) paras 153–57.
166 ibid. para 156.
167 ibid. para 157.
168 Revised Draft Agreement (n 140).
169 ibid art 20.
170 Takei (n 30) 28.

submit to international authority.[171] On the contrary, coastal States, and in particular developing States, proposed that their jurisdiction be expanded further seawards. This included the 1972 Draft articles on exclusive economic zone concept, submitted by Kenya.[172] The EEZ concept would provide for a more just and equitable distribution of marine resources, it was argued. A Kenyan delegate stated '... We must find new concepts to resolve existing conflicts of interests in the sea, so that [a] fair and equitable framework for the exploitation of the seas is created'.[173] The concept implied that the coastal States would enjoy sovereign rights over the natural resources – living and non-living – within 200 nautical miles measured from the baselines.[174]

### 3.3.2 LOSC: Preferential Rights for Coastal States?

The establishment of the EEZ also transformed the freedom of fishing on the high seas.[175] Although most commercial fisheries are undertaken within 200 nautical miles, some fish stocks straddle into adjacent areas of the high seas or migrate between areas within and beyond national jurisdiction.[176] This raised questions on how rights and interests of the coastal State in respect of such transboundary resources (known as straddling fish stocks and highly migratory fish stocks) should be accommodated and whether they would involve preferential rights in areas of the high seas adjacent to their EEZs.[177] The background was that the freedom of fishing on the high seas under the LOSC is '... subject to the rights, duties as well as the interests of coastal States provided for, *inter alia* in article 63 paragraph 2, and articles 64 to 67 ...'[178] Unsurprisingly,

---

171 Parzival Copes, 'The impact of UNCLOS III on management of the world's fisheries' (1981) 5 Marine Policy 217, 220.

172 Draft articles on exclusive economic zone concept, submitted by Kenya, in Report of the Committee on the Peaceful Uses of the Sea-Bed and the Ocean Floor beyond the Limits of National Jurisdiction, Twenty-seventh Session, suppl 21, UN Doc A/8721, 180–82, referred to by Satya N Nandan, 'The Exclusive Economic Zone: An Historical Perspective' in *Law of the Sea – Essays in Memory of Juan Carroz* (FAO 1987) available at <www.fao.org/3/s5280T/s5280t00.htm#Contents> accessed 22 July 2021.

173 Referred to by Anand, 'Winds of change' (n 47) 45–46.

174 Draft articles on exclusive economic zone concept (n 172) arts II and VII.

175 Barbara Kwiatkowska, 'The High Seas Fisheries Regime: At a Point of No Return' (1993) 8 The International Journal of Marine and Coastal Law 327.

176 U Rashid Sumaila and others, 'Winners and losers in a world where the high seas is closed to fishing' (2015) 5 Scientific Reports Article no 8481. They estimate (at 3) that 42% of fish stocks analysed are straddling and that 10% of catches are taken in adjacent areas of the high seas.

177 ibid.

178 LOSC art 116(b). Art 63(2) regulates the duty to cooperate of coastal States and States fishing on the high seas on management of straddling fish stocks in adjacent areas of the high

the provision was subject to different interpretations, prompting Kwiatkowska to describe the rights of coastal States in areas beyond 200 nautical miles as 'one of the unfinished businesses of UNCLOS III'.[179] Burke probably offered the most radical interpretation arguing that the freedom to harvest straddling fish stocks on the high seas was subjected to the sovereign rights of the relevant coastal States.[180]

Other writers have a more nuanced reading of these provisions. According to Nandan and others, the provision builds on the premise that the '… marine ecosystem is a physical continuum which has been subdivided by juridical boundaries …'[181] The purpose, they argued, of conditioning the high seas fisheries to duties of conservation and cooperation was to ensure sustainable fish stocks as well as maintaining the balance between the interests of the coastal States and those of the other States.[182] Subjecting the right to fish on the high seas to the right and interests of coastal States could be seen as an application of the general duty to have due regard to the interests of other States.[183]

This unfinished business probably contributed to disputes between flag States and coastal States over the harvesting of straddling and highly migratory fish stocks in adjacent areas of the high seas.[184] Coastal States were concerned that the activities of distant water fishing fleets undermined their efforts to manage the fish stocks within their EEZ. One example is the Turbot war between Canada and EU following the arrest of the Spanish fishing vessel *Estai* on the high seas of the Grand Banks off Newfoundland.[185]

---

seas. Art 64 involves obligation to cooperate between coastal States and States fishing on the high seas on the management of highly migratory species (which are listed in Annex I of the LOSC).

179 Kwiatkowska (n 175) 327.

180 William T Burke, *The New International Law of Fisheries. UNCLOS 1982 and Beyond* (Oxford University Press 1994) 132–36.

181 Satya Nandan and others, *The United Nations Convention on the Law of the Sea. A Commentary. Articles 86-132 and Documentary Annexes Vol. III* (Martinus Nijhoff 1985) 285.

182 ibid.

183 ibid.

184 Peter G G Davies and Cathrine Redgwell, 'The International Legal Regulation of Straddling Fish Stocks' (1997) 67 The British Yearbook of International Law 199, 200–02.

185 Christopher C Joyner and Alejandro Alvarez von Gustedt, 'The Turbot War of 1995: Lessons for the Law of the Sea' (1996) 11 International Journal of Marine & Coastal Law 425, 444–45.

### 3.3.2 The Compatibility Requirement: Balancing Coastal States Sovereign Rights and Freedom of Fishing

#### 3.3.2.1 *A Short Introduction to the Fish Stocks Agreement*

The 1992 Rio Conference called for convening an intergovernmental conference.[186] Its mandate was to identify and assess existing problems related to the conservation and management of straddling and highly migratory fish stocks and to consider means of improving cooperation on fisheries among States, and to formulate appropriate recommendations.[187] This resulted in the adoption of the 1995 UNFSA.[188]

Under the UNFSA, coastal States and States fishing on the transboundary fish stocks in adjacent areas of the high seas are required to cooperate on the conservation and management of these stocks through competent Regional Fisheries Management Organization (RFMO).[189] States shall either become member of the RFMO or accept to apply its regulatory measures.[190] The adjacent coastal States may influence the conservation and management of the stocks on the high seas as members of the relevant RFMO.

The UNFSA is applicable to straddling fish stocks and highly migratory fish stocks in adjacent areas of the high seas.[191] As these stocks are transboundary, some of its provisions are made applicable to the conservation and management of these stocks in AWNJ.[192] This includes the general principles (including long-term sustainability and the duty to protect marine biodiversity) and the obligation to apply the precautionary approach.[193] The challenge is to ensure common understanding and application of these norms across the jurisdictions and some form of coordination between the regulatory measures adopted by the coastal State and those agreed through the RFMO. The duty of coastal States and the States fishing on the high seas to cooperate with the purpose of achieving compatibility between the measures is the remedy.[194]

---

186 Agenda 21, Chapter 17 Protection of the Oceans, Report of the United Nations Conference on the Environment and Development, Annex II, UN Doc A/CONF.151/26 (vol. II), para 17.49.

187 UNGA Res 47/192, United Nations Conference on Straddling Fish Stocks and Highly Migratory Fish Stocks.

188 Full title: Agreement for the Implementation of the Provisions of the United Nations Convention on the Law of the Sea of 10 December 1982 relating to the Conservation and Management of Straddling Fish Stocks and Highly Migratory Fish Stocks (n 55).

189 UNFSA art 8.

190 ibid art 8(3).

191 ibid art 3(1).

192 ibid art 3.

193 ibid arts 5 and 6.

194 ibid art 7(2).

#### 3.3.2.2 *Compatibility*

The compatibility requirement was one of the most challenging themes to address during the negotiations, together with finding a balance between the freedom of fishing and States' sovereign rights.[195] States agreed on the need for coordination of measures but disagreed on how to achieve such coordination. Coastal States submitted a proposal that meant that the measures agreed through a RFMO for the high seas were not to have harmful effects on the stock in AWNJ.[196] Flag States such as Japan favoured a more balanced approach, arguing that the principle of due regard should inform the compatibility requirement.[197] A commentator gave this striking description of the dilemma:

> ... Should the high seas rules be made or altered to conform to pre-existing EEZ rules (which could be seen as an extension of the coastal State control beyond 200 miles)? Should coastal States establish EEZ rules compatible with high seas rules adopted multilaterally (which could be seen as infringement on coastal State jurisdiction)?[198]

The compatibility requirement provides for the co-existence of two different regimes.[199] Five different factors supplement the compatibility requirement under an overall prerequisite that the measures in total do not result in harmful effects on the living marine resources as a whole.[200]

Does this arrangement provide priority to coastal States' interests? The measures agreed for the high seas are not to undermine the effectiveness of the measures adopted by the coastal State, suggesting some sort of priority.[201] However, the coastal State is to take into account the measures adopted or agreed for the same stock in adjacent areas of the high seas.[202] These seemingly

---

195 David Balton, 'Strengthening the law of the sea: The new agreement on straddling fish stocks and highly migratory fish stocks' (1996) 27 Ocean Development & International Law 125, 137.

196 Draft Convention on the Conservation and Management of Straddling Fish Stocks and Highly Migratory Fish Stocks on the High Seas (Argentina, Canada, Chile, Iceland and New Zealand) UN Doc A/Conf.164/L.11/Rev. 1.

197 Comments on compatibility and coherence between national and international conservation measures for the same stock (Japan) UN Doc A/Conf.164/L.28.

198 Balton (n 195) 137.

199 Tore Henriksen, Geir Hønneland and Are Sydnes, *Law and Politics in Ocean Governance. The UN Fish Stocks Agreement and Regional Fisheries Management Regimes* (Martinus Nijhoff 2006) 31.

200 UNFSA art 7(2)(a)–(e) whereas the limits on the total pressure follows from art 7(2) (f).

201 ibid art 7(2)(a).

202 ibid art 7(2)(b) and (c).

contradicting factors are criticized for not providing a clear understanding of the requirements.[203] Others have warned against reading too many details into the requirement because it is to be applied in different regions under changing circumstances.[204] In a more recent paper it is argued that the UNFSA does not provide the coastal State with the means to dictate the regulation of high seas fisheries.[205]

The compatibility requirement primarily calls for a more coherent conservation and management of transboundary fish stocks. An example is the dependency factor, providing guidelines on the distribution of fishing opportunities and practices between coastal States and the States fishing in adjacent areas of the high seas, *inter alia* based on their respective dependency on the stocks in question.[206] The overall duty to ensure that the effects of the measures do not have harmful impact on the living marine resources as a whole means that their duty to conserve the living marine resources is to downplay juridical boundaries.[207]

### 3.3.3 The Compatibility Requirement: An Example for the BBNJ Process to Follow?

The relationship between AWNJ and ABNJ, specifically the role of the coastal State in managing adjacent areas of the high seas is also relevant in the BBNJ process. MGRs, ABMTs as well as EIAs, three of the themes of the ongoing negotiations, have implications for areas within national jurisdiction.[208] Arguments from the 1990s on straddling and highly migratory fish stocks can be recognised in the so-called adjacency debate. Adjacency is not only used as a geographical concept. In the debate, adjacency relates to the role and interests of the coastal State in relation to the activities of the ABNJ.[209] Following the same line of argument as Burke it has been argued that '… extending the

203 Rosemary Rayfuse, 'The Interrelationship between the Global Instruments of International Fisheries Law' in Ellen Hey (ed) *Developments in International Fisheries Law* (Kluwer Law International 1999) 134.

204 Alex G Oude Elferink, 'The Determination of Compatible Conservation and Management Measures for Straddling and Highly Migratory Fish Stocks' (2001) 5 Max Planck Yearbook of United Nations Law 551, 603.

205 Mossop and Schofield (n 4) 3.

206 UNFSA art 7(2)(c).

207 ibid art 7(2)(f).

208 International legally binding instrument under the United Nations Convention on the Law of the Sea on the conservation and sustainable use of marine biological diversity of areas beyond national jurisdiction, UNGA Res 72/249 para 2.

209 Joanna Mossop and Clive Schofield (n 4) 1–2.

rights of coastal States to have primary responsibility in conservation of their migratory and straddling biodiversity in ABNJ is not only consistent with existing principles in international law [...] but would likely result in better stewardship of those resources ...'[210] The lessons from disputes on transboundary fish stocks is that there is a need for clearer and more specific regulations of the rights, interests and obligations of the adjacent coastal State(s).

The compatibility requirement may be viewed as part of the wider development described by Broggatio and others[211] as operationalization of the freedoms of the high seas. It is not happening as 'a *Mare Clausum* type of policy', but rather it is a recognition that there is a further need for sharing common resources. Instead of sharing the ocean space freely through open access, States are sharing its natural resources in an organised and regulated way.[212]

The debate on compatibility requirement broadens the context of the adjacency debate in the BBNJ process. It seems clear that the coastal State does not enjoy preferential rights of any sort in the governance of adjacent high seas fisheries. Compatibility appears as more balanced, introducing biological as well as socio-legal criteria, located within an overall frame where conservation of the living marine resources is the overall goal or duty. Importantly, and in contrast to the BBNJ process, the coastal State does not only have rights, but also obligations under the Fish Stocks Agreement. In the BBNJ process, as the primary focus is on the ABNJ, the emphasis is on preventing negative effects of measures taken in the ABNJ on the rights and jurisdiction of adjacent coastal States.[213] These obligations relate to transboundary MGRS (duty of due regard), ABMTS (duty not to undermine the effectiveness of coastal State policy), and EIAS (take into account possible impacts of activities in AWNJ).[214] The rights and interests of the coastal States are further to be safeguarded through procedures for notification and consultation and involvement in benefit sharing. As noted by Mossop and Schofield, the proposal differs from the compatibility requirement as the duty not to undermine is not balanced by a similar

210 D C Dunn and others, 'Adjacency: How legal precedent, ecological connectivity, and Traditional Knowledge inform our understanding of proximity' (2017) Nereus Scientific & Technical Briefs on ABNJ series 9, available at <http://archives.nereusprogram.org/tag/Nereus-Scientific-&-Technical-Briefs-on-ABNJ-series/> accessed December 2020.

211 Arianna Broggatio and others, 'Mare Geneticum: Balancing Governance of Marine Genetic Resources in international waters' (2018) 33 International Journal of Marine and Coastal Law 3, 5–6.

212 ibid.

213 Revised Draft Agreement, eg art 15(4) on ABMTS.

214 Revised Draft Agreement, arts 9(2), 15(4) and 26(2), respectively.

duty of the coastal State.[215] The Revised Draft Agreement is only applicable to ABNJ, consistent with the mandate given by the UNGA.[216] Consequently, a legally binding instrument on conservation and sustainable use of BBNJ will not include any obligations on the coastal States in AWNJ. Even if the Revised Draft Agreement includes principles such as ecosystem approach and integrated approach, implying a need for cooperation between coastal States somehow involving the parts of the same ecosystems, species, and habitats under their jurisdiction, it does not provide any answers as to how.

## 4 Concluding Remarks

The high seas and its freedoms have been a central element in the law of the sea from the early 1600s till the present, including the on-going BBNJ process. However, the character and content of the high seas regime has changed from a simple regime to a complex set of regimes.

The purpose of this chapter has been to map the debate on the status of ABNJ throughout the modern history of law of the sea and in particular assess if and how it is reflected and relevant in the BBNJ process. The debate has been mapped in regard of two themes: the legal status of the natural resources of the seabed and the role or interests of the coastal State in governance of ABNJ (adjacency). The mapping was based on two hypotheses or rather assumptions, on what activates, drives and/or permeates the debate: *First*, the struggle of States for territory, in the context of oceans, ensuring access to the oceans for transport and for the utilisation of the marine resources and the competition between the exercise of territorial authority in the form of exclusive rights over the sea and the idea of the freedoms of the seas. *Second*, fundamental notions of the law of the sea have been challenged and has prompted some evolution of the law in times of globalization, as indicated in the following paragraphs.

The freedoms of the high seas prevailed for centuries because they provided a few major maritime States with ample access to space and resources. The freedoms provided them with benefits equivalent with those of a territory. These privileges have particularly been challenged during the last 75 years, leading to the evolution of the law of the sea. This chapter maps several phases of this evolution. The first phase, inaugurated in 1945 (section 2) which was characterised by the extension of AWNJ (section 2.2), driven by new technology and

215 Mossop and Schofield (n 4) 6.
216 Revised Draft Agreement art 3(1).

increased knowledge, made the oceans available to more States and introduced them to new resources and consequently intensified competition between States over space and resources. State practice and subsequent codification came primarily as a recognition that the freedoms of the high seas did not provide adequate security in regard of the access to resources and control its thus, a need to provide the States with exclusive or at least preferential rights. In the codification process (section 2.3) proposals for managing the marine resources of the high seas on behalf of world community interests were not seriously considered. The status quo prevailed, the law adapted to State practice and not vice versa. The interests of the individual State prevailed over the interests of the community.

The second phase (section 3) is characterised by the entry into the world community of new and mostly developing States, which affected the debate in different ways. Globalization – in terms of integrating States in the world community with more diverse interests – resulted in broadening the set of values in the law of the sea debate. New arrivals were proponents of community interests, as reflected by the CHM concept. The idea of community interests had earlier been rejected in favour of bilateral/individual interests of States. The developing States called for a more just legal order for the oceans, where States irrespective of their capacities and level of development were ensured access to their natural resources and their benefits. The status of the seabed and its resources as CMH would provide them with access to the governance, utilization, and benefits of these natural resources, which otherwise would not be possible under the 'first come, first served' consequences of the freedom of the high seas principle. Such re-distribution of access to the resources would provide them with benefits equivalent to the benefits of a territory. In parallel, developing States and developed States reached compromises on extended sovereignty and sovereign rights over the natural resources of their coastal waters through an extended territorial sea, the EEZ and continental shelf. This extension of the jurisdiction of coastal States at the expense of the high seas freedoms can also be viewed as a contribution to a more just and equitable legal regime. This was less controversial as developed States were also interested in extending their national jurisdiction. More contentious was the proposed CHM status of the deep-sea bed which clashed with the economic liberalism that had been the dominating the freedom of the high seas' dogma (section 3.2). The CHM was incorporated into the LOSC, but the success was short-lived. Important elements of the CHM were watered-down through the 1994 Implementation Agreement to safeguard economic liberalism: Activities were to be based on commercial conditions, profits should come to those investing in technology and providing funding.

There is a similar debate in the BBNJ process in regard of MGRs (section 3.2.2) where developing States are arguing their CHM status, whereas developed States claim that MGRs are part of the freedoms of the high seas. Many of the arguments may be recognised from the negotiations of UNCLOS III: A regime that promotes the core values of the CHM, such as equity, preferential treatment, transfer of knowledge and technology and benefit sharing, or a regime that facilitates the freedom to explore and exploit MGRs and where the profits fall to those investing/taking the financial risks. However, CHM is not a clear-cut legal concept, particularly following the amendments to the deep-sea bed regime made through the Implementation Agreement. Benefit sharing appears the main element of the CHM. Unless the intention is to reintroduce CHM in its original format, questions may be raised about the usefulness of including it as a principle in an international legal instrument on the conservation and sustainable use of BBNJ. Would the status of MGRs as CHM be more of symbolic than have a real value? Could States achieve the same result through a less principled approach, not defining its status, either as CHM or as part of the freedoms of the high seas? Or is the symbolic value as CHM more important for developing States? The past law of the sea negotiations seems to favour the interests of economic liberalism. States with the economic, technological and personnel capacity to exploit and explore MGRs, although in a minority, are in a position to ignore solutions that conflict with their interests. What is the value of an instrument not applicable to those States? Will the interests of universally applicable norms prevail, again? The description of Friedheim of the first period as focusing on solving problems rather than considering principles may still be the dominant feature.[217]

The scope of preferential treatment of developing States, an element of CHM, was addressed in the 2011 Advisory Opinion of the ITLOS SDC (section 3.2.2). Preferential treatment does not apply to the due diligence obligations of the sponsoring State. They may be subject to the same obligations as developed States. This may deter developing States from getting actively involved in deep-sea mining activities. They are likely to meet similar obstacles in participating in exploration and exploitation of MGRs. The obligations of developed States to provide for technological, personnel and financial assistance are likely to remain of a hortatory character and thus not provide for building adequate capacity.

The second theme of the chapter is adjacency or the role of the coastal State in the adjacent areas of the high seas – specifically whether it enjoyed some sort

217 Friedheim (n 23) 19.

of special rights or preferential rights was primarily addressed in section 3.3. However, it came to the forefront with the 1945 Truman proclamation (section 2.2). The adjacency perspective was a driver for the extension of AWNJ through the continental shelf, subsequently by exclusive fisheries zones and the 200 nautical mile EEZ. These maritime zones provided coastal States with exclusive rights, a better solution for them than having preferential rights in adjacent areas of the high seas or having actively to occupy and control an area of the seabed. Following the adoption of the LOSC, there were different opinions as discussed in section 3.3.2 on whether the coastal State enjoyed special or preferential rights in the management of transboundary living resources in areas of the high seas adjacent to the EEZ. The 1995 UNFSA has contributed to the clarification on how to ensure coordination of conservation of marine living resources subjected to two different regimes, consistent with an ecosystem approach. The compatibility requirement (section 3.3.2) seems to provide for a balancing of the interests, and not providing the coastal State with any preferential rights. There are similar transboundary challenges in the BBNJ process discussed in section 3.3.3, as MGRs may be transboundary and a MPA in ABNJ may affect coastal States' rights and jurisdictions and vice versa. This raises questions whether and how coastal States should be involved, from having an active role in the governance of the adjacent ABNJ to a more 'passive' duty of other States not to take actions in ABNJ that undermine coastal States' sovereign rights and jurisdiction in adjacent AWNJ. Differently from transboundary marine living resources, the on-going debate seems to only apply to impacts of activities in ABNJ or measures to be adopted in ABNJ on the national jurisdiction of coastal States. There seems to be a consensus that a new legally binding instrument resulting from the BBNJ process is only applicable to ABNJ. However, such juridical boundaries are at odds with principles such as ecosystem approach and integrated approach, which are included in the Revised Draft Agreement (although in brackets).[218] The obligations of coastal States in regard of ABNJ would then have to be based on their obligations under the LOSC, such as Article 194 paragraph 5 and Article 197 as well as other pertinent obligations, including those contained in Article 8 of the CBD.

The reason for restricting the BBNJ process to ABNJ is probably that a legally binding instrument *inter alia* providing basis for the adoption of ABMTs may potentially impact the sovereign rights and interests of coastal States. In contrast to fisheries management, coastal States, and States with interests in ABNJ do not necessarily have concurrent interests in more extensive protection of

218 Revised Draft Agreement art 5(f) and (g) – in brackets.

the marine environment through such means as an MPA. It would be difficult for a coastal State to ignore the establishment of an MPA in an adjacent area of an ABNJ, even if this would lead to costs in form of restrictions in access to and exploitation of marine resources. Furthermore, the coastal State has a separate obligation under Article 194 paragraph 5 of the LOSC to protect fragile ecosystems, habitats of threatened or endangered species and other forms of marine life. Thus, it would be problematic to disregard measures taken in ABNJ to protect the same ecosystems or habitats. Thus, applying a similar solution as the UNFSA, eg requiring some sort of compatibility between the environmental protection of the coastal State and of the adjacent ABNJ would be a way of developing measures to protect marine biodiversity straddling/across jurisdictional boundaries.

The BBNJ process, like past law of the sea negotiations, does not seem to provide room for any fundamental rethinking or transformation of the law of the sea, but seems locked to the status quo and opening only for minor amendments or gradual evolution, consistent with the interests of the major States. A fundamental rethinking would require community interests such as the protection of the marine environment – to be prioritized at the expense of the territoriality approach of States. The SDC in its Advisory Opinion recognised that the protection of the marine environment is a community interest – a duty *erga omnes*. However, the law of the sea provides few venues for promoting such interests, if adequate. It is still to a large degree left to the individual State to enforce the compliance with these obligations, within a system that primarily is constructed for bilateral interaction.

Future debates on the development of the law of the sea are likely to follow the same pattern as those presented here. However, with increasing negative effects of climate change on the oceans, marine species and ecosystems, the question is whether the debate will take another direction, giving environmental protection and justice a stronger voice and the recognition of the need for more coherent approaches that challenge the law of the sea. Although not new, recent calls for other ethos or approaches such as 'World Ocean Public Trust', public trusteeship, Ocean Trust or stewardship may diversify the future debate.[219] It would require a recognition that continuing the pursuit

219 Montserrat Gorina-Ysern, 'World Ocean Public Trust: High Seas Fisheries after Grotius – Towards a New Ocean Ethos' (2004) 34 Golden Gate University Law Review 645; Montserrat Gorina-Ysern, Kristina Gjerde and Michael Orbach, 'Ocean Governance: A New Ethos through a World Ocean Public Trust' in Linda Glover and Sylvia Earle (eds), *Defying Ocean's End: An Agenda for Action* (Island Press 2004); Peter H Sand, 'Sovereignty Bounded: Public Trusteeship for Common Pool Resources?' (2004) 4 Global Environmental Politics 47,

of economic liberalism is likely to lead to irreversible damage to the oceans, marine species, ecosystems and the marine environment.

48; Rosemary Rayfuse and Robin Warner, 'Securing a Sustainable Future for the Oceans Beyond National Jurisdiction: The Legal Basis for an Integrated Cross-Sectoral Regime for High Seas Governance for the 21st Century' (2008) 23 The International Journal of Marine & Coastal Law 399; Fran Humphries, 'A Stewardship Approach to Legitimate Interests in Deep Sea Genetic Resources for Use in Aquaculture' (2017) 40 University of New South Wales Law Journal 27; Mary Turnipseed and others, 'Using the public trust doctrine to achieve ocean stewardship' in Christina Voigt (ed), *Rule of Law for Nature New Dimensions and Ideas in Environmental Law* (Cambridge University Press 2013) 365–79.

CHAPTER 5

# Principled Challenges

## *Between Collective Interest and Individual Freedom*

*Lan Ngoc Nguyen*

## 1 Introduction

While the high seas and the Area are both known as areas beyond national jurisdiction (ABNJ), their underpinning legal regime drastically differs in nature. The high seas are governed by the long-standing principle of freedom of the high seas, which adopts a laissez-faire approach, allowing States to freely exercise their rights and freedom subject to only some limited restrictions. The Area is, in contrast, governed by the more recent principle of common heritage of mankind (CHM). Included in the 1982 United Nations Convention on the Law of the Sea (LOSC), this principle posits that 'all rights in the resources of the Area are vested in mankind as a whole'[1] whose management would be put under an international administration, the International Seabed Authority—acting on behalf of humankind. As such, the principle of CHM shifts the focus from States' individual freedom to protecting collective interests in the commons.

In recent decades, these two important principles have faced serious challenges. To illustrate these challenges, this chapter will focus, for the freedom of the high seas, on the freedom of fishing. The 1995 UN Fish Stocks Agreement (UNFSA) and the existence of various regional fisheries management organisations (RFMOs) around the world have drastically reduced the scope of the freedom of fishing in the high seas. Yet, fish stocks are still in decline and unsustainable fishing practices are still rampant, which begs the question of whether the freedom of fishing as part of the freedom of the high seas still appropriate and should be preserved. The CHM principle, for its part, has been weakened by the 1994 Implementing Agreement to Part XI of the LOSC. In addition, renewed debates on CHM have also emerged, with questions raised over whether and to what extent this principle could evolve beyond the current regulation under LOSC to cover also biodiversity in ABNJ. All these

1 United Nations Convention on the Law of the Sea (opened for signature 10 December 1982, entered into force 16 November 1994) 1833 UNTS 3 (LOSC) art 137.

 | DOI:10.1163/9789004506367_006

developments taken together result in a current framework for ABNJ which oscillates between concerns for preserving individual freedom and enhancing collective resource management.

Against this background, this chapter seeks to examine the development and current application of freedom of the high seas and CHM in order to understand the extent to which they still safeguard individual freedom and collective interests in common areas of the sea, and to explore the role that these concepts may play in the new model of governance for ABNJ that is emerging through the ongoing negotiation on biodiversity beyond national jurisdiction (BBNJ process). To that end, Part 2 and Part 3 will respectively review the normative content of freedom of the high seas and CHM and analyse the current challenges that have arisen in the application of these concepts. Based on this discussion, Part 4 will explore whether, in light of the way in which freedom of the high seas and CHM are currently applied, the dichotomy between the two concepts can still be maintained. Part 5 will follow with an examination of the BBNJ process to understand the implication of these concepts in the new legal instrument, in order to have an indication of the balance to be struck between individual freedom and collective interests in the future regulatory framework for the ocean commons.

## 2 Freedom of the High Seas: The Scope of Individual Freedom and Its Application

### 2.1 *Scope and Normative Content of the 'Freedom of the High Seas'*

Freedom of the high seas is one of the oldest principles of law of the sea. Credited to Hugo Grotius and his famous Mare Liberum doctrine, the principle of freedom of the high seas in its modern form has come a long way since then. According to Grotius, '[t]he sea is common to all, because it is so limitless it cannot become a possession of any one, and because it is adapted for the use of all, whether we consider [it] from the point of view of navigation or fisheries'.[2] As observed by Young, '[t]he core of Grotius's argument is that "things which cannot be reduced to possession or are in infinite supply and thus suffice for the common use of all" are common property'.[3] The classification of the high seas as 'common property' is but one way of classifying the

2 As quoted in Alexander Proelss (ed), *United Nations Convention on the Law of the Sea: A Commentary* (Hart 2017) 679.

3 Michaela Young, 'Then and Now: Reappraising Freedom of the Seas in Modern Law of the Sea' (2016) 47(2) Ocean Development & International Law 165.

high seas. De Lucia, for example, argues that Grotius' freedom of the high seas is based on the Roman concept of *res communes omnium*, indicating 'a set of things—goods—that are common to all in the sense of not falling under ownership of any individual, nor of any particular political community, but also, importantly, of not being susceptible of individual or collective ownership'.[4] Thus, instead of being common property, the high seas and its resources are no-one's property. While there may be different views on its underlying conceptual foundation, what remains is that the doctrine of freedom of the high seas seeks to ensure open access to resources at sea for all. In practice, however, open access did not mean equal access for all States, as access usually corresponded to States' technological and financial resources.[5] Thus, as explained by Henriksen in chapter 4 of this volume, the law was used by powerful States as a means to promote national interests and to legitimize the use of power. As such, the emphasis of the freedoms of the high seas was on securing the ability of States to project their power at sea, in other words, to protect individual freedom. The growing power of maritime States ensured that the freedom of the high seas prevailed as the dominating paradigm for over two centuries.[6]

In the modern law of the sea, freedom of the high seas is encapsulated in Article 87 of the LOSC. Paragraph (1) of this article again confirms that 'the high seas are open to all States'. However, as argued by Scovazzi, '[t]he erosion of the principle of freedom of the sea, as far as new interests and activities required a specific regulation, has been the main trend in the evolution of international law of the sea'.[7] In other words, individual freedom in the high seas has increasingly been restricted. As mentioned in the Introduction, due to limited space, this chapter will focus on freedom of fishing in the high sea, and use this freedom to examine the way in which and the extent to which individual freedom in the high seas has 'eroded'. Freedom of fishing has been chosen for two reasons. First, fishing is one of the oldest freedoms exercised in the high seas, and one which has gone through many developments and arguably more eroded. Thus, an examination of the freedom of fishing will help to illustrate whether and to what extent individual freedoms in the high

---

4 Vito De Lucia, 'Ocean Commons, Law of the Sea and Rights for the Sea' (2019) 32(1) Canadian Journal of Law & Jurisprudence 45.

5 Jutta Brunnée, 'Common Areas, Common Heritage, and Common Concern' in Daniel Bodansky, Jutta Brunnée and Ellen Hey (eds), *The Oxford Handbook of International Environmental Law* (OUP 2008) 562.

6 See Henriksen (ch 4) in this volume.

7 Tullio Scovazzi, *The Evolution of International Law of the Sea: New Issues, New Challenges* (vol 286, Hague Academy of International Law, Recueil des cours, 2001) 39.

seas have developed. Second, as fishing has significant impacts in ABNJ,[8] an examination of the freedom of fishing in the high seas may help shed light on the future of individual freedoms in ABNJ, including on the negotiations in the BBNJ process.

Under LOSC, all States may license vessels to fish in the high seas. However, the exercise of this freedom is also not without restrictions. These restrictions can be found first in the chapeau of Article 87, which states, 'freedom of the high seas is exercised under the conditions laid down by this Convention and by other rules of international law'. The conditions mentioned in the chapeau are specified for each type of freedom, in each of the sub-paragraphs of Article 87(1). In relation to the freedom of fishing, sub-paragraph (e) states that this freedom is 'subject to the conditions laid down in section 2' which deals with the conservation and management of the living resources of the high seas. Paragraph (2) of Article 87 further imposes another restriction, namely the obligation of due regard. The three groups of conditions mean that freedoms of the high seas are not unfettered. Therefore, in order to understand the scope of the freedoms of fishing, these conditions must be considered. It is worth noting that from the beginning, the principle of freedom of fishing was not expected to be unlimited. While Grotius used navigation and fishing to demonstrate that the sea was susceptible to common use,[9] he still made a distinction between these two freedoms based on the natural resources that enable them, ie the water and the fish—the latter being exhaustible.[10] As contended by Young, 'Grotius implicitly recognizes … that prohibitions or limitations on the right to fish are conceivable'.[11]

As was made clear by the International Law Commission (ILC): '[T]he law of the high seas contains certain rules … which are designed not to limit or restrict the freedom of the high seas, but to safeguard its exercise in the interests of the entire international community'.[12] It follows that in the high seas, where the underlying principle is that of freedom of the international community, a balance still has to be struck between Sates' individual freedom

8 Glen Wright and others, 'The long and winding road: negotiating a treaty for the conservation and sustainable use of marine biodiversity in areas beyond national jurisdiction' (2018) IDDRI, Studies N°08 available at <www2.ecolex.org/server2neu.php/libcat/docs/LI/MON-093956.pdf> accessed 27 July 2021.

9 Young (n 3) 173.

10 ibid 174.

11 ibid 174.

12 ILC, Report of the International Law Commission: Commentaries to the Articles Concerning the Law of the Sea, UN Doc A/3159 (1956), GAOR 11th Session Suppl. 9, 12, 24 (art 27).

and collective interests of the international community. However, a question that arises is: what are the 'interests of the entire international community' that these conditions purport to safeguard? Interestingly, during the First United Nations Conference on the Law of the Sea, while high seas fisheries conservation was included within the high seas draft articles prepared by the ILC, this issue was eventually addressed in a separate convention, ie the 1958 Convention on Fishing and Conservation of the Living Resources in the High Seas.[13] As a result, the freedom to fish in the 1958 Convention on the High Seas was recognised without qualification.[14] The 1958 Convention on Fishing and Conservation of the Living Resources in the High Seas itself contains obligations that are similar to those subsequently found under LOSC. The nature of the conditions for the exercise of the freedom of fishing under LOSC seems to suggest that the 'interests of the entire international community' would be first and foremost in the conservation of living resources.

It is then pertinent to unpack the scope of the conservation obligations in the high seas to understand the scope of collective interests in the high seas. Article 2 of the 1958 Convention on Fishing and Conservation of the Living Resources in the High Seas defines conservation as 'the aggregate of the measures rendering possible the optimum sustainable yield from those resources so as to secure a maximum supply of food and other marine products' and requires conservation programmes to be formulated 'with a view to securing in the first place a supply of food for human consumption'. In the commentaries to the draft articles of the law of the sea, the ILC observed that existing law provided no effective protection of marine fauna against waste or extermination, and this constituted 'a danger to the food supply of the world'.[15] By contrast, Article 119 of the LOSC on conservation of living resources in the high seas requires conservation measures to take into account 'the effects on species associated with or dependent upon harvested species with a view to maintaining or restoring populations of such associated or dependent species above levels at which their reproduction may become seriously threatened'. It has therefore been argued that LOSC places greater emphasis on conserving

13 Donald Rothwell and Tim Stephens, *The International Law of the Sea* (Hart 2016) 162. Convention on Fishing and Conservation of the Living Resources of the High Seas (opened for signature 29 April 1958, entered into force 20 March 1966) 559 UNTS 285.

14 Rothwell and Stephens (ibid) 166. Convention on the High Seas (opened for signature 29 April 1958, entered into force 30 September 1962) 450 UNTS 11.

15 Rothwell and Stephens (n 13) 318.

marine living resources as part of protecting marine biodiversity as a whole, as opposed to merely serving anthropocentric purposes.[16]

However, the obligations to conserve living resources in the high seas under LOSC mainly take the form of the obligation of due diligence under Article 192, which applies to all maritime zones and the obligation to cooperate. According to the *South China Sea* arbitral tribunal, Article 192 of the LOSC, read in conjunction with its Article 194(5), imposes on flag States a due diligence obligation to prevent illegal fishing and to prevent harvesting endangered species and/or their habitat.[17] In addition, Articles 117 and 118 of the LOSC include two types of obligations: the obligation to cooperate and negotiate with other States in the conservation of living resources in the high seas and the obligation to cooperate to establish subregional or regional fisheries organizations. No further guidance under LOSC is provided on the contours and content of this obligation to cooperate. The duty to cooperate to establish subregional or regional fisheries organizations under Article 118 is clarified in the 1995 UNFSA. Article 8 specifies the contours of the obligation to cooperate in the high seas, among which Paragraph (4) provides that only those States that agree to participate in conservation and management measures adopted by a particular RFMO have access to the resources to which the measures apply.

Beyond specifying the duty to cooperate, the UNFSA includes further limits to the freedom of the high seas. It elaborates at great length the duties of the flag State and makes more stringent the obligation of flag States to exercise control over vessels flying their flags in the high seas. Moreover, it also contains the precautionary approach as one of its general principles. UNFSA requires States when applying the precautionary approach to 'take into account ... the impact of fishing activities on non-target and associated or dependent species'[18] and 'adopt plans which are necessary to ensure the conservation of such species and to protect habitats of special concern'.[19] As a result, the UNFSA seems to take a step further than LOSC, shifting more clearly the focus of conservation measures to protecting biodiversity and maintaining ecosystem integrity.[20] In contrast, under LOSC, while the conservation of marine living resources is part

16 Ellen Hey, 'The Fisheries Provisions of the LOS Convention' in Ellen Hey (ed), *Developments in International Fisheries Law* (Kluwer Law International 1999) 28.

17 *South China Sea (Philippines v China)*, Arbitral Award on Merits (12 July 2016) paras 942 and 956.

18 UNFSA art 6(3)(c).

19 ibid art 6(3)(d).

20 Daniela Diz Pereira Pinto, *Fisheries Management in Areas beyond National Jurisdiction: The Impact of Ecosystem Based Law-Making* (Brill 2012) 26.

and parcel of the protection and preservation of the marine environment,[21] as analysed above, the obligations found in Part XII are worded in such a general manner that they do not form the precondition for undertaking fishing activities in the high seas. The UNFSA thus in essence imposes restrictions on the freedom of fishing that go beyond LOSC.

In sum, this section has outlined the normative content of the freedom of fishing, and examined how the principle of freedom of fishing on the high seas has gone through a process of dilution. The conditions imposed upon the freedom of fishing under LOSC, further elaborated under other international agreements, including the UNFSA, seek to balance the exercise of the freedom with the collective interests of conserving marine living resources. The purpose of the conservation of marine living resources seems to have also evolved over the past decades, focusing on recognizing the value of the resources as part of marine biodiversity.[22] However, it is arguable that the conservation of living resources, while being an important element of the protection of the marine environment, does not only serve to protect the marine environment per se. Given the economic interests that underly the freedom of fishing since Grotius' day, the conservation of living resources also aims to protect the maintenance of long-term access to resources for all States. Here, collective interests, ie the conservation of marine living resources, enable the exercise of individual freedoms, ie the right to fish.

### 2.2 *What Remains of the Freedom of Fishing?*

As discussed, the freedom of fishing in the high seas is not unqualified and there are increasing restrictions on the freedom of fishing, which come in the

---

21 Both ITLOS in *Southern Bluefin Tuna* and the Annex VII tribunal in *Chagos MPA* regarded the conservation of marine living resources, despite not explicitly provided for in Part XII, as a component of marine environment protection. See *Southern Bluefin Tuna Cases (provisional measures) (New Zealand v. Japan; Australia v. Japan)* (27 August 1999) ITLOS 3 and 4, 280, para 70; *Chagos Marine Protected Area Arbitration (Mauritius v United Kingdom)* (Award, 18 March 2015) PCA Case 2011–03, para 538 available at <http://www.pca-cpa.org/MU-UK%2020150318%20Awardd4b1.pdf?fil_id=2899> accessed 25 September 2018.

22 The focus on fisheries for its biodiversity value in the UNFSA could partly be explained by the fact that the UNFSA was a product of the 1990s. Therefore, it was heavily influenced by the 1992 United Nations Conference on Environment and Development, which resulted in the Rio Declaration and, among others, the Convention on Biological Diversity (CBD). The main objectives of the CBD included the conservation of biological diversity and the sustainable use of the components of biological diversity. See Pierre-Marie Dupuy and Jorge E Vinuales, *International Environmental Law* (2nd edn, Cambridge University Press 2018) 14.

form of the obligation to cooperate to take conservation measures. Under the UNFSA, the obligation to take conservation measures has now become the precondition for the right to fish.

However, while the UNFSA is an implementing agreement of LOSC, it is an international treaty in its own right. This means that States that are not parties to the UNFSA are not bound by the obligation under Article 8(4) of the UNFSA. For these states, the freedom of fishing in the high seas remains intact, subject only to the general obligations under Articles 117 and 118 of the LOSC. To date, the number of state parties to the UNFSA is 91,[23] much lower than that of LOSC which numbers at 168.[24] Moreover, the UNFSA only covers straddling and highly migratory stocks, not all fish stocks that occur in the high seas. In addition, not all high seas are managed by a regional or subregional fisheries management organisation, namely areas in the Central and Southwest Atlantic.[25] Even for those regions where there is an RFMO, compliance is not always guaranteed and compromises often have to be made amongst the members, rendering conservation measures ineffective.[26] Enforcement also remains a weakness for RFMOs vis-à-vis non-member States.[27]

Taken together, these factors mean that the restrictions on the freedom of fishing in the high sea as imposed under the UNFSA may sound more impressive than they really are. The nature of the conservation obligations under both LOSC and UNFSA also means that the freedom of fishing, while regulated, still remains largely intact in the high seas. Individual freedom thus still seems to prevail over collective interests in the high seas. As a result, fishing in the high seas still takes place in an unsustainable manner.[28] While most of the negative

23 United Nations Agreement for the Implementation of the Provisions of the United Nations Convention on the Law of the Sea of 10 December 1982 relating to the Conservation and Management of Straddling Fish Stocks and Highly Migratory Fish Stocks (opened for signature 4 August 1995, entered into force 11 December 2001) 2167 UNTS 3 (UNFSA).

24 See LOSC.

25 See FAO, Regional fisheries management organizations and deep-sea fisheries available at <www.fao.org/fishery/topic/166304/en> accessed 27 July 2021.

26 James McDonald, 'Governing Fisheries in the High Seas' JSTOR Daily (5 October 2018) available at <https://daily.jstor.org/governing-fisheries-in-the-high-seas/> accessed 27 July 2021.

27 Gordon R Munro, 'Internationally shared fish stocks, the high seas, and property rights in fisheries' (2007) 22(4) Marine Resource Economics 425; Rosemary Gail Rayfuse, 'Countermeasures and High Seas Fisheries Enforcement' (2005) 51 Netherlands International Law Review 41.

28 According to a study, 'more than half of the world's ocean is under industrial-scale harvest, spanning an area four times that covered by land-based agriculture'. See David A Kroodsma and others, 'Tracking the global footprint of fisheries' (2018) Science 359, 904–08. Another study in 2016 estimated that by 2050, 88% of fish stocks will be

effects of fisheries occur within EEZ, there is no denying the overexploitation in the high seas is a reality, leading to what is commonly referred to as 'tragedy of the commons' which posits that in open access systems, there is incentive for individual overexploitation as each individual enjoys the benefit of exploiting the resource to its maximum, while the cost of this increased utilization is spread out over all users.[29] This overexploitation is caused by the underlying understanding that the commons, in this case the ocean commons beyond national jurisdiction, is *res communes* and thus open and free to all individual uses. While in the high seas, the individual freedom of fishing is sought to be balanced with the collective interests of conservation of living resources, the obligations relating the latter are currently not enough to limit the benefits of exploiting the resources on an individual basis.

Faced with this reality, there have been numerous calls for more stringent measures to further restrict the freedom of fishing in the high seas. These measures include first and foremost strengthening the efficiency of RFMOs, ranging from improving participation in RFMOs, increasing the quality of RFMO performance reviews, promoting cooperation and coordination between RFMOs.[30] These measures help to overcome the gap that exists between the formal legal and institutional development brought about by UNFSA and the effectiveness of measures undertaken by RFMOs to monitor, control and enforce fishing practices at sea.[31] In addition to improving the work of RFMOs in general, some RFMOs have also taken steps to restrict the freedom of fishing in the high seas. For example, the 1994 Bering Sea Pollock Convention, in response to the collapse of the pollock, imposes a moratorium on fishing in the high seas of the Bering Sea. More recently, the Agreement to Prevent Unregulated High Seas Fisheries in the Central Arctic Ocean (CAOFA), concluded in 2018, imposes a moratorium on 'unregulated' commercial fishing in 'the single high seas portion of the central Arctic Ocean'. Recognising that 'commercial fishing is unlikely to become viable in the high seas portion of the central Arctic Ocean in the near future', CAOFA essentially adopts a precautionary approach

overfished if current trends continue. Christopher Costello and others, 'Global fishery prospects under contrasting management regimes' (2016) 113(18) PNAS 5125 available at <www.pnas.org/content/113/18/5125> accessed 27 July 2021.

29 See Dalaker (ch 12) in this volume.

30 See James Harrison, 'Key Challenges Relating to the Governance of Regional Fisheries' in Richard Caddell and Erik J Molenaar (eds), *Strengthening International Fisheries Law in an Era of Changing Oceans* (Hart 2019).

31 These measures include, inter alia, data collecting and reporting (UNFSA art 10), at-sea boarding and inspection (art 18(3)(g)(i)), RFMO registers (art 18(3)(c)), catch documentation and trade measures.

and is considered 'an important step in gradual transformation of the freedom of the high seas'.[32]

Proposals have also been made to establish marine protected areas (MPAs) in the high seas, in which fishing is prohibited or restricted in order to help 'conserve the biological diversity and productivity (including ecological life support systems) of the oceans'.[33] Notwithstanding the benefits that these MPAs bring to conservation of living resources and biodiversity, the fact remains that there is no comprehensive legal instrument or legal basis to allow States to establish MPAs in the high seas. Most of them are established under the auspices of RFMOs,[34] which in turn only have the competence in specific areas of the oceans or activities and generally lack efficient control and enforcement scheme to effectively implement MPAs in the high seas.[35] Moreover, within certain RFMOs, the establishment of MPAs has not been without controversy due to the competing interests between pro-exploitation and pro-conservation States.[36] As a result, restriction of the freedom of fishing via the adoption of MPAs in the high seas can hardly be described as comprehensive nor certain. Instead, it resembles patchwork attempts to regulate access to sources. These attempts are very much still dependent on the political will of States, which in turn is informed by their individual interests.

In general, freedom of fishing in the high seas remains an important principle in the law of the sea and is widely exercised in practice. However, due to the negative effects of unsustainable fishing, there is increased acknowledgement of and thus a trend towards challenging the laissez-faire exercise of freedom of fishing in the high seas in favour of conservation goals. This is manifested

32 Erik J Molenaar, 'The CAOF Agreement: Key Issues of International Fisheries Law', Presentation at Conference New Knowledge and Changing Circumstances in the Law of the Sea, Reykjavik, 28–30 June 2018. See also Valentin J Schatz, Alexander Proelss and Nengye Liu, 'The 2018 Agreement to Prevent Unregulated High Seas Fisheries in the Central Arctic Ocean: A Critical Analysis' (2019) 34(2) The International Journal of Marine and Coastal Law 195.

33 PEW Charitable Trust, 'Marine Protected Areas Beyond National Jurisdiction' available at <www.pewtrusts.org/-/media/assets/2016/03/high-seas-mpa-policy-brief.pdf> accessed 27 July 2021.

34 See <www.fao.org/fishery/topic/16204/en> accessed 27 July 2021. Note, however, that MPAs are also established beyond the auspices of RFMOs and under other regional mechanisms such as OSPAR. See <www.ospar.org/work-areas/bdc/marine-protected-areas> accessed 27 July 2021.

35 ibid.

36 See for example, the discussions at CCAMLR. See also Klaus Dodds, Alan D Hemmings and Peder Roberts, *Handbook on the Politics of Antarctica* (Edward Elgar 2017) 177; Jennifer Jacquet and others, '"Rational use" in Antarctic waters' (2016) 63 Marine Policy 28.

in the UNFSA itself—for all its shortcomings—as well more recent measures taken by RFMOs. What these measures have in common is the introduction of more regulated access to resources, as opposed to free access for all States.

## 3 Common Heritage of Mankind

### 3.1 *Scope and Content of 'Common Heritage of Mankind'*

In the context of the law of the sea, the concept of CHM is found in relation to the seabed beyond national jurisdiction, ie the Area. Compared to the principle of freedom of the high sea, the concept of CHM is much younger. Its origin may be traced back to the proposal made by the Maltese Ambassador Arvid Pardo during a debate over the status of the seabed of the high seas in 1967 that the seabed and ocean floor 'underlying the seas beyond the limits of present national jurisdiction' be designated 'the common heritage of mankind'.[37] As described by Henriksen in chapter 4 of this book, '[h]is intervention was part of a broader movement both to stop the tendency of creeping national jurisdiction into ABNJ and to redefine its *res communis* character which benefited only a few States'.[38] This underscores the observation made above that the concept of *res communis,* when applied to ABNJ, allows for open access, but not equal access for all States. Equity is thus not guaranteed when applying the *res communis* conceptual foundation to ABNJ. CHM seeks to remedy this shortcoming and brings equity to centre stage.[39] The driving force behind CHM was the emergence of the New International Economic Order that came about as a result of the increasing number of new states gaining independence and thus determined to have a say in shaping a new international legal order.[40] As Ranganathan observed, CHM not only facilitated developing States' effective participation in the activity of seabed mining, but more importantly their participation in its administration. The latter is particularly noteworthy as it demonstrated a defiance of 'the existing order in which developing states

37 Arvid Pardo, UN General Assembly, First Committee, 1515th Meeting 1 November 1967 A/C.1/PV.L515, paras 10(a) and 13.

38 See Henriksen (ch 4) in this volume.

39 Rothwell and Stephens (n 13) 134.

40 See for example, Kemal Baslar, *The Concept of the Common Heritage of Mankind in International Law* (Martinus Nijhoff 1998) 201–16; Bradley Larschan and Bonnie C Brennan, 'The Common Heritage of Mankind Principle in International Law' (1983) 21 Columbia Journal of Transnational Law 305.

remained passive recipients of aid and consumers of products manufactured elsewhere'.[41]

It seems quite clear that with the concept of CHM, individual freedom has to make way for broader community or collective interests. So here, the need to balance individual freedom and collective interests is no longer present, at least in theory, as the latter assumes priority. What remains to be determined is the extent to which individual states need to invest or contribute to the collective interests, which in turn, informs the operationalisation of the different components of CHM, such as arrangements for transfer of technology. But the question that arises is: what are these collective interests? The discussion so far seems to suggest that collective interests simply mean the inclusion of the interests of all States, particularly developing States, with the emphasis on ensuring equity for all States involved in activities in the seabed. However, is that all there is to it? Does the term CHM itself not encompass more than the interests of States?

To answer this question, it is useful to take a closer look at the conceptual foundation as well as the historical development of the concept. According to Baslar, CHM is rooted in natural law, which generally holds that 'certain basic principles and obligations ... derive from natural law binding states and the international community as a whole, equally and unconditionally'.[42] Under natural law, the spirit of CHM is framed in the stewardship theology,[43] which contradicts with the notion of *res communis*, which is 'based primarily upon successful sharing rather than conservation itself'.[44] The essence of the stewardship ethic, as interpreted by Baslar, is that it is human-centred, which means that human beings 'have responsibilities not only for other creatures, but also for the generations to come'.[45] He further argues that when looking at a 'modernised version of natural law', meaning the natural law developed after the Second World War, there is an increasingly clear 'departure from a state-centric international legal system to a human-centric law of mankind'.[46] Baslar thus seems to suggest that CHM as a concept steers the attention away from the interests of States per se, and instead focuses on something greater—humankind.

41 Surabhi Ranganathan, 'The Law of the Sea and Natural Resources' in Eyal Benvenisti and Georg Nolte (eds), *Community Interests Across International Law* (Oxford University Press 2018) 126.
42 Baslar (n 40) 14.
43 ibid 15.
44 ibid 16.
45 ibid.
46 ibid 22.

Ranganathan acknowledges that 'certain ocean issues ... stemming from the common nature of the ocean, engage the collective interest of the international community as a whole and pose collective-action problems to be resolved on multilateral platforms'.[47] These collective-action problems then give rise to community obligations, which operate vis-à-vis the whole community of states. According to Ranganathan, CHM expresses 'an even more expansive understanding of community obligations'.[48] While using the rhetoric of states, what her argument shares with that of Baslar is the acknowledgment that CHM embraces interests that go beyond the mere goal of sharing resources amongst states and instead points to community obligations that foster protection of natural resources and equitable sharing.[49]

The historical development of CHM in the modern law of the sea, however, shows that access to and sharing of resources in ABNJ were precisely the focus in the emergence of this concept. While developed States did not oppose to the concept of CHM itself, recognising that the free-for-all, open-access regime was no longer tenable, there were vast differences between developed and developing states on how to give content to CHM. Developed states understand CHM to allow the 'common use of designated areas while upholding traditional concepts such as freedom of the high seas and freedom of exploration'.[50] In contrast, developing countries view CHM as having three goals: prevention of monopolization in these areas by developed nations at the expense of nations that lack technology or financing, the direct participation of developing nations in the international management of resource extraction, and favourable distribution of economic benefits to developing nations.[51]

Developing States initially gained advantage, manifested in the original Part XI containing provisions which gave the International Seabed Authority (ISA) extensive capacity to regulate seabed mining, as well as the special status given to the Enterprise—the commercial arm of the ISA—as compared to private contractors and other provisions relating to the transfer of mining technologies from developed States to the Enterprise and developing states.[52] However,

47 Ranganathan (n 41) 124.

48 ibid.

49 ibid 134.

50 Harminderpal Singh Rana, 'The "Common Heritage of Mankind" & the Final Frontier: A Revaluation of Values Constituting the International Legal Regime for Outer Space Activities' (1994) 26 Rutgers Law Journal 225, 230.

51 Seokwoo Lee and Jeong Woo Kim, 'Applying the Principle of the Common Heritage of Mankind: An East Asian Perspective' in Keyuan Zou (ed), *Global Commons and the Law of the Sea: Maritime Cooperation in East Asia* (Brill 2018).

52 Rothwell and Stephens (n 13) 136.

this was but a pyrrhic victory as most developed States involved or interested in deep seabed mining did not accept this outcome. As a result of the complex negotiations and the bargaining involved therein, the content of CHM went through a process of radical change. It was watered down substantially through the 1994 Agreement relating to the Implementation of Part XI of the United Nations Convention on the Law of the Sea of 10 December 1982 (1994 Implementing Agreement)[53] in order to appeal to major industrial, developed States. What is ironic is that while the philosophical foundation of CHM underlies the protection of interests transcending those of States, in practice the development of this concept is weighed down precisely by the need to balance States' interests. In other words, individual interests were omnipresent.

As it now stands in the 1994 Implementing Agreement, CHM is 'not as visionary as Pardo's original conception of [CHM]'.[54] The concept of CHM is not defined anywhere under LOSC, even though it is incorporated into its Article 136, which states that 'the Area and its resources are the common heritage of mankind'. Based on Articles 137, 140, 141 and 145 of the LOSC, however, the concept of CHM essentially encapsulates the following principles: (i) the seabed must be used for peaceful purposes; (ii) the Area and its resources are not subject to appropriation and 'are vested in mankind as a whole'; (iii) the Area and its resources are subject to common management by an international body-the ISA who acts on behalf of humankind, and (iv) the benefits of deep seabed mining will be shared equitably.

Despite the existence of these articles, the meaning of each component is not all clear. In the *Advisory Opinion on Activities in the Area*, while the Seabed Disputes Chamber (SDC) of the International Tribunal for the Law of the Sea (ITLOS) based the interpretation of the sponsoring States' obligations in the Area on CHM, it did little in clarifying its content. The reference to CHM seemed simply to mean the Area and resources.[55] Looking at the components of CHM, it would seem that components (i) and (ii) do not raise much controversy as they were in principle widely accepted by all States. Components (iii) and (iv) are much vaguer, though not so much in relation to the idea behind them, but in how they are to be implemented due to the much watered down version of CHM in 1994 Implementing Agreement as discussed above. As a result, while

53 Agreement relating to the implementation of Part XI of the United Nations Convention on the Law of the Sea of 10 December 1982 (signed 18 July 1994, entered in force 16 November 1994) 1836 UNTS 3 (1994 Implementing Agreement).

54 Rothwell and Stephens (n 13) 141.

55 *Responsibilities and obligations of States with respect to Activities in the Area* (Advisory Opinion, 1 February 2011) ITLOS Reports 2011, 10, paras 148, 179.

equitable sharing of financial and other economic benefits derived from activities in the Area remains as a guiding principle,[56] the details regarding how it is to be implemented are not clearly spelled out. The requirement for compulsory transfer of technology from a contractor to the Enterprise or to developing country miners[57] was replaced with a more general duty to facilitate the acquisition of deep seabed technology and provision of economic assistance. Similarly, it was not debated that the resources would be under collective management through the establishment of an international body, the ISA. In fact, the ISA epitomizes the idea of protection of collective interests by placing 'exploitation of resources under common management'.[58] However, the functions of the ISA have been substantially altered. For example, while the Assembly is the plenary body of the ISA, a 'decision of the Assembly on any matter for which the Council also has competence ... shall be based on the recommendations of the Council'.[59] This provision has limited the power of the Assembly and has given industrialised states—whose interests are much better reflected in the Council due to the requirement of representation from different groups of states—more control in the decision-making process. In terms of its functioning, the ISA is to operate in a cost-effective manner.[60] This is most evident in the changes that were made to the Enterprise, which no longer enjoys the privileges that were granted to it under LOSC Part XI.[61] The changes made to the ISA further buttress the observation made above that CHM as it currently stands in the law of the sea merely revolves around the interests of States and the need to balance these interests in a way that is acceptable to all States.

In short, while CHM underpins the legal regime of the Area, relevant provisions of the 1994 Implementing Agreement present a version of CHM that is much weaker than what its conceptual foundation suggests and what its earlier proponents wanted to achieve. This concept is now realised mainly through the establishment of the ISA, which acts on behalf of humankind to regulate activities concerning mineral resources in the Area. The ISA thus epitomizes the protection of collective interests in the Area. However, what these

---

56 LOSC arts 140(2), 155 and 160.

57 Annex III, art 5.

58 Pierre-Marie Dupuy and Jorge E Viñuales, *International Environmental Law* (2nd edn, Cambridge University Press 2018) 96.

59 1994 Implementing Agreement section 3(4).

60 ibid section 1(2).

61 ibid section 2(4). The privileges that the Enterprise enjoyed are included in, inter alias, art 153(3) and Annex III, art 3(5).

collective interests are, to whom they belong and how they are to be protected are not all clear.

### 3.2 *What Remains of CHM?*

While the main problems with the principle of freedom of fishing in the high seas lie in the imbalance between exploitation and conservation of resources, the challenges posed to the concept of CHM include: (i) the uncertainty regarding what each of the components of the concept encompasses, (ii) how these components are to be operationalised in practice; and, more recently (iii) whether CHM can or should be extended to living resources.

First, one of the most salient features of the application of CHM is the establishment of the ISA. The ISA represents the collective efforts of humankind to protect common interests. These common interests are mainly manifested in the exploitation of the resources which are 'vested in mankind as a whole' and for the benefit of humankind. As the term 'resources' within the meaning of Part XI only refers to non-living resources, ie minerals, the ISA is only mandated to deal with a specific activity, namely, mining. This means that it was not envisioned nor designed to be a vehicle to deal with other aspects of governance in the Area. More importantly, the question that arises is who is 'mankind'? Article 140 entitled 'benefit of mankind' does not define this term. It refers instead to States 'irrespective of the geographical location' and 'whether coastal or land-locked'. It further provides that activities in the Area also need to 'tak[e] into particular consideration the interests and needs of developing States and of peoples who have not attained full independence or other self-governing status'. So here, it would seem that 'mankind' is equated to first and foremost States, then peoples.

In practice, participation in the ISA is limited only to States according to Article 157.[62] It is true that participation in the Council of the ISA is according

---

62 The ISA welcomes observers which include non-governmental organisations. See <www.isa.org.jm/observers> accessed 27 July 2021. However, according to a study on transparency at ISA, it is not clear the extent to which observers can play a meaningful role in the operation of ISA. Acceptance of observers to the ISA is by consensus, and therefore a minority of Parties can potentially block an observer's application from being accepted. While Meetings of the Assembly and Council are generally open to observers, meetings of the Legal and Technical Commission (LTC) and the Finance Committee are not. Only when invited by the Chair and approved by the Assembly, may observers make an intervention in Assembly, while in the Council they may only participate upon the Council's invitation and only 'on questions affecting them or within the scope of their activities'. See Jeff A Ardron, 'Transparency in the operations of the International Seabed Authority: An initial assessment' (2018) 95 Marine Policy 324.

to different groups representing the interests of different stakeholders, namely consumers, exporters, investors and developing States and special interests. The fact that all these interests are presented in the executive organ of the ISA may represent an effort to ensure that deep seabed mining is conducted with the interests of all stakeholders in mind, thus serving the interests of all States. However, as States are the only participants in the decision-making process at the Assembly and in the implementation process at the Council, the term 'mankind' now seems to be synonymous with 'States' which act 'primarily in their national interest' with 'no discernible common direction or vision'.[63] The State-centric approach in the operation of the ISA is further exacerbated by the lack of transparency, particularly concerning access to the Legal and Technical Commission meetings, data, and information to assess whether a Contractor has met its obligations.[64] For example, the ISA to date has not consulted the public regarding assessing possible environmental impacts of deep seabed mining exploration applications and the awarding of exploration contracts. Instead, it has relied exclusively on the recommendations of its Legal and Technical Commission, whose work, as mentioned, is not open to public scrutiny.[65] Civil society, for example, is not given the opportunity to request for appeal or review of the ISA's decisions, which seems to be at odds with the principle of public participation well established under international law.[66] It should be noted that the ISA is in the process of developing a Communications and Stakeholder Engagement Strategy, which aims to '[facilitate] open, meaningful and constructive dialogue, including on stakeholder expectations'.[67] Whether this Strategy will allow for the work of the ISA to move beyond the State-centric approach mentioned above remains to be seen. Commenting on the Zero Draft of this Strategy, the PEW Charitable Trust, for example,

63 Sabine Christiansen and others, 'Towards a Contemporary Vision for the Global Seafloor: Implementing the Common Heritage of Mankind' (2019) 45 Publication Series Ecology (Heinrich-Böll-Stiftung e.V.) 35 available at <www.boell.de/en/2019/11/11/towards-contemporary-vision-global-seafloor-implementing-common-heritage-mankind> accessed 27 July 2021.

64 Jeff A Ardrona, Henry A Ruhl and Daniel O B Jones, 'Incorporating transparency into the governance of deep-seabed mining in the Area beyond national jurisdiction' (2018) 89 Marine Policy 58.

65 ibid.

66 See Leslie-Anne Duvic-Paoli, 'The Status of the Right to Public Participation in International Environmental Law: An Analysis of the Jurisprudence' (2012) 23(1) Yearbook of International Environmental Law 80.

67 ISA, Communications and Stakeholder Engagement Strategy (Zero Draft) available at <https://isa.org.jm/files/files/documents/Draft_Comms_and_Stakeholder_Engagement_Strategy.pdf> accessed 27 July 2021.

remarked that '[i]t does not reflect what is needed: an explanation of the principles and strategic approaches that could improve information sharing, consultations and public participation at an increasingly important international organization'.[68]

The approach of the SDC in the *Advisory Opinion on Activities in the Area* seems to further highlight the narrow understanding of 'mankind'. When examining sponsoring States' obligations in the Area, the SDC held that:

> The role of the sponsoring State, as set out in the Convention, contributes to the realization of the common interest of all States in the proper application of the principle of the common heritage of mankind which requires faithful compliance with the obligations set out in Part XI.[69]

Here, the application of CHM is considered as part of the goal to realise 'the common interests of all States' to apply the principle. While the concept itself refers to 'mankind', the SDC viewed its application merely from the perspective of States. This rather narrow view of whose interests are at stake is further underlined by the fact that the SDC declined to grant requests made by two non-governmental organisations, namely Greenpeace International and World Wide Fund for Nature to submit written statements or participate in the advisor proceedings as *amici curiae*.[70] In the end, only States and international organisations—comprised of States—were allowed to participate in the proceedings. While this decision was explained by a failure to comply with the procedural rules, ie Article 133 of the Rules of the Tribunal,[71] the SDC's decision and this article itself again reaffirm the central role that States' interests play, at least in the implementation of the CHM. As a result, as observed by one scholar, 'the common heritage of mankind principle has been reduced to merely another instance of commonly managed access to a resource, in which no one State offends another, and therefore all applications are likely to go through, whether or not they benefit the common heritage'.[72]

68 The PEW Charitable Trusts, 'Comments to the Zero Draft of the Communications and Stakeholder Engagement Strategy' (28 January 2021) available at <www.pewtrusts.org/-/media/assets/2021/01/isa-stakeholder-strategy-comments-pew_jan-2021.pdf> accessed 27 July 2021.

69 *Advisory Opinion on Activities in the Area* (n 55) para 76.

70 ibid 14.

71 ibid.

72 Christiansen and others (n 63) 35.

While not envisioned at the time when LOSC was being negotiated, the term 'mankind' should now encompass a broader category of beneficiaries than States, and should include the interests of future generations.[73] This argument then incorporates into CHM the principle of inter-generational equity, which 'articulates a concept of fairness among generations in the use and conservation of the environment and its natural resources'.[74] As argued by Tladi, the inter-generational equity element of CHM does not only require the protection, conservation, and preservation of marine biological diversity in ABNJ but more importantly, that this should be done with a forward-looking approach, bearing in mind the interests of future generations.[75] As the principle of intergenerational equity is the foundation of sustainable development, it also establishes a close link between CHM and sustainable development and reflects sustainable development in the exploitation and utilization of resources. Sustainable development therefore reflects within the scope of CHM a balance between the common interest to protect the marine environment of the seabed and the individual interest of States to engage in resource extraction.

In practice, inadequate attention is paid to the protection of the marine environment in the application of CHM. This is particularly worrying in light of the fact that '[g]iven the very slow natural rates of recovery in most deep-sea ecosystems targeted for mining, loss of biodiversity in the deep sea is inevitable and may be considered to be 'forever' on human time scales. In effect, the actions of one generation will affect the common heritage of humankind for many generations to come'.[76] The legal framework exists. Article 145 of the LOSC requires that '[n]ecessary measures shall be taken with respect to activities in the Area to ensure effective protection for the marine environment from

73 Rüdiger Wolfrum, 'The Common Heritage of Mankind' *Max Planck Encyclopedia of Public International Law* available at <www.zaoerv.de/43_1983/43_1983_2_a_312_337.pdf> accessed 27 July 2021. See also Christopher C Joyner, 'Legal Implications of the Concept of the Common Heritage of Mankind' (1986) 35(1) The International and Comparative Law Quarterly 190, 190; Alexandre Kiss, 'The Common Heritage of Mankind: Utopia or Reality?' (1985) 40 International Journal 423, 423–24.

74 Edith Brown Weiss, 'Intergenerational Equity' (2013) *Max Planck Encyclopedias of International Law* available at <https://opil.ouplaw.com/view/10.1093/law:epil/9780199231690/law-9780199231690-e1421?print=pdf> accessed 27 July 2021.

75 Dire Tladi, 'The Common Heritage of Mankind and the Proposed Treaty on Biodiversity in Areas beyond National Jurisdiction: The Choice between Pragmatism and Sustainability' (2015) 25(1) Yearbook of international Environmental Law 113, 129.

76 Holly J Niner and others, 'Deep-Sea Mining With No Net Loss of Biodiversity—An Impossible Aim' Frontiers in Marine Science (01 March 2018) available at <https://doi.org/10.3389/fmars.2018.00053> accessed 27 July 2021.

harmful effects which may arise from such activities'. The Mining Code developed by the ISA includes principles of environmental protection, including the principle of precaution, which is not found under LOSC itself, to guide the exploration activities of the mineral resources. The SDC in its *Advisory Opinion on Activities in the Area* confirmed that sponsoring States, in order to fulfil their obligations under Article 139 of the LOSC, need to discharge of various obligations to protect the marine environment. However, the ISA itself has not determined which measures will be taken to give effect to environmental aspects of the CHM concept.[77] In practice, it has been argued that when reviewing exploration applications, the ISA does not prioritise the marine environment and does not acknowledge MPAs or ecologically or biologically significant marine areas.[78]

Finally, an important question relating to the application of CHM in recent years has been whether CHM applies to the exploitation of marine genetic resources (MGRs). Article 136 of the LOSC states that '[t]he Area and its resources are the common heritage of mankind' and the term 'resources', in turn, is defined under Article 133 as 'all solid, liquid or gaseous mineral resources in situ in the Area at or beneath the seabed, including polymetallic nodules'. However, the deep seabed is home not only to mineral resources, but also to complex biodiversity. Deep seabed biodiversity has attracted attention not only due to its intrinsic value as part of the marine environment, but increasingly due to the considerable potential scientific and economic value derived or perceived to derive from marine organisms, including MGRs. Whether substantiated or not, MGRs and biotechnologies developed and commercialized on the basis of MGRs are expected to bring enormous benefits.[79] These benefits have sparked debates regarding the regime applicable to the exploitation of MGRs found in ABNJ, namely high sea freedom or CHM. A restrictive understanding of the term 'resources' within the meaning of Article 136 suggests that it

77 Aline Jaeckel, Kristina M Gjerde and Jeff A Ardron, 'Conserving the common heritage of humankind—Options for the deep-seabed mining regime' (2017) 78 Marine Policy 157.

78 Christiansen and others (n 61) 54. See also IISD, Earth Negotiations Bulletin 25(151) (21 August 2017) which reported, inter alia, that during the 23rd session of the ISA, the LTC pointed to the absence of binding rules in relation to EBSAs in response to a call from States to address the issue of impacts on EBSAs in … applications for approval of work plans and extension of exploration contracts, as well as in the exploration regulations.

79 Konrad Jan Marciniak, 'Marine Genetic Resources: Do They Form Part of the Common Heritage of Mankind Principle?' in Lawrence Martin, Constantios Salonidis and Christina Hioureas (eds), *Natural Resources and the Law of the Sea: Exploration, Allocation, Exploitation of Natural Resources in Areas under National Jurisdiction and Beyond* (Juris Publishing 2017) 373–406.

only includes non-living resources, and thus CHM would not be applicable. However, different views have been expressed on this matter. Oude Elferink, for example, argues that Article 133 does not provide an exhaustive definition of 'resources but merely one specific category of resources for the purposes of Part XI'. Consequently, this article 'does not exclude living resources or other non-mineral resources from the scope of application of Part XI'.[80] States are also equally divided on which principle should apply to access to and exploitation of MGRs.[81] Some developed States, such as the United States, Japan, the EU have argued that the concept of resources under LOSC does not encompass MGRs, thus MGRs cannot be considered CHM, and instead freedom of fishing should be applicable.[82] On the other hand, developing States argue that what falls under the concept of CHM is not only resources but also the Area, which includes living resources that live on the deep seabed.[83]

In short, the core elements of CHM which distinguish it from freedom of the high seas are access to resources accompanied with community obligations in the form of equitable sharing and protection of the resources. However, there is still uncertainty regarding what these components mean. More importantly, these components seem to have been diluted. What remains of CHM as it is currently being applied is merely restriction on free access to the resources and instead placing the resources under common management. Equitable sharing, which forms the foundation for the development of the concept, remains uncontroversial in the abstract, but is only a hollow form of itself in practice. The term 'mankind' is now being applied as if it only contains States.

---

80 Alex Oude Elferink, 'The Regime of the Area: Delineating the Scope of Application of the Common Heritage Principle and Freedom of the High Seas' (2007) 22(1) The International Journal of Marine and Coastal Law 143, 152.

81 For a more detailed discussion on the debate about the legal status of MGRs, see Henriksen (ch 4) in this volume, part 3.2.2.

82 See eg, The International Institute for Sustainable Development, 'Summary of the First Session of the Intergovernmental Conference on an Internationally Legally Binding Instrument Under the UN Convention on the Law of the Sea on the Conservation and Sustainable Use of Marine Biodiversity of Areas Beyond National Jurisdiction' (2018) 25(179) Earth Negotiations Bulletin 1, 3. Verena Grafin von Roedern, European Union, statement at the United Nations Open-ended Informal Consultative Process on Oceans and the Law of the Sea: Statement on behalf of the European Union by the Representative of Germany (28 June 2007). Note also that the Secretariat of the CBD prepared a Note on bioprospecting for the genetic resources of the deep seabed, in which it also classified MGR as living resources subject to freedom of fishing.

83 See 'Letter Dated 25 July 2014 from the Co-Chairs of the Ad Hoc Open- Ended Informal Working Group to the President of the General Assembly' (17 September 2014) UN Doc A/69/177.

The protection of the resources and the marine environment has not been of prime concern.

## 4 Dichotomy without a Difference?

The freedom of fishing and CHM, while sharing the underlying acknowledgement of ABNJ as global commons, adopt drastically different approaches to resource management. As a result, they may be perceived as two contrasting principles governing resources in ABNJ. However, the above discussion shows that the gap in the application of the two principles has increasingly narrowed. The dichotomy between freedom of the high seas and CHM, therefore, is not as pronounced as perceived, and may have altogether faded.

The main differences between freedom of fishing and CHM lie in the extent, rationale for and nature of the restrictions on the exercise of individual freedom in common areas. The freedom of fishing ensures that all States have individual access to living resources in the high seas. In contrast, under CHM, there is no individual freedom to access resources in the Area; access is instead managed through the operation of an international body. In terms of the rationale for the restrictions, the conditions which restrict the freedom of fishing primarily aim at coordinating the exercise of such a freedom and maintaining access to all States, thus still focusing on individual interests. These restrictions do not take into account discrepancies in technological and financial capacities of states to have access to the resources, nor do they require that the use of resources benefits all states in the high seas. On the other hand, the restrictions imposed upon the utilization of the deep seabed are not merely meant to protect equal access to resources for individual States, but to protect the interests of humankind.[84] CHM thus embraces the notion of equity much more clearly, particularly in the operation of the ISA and the requirement of benefit-sharing. The protection of collective interests is therefore more prominent in the concept of CHM, at least in theory. Third, the nature of the collective interests differs. Collective interests that are to be balanced with freedom of fishing in the high seas are to ensure and maintain equal access for all States, while regulated access through the ISA in the Area is to ensure that activities undertaken in the Area are for the benefit of humankind. The collective interests associated with the former could be described as an aggerate of individual interests, whereas the latter goes beyond

84 Rüdiger Wolfrum, 'Identifying Community Interests in International Law: Common Spaces and Beyond' in Benvenisti and Nolte (n 41).

individual interests. It follows that while RFMOs may be similar to the ISA in their function of overseeing access to resources, they only do so to secure the interests of their respective members. They do not represent the interests of the broader international community and equity does not play such an important role. Regulated access through RFMOs, therefore, does not have to adhere to the requirement of equitable sharing of the benefits of the resources.

However, these differences have now narrowed due to two concurrent trends. The freedom of fishing is placed under increasing restriction in the form of the obligation to conserve living resources. In high seas areas in which there are RFMOs, access to the resources is regulated by the rules of the RFMO. Thus, the regime of freedom of fishing as currently set up is no longer the free exercise of individual freedom, but increasingly more about achieving regulated access for operators. This makes the regime in essence not that different from deep seabed mining. Moreover, collective interests in ABNJ are starting to merge as well. As explained in section 2.1, there is an increasingly stronger emphasis on the conservation of living resources for their intrinsic value as part of marine biodiversity, as opposed to merely resources to serve human needs. It follows that, as RFMOs serve as regional mechanisms to implement the obligations to conserve the marine living resources, they help to ensure the collective interests in ABNJ. At the same time, the collective interests in the Area, as explained in section 3.1, exist more in theory than in practice. The way that CHM is currently regulated and applied in reality, as a result of the compromises between States during the negotiation of LOSC and the 1994 Implementing Agreement, shows that the interests of States still occupy a central role in application of CHM. Protecting collective interests might have been the goal of at the outset, but ultimately the operation of the concept indicates a return to individual interests. Taken together, the increasing attention to collective interests in the high seas and the return to individual interests in the Area mean that the line drawn between collective interests that are present in the regime for the high seas and the Area are not as marked as made out to be.

That said, one major difference still seems to stand, namely the role of equity, including both intra-generational and inter-generational equity, as part of collective interests for CHM. This element is absent in high seas fishing. Regarding intra-generational equity, it must be acknowledged that the UNFSA dedicates a Part to recognising the special requirements of developing States in the conservation and management of straddling fish stocks and highly migratory fish stocks.[85] This entails, inter alia, the obligation to cooperate

---

85 UNFSA art 24.

and assist developing states in participating in high seas fisheries,[86] including 'the provision of financial assistance, assistance relating to human resources development, technical assistance, transfer of technology'.[87] However, as some authors have pointed out, the influence of these provisions on the extent to which developing States have a right to the allocation of fishing opportunities is still unclear. States parties only have to take into account the criteria listed in the UNFSA or developed by RFMOs, and there is no indication of how they should apply.[88] The mention of the needs of different stakeholders in allocating fishing opportunities does not seem to amount to equity. In contrast, intragenerational equity as part of CHM concerns at least two other aspects that are missing in high seas fisheries, namely (i) the focus on the sharing of the benefits derived from exploitation of the resources and (ii) the ability of developing States to have a say in the administration of the resources, instead of being merely placed at the receiving end of the decision-making process. It is also worth mentioning that explicit references to equity, or equitable results, in the allocation criteria or processes 'were consistently deleted from earlier drafts' of international instruments highlighting the need for RFMOs to develop allocation criteria, preferring references to existing international law or transparency.[89] It follows that while freedom of the high seas may not be completely devoid of regard for equity, there is still a gap, at least in theory, between how equity is being realised as part of high seas freedom and as part of CHM.

Simiarly, inter-generational equity, whose focus is on the conservation and preservation of the environment for future generations, is not the main concern of the freedom of fishing. While, as explained above, increasing attention is given to the importance of conservation measures in the high seas coupled with a higher level of appreciation for the value of living resources as part of marine biodiversity, the main goal of conservation measures still leans towards maintaining the fish stocks for exploitation by States in the current generation without much regard for the interests of future generations. While the application of CHM in reality may seem to indicate a lack of adequate attention to the conservation and protection of the marine environment, and regard for the

86 ibid art 25(1)(b).
87 ibid art 25(2).
88 Maria Cecilia Engler-Palma, 'Allocation of Fishing Opportunities in Regional Fisheries Management Organizations: From Power to Law?' in Dawn A Russell and David L VanderZwaag (ed.), *Recasting Transboundary Fisheries Management Arrangements in Light of Sustainability Principles: Canadian and International Perspectives* (Brill 2010). See also Oude Elferink and Kerr (ch 7) in this volume.
89 Engler-Palma (ibid) 494 and 501.

interests of future generation, this does not negate the fact that inter-generational equity forms part of the collective interests of CHM.

In sum, given the narrowing gap between the two concepts, high seas freedoms and CHM can no longer be viewed as two opposing concepts, at least in respect of resources, but are rather aligned along a gradient of fading differences. In ABNJ, access to resources is no longer free but instead regulated, albeit under different models. Going forward, therefore, the question as to which principle should apply should not be the primary concern. The more important question that needs to be fleshed out is what regulated access to resources will look like. Another pertinent question is which international body will assume the function of joint management, something more akin to RFMOs or something like the ISA? Finally, the role that equity should play in the regulation of resources should also be addressed.

## 5 Going Forward: The Future of the Dichotomy in ABNJ

The new international legally binding instrument that is the intended outcome of the ongoing BBNJ process (BBNJ Agreement) presents an opportunity to clarify the regime applicable to ABNJ with regards to the conservation of marine biodiversity. The Draft Text of an Agreement Under the United Nations Convention on the Law of the Sea on the Conservation and Sustainable Use of Marine Biological Diversity of Areas Beyond National Jurisdiction (the Draft Agreement), despite its many brackets which indicate the lack of agreement, provides some indication as to how the new BBNJ Agreement may impact on freedom of fishing and/or CHM. In the Draft Agreement of 17 May 2019, which was later revised, Article 5 entitled General principles and approaches makes no mention of high seas freedom or CHM.[90] However, elements of the latter can be seen in various provisions of the Draft Agreement. For example, in dealing with MGRs, Article 9 states that '[n]o State shall claim or exercise sovereignty or sovereign rights over marine genetic resources of areas beyond national jurisdiction' and that '[t]he utilization of marine genetic resources of areas beyond national jurisdiction shall be for the benefit of mankind as a whole, taking into consideration the interests and needs of developing States, in particular the least developed countries, landlocked developing countries, geographically

90 Draft text of an agreement under the United Nations Convention on the Law of the Sea on the conservation and sustainable use of marine biological diversity of areas beyond national jurisdiction (17 May 2019) UN Doc A/CONF.232/2019/6 (Draft Agreement) available at <https://digitallibrary.un.org/record/3811328?ln=en> accessed 27 July 2021.

disadvantaged States, small island developing States, coastal African States and developing middle-income countries'. Non-appropriation and utilization of resources for the benefit of humankind are two of the core elements of CHM.

Article 4 of the Draft Agreement states that the ILBI shall not 'prejudice the rights, jurisdiction and duties' under LOSC. At first glance, this article suggests that the ILBI would not contain any provisions which purport to further restrict the freedom of fishing in the high seas. However, the UNFSA contains the same provision, but it still in fact limits high seas freedom. Thus, such a reading may be premature. The ILBI will, for example, contain provisions on area-based management tools (ABMTS), including MPAS, and environmental impact assessments (EIAS), which will have an impact of high seas fishing. While it is not clear how the relevant provisions are to be implemented, it could be argued that the fact that ABMTS and EIAS are part of the package deal from the beginning suggests the drafters had always envisioned some sort of restriction to high seas freedom in the ILBI. There remains considerable debate regarding the details for the adoption of MPAS, including who should adopt MPAS and who should decide on the specific measures, and how ABMTS under the ILBI interact with existing MPAS developed by regional bodies. A more robust framework to strengthen and coordinate MPAS to overcome the shortcomings of the patchwork that currently exists, as discussed in section 2.1, will certainly be desirable to fulfil the goal of conservation of marine biodiversity in ABNJ. This would mean, at the same time, strengthening restrictions on freedom of fishing in the high seas. However, the requirement under Article 4, without brackets, that the ILBI 'does not undermine relevant legal instruments and frameworks and relevant global, regional, subregional and sectoral bodies' has been argued to pose difficulties for such a desire.[91]

In the Revised Draft Agreement of 27 November 2019, some important changes were made.[92] Most noticeably, CHM has now made its way into Article 5, albeit still in brackets. The inclusion of CHM in the Revised Draft

91 See eg, Zoe Scanlon, 'The Art of "Not Undermining": Possibilities Within Existing Architecture to Improve Environmental Protections in Areas Beyond National Jurisdiction' (2018) 75(1) ICES Journal of Marine Science 405; Vito De Lucia, 'Reflecting on the meaning of "not undermining" ahead of IGC-2' NCLOS Blog (21 March 2019) available at <https://site.uit.no/jclos/files/2019/03/JCLOS-Blog-21.3.2019-Reflecting-on-the-meaning-of-not-undermining-ahead-of-IGC-2-3.pdf> accessed 27 July 2021.

92 Revised draft text of an agreement under the United Nations Convention on the Law of the Sea on the conservation and sustainable use of marine biological diversity of areas beyond national jurisdiction (17 November 2019) UN Doc A/CONF.232/2020/3 (Revised Draft Agreement) available at <https://undocs.org/en/a/conf.232/2020/3> accessed 27 July 2021.

Agreement was the result of strong reactions from developing States during the third session of the inter-governmental conference, with one describing the lack of CHM in the ILBI as 'giving life to a treaty of this importance without a soul, or like putting a ship in the water without a navigational instrument.[93] However, the textual proposals submitted by States in response to the Revised Draft Agreement confirm that the division amongst States surrounding CHM will remain a bone of contention. Developed States continue to oppose to the inclusion of CHM,[94] while developing States continue to endorse CHM,[95] which means that the incorporation of CHM into the ILBI is not at all guaranteed.

Even if CHM were to be included, it is still not clear what implications it would have. The first question is to what kind of resources will it apply? Article 8 of the Revised Draft Agreement indicates that the Agreement or Part will not apply to fish and other biological resources as commodity. Thus, it is clear that it will not be CHM but freedom of high seas that will continue to apply to most exploitation activities of living resources, at least fish harvested as a commodity.

In relation to MGRS, while CHM is not specifically mentioned in Part III concerning MGRS, it would seem that, as a general principle contained in Article 5, it would apply to MGRS. The application of CHM to MGRS would result in the exploitation of these resources being subject to the requirement of non-appropriation. The question remains whether MGRS would then fall under the management of the ISA. As LOSC does not give the ISA a mandate over MGRS, such management would need to be explicitly provided for by the ILBI. Perhaps most importantly for developing States, the application of CHM to MGRS would mean that the benefits from exploitation will be shared equitably. While the meaning of 'equitable sharing' as a component of CHM has been watered down substantially under the 1994 Implementing Agreement, it at

93 Vito De Lucia, 'The Question of the Common Heritage of Mankind and the Negotiations towards a Global Treaty on Marine Biodiversity in Areas Beyond National Jurisdiction: No End in Sight?' (2020) 16(2) McGill Journal of Sustainable Development Law 140.

94 These States include, for example, the EU and member States, Monaco, Republic of Korea, the United States. See Textual proposals submitted by delegations by 20 February 2020, for consideration at the fourth session of the Intergovernmental conference on an international legally binding instrument under the United Nations Convention on the Law of the Sea on the conservation and sustainable use of marine biological diversity of areas beyond national jurisdiction (the Conference), in response to the invitation by the President of the Conference in her Note of 18 November 2019 (UN Doc A/CONF.232/2020/3) available at <www.un.org/bbnj/sites/www.un.org.bbnj/files/textual_proposals_compilation_article-by-article_-_15_april_2020.pdf> accessed 27 July 2021.

95 ibid. These States include Core Latin America Group, South Africa, Pakistan (proposing specifically that MGR in ABNJ fall under the common heritage regime and definition).

least ensures that some kind of sharing is envisioned. This is a much more desirable outcome for developing States than if the freedom of the high seas principle were to apply, as advocated by developed States. The application of the principle of freedom of fishing to MGRs would mean all States would have free access to these resources, subject only to the general obligation to conserve these resources. However, how equitable sharing will be implemented again remains to be seen and will depend on the specific content of ILBI on this point.

But even if CHM were to apply to MGRs, it is still not clear what this entails. Similar to the Draft Agreement, the Revised Draft Agreement still contains in Article 9 the requirements that MGRs are not subject to claims of sovereignty and appropriation, and that the utilization of MGRs of ABNJ shall be for the benefit of humankind as a whole. These components of CHM are therefore firmly established. However, the requirement of non-appropriation raises questions when it comes to marine scientific research activities in the Area under Article 143 of the LOSC, which reiterates that such activities must be for peaceful purposes and for the benefit of humankind as a whole. Commentators have observed that samples of organisms that have been gathered in connection with marine scientific research may be of commercial interest because of their genetic material.[96] Does the requirement on non-appropriation and more specifically that marine scientific activities should serve the benefit of humankind under Article 143 then restrict acquiring exclusive rights to that genetic material? In the same vein, if CHM were to apply to MGRs, does this mean that the activities relating to MGRs will be placed under a regime of common management by an international body similar to mining activities? Article 10 of the Revised Draft Agreement seems to show that a common management regime for MGRs is not envisioned. This article instead provides for a system of license or permit to be issued by individual States under the terms and conditions provided therein. There is no indication of the involvement of any international body, except for the secretariat of the Agreement, whose function is to receive prior and/or post-cruise notification of the collection of and/or access to and utilization of MGRs. The textual proposals submitted by States indicate a strong objection even to the requirement of prior notification to the secretariat.[97] Finally, will benefits arising from activities concerning MGRs

96 Oude Elferink (n 80).

97 For example, the European Union, the United States in relation to art 10, the European Union, the United States and Israel in relation to art 13. See Textual proposals submitted by delegations by 20 February 2020, for consideration at the fourth session of the Intergovernmental conference on an international legally binding instrument under

be subject to the requirement of equitable benefit sharing? Fair and equitable sharing of benefits arising from activities relating to MGRs is already provided for as one of the objectives of Part III and in a separate Article 11. However, it should be noted that Article 11 itself is still in brackets, and again the textual proposals submitted by the delegations show that not all States are in favour of establishing a compulsory benefit sharing mechanism nor is it clear what this mechanism will look like, particularly whether benefits will include both monetary and non-monetary benefits.

As analyzed above, in light of the narrowing gap between freedom of the high seas in relation to resources and CHM, the regime for ABNJ essentially boils down to regulated access to resources. The question of course remains: regulated by whom, which relates to the institutional design of the ILBI.[98] This question is, in turn, closely linked to the question of which collective interests should be protected as this underlines the whole debate regarding whether and how CHM should be included in the ILBI. To recall, the collective interests associated with freedom of the high seas include primarily the maintenance of long-term access to resources which also require the taking of conservation measures. The scope of collective interests as part of CHM is broader, at the core of which is the notion of equity, including intra-generational and inter-generational equity. Focusing on how these different aspects of equity are to be fleshed out in the ILBI will allow the discussion to move past the ideological impasse in order to achieve a more effective regime for ABNJ.

In the current Revised Draft Agreement, both elements of equity seem to be present, but the debate has focused to a much greater extent on intra-generational equity. Equitable sharing of benefits in relation to MGRs has been the bone of contention throughout the negotiation and is unlikely to be easily resolved, particularly in light of the diverging opinions that have been expressed to the Revised Draft Agreement. It has been observed 'there is general agreement that recognition of MGRs as common heritage of mankind is not a prerequisite for the establishment of benefit-sharing obligations'.[99] This

the United Nations Convention on the Law of the Sea on the conservation and sustainable use of marine biological diversity of areas beyond national jurisdiction (the Conference), in response to the invitation by the President of the Conference in her Note of 18 November 2019 (UN Doc A/CONF.232/2020/3).

98 See Dalaker (ch 12) in this volume.

99 Klaudija Cremers and others, 'A Preliminary Analysis of the Draft High Seas Biodiversity Treaty' IDDR Study (January 2020) available at <https://www.iddri.org/sites/default/files/PDF/Publications/Catalogue%20Iddri/Etude/202001-ST0120-high%20seas.pdf> accessed 27 July 2021.

again reiterates the argument that it may be unproductive to get tied down in the debate over which label to use, as long as the ILBI does not lose sight of the collective interests be to protected. On the other hand, focusing on the mechanism for benefit-sharing as opposed to the principle that underlies it has been advocated as the pragmatic solution,[100] but it could be said to be a diverging tactic to avoid the inclusion of CHM as a guiding principle for the whole agreement. It is important, particularly for developing States, that the ILBI, while not bogged down with labels, would not suffer the same fate as the 1994 Implementing Agreement which, in order to appease developed States, renders the requirement of equitable benefit much less stringent. Intra-generational equity is, moreover, not only about benefit-sharing. Capacity-building and transfer of technology also play an important part in ensuring equity and thus should also be given due attention. The absence of any mention of CHM might allow the negotiations to proceed at a quicker pace, but may fragmentize the framework that deals with ABNJ as different issues of the package deal may be treated under different arrangements—similar to the current reality that the future agreement aims to rectify. Moreover, merely focusing on benefit-sharing mechanisms without CHM moves the discussion back to States' individual interests, without paying due consideration to the second element of equity, namely inter-generational equity.

Inter-generational equity has received much less attention during the IGC. To recall, the 'inter-generational equity element reminds us that, more than just being about benefit sharing, the common heritage of mankind requires us to protect, conserve, and preserve marine biological diversity in areas of the ocean and ocean floor beyond national jurisdiction'.[101] The protection of biological diversity seems to be present in the very rationale for the negotiation of the ILBI itself, as the protection, conservation and preservation of marine biological diversity in ABNJ is the exact purpose of the ILBI. In terms of content, it seems to also be present in the parts relating to measures aimed at strengthening the conservation of biodiversity, such as ABMTs, including MPAs and EIAs. Details regarding the implementation of each of the components are still elusive, thus it is still open to question the extent to which they will be effectively integrated into the overall governance of ANBJ. Moreover, the Revised Draft Agreement, unlike the Draft Agreement, also reintroduces

100 Kentaro Nishimoto, 'Marine Genetic Resources in Areas Beyond National Jurisdiction: Finding Ways Towards A Pragmatic Solution', Presentation Delivered at the Workshop on Biodiversity Beyond National Jurisdiction: Towards the Development of a Balanced, Effective and Universal International Agreement (February 2019, Malmö, Sweden).

101 Tladi (n 75) 128.

the ecosystem approach as one of the general principles in Article 5. The ecosystem approach has been adopted by various international agreements as a strategy for 'integrated management of land, water and living resources'.[102] However, the ecosystem approach in itself is not free of ambiguities,[103] which then begs the question of what added value it will bring to promoting the conservation of biodiversity. It is interesting perhaps to point out at this juncture, however, that the ecosystem approach has been described as 'a tool to achieve sustainable development'.[104] The inclusion of the ecosystem approach would then, adopting the narrative of inter-generational equity of Tladi, at least promote the protection of collective interests inherently captured under CHM.

In short, the governance regime for ABNJ going forward should not be one which is overly concerned with the issue of which guiding principle will be applied. Given the narrowing gap between high seas freedom and CHM, having one or the other included in the future the ILBI will not shed much light on the regime to be applied to resources in ABNJ. At the same time, it must be acknowledged that in light of the state of biodiversity in ABNJ, it is no longer possible to allow for individual freedom to be exercised in an unregulated manner. Individual freedom must therefore give way to collective interests. What is important, therefore, is for the new regulatory regime for ABNJ not to lose sight of what these collective interests should be. It is argued that the collective interests that need to be protected should draw inspiration from CHM and should thus be based on consideration of equity, both intra-generational and inter-generational equity. This would translate into a regime which gives due consideration to not only ensuring equitable access to resources and sharing of benefits amongst stakeholders, but also a proper regime to conserve and protect marine biodiversity for future generations. Civil societies would seem to be in a good position to represent considerations of equity, and draw proper attention to the protection of marine biodiversity itself.[105] The details to be fleshed out in the corresponding parts of the ILBI should reflect these

---

102 Decision V/6 'Ecosystem Approach', Nairobi, 15–26 May 2000, UNEP/CBD/COP/DEC/V/6.

103 See, more generally, Vito De Lucia, *The 'Ecosystem Approach' in International Environmental Law Genealogy and Biopolitics* (Routledge 2019).

104 Vito De Lucia, 'Competing Narratives and Complex Genealogies: The Ecosystem Approach in International Environmental Law' (2015) 27(1) Journal of Environmental Law 91.

105 Robert Blasiak and others, 'The role of NGOs in negotiating the use of biodiversity in marine areas beyond national jurisdiction' (2017) 8 Marine Policy 1. Interestingly, according to this study, some governments 'felt that NGOs were disproportionately focused on conservation issues, in contrast with the General Assembly mandate to consider both conservation and sustainable use, and the entire package of issues'.

collective interests to the largest extent possible. As it currently stands, however, power play dictated by individual interests seems to still dominate the discussion.

## 6 Conclusion

This chapter has examined the exercise of individual freedom and protection of collective interests in the oceans space that are considered ABNJ, namely the high seas and the Area. The chapter touches upon all the framing themes of this project, namely, justice, space, power, knowledge. In terms of space, the chapter has shown that ABNJ is usually used as a convenient shorthand for both the high seas and the Area, which are ocean spaces considered as common areas underpinned by the concept of *res communes*. However, it should be borne in mind that the legal regime that regulates these respective oceans space differs, illustrating a different balance between individual freedom and collective interests. Individual freedoms dominate the high seas. In the case of freedom of fishing, all States are free to exploit living resources, and collective interests exist as conditions for the exercise of this freedoms primarily aimed at the conservation marine living resources. In the Area, individual freedom takes a back seat and collective interests prevail with the application of CHM. The requirement that the activities must be carried out for the benefit of humankind thus introduces a broader category of collective interests, one which transcends the mere interests of individual States.

Knowledge, power and justice, in different ways, explain the different legal regimes that regulate the high seas and the Area. Knowledge, or to be more precise, the increasing acquisition of knowledge, plays an important role in the formation of the legal framework regulating ABNJ. This is manifested both in the knowledge gained *about* resources at sea and knowledge gained *by* those taking part or should like to take part in exploiting the resources. With regards to the former, knowledge about the existence and the condition of the resources in ABNJ drove the negotiations on and underlie the stalemates behind the regime to exploit these resources. Clear examples include increased understanding about ocean biodiversity and ecosystem, new discovery of MGRs and understanding of their potentials—all constituting the driving force behind the ongoing BBNJ process. In terms of the holder of the knowledge, the capacity of developing States to take part in both the construction of the legal framework for ABNJ and to participate in the conservation and exploitation resources in ABNJ in practice hinges partly upon the knowledge that they possess about the resources. This, in turn, explains why capacity building and transfer of technology was chosen as one of the items of the package deal for the BBNJ Agreement.

Justice—or the lack thereof—informs the different collective interests that are protected in the high seas and in the Area. In the high seas, collective interests are in the form of conserving marine living resources, with the primary aim of ensuring all States' ability to have long-term access to the resources but without consideration for the differences in States' capacity to do so. Even with new developments in high seas fisheries, the need for equitable access is not a major concern in the work of RFMOs, let alone equitable sharing of benefits. In contrast, the collective interests that CHM purports to protect are much more grounded in consideration of justice. This is manifested in equity, including both intra- and inter-generational equity. The former allows developing States to not only take part in but also be involved in the administration of mining activities, and more importantly, facilitates the equitable sharing of benefits amongst stakeholders. The latter incorporates into CHM the protection, conservation, and preservation of marine biological diversity for the interests of future generations

Power underlies the emergence of freedom of the high seas. The doctrine of freedom of high seas was proposed in order to allow maritime States at the time to project their power in the oceans. It was the growing power of maritime States that maintained the prevalence of this doctrine for activities in common areas for centuries. This power play is, however, inherently inequitable. While on the surface it allows for all States to have access to resources in the commons, in reality it favours only those with sufficient capacity to do so. States without the means and resources are therefore left out and left behind. It is the lack of any consideration for equity that prompted developing States, comprising primarily of newly independent States pushing for a new economic order, to rally behind the CHM. In other words, if high seas freedoms emerged and prevailed thanks to power play, CHM came about to rectify the injustices brought by power play. It follows that equity—or the lack thereof—formed the main impetus behind the emergence of CHM to regulate ocean space. However, after the concept was introduced, its development was dictated again by the pull of power. The negotiations of LOSC and particularly Part XI on the Area became a battle ground for ideological contests between developed and developing States. In this process, the ideals behind CHM were gradually lost and replaced by a legal regime that appealed best to developed States in order to secure their participation. Here again, power played a major role in the distribution of rights and obligations in the seabed.

Finally, as mentioned at the start of the paper, the framework for ABNJ has oscillated between concerns for preserving individual freedom and enhancing collective resource management. However, neither of these approaches is in practice still intact or desirable. Due to the increasing restrictions on freedom of fishing on the one hand, and the watered down application of CHM on the other, what the two regimes essentially boil down to in practice is regulated access to resources. These regulations are aimed at restricting the exercise of individual freedom in favour of protecting collective interests. As a result, this chapter has argued that the future regulatory framework for ABNJ should not be tied down with the question as to which principle should be applicable. It should instead focus on how access to resources in ABNJ should be collectively regulated. This, in turn, should be informed by the collective interests that the new regime seeks to protect, which must be guided by consideration of equity. The revised draft of the BBNJ Agreement that is the outcome of the ongoing multilateral negotiations contains elements reflecting equiy. However, similar to the negotiations of LOSC and Part XI, power continues to play a prominent role in the BBNJ process. The interests of individual or groups of States seem to be the dominating driving force behind the discussions, resulting a rift between, once again, developed and developing States regarding the principle to be applied in ABNJ, particularly with regards to MGRS, posing serious questions as to whether the ILBI will eventually pursue the goal that it was set out achieve. It is important that the future regime for ABNJ should not suffer the fate of Part XI, succumbing to power play at the expense of equity and justice.

CHAPTER 6

# Thinking about Ocean Governance

*By Whom, for Whom?*

*Margherita Paola Poto*

Rinses, washes,
roars, pops, crashes,
roars, laughs, sings,
accords, disagrees,
all welcomes and merges
acute dissonances
in her scrolls
deep,
free and beautiful,
numerous and crazy,
mighty and soft,
living creature
who enjoys
of her mystery
fleeting.

from *The Wave*, G. D'ANNUNZIO

## 1 Introduction*

Irreversible changes to the oceans, with consequent disastrous effects on life on Earth, are real.[1] Ocean governance can live up to its name in a meaningful

* I would like to thank Susan Hoivik for her thoughtful work of proofreading and for sharing a part of her journey in it. My thanks also go to the editors, whose comments helped sharpen my mind and improve the quality of my thoughts on this subject matter, and to Mana Tugend, for her precious work as editorial assistant.

1 The Intergovernmental Panel on Climate Change *A Special Report on the Ocean and Cryosphere in a Changing Climate* (IPCC 2019) available at <www.ipcc.ch/site/assets/uploads/sites/3/2019/12/SROCC_FullReport_FINAL.pdf> accessed 7 October 2021.

 | DOI:10.1163/9789004506367_007

way only through the recognition of the sacredness of water, the interconnectedness of all life, and the importance of protecting and caring about the oceans.[2]

Current strategies for tackling the ocean crisis with the means offered by general international law and the law of the sea regime have evoked widespread critical concern regarding their adequacy, integration, and effectiveness for dealing with environmental challenges.[3] Understanding 'governance' as including the ability of responding to environmental threats (response-ability),[4] this chapter analyses an ocean-centred model of governance that puts participation at the forefront. This understanding forms the basic premise of the chapter: ocean governance must ensure that we are responsibly and collectively contributing to a functioning and healthy ocean system. Reorienting and restructuring the actor framework of ocean governance towards an inclusive and integrated system in the context of water care and protection is part of the constructive legal response that this chapter aims to offer to the environmental crisis.

Therefore, the analysis takes on a subject–actor perspective, focusing on the importance of a system of governance that reaches out to *all* actors involved in ocean protection and stewardship,[5] and contributes to the construction of

2 This is inspired by the words of the Assembly of Nations <www.afn.ca/honoring-water/> accessed 7 October 2021.

3 For a broad and substantiated analysis on the inadequacy of tackling climate change through international (environmental) law see Cinnamon Carlarne, 'Delinking International Environmental Law & Climate Change' (2014) 4 Michigan Journal of Environmental & Administrative Law 1 available at <http://repository.law.umich.edu/mjeal/vol4/iss1/1> accessed 7 October 2021. Carlarne (at 4) argues that climate change is an issue of such scale and complexity that it defies resolution through the constrained channels of an international environmental treaty. It is a challenge rooted in our models of development, capitalism, free trade, and state sovereignty, and we are no more likely to be able to "solve" it with the tools of international environmental law alone than we are likely to be able to solve it using any type of linear approach that ignores the economic and socio-legal realities that shape the field. Yet, we continue to characterize and approach climate change "just like any other international environmental problem".

4 I take here the true meaning of responsibility as being response-able or having the ability to respond as expressed in <www.thoughtfortoday.org.uk/> accessed 7 October 2021.

5 I here differentiate (environmental or ocean-centred) governance as a broad concept and stewardship as a narrower concept, with a less explored history in the field of environmental law. *Governance* has several declinations, in the field of public law and administrative law (and I include environmental law as a part of it), and it is used in different ways to discuss topics as different as the formation and consolidation of core principles such as good administration (here the reference to 'good' governance), which include transparency and participation. In a previous work, I have explored the meaning of good

a model that can respond to climate threats more effectively than the State-centred system has been able to do. The centrality of the oceans stands in contrast to the mainstream regulatory approach of the law of the sea, with its emphasis on the sovereign rights of States, based on the presumption of the sea's exploitable value. Admittedly, the dichotomy is over-emphasized here, with the expression 'ocean-centred governance' used to refer to the ocean-centric system, while the State-centred system is referred to as 'law of the sea', with a legal grounding in the 1982 UN Convention on the Law of the Sea (LOSC).[6] The terms ocean(s), sea(s), marine environment, and water are used interchangeably.

In this vein, the chapter also takes a critical approach to the LOSC, observing how it relies on the assumption of a separation and superiority of humans over nature. This has generated top-down regulatory patterns, with sovereign States at the top level and exploitable marine resources at the bottom.[7] The LOSC epitomizes such an approach, by stating the obligation for States to protect and preserve the marine environment, only to downgrade that obligation as an ancillary consequence of the sovereign right to exploit these natural resources (Article 193, Part XII).[8] The sovereign right of the States as a clear logical priority over

---

governance essentially as a 'participatory' and 'inclusive' system, where the public interest is reached by means of an effective engagement and participation of all interested parties. See Margherita Paola Poto and Lara Fornabaio, 'Participation as the essence of good governance: some general reflections and a case study on the Arctic Council' (2018) 8 Arctic Review on Law and Politics 139. *Stewardship*, by contrast to governance, is a word with a more limited history in environmental law. While the word was introduced by Aldo Leopold in 1949 to define the responsible use and protection of the environment, see Aldo Leopold, *A Sand County Almanac* (Oxford University Press 1949) it was not until the 1992 UN Conference on Environment and Development (UNCED) in Rio de Janeiro that environmental stewardship became global in scale, see Robert Falkner and Barry Buzan 'The emergence of environmental stewardship as a primary institution of global international society', (2018) 25(1) European Journal of International Relations 131. In this contribution, governance and stewardship will be kept separate, in such a way that governance is seen as the structure and stewardship as one of the activities developed in a system of good governance. For analogous reflections in the field of health law, see Scott L Greer, 'Organization and Governance: Stewardship and Governance in Health Systems' in Adrian Levy and others (eds), *Health Services Evaluation. Health Services Research* (Springer 2019).

6 United Nations Convention on the Law of the Sea (signed 10 December 1982, entered into force 16 November 1994) 1833 UNTS 396 (LOSC).

7 Edith Brown Weiss, 'The evolution of international environmental law' (2011) 54 Japanese Yearbook of International Law 1.

8 LOSC art 193, Part XII on *Sovereign right of States to exploit their natural resources* states that, 'States have the sovereign right to exploit their natural resources pursuant to their environmental policies and in accordance with their duty to protect and preserve the

the duty to protect Stated only in Part XII of the Convention, and only at the end of Article 193. The formulation of the article itself is such that firstly the right to exploit is once again reiterated, and then only secondly comes the affirmation of the duty to protect. Therefore, the duty to protect is not independently and unconditionally defined, and very little can do the expression 'in accordance to their duty' to mitigate the priority given to the right to exploit. The right to exploit the ocean is at the core of the LOSC, the duty to protect at the periphery. This logic permeates the LOSC implementing measures and the mandates of the law of the sea's institutions; it remained unchanged even after the regulatory system intersected the climate change regulatory framework with the approval of Agenda 21, where an action plan for sustainable development was introduced.[9] The unchanged focus on the regulation of human activities and the consequent growth of such activities has brought a considerable increase in new, specialized subareas and actors at the intersection of the law of the sea and environmental protection.[10] This proliferation of rules, actors and areas of regulation has exacerbated existing inequalities and imbalances between the actors involved in decision-making, without offering concrete solutions to the environmental challenges.[11]

---

marine environment'. Nilufer Oral, 'Implementing Part XII of the 1982 UN Law of the Sea Convention and the role of international courts' in Nerina Boschiero and others (eds), *International Courts and the Development of International Law* (Springer 2013) 403–423. For a critical analysis of the law of the sea's institutional framework, see Margherita Paola Poto, 'The Law of the Sea and its institutions: Today's hermeneutic approach and some suggestions for an ocean-centred governance model' in Elise Johansen, Signe V Busch and Ingvild Ulrikke Jakobsen (eds), *The Law of the Sea and Climate Change: Solutions and Constraints* (Cambridge University Press 2020). For future scenarios of the institutional framework of the oceans see Alex G Oude Elferink, 'Exploring the future of the institutional landscape of the oceans beyond national jurisdiction' (2019) 28(3) Review of European, Comparative & International Environmental Law 236.

9 United Nations Conference on Environment & Development, Rio de Janerio, Brazil, 3–14 June 1992, Agenda 21 available at <https://sustainabledevelopment.un.org/content/documents/Agenda21.pdf> accessed 7 October 2021.

10 Anne Peters 'The refinement of international law: From fragmentation to regime interaction and politicization' (2017) 15(3) International Journal of Constitutional Law 671.

11 See Weiss (n 7). Noteworthy is the case of the 1992 Convention on Biological Diversity (CBD), frequently mentioned as *the* instrument that introduced and reflected an integrated approach to the protection of marine biodiversity, in coordination with the LOSC regime. Rüdiger Wolfrum and Nele Matz, 'The interplay of the United Nations Convention on the Law of the Sea and the Convention on Biological Diversity' in Jochen A Frowein and Rüdiger Wolfrum (eds), *Max Planck Yearbook of United Nations Law* (Kluwer Law International 2000) 445–80. WWF Report, *Protecting our Ocean: Europe's Challenges to Meet the 2020 Deadlines*, notes the substantial failure of 19 of 23 EU member states to

The chapter explores the possibility to develop the ocean-centred governance within a participatory-constructed frame, where actors other than States contribute to its ontology and formation, so as to provide a constructive response to the critical approach. Such a participatory-constructed frame takes into account indigenous legal orders that have recognized the ocean as an inseparable part of life on Earth. Examples of this understanding are found in indigenous marine communities all over the world.[12] They all acknowledge the unconditional value of water, independent from any economic appraisal. Coastal and marine peoples see the oceans in terms of connections: between land and sea, earth and sky, day and night, between the spiritual and physical past, present and future, and between knowledge and practice, people and places.[13] Such views have often been marginalized and stigmatized as insufficiently objective and not scientifically testable.[14] Nonetheless, indigenous

---

comply with the CBD, hinting that the Convention itself has not been effective for protection of the marine environment available at <http://d2ouvy59p0dg6k.cloudfront.net/downloads/protecting_our_ocean_pdf> accessed 7 October 2021. The low level of integration of the CBD has been reported by coastal communities of New Zealand which have also expressed concern about the effects of the Convention on indigenous rights and consultation rights, see Report CBD Response 2019 *Te Ohu Kaimoana's response to the Secretariat for the Convention on Biological Diversity on the priorities for negotiations on a new framework for implementing the Convention on Biological Diversity* available at <https://teohu.maori.nz/wp-content/uploads/2019/06/Convention-on-Biological-Diversity-Response.pdf> accessed 7 October 2021.

12 Jon Altman and Sue Jackson, 'Indigenous land and sea management' in Steve Morton, David Lindenmayer and Stephen Dovers (eds), *Ten Commitments Revisited, Securing Australia's Future Environment* (CSIRO 2014); Te Ahukaramu Charles Royal, *Indigenous Worldviews: A Comparative Study. A Report on Research in Progress* (Wānanaga-o-Raukawa 2002).

13 See for example Garth R Harmsworth (Te Arawa, Ngāti Tūwharetoa, Ngāti Raukawa) and Shaun Awatere (Ngāti Porou), 'Indigenous Māori knowledge and perspectives of ecosystems' in John R Dymond (ed), *Ecosystem Services in New Zealand: Conditions and Trends* (Manaaki Whenua Press 2013); Gregory Cajete, *Native Science: Natural Laws of Interdependence* (Clear Light Publishers 1999). See also *Assessment Report: Sea Country – an Indigenous Perspective* (National Oceans Office 2002 Hobart) available at <www.environment.gov.au/system/files/resources/271c0bfc-34a2-4c6c9b0201204ebc0f43/files/indigenous.pdf> accessed 7 October 2021; Jörg Korff, *Meaning of Land to Aboriginal People*, October 2019 available at <www.creativespirits.info/aboriginalculture/land/meaning-of-land-to-aboriginal-people> accessed 7 October 2021.

14 For an example of marginalization and stigmatization of indigenous coastal peoples' knowledge see the recent study of Carrie Oloriz, and Brenda Parlee 'Towards Biocultural Conservation: Local and Indigenous Knowledge, Cultural Values and Governance of the White Sturgeon (Canada)' (2020) 12 *Sustainability* 7320. For the difficulties to recognize scientificity to marine traditional and indigenous knowledge, see Fikres Berkes, Johan Colding and Carl Folke, 'Rediscovery of traditional ecological knowledge as adaptive management' (2000) 10(5) Ecological Applications 1251. For a broad overview of the

systems have strived to maintain their solidity, continually sustaining the ocean ecosystems.[15] Integrating indigenous and marine communities' laws is an essential support column of an ocean-centred governance that responsibly and collectively safeguards and protects the marine environment.

This chapter retraces the steps of the recognition and evolution of environmental participatory rights in international law (participatory or procedural rights *for* nature, PRfN),[16] the implications of extending such rights to the carriers of 'nature-centred views', by recognizing legal personhood to nature (or substantive rights *of* nature, nature's rights, RoN), and ultimately by critically reflecting on the possibility to extend the discourse of the ocean rights to marine biodiversity in areas beyond national jurisdiction (BBNJ).

The need to expand the horizons of investigation beyond spatio-temporal coordinates, thinking in terms of a global and *therefore*[17] fluid arena, sets the scene for the construction of the ocean-centred governance model.

Section 1 traces the chronological evolution of the participatory rights *for* nature (PRfN), noting how they can contribute to the shaping of an overarching environmental governance system[18] that attributes a prominent role to nature, by giving voice to her defenders.[19]

---

stigmatization of indigenous knowledge from an indigenous perspective, see Linda Tuhiwai Smith, *Decolonizing Methodologies. Research and Indigenous Peoples* (University of Otago Press 1999).

15 Royal (n 12) 353.

16 For clarity, here I will focus on the distinction between *participatory* rights *for* nature and rights *of* nature, the latter intended as *substantive* rights *of* nature, and synonym of nature's rights. I acknowledge that there is also a further distinction in literature, within the category of nature's rights, between rights for nature (RfN) and rights of nature (RoN), where RfN considers rights as a legal tool that can be used to protect nature, for example in the form of assigning legal personhood to nature and natural elements, while RoN considers rights as based on a moral and intrinsic quality of nature. On the application of these two declinations of nature's rights to the ocean, see Vito De Lucia, 'Ocean commons, Law of the Sea and Rights *for* the Sea' (2019) 32 Canadian Journal of Law & Jurisprudence 45, 53.

17 For the connection between the terms 'global' and 'fluid' see n 24.

18 That an overarching system of governance and environmental participation is central to decision-making for areas beyond national jurisdiction (ABNJ) has been reiterated throughout the BBNJ process. See for example Kristina Gjerde and others, 'Conservation and sustainable use of marine biodiversity in Areas Beyond National Jurisdiction: Options for underpinning a strong global BBNJ Agreement through regional and sectoral governance' (2018) STRONG High Seas Project 17 available at <www.prog-ocean.org/wp-content/uploads/2018/08/STRONG-High-Seas-Policy-Brief_Options-for-underpinning-BBNJ-agreement.pdf> accessed 7 October 2021.

19 I argue elsewhere that participation is the core principle of good governance, Poto and Fornabaio (n 5). See also UNESCAP, 'What is Good Governance?' (2009) available at <www.unescap.org/sites/default/files/good-governance.pdf> accessed 7 October 2021.

Ascertaining the instrumental role of PRfN in facilitating the development of RoN, Section 2 focuses on two cases of the rights *of* nature concerning water – implicitly (New Zealand) and explicitly (India). In New Zealand, the indigenous system of water governance now enjoys full legal recognition, with rivers defined as living entities. In India, the legal personhood of the Ganga (Ganges) and Yamuna rivers, and of their glaciers was first acknowledged by the High Court of the river regions of Uttarakhand but later withdrawn by the Indian Supreme Court.[20]

Section 3, noting the problematic nature of the recognition of rights *of* nature, analyses some of its basic tenets (rights-bearer entities, connectivity, right and duties, representation) applied to ocean governance, to areas beyond national jurisdiction (ABNJ) and BBNJ, and suggests some further critical reflections on this approach.[21]

The conclusion takes a slightly radical tone, though still recognizing the validity of the instrumental consequences of the human-constructed category of nature rights that helps protect nature. In the global order of the 21st century, the deployment of rights (be they *for* or *of* nature) makes sense only if taken in the instrumental and liminal dimension, concretized in the need to re-affirm and regulate human obligations towards nature.

Thinking in these terms not only does justice to the nonhuman but could help us reimagine our State of being more richly and openly. Given all that is at stake, nothing less than a radical re-storying will do; and laws and rights – for too long tools of human privilege and exceptionalism – need to be re-imagined if they are to play a full role in human-nonhuman struggles for a future worth living.[22]

---

20 For an updated overview of the rights of water and rivers see the Report from Cyrus R Vance Center for International Justice, Earth Law Center, and International Rivers, *Rights of Rivers* available at <https://3waryu2g9363hdvii1ci666p-wpengine.netdna-ssl.com/wp-content/uploads/sites/86/2020/09/Right-of-Rivers-Report-V3-Digital-compressed.pdf> accessed 7 October 2021.

21 Harriet Harden-Davies and others, 'Rights of Nature: Perspectives for Global Ocean Stewardship' (2020) 122 Marine Policy 104059, 3. See also the Revised Draft Text of an Agreement under the United Nations Convention on the Law of the Sea on the Conservation and Sustainable Use of Marine Biological Diversity of Areas beyond National Jurisdiction, 27 November 2019 available at <https://www.un.org/bbnj/sites/www.un.org.bbnj/files/revised_draft_text_a.conf_.232.2020.11_advance_unedited_version.pdf> accessed 7 October 2021.

22 Anna Grear, 'It's wrongheaded to protect nature with human-style rights' (2019) Aeon available at <https://aeon.co/ideas/its-wrongheaded-to-protect-nature-with-human-style-rights> accessed 7 October 2021.

## 2 Background

Thinking globally[23] has contributed to forging the polycentric, fluid,[24] all-round, and encompassing characteristics of governance. Global thinking has fascinating origins that can help move away from the straitjacket of Western-centric legal classifications. In the realm of law, it led to the progressive observation of the interactions of legal cultures as a growing interconnected web, in which spatiotemporal coordinates[25] assume new meanings and are complemented by other variables, such as the no-space and the a-temporal dimensions of cyberspace.[26] The actors involved in the new inter-*actions* shift from a flat conception of territoriality to a cyber-space, with the characteristics of inter-connectivity, virtuality, expansion, and ambiguity.[27] In this global world, barriers are overcome and the relationships between past, present, and future redefined.[28] In law as well in other disciplines, overcoming spatiotemporally

---

23 The expression alludes to the work of Mark Juergensmeyer (ed), *Thinking Globally: A Global Studies Reader* (University of California Press 2014). The author reminds that some global studies scholars avoid the term 'globalization' because it can be interpreted as an acritical promotion of Western economic models; other scholars prefer the use of 'critical global studies', positioning their research in the critics of economic models of globalization. In this contribution, I chose to adopt the terms 'global/globally' in the attempt to neutralize the political implications of the term 'globalization' to the fullest possible extent. The term 'global' is here synonym of a round, multidimensional, *as fluid as the ocean*, system.

24 The term echoes the 'liquid modernity' of Zygmunt Bauman, who, in an interview with Simon Tabet, noted the transient characteristics of the expression, used to denote a new kind of society, a state of the *interregnum*: 'it is indeed used, in contemporary political language, as a name for the passage from one known state to another known state'. Simon Tabet, 'Interview with Zygmunt Bauman: From the modern project to the liquid world' (2017) 34(7–8) Theory, Culture & Society 131. In our case, from the familiar state-sovereignty model to a pluri-actor or polycentric system of governance.

25 Massimo Meccarelli and María Julia Solla Sastre, 'Spatial and temporal dimensions for legal history: an introduction' in Massimo Meccarelli and María Julia Solla Sastre (eds), *Spatial and Temporal Dimensions for Legal History: Research Experiences and Itineraries, Global Perspectives on Legal History* (Max Planck Institute for European Legal History 2016) 5.

26 Governance and cybernetics share the same roots, from the ancient Greek verb *kybernao*, 'steering a ship'. See Poto (n 8).

27 See <http://airpower.airforce.gov.au/APDC/media/PDF-Files/Pathfinder/PF157-What-is-Cyberspace-Examining-its-Characteristics.pdf> accessed 7 October 2021; Mark Federman, *The Cultural Paradox of the Global Village* (McLuhan Program in Culture and Technology 2006) available at <http://individual.utoronto.ca/markfederman/CulturalParadoxOfTheGlobalVillage.pdf> accessed 21 May 2021.

28 ibid.

coordinates also means overcoming the Western-centred perspective.[29] In this sense, thinking global contributes to building a useful bridge to other viewpoints, restoring and reducing marginalization, and strengthening long-term collective resilience to climatic threats.

That thinking global offers opportunities for re-conceptualizing and re-orienting international law is particularly evident in the case of the law of the sea's regime. After the 1992 Rio Declaration on Environment and Development,[30] considerations of the protection and preservation of the marine environment shifted from a functionalist to a teleological perspective: from being a condition that limited the rights to exploit nature, to the final objective for States to pursue. Moreover, the linear, State-oriented dimension of the protection was expanded to embrace a multi-stakeholder approach.

As a shared global objective, environmental protection has helped to provide a new space for actors and their relationships with the sea. Gradually, the scope of ocean governance has moved beyond the need to regulate the seas as an inter-State affair, pushing the debate in the direction of defining the oceans as *global* commons.[31]

## 3 How Participatory Rights *for* Nature (PRfN) Contribute to Eroding the Exclusiveness of State Sovereignty

Recognition of the need for new actors in decision-making is a process that, in environmental law, started from within, to then expand and guide administrative law on the path to participatory democracy,[32] and was spurred by the need of environmental law to engage with the vast number of interested parties in public decisions. Hereafter I recap the steps that led to the recognition of procedural and then substantive nature rights. The tool of access rights enabled new viewpoints, facilitating the entry of substantive rights to the procedural-rights-carriers, and contributing to eroding the exclusiveness of State-sovereign

29 Michel Foucault and Jan Miskowiec, 'Of other spaces' (1986) 16(1) *Diacritics* 22.

30 UN Doc A/CONF.151/26 (vol. I) 31 ILM 874 (1992).

31 *De Lucia* (n 16). See also Keyuan Zou (ed), *Global Commons and the Law of the Sea* (Brill 2018).

32 On the history of how the participatory rights movement started from international environmental law and influenced the other sectors of public – international and domestic – law see Roberto Caranta, Anna Gerbrandy and Bilun Mueller (eds), *The Making of a New European Legal Culture: The Aarhus Convention* (Europa Law Publishing 2018).

actors in environmental decision-making. Recognizing substantive rights to the procedural-rights-carriers is a process that also involves the ocean-defenders[33] and therefore a brief recapitulation of the main milestones of such a process is particularly relevant in the context of ocean governance.

### 3.1 *PRfN: The Foundation Stone*

The foundation stone of a participatory-constructed framework in environmental governance was laid in an international environmental law treaty. The 1998 Århus Convention (AC)[34] – 'the most ambitious venture in [...] environmental democracy'–[35] recognizes environmental rights to non-State actors, introducing the concept of access rights for the public, and dramatically changing the actor dynamics in international negotiations. The crowning achievement of these participatory negotiations came with the recognition of the fundamental right for every person 'to live in an environment adequate to his or her health and well-being', and in 'the duty, both individually and association with others, to protect and improve the environment'.[36] The right of access to information, the right to participate in decision-making, and the right of access to justice in environmental matters are the logical consequences of this recognition.

More specifically as to the content, the second part of the AC, known as the 'Second Pillar', covers three domains: 1) participation in the authorization procedure for certain specific activities, mainly of industrial nature (Article 6); 2) participation in the formulation of environmental plans, programs, environmental policies as well as legislation, binding regulation and standards and legislation that may have a significant effect on the environment (Articles 7 and 8); and 3) participation in decisions concerning the deliberate release of genetically modified organisms into the environment.

33 For an example among many see Earth Law Center available at <www.earthlawcenter.org/salish-sea-initiative> accessed 7 October 2021.

34 The Aarhus (Århus in Danish) Convention is hereinafter abbreviated as AC. Note that authors and legislation cited in this chapter may also refer to it as the Aarhus/Århus Convention or the Convention.

35 United Nations Economic Commission for Europe (UNECE), *The Århus Convention: An Implementation Guide* (2nd edn 2014) available at <http://www.unece.org/fileadmin/DAM/env/pp/Publications/Aarhus_Implementation_Guide_interactive_eng.pdf> accessed 7 October 2021.

36 Preamble of the AC. The full text of the Convention is available at <www.unece.org/env/pp/treatytext.html> accessed 7 October 2021.

The shortcoming of the AC is found in its strictly procedural content, limited to public participation in environmental decision-making, access to justice and information. 'The Aarhus Convention is important in the present debate because […] it gives particular emphasis to public interest activism by NGOs. But […] while the Convention endorses the right to live in an adequate environment, it stops short, however, of providing the means for citizens directly to invoke this right'.[37]

Despite the effort to come closer to effective participation *for* the environment (rights for the environment), there remained fundamental flaws in the AC. In Europe (or the Western part of the world), the process remained restricted to Western constructs of the procedural rights' narrative. The AC heritage was collected by Latin America, which, not coincidentally, happens to also be one of the regions where nature's rights movement took place, at the indigenous initiative.

### 3.2 *Indigenous Countries and Indigenous Parties Carry Forward the Process of PRfN*

The Escazú Agreement (EA),[38] negotiated twenty years after the AC to ensure its continuity and application to the Latin American and Caribbean nations, opened decision-making to new actors and their views on nature, consequently expanding the horizons of rights from merely participatory to substantive. Passing the baton of environmental decision-making to the carriers of nature-centred views has opened perspectives for the gradual recognition of the rights of nature also at the international level. The EA[39] brought forward the discourse on actors involved in environmental decision-making,[40]

37 Alan Boyle, 'Human Rights or Environmental Rights? A Reassessment' (2006) 18(3) Fordham Environmental Law Review 471.

38 Regional Agreement on Access to Information, Public Participation and Justice in Environmental Matters in Latin America and the Caribbean, 4 March 2020 available at <https://treaties.un.org/doc/Treaties/2018/03/20180312%2003-04%20PM/CTC-XXVII-18.pdf> accessed 7 October 2021. The agreement entered into force on 22 April 2021 (the Earth Day).

39 See <https://treaties.un.org/pages/ViewDetails.aspx?src=TREATY&mtdsg_no=XXVII-18&chapter=27&clang=en> accessed 7 October 2021.

40 Prior to the EA, several initiatives – not all of them not binding, however – have been conducted in Latin America to promote and protect rights for nature and rights of nature: here we may note the Peoples' World Conference on Climate Change and the Rights of Mother Earth, hosted by the Plurinational State of Bolivia in Cochabamba, 20–22 April 2010, followed by the Universal Declaration of the Rights of Mother Earth. See UNGA Resolution 73/235 available at <www.un.org/pga/73/wp-content/uploads/sites/53/2019/04/A.RES_.73.235.pdf> accessed 7 October 2021.

recognizing 'the important work of the public and of human rights defenders in environmental matters for strengthening democracy, access rights and sustainable development'.[41]

An effective democracy must include those groups of people who have traditionally been under-represented in participatory processes. For this reason, Article 2 of the EA defines groups whose access rights are now recognized for the first time:

> ... (e) Persons or groups in vulnerable situations' means those persons or groups that face particular difficulties in fully exercising the access rights recognized in the present Agreement, because of circumstances or conditions identified within each Party's national context and in accordance with its international obligations. [42]

In the words of the Executive Secretary of the Economic Commission for Latin America and the Caribbean (ECLAC), Alicia Bárcena, Article 2 is the expression of a 'new integration paradigm'[43] that helps address social asymmetries and climate emergency.[44] Moreover, as she expressly affirms, this recognition gives a human face to participation: 'the face of women, youth, indigenous peoples', adding that the parties to the Agreement have the 'duty to protect them and never forget the human face of those affected by the impacts of climate change'.[45]

Let me offer two brief comments that can help develop the discourse on participatory environmental rights further in line with the need to recognize, redistribute, and represent the rights of actors who are interested, but not always involved.

First, bringing women, youth, and indigenous peoples together as environmental actors expands the participatory process initiated under the AC, towards an effective participatory approach in a system of accountable, responsive, and inclusive environmental governance.[46]

---

41 See Regional Agreement on Access to Information, Public Participation and Justice in Environmental Matters in Latin America and the Caribbean (n 38).

42 ibid.

43 Press Release of the Economic Commission for Latin America and the Caribbean of 11 October 2019 available at <https://www.cepal.org/en/pressreleases/latin-american-and-caribbean-countries-call-prompt-entry-force-escazu-agreement> accessed 7 October 2021.

44 ibid.

45 ibid.

46 See 'What Does It Mean To Leave No One Behind? A UNDP discussion paper and framework for implementation July 2018' available at <www.undp.org/content/dam/undp/library/Sustainable%20Development/2030%20Agenda/Discussion_Paper_LNOB_EN_lres.pdf> accessed 7 October 2021.

Second, the duty to protect vulnerable groups enables the participation of indigenous groups.[47] Integrating the experiences and observations of indigenous peoples in environmental governance implies placing nature itself at the centre of investigation and protection. This marks another step forward, another explicit recognition of the fundamental rights of non-State actors – not only as passive receivers of legal protection but as proactive decision-makers in environmental decisions that concern them.

In conclusion, AC and EA are the two predecessors for the recognition of participatory rights to nature-defenders, and ultimately for the recognition of nature rights at the international level: the former, with a scope covering both regional (EU[48]) and domestic settings, the second specifically referring to nature-centred visions (even though for the moment only focusing on a domestic setting) and expanding the connection between non-State actors (indigenous- and nature-rights carriers) and the nature-actor. These two agreements prepared the terrain for the discourse of nature rights, applicable also to the ocean. They apply to the environment as a whole, and they are the ancestors at the international law level of the acknowledgment of nature-centred visions, paving the way also for ocean-centred voices.

## 4 How the Rights *of* Nature Narrative Help Shift the Focal Centre to Nature

The emerging legal recognition of 'other than human entities' (with the affirmation of their legal standing and consequent rights) has been progressively facilitated by the recognition of instrumental and procedural rights to groups

47 The EA is the first agreement of its kind because it engaged representative of indigenous groups and civil society organizations, and included them as beneficiaries of the Agreement provisions. One example among many the participation of the organization DAR (Derecho, Ambiente y Recursos Naturales) committed to building and strengthening environmental governance and promoting the exercise of human rights in the Amazon Basin. DAR focuses on issues of environmental policy and legislation, indigenous peoples' rights, climate change and investment and good governance in the areas of infrastructure and extractive industries, see <https://civicus.org/index.php/media-resources/news/interviews/3728-escazu-the-work-of-civil-society-made-a-huge-difference> accessed 7 October 2021.

48 The EU is a party to the Convention since May 2005. For all the implementing regulations and directives, which include the Water Framework Directive, see <https://ec.europa.eu/environment/aarhus/legislation.htm> accessed 7 October 2021.

of people and knowledge-keepers who have shared their understandings of nature's laws.[49] This has led to the emergence of a revitalizing eco-spiritual consciousness paradigm around the world.

In this section, I follow the steps in such recognition, noting some milestones in the setting of a rights-based approach: 1) broad international recognition, albeit only from a soft-law perspective, of the rights *of* nature (with the example of Harmony with Nature); 2) progressive national-level recognition of the rights of bodies of water, conveyed through indigenous and local voices and engagement (with the examples of the Māori legal order, and the controversial case of the Ganga and Yamuna rivers and glaciers in India). The findings of this investigation will lead to critical reflections on future recognition of rights of the ocean within a system of marine environmental governance.

### 4.1 *Recognition of the RoN*

Recognizing the inherent rights of nature has been a process that has followed many steps, although not always linearly. It builds on the shared understanding of the fundamental and non-anthropocentric relationship between human beings and the natural world.

Since 2009, Harmony with Nature, the UN Platform for recognition of the rights of nature, has developed, under the leadership of the Plurinational State of Bolivia. There has been intense activity, with negotiations, intergovernmental dialogue, and mapping of the recognition of the rights of nature at the national level.[50] This mapping has involved seventeen legal cultures that have progressively moved toward such acknowledgment through constitutions, national statutes, and local laws.[51]

Various criteria have been followed in the categorization of such recognition:

a. legal basis: sometimes defined as human responsibilities/constitutional duties
b. ensuring how responsibility is upheld: sometimes defined as legal personhood, sometimes as legal guardianship
c. creating personhood/guardianship (by court/statute)
d. elaborating the concept of duties imposed for current and future generations

---

49 Here the expression hints at the laws of nature as used by Gregory Cajete, *Native Science: Natural Laws of Interdependence* (Clear Light Publishers 2000).

50 United Nations Harmony With Nature available at <www.harmonywithnatureun.org/> accessed 7 October 2021.

51 See United Nations Hamony With Nature. *Rights of Nature* available at <www.harmonywithnatureun.org/rightsOfNature/> accessed 7 October 2021.

e. establishing a new relationship with nature, by recognizing an ancestral relationship.[52]

Hereafter I focus on two cases where the recognition of the RoN stems from a water-centred context: New Zealand, where indigenous views have been fully embraced in a normative Act and water is accorded the status of a living being (with the example of the three Acts in New Zealand); India, with the case of the Ganga/Ganges River, its tributary Yamuna and the glaciers Gangotri and Yamunotri, where legal personality was recognized by the High Court of Uttarakhand, only to be quashed a few months later by the Supreme Court, on grounds of implementation difficulties.[53]

The two cases are relevant for many reasons: they both originate from participatory movements (PRfN); they are interconnected (the High Court Judges of Uttarakhand formulated their judgment based on the New Zealand case), and therefore contain elements of the above-mentioned criteria; they provide examples for reflection to the discourse on ABNJ/BBNJ.

Before delving into the analysis of the two cases, I briefly point out here how in both cases PRfN played an instrumental role in the process that culminated in the recognition of a water-centric system of governance. In the case of New Zealand, the indigenous Wanganui Iwi had been petitioning for their rights ever since the 1840 Treaty of Waitangi and succeeded only in 2017.[54] The first main step was the recognition by the Waitangi Tribunal of a resort to the Waitangi Treaty that clarified the 'question of recognition and *mana*' (authority/power), in 1994.[55] Only twenty years later did the Wanganui Iwi and the Crown start negotiating the Acts that are now in place and that, through indigenous participation, recognized the Whanganui River as a living entity. In the case of the Ganga River, civil society and several environmental organizations, led by the National Ganga Rights Movement (NGRM), initiated the process that culminated with the Court decision. The NGRM called for a new form of environmental governance with the sacred river at its centre, highlighting the need for a new legal system where ecosystems and natural communities had inalienable rights to exist and flourish.[56]

---

52 ibid.

53 Stefan Knauß, 'Conceptualizing human stewardship in the Anthropocene: the rights of nature in Ecuador, New Zealand and India' (2018) 31 Journal of Agricultural and Environmental Ethics 703.

54 Elaine Hsiao, 'Whanganui River Agreement: indigenous rights and rights of nature' (2012) 42(6) Environmental Policy and Law 371.

55 ibid 372.

56 National Ganga Rights Movement. *The Ganga Rights Act* <www.gangarights.org/ganga-right-act/> accessed 7 October 2021.

### 4.2 *New Zealand: Integrated and Indivisible Living Ancestors*

Three acts – the Tūtohu Whakatupuam, the Ruruku Whakatupua, and the Te Awa Tupua Act – stand as the three-tier legal foundations of the recognition of the Whanganui River as a living entity, marking the successful conclusion of one of the longest-standing legal battles in New Zealand's history. The resultant agreement, discussed officially in 2012, finalized by the Crown and the indigenous Whanganui Iwi in 2012, and implemented in 2017, showcases the harmonization of indigenous and non-indigenous views on the oneness of nature and human beings.[57]

As also in the Indian case, these acts build on four foundation stones: 1) connectivity of the River with all the natural elements; 2) connectivity with the health and well-being of human communities; 3) a guardianship system; 4) an implementation strategy.

The first foundation stone defines the *Te Awa Tupua* as a living, actual ancestor that includes the various elements of nature and goes beyond the territorial delimitation of waters and land.[58] Te Awa Tupua includes the main Whanganui River and its tributaries, from which two principal ancestors, the Paerangi and the Ruatipua, draw their life-force. It includes all the elements

57 Indigenous claims over the river have been the subject of petitions to the New Zealand Parliament, of reports by a Royal Commission and by the Waitangi Tribunal, as well as of numerous court cases 1938–2010, although the first claim dates back to 1840. See Catherine J Iorns Magallanes, 'Nature as an ancestor: two examples of legal personality for nature in New Zealand' (2015) in VertigO – la revue électronique en sciences de l'environnement, Hors-série 22.

58 For the definition of Te Awa Tupua see Part II available at <www.legislation.govt.nz/act/public/2017/0007/latest/whole.html> accessed 7 October 2021. Part of the literature saw in this recognition the affirmation of the legal personality of the Te Awa Tupua. The concept of applying 'legal personality' to natural resources was introduced in the 1970s by a US professor of law, Christopher Stone. Stone proposed that legal rights be given to 'forests, oceans, rivers and other so-called 'natural objects' in the environment – indeed, to the natural environment as a whole'. He also discussed the various other non-human objects that have been accorded legal personality, such as companies as early as 1897. Christopher Stone, *Should Trees Have Standing? Toward Legal Rights for Natural Objects* (3rd edn, Oxford University Press 2010). Since the Agreement does not expressly refer to the Te Awa Tupua as a 'legal person', I have chosen not to apply this terminology to it here. We may note two etymological ties: one from the Latin (and Etruscan) word *persona*, used to denote the mask that human actors used to interpret different characters; and evoking a slightly different meaning: from *per-sonare*, 'talking through'. Both origins indicate a tool or an instrument through which one may represent/hide or give voice to something. However, they both evoke an anthropocentric vision, reflecting a Western-centric perspective not always appropriate when referring to actors with little in common with Western legal traditions.

of nature, in their physical and metaphysical interconnections, from Mount Tongariro, where the Whanganui River has its source, to the Tasman Sea, where it has its estuary.

As the second foundation stone, there is the recognition of peoples, river tributaries, mountains, and sea as interrelated among and across each other, forming one inseparable entity. This is the *Te Awa Tupua Mai i te Kahui Maunga ki Tangaroa*: the integrated, indivisible view of the living being (in biophysical and metaphysical terms, from the mountain to the sea). Together with the recognition of an integrated and indivisible living being and its lineage, the Agreement acknowledges that the health and wellbeing of the River and its people are the same, and as such shall be treated and protected: 'Ko au te Awa, ko te Awa ko au: the health and well being of the river coincides with the health and wellbeing of people'.[59]

The Te Awa Tupua has a metaphysical dimension, beyond space and time. This generates a duty to respect the holistic entity by establishing a reciprocal relation.[60] This relationship in legal terms, with rights and duties, and indicating how the responsibility towards the living entity, is upheld.[61] Such responsibility is expressed with the concept of *kaitiakitanga,* which includes a guardianship system (third foundation stone), Te Pou Tupua, formed by one Māori representative appointed by the Iwi peoples, and by one guardian appointed by the Crown, as well as the collective responsibility of all the peoples to protect the kinship bond embodied by the River. The agreement recognizes that no-one owns the River: the River owns itself.

The final part of the Agreement concerns strategizing around the *oneness* of the River: identifying the issues involved, strategies for addressing them, and recommended actions for implementation (fourth foundation stone). The two Guardians (Te Pou) are charged with promoting, protecting, acting, and speaking on behalf of the River, supported by an advisory board, and a strategy group

59 On the wellbeing approach adopted by New Zealand see Dan Weijers and Philip S Morrison, 'Wellbeing and public policy: Can New Zealand be a leading light for the 'wellbeing approach'? Reflections on the Third International Conference on Wellbeing and Public Policy, Beehive and Victoria University of Wellington, 5–7 September 2018' (2018) 14(4) Policy Quarterly 3.

60 Wouter Blankestijn and Anna Martin, 'Testing the (legal) waters: interpreting the political representation of a river with rights in New Zealand – *'Let's talk to the river, instead of talking about the river'* (Master's Thesis, Faculty of Natural Resources and Agricultural Sciences, Department of Urban and Rural Development 2018) available at <https://pdfs.semanticscholar.org/efe5/2495593f9a6d12b1e147c5ced5040d37644b.pdf> accessed 7 October 2021.

61 In March 2017, when the Act was officially signed.

formed by representatives of the Iwi, local government, and interested parties that co-govern inclusively and openly.

From the Māori law, it emerges how the centrality of water and nature does not rely on Western legal constructs but reflects an indigenous system of governance that sees water as a living being, where there are empathy and identification between the animal, human world, and the vegetable world. The next case, of the Ganga River, makes clear the highly problematic nature – indeed, the logical impossibility – of attributing Western categories to water.

### 4.3 *India: Is Water a Living Entity?*

On 20 March 2017, the High Court of Uttarakhand in northern India, the region of the holy Ganga and Yamuna rivers, declared that the Rivers Ganga and Yamuna, with all their tributaries and watercourses, to be juristic/legal persons/living entities, having the status of a legal person, with the consequent recognition of rights, duties, and liabilities of a living person. This was done to preserve and conserve these two sacred rivers.[62] After being presented with information regarding the New Zealand case, the Judge developed the motivation and articulated the Indian category of RoN, taking into account that deities in India are to be considered juristic persons. Similarly to the case of New Zealand, this view enjoyed the support of civil society: the initiative was backed by NGOs; and, only a few years before the High Court decision, the Community Environmental Legal Defence Fund and a group of religious leaders of various faiths had issued a similar declaration regarding sacred rivers.[63]

This widely supported position was rooted in the deep connection that Hinduism established singularly and collectively with the rivers Ganga and Yamuna, the core of the spiritual and physical sustenance of much of the population of India. The rivers, as in the case of New Zealand, are considered as an integral part of the community, breathing, living, and sustaining them 'from the mountains to the sea' (first and second foundation-stones).

Also, the High Court Judge appointed three guardians – the director of Namami Gange (the national-level Clean Ganga Programme), the chief secretary of the State of Uttarakhand, and the advocate general of the State – as 'persons *in loco parentis* to protect, conserve and preserve the Rivers Ganga and Yamuna and their tributaries'[64] (third foundation stone). Ten days later,

62 For a detailed analysis of the Court decisions and their implications at religious level see Kelly D Alley, 'River goddesses, personhood and rights of nature: implications for spiritual ecology' (2019) 10(9) Religions 502.

63 ibid.

64 Order dated 20 March 2017 in Writ Petition (PIL) No. 126 of 2014, *Mohd. Salim v State of Uttarakhand and others* 11–12.

in the *Miglani* case, the same bench designated also the glaciers, lakes, and wetlands of these basins as 'legal persons'.[65]

The fourth foundation stone in the strategy to implement such decisions proved to be the Achilles' heel of the decision: the state submitted its appeals before the Supreme Court, seeking to overturn the rulings of the High Court.

In particular, the State's alleged motivation was related to a contingent controversy regarding the officers named as stewards, who, in the opinion of the Government, could not be mandated to act as guardians. As a consequence, the Supreme Court granted the State's petition, stating: 'The order had put the State government in a quandary. Since the rivers flow through several States, only the Centre could frame rules for their management. The ruling also raised questions like whether the victim of a flood in the rivers can sue the State for damages and also about whether the State and its officers will be liable in case of pollution in the rivers in another State through which it flows'.[66] State and central governments appeared interested in avoiding liability and responsibility for the grievances and criminal charges that people could bring to them in the name of Ganga's rights.

---

65 Writ Petition PIL No. 140 of 2015, *Lalit Miglani v. State of Uttarakhand*, declared glaciers, including Gangotri and Yamunotri, rivers, streams, rivulets, lakes, air, meadows, dales, jungles, forests wetlands, grasslands, springs and waterfalls as legal persons.

66 As reported in Alley (see n 62 *supra*), a copy of the original pleading is difficult to obtain because the case is still *sub-judice.* Here I can only quote the report published in *The Times of India*:

> The state government contended that the two holy rivers played a very important role in supporting the life and well-being of people in the country but that could [was] not a ground to declared them as living entities. "Only to protect the faith of the society river Ganga and Yamuna cannot be declared as legal person," the state government said in its petition. "If there arises any dispute in respect any kind of different illegalities being committed in other states, then how can the Chief Secretary pass any instruction against any other states or Centre", it said. The government said that Centre had been given the right under the constitution to frame rules for efficacious management of all the interstate rivers and the HC did not examine the provision while passing the order. "The High Court has gravely erred in declaring Ganga and Yamuna as legal person/living entity. Hence, in case of coming of flood vis-à-vis someone dying in these rivers due to such flood, therefore, the effective party can file suit for damages against the Chief Secretary of the State and then in that case State Government will be liable to bear such financial burden", the petition said.

See <https://timesofindia.indiatimes.com/india/sc-stays-uttrakhand-hc-order-declaring-ganga-yamuna-as-living-entities/articleshow/59494002.cms> accessed 7 October 2021.

## 5 From the Governance of the Oceans to Ocean-centred Governance

A participatory-constructed framework, with the evolution of PRfN in the AC, followed by the expansion to indigenous views in the EA and the growing recognition of nature and water as a living being, paved the way to the modelling of water-centred governance as it also seems to take form in the BBNJ negotiations.

After ascertaining the instrumental role of PRfN in the development of the RoN, my analysis developed a new baseline for the integration and convergence of participatory and substantive rights. In numerous legal orders worldwide, water now enjoys full legal recognition as a living entity or entity with legal personality (Harmony with Nature; New Zealand and India).

Despite the problematic implications associated with the RoN (ie the risk of anthropocentrism), the benefit of promoting, and therefore protecting water-centred visions, is twofold. On the one side, it offers an effective way to protect the environment and to develop responses to threats affecting water. On the other side, it heals wounds (to humans and non-humans) experienced by the people displaced due to water scarcity, by recognizing their rights to water, and the deeper connection that exists between them and the natural environment.

From this perspective, re-thinking ocean governance in terms of a participatory-framed system of governance,[67] grounded in the values of pluri-actor participation, has the logical implication of considering the ocean as one of the actors in environmental governance.

That the ocean needs to be stewarded in a pluri-actor system has been brought forward in the BBNJ negotiations and now the stewardship of the ocean is stated in the BBNJ Preamble.[68] Going up and beyond the formulation of the BBNJ Preamble would lead to the direction where all are actors, all are interconnected, all have rights that correspond to obligations for the other inter-actors. At the centre of the participatory-framed governance, the sea fulfils her duty to generate and sustain life – as she has done from the dawn of time.[69] Surely it goes without saying that we humans have to protect her.

---

67 See Dalaker (ch 12) in this volume.

68 The draft text Preamble of the BBNJ agreement conveys a desire of states to 'to act as stewards of the ocean in areas beyond national jurisdiction on behalf of present and future generations' available at <www.un.org/bbnj/sites/www.un.org.bbnj/files/revised_draft_text_a.conf_.232.2020.11_advance_unedited_version.pdf> accessed 7 October 2021.

69 The choice of a feminine pronoun for the ocean is not coincidental. I subscribe here what Glennon Doyle says in her book *Untamed* (Vermillion 2020 247) about God, and apply it to the ocean. Similarly to what she thinks of God, I think that it is ridiculous that the ocean, as a fluid living being, could be gendered. But as long as the expression of ocean as

### 5.1 *Research Results in the Context of the Negotiations of a Treaty on Marine Biodiversity in ABNJ: The Explored and the Untold*

Moving from the understanding of PRfN as the necessary preliminary step towards the recognition of RoN, and consequently, towards the recognition of the ocean as a living being, I now expand my reflection on the implications that can be drawn when applying the milestones of the described process to the discussion brought forward in the negotiations of a treaty on marine biodiversity in ABNJ. What happens when we acknowledge that the ocean is at the centre of the system of governance and that the State-centred vision cannot be used as the only valid argument to protect the marine environment, because it is inevitably and primarily used to *jus*tify[70] the exploitation of the sea (at least as it stands still now in Part XII, Article 193 of the LOSC[71])?

Harriet Harden-Davies and others look at how a RoN perspective might inform the BBNJ agreement, in light of what they call the 'four defining characteristics of Rights of Nature Approaches', and namely: rights, connectivity, reciprocity, and representation.[72] Their argumentation has four foregrounding consequences that reflect the foundation stones examined in the evolution of PRfN and RoN, and contribute to mould ocean governance in the shell of ABNJ and BBNJ.[73] Nature is a right-bearing entity; all elements in nature are interconnected; the recognition of nature rights implies recognition of responsibilities for the humans to respect, restore and regenerate nature; implementation is needed to execute such responsibilities, and States should not be the only actors to speak for nature.

This fourfold structure seems to be moulded around the elements of the story of PRfN and RoN that I narrated in the sections above, and at the same time gives a sense of circular – or wavy – motion to it. PRfN are instrumental to RoN, and yet their function does not extinguish in such a recognition, but they resurge and get back to being relevant again in the development of forms of representation to nature's rights. And representation comes in the form of participatory rights for nature: participation in decision-making, but also participation in the justice system, the form of access to justice on behalf of nature.

---

a woman is 'unimaginable to many – and as long as women continue to be undervalued and abused and controlled here on Earth – I will keep using it' (ibid 247).

70 Here reference is done to the etymology of the verb 'justify': 'c. 1300, "to administer justice" late 14c., "to show (something) to be just or right" '. See the Online Etymology Dictionary available at <www.etymonline.com/word/justify> accessed 7 October 2021.

71 See Introduction.

72 Harden-Davies (n 21) 3.

73 ibid 7.

Similarly, rights and duties are two complementary and recurring waves. As said above, if rights *for* nature are instrumental to the recognition and (then) protection of rights *of* nature, these latter are meaningful and instrumental to think in terms of *duties towards* nature. It is interesting to note how these characteristics are also the foundation stones highlighted in the New Zealand and Indian systems: 1) connectivity of water with all the natural elements (rivers from springs to the sea, tributaries, watercourses, glaciers); 2) connectivity between water's health and rights, and well-being and rights of human communities; 3) a guardianship system that supervises and implements the duties towards the water; 4) an implementation strategy based on model integration, which includes the assignment of the role of ocean stewards to nature defenders (indigenous peoples among others), and the integration of divergent legal orders (Western and indigenous) within one interconnected fabric. Such legal fabric, rooted in common values (rights, connectivity, reciprocity, and representation), can inform a new ontology of ocean-centred governance.

### 5.2 *A Perspective* De Jure Condendo*: Some Ideas on the Inclusion of RoN in the Draft of the* BBNJ *Agreement*

As said, the draft agreement on BBNJ seems to open prospects for the inclusion of RoN and ocean rights in the regulation of the sea. The opening is still very timid and defined in blurry terms, and it could be strengthened if the provisions were clearer on certain aspects.

In particular, it would be advisable for the text to refine the choice of words, actors, roles, and provisions, integrating content from indigenous and marine cosmovisions.

To support a transition towards a participatory and ocean-centric governance, it could be helpful to act on different levels: 1) systematizing the provisions and demonstrating an effort to integrate the international regulations with the nature-centred instruments already existing at different levels; 2) coordinating the role of institutions and actors, including non-State participants at all levels of decision-making; 3) integrating into the fabric of the agreement a specific reference to RoN and to the rights of the ocean in particular, tying nature rights with duties and obligations of States and communities to protect and restore the marine environment; 4) revisiting the adoption of certain terms (State sovereignty, sustainable development) that reflect Western ideological hegemony of the human domination over nature.[74]

74 Alex Geisinger, 'Sustainable Development and the Domination of Nature: Spreading The Seed of the Western Ideology of Nature' (1999) 27 Boston College Environmental Affairs Law Review 43.

As for suggestion 1), the integration with the pre-existing legal provisions is a necessary step to demonstrate the integrity of intentions to effectively pursue that 'universal participation' mentioned in the Preamble. In particular, an explicit reference to the diverse corpus of legal provisions focusing on nature-centred visions would restitute a systematic integral and authentic vision to the regulatory framework (eg with an express reference to the participatory approaches embedded in the AC and the EA from the procedural viewpoint; to the Harmony with Nature's initiative and to the domestic law that already acknowledged RoN and water rights). Recognizing the key role played by indigenous knowledge in the positivization of ocean-centrism and ocean protection would help restore both nature and indigenous rights (to be heard, to participate, and be included *also* in the role of legislators).[75]

As for suggestion 2), the knitting of legal constructs from Western and non-Western legal orders should translate into effective solutions of cooperation at the institutional level. Starting from the Preamble, the affirmation of the States as only stewards of the oceans should be integrated by the intention of establishing a board of stewards or custodians, one that acknowledges and includes the already existing mechanisms of protection. Here again, it would be advisable to follow the already existing institutional mechanisms (such as the one established by the international agreement of the Whanganui River), to live up to the aim of achieving 'universal participation', expressed in the Preamble. Consequently, Part VI on Institutional Arrangements could be revisited in the same light, indicating as institutions *also* actors that – according to the sovereignty mechanisms – do not qualify yet as such.[76]

As for suggestion 3), enshrining in the treaty legal provisions on PRfN, RoN, ocean rights, and consequential duties of all human actors to fulfil the obligations to protect the sea, could be enabled by following the example of the Charter of Rights of the EU, elaborated by Michele Carducci and al.[77] This could be done, for example, starting with the inclusion of a definition of PRfN, RoN, duties, responsibilities of States and private parties, expanding the glossary of the current Article 1. A Charter of Rights embedded in the fabric of the Treaty would require an intense restructuring effort of Part IV, now dedicated to the

75 On the legislative tools of the Indigenous Environmental Justice see Margherita Paola Poto and Endalew Lijalem Enyew, 'Nature Protection, Indigenous Rights, and Climate Action' in Hans Christian Bugge (ed), *Klimarettsbok* (Universitetsforlaget, UiO 2021) 155–74.

76 For an extensive interpretation of the concept of law of the sea institutions, one that includes indigenous marine communities and possibly the ocean, see Poto (n 8).

77 Michele Carducci and others, *Towards an EU Charter of the Fundamental Rights of Nature. Study* (European Economic and Social Committee 2020) available at <www.eesc.europa.eu/sites/default/files/files/qe-03-20-586-en-n.pdf> accessed 7 October 2021.

Environmental Impact Assessments (EIAs). As it stands now, the formulation replicates the uni-directional administrative procedure governed by States that have the last word on the final decision, and thus the mere discretionary power to accept or dismiss the opinion of non-State actors on the environmental impacts of the act. Re-writing the EIAs provisions by reformulating the participatory process as a space of knowledge co-creation rather than a merely procedural guarantee,[78] would demonstrate the willingness to revitalize the role of PRfN as functionally supportive to RoN and ultimately rebalance the powers between decision-makers. In addition, a mechanism of liability in case of violation of procedural and substantive rights would help create a system of control, responsibility, and liability and testify that the instances of climate justice are taken into account also at a legislative level.[79]

More in general, and in continuity with the aim to orientate the legal provisions towards the effective protection of the oceans, a substantial linguistic revision of the terminology adopted in the Treaty could help achieve integrity of ocean visions (Western and non-Western): in the Preamble, before the recognition of State sovereignty, the centrality of the oceans for all life should be acknowledged. And more: the sovereignty of States over the oceans should be preceded by the overarching principle of sovereignty of the oceans over human life and of self-determination of all people; the words 'sustainable development' could be replaced or at least accompanied by a reference to the respect of all living beings, of past, present and future generations.

In sum, a substantive revision of the draft towards a participatory and ocean-centred model of governance is needed to shift a change of ecological consciousness.

## 6 Conclusions

Building on the need to elaborate effective regulatory responses to the ocean threats, this chapter has moved the rights-based approach forward by

---

78 Romina Rodela and Åsa Gerger Swartling, 'Environmental governance in an increasingly complex world: Reflections on transdisciplinary collaborations for knowledge coproduction and learning' (2019) 29(2) Environmental policy and governance 83. Wolfram Mauser and others, 'Transdisciplinary global change research: the co-creation of knowledge for sustainability' (2013) 5(3–4) Current Opinion in Environmental Sustainability 420.

79 For further references see Margherita Paola Poto, *Salvare la nostra casa comune è l'Affaire du Siècle*, note to Tribunale Amministrativo di Parigi, IV Sez. I Camera, 3 February 2021, Association Oxfam France, Association Notre Affaire À Tous, Fondation Pour La Nature Et L'Homme, Association Greenpeace France, Resp. Civ. and Prev. (2021) 4, 1047.

demonstrating how the recognition and deployment of rights (be they *for* or *of* nature) has procedural and liminal dimensions: to develop a participatory framed governance and to re-affirm and regulate human duties towards nature.

Moreover, the critical analysis of the current law of the sea framework spurred some critical reflections and helped move the focus towards other ocean legal orders that focus on the centrality of water rather than on the superiority of human beings over water.

The lessons learned from New Zealand and Indian cases highlight the central importance of water and its sacredness, moving forward the logic of rights and duties, a logic that is exclusively embedded in Western-legal constructs.

Integrating indigenous laws to uproot any resources-exploitation allusion in the construction of an ocean-centred model of governance can help disentangle regulation from the logic of Western constructs and contribute to unify and interconnect human and non-human components, in a way that responds to the environmental threats of our time. Such new thinking understands the interconnectedness of living systems, be they living organisms, social systems, or ecosystems.

Although the narrative of ocean rights has the potential to lead to encouraging partial results, such results encounter the obstacle of the current LOSC formulation of the sea as an exploitable resource. If such a formulation remains the platform from where the negotiations of a treaty of marine biodiversity in ABNJ stem, it risks becoming a stumbling stone in the development of ocean-centred governance. Instead of preventing the disentanglement of State sovereignty from ocean exploitation and resource extraction, it risks overshadowing the values of ocean protection and care. The same reasoning on the need to look at the narrative of rights only from an instrumental perspective applies a fortiori when approaching the need to regulate 'States' sovereign rights' in ABNJ. States' sovereignty and States' rights over nature do not have happy precedents in history. Under the State-framed resource sovereignty, the negotiation of 'package deals' to make sustainable protection and use of the marine biological diversity in ABNJ resonates with some of the dynamics of modern State colonialism, described as the phenomenon where the resources of a country were exploited by another country.[80] Under the aegis of LOSC, 'conservation and sustainable *use*' does not sound too dissimilar from 'resource exploitation'. The same expression 'areas beyond national jurisdiction' has a remarkable

80 Harry Magdoff, Charles E Nowell and Richard A Webster, 'Western colonialism' (Encyclopedia Britannica 2020) available at <www.britannica.com/topic/Western-colonialism> accessed 7 October 2021.

resemblance with space (country) we like to imagine as uninhabited and probably wild.

Though the doubt remains as to whether the BBNJ negotiations are whitewashing history, and green/blue washing domination with many labels (protection, stewardship, and even nature's rights), the hope is still that the negotiations on a treaty on marine biodiversity in ABNJ will go in the direction of including elements of an ocean-centric model where the human communities responsibly protect the oceans.[81]

Liberating our minds from the yoke of domination, listening to the ocean, and to the peoples that listen to her from time immemorial – and by doing so honouring the ocean's sacredness – are the only ways to finally realize that the ocean owns us and not the reverse.[82] Let's think *with* the ocean, and stop thinking about her.

> Sciacqua, sciaborda,
> scroscia, schiocca, schianta,
> romba, ride, canta,
> accorda, discorda,
> tutte accoglie e fonde
> le dissonanze acute
> nelle sue volute
> profonde,
> libera e bella, numerosa e folle,
> possente e molle,
> creatura viva
> che gode
> del suo mistero
> fugace
>
> (original excerpt from *L'Onda*, G D'ANNUNZIO)

81 See Endalew Lijalem Enyew and Nigel Bankes, 'Interaction between the Law of the Sea and the Rights of Indigenous Peoples' in Nele Matz-Luck, Øystein Jensen and Elise Johansen (eds), *The Law of the Sea: Normative Context and Interactions with Other Legal Regimes* (Hart Publishing 2021) (forthcoming).

82 This last expression is inspired by the video 'The land owns us' created by the Global Oneness Project available at <https://www.youtube.com/watch?v=w0sWIVR1hXw> accessed 7 October 2021.

CHAPTER 7

# Finding a Home for BBNJ – The CBD, the LOSC, and the General Assembly

*Complementary Alternatives?*

*Alex Oude Elferink and Baine P Kerr*

## 1 Introduction*

The sustainable use and conservation of biological diversity beyond national jurisdiction (BBNJ) has been one of the main issues in the law of the sea and ocean governance the last couple of decades. Looking at the work under the aegis of the United Nations General Assembly on that issue (hereafter BBNJ process), it is clear that there have been significant overlaps with the work in other international frameworks, in particular the Convention on Biological Diversity (CBD).[1] The CBD has been addressing all issues addressed at the BBNJ process (area-based management tools (ABMTS), including marine protected areas (MPAS); environmental assessments; access and benefit sharing in relation to marine genetic resources (MGRS) of BBNJ; and capacity building and transfer of technology). This chapter seeks to reconstruct the interactions between the CBD and the United Nations General Assembly (UNGA or General Assembly) in relation to the development of a comprehensive regime for BBNJ.[2]

* The authors want to thank the editors and the participants at the workshop *International Law and Marine Areas beyond National Jurisdiction: Current Status and Future Trends* (Utrecht, 3–4 December 2019) for their comments on an earlier version of this chapter). We want to thank Catherine Blanchard for helping us finding our way in developing the story line of this chapter.

1 Convention on Biological Diversity (adopted 5 June 1992, entered into force 29 December 1993) 1760 UNTS 79 (CBD). See also Catherine Blanchard and others, 'Three Structural Pillars of the Future International Legally Binding Instrument on the Conservation and Sustainable Use of Marine Biodiversity of Areas Beyond National Jurisdiction' in Marta Chantal Ribeiro and others (eds), *Global Challenges and the Law of the Sea* (Springer 2020) 352–78, 362–63.

2 While it should be acknowledged that BBNJ also has been addressed in the context of other global and regional fora, it is submitted that only the CBD and the UNGA were an option for

 | DOI:10.1163/9789004506367_008

The focus will be on the period between the middle of the 1990s, when the issue first was considered in both fora, and the first decade of this century. Subsequently, the respective roles of the CBD and the General Assembly became settled. The General Assembly was driving the process of developing a regime for BBNJ, while the CBD was focusing on scientific and technical inputs into that process. These interactions between the General Assembly and the CBD link directly to the overall theme of the book project, which is concerned with different visions of the ocean. On the one hand, the CBD's environmental focus and its emphasis on fair and equitable benefit sharing of genetic resources. On the other hand, the General Assembly has approached this issue primarily from a law of the sea perspective, which has a broader focus and articulates interests in light of the broader focus.

The chapter is set up as follows. When the CBD started considering the issue of BBNJ, the relationship between the CBD and the United Nations Convention on the Law of the Sea (LOSC),[3] which both are relevant to regulating BBNJ, immediately came to the fore. This eventually resulted in a Study on the relationship between the two instruments in 2003.[4] The following year, the General Assembly established the Ad hoc Working Group, initiating the BBNJ process. Section 2 of this chapter looks at developments in the period up to 2004, and in particular focusses on the Study on the relationship between the CBD and the LOSC. Section 3 considers how the establishment of the Ad hoc Working Group impacted on the work of the CBD on BBNJ. Section 4 reflects on the question of what may explain the choice for developing the regime of BBNJ through the BBNJ process instead of the CBD. Finally, section 5 by way of conclusion discusses the findings of the chapter in the light of the themes of the book project.

---

developing a comprehensive regime. The CBD because of its centrality in the biodiversity regime and the General Assembly because of its primary role in reviewing ocean policy and law of the sea. Consequently, developments in other bodies and instruments will not be considered in the present chapter.

3 United Nations Convention on the Law of the Sea Law (signed 10 December 1982, entered into force 16 November 1994) 1833 UNTS 3 (LOSC).

4 Study of the relationship between the Convention on Biological Diversity and the United Nations Convention on the Law of the Sea with regard to the conservation and sustainable use of genetic resources on the deep seabed (decision II/10 of the Conference of the Parties to the Convention on Biological Diversity) UNEP/CBD/SBSTTA/8/INF/3/Rev.1 (hereafter Study or Study on the relationship between the CBD and the LOSC).

## 2 Determining the Relationship between the CBD and the LOSC

### 2.1 *The Early Years*

The interest in developing a regime specifically dealing with BBNJ can be traced back to the middle of the 1990s. The CBD Subsidiary Body on Scientific, Technical and Technological Advice (SBSTTA) considered the issue of conservation and sustainable use of coastal and marine biological diversity at its first session in September of 1995.[5] Recommendation I/8 of the SBSTTA observes that the next session of the SBSTTA should 'also address the questions related to bio-prospecting on the deep sea bed, including access to its genetic resources'.[6] During the discussion relating to the issue of conservation and sustainable use of coastal and marine biological diversity, the representative of the United States observed that 'the issue of bio-prospecting on the deep sea bed should be out of the scope of the Convention'.[7] Recommendation I/8 did not endorse this point, but did point out that national legislation of Parties to the CBD needs to be in conformity with the CBD and other instruments, including the LOSC.[8]

These developments at the CBD were reported to the 50th session of the General Assembly by the United Nations Secretary-General.[9] The report also pointed out that the CBD, 'even as supplemented by certain provisions of the [LOSC]' did not 'provide a coherent and comprehensive regime appropriate to the particularities of marine life-forms'.[10] The General Assembly's Resolution on the law of the sea for the year 1995 does not make any reference to the conservation and sustainable use of marine biodiversity.[11]

The second Conference of Parties (COP) of the CBD in November of 1995, acting on SBSTTA Recommendation I/8, requested the Executive Secretary of the CBD to undertake a study of the relationship between the CBD and the

5 The SBSTTA had been requested by the first COP to provide 'advice on the scientific, technical and technological aspects of the conservation and sustainable use of coastal and marine biological diversity' (CBD COP Decision I/7, UNEP/CBD/COP/DEC/I/7, 2, para 5.5.3).

6 Report of the First Meeting of the Subsidiary Body on Scientific, Technical and Technological Advice, UNEP/CBD/COP/2/5, 36, para 2.

7 ibid 15–16, para 75.

8 ibid 40, para 12(e).

9 Report of the Secretary-General, Law of the Sea, 1 November 1995, UN Doc A/50/713. For a discussion of developments in relation to BBNJ at the United Nations, see Fernanda Millicay, 'A Legal Regime for Biodiversity of the Area' in Myron Nordquist and others (eds), *Law, Science, and Ocean Management* (Brill 2007).

10 ibid 52, para 203.

11 See Resolution Adopted by the General Assembly, 22 December 1995, UN Doc A/RES/50/23.

LOSC in consultation with the then Office for Ocean Affairs and the Law of the Sea of the United Nations Secretariat 'with regard to the conservation and sustainable use of genetic resources on the deep seabed'.[12] COP Decision II/10 indicates that the Study was to be carried out 'with a view to enabling the [SBSTTA] to address at future meetings, as appropriate, the scientific, technical, and technological issues relating to bio-prospecting of genetic resources on the deep seabed'.[13] At first sight, this purpose might suggest a narrow focus of the CBD in relation to a future regime for MGRs. However, reference is to the mandate of the SBSTTA, and the COP on the basis of the recommendations of the SBSTTA might have decided to deal with this issue in a comprehensive manner.

The United Nations Secretary-General in 1996 again reported on developments at the CBD to the General Assembly.[14] According to the report, COP Decision II/10 'demonstrate[s] the increasing attention that States are giving to the need to ensure uniformity and compatibility between the [LOSC] and subsequent legal developments'.[15] The issue of access to genetic resources was relevant to different matters addressed by the LOSC, such as

> [The] protection and preservation of the marine environment, including that of the international seabed area, … the application of the consent regime for marine scientific research, the regime for protected areas in the exclusive economic zone, the duties of conservation and management of

---

12 CBD COP Decision II/10, UNEP/CBD/COP/2/19, 16, para 12.

13 ibid.

14 Report of the Secretary-General, Law of the Sea, 1 November 1996, UN Doc A/51/645. As the report indicates, the Secretary-General also reported on this matter to the Meeting of States Parties to the LOSC (ibid para 230). The report to the Meeting contains less detail than the Secretary-General's report on the law of the sea (see Report of the Secretary-General under article 319 of the United Nations Convention on the Law of the Sea, 11 April 1996 ((SPLOS/6), paras 41–46) and the Meeting did not take any specific follow-up actions in relation to the report (see SPLOS/14). It may be noted that the Meeting has played a very limited role in relation to reviewing development in relation to oceans and law of the sea as compared to the General Assembly. See Tullio Treves, 'The General Assembly and the Meeting of the States Parties in the Implementation of the LOS Convention' in Alex Oude Elferink (ed), *Stability and Change in the Law of the Sea* (Martinus Nijhoff 2005); Alex Oude Elferink, 'Reviewing the Implementation of the LOS Convention: the Role of the United Nations General Assembly and the Meeting of States Parties' in Alex Oude Elferink and Donald R Rothwell (eds), *Oceans Management in the 21st Century: Institutional Frameworks and Responses* (Martinus Nijhoff 2004).

15 UN Doc A/51/645 (n 14) para 189.

> the living resources of the high seas, and the sustainable development of living marine resources generally. [16]

The report pointed to the need for the development of a regime for MGRs in the Area.[17] The Secretary-General's report submitted that the proposed study on genetic resources 'will be of equal, or possibly greater importance to States Parties to the [LOSC], as well as to Member States in the General Assembly reviewing the overall implementation of the Convention and the implications of current trends and developments for the law of the sea' as compared to the importance for the States Parties to the CBD.[18] The report concludes that the issue of genetic resources in the Area might not only raise questions about the applicable legal regime and its further development, but also 'as to the appropriate intergovernmental forum for [addressing the issue], as well as other institutional issues, including coordination among treaty bodies and the competent international organizations'.[19] The difference between the CBD and the Secretary-General's report in approaching the issue at hand is notable. While the former is silent on the broader policy implications of the issue, these are central to the latter.[20] As was the case for the previous year, the General Assembly Resolution on the law of the sea of 1996 does not refer to the issue of biodiversity or the specific matter of MGRs of the Area.[21]

The Secretariat of the CBD prepared a note on bioprospecting of the genetic resources of the deep seabed for the second session of the SBSTTA in September 1996.[22] The note observes that it had been presented to the Office for Oceans Affairs and the Law of the Sea and was a 'preliminary investigation'.[23] The note continued that '[i]n this sense it represents no more than a preparatory step

16 ibid para 231.
17 ibid.
18 ibid.
19 ibid para 232.
20 The Secretary-General's report in discussing the issue of choosing the appropriate forum and coordination between instruments observes that some of these issues have been considered at the CBD, ibid para 232. The document to which reference is made is a note prepared by the Executive Secretariat of the CBD entitled Modalities for Enhanced Cooperation with Relevant Biodiversity-Related Bodies (Note by the Executive Secretary, 21 September 1996, UNEP/CBD/COP/3/35). The document does not specifically address MGRs in ABNJ, and narrowly focusses on practical modalities for cooperation, without touching upon policy choices that might have involved in shaping this cooperation.
21 See Resolution Adopted by the General Assembly, 17 January 1997, UN Doc A/RES/51/34.
22 Provisional Agenda, SBSTTA, UNEP/CBD/SBSTTA/2/15.
23 UNEP/CBD/SBSTTA/2/15, 2, para 5.

for the study requested by the … COP'.[24] Notwithstanding this cautionary note, the agenda item '3.12.2 Bio-prospecting of genetic resources of the deep seabed' included in the provisional agenda of the SBSTTA was removed, since the Secretariat had not been able to consult with the Office for Oceans Affairs and the Law of the Sea to allow coordination of their positions.[25]

In subsequent years, the issue of MGR in areas beyond national jurisdiction (ABNJ) and BBNJ in general received limited attention in the reports on the law of the sea and oceans of the Secretary-General.[26] The report for 2000 recalled the Secretary-General's reports of the years 1995 and 1996, which had identified the legal and policy issues in relation to marine biodiversity and genetic resources of the deep seabed in ABNJ.[27]

### 2.2 *The Study on the Relationship between the CBD and the LOSC*

The Study on the relationship between the CBD and the LOSC as regards the conversation and sustainable use of MGRs of the deep seabed in ABNJ became available in early 2003.[28] In view of the fact that the Study, as will be further discussed below, likely contributed to initiating the BBNJ process under the

24 ibid. For a brief discussion of the content of the note see further below n 28 and 63.

25 See Recommendations of the SBSTTA at its Second Meeting, UNEP/CBD/COP/3/3, 5–7, para 14. The provisional agenda is reproduced in Provisional Agenda of the SBSTTA, 15 August 1996, UNEP/CBD/SBSTTA/2/1/Rev.1, and agenda item 3.12.2 appears at ibid 3.

26 For instance, the report for 1998 refers to an international conference co-organized by the FAO, which flagged the need to look at the issue of 'the sharing of benefits from the exploitation of aquatic genetic resources found outside areas of national jurisdiction' (Report of the Secretary-General, Oceans and the Law of the Sea, 5 October 1998, UN Doc A/53/456, para 310).

27 Report of the Secretary-General, Oceans and the Law of the Sea, 20 March 2000, UN Doc A/55/61, para 136.

28 Study (n 4). As was observed above, the Secretariat of the CBD had prepared a Note containing a 'preliminary investigation', which it had presented to the SBSTTA in 1996. The Note already prefigures most of the argument contained in the Study. However, where the Study is strongly focused on building the case for equitable access and benefit sharing and, in that connection, submits that all resources of the Area are part of the common heritage of mankind (see further below), the Note submits that:

> The regime for the Area makes no reference to genetic resources. As a result, it is not clear how [the LOSC] may apply to the Area's genetic resources. The most plausible interpretation is that, as with all resources of the high seas other than mineral resources, they are freely accessible, open-access resources appropriable by anyone who collects them. These types of resources are governed by a number of broad principles included under the rubric of the freedom to fish, UNEP/CBD/SBSTTA/2/15, 3, para 11 (footnotes omitted).

aegis of the General Assembly, it is of interest to determine how it frames the regulatory scope of both instruments and their relationship in some detail.[29]

In assessing the relationship between the LOSC and the CBD, the Study starts by referring to the General Assembly's recognition of the centrality of the LOSC in ocean governance, providing the 'legal framework within which all activities in the oceans and seas must be carried out, and with which these activities should be consistent'.[30] The fact that the LOSC does not refer to sustainable use, which is central to the regime of the CBD is explained by the fact that the 'concept only became current after the adoption of the Convention'.[31] However, the Study submits that Article 119 of the Convention provides evidence of an implicit recognition in the Convention of sustainable use.[32] Interestingly, it also submits that the CBD complements the LOSC 'in explicitly providing for the conservation of biological diversity, the sustainable use of its components and the fair and equitable sharing of benefits arising out of the use of genetic resources'.[33] Apart from suggesting complementarity, it may be noted that these arguments point to a possible tension between the two regimes. Article 119 is placed in Part VII of the LOSC, regulating the freedoms of the high seas, which are not based on fair and equitable sharing of resources. The Study further posits that the CBD and the LOSC are mutually supportive as they both envisage an ecosystem approach.[34]

The Study also considers the relationship provisions contained in Articles 237 and 311 of the LOSC and Article 22 of the CBD. The latter article, read in conjunction with Article 311 of the LOSC, implies that the implementation of the CBD 'must be compatible' with the LOSC.[35] The Study submits that achieving such compatibility should not be a problem, as the CBD 'is an elaboration of some of the general principles of the [LOSC]', in which connection reference is made to Article 237(1) of the LOSC.[36] The Study does not further develop

29 For a discussion of the Study and its consideration at the CBD, see Millicay (n 9) 784–86. An introductory note to the Study recalls that it was prepared pursuant to paragraph 12 of CBD COP Decision II/10 (ibid 1). As paragraph 12 indicates, the Study was to be prepared by the Executive Secretary to the CBD in consultation with the then Office for Oceans Affairs and Law of the Sea of the United Nations Secretariat. The Study does not provide any indication of what these consultations entailed and how they impacted on the preparation of the Study by the Executive Secretariat.

30 Study (n 4) 6, para 13.

31 ibid 6, para 14.

32 ibid.

33 ibid.

34 ibid para 16.

35 ibid 7, para 18.

36 ibid.

the implications of the compatibility requirement. It certainly could be argued that it would not have excluded the CBD from developing a regime for BBNJ that in regulating high seas freedoms would have curtailed the scope for unilateralism of individual States. This might have involved mechanisms for access and benefit sharing or the designation and management of MPAs.[37]

A large part of the Study is devoted to providing an overview of the legal regime of the LOSC (paras 19–69) and the relevant provisions of the CBD (paras 68–102). The discussion of the LOSC might reflect a certain unease with the Convention's regulation of the use of marine living resources in relation to their applicability to MGRs. The Study observes that that the LOSC 'does not specifically address [MGRs]. However, since such resources are biological resources, the jurisdictional framework set forth in the [LOSC] that governs marine living resources applies to them'.[38] The CBD recognizes the LOSC framework and has regulated genetic recourses within national jurisdiction accordingly.[39] In relation to genetic resources in ABNJ, the Study submits that both the LOSC and the CBD '*inter alia*, recognize the importance of cooperation among States in respect of the conservation and sustainable use of living resources'.[40] A subsequent discussion of the regime of the Area again suggests a certain unease about the possible implications of the LOSC's jurisdictional framework for regulating the access to (and benefit sharing of) MGRs in ABNJ. At the same time, that argument indicates how the Study views the direction the development of a specific regime for MGRs should take:

37 In this connection reference may be had to the Fish Stocks Agreement (UNFSA). Its relationship provision provides that 'Nothing in this Agreement shall prejudice the rights, jurisdiction and duties of States under the Convention. This Agreement shall be interpreted and applied in the context of and in a manner consistent with the "LOSC"'. (Agreement for the Implementation of the Provisions of the United Nations Convention on the Law of the Sea of 10 December 1982 relating to the Conservation and Management of Straddling Fish Stocks and Highly Migratory Fish Stocks (signed 4 August 1995, entered into force 11 December 2001) 2167 UNTS 3.) The UNFSA details the obligations of States fishing on the high seas and thus curtails the discretionary decision-making power of individual States existing under Part VII of the LOSC. It may moreover be noted that the Study submits that the CBD could contribute to protecting BBNJ through the establishment on MPAs. The Study in that connection also points to the difficulties involved in establishing MPAs in ABNJ, but that does not detract from the Study's proposition that the CBD could be used in this regard (Study (n 4) 22–23, paras 85–90).

38 Study (n 4) 8, para 21.

39 ibid.

40 ibid 8, para 21.

> It is worth noting that the regime for access and management of living resources under the [LOSC] provides for resources and related activities and uses that were current at the time of the negotiations, primarily fisheries and fishing activities for consumption. Such provisions are therefore based on the specific characteristics of such resources and activities, and take into account the historic development of the regime for fisheries. A more recent development is the understanding of the value of marine biodiversity and ecosystems and of the need to protect and manage them in a sustainable manner using new approaches and considerations …
>
> While the International Seabed Authority has a clear mandate to deal with the impact of mining on biodiversity and the rules are clear in relation to marine scientific research in the Area, it is not clear what legal regime applies to bioprospecting for genetic resources in the Area. What is certain, however, is that the Area and the resources of the Area whose existence and value was known by the negotiators of the [LOSC] are the common heritage of mankind.[41]

In discussing the specifics of the regime applicable to the Area, the Study observes that no specific rules are in place for the sustainable use and conservation of its biodiversity, apart from those dealing with marine scientific research and the protection and preservation of the marine environment.[42]

The Study's discussion of the CBD starts by considering its jurisdictional scope. Article 4 of the CBD provides that in relation to ABNJ it is only applicable to processes or activities under the jurisdiction or control of Contracting Parties and not components of biodiversity, as is the case for areas within national jurisdiction (AWNJ). The Study relies on this distinction for arguing that in ABNJ, 'Parties have no obligation with respect to the conservation and sustainable use of specific components of biological diversity'.[43] However, bioprospecting for genetic resources carried out by a national of a Contracting Party, is an activity that would take place under the jurisdiction or control of that Contracting Party that would impact a 'component' of biodiversity, specifically, MGRs.[44] Be that as it may, the Study does not consider that option, which could easily have led to a different assessment of the future role of the CBD.

41 ibid 28–29, paras 109 and 111 (footnotes omitted).

42 ibid 11, para 37.

43 Study (n 4) 19, para 70.

44 See also Daniela Diz, *Unravelling the Intricacies of Marine Biodiversity Conservation and its Sustainable Use: An Overview of Global Frameworks and Applicable Concepts* (University of Edinburgh School of Law Research Paper Series, No 2016/11) 10–11; Charlotte Salpin 'Marine genetic resources of areas beyond national jurisdiction: Soul searching and the

Based on its assessment of the implications of the jurisdictional scope of the CBD, the Study concludes that a future regime for genetic resource of the Area 'can only be addressed *comprehensively* through further cooperative initiatives amongst Parties and Governments'.[45] The Study seems to consider that this cannot be achieved through the CBD, as the quoted text is preceded by the proviso '[g]iven the limitations in the relevant provisions of the Convention', ie Article 4.[46] It may be questioned whether Articles 4 and 5 of the CBD exclude its Contracting Parties from comprehensively dealing with the regime for MGRs in ABNJ. As is argued above, Article 4 is applicable to activities in ABNJ impacting on biodiversity, which includes activities targeting MGRs, and Article 5 does not exclude cooperation between the parties of the CBD under the framework of the Convention. The practice of the CBD indicates the phrase 'matters of mutual interest' has been interpreted broadly to include cooperation in relation to ABNJ, as illustrated by its work related to ecologically or biologically significant areas (EBSAs) discussed in section 3.1 below.

Although according to the Study the CBD itself is not the proper regulatory framework, the principles and concepts it contains are of relevance.[47] The Study among others discusses the role of the CBD in relation to direct regulation of deep seabed activities, the indirect regulation of such activities through the establishment of MPAs, the general framework for the sustainable use of genetic resources and the fair and equitable sharing of benefits.[48] In relation to the latter point, it is submitted that both the LOSC and the CBD contain the idea of equity in relation to the use of marine living recourse.[49] The principles of the CBD could assist in dealing with 'issues of equity regarding access to and the exploitation of [genetic] resources'.[50]

The final part of the Study is concerned with recommendations regarding the development of a specific regime for MGRs of the Area. The starting point in this respect is provided by the conclusion that neither the CBD nor the LOSC 'provide a specific legal regime for commercially oriented activities relating to [MGRs] on the high seas and in the Area'.[51] In view of the fact that activities

art of balance' in Elisa Morgera and Kati Kulovesi (eds), *Research handbook on international law and natural resources* (Elgar 2016) 418; Blanchard (n 1) 363.

45 Study (n 4) 19, para 72 (emphasis provided).

46 ibid.

47 ibid para 72.

48 ibid 20–26, paras 77–100.

49 ibid 25, paras 97–98.

50 ibid 26, para 100.

51 ibid 26, para 103.

are already taking place, it is recommended that such a regime should be developed.[52]

The Study submits that the objectives of the CBD and the LOSC are similar.[53] Both seek to achieve sustainable use and conservation and provide for equitable sharing mechanisms. The Study at this point recognizes that the LOSC only provides for such a mechanism in relation to the mineral resources of the Area,[54] confirming the discrepancy with the CBD as regards spatial application and substantive regime. The Study observes that it is not certain whether those 'objectives can be effectively achieved concerning deep seabed genetic resources, which do not fall per se within the scope of either instrument, but the exploitation of which is relevant to both'.[55] As an alternative a specific legal regime could be elaborated. According to the Study, this would first require a clarification of the status of MGRs.[56] In this context, the LOSC would provide the basic legal framework, which could be complemented by the principles of the CBD.[57] A major shortcoming of the CBD is that its benefit-sharing mechanisms are not applicable to common resources in ABNJ.[58] These requirements would seem to pose a major obstacle to dealing comprehensively with BBNJ under the CBD. Defining the status of genetic resources arguably requires a clarification of the LOSC's basic jurisdictional framework. However, such jurisdictional issues – the unclarified interaction between the regime for marine scientific research and the access to genetic resources in AWNJ – have not prevented the development of the CBD's Nagoya Protocol. Its Article 10 indicates that the common pool nature of ABNJ resources also does not constitute a fundamental objection to using the CBD framework for dealing with an access and benefit regime for BBNJ.[59]

The Study ends by offering three options for dealing with the governance of BBNJ. First, maintaining the *status quo*. However, that option does not guarantee the sustainable use and conservation of the resources, which 'would be contrary to the regulatory intent of the [LOSC] as a whole, and would run counter to the specific regime of the Area'.[60] Second, a special regime could be

52 ibid. The Study sets out a number of arguments in support of this position (see ibid).
53 ibid 26, para 104.
54 ibid 27, para 104.
55 ibid 27, para 105.
56 ibid.
57 ibid. See also ibid para 107.
58 ibid para 105.
59 See also above for the discussion of the relationship clauses contained in the art 22 of the CBD and arts 237 and 311 of the LOSC. On the Nagoya Protocol see also below.
60 Study (n 4) 29, para 114.

tailored on the detailed regime for mineral resources contained in Part XI of the LOSC.[61] In discussing this approach, the Study submits that the only reason for excluding living resources from the regulatory scope of Part XI is that their existence was largely unknown at the time the LOSC was negotiated.[62] Thirdly, and this might seem surprising in light of the Study's preceding analysis, the CBD is presented as an equally viable alternative.[63]

### 2.3 *The Follow-up to the Study on the Relationship between the CBD and the LOSC*

The Study was submitted for consideration to the SBSTTA together with a note of the Executive Secretary, which summarizes the Study and contains suggestions for recommendations the SBSTTA might forward for consideration by the CBD COP.[64] These suggested recommendations among others included the following items:

- to request the Executive Secretary to look at the options for assessing monitoring the status of genetic resources on the seabed of ABNJ in collaboration with relevant organizations; and
- to invite the General Assembly to call upon relevant organizations 'to review issues relating to the conservation and sustainable use of genetic resources of the deep seabed [of ABNJ] and make appropriate recommendations to the General Assembly regarding appropriate actions'.[65]

Both these suggested recommendations were included in the SBSTTA's recommendation on marine and coastal biodiversity to the COP, but the first one was significantly amended. The SBSTTA included the request to compile and synthesize relevant information 'with a view to addressing processes and activities under Article 4(b) of the [CBD]'.[66] This reference to Article 4(b) could be considered as an implied claim that the CBD should have primary responsibility

61 ibid 29–31, paras 115–23.
62 ibid 30, para 117.
63 ibid 32, paras 124–26.
64 Revised Note by the Executive Secretary, SBSTTA, 20 February 2003, UNEP/CBD/SBSTTA/8/9/Add.3/Rev.1.
65 ibid 4.
66 Recommendations Adopted by SBSTTA at Its Eight Meeting (Recommendation VIII/3), UNEP/CBD/COP/7/3, Section D, 63. Conservation and sustainable use of deep seabed genetic resources beyond national jurisdiction: study of the relationship between the Convention on Biological Diversity and the United Nations Convention on the Law of the Sea.

for addressing issues related to conservation and use of the genetic resources of the Area.[67]

The Study was also mentioned in the United Nations Secretary-General's 2003 report on oceans and law of the sea. The report highlighted the Study's conclusions that the CBD and the LOSC were mutually supportive and complementary and that 'there is an important legal lacuna with respect to commercially oriented activities relating to [MGRs] in deep seabed [of ABNJ]'.[68] The report submitted that this entailed 'the risk of their overexploitation without due regard to conservation and equity imperatives'.[69] The General Assembly in Resolution 58/240 on oceans and the law of the sea invited the relevant instruments to identify the risks and threats to BBNJ and how these instruments could be used to address them consistent with international law and the LOSC. The Secretary-General was requested to report on the matter to the General Assembly in his next report on oceans and the law of the sea.[70]

CBD COP 7 addressed the Study and the recommendations of the SBSTTA in its Decision VII/5. The decision requests the Executive Secretary to look at the options for assessing and monitoring the status of genetic resources on the seabed of ABNJ in collaboration with relevant organizations, but it excluded the SBSTTA's reference to Article 4(b) of the CBD. In addition, the decision welcomed General Assembly Resolution 58/240, which had been adopted after the SBSTTA had drafted its recommendations to the COP. The COP invited the General Assembly to take upon itself the task of coordinating work in relation to the conservation and sustainable use of genetic resources in ABNJ.[71]

The United Nations Secretary-General in an addendum to his 2004 report on oceans and law of the sea dealt comprehensively with the request of the General Assembly to report on the risks and threats to biodiversity in ABNJ and the existing regulatory frameworks. After describing ecosystems and biodiversity in ABNJ and the risks and threats posed to them, the addendum considers the legal and policy framework,[72] concluding that:

---

67 A report on the meeting indicates the existence of different views in the SBSTTA as regards the appropriate forum for dealing with the issue (*Earth Negotiations Bulletin* Vol 9, No 252, 2003, 12).

68 Report of the Secretary-General on Oceans and Law of the Sea, 3 March 2003, UN Doc A/58/65, 46, para 147.

69 ibid.

70 Resolution adopted by the General Assembly on 23 December 2003, UN Doc A/RES/58/240, 10, para 52.

71 Decision Adopted by the COP to the CBD at Its Seventh Meeting, Decision Five, 13 April 2004, UNEP/CBD/COP/DEC/VII/5.

72 Report of the Secretary-General, Oceans and Law of the Sea, Addendum, 18 August 2004, UN Doc A/59/62/Add.1, 45–79. These same issues are also considered in the report itself,

> [The LOSC] sets out a legal framework within which all activities in the oceans are to be conducted, including in areas beyond national jurisdiction. This general legal framework is supplemented by a number of international instruments adopted at the global and regional levels. Effective implementation of the relevant provisions of [the LOSC] and those instruments, within the scope of their regulatory mechanisms, is essential to conserve and manage vulnerable marine ecosystems and [BBNJ]. Nevertheless, it appears that additional steps are needed. The General Assembly may therefore consider what further action is required[.][73]

In response to this call for action, the General Assembly established the Ad hoc Working Group.[74] The mandate of the Ad hoc Working Group was formulated in broad terms and did not imply any specific choice as regards the legal framework for elaborating the regime for the conservation and sustainable use of BBNJ:[75]

> To indicate, where appropriate, possible options and approaches to promote international cooperation and coordination for the conservation and sustainable use of marine biological diversity beyond areas of national jurisdiction.[76]

CBD COP 8, which was held in 2006, reconfirms the CBD's secondary role in relation to the development of the regime for the sustainable use and conservation of BBNJ. In Decision VIII/21, the COP:

> *Recognizes also* that the [LOSC] regulates activities in [ABNJ], and *urges* Parties and other States to cooperate within the relevant international

which was issued previously (see Report of the Secretary-General, Oceans and Law of the Sea, 4 March 2004, UN Doc A/59/62, 59–68, paras 229–66).

73 UN Doc A/59/62/Add.1, 80, para 318.

74 Resolution adopted by the General Assembly on 17 November 2004, UN Doc A/RES/59/24, 13, para 73. According to a report on the first meeting of the Ad hoc Working Group there was broad support for the United Nations General Assembly taking the lead in the development of the regime for BBNJ. Only Venezuela and the Russian Federation submitted the CBD should have been given priority (*Earth Negotiations Bulletin* Vol 25, No 25, 9.) Other participants did refer to the role of the CBD in providing scientific and technical input (ibid).

75 See ibid 14, para 73(a)–(d).

76 ibid para 73(d). For a detailed discussion of the work of the Ad hoc Working Group and the legal issues involved see eg Salpin (n 44).

> and/or regional organizations in order to promote the conservation, management and sustainable use of marine biodiversity in [ABNJ], including deep seabed genetic resources.[77]

The call upon Contracting Parties to cooperate indicates that this is an individual responsibility, which, although it flows from Article 5 of the CBD, indicates that this is not a matter to be addressed by the COP as such.[78]

## 3 Developments in Relation to BBNJ at the CBD following the Establishment of the Ad Hoc Working Group

The Ad hoc Working Group started its work in 2006 and initially met biennially and made little progress. The package of issues that is currently subject of negotiations at the IGC was only finally agreed upon in 2011.[79] In 2015, the Ad hoc Working Group wrapped up its work, recommending to the General Assembly that it '[d]ecide to develop an international legally binding instrument under the [LOSC] on the conservation and sustainable use of marine biological diversity of areas beyond national jurisdiction'.[80] This resulted in the General Assembly establishing a Preparatory Committee and subsequently the Inter-governmental Conference (IGC). Notwithstanding the BBNJ process, the CBD continued paying attention to all four of the elements of the package at the BBNJ process. The present section identifies relevant work of the CBD on these individual elements of the BBNJ package: ABMTs, including MPAs; EIAs; MGRs; and capacity building and transfer of technology. This analysis serves the purpose of establishing how these developments may have impacted (and may continue to impact) the BBNJ process. In addition to looking at the CBD, the subsections that follow will also briefly look at the relevant provisions of the LOSC to allow comparing

77 Decision Adopted by the COP of the CBD at Its Eighth Meeting, Decision VIII/21, UNEP/CBD/COP/DEC/VIII/21, 2, para 6.

78 See also Study (n 4) 19, paras 70–71.

79 See eg David Freestone 'The UN Process to Develop an International Legally Binding Instrument under the 1982 Law of the Sea Convention: Issues and Challenges' in David Freestone (ed), *Conserving Biodiversity in Areas beyond National Jurisdiction* (Brill 2019) 17.

80 Letter dated 13 February 2015 from the Co-Chairs of the Ad Hoc Open-ended Informal Working Group to the President of the General Assembly, UN Doc A/69/780, Annex I.1(e).

the two conventions as regards their 'regulatory potential' in relation to BBNJ.[81]

An issue that is relevant to all of the elements of the package is the institutional architecture of the CBD and the LOSC. The CBD has the institutional structure that is typical to multilateral environmental agreements, with a COP at its apex that is supported by the SBSTTA and other subsidiary bodies and working groups that have been set up on an ad hoc basis. Another possibility is the convening of various expert groups. The LOSC has much more limited institutional arrangements. The International Seabed Authority (ISA) is set up to regulate mining in the Area, including its environmental impacts, but has no mandate to deal with other aspects of the sustainable use and conservation of BBNJ. The Meeting of States Parties of the LOSC has limited functions and attempts to broaden its mandate in the 1990s were unsuccessful.[82] Contrary to the CBD, the current institutional framework of the LOSC hardly can be said to allow addressing issues of BBNJ in a comprehensive manner at the global level.

### 3.1 *Area-based Management Tools and Marine Protected Areas*

The CBD deals explicitly with the establishment of MPAs in its Article 8, which requires States parties among others to 'establish a system of protected areas or areas where special measures need to be taken to conserve biological diversity'.[83] Although there might be some uncertainty about the scope of application of Article 8, it provides a basis for establishing MPAs in ABNJ.[84] The LOSC does not explicitly refer to ABMTs and MPAs. However, Article 194(5), dealing with rare and fragile ecosystems and marine life, has been considered to provide a legal basis for establishing ABMTs or MPAs in ABNJ.[85] In addition, the provisions of the Convention dealing with specific activities also allow for the adoption of ABMTs.[86] However, those provisions are lacking the specific detail that is provided by Article 8 of the CBD.

At the political level, the international community committed itself to establishing a coherent network of MPAs by 2012 at the World Summit on

---

81 The term 'regulatory potential' is used here to refer to the substantive rules and procedural mechanism that are (potentially) applicable/available in relation to the sustainable use and conservation of BBNJ.

82 See eg Treves (n 14); Oude Elferink (n 14).

83 CBD art 8(a).

84 See eg Petra Drankier, 'Marine Protected Areas in Areas beyond National Jurisdiction' (2012) 27 International Journal of Marine and Coastal Law 296–97.

85 See eg Alex Oude Elferink, 'Coastal States and MPAs in ABNJ: Ensuring Consistency with the LOSC' (2018) 33 International Journal of Marine and Coastal Law 445.

86 See, for instance, LOSC arts 118 and 211.

Sustainable Development (WSSD) in 2002. Three basic requirements were identified in relation to this goal: the network of MPAs has to be coherent and representative, consistent with international law and based on scientific information.[87] This political commitment was quantified at the 2010 CBD COP, where the Contracting Parties adopted the Aichi Targets, which called for at least 10 percent of the world's coastal and marine areas to be conserved by 2020 by either ABMTs or MPAs.[88]

The work of the CBD on MPAS indicates the impact of the BBNJ process. A decision on protected areas of the 2004 COP indicates that the issue of MPAS in ABNJ would be part of the CBD's plan of work on protected areas.[89] The decision observes that the CBD's ecosystem approach and the fact that relevant ecosystems extend beyond national boundaries 'presents a strong argument for and adds complexity to the establishment of transboundary protected areas and protected areas in [ABNJ]'.[90] The decision views the relationship with the UNGA as requiring collaboration on the basis of equality.[91] Two subsequent decisions, from respectively 2006 and 2008, reflect a different view on the CBD's role. Both decisions recognize the General Assembly's 'central role in addressing issues relating to the conservation and sustainable use of [BBNJ]'[92] and frame the role of the CBD in relation to BBNJ as being in support of the work of the General Assembly.[93] In 2010 the CBD COP voiced concern

87 Plan of Implementation of the World Summit on Sustainable Development, Johannesburg, 4 September 2002; Report of the World Summit on Sustainable Development, Johannesburg, South Africa, 26 August–4 September 2002 (United Nations publication, Sales No. E.03.II.A.1 and corrigendum), Resolution 2, para 32(c).

88 Decision Adopted by the COP of the CBD at Its 10th Meeting 10, Decision X/2, Annex IV, UNEP/CBD/COP/DEC/X/2. For a further discussion on the relationship between ABMTs and MPAs in this connection and more in general see ch 8 in this volume.

89 Decision of the COP of the CBD at its Seventh Meeting, Decision VII/28, UNEP/CBD/COP/DEC/VII/8, see eg para 18, 29(a) and Annex, Section II at 7. However, at the time Parties to the CBD already differed over the question whether the CBD should be dealing with MPAs in ABNJ (see *Earth Negotiations Bulletin* Vol 9, No 252, 2003, 12).

90 ibid Annex, Section II at 7.

91 ibid 11, para 1.3.2. which reads:

> Collaborate with other Parties and relevant partners through the United Nations Informal Consultative Process on the Law of the Sea (UNICPOLOS) to establish and manage protected areas in marine areas beyond the limits of national jurisdiction, in accordance with international law, including the [LOSC], and based on scientific information.

92 Decision by COP of the CBD at Its Eighth Meeting, Decision VIII/24, UNEP/CBD/COP/DEC/VIII/24, para 42; Decision by COP of the CBD at Its Ninth Meeting, Decision IX/20, UNEP/CBD/COP/DEC/IX/20, 1st preambular consideration.

93 UNEP/CBD/COP/DEC/VIII/24, para 34; UNEP/CBD/COP/DEC/IX/20, 5th preambular consideration. See also Daniel Dunn and others, 'The Convention on Biological Diversity's

about the slow progress of the BBNJ process in relation to the topic of MPAs.[94] Subsequent COPs have not revisited this issue.

Consistent with its supporting role in relation to the General Assembly, the CBD has been working on the establishment of specific scientific and technical criteria for EBSAs, including in marine areas.[95] The CBD COP in 2008 stated its key role was providing scientific and 'technical information and advice relating to marine biological diversity, the application of the ecosystem approach and the precautionary approach'. To that end, it adopted a decision defining EBSA criteria for ocean areas in need of protection.[96] The COP requested the Executive Secretary to forward the decision to 'relevant General Assembly processes',[97] ie primarily the Ad hoc Working Group, and decided convening an expert workshop on EBSAs, that 'shall not consider issues relating to management and only provides scientific and technical information and guidance'.[98] In addition to establishing criteria for EBSA identification, ongoing regional workshops have generated a large number of data sets that have resulted in detailed mapping of EBSAs.[99] In its capacity as an observer to the BBNJ process, the CBD Secretariat has presented its work on EBSAs to BBNJ participants.[100]

### 3.2 *Environmental Assessments*[101]

The CBD addresses environmental assessments in its Article 14. Although being somewhat more specific than the relevant provisions of the LOSC, Article 14

---

Ecologically or Biologically Significant Areas: Origins, development, and current status' (2014) 49 Marine Policy 138–39.

94 Decision by COP of the CBD at Its Tenth Meeting, Decision 29, UNEP/CBD/COP/DEC/X/29, para 33.

95 See also Robin Warner, *Protecting the Oceans Beyond National Jurisdiction: Strengthening the International Law Framework* (Brill 2009) 214.

96 UNEP/CBD/COP/DEC/IX/20, Annex I; II.

97 UNEP/CBD/COP/DEC/IX/20, 4, para 14.

98 ibid 4, para 19. Subsequent decisions have emphasized that 'the identification of ecologically or biologically significant marine areas and the selection of conservation and management measures is a matter for States and competent intergovernmental organizations'. (CBD COP Decision X/29, para 26; CBD COP Decision XI/17, para 6).

99 See generally Nicholas Bax and others, 'Results of Efforts by the Convention on Biological Diversity to Describe Ecologically or Biologically Significant Marine Areas' (2015) 30(3) Conservation Biology 571; Dunn (n 93) 137–45.

100 See eg IISD Reporting Service, 'Coverage of Side Events at BBNJ' 5–6 September 2018 <https://enb.iisd.org/oceans/bbnj/igc1/side-events/5sep.html> accessed 25 April 2021.

101 We acknowledge that legal text both refer to environmental assessment and EIAs. For the purposes of this chapter, any difference that may exist between these two terms is not relevant and should not be read into the use of ether of these terms in the chapter.

also fails to add specificity to the regime for environmental assessment. Similar to its approach to EBSAs, the CBD has played a proactive role in addressing environmental assessments in ABNJ in a way that sought to develop normative guidance based on scientific principles, while deferring legal and policy decisions to the BBNJ process.[102] Starting with the 2009 Manila working group, the CBD decided that it would develop voluntary environmental assessment guidelines that would inform the BBNJ process with technical information.[103] Voluntary guidelines on environmental and strategic impact assessments were finalized by the SBSTTA in 2012.[104] The CBD COP has taken note of both sets of guidelines, while emphasizing that the guidelines were 'without prejudice to the ongoing consideration of biodiversity' in the BBNJ process. It requested that the Executive Secretary forward the guidelines to the General Assembly, and encouraged States and international organizations to use the guidelines 'in accordance with national and international law', including the LOSC.[105]

The LOSC includes a number of general obligations in relation to environmental assessments in Articles 204–206. Some clarification of these provisions of the LOSC have been achieved through the law of the sea case law,[106] but with the exception of mining in the Area, the Convention has not accomplished a clear and comprehensive framework for carrying out and following up impact assessments.[107] Apart from the ISA, the LOSC does not dispose of an institutional framework that could assist in the elaboration of such a framework.

---

102 For a discussion of the CBDs work in relation tor EIA in ABNJ see also Alex Oude Elferink 'Environmental Impact Assessment in Areas Beyond National Jurisdiction' (2012) 27 International Journal of Marine and Coastal Law 449–480 at 464–465.

103 Warner (n 95) 337–38. The CBD's work on assessments for ABNJ built on its earlier development of voluntary guidelines that applied to biodiversity generally, including in marine and coastal ecosystems. (ibid 322–23. See Decision of the COP of the CBD at Its Eighth Meeting, Decision 27, Addendum 2, UNEP/CBD/COP/8/27/Add.2.).

104 The annotated guidelines are contained in an annex of document entitled 'Note by the Executive Secretary' 12 August 2012, UNEP/CBD/COP/11/23.

105 Decision of the COP of the CBD at Its Eleventh Meeting, Decision XI/18, UNEP/CBD/COP/11/18, Part B, paras 1–3.

106 See eg *In the Matter of the South China Sea Arbitration* (*Philippines v. China*) [2016] PCA, Arbitral Award, para 991.

107 *Responsibilities and Obligations of States Sponsoring Persons and Entities With Respect to Activities in the Area* (Advisory Opinion, Judgment of 1 February 2011) ITLOS, paras 148–49. Customary law is equally lacking in specific as regards the obligations in relation to environmental impact assessment, see *Pulp Mills on the River Uruguay* (*Argentina v. Uruguay*) [2011] ICJ Rep 14, para 205.

### 3.3 *Marine Genetic Resources*

Access and benefit sharing in relation to genetic resources in AWNJ is addressed in general terms in the CBD, and a specific regime for access and benefit sharing has been established through its 2010 Nagoya Protocol. Neither the CBD nor the Nagoya Protocol envisage specific mechanisms for access and benefit sharing in relation to MGRs of ABNJ. However, the CBD does not exclude the development of such a mechanism.[108] The negotiations leading up to the Nagoya Protocol also show some support for this proposition.[109] Article 10 of the Protocol provides that:

> Parties shall consider the need for and modalities of a global multilateral benefit-sharing mechanism to address the fair and equitable sharing of benefits derived from the utilization of genetic resources and traditional knowledge associated with genetic resources that occur in transboundary situations or for which it is not possible to grant or obtain prior informed consent ...[110]

---

108 CBD art 1 states that its objectives include 'fair and equitable sharing of the benefits arising out of the utilization of genetic resources, including by appropriate access to genetic resources'. This objective is not limited in spatial terms. Art 5 provides that the Convention is applicable to activities in ABNJ. Accessing genetic resources is an activity and benefit sharing a modality of such access. Art 28 on protocols to the Convention is broadly formulated and allows for the conclusion of a protocol dealing with this issue, see Dire Tladi, 'The Common Heritage of Mankind and the Proposed Treaty on Biodiversity in Areas beyond National Jurisdiction: The Choice between Pragmatism and Sustainability' (2015) 25 Yearbook of International Environmental Law 120.

109 The Pacific regional group of states consultation indicated those states wanted high seas pockets completely surrounded by EEZ's to be covered by the Protocol, see Ad hoc Open Ended Working Group on Access and Benefit Sharing, 'Final Report of the Regional Consultations for the Pacific on Access and Benefit Sharing' UNEP/CBD/WG-ABS/9/INF/5, 9. The African Group of States reportedly submitted an informal white paper that advocated including a 'global multilateral benefit-sharing mechanism' within the Protocol that could address genetic resources in ABNJ, see Thomas Greiber, 'Access and Benefit Sharing in Relation to Marine Genetic Resources from Areas Beyond National Jurisdiction A Possible Way Forward' Research Project for Federal Agency for Nature Conservation and IUCN (2011) 34. Other States indicated that they favored the exclusion of genetic resources in ABNJ from the scope of the Protocol, see eg Commentary of Mexico to a draft of the Protocol, CBD Ad hoc Informal Working Group on Access and Benefit Sharing, 'Compilation of Submissions in Respect to Legal Regime on Access and Benefit Sharing' 2 February 2009, UNEP/CBD/WG-ABS/7/INF/1, 40–41.

110 The Preamble of the Protocol recognizes that innovative solutions are required to address this issue. There has been some scholarly analysis on how the Protocol could be used to address MGRs in ABNJ, see Greiber (n 108) 31–34. See also Morten Walløe Tvedt and Ane E Jørem, 'Bioprospecting in the High Seas: Regulatory Options for Benefit Sharing' (2013) 16(3–4) The Journal of World Intellectual Property 160.

However, according to the CBD Secretariat, the inclusion of ABNJ in the Protocol was not discussed 'in depth'.[111]

After the adoption of the Nagoya Protocol, the development of an Article 10 mechanism has been considered, but with limited support for including genetic resources in ABNJ in its scope.[112] In their formal submissions to the Nagoya Protocol's intergovernmental committee, and later, its COP, States expressed a range of views in this respect. The African Group submitted that the global mechanism should regulate MGRS accessed in ABNJ.[113] Canada stated that the parties should consider situations where genetic resources are accessed in areas outside national jurisdictions in connection with a global mechanism.[114] The European Union did not take an express position on the mechanism's scope, but stressed the need for the mechanism in general, and the importance of considering how it would relate to other legal instruments, in particular the LOSC.[115] In 2014, Argentina voiced concern that the mechanism might be a way to regulate genetic resources in ABNJ, and stated that it would oppose that outcome.[116] Following the 2014 intergovernmental committee meeting and first Protocol COP, the Parties invited further discussion and instructed the Executive Secretary to further study the need for and modalities of the mechanism.[117] It appears these issues were not finally resolved, but

111 CBD Ad hoc Informal Working Group on Access and Benefit Sharing, 'Overview of Recent Developments at the International Level Related to Access and Benefit Sharing' UNEP/CBD/WG-ABS/6/INF/3, 10.

112 As is observed by Tladi (n 108) 120.

The adoption by the UNGA of a process that could lead to the adoption of such an implementation agreement under UNCLOS makes the extension of the Nagoya Protocol to cover genetic resources in areas beyond national jurisdiction all the less likely.

113 African Group Submission on The need for and modalities of a Global Multilateral Benefit-Sharing Mechanism (Art 10) Prepared for the Second Meeting of the Intergovernmental Committee for the Nagoya Protocol (ICNP 2) <www.cbd.int/abs/submissions/icnp-2/african-group-en.pdf> accessed 25 April 2021, 2.

114 Government of Canada Submission to the Secretariat of the Convention on Biological Diversity on a Global Multilateral Benefit Sharing Mechanism under art 10 of the Nagoya Protocol on Access to Genetic Resources and the Fair and Equitable Sharing of Benefits arising from their Utilization <www.cbd.int/abs/submissions/icnp-2/canada-en.pdf> accessed 25 April 2021, 1.

115 EU submission in response to CBD notification 2011–142 on awareness-raising and new issues to be addressed by the ICNP-2 <www.cbd.int/abs/submissions/icnp-2/eu-en.pdf> accessed 25 April 2021, 5–6.

116 Report of the Third Meeting of the Open Ended Ad hoc Intergovernmental Committee for the Nagoya Protocol, 14 April 2014, UNEP/CBD/COP/12/6, 7.

117 Decision of the Nagoya Protocol COP, 20 October 2014, UNEP/CBD/NP/COP-MOP/DEC/1/10.

submissions to subsequent Protocol COPs did not focus on the potential application of the mechanism to ABNJ.[118] The 2016 COP considered other aspects of the mechanism and invited further dialogue, as did the 2018 COP.[119] As of writing, no Article 10 mechanism has been established.[120]

The LOSC does not explicitly address the issue of MGRs and different views have been advanced in relation to their status under the Convention. On the one hand, it has been argued that access to these resources is part of the freedom of the high seas. On the other hand, it has been submitted that the living resources of the Area are part of the Area and as such are part of the common heritage regime, even though Part XI only sets up a specific regime for mineral resources.[121]

### 3.4 *Capacity Building and Transfer of Technology*

Capacity building and the transfer of technology go to the heart of the sustainable use and conservation of the ocean.[122] Without the requisite capacity and access to technology, States in particular developing States, will not be able to implement policies that ensure sustainability.[123] These needs were already recognized by the drafters of the LOSC. Part XIV of the Convention is

118 See generally Note by Executive Secretary of the Subsidiary Body on Implementation of the CBD on Submissions regarding Art 10 Mechanism, 18 May 2018, CBD/SBI/2/5.

119 Decision by the Nagoya Protocol COP at Its Third Meeting, Decision 3/13, CBD/NP/MOP/DEC/3/13.

120 See CBD Website on Art 10 mechanism <www.cbd.int/abs/art10-whatdone.shtml> accessed 25 April 2021.

121 See further eg Marie Bourrel and others, 'The Common Heritage of Mankind as a Means to Assess and Advance Equity in Deepsea Mining' (2018) 95 Marine Policy 311, 314.

122 Capacity is complex concept, with different dimensions. The World Bank has provided the following description 'the ability of individuals, institutions and societies to solve problems, make informed choices, define their priorities and plan their futures. The objective of aid assistance is to help developing countries build capacities that boost their ability to achieve their development goals'. (Report of the Secretary-General, Oceans and Law of the Sea, 29 March 2010, UN Doc A65/69, para 17).

123 See eg ibid para 34. As this report also observes '[n]o comprehensive assessment has been carried out at the global level of the capacity-building needs of States in relation to ocean affairs and the law of the sea, including marine science' (ibid). Notwithstanding continued efforts at capacity building, the above findings no doubt remain relevant today. As a 2019 report by the Secretary-General observes:

> However, significant knowledge and capacity gaps remain to be filled. For example, UNEP reported that there were insufficient data to assess progress with respect to 68 per cent of the 93 environment -related indicators of the Sustainable Development Goals (Report by the Secretary-General, Oceans and Law of the Sea, 11 September 2019 (UN Doc A/74/350).

dedicated to the transfer of marine technology. The Convention does not refer explicitly to capacity building, but as has been observed 'it contains over 25 references to the need to help developing States and take their concerns into account'.[124] At the same time, the continued focus on these topics indicates that Part XIV and the Convention's calls to assist developing States have led to limited results. A 2007 review of the accomplishment in relation to capacity building and transfer of technology rhetorically asked, 'Has the Normative Framework Set Down by the [LOSC] Failed?'[125] Long identifies a number of factors explaining this failure. First, the lack of basic capacities in developing States to take advantage of the opportunities the Convention is offering to them.[126] Secondly, 'weak institutional structures at both national and international levels [make] it difficult to implement the broader principles of international cooperation and benefit sharing enshrined by the [LOSC]'.[127] This latter point identifies what may be a critical defect in the legal regime as contained in the LOSC. Its broadly stated principles are sound, but will remain ineffective if specific timelines, rules and specific mechanisms for implementation and review are lacking.[128] As is argued by Harden-Davies and Gjerde, the BBNJ Agreement could be used to give greater effect to the existing LOSC regime by making the existing obligations more specific. The CBD, its Nagoya Protocol and other relevant instruments provide an inspiration in that connection.[129]

124 UN Doc A/65/69, para 8. In addition, provisions that do not explicitly refer to the special needs of developing States, may also be relevant in this respect. This for instance concerns the provision of Part XIII of LOSC concerning the rights of the coastal State to participate in and be informed about marine scientific research in its exclusive economic zone and continental shelf (LOSC art 249). At the same time, this provision reconfirms that to effectively reap the benefits of these rights, the coastal State has to have the necessary capacities.

125 Ronán Long, 'Marine Science Capacity Building and Technology Transfer: Rights and Duties Go Hand in Hand Under the 1982 UNCLOS' in Myron H Nordquist and others (eds), *Law, Science & Ocean Management* (Brill 2007) 307.

126 ibid 307–08.

127 ibid 308.

128 A similar conclusion is likely justified in relation to the provisions of the UNFSA on capacity building. The report of the President of the 2016 resumed Review Conference of the Agreement, makes a number of reference to capacity building, but lacks any reference to a comprehensive approach or assessment in this respect (see Review Conference on the Agreement for the Implementation of the Provisions of the United Nations Convention on the Law of the Sea of 10 December 1982 relating to the Conservation and Management of Straddling Fish Stocks and Highly Migratory Fish Stocks, 1 August 2016, UN Doc A/CONF.210/2016/5, *passim*).

129 Harriett R Harden-Davies and Kristina Gjerde, 'Building Scientific and Technological Capacity: a Role for Benefit-sharing in the Conservation and Sustainable Use of Marine Biodiversity beyond National Jurisdiction' (2019) 33 Ocean Yearbook 392–98.

Transfer of technology and appropriate funding are specifically identified as means for achieving fair and equitable sharing of the benefits resulting from the use of genetic resources, one of the three objectives of the CBD.[130] Articles 16 to 21 of the CBD elaborate this general reference to transfer of technology and funding. While Part XIV of the LOSC is general in nature, the relevant provisions of the CBD are in part directly linked to providing access to genetic resources.[131] However, it should be noted that these provisions are based on the proprietary rights of the developing State concerned and are not applicable as such to ABNJ.[132] The CBD's Nagoya Protocol addresses capacity building and transfer of technology respectively in Articles 22 and 23. Article 22 identifies areas for capacity building in support of the implementation of the Protocol. Article 23 requires parties to cooperate and collaborate on transfer of technology in accordance with the relevant articles of the Convention as a means to achieving the objective of the Protocol. The CBD COP in its decisions on marine and coastal biodiversity has also highlighted the need for capacity building and transfer of technology in relation to BBNJ.[133]

## 4 What May Explain the Choice for the BBNJ Process?

The preceding analysis indicates that it would not seem to be too difficult to build a convincing case that a detailed regime for the sustainable use and conservation of BBNJ could well have taken place in the framework of the CBD. The sustainable use and conservation of biodiversity is the core business of the CBD, and the CBD as a matter of fact has been addressing all of the elements of the package that provided the basis for the current negotiations at the IGC. In addition, the CBD might have been able to conclude the negotiations on that package in a shorter time frame than that of the still ongoing BBNJ process. Opting for the CBD likely would have avoided much of the exploratory consultations that took place in the Ad hoc Working Group. At the time the Working Group was holding its biennial meetings, the CBD was making significant progress on elements of the package through *inter alia* the EBSA process

130 CBD art 1.

131 See CBD art 16(3).

132 The CBD has specific programs for capacity building and for technology transfer and technological and scientific cooperation. See further CBD Secretariat *Thematic Programmes and Cross-Cutting Issues* <www.cbd.int/programmes/> accessed 25 April 2021.

133 See eg COP of the CBD at its Eighth Meeting, Decision VIII/21, UNEP/CBD/COP/DEC/VIII/21, 2, para 9.

and the work on environmental assessments in ABNJ. So, why the choice for the BBNJ process?

In answering the question why the UNGA-led BBNJ process, with its law of the sea focus, was preferred instead of according the CBD a central role in developing the regime for BBNJ, the sequence of events at the CBD and the UNGA provides some indications.[134] The issue was taken up by the CBD during the first meetings of the COP and the SBSTTA, but there was an immediate recognition of the need to further explore the implications of the relationship between the CBD and the LOSC. It was moreover accepted that this required the involvement of the then Office of Oceans and Law of the Sea of the United Nations Secretariat. Although the issue was included in the Secretary-General's report on the law of sea to the General Assembly, which argued the importance of the issue for the law of the sea, the General Assembly did not immediately pick up the issue. The initial recognition that the Office of Oceans and Law of the Sea had to be involved, was a reason for the SBSTTA to not deal with the legal issues involved when the CBD secretariat submitted a 'preliminary investigation' on the issue in 1996. The SBSTTA only picked up the issue again and reported back to the CBD COP after the Study on the relationship between the CBD and the LOSC had been finished in 2003. The SBSTTA's recommendations to the COP, while referring to Article 4(b) of the Convention, might seem to have held the potential of a central role for the CBD in developing the legal regime for BBNJ. However, the General Assembly in the meantime also had started monitoring this issue more actively and, prior to the relevant COP meeting, adopted its Resolution 58/240, which requested other instruments to report on the issue to the Secretary-General and the latter to report back to the General Assembly. The CBD COP in its subsequent decision on marine and coastal diversity refrained from referring to Article 4(b) of the CBD and, while referring to Resolution 58/240, deferred to the General Assembly as the central body for dealing with BBNJ.[135]

---

134 We note that this section examines a 'relational form of regime interaction' between the CBD and UNGA that is more collaborative than conflictual, Jeffrey Dunoff, 'A New Approach to Regime Interaction' in Margaret A Young (ed), *Regime Interaction in International Law: Facing Fragmentation* (Cambridge University Press 2012) 158. See also Margaret A Young and Andrew Friedman 'Biodiversity Beyond National Jurisdiction: Regimes and Their Interaction' (2018) 112 AJIL Unbound 123.

135 One of the persons with whom we informally discussed our views on the relationship between the CBD COP and the UNGA mentioned that the number of delegation members with a law of the sea and/or foreign affairs background attending the CBD COP seemed to increase at the COPs up to and including COP 7 as compared to the number of delegation members from ministries of the environment. This might indicate that law of the sea interests in contracting parties to the CBD did not want to entrust the issue to the CBD,

At the same time, as the preceding analysis demonstrates, the CBD remained concerned with the various elements that eventually became included in the BBNJ package. That involvement would seem to be relevant for a number of reasons. First, it demonstrated the capacity of the CBD for dealing with these issues. In case the BBNJ process would have continued stalling, the CBD would have offered an alternative. Second, the CBD contributed to developing aspects of the BBNJ package beyond the BBNJ process. This is probably most vividly illustrated by the regional implementation of the EBSA process, where EBSA workshops sought input and collaboration from bodies such as the OSPAR Commission and regional fisheries management organizations to facilitate the 'description' of EBSAs.[136] The CBD's work on environmental assessments also contributed to identifying the specific requirements in relation to ABNJ. As discussed above, the CBD's COP convened an expert workshop expressly mandated to examine assessments for activities and processes in ABNJ.[137]

The General Assembly's involvement in addressing the regime for BBNJ likely made the choice for a focus on the development of an instrument under the LOSC inevitable. The issue of BBNJ was included in the Secretary-General's reports on oceans and law of the sea and the General Assembly dealt with the

---

with its focus on the environment. To assess whether there actually was a relative increase in the representation of delegates with a law of the sea and/or foreign affairs background, we compared the composition of delegations at CBD COPs 4 to 8. In that connection, we would like to thank Johanna Bürkert for her compiling the relevant information. An assumption we have made is that persons from ministries of foreign affairs in these kinds of meetings typically will represent broader foreign policy interests, including the public international law/law of the sea context, in which cooperation in the framework of the CBD takes place. While the number of delegates from ministries of the environment at COPs 5, 6 and 7 was respectively 348, 442 and 466 for ministries of foreign affairs these figures respectively are 43, 58 and 100. Otherwise stated, for the former category there was an increase of 25% between 2000 and 2004, for the latter this concerned an increase of 133%. Although these figures obviously only tell part of the story, they can be taken as corroborating the observation of our resource person.

136 See Report of Regional Workshop to Facilitate Description of EBSA's in the Northeast Atlantic Ocean 8 November 2019, CBD/EBSA/WS/2019/1/4. Although the EBSA process has capacity for addressing these issues, it likewise faces similar challenges to the BBNJ process, with disagreements at the 2018 CBD COP about the relative legal position of LOSC and regional bodies, and a lack of consensus about EBSA modalities (See *Earth Negotiations Bulletin*, Vol 9, No 725, 15), parties disagree about LOSC as the framework for all ocean activities and EBSA modification, identification, and process modalities; Decision Adopted by the COP of the CDB at its Fourteenth Meeting, Decision 14/2, CBD/COP/14/14, 100, 122, 127 (COP decision recalling UNGA Resolution on law of the sea and LOSC and bracketing annex on modalities).

137 See section 2.1; UNEP/CBD/COP/11/23.

issue in the context of its resolutions on oceans and law of the sea, involving government representatives with an affinity for the significance of the LOSC for ocean governance having the conviction that the Convention's integrity had to be safeguarded,[138] who at the same time may have been less involved in the CBD. The two implementation agreements to the LOSC that had been concluded in the 1990s had shown that the law of the sea regime could be further developed without reliance on the cumbersome amendment procedure contained in the Convention. Finally, Part XI provided a model for equitable access and benefit sharing that might be adapted to the issue of MGRs.[139] The attraction of this model may have been further enhanced by the fact that most genetic resources with potential commercial value are located on the seabed, downplaying the importance of and possibilities to rely on the regime of freedom of the high seas as an alternative approach offered by the LOSC to regulate the access to these resources.

The choice between the CBD and the LOSC may also be assessed from a legal perspective. Did the issues that would need to be addressed in developing a regime for BBNJ require dealing with it under the LOSC, instead of the CBD? The Study on the relationship between the two conventions identifies arguments for and against the use of both. Although the above analysis of the Study indicates that some doubts may be entertained about some of its specific arguments, that does not detract from the overall conclusion that a legal perspective does not offer conclusive arguments for choosing either the CBD or the LOSC as the framework for developing the regime for BBNJ.

## 5 Concluding Thoughts – The Interaction between the CBD and the LOSC in Light of the Themes of the Book Project

The editors of this book project requested the authors of the individual chapters to consider how their topic 'relate[s] to different visions of the oceans, and to the framing themes identified above, that is, justice, space, power,

138 See also Alan J C Simcock 'The UN Open-ended Informal Consultative Process on Oceans and the Law of the Sea (UNICPOLOS) – Current Status' in Hjalmar Thiel and J Anthony Koslow (eds), *Managing Risks to Biodiversity and the Environment on the High Sea, Including Tools Such as Marine Protected Areas – Scientific Requirements and Legal Aspects* (Proceedings of the Expert Workshop held at the International Academy for Nature Conservation Isle of Vilm, Germany, 27 February–4 March 2001, BfN-Skripten 43, German Federal Agency for Nature Conservation Bonn 2001) 134–35.

139 The authors would like to thank Daniela Diz for suggesting this point. See also Millicay (n 9) 832.

knowledge?'[140] The first theme, justice, is framed as meaning 'questions of distribution in relation to access to and utilization of marine resources'.[141] The CBD and the LOSC provide different perspectives on justice. The LOSC in relation to ABNJ distinguishes between regime for the freedom of the high seas, which is premised on open access and limited attention to issues of distributional fairness, and the regime of the Area, which provides for equitable access and benefit sharing of its mineral resources. The Convention fails to provide for clarity in relation to the living resources of the Area in this respect. On the other hand, one of the objectives of the CBD is 'the fair and equitable sharing of the benefits arising out of the utilization of genetic resources'.[142] The CBD represents a broader vision of ocean justice and allows States to argue that the CBD implies a recognition that the freedom of the high seas needs to be regulated in line with this objective.[143] The two conventions probably are more aligned as regards other aspects of justice, such as inter- and intra-generational and environmental justice. To the extent that these concepts are not included explicitly in the LOSC and the CBD, they have been incorporated in both instruments through the subsequent development of general international law and supported by political commitment of the international community.

The theme of power is defined as 'the way power is distributed and how it affects decision making, the distribution of rights and obligations, jurisdiction over ocean areas as well as activities, and participation in the relevant legal and governance processes'.[144] Recourse to the General Assembly for elaborating the regime of BBNJ may be explained by that body's central role in international policy making in relation to oceans and law of the sea. At the same time, the CBD itself recognized the significance of the General Assembly, and made the relationship between the CBD and the LOSC a focal point of the discussion. A different frame could also have been imagined, and might have resulted in another dynamic. For instance, the Executive Secretary could have been requested to prepare a Study on how the CBD might address the sustainable use and conservation of BBNJ in accordance with its objectives and the scope of the Convention. In a study of that nature, the relationship with the LOSC could have been addressed through the lens of Article 22 of the CBD. As was argued above, Article 22 does not impede the development of a regime

140 See ch 1 (this volume).

141 ibid.

142 CBD art 1.

143 This latter point also raises the need to consider the relationship clauses of the CBD and the LOSC, which will be further discussed below.

144 See ch 1 (this volume).

that regulates and conditions high seas freedoms, as is also witnessed by other specific regimes that have been developed after the adoption of the LOSC.

Another point that is illustrated by the Study on the relationship between the CBD and the LOSC is the power of international bureaucracies to influence the framing of issues. It also illustrates how legal arguments may be used to frame issues and impact upon the further development of the future legal regime of the oceans. The current development of the BBNJ Agreement illustrates that the issue area that needs to be regulated also impacts decision making. Although the agreement likely will be an implementation agreement to the LOSC, the institutional arrangements envisaged by the draft agreement make it akin to multilateral environmental agreements, and differentiate it from the LOSC.

The third theme of the project, space, involves 'reference ... to the way space is understood and regulated in the law of the sea with regards to ABNJ'.[145] Where the LOSC provides for two regimes in respect of ABNJ, with a different spatial scope of application, and different core principles – freedom of the high seas and common heritage of mankind – the CBD refers to ABNJ as a single space, to which the CBD's substantive provisions in principle apply without distinction. In view of the CBD's emphasis on community interests in formulating its objectives, this approach to ocean space may contribute to further downplaying the role of individual high seas freedoms and foregrounding international governance approaches.

The fourth theme of the project is meant to 'capture ... knowledge, or its lack, plays in the construction of legal principles and regimes etc'.[146] Knowledge, and the lack thereof, has been a main driver in the development of the regime for BBNJ. The Study on the relationship between the CBD and the LOSC is most likely right in arguing that, had knowledge about the presence and value of MGRs been known at the time the LOSC was negotiated, these resources of the Area would have been included explicitly in the common heritage regime. Increased knowledge about these resources and the capabilities to exploit them in the 1990s led the CBD and subsequently the UNGA to making this knowledge widely available throughout the international community and garnering support for the creation of a specific regime.[147] Another example of the

145 ibid.

146 ibid.

147 See also Charlotte Salpin and Valentina Germani 'The Status of High Seas Biodiversity in International Policy and Law' in Pierre Jacquet and others (eds), *A Planet for Life – Oceans: The New Frontier* (TERI Press 2011) 194–96; *Earth Negotiations Bulletin* Vol 9, No 252, 12.

importance of knowledge to the BBNJ process is provided by the CBD's work on EBSAs. The identification of EBSAs on the basis of the scientific criteria and guidance has generated a significant increase in awareness about ecosystems that are critical to maintaining the ocean's biodiversity and provide a steppingstone to establishing a representative network of MPAs. The significance of knowledge to the BBNJ process as such is recognized by the inclusion of capacity building and transfer of technology as one of the issues of the BBNJ package.

To put the above remarks in perspective, it should be realized that BBNJ process was never intended to fundamentally remap legal ocean space. The General Assembly in defining the mandate of the IGC has provided that the 'work and results of the conference should be fully consistent with the provisions' of the LOSC.[148] Similarly, in terms of justice, power and knowledge, the BBNJ process is unlikely to lead to a departure of the current trajectory of the law of the sea. True, the regime for access and benefit sharing may imply some distributional justice. However, in general a future BBNJ Agreement unlikely will result in a redistribution of power between the actors with interests in ABNJ. The same actors will remain competent to regulate ocean activities, albeit under stricter environmental regulation. Perhaps the major innovation of a future BBNJ Agreement would be in the dissemination of knowledge about the oceans. The clearing house mechanism(s) that is/are envisaged by the draft agreement, coupled with the development of new technologies, which have the potential to exponentially increase humanity's knowledge base, may lead to a (much) more even distribution of knowledge within the international community, including among non-State actors.

Finishing with the question that is posed in the chapter title, it is without doubt possible to subscribe to the view of the Study on the relationship between the CBD and the LOSC that both are complementary and mutually supportive.[149] What counts most in elaborating an effective regime for BBNJ will be the content of a BBNJ Agreement, not the framework in which it was negotiated. The current draft suggests that a BBNJ Agreement will share many characteristics with multilateral environmental agreements and less so with the LOSC and the Fish Stocks Agreement, one of its other implementation agreements.[150] That approach may contribute to addressing the lack of a

148 Resolution adopted by the General Assembly on 24 December 2017, UN Doc A/72/249.

149 See also Blanchard (n 1) 365–67.

150 It could be argued that in the current negotiations the relationship between the rights and obligations of coastal States and the rights and obligations is one of the major controversial issues and is a law of the sea matter that should not be addressed in an environmental law context. However, as the current draft of the BBNJ Agreement states,

dedicated environmental institutional framework under the LOSC and contribute to the systemic integration of international law.

---

it 'shall be interpreted and applied in the context of and in a manner consistent with the Convention' (Draft text of an agreement under the United Nations Convention on the Law of the Sea on the conservation and sustainable use of marine biological diversity of areas beyond national jurisdiction, 17 May 2019, A/CONF.232/2019/6 Annex, art 4(1); see also ibid, art 4(2)). As art 22 of the CBD illustrates a similar savings clause could have been included in an instrument negotiated in an environmental law context. Such a treaty could also have further detailed the rights and obligations of States in relation to BBNJ, while respecting the jurisdictional framework of the LOSC. Again, reference may be had to the more detailed rights and obligations of States in relation to marine biodiversity as contained in the CBD as compared to the LOSC. For a further discussion concerning the use of either the LOSC or the CBD as a framework for dealing with BBNJ, see Tvedt and Jørem (n 110) 159–61.

CHAPTER 8

# Protecting the Environment of ABNJ through Marine Protected Areas and Area-based Management Tools

## *Is the Glass Half Empty or Half Full and Whose Glass Is It Anyway?*

*Alex Oude Elferink*

## 1 Introduction*

Existing political commitments and the current negotiation on an Agreement under the United Nations Convention on the Law of the Sea on the conservation and sustainable use of marine biological diversity of areas beyond national jurisdiction (BBNJ Agreement) indicate that there is widespread support for using marine protected areas (MPAs) and area-based management tools (ABMTs) to protect the environment of ABNJ. In drafts of the BBNJ Agreement that have been presented thus far, MPAs and ABMTs are closely related. Reference is generally made to 'area-based management tools, including marine protected areas'. However, ABMTs and MPAs are two distinct terms that differ conceptually – one is a tool applicable to a specific area and the other characterizes the nature of a specific area – and their purpose is not the same.[1] ABMTs are primarily intended to regulate specific activities at a

* I would like to thank Vito De Lucia, Lan Nguyen, Erik Molenaar and Catherine Blanchard for their comments on an earlier version of this chapter.

1 See also Elizabeth M De Santo, 'Implementation challenges of area-based management tools (ABMTs) for biodiversity beyond national jurisdiction (BBNJ)' (2018) 97 Marine Policy 34, 34–35. The terms 'ABMTs' and 'MPAs' are defined in the Revised draft text of the agreement under the United Nations Convention on the Law of the Sea on the conservation and sustainable use of marine biological diversity of areas beyond national jurisdiction (Advance unedited version (27 November 2019) (Revised Draft Agreement; available at <www.un.org/bbnj/sites/www.un.org.bbnj/files/revised_draft_text_a.conf_.232.2020.11_advance_unedited_version.pdf> accessed 11 May 2021), Annex, arts 1(3) and 1(10). For a brief discussion of these provisions see below text n 37 and following; see also Erik Molenaar, 'Multilateral Creeping Coastal State Jurisdiction and the BBNJ Negotiations' (2021) 36 International Journal of Marine and Coastal Law 5, 39–40. The overlap of these definitions and the conflation of MPAs and ABMTs in art 1(3) might be used to argue that the present distinction between MPAs and ABMTs is not justified. As different categories in the *IUCN Protected Area Categories System* indicate, there are huge difference between these various categories (see *Protected*

 | DOI:10.1163/9789004506367_009

sectoral level, and their primary objective may be different from the protection of the marine environment. On the other hand, MPAs have the protection of the marine environment as their primary objective and may involve the regulation of different activities to also address cumulative impacts.

The present chapter is intended to further explore the relationship between ABMTs and MPAs. In order to do so, section 2 will first consider the development of the general framework applicable to both instruments, starting from the United Nations Convention on the law of the sea (LOSC)[2] and ending with a discussion of the Revised Draft Agreement, the current negotiating text for the BBNJ Agreement. Section 3 will consider the practice in relation to ABMTs and MPAs of a number of specific instruments and bodies. This section, among others, will consider how this practice relates to the development of the general framework as discussed in section 2 and what kind of legal issues have come to the fore in specific instruments and bodies. Section 4 provides a synthesis of the two preceding sections and discusses that synthesis in the framework of the overarching themes of the current volume. In light of these themes, the analysis in sections 2 and 3 will include a brief discussion of the legal bases for adopting MPAs and ABMTs, decision-making procedures, the mandate of the instruments and bodies concerned, and the role of knowledge in relation to the establishment of MPAs and ABMTs.[3] Apart from exploring the relationship between MPAs and ABMTs, this analysis will also allow assessing the progress the international community has been making in achieving existing political commitments in relation to the protection of the marine environment through these two instruments. Both these strands of the chapter's narrative will be revisited and further discussed in its final section.

*Area Categories* available at <www.iucn.org/theme/protected-areas/about/protected-area-categories> accessed 22 April 2021). In that sense, it is submitted that it would be possible to speak of a sliding scale, with IUCN category Ia 'Strict nature reserve' on the one side and an ABMT that regulates an activity to optimize use but without clear nature conservation benefits on the other. Sliding as it may be, both ends of the scale have very different implications. In any case, the conflation of MPAs and ABMTs in Revised Draft Agreement art 1(3) is a political choice that does not efface the different implications of both concepts as set out here in the main text.

2 United Nations Convention on the Law of the Sea (opened for signature 10 December 1982, entered into force 16 November 1994) 1833 UNTS 3.

3 Due to the constraints a chapter-length analysis imposes, issues in relation to the management of MPAs and ABMTs will not be discussed.

## 2 Attributing Rights and Obligations in Relation to MPAs and ABMTs

The LOSC provides the logical starting point for assessing the rights and obligations in relation to the MPAs and ABMTs in ABNJ at the global level. The Convention continues to be recognized as the fundamental legal framework applicable to the oceans as currently reaffirmed by the BBNJ process.[4]

The LOSC does not employ the terms MPAs and ABMTs, but in a number of instances does point to the need or alludes to the potential of using these spatial management tools.[5] In addition, the LOSC's references to the right or obligation to regulate may also include the adoption of ABMTs or MPAs.[6] Without the need to go into a detailed discussion of all relevant provisions of the LOSC, a number of general points may be made about the regulatory framework provided by the LOSC. It is trite knowledge that the LOSC mostly takes a sectoral approach in regulating activities in the marine environment. Consequently, user States, which are involved in managing these activities, have a central role in standard setting, including in adopting ABMTs, (potentially) marginalizing other interests. The establishment of MPAs holistically protecting the marine environment from human impacts under this approach becomes problematic, to say the least. The LOSC does not endow any body with a competence to assess the need for comprehensive protection and mechanisms for cross-sectoral coordination are also lacking.

The centrality of user States is aptly illustrated by the LOSC's approach to high seas fisheries. The power to regulate fisheries is entrusted to States whose nationals are engaged in fishing activities.[7] It is these States that are required to cooperate in the adoption of conservation and management measures, which may include ABMTs. The focus on user interests is reconfirmed by the focus on the living resources that are subject to exploitation.[8] A similar focus on user interests applies in the case of mining activities in the Area, in respect of which the International Seabed Authority (ISA) has a central coordinating role. The Convention accords the ISA a broad regulatory mandate that also allows using ABMTs to protect the marine environment from harmful effects that may arise

4 See eg the relationship clauses contained in Revised Draft Agreement art 4(1). The term BBNJ process is used as a shorthand for referring to the work under the aegis of the United Nations General Assembly on the issue of biodiversity beyond national jurisdiction (BBNJ).
5 See eg LOSC arts 162(2)(x) and 194(5).
6 See eg ibid arts 117 and 194(1).
7 ibid arts 116 and 117.
8 ibid arts 118 and 119.

from mining activities.[9] Both in the case of fisheries and mining, the LOSC does not contain rules that contain specific guidance on the generation of knowledge that will be required to assess the need for ABMTs or MPAs. In the case of fisheries, the relevant provisions, among others, refer to the 'best scientific evidence'.[10] The obligation to gather relevant information rests on the States involved in fishing activities.[11] Article 145, defining the environmental mandate of the ISA refers to the 'necessary measures', without specifying how the relevant knowledge base has to be generated.

Part XII of the LOSC, which addresses the protection and the preservation of the marine environment is also largely based on a sectoral approach. This is particularly the case for section 5, which deals with international standard setting on a 'source-by-source' basis in consecutive articles. The focus on the regulation of individual activities to protect and preserve the marine environment is also apparent from the general provisions of Part XII, section 1.[12] At the same time, Article 192 imposes a general duty on States 'to protect and preserve the marine environment' and their sovereign right to exploit their natural resources has to be exercised 'in accordance with their duty to protect and preserve the marine environment'.[13] Section 1 of Part XII arguably also provides a basis for going beyond ABMTs regulating activities on a sectoral basis. Article 194(5) provides that States are required to take measures 'necessary to protect and preserve rare or fragile ecosystems as well as the habitat of depleted, threatened or endangered species and other forms of marine life'. In addition, Article 197 contains a generally-worded provision on global and regional cooperation in relation to the protection and the preservation of the marine environment. That obligation also extends to the issues addressed by Article 194(5).[14] At the same time, the practical importance of these provisions should not be overstated. Both are formulated in a general manner and do not provide any specific guidance beyond the requirement that in case it is concluded that measures are necessary, they have to be taken.[15] Article 194(5) moreover

9 ibid art 145; see also ibid art 162(2)(x), which provides that the Council shall 'disapprove areas for exploitation by contractors or the Enterprise in cases where substantial evidence indicates the risk of serious harm to the marine environment'.

10 ibid art 119(1)(a).

11 ibid arts 119–120.

12 See eg ibid arts 194, paras (1) to (3).

13 For a contrary view see the discussion in Poto (ch 6) in this volume.

14 For a further discussion of the relevance of arts 194 and 197 for MPAs in ABNJ see, eg, Ingvild Ulrikke Jakobsen, *Marine Protected Areas in International Law: An Arctic Perspective* (Brill 2016) 51–53.

15 See also Jeff A Ardron and others, 'The sustainable use and conservation of biodiversity in ABNJ: What can be achieved using existing international agreements' (2014) 49 Marine

is conditioned by Article 194(4), which provides that in taking measures States 'shall refrain from unjustifiable interference with activities carried out by other States in the exercise of their rights and in pursuance of their duties in conformity with this Convention'. In other words, this indicates that States engaged in activities in the marine environment in this case will also have a say in determining the content of specific measures. Finally, Article 194(5) does not entail a duty to protect and preserve fragile ecosystems and habitats as such, but in the context of regulating activities in the marine environment.[16] That is, it is an obligation that first of all rests on user States. As far as the generation of knowledge is concerned, Part XII similarly attributes primary responsibility to States engaged in activities.[17]

The Convention on Biological Diversity (CBD), which was adopted at the United Nations Conference on Environment and Development (Rio Conference) in 1992, does explicitly refer to the establishment of protected areas.[18] Article 8 requires contracting parties to '[e]stablish a system of protected areas or areas where special measures need to be taken to conserve biological diversity'.[19] This Article moves the obligation to establish protected areas significantly beyond the language of Article 194(5) of the LOSC. In particular, the reference to 'a system' implies the need to establish a coherent network of areas.[20] The reference to 'biodiversity' is more comprehensive than the reference to 'rare or fragile ecosystems as well as the habitat of depleted, threatened or endangered species and other forms of marine life' contained

---

Policy 98, 106; Glen Wright, Julien Rochette and Elisabeth Druel, 'Marine protected areas in areas beyond national jurisdiction' in Rosemary Rayfuse (ed.), *Research Handbook on International Marine Environmental Law* (Elgar 2015) 272–73.

16 LOSC art 194(5) refers to 'measures taken in accordance with this Part'. The focus of Part XII is almost wholly on the prevention, reduction and control of pollution.

17 See eg LOSC arts 204 and 206.

18 Convention on Biological Diversity (signed 5 June 1992, entered in force 29 December 1993) 1760 UNTS 79 art 8. Agenda 21 (available at <https://sustainabledevelopment.un.org/content/documents/Agenda21.pdf> accessed 11 May 2021), which was also adopted at the same time, in ch 17, dealing with the protection of the oceans, does not make such an explicit reference, although para 17.22 not only refers to the prevention, reduction and control of pollution, but also to the requirement to prevent, reduce and control degradation of the marine environment, indicating that in this connection it 'is necessary to … [a]pply preventive, precautionary and anticipatory approaches. In general, Agenda 21 is largely focused on the regulation of activities.

19 The CBD defines a 'protected area' as 'a geographically defined area which is designated or regulated and managed to achieve specific conservation objectives' (CBD art 2).

20 See further Lyle Glowka and others, *A Guide to the Convention on Biological Diversity* (IUCN – The World Conservation Union 1994) 39.

in Article 194(5).[21] In addition, Article 8(b) requires contracting parties to '[d]evelop, where necessary, guidelines for the selection, establishment and management of the areas concerned'. At the same time, it may be noted that the CBD's definition of protected areas allows for adopting different levels of protection.[22] This implies that, in managing these areas, user interest will likely be factored in, and in particular established interests may be expected to have a strong voice. Furthermore, the CBD was neither accorded the regulatory authority to deal with many aspects of the sustainable use and conservation of biodiversity nor a coordinating role in relation to the sectoral bodies that have such authority. Finally, although it has been submitted that Article 8 is also applicable to ABNJ,[23] Article 4 provides that in ABNJ the Convention applies to 'processes and activities' and not to biological diversity as such. Although that focus does not prevent taking protective actions,[24] it could be used to argue that use and user States should play a prominent role in adopting such measures.

A similar shift towards wider environmental concerns is witnessed by the Fish Stocks Agreement, which was adopted in 1995 in the wake of the Rio Conference.[25] The Agreement among others incorporates the precautionary approach and refers to the need to protect biodiversity and the need of assessing not only the impacts of fishing, but also those of other human activities and environmental factors.[26] Perhaps most importantly, the Fish Stocks Agreement (UNFSA) further elaborates the duty to cooperate on high seas fisheries through the participation in or collaboration with regional fisheries management organizations and arrangements. The fact that having a 'real interest' provides the basis for participation,[27] seemingly further cements the central role of user States, which was already contained in the LOSC, in fisheries management.[28]

21 Arguably, the reference to 'other forms of marine life' could be said to imply that art 194(5) is formulated in a similarly inclusive manner.

22 See further Glowka (n 20) 22–23 and 39.

23 See Oude Elferink and Kerr (ch 7) in this volume.

24 See also ibid.

25 United Nations Agreement for the Implementation of the Provisions of the United Nations Convention on the Law of the Sea of 10 December 1982 relating to the Conservation and Management of Straddling Fish Stocks and Highly Migratory Fish Stocks (opened for signature 4 August 1995, entered into force 11 December 2001) 2167 UNTS 3 (UNFSA).

26 ibid art 5.

27 ibid art 8(3).

28 For a nuanced discussion of the implications of the concept of 'real interest' see Erik Molenaar, 'The Concept of "Real Interest" and Other Aspects of Co-operation through Regional Fisheries Management Mechanisms' (2000) (15) International Journal of Marine and Coastal Law 475. Although Molenaar submits that the concept may not exclude other

At the political level, the international community committed itself to establishing MPAs, including representative networks by 2012 at the World Summit on Sustainable Development (WSSD) in 2002.[29] Three basic requirements were identified in relation to this goal: the networks of MPAs had to be representative, consistent with international law and based on scientific information.[30] This political commitment was further operationalized through Target 11 of the Aichi Targets adopted by the 2010 CBD Conference of the Parties (COP), which called for at least 10 percent of the world's coastal and marine areas to be conserved by 2020.[31] In particular, Target 11 provides that:

> especially areas of particular importance for biodiversity and ecosystem services, are conserved through effectively and equitably managed, ecologically representative and well connected systems of protected areas and other effective area-based conservation measures, and integrated into the wider landscapes and seascapes.[32]

A comparison of the WSSD outcome and Aichi Target 11 indicates a shift away from the concept of MPAs. While the WSSD outcome refers to representative networks of MPAs, Aichi Target 11 indicates that both MPAs and other ABMTS may be used to meet the 10 percent conservation target.[33]

---

than fishing interests from being represented in RFMOs, he at the same time provides a number of arguments indicating the close link between the concept and fishing interests (ibid 529–31). The current participation in RFMOs does not point towards a diversification of membership following the adoption of UNFSA (relevant information may be accessed through the webpage *Regional Fishery Bodies* (*RFB*) available at <www.fao.org/fishery/rfb/en> accessed 29 April 2021).

29 The skeleton of this paragraph is based on a paragraph included in Oude Elferink and Kerr (ch 7) in this volume.

30 Plan of Implementation of the World Summit on Sustainable Development, Johannesburg, 4 September 2002; (Report of the World Summit on Sustainable Development, Johannesburg, South Africa, 26 August–4 September 2002 (United Nations publication, Sales No. E.03.II.A.1 and corrigendum), Res 2, para 32(c).

31 Decision Adopted by the Conference of Parties of the CBD at Its 10th Meeting, Decision X/2, Annex IV (UNEP/CBD/COP/DEC/X/2).

32 Almost identical language is included in para 2(c) of the Leaders' Pledge for Nature; United to Reverse Biodiversity Loss by 2030 for Sustainable Development, which was adopted at the United Nations Summit on Biodiversity on 28 September 2020 available at <www.leaderspledgefornature.org/> accessed 10 March 2021.

33 Two points might be raised in this connection: First, Aichi Target 11 may be read in different ways. The qualifying phrase 'effectively and equitably managed, ecologically representative and well connected systems' may be read as referring to both MPAs and ABMTS or referring only to MPAs. The use of the word 'and' instead of the word 'or' suggests that former interpretation is more likely (see also *South China Sea* (*Philippines v China*)

MPAS and ABMTS have figured prominently in the debate concerning the conservation and sustainable use of BBNJ throughout the BBNJ process. Already during the first meeting of the so-called Ad hoc Working Group, there was broad agreement that '[ABMTS], including [MPAS] and temporal and spatial closures for fisheries management' constituted a 'key tool to improve integrated conservation and sustainable use' of BBNJ.[34] That is, already at the start of the BBNJ process, MPAS were classified as a subset of ABMTS.[35] Interestingly, non-governmental organizations presented a different perspective, arguing for 'a global network of marine protected areas, including both strictly protected areas and multi-use areas'.[36]

The current Revised Draft Agreement generally maintains the link between ABMTS and MPAS, using the formulation 'area-based management tools, including marine protected areas'.[37] Only in two instances does the Revised Draft Agreement refer to MPAS separately, and not as a subset of ABMTS. Article 1(10) provides a definition of the term 'MPA'. This definition quite closely resembles the definition of the term 'ABMTS, including MPAS' contained in Article 1(3), although arguably the focus of Article 1(10) is holistic, while Article 1(3) focuses on the regulation of specific activities.[38] The second separate reference to

(Award on Jurisdiction and Admissibility, 29 October 2015) PCA on Merits, paras 493–97). Secondly, the WSSD outcome also refers to MPAS in the context of a broader set of measures for managing and conserving the oceans. However, in this case a specific linkage to ABMTS similar to Aichi Target 11 is missing (see Plan of Implementation (n 30) para 32).

34 Report of the Ad Hoc Open-ended Informal Working Group to study issues relating to the conservation and sustainable use of marine biological diversity beyond areas of national jurisdiction; Transmittal letter dated 9 March 2006 from the Co-Chairpersons of the Working Group to the President of the General Assembly (UN Doc A/61/65) para 59.

35 For a discussion of the relationship between the two concepts see also n 1.

36 Report (n 34) para 58. The only non-governmental organization that is mentioned in the summary of the debate on this point in Earth Negotiations Bulletin is Greenpeace (see 25(25) Earth Negotiations Bulletin 4).

37 Revised Draft Agreement, *passim*. A number of delegations have proposed to delete the phrase 'including marine protected areas' from the definition of ABMTS contained in Revised Draft Agreement art 1(3) (see Textual proposals submitted by delegations by 20 February 2020, for consideration at the fourth session of the Intergovernmental conference on an international legally binding instrument under the United Nations Convention on the Law of the Sea on the conservation and sustainable use of marine biological diversity of areas beyond national jurisdiction, in response to the invitation by the President of the Conference in her Note of 18 November 2019 (UN Doc A/CONF.232/2020/3) available at <www.un.org/bbnj/sites/www.un.org.bbnj/files/textual_proposals_compilation_article-by-article_-_15_april_2020.pdf> accessed 22 April 2021 11, 17–18.

38 The reference to 'conservation and sustainable use objectives' might be taken as indicating that an MPA should allow sustainable use of the area concerned. However, it is submitted that achieving sustainable use objectives in the broader marine environment may require closing certain areas to all human activities.

MPAS is in Article 14 of the Revised Draft Agreement, which sets out the objectives of its Part III, dealing with ABMTS, including MPAS. Article 14(d) provides that one of the objectives is to '[(d) Establish a system of ecologically representative marine protected areas that are connected [and effectively and equitably managed];]'.[39] Article 14(d) is an alternative to square bracketed Article 14(c), which provides for use and conservation of areas requiring protection by either ABMTS or MPAS. The choice for the approach contained in Article 14(d) in the final text of the Agreement would recognize that Part III cannot be effectively implemented by only adopting single-sector ABMTS. At the same time, the fact that the text of the Revised Draft Agreement in general refers to ABMTS and MPAS in conjunction and does not seem to provide clear guidance as to when either of these instruments should be used, indicates that the objective contained in current Article 14(d), if maintained in its current setting, in the specific case may result in discussions about whether designation of an area as an MPA is justified, or whether specific ABMTS would suffice.[40]

The Revised Draft Agreement contains detailed rules for the identification, designation and management (including monitoring and review) of areas that require a higher level of protection through ABMTS/MPAS. It is beyond the purposes of this chapter to go into a detailed discussion of Part III.[41] However, a couple of points may be observed. First, the objectives of Part III, which are listed in Article 14 and currently all are in square brackets, stress the need for a 'holistic and cross-sectoral approach'. However, the importance of this objective arguably is downplayed by the fact that it is not presented as a free-standing

39 The use of square brackets in the text of the Revised Draft Agreement is explained as follows in a Note by the President of the Intergovernmental conference on an international legally binding instrument under the United Nations Convention on the Law of the Sea on the conservation and sustainable use of marine biological diversity of areas beyond national jurisdiction (IGC), preceding that text:

> Square brackets have been used to indicate the following: (a) there are two or more alternative options within a provision; and (b) support has been expressed for a "no text" option, either within a provision or in relation to a provision as a whole. However, the absence of square brackets does not imply agreement on the ideas or specific language reflected in a provision. Equally, text that has not been revised should not be taken as indicating agreement on the unrevised text (Revised Draft Agreement (n 1) at Note by the President, para 7).

40 The EU has proposed to merge arts 14(c) and (d) of the Revised Draft Agreement and make it the first objective of art 14. The EU text would require setting up 'a network of ecologically representative marine protected areas that are ecologically connected and effectively as well as equitably managed' (see Textual proposals (n 37) 133).

41 In addition, much of the text at present is in square brackets, making a detailed discussion on the final outcome speculative.

objective, but as an outcome of enhanced international cooperation and coordination.[42] The other objectives display a certain tension between conservation and use. For instance, Article 14(h) refers to the safeguarding of 'aesthetic, natural or wilderness values', while Article 14(f) mentions the supporting of 'food security and other socioeconomic objectives'. While such a dual focus is in line with Part III's coverage of ABMTs, including MPAs, it allows foregrounding economic interests over conservation objectives and objecting against strict protective measures, including MPAs closed to human activities, because it allows arguing that ABMTs ensure meeting the objectives of Part III.

Draft Article 15 on international cooperation and coordination largely makes these activities complementary to the work being undertaken in the framework of existing instruments and frameworks. Article 15 moreover has to be read in light of the general relationship clause contained in Article 4(3) of the Revised Draft Agreement, which provides that the 'Agreement shall be interpreted and applied in a manner that [respects the competences of and] does not undermine relevant legal instruments and frameworks and relevant global, regional, subregional and sectoral bodies'.[43] Depending on how the 'not undermine' requirement will play out in practice, it may to a lesser or larger degree complicate a holistic approach to the conservation and sustainable use of BBNJ. In this connection, it may also be noted that the Revised Draft Agreement gives the COP a rather weak coordinating role in relation to other instruments, frameworks and bodies.[44]

Article 15(4) furthermore provides that measures under Part III 'shall not undermine the effectiveness of measures adopted by coastal States in adjacent areas within national jurisdiction [(AWNJ)] and shall have due regard for the rights, duties and legitimate interests of all States'. Articles 16 to 18 contain detailed provisions on respectively the identification of areas, proposals on ABMTs, including MPAs, and consultation on and assessment of proposals. These Articles, among others, create procedures for operationalizing the requirements in relation to existing frameworks and instruments and coastal States as defined in general terms in preceding Articles. The initiative to identify specific areas and formulate proposals rests with individual States. In that

42 See Revised Draft Agreement art 14(a).

43 For a further discussion on the 'not undermine' requirement see eg Vito De Lucia and Philip Peter Nickels, 'Reflecting on the Role of the Arctic Council vis-à-vis a Future International Legally Binding Instrument on Biodiversity in Areas Beyond National Jurisdiction' (2020) 11 Arctic Review on Law and Politics 189.

44 See Revised Draft Agreement art 48(4)(c). For a further discussion of this provision see also Barnes (ch 10) in this volume.

sense the procedure could be used pro-actively both by States primarily pursuing conservationist objectives or by States that want to secure access to an area by focusing on ABMTs. The consultation procedure contained in Article 18 is inclusive and proponents of proposals are bound to 'consider the contributions received during the consultation period and shall either revise the proposal accordingly or continue the consultation process'.[45] However, consultations cannot be dragged out for an indefinite period of time, as they are time-bound.[46] The fact that it is up to the proponents of a proposal to revise it on the basis of the consultation, would give them some leeway in case of continued disagreement over the content of the proposal.[47] Proposals as revised will be assessed by the scientific and technical body and be forwarded to the COP for taking a decision.[48] Text that currently still is in square brackets indicates that decisions of the COP in principle shall be taken by consensus. Only if all efforts to reach consensus have been exhausted, decision-making will be non-consensual.[49] The monitoring and review procedures contained in Article 21 of the Revised Draft Agreement may contribute to the effectiveness of the measures adopted under Part III. Although it is upon States parties to report on implementation, the reporting shall be made publicly available by the Agreement secretariat. This should facilitate the input from other actors in the review of existing measures.

## 3 Practice in Relation to MPAs and ABMTs

### 3.1 *Introduction*

There is a wealth of practice of global and regional frameworks, instruments and bodies in relation to MPAs and ABMTs. It is beyond to scope of a book chapter to present a comprehensive discussion of such practice. At the same time, in considering the approach to this section, I felt that providing a general overview of all relevant practice would only be skimming the surface and not provide a meaningful basis for discussion. For that reason, I have chosen to

45 Revised Draft Agreement art 18(4).

46 ibid art 18(5). However, no specific time frame is mentioned in this connection. The elaboration of the modalities for the consultations is deferred to a decision after the entry into force of the Agreement, see ibid art 18(7).

47 This aspect of the consultation process may also be subject to further clarification through the procedure envisaged by Revised Draft Agreement art 18(7).

48 ibid arts 18(6) and 19.

49 ibid art 48(3 bis).

focus on certain aspects of the practice of a number of bodies and instruments and in this way provide the reader with a more detailed discussion of the pertinent issues. Sections 3.2 and 3.3 respectively discuss the ISA and the CBD's work on EBSAs, both relevant examples of developments at the global level, while section 3.4. discusses two specific regions, the Northeast Atlantic Ocean and the Southern Ocean, involving respectively the OSPAR Convention[50] and the OSPAR Commission, and the CAMLR Convention[51] and the Commission for the Conservation of Antarctic Marine Living Resources (CCAMLR).

### 3.2 *The ISA and Mining in the Area*

Apart from fisheries, and perhaps shipping, mining potentially is the activity *in* ABNJ that may have most impact on the marine environment and BBNJ.[52] The ISA currently has concluded 30 exploration contracts with 21 contractors in areas in the Atlantic, Indian and Pacific Oceans.[53] Although, according to Secretary-General Lodge of the ISA, in 2018 exploration contracts only covered less than 1 per cent of the Area,[54] localized impacts may be significant and may extend beyond the area covered by an exploration contract or future exploitation contracts.[55] The ISA, like other sectoral bodies, seemingly is concerned about the impact the future BBNJ Agreement might have on its mandate. Secretary-General Lodge at the first session of the IGC in 2018 argued that the ISA, having specialized knowledge, was best placed to develop ABMTs

50 Convention for the Protection of the Marine Environment of the North-East Atlantic (opened for signatures 22 September 1992, entered into force 25 March 1998) (OSPAR Convention).

51 Convention on the Conservation of Antarctic Marine Living Resources (opened for signature 20 May 1980, entered into force 7 April 1982) (CAMLR Convention).

52 See further Kathryn A Miller and others, 'An Overview of Seabed Mining Including the Current State of Development, Environmental Impacts, and Knowledge Gaps' (2018) 4 Frontiers in Marine Science 418.

53 For a list of these contractors see *Exploration Contracts* available at <www.isa.org.jm/exploration-contracts> accessed 3 March 2021.

54 Statement on Measures such as Area-based Management Tools at the Intergovernmental Conference on an international legally binding instrument under the United biological diversity of areas beyond national jurisdiction. Section III (4) of the President's aid to discussions (UN Doc A/CONF.232/2018/3); 7 September 2018, New York available at <www.isa.org.jm/files/documents/EN/BBNJ/2018/Stats/ABMT.pdf> accessed 3 March 2021.

55 In addition, it should be realized that BBNJ is also localized. For instance, one source reports that active hydrothermal vent fields in total cover some 50 square kilometers: The Pew Charitable Trusts, *Deep-Sea Mining on Hydrothermal Vents Threatens Biodiversity Protections could safeguard ecosystems that lie beyond national jurisdiction* (2019) available at <www.pewtrusts.org/-/media/assets/2019/09/deep-sea_mining_on_hydrothermal_vents_fact_sheet_v1.pdf> accessed 3 March 2021).

in relation to mining activities in the Area.[56] Perhaps not surprisingly, in that connection he referred to the 'risk of undermining the careful balance of competences established in the [LOSC]'.[57]

Whether the ISA is properly equipped to carry out its environmental mandate at the moment may be open to questioning. This was, among others, highlighted by the first periodic review of the functioning of the mining regime and the ISA. Two of the recommendations respectively dealt with enhancing the environmental expertise of the secretariat and more extensive engagement of the ISA with the deep-sea scientific community and deep-sea scientific projects.[58] Another recommendation was to set up an environmental working group under the Legal and Technical Commission (LTC).[59] All of these recommendations were endorsed by the Assembly of the ISA.[60] According to a report on the meeting, NGOs were critical of the latter recommendation, as it would not create 'a self-standing body with the necessary expertise, which is the usual feature of other multilateral environmental agreements'.[61] Recent reports on the work of the ISA express continued concern about whether the ISA is properly equipped to deal with environmental aspect of mining activities in the Area.[62] All these considerations point to the importance of creating an adequate knowledge base and the involvement of relevant stakeholders. In that connection, it should also be realized that much of the relevant data is generated by the users that engage in the activities having potentially adverse impact on the marine environment.[63] It is essential that the ISA guarantees

56 Statement (n 54) 2.

57 ibid. At the same time, Lodge acknowledged the need for cooperation, referring to the existing cooperation of the ISA with global and regional organizations (ibid).

58 See ISBA/23/A/5/Rev.1, recommendations 6 and 7.

59 See ibid recommendation 14.

60 See ISBA/23/A/13, sections E.5, G.1 and H.

61 See 25(151) Earth Negotiations Bulletin 17.

62 See 25(185) Earth Negotiations Bulletin 11; Andrew Friedman, 'After Chaotic Year, Seabed Mining Oversight Body Must Strengthen Policies' The Pew Charitable Trusts (12 February 2021) available at <www.pewtrusts.org/en/research-and-analysis/articles/2021/02/11/after-chaotic-year-seabed-mining-oversight-body-must-strengthen-policies> accessed 25 July 2021.

63 For instance, ISA Secretary-General Lodge has observed that in particular the scope of environment baseline studies by contractors in the exploration phase 'would determine the success of [regional environmental management plans]' *Developing a Framework for Regional Environmental Management Plans for Polymetallic Sulphide Deposits on Mid-Ocean Ridges* (ISA Technical Study No. 22) 12. See also Michael Lodge, 'Measures such as area-based management tools, including marine protected areas' (Statement to the Intergovernmental Conference on an international legally binding instrument under the United Nations Convention on the Law of the Sea on the conservation and

that relevant data will be gathered, shared with the ISA and relevant stakeholders and be acted upon.[64]

Over the last decade, the ISA has gradually developed a spatial management approach, in particular through regional environmental management plan (REMPs) and areas of particular environmental interest (APEIs).[65] That development has been lagging behind the regulation of mining activities in general. Interestingly, as has also been acknowledged by the ISA, the initiative for gathering scientific information in relation to the development of environmental management plans in the middle of the last decade had been taken by contractors and other stakeholders, not the ISA itself.[66] These initiatives may have contributed to the ISA pursuing this matter more actively. As the Preliminary Strategy in relation to the development of REMPs observes:

> While external scientific initiatives are to be welcomed, it is considered important, given the mandate and role of the Authority, including in relation to the conduct of marine scientific research in the Area, that regional environmental management plans be developed under the auspices of the Authority, in a transparent manner, and with the full engagement of the relevant organs of the Authority.[67]

---

sustainable use of marine biological diversity of areas beyond national jurisdiction, Friday 7 September 2018) 2.

64 It may be noted that the ISA is in the process of developing a Communications and Stakeholder Engagement Strategy (a draft of the Strategy, which was circulated in early December of 2020) is available at <https://isa.org.jm/files/files/documents/Draft_Comms_and_Stakeholder_Engagement_Strategy.pdf> accessed 8 March 2021. For a critical review of the draft Strategy see the letter of 28 January 2021 of Andrew Friedman, 'Seabed Mining Project' The Pew Charitable Trusts (available at <www.pewtrusts.org/en/research-and-analysis/speeches-and-testimony/2021/01/28/pew-suggests-ways-to-improve-stakeholder-engagement-at-the-international-seabed-authority> accessed 8 March 2021).

65 While the ISA has characterized REMPs as a type of ABMTs, REMPs are at the same time intended to allow for the adoption of ABMTs for specific areas in the region concerned (ISBA/24/C/3), para 5). This includes APEIs, which offer a higher level of protection than surrounding areas. The Secretary-General of the ISA has observed that the designation of APEIs helps the Authority 'to meet internationally agreed targets, such as Aichi Biodiversity Target 11' (ibid paras 5–6).

66 ISBA/24/C/3, para 8.

67 ibid.

The first REMP, for the Clarion-Clipperton Zone (CCZ) in the Pacific Ocean, was only adopted by the ISA in 2012.[68] More recently, the ISA started the process of elaborating REMPs for other regions.[69] Both for the CCZ and other areas, the ISA had already concluded exploration contracts previously. The mandate of the ISA to develop and designate REMPs is provided by Articles 145 and 162(1) of the LOSC. The latter provision empowers the Council to develop specific policies in relation to 'any question or matter within the competence of the Authority'.[70] This mandate has not been open to question, but questions do exist in relation to the status of REMPs and their relationship to the (draft) regulations for the exploitation of minerals.[71]

Prior to the decisions of the ISA Council on the environmental management plan for the CCZ, the ISA had not adopted a general framework in relation to the purposes and content of such plans. Those decisions explain the reason for adopting the plan for the CCZ in the following terms:

> *Considering* that the implementation of a comprehensive environmental management plan at the regional level is one of the measures appropriate and necessary to ensure effective protection of the marine environment of [the CCZ] from harmful effects that may arise from activities in the Area and that such a plan should include provision for the establishment of a representative network of [APEIs].[72]

In its Preliminary Strategy for the development REMPs adopted in 2017, the objective of REMPs and APEIs was further elaborated, as providing the ISA, contractors and sponsoring States:

> with a proactive area-based management tool to support informed decision-making that balances resource development with conservation. [REMPs] provide the Authority with a clear and consistent mechanism to identify particular areas thought to be representative of the full range of habitats, biodiversity and ecosystem structures and functions within

68 Decision of the Council relating to an environmental management plan for the Clarion-Clipperton Zone (ISBA/18/C/22). For a further discussion of the legal framework in relation to REMPs see ISBA/17/LTC/7 and ISBA/18/C/11.

69 See further below.

70 See eg ISBA/18/C/22, 2nd and 3rd preambular consideration.

71 For further discussion of this point see below.

72 ISBA/17/C/19, 6th preambular consideration; ISBA/18/C/22, 6th preambular consideration.

> the relevant management area, and provide those areas with appropriate levels of protection, thus helping the Authority to meet internationally agreed targets, such as Aichi Biodiversity Target 11.[73]

As their definition and objectives indicates, APEIs are similar to ABMTs as defined in the Revised Draft Agreement. REMPs seek to balance conservation and use from a mining perspective.

The starting point for the designation of APEIs in the REMP for the CCZ was a workshop that was convened in Honolulu is 2007.[74] According to Wedding and others, the workshop identified three scenarios for the designation of 9 MPAs in the CCZ.[75] This identification was done on the basis of 'guiding scientific principles developed at the workshop' while minimizing overlap with areas of contractors and reserved areas[76] and 'mitigate[ing] the potential impact of sediment plumes from deep-sea mining'.[77] Under all three proposed scenarios, the MPAs did not overlap with areas of contractors, but a number of them overlapped to a considerable extent with reserved areas.[78] The summary of the workshop provided by an LTC document does not present the three scenarios as developed by the workshop, but instead includes a figure that 'shows one of many options for location of preservation reference areas'.[79] Only one of these areas overlapped in part with reserved areas.[80]

The LTC, '[a]fter an initial review of the workshop outcomes, [amended] the locations of the proposed [APEIs] … in the light of the current distribution of contracts and reserved areas'.[81] The document concerned does not provide a further explanation in this connection. The APEIs in the REMP as elaborated

73 ISBA/24/C/3, para 5.

74 See ISBA/14/LTC/2, para 1; Lisa M Wedding and others, *From principles to practice: a spatial approach to systematic conservation planning in the deep sea* (Proceedings of the Royal Society B 2013) 3 and 8.

75 ibid 7 and figure 3.

76 Applications for exploration by (contractors sponsored by) a developed State must contain two areas that can be mined, one of which will be set aside for mining by developing States or the Enterprise, the organ of the ISA that is to carry out mining operations (see LOSC, Annex III, art 8).

77 Wedding (n 74) 7.

78 ibid figure 3.

79 ISBA/14/LTC/2, 4, figure 2. The references to MPAs, preservation reference areas and APEIs might suggest that this concerns different types of areas. However, this rather concerns an inconsistent use of terminology to refer to the same type of areas, albeit located differently geospatially. See also ISBA/17/LTC/7, para 26.

80 ISBA/14/LTC/2, 4, figure 2.

81 ISBA/17/LTC/7, 8.

by the LTC and endorsed by the Council, do not have any overlap with areas of contractors or reserved areas.[82] The decision of the Council on the location of APEIs in the REMP CCZ suggests that the contractual rights of contractors, 'in particular their security of tenure over areas allocated for exploration',[83] may have been an important consideration in this respect. Designating parts of reserved areas as APEIs, potentially closing them for future mining activities, might arguably be said as resulting in contractors not meeting their obligations in relation to reserved areas as defined in the LOSC.[84]

The REMP CCZ was initially adopted for a period of three years and was reviewed by the LTC in 2016.[85] The review, among others, notes that many of the proposed actions under the REMP remain to be implemented, that additional data in relation to the APEIs indicates that their location may not be optimal and suggests the establishment of two additional APEIs for areas that are not covered well.[86]

Following the approval of the REMP CCZ, the ISA has been considering the development of REMPs for other regions, in first instance focusing on areas covered by exploration contracts.[87] Little progress was made on this matter until the end of 2017.[88] In January 2018, the Secretary-General of the ISA presented the Preliminary Strategy for the development of regional environmental management plans for the Area.[89] On the basis of the budgetary and other constraints the Authority was facing in developing REMPs, the Strategy envisaged that work would start in relation to the 'Mid-Atlantic Ridge, the Indian Ocean triple junction ridge and nodule-bearing province, as well as the North-west Pacific and South Atlantic for seamounts'.[90] This selection was made taking into account current exploration activities in the Area.[91] Since

82 See ISBA/17/LTC/7, 17, figure II; ISBA/18/C/22, 5, figure 'Exploration areas, areas reserved for the authority and areas of particular environmental interest in the Clarion-Clipperton Fracture Zone'.

83 ISBA/18/C/22, 7th preambular consideration.

84 See LOSC, Annex III, Article 8.

85 See ISBA/22/LTC/12.

86 See ibid, paras 13 and 17–19. A 2019 workshop further considered the issues in relation to the designation of these two additional APEIs. The results of this workshop will be taken into consideration by the LTC in its future work on additional APEIs in the CCZ (see *Environmental Management Plan* available at <www.isa.org.jm/minerals/environmental-management-plan-clarion-clipperton-zone> accessed 25 July 2021.

87 See ISBA/24/C/3 para 3.

88 See ibid para 4.

89 ISBA/24/C/3. Subsequently, the development of REMPs was included in the Authority's strategic plan for the period 2019–2023 (see ISBA/24/A/10, 10, Strategic direction 3.2).

90 ISBA/24/C/3, paras 9–12.

91 ibid para 12.

January 2018 the Authority has, among others, been partnering a number of workshops for developing REMPS for specific regions.[92] The outcomes of a June 2018 Workshop relating to REMPS for polymetallic sulphide deposits on mid-ocean ridges indicates that the question of the location of APEIS in relation to contract areas and reserved areas remain a topic needing further consideration.[93] More in general, the outcomes of this workshop indicated that many of the parameters for assessing the effectiveness of REMPS remained to be developed.[94]

Although the Authority has prepared a guidance document in relation to the development of REMPS,[95] there have been criticisms that there is not a standardized approach setting out the requirements for the procedure for the development of REMPS and their content.[96] Germany, the Netherlands and Costa Rica addressed this issue in a proposal that was considered by the Council in January 2020.[97] In response, the Council requested the LTC to develop 'a standardized approach, including a template with indicative elements' in relation to the requirements for REMPS.[98] During the discussion of this matter there was considerable support for a standardized approach.[99]

Recent discussions at the ISA have also touched upon the questions whether REMPS should be mandatory and binding, and should be in place prior to the issuance of exploitation contracts.[100] Both these positions have received support, but are not generally accepted.[101] These questions also touch upon the relationship between the regulations for the exploitation of

---

92 See an overview see ISBA/25/C/3.

93 ISA Technical Study No. 22 (n 63) 22. See also ibid 12–13.

94 ibid 28.

95 *Guidance to facilitate the development of regional environmental management plans* available at <www.isa.org.jm/files/files/documents/remp_guidance_.pdf> accessed 10 March 2021.

96 See Andrew Friedman, 'Global leaders must act to protect ocean life from seabed mining impacts' The Pew Charitable Trusts (12 November 2020) available at <www.pewtrusts.org/en/research-and-analysis/articles/2020/11/12/global-leaders-must-act-to-protect-ocean-life-from-seabed-mining-impacts> accessed 10 May 2021; Harald Ginzky, Pradeep A Singh and Till Markus, 'Strengthening the International Seabed Authority's knowledge-base: Addressing uncertainties to enhance decision-making' (2020) 114 Marine Policy 103823, 9.

97 See ISBA/26/C/6 and ISBA/26/C/7.

98 See ISBA/26/C/10, para 1; ISBA/26/C/7.

99 See 25(224) Earth Negotiations Bulletin 7.

100 For a discussion of the status of REMPS and their relationship to the (draft) exploitation regulations see also ISBA/25/C/4.

101 See 25(185) Earth Negotiations Bulletin 5 and 11; 25(224) Earth Negotiations Bulletin 7 and 12.

mineral resources, which are being developed by the ISA, and REMPS.[102] The proposal of Germany, the Netherlands and Costa Rica on REMPS as a matter of fact aimed at making the proposed approach part of the draft regulations. In the debate, opposition to this approach argued that this might delay the timeline for adopting the exploitation regulations.[103] As noted above, the Council referred further consideration of the approach to REMPS to the LTC, instead of considering it further in its consideration of the draft exploitation regulations. The current draft exploitation regulations do include several references to REMPS. They are mentioned as part of the framework for providing effective protection of the marine environment in accordance with Article 145 of the LOSC.[104] Environmental impact statements to be prepared prior to mining operations are required to be '[i]n accordance with the objectives and measures of the relevant regional environmental management plan'.[105] The same condition applies to the Environmental Management and Monitoring Plan that is to be prepared prior to such activities and Closure plans.[106] These references to REMPS in the draft exploitation regulations point to the need to have a REMP in place before the planning of exploitation in a specific area starts and the need to have standardized procedures in relation to the elaboration and the need to elaborate clearly the requirements that flow from a REMP for operators.[107]

### 3.3 *The CBD and EBSAS*

As discussed in chapter 7 of this volume, the CBD has played a significant role in getting the BBNJ process on track and, as is argued in that chapter, its mandate would have allowed it to play a significant role in setting up mechanisms for international cooperation on all elements of the package on the table at the BBNJ process, including MPAS and ABMTS. As is also detailed in chapter 7, the CBD's role in relation to MPAS and ABMTS, apart from adopting Aichi Target 11, in practice has been limited mostly to developing criteria for the identification

102 See ibid.

103 See 25(224) Earth Negotiations Bulletin 12.

104 Draft regulations on exploitation of mineral resources in the Area (ISBA/25/C/WP.1), Regulation 2(e).

105 ibid Regulation 47(3)(c).

106 ibid Regulation 48(3)(b); ibid Annex VIII, para 1. A Closure Plan 'shall set out the responsibilities and actions of a Contractor for the decommissioning and closure of activities in a Mining Area' (ibid Regulation 59(1)).

107 See also Ginzky (n 96) 9.

of EBSAs and being involved in regional workshops for considering the designation of specific areas meeting these criteria as EBSAs.[108]

Identification of an area as an EBSA in itself does not give that area protected status, but provides an indication that such an area may require/should be protected by ABMTs or designation as an MPA.[109] However, EBSA status does not automatically trigger a procedure for MPA designation or the taking of protective measures.[110] Discussions during the 23rd session of the Council of the ISA in 2017 illustrate the implications of this situation. The Netherlands reportedly

> called for the Council to consider the work of other multilateral environmental agreements, including the CBD, and requested the LTC to address the issue of impacts on EBSAs in … applications for approval of work plans and extension of exploration contracts, as well as in the exploration regulations.[111]

In reply, the LTC chair pointed to the absence of binding rules in relation to EBSAs. Furthermore, Argentina reportedly voiced opposition against incorporating criteria from other international instruments in the regulatory framework of the ISA provided by the LOSC.[112]

Several factors may have contributed to the specific role of the CBD in relation to MPAs and ABMTs. Although the CBD clearly spells out the obligations of States parties in relation to the designation of MPAs, it does not provide a clear mandate of the CBD in that connection. In addition, the CBD mandate does not directly allow regulating activities taking place in the marine environment, for which other instruments and bodies have primary responsibility. On the other hand, the CBD's role in relation to EBSAs is much more easily justified under its mandate and its role in the generation and dissemination of knowledge in relation to BBNJ.[113]

---

108 For a further discussion of the EBSA process see eg Daniel C Dunn and others, 'The Convention on Biological Diversity's Ecologically or Biologically Significant Areas: Origins, development, and current status' (2014) 49 Marine Policy 137.

109 See also Sarah M Watson, *Sustainable Development Goal 14's Marine Protected Area Target—Is it 'SMART' Enough to Conserve Marine Biodiversity in Areas Beyond National Jurisdiction?* 20–21, available at <https://globalgoalsproject.eu/globalgoals2020/wp-content/uploads/2020/06/GlobalGoals2020_Watson.pdf> accessed 28 April 2021.

110 A detailed discussion of the (possible) legal implications of the designation of an area as and EBSA is beyond the scope of this chapter.

111 25(151) Earth Negotiations Bulletin 7.

112 ibid.

113 See CBD arts 23(4)(b) and 25.

### 3.4 *Regional Practice of the OSPAR Convention and the OSPAR Commission and the CAMLR Convention and CCAMLR*[114]

#### 3.4.1 The OSPAR Convention and the OSPAR Commission[115]

The spatial scope of application of the OSPAR Convention is the North-East Atlantic and includes extensive areas of ABNJ.[116] In this connection, Article 1(a) provides that the Maritime Area includes 'the sea beyond and adjacent to the territorial sea under the jurisdiction of the coastal state to *the extent recognised by international law*'.[117] In 1998, the Contracting Parties to the OSPAR Convention concluded Annex V to the Convention concerned with biodiversity.[118] Annex V requires the Contracting Parties to 'develop means, *consistent with international law,* for instituting protective, conservation, restorative or precautionary measures related to specific areas or sites or related to particular species or habitats'.[119] Annex V also provides that it is intended to implement the obligations of the States parties under the CBD. In this connection, Annex V does not refer explicitly to Article 8 of the CBD dealing with MPAs.[120] However, the Annex's reference to the obligations under Article 6(a) of the CBD implies a cross-reference to Article 8.

During the BBNJ process, some concern has been expressed as regards the propriety of the OSPAR Commission designating MPAs in the high seas:

> the view was expressed that the OSPAR Convention and other regional seas conventions did not have the competence under the United Nations Convention on the Law of the Sea, nor the legitimacy, to take measures in

---

114 For a discussion of the experience of these regions in dealing with MPAs in ABNJ see also eg Wen Duan, 'The International Legal Regime Relating to Marine Protected Areas in Areas Beyond National Jurisdiction: Identifying and Addressing Gaps' (PhD Manuscript, Utrecht University 2021) 64–95 and 176–206; Nele Matz-Lück and Johannes Fuchs, 'The impact of OSPAR on protected area management beyond national jurisdiction: Effective regional cooperation or a network of paper parks?' (2014) 49 Marine Policy 155; Wright and others (n 15) 279–83.

115 The discussion of OSPAR in part is based on Alex G Oude Elferink, 'Coastal States and MPAs in ABNJ: Ensuring Consistency with the LOSC' (2018) International Journal of Marine & Coastal Law 437, 457–60.

116 OSPAR Convention art 1(a).

117 Emphasis added.

118 Annex V on the Protection and Conservation of the Ecosystems and Biological Diversity of the Maritime Area (opened for signature 23 July 1998; entered into force 30 August 2000) available at <www.ospar.org/site/assets/files/1290/ospar_convention_e_updated_text_in_2007_no_revs.pdf> accessed 25 July 2021.

119 ibid art 3(1)(b)(ii) (emphasis added).

120 ibid art 2. CBD art 6(a) refers to the 'measures set out in this Convention relevant to the Contracting Party concerned', which in this case includes the measures listed in art 8.

areas beyond national jurisdiction such as the establishment of marine protected areas.[121]

Although Article 197 of the LOSC in combination with Article 194(5) arguably offers a basis for the establishment of MPAs[122] and, as discussed in the preceding paragraph, OSPAR States parties rely on international law to justify their actions, this statement points to the existence of different views in this regard.

Following the adoption of Annex V, the OSPAR Contracting Parties have worked towards the designation of a network of MPAs in their maritime zones and in ABNJ of the Maritime Area. Two OSPAR documents from 2003 set up a framework for the designation of MPAs. This concerned OSPAR Recommendation 2003/3 on a Network of Marine Protected Areas[123] and the 2003 Strategies of the OSPAR Commission for the Protection of the Marine Environment of the North-East Atlantic.[124] Any Contracting Party may take the initiative to make a proposal to the OSPAR Commission to include MPAs in ABNJ in the OSPAR Network.[125] In practice, Contracting Parties have collaborated with NGOs in preparing proposals for MPAs in ABNJ.[126] Recommendation 2003/3, like Annex V, provides that the establishment of MPAs has to be consistent with international law, and adds that it has to be based on scientific information.[127] The Guidelines for the Identification and Selection of Marine Protected Areas in the OSPAR Maritime Area contained in OSPAR Agreement

121 Intersessional workshops aimed at improving understanding of the issues and clarifying key questions as an input to the work of the Working Group in accordance with the terms of reference annexed to General Assembly Res 67/78; Summary of proceedings prepared by the Co-Chairs of the Working Group (UN Doc A/AC.276/6), para 89. Similar concerns have been expressed by Ukraine in CCAMLR see Wright and others (n 15) 281.

122 Also see above. The 2010 OSPAR Strategy also refers to LOSC art 197 as the basis for cooperation on the protection of the marine environment, including that in ABNJ and submits that to achieve its objectives, OSPAR may designate MPAs in ABNJ (The North-East Atlantic Environment Strategy. OSPAR Agreement 2010–3, paras 1.1, 3.1 and 4.4 available at <www.ospar.org/site/assets/files/1200/ospar_strategy.pdf> accessed 25 July 2021.

123 OSPAR Recommendation 2003/3 on a Network of Marine Protected Areas (Summary Record OSPAR 2003; OSPAR 03/17/1-E, Annex 9).

124 2003 Strategies of the OSPAR Commission for the Protection of the Marine Environment of the North-East Atlantic (Summary Record OSPAR 03/17/1-E, Annex 31).

125 See ibid paras 2.4-2.9, which contain the relevant amendments.

126 See eg, Sabine Christiansen, 'Marine Protected Areas in areas beyond national jurisdiction; Proposed High Seas MPAs in the North East Atlantic by WWF 1998–2006' WWF NEAME (August 2007) available at <www.cbd.int/doc/meetings/mar/ewsebm-01/other/ewsebm-01-wwf-en.pdf> accessed 22 March 2021.

127 OSPAR Recommendation 2003/3 on a Network of Marine Protected Areas, 5th preambular consideration available at <www.ospar.org/documents?d=32867> accessed 11 May 2021.

2003/17 as amended in 2007 indicate that the criteria for selection as an MPA should be considered and assessed 'based on best available scientific expertise and knowledge'.[128]

The OSPAR Commission has thus far included seven MPAs in ABNJ within the OSPAR Network.[129] Two of the MPAs designated by the OSPAR Commission in 2010 (Charlie-Gibbs South Marine Protected Area; Milne Seamount Complex Marine Protected Area) comprise the water column and seabed, which are both part of ABNJ. The other four areas designated in 2010 only concern the high seas water column superjacent to the continental shelf beyond 200 nautical miles of Portugal. All six decisions provide that they 'shall apply without prejudice to the rights and obligations of coastal States, other States and international organisations in accordance with [the LOSC] and customary international law'.[130]

In addition, the Preamble of all six decisions recognizes that they do not prejudice the rights of coastal States over their continental shelf.[131] In the case of the MPAs superjacent to the Portuguese continental shelf, the Preamble adds that the procedure for designation is not intended to set a precedent for such MPAs and that future designations 'will be decided on a case by case basis'.[132] The general safeguarding clause of the 2012 decision on the Charlie-Gibbs North High Seas MPA, which covers waters superjacent to the continental shelf of Iceland, is identical to that of the six 2010 decisions.[133] The rights of the coastal State are in addition safeguarded in more specific terms in the

---

128 Guidelines for the Identification and Selection of Marine Protected Areas in the OSPAR Maritime Area contained in OSPAR Agreement 2003/17 as amended in 2007, Appendix 1 available at <www.ospar.org/documents?d=32398> accessed 25 July 2021. The Guidelines are incorporated in Recommendation 2003/3 by cross-references in OSPAR Recommendation 2003/3 (n 123) paras 1.1 and 3.1.

129 OSPAR Decision 2010/2 on the establishment of the Charlie-Gibbs South Marine Protected Area (OSPAR 10/23/1-E, Annex 36); OSPAR Decision 2010/1 on the Establishment of the Milne Seamount Complex Marine Protected Area (ibid Annex 34); OSPAR Decision 2010/3 on the Establishment of the Altair Seamount High Seas Marine Protected Area (ibid Annex 38); OSPAR Decision 2010/4 on the Establishment of the Antialtair Seamount High Seas Marine Protected Area (ibid Annex 40); OSPAR Decision 2010/5 on the Establishment of the Josephine Seamount High Seas Marine Protected Area (ibid Annex 42); OSPAR Decision 2010/6 on the Establishment of the MAR North of the Azores High Seas Marine Protected Area (ibid Annex 44); OSPAR Decision 2012/1 on the establishment of the Charlie-Gibbs North High Seas Marine Protected Area (OSPAR 12/22/1, Annex 6).

130 OSPAR Decisions 2010/1 and 2010/2 (ibid) para 2.2; OSPAR Decisions 2010/3 to 2010/6 (n 129) para 2.3.

131 OSPAR Decisions 2010/1 to 2010/6 (n 129) preamble.

132 OSPAR Decisions 2010/3 to 2010/6 (n 129) preamble.

133 OSPAR Decision 2012/1 (n 129) para 2.3.

body of the decision.[134] The preambular considerations of the 2012 decision are more elaborate on the point of the rights of the coastal State and other States than the 2010 decisions, but essentially confirm that the rights of the coastal State over its continental shelf and other States in the superjacent waters are defined in the LOSC.[135] The difference in wording between the 2010 and 2012 decisions is likely explained by the differences in approach of the coastal States concerned. Portugal has designated the parts of its continental shelf overlain by the water column concerned as MPAS, but Iceland has not.[136]

A proposal to the OSPAR Commission to designate an MPA in ABNJ in the part of the Maritime Area in the Arctic Ocean, identified as the OSPAR Arctic Ice High Seas MPA, failed, due to the opposition of Denmark, Iceland and Norway, who are both members the OSPAR Commission and the Arctic Council. During an OSPAR Commission Heads of Delegation meeting, the contracting parties agreed to not further consider the proposal for designation, but instead to refer it to the Arctic Council for information.[137] This implied the proposal likely would be shelved.[138] The Arctic Council does not have the required competence to designate MPAS in ABNJ and it seems excluded that it would have referred the matter back to the OSPAR Commission.[139]

At the 2016 meeting of the OSPAR Commission following the Heads of Delegation meeting, the issue was further discussed. Contracting parties disagreed about whether an MPA designation was the right means to protect the area concerned.[140] Denmark, Iceland and Norway justified their position by pointing out that all relevant Arctic Ocean coastal States had to be involved, including the US, Canada and the Russian Federation,[141] which are not

134 ibid para 2.2.

135 ibid preamble.

136 For a further consideration of this point see Matz-Lück and Fuchs (n 114) 161–62.

137 Meeting of the OSPAR Commission (OSPAR); Tenerife: 20–24 June 2016; Summary Record; Agenda Item 20 (OSPAR 16/20/1-E) para 6.24.

138 In this context, it should be noted that the PAME Workgroup of the Arctic Council had prepared the *Framework for a Pan-Arctic Network of Marine Protected Areas* in April of 2015 available at <https://pame.is/images/03_Projects/MPA/MPA_Report.pdf> accessed 22 April 2021. Although the framework recognizes linkages to ABNJ, its focus is on MPA networks within the EEZS of the Arctic States (ibid 5 and 11).

139 An enquiry of the author with the Arctic Council Secretariat (emails of 22 April 2021 and 10 May 2021; on file with the author) concerning whether the Arctic Council took any follow-up action upon receiving the information forwarded by the OSPAR Commission did not lead to a reaction from the secretariat.

140 Summary Record (n 137) para 6.27.

141 This position is in line with the claim of the Arctic States concerning their shared stewardship role in relation to the Arctic Ocean including its ABNJ as reflected in the Ilulissat Declaration (adopted 28 May 2008) at the Arctic Ocean Conference, available at

contracting parties to the OSPAR Convention. In this connection, Article 76 of the LOSC was also invoked.[142] In case the submissions of the coastal States to the Commission on the Limits of the Continental Shelf (CLCS) under Article 76(8) will be accepted, most of the seabed of the central Arctic Ocean beyond 200 nautical miles will be part of the continental shelf of the coastal States. Moreover, it was submitted that 'Arctic marine ecosystems [had to be assessed] in a coherent manner'. For these reasons the Arctic Council should take the lead in considering this issue.[143] Whether these arguments are fully convincing is open to doubt. First, as discussed above, OSPAR practice in designating MPAS in ABNJ has been careful in safeguarding the rights of coastal States over their continental shelf. These safeguarding clauses were acceptable to all OSPAR contracting parties, including Denmark, Iceland and Norway, which all had an interest in this matter.[144] Second, whether the designation of an area that meets the criteria for MPA designation by the OSPAR Commission threatens a coherent approach to Arctic ecosystems is questionable.[145] Other States disagreed that the Arctic Council should be given primacy, pointing to the clear mandate of the OSPAR Commission for the whole Maritime Area, including in the Arctic Ocean.[146] Denmark, Iceland and Norway indicated that they could not agree to reopening the issue at future OSPAR Convention meetings.[147] Reportedly, Norway even threatened to withdraw from the OSPAR Convention.[148]

The OSPAR Commission does not have the competence to comprehensively regulate activities in the MPAS in ABNJ it has designated. For instance, fisheries are regulated by the relevant RFMOS, in particular NEAFC, and the regulation of mining at the international level is the exclusive competence of the ISA. To ensure a comprehensive approach to the management of OSPAR MPAS in ABNJ, the OSPAR Commission has sought to establish cooperation

---

<www.regjeringen.no/globalassets/upload/ud/080525_arctic_ocean_conference-_outcome.pdf> accessed 10 April 2021.

142 Summary Record (n 137) para 6.27.

143 ibid.

144 Denmark, Iceland and Norway have made submissions to the CLCS in relation to their continental shelf in the Maritime Area, and, as was discussed above, one of the previous MPA designations by the OSPAR Commission, the Charlie-Gibbs North High Seas MPA, is superjacent to the Icelandic continental shelf.

145 The *Framework for a Pan-Arctic Network of Marine Protected Areas* prepared by the PAME Workgroup of the Arctic Council suggests that the Council at the time also may not have had a comprehensive approach (see further above n 138).

146 Summary Record (n 137) para 6.27.

147 ibid para 6.30.

148 See Robin des Bois, *OSPAR loses the Arctic* (22 March 2017) available at <https://robindesbois.org/en/ospar-perd-le-nord-5/> accessed 11 March 2021.

with other relevant international instruments and organizations.[149] After a detailed analysis of the existing bilateral arrangements, Duan concludes that they in general remain 'to be operationalised by further concrete joint working arrangements'.[150] This conclusion does not apply to the so-called Collective Arrangement, which the OSPAR Commission and NEAFC concluded in 2014.[151] The Collective Arrangement is intended to achieve cooperation between all competent international institutions and instruments that have the competence to regulate human activities in the North-East Atlantic. The Collective Arrangement was one of the results of the aspiration of the OSPAR Commission and NEAFC to reach policy coherence. Although NEAFC and the OSPAR Commission have sought to include other institutions and instruments in the Collective Arrangement since 2010, they remain the only two participants to date.[152]

### 3.4.2 The CAMLR Convention and CCAMLR

The spatial scope of the CAMLR Convention consists of Antarctic waters up to the Antarctic Convergence as defined by the Convention.[153] Due to the existence of the Antarctic Treaty and its 'freezing' of claims to territory in the Antarctic continent,[154] most waters included in the spatial scope of application of the CAMLR Convention in practice are treated as high seas. CCAMLR has been set up as the main regulatory body under the Convention. There has been debate over the nature of the Convention and the Commission, ie, whether it is an RFMO or something different, eg a regional seas program.[155] Molenaar argues in detail that the Commission is best classified as the former, mainly because its mandate is mostly limited to fisheries and fisheries-related

149 For a detailed overview see Duan (n 114) 176–96.

150 ibid 217.

151 Collective Arrangement between competent international organisations on cooperation and coordination regarding selected areas in areas beyond national jurisdiction in the North-East Atlantic. An updated version of the Collective Arrangement is available at <www.ospar.org/documents?v=33030> accessed 15 March 2021); for a further discussion see Duan (n 114) 186–89.

152 *Collective Arrangement* available at <www.ospar.org/about/international-cooperation/collective-arrangement> accessed 15 March 2021.

153 CAMLR Convention arts I(1) and I(4).

154 Antarctic Treaty (adopted on 1 December 1959, entered into force 23 June 1961) 402 UNTS 71, art IV. CAMLR Convention art IV reaffirms the obligations that parties to the Antarctic Treaty have undertaken under Antarctic Treaty art IV.

155 Erik Molenaar, 'Regional Fisheries Management Organizations' in Marta Chantal Ribeiro, Fernando Loureiro Bastos and Tore Henriksen (eds.), *Global Challenges and the Law of the Sea* (Springer 2020) 81–109, 93.

activities.[156] At the same time, contrary to other RFMOs, States do not have to engage in fishing in the Convention Area to be members of CCAMLR and the objective of the CAMLR Convention is phrased more broadly than that of 'typical' RFMOs, as being, as per Article II of the Convention, 'the conservation of Antarctic marine living resources', with the term 'conservation' including rational use.[157]

The somewhat atypical nature of CCAMLR as compared to other RFMOs is also reflected in its approach to ABMTs and MPAs. While other RFMOs have focused on ABMTs to regulate the impact of fishing activities on the marine environment,[158] CCAMLR has set up a process for establishing MPAs and a number of MPAs in the CAMLR Convention Area have been established. As the *General framework for the establishment of CCAMLR Marine Protected Areas* (General framework), which was adopted in 2011, indicates:

> CCAMLR MPAs aim to contribute to sustaining ecosystem structure and function, including in areas outside the MPAs, maintain the ability to adapt in the face of climate change, and reduce the potential for invasion by alien species, as a result of human activity.[159]

The General framework indicates that the basis for the Commission's mandate to adopt measures establishing MPAs is Article IX(2)(g) of the Convention, which provides that measures may include measures concerning 'the designation of the opening and closing of areas, regions or sub-regions for purposes of

---

156 ibid 96ff. Molenaar also submits that CCAMLR is 'more than an RFMO'. However, that conclusion is not based on its subject-matter competence, but its being a part of the Antarctic Treaty System (see ibid 96). As is observed by Rayfuse, 'while CCAMLR may be something more than a *normal* RFMO, it functions as at least a *normal* RFMO' (Rosemary Rayfuse, 'Regional Fisheries Management Organizations' in Donald R Rothwell and others (eds.), *The Oxford Handbook of the Law of the Sea* (Oxford University Press 2015) 450 (emphasis in the original).

157 Molenaar, 'Regional Fisheries Management Organizations' (n 155) 92–93.

158 See eg, NEAFC Recommendation 19:2014 on area management measures for the protection of vulnerable marine ecosystems in the NEAFC Regulatory Area, as amended, available at <www.neafc.org/system/files/Recommendation-19-2014-VME-protection-as-amended-by-%20Rec-09-2015-Rec-10-2018-Rec-10-2021.pdf> accessed 16 March 2021; SEAFO Conservation Measure 30/15 on Bottom Fishing Activities and Vulnerable Marine Ecosystems in the SEAFO Convention Area, available at <www.seafo.org/media/8933d489-854c-4c99-895e-66573c7010a4/SEAFOweb/CM/open/eng/CM30-15_pdf> accessed 16 March 2021.

159 Conservation measure 91-04 (2011); General framework for the establishment of CCAMLR Marine Protected Areas, 6th preambular consideration; see also ibid 1st preambular consideration and para 2.

scientific study or conservation, including special areas for protection and scientific study'.[160] The General framework also refers to Article II of the CAMLR Convention, explicitly recalling that 'conservation includes rational use'.[161] Conservation measures of the Commission relevant to MPAs 'shall be adopted and implemented consistent with international law, including as reflected in the [LOSC] … [and] shall be established on the basis of the best available scientific evidence'.[162] Unlike Annex V to the OSPAR Convention, the General framework does not refer to the obligations of the member States of CCAMLR under the CBD.[163] However, it does refer to 'the aim of conserving marine biodiversity in the Convention Area' and 'the decision at the [WSSD] in 2002 to achieve a representative network of MPAs by 2012'.[164]

Notwithstanding the agreement of the members of CCAMLR on the General framework, the discussions on the adoption of conservation measures establishing specific MPAs in most cases have been arduous and time-consuming.[165] This is mostly explained by the existence of different perspectives on the right balance between fishing and conservation, while conservation measures can only be adopted by consensus.[166] It might be argued that the opposition between conservationist and fishing interests is included in the General framework itself by its reconfirmation of the inclusion of rational use as part of conservation under Article II of the Convention. Although that reference recalls the general objectives of the Convention, in the framework of a measure setting out the procedure for establishing MPAs it seems somewhat out of place. The reference to rational use is included in the chapeau of the list of objectives in relation to MPAs to be established by CCAMLR.[167] That reference could be used by fishing interests to argue that rational use is one of the main objectives in managing MPAs. At the same time, the other objectives listed by the General

160 ibid 2nd preambular consideration.

161 ibid para 2.

162 ibid paras 1–2.

163 This might be explained by the fact that not all members to the Commission are parties to the CBD.

164 ibid 1st preambular consideration.

165 See further Cassandra Brooks, 'Why are talks over an East Antarctic marine park still deadlocked?' The Conversation (3 November 2017) available at <https://theconversation.com/why-are-talks-over-an-east-antarctic-marine-park-still-deadlocked-86681> accessed 29 April 2021; Klaus Dodds and Cassandra Brooks, 'Antarctic Geopolitics and the Ross Sea Marine Protected Area' E-International Relations (20 February 2018) available at <www.e-ir.info/2018/02/20/antarctic-geopolitics-and-the-ross-sea-marine-protected-area/> accessed 10 March 2021.

166 CAMLR Convention art XII(1).

167 Conservation measure 91-04 (n 159) para 2.

framework have a clear focus on the protection and preservation of biodiversity, habitats and ecosystems.[168]

Proposals for MPAs to CCAMLR in general have been made by States having an interest in conservation, while all Antarctic claimant States have been involved in one or more proposals. States with fishing interests opposed (certain aspects of) these proposals.[169] In the case of the Ross Sea MPA, which currently is the largest MPA in the world and which was adopted in 2016,[170] the consideration of the proposal by CCAMLR led to a gradual diminution of the spatial extent of the MPA and the inclusion of a Special Research Zone and a Krill Research Zone.[171] In both these zones members of the Commission are allowed to fish for Antarctic krill and in the Special Research Zone for *Dissostichus* spp. (toothfish) under the conditions set out in conservation measure 95-01 (2016).[172]

At the 2020 meeting of CCAMLR three proposals for MPAs were on the table, for the Antarctic Peninsula (Domain I), the Weddell Sea and East Antarctica. No decision was taken at the meeting and the proposals will be further considered during the next meeting of CCAMLR, which is scheduled to take place in October of 2021.[173] The proposal for the East Antarctic MPA has been under consideration since 2012. As originally proposed, the MPA would have covered 1.8 square million kilometers and included a network of seven areas. At present, the proposed MPA has an extent of some 1 million square kilometers and includes three separate areas.[174] The main opponents of the establishment of these three MPAs in their current form are the Russian Federation and China. Both have relied on the Convention's inclusion of rational use in conservation in the General framework's objective.[175] In that connection, China has also

---

168 ibid.

169 See Dodds and Brooks (n 165).

170 Conservation measure 91-05 (2016), Ross Sea region marine protected area.

171 The revised joint proposal New Zealand and the US submitted in 2012 covered an area of about 2.27 million km$^2$ (see Report of the Thirty-First Meeting of the Commission (CCAMLR-XXXI) para 7.70). The Ross Sea MPA as designated covers 1.55 million km$^2$ (*Ross Sea region Marine Protected Area* available at <www.doc.govt.nz/about-us/international-agreements/antarctica-treaty-system/ross-sea-region-marine-protected-area/> accessed 22 March 2021).

172 Conservation measure 91-05 (n 170) paras 5–9 and 11.

173 For the discussion on the proposals at the 39th meeting of the Commission see Report of the Thirty-Ninth Meeting of the Commission (CCAMLR-39) paras 8.19–8.44; see also ibid paras 8.16–8.18.

174 See Brooks (n 165).

175 See CCAMLR-39 (n 172) paras 8.29 and 8.31; Report of the Thirty-Eighth Meeting of the Commission (CCAMLR-38) para 6.56.

referred to the fact that 'MPAs are tools and not objectives in their own'.[176] Both the Russian Federation and China have also observed that further scientific data was required to justify the establishment of the additional MPAs.[177] Proponents of the MPA proposals during the 39th meeting of the Commission reiterated that they were based on the best available science.[178] France in relation to the East Antarctic MPA recalled that CCAMLR's Scientific Committee both in 2011 and 2013 had concluded that it was based on the best available science.[179] China and the Russian Federation have also argued that MPAS should not be established in haste, but that more fundamental issues should be considered first.[180] The Russian Federation in that connection proposed 'to develop an agreed definition of the term "MPA", which may be designated in the CAMLR Convention Area, without prejudice to the [LOSC]'.[181] It may be questioned whether these suggestions are genuinely intended to help moving the debate forward or are intended to stall a decision on the specific MPA proposals. Taking into account that the protection of species, habitats and ecosystems was already included in the LOSC and the original target for a representative network of MPAs covering 10% of the ocean was 2012, it is difficult to argue that the international community has been acting in haste, not having met that target in 2020. Requiring more science in relation to a proposal that is based on the best available science also does not accord with existing legal

176 See CCAMLR-38 (ibid) para 6.56. See also CCAMLR-39 (n 173) para 8.31. It may be noted that this latter statement seems to be, or rather is, backtracking on the consensus expressed in Conservation measure 91-04 (2011) to the effect that:

> Recalling its endorsement of the work program of the Scientific Committee to develop a representative system of Antarctic Marine Protected Areas (MPAs) with the aim of conserving marine biodiversity in the Convention Area, and in accordance with the decision at the World Summit on Sustainable Development (WSSD) in 2002 to achieve a representative network of MPAs by 2012 (Conservation measure 91-04, note 159 at 1st preambular paragraph).

177 See eg CCAMLR-38 (n 175) para 6.43; CCAMLR-39 (n 173) para 8.29.

178 See ibid paras 8.21–8.22, 8.25–8.27.

179 ibid para 8.27.

180 See CCAMLR-38 (n 175) para 6.56; CCAMLR-39 (n 173) para 8.29. As observed by China:

> Many practical and policy issues associated with establishing MPAs necessitate a pace allowing a well weighted pragmatic approach to decision-making, with a hasty approach may be detrimental to the purpose. CCAMLR's leading role should be represented by the quality of the MPAs designated, in order to give effect to the objective and principles of the Convention, rather than the speed, number and size of MPAs. In the 10th anniversary of our first MPA, we strongly feel that it is the right time for all CCAMLR Members to take stock, to draw experience and lessons from our past practice, and to build common ground to facilitate future progress.

181 CCAMLR-39 (n 173) para 8.29.

and political commitments. It is also difficult to grasp why there is a need for an agreed definition of MPAs in the context of the CAMLR Convention at this point in time. CCAMLR has developed a comprehensive framework for establishing and managing MPAs without such a definition. Moreover, a definition of MPAs is likely to be included in the BBNJ Agreement , raising the question why CCAMLR would need to duplicate the work of the IGC.

## 4 Discussion and Assessment

As the title of this chapter asks, is the glass half empty or half full as concerns the protection of the marine environment in ABNJ through MPAs and ABMTs? One could well argue that the legal framework for the establishment and management of MPAs and ABMTs and practice in relation to the same have shown a remarkable development since the adoption of the LOSC in 1982. This applies not only to AWNJ, but also to ABNJ. The LOSC provides the basis for ABMTs in relation to specific activities, and impliedly provides for the establishment of MPAs. One could further argue that the BBNJ process is likely on the way to adopting an implementation agreement to the LOSC that will provide detailed rules for the identification, designation/adoption and management of ABMTs and MPAs. Global and regional organizations have been adopting ABMTs for specific activities. In particular, the OSPAR Commission and CCAMLR have established a number of MPAs in ABNJ and are acquiring experience with managing these areas in cooperation with other relevant instruments, bodies and frameworks. That experience that may assist other regions in developing similar initiatives in ABNJ.

On the other hand, it could equally well be argued that the development of a legal framework for MPAs and ABMTs has been excruciatingly slow, has known considerable setbacks and may never meet the targets that are required to effectively protect and preserve marine ecosystems and biodiversity. To start with a bird's eye perspective, according to the International Union for Conservation of Nature (IUCN):

> MPAs ... currently cover about 6.35% of the ocean. However only just over 1.89% of that area is covered by exclusively no-take MPAs that do not allow any fishing, mining, drilling, or other extractive activities. This is far from the commitments of States made in relation to the Convention on Biological Diversity's (CBD) Aichi Target 11 of 10% MPA coverage by 2020, and even further from the recommendations made at the IUCN World

> Parks Congress 2014 that at least 30% no-take MPA coverage worldwide is needed.[182]

As the analysis in section 2 indicates, there arguably has been a shift away from MPAs towards ABMTs at the conceptual level. While the CBD and the political commitments at the 2002 WSSD could be said to have emphasized the significance of MPAs, MPAs seemingly are a subset of ABMTs in the Revised Draft Agreement. Although it could be argued that neither the CBD nor the WSSD commitments implied an exclusive focus on MPAs, it is submitted that this shift is not without importance. ABMTs, being tools to manage activities, imply a focus on (optimizing) use, while MPAs, being areas that require protection, imply a focus on conservation, without necessarily having to accommodate current or future use.[183] Formulated somewhat differently, ABMTs can be characterized as 'free-standing', ie, they have a specific activity as their object, without looking holistically at the state of the environment, while MPAs require the consideration of a set of measures that are needed to achieve a certain state of the environment.

The discussion of practice in relation to MPAs and ABMTs in section 3 illustrates some of the reasons why the international community has failed to meet Aichi Target 11. Preliminarily, it may be noted that apart from the examples discussed in that section, regional cooperation on the preservation and protection of the marine environment is mostly limited to AWNJ. The regional EBSA workshops co-organized by the CBD Secretariat have led to the identification of EBSAs in ABNJ in many regions, but that identification for the moment has received limited follow-up actions.[184] As the above discussion in relation to EBSAs indicates, that may at least in part be due to the status of the EBSA process, ie the absence of specific obligations that flow from EBSA status of an area in terms of regulating activities or MPA designation. The existing regional practice identifies a number of factors that have contributed to the slow progress in

---

182 IUCN Issues Brief *Marine protected areas and climate change* available at <www.iucn.org/resources/issues-briefs/marine-protected-areas-and-climate-change> accessed 17 March 2021. See also Resolution WCC-2016-Res-047-EN Advancing conservation and sustainable use of biological diversity in areas beyond national jurisdiction adopted at the 2016 IUCN World Conservation Congress (*IUCN Resolutions, Recommendations and other Decisions World Conservation Congress; Honolulu, Hawai'i, United States of America6–10 September 2016*, 112–13). For a further discussion of the significance of the 30% no-take MPA coverage in relation to MPAs in ABNJ see below n 191.

183 See also above text at n 38.

184 See also Dunn and others (n 108) 42.

establishing MPAs as opposed to ABMTs. These factors will be further discussed in revisiting the central themes of the current volume.

As the introductory chapter to this volume indicates, these four themes that frame the project are justice, space, knowledge and power. Justice, understood in terms of access and utilization of marine resources, both in terms of intra- and intergeneration equity, is obviously central to the issue of MPAs and ABMTs. In the context of ABMTs and in particular (no-take) MPAs, it is also, or even rather, an issue of denying access. Denying access to current activities will contribute to the conservation of ecosystems, habitats and biodiversity and safeguarding and rebuilding a healthy ocean for future generations. As the current discussion indicates, the balance seemingly is weighed against future generations and maintaining the ocean for future sustainable use. For instance, both the practice in the ISA and CCAMLR indicate how user interests impact significantly on the selection and designation of ABMTs/MPAs. Giving a meaningful voice to future generations, or, as is apparent from the discussion in chapter 6 of this volume, the ocean, remains a task that the power structure in which current international law operates makes difficult if not impossible to address. Even in the presence of political commitments of the international community to take action on MPAs and ABMTs, albeit falling short of what may be actually needed to effectively conserve BBNJ, implementation remains haphazard due to interests at play and the decision-making structures.

MPAs and ABMTs, being spatial instruments, are intrinsic to the theme of space. As already mentioned, how ocean space is currently used or may be used is an important factor in shaping the process of identifying, designating and managing MPAs and ABMTs. At a more fundamental level, the spatial division of the ocean in AWNJ and ABNJ is a critical factor in the developing regime for MPAs and ABMTs. On the one hand, coastal States are seeking to safeguard their perceived rights and interests by getting a say on MPAs and ABMTs in ABNJ as coastal States. The practice in the OSPAR Convention, both as regards the designation of MPAs in the OSPAR Maritime Area in the North East Atlantic, and the failure to designate an MPA in the OSPAR Maritime Area in the Arctic Ocean, attest to how coastal States may weigh in in practice. Perhaps one could say that the proposal for an MPA in the Arctic Ocean was bound to fail due to the geopolitical considerations that seemingly inspired Denmark, Iceland and Norway, but one may at the same time pose the question how their approach relates to their legal commitments under the OSPAR Convention. On the other hand, ABNJ remain characterized by a decentralized and mostly sectoral approach. As is apparent from the practice of the ISA and RFMOs, this is less of a problem in relation to ABMTs applying to specific activities. Such sectoral mandates are already clearly defined in positive law. The establishment of MPAs by regional bodies, with a limited mandate, may be objected against by raising questions of legitimacy and requires setting up cooperation with other bodies and instruments having relevant regulatory competence and securing the cooperation of relevant third States.[185] The future BBNJ Agreement may contribute to resolving both of these issues by providing a further legal basis for a holistic approach to the conservation and use of ABNJ and requiring States parties to coordinate their actions across the sectoral and regional instruments in which they are participating.

Knowledge has been recognized as being central to the identification, establishment and management of MPAs and ABMTs. This makes it critical to establish what information is required, who is responsible for gathering it, and how it will be disseminated.[186] These questions are all the more relevant because much of the information concerned is being gathered in the execution of activities. The current legal framework provides that decisions are taken on the basis of the best available science. Moreover, the precautionary approach is relevant to regulating activities in the absence of sufficient scientific data concerning harmful impacts. Notwithstanding these general parameters, the discussion of CCAMLR shows that certain States have been attempting to defer decisions from being taken while justifying this by the absence of sufficient scientific data. Although urging for additional scientific data might seem to be laudable, it is difficult to square with the applicable legal framework. In light of the challenges to building a knowledge base for ABNJ, this approach likely will make the realization of the political commitments in relation to MPAs and ABMTs, which, it should be realized, not only includes a commitment to give a specific percentage of the ocean protected status, but also identifies qualitative objectives, a moving target. The building of an additional knowledge base in many cases likely will go hand in hand with new activities, which will lead to generating further vested interests that may block the adoption of protective measures.

The current chapter allows to identify a number of angles to the theme of power in relation to the issue of MPAs and ABMTs in ABNJ. First of all, while in AWNJ this issue is primarily the competence of individual coastal States, in ABNJ a variety of instruments and bodies deals with MPAs and ABMTs. As regards the competence of these instruments and bodies, a divide exists between ABMTs and MPAs. Although the LOSC does not explicitly refer to ABMTs, the

185 As is discussed in section 3.4, both Annex V to the OSPAR Convention and the General framework of the CCAMLR refer to relevant global instruments that can be said to justify the establishment of MPAs, including in ABNJ.

186 See also the discussion in Morgera (ch 9) in this volume.

general competence of the sectoral bodies concerned, such as RFMOs and the ISA, comprises the competence to adopt ABMTs. The LOSC does not create a similar competence to identify, designate and manage MPAs.[187] In that sense, the division of decision-making power under the LOSC made the development of a comprehensive approach to the protection and the preservation of the marine environment in particular in ABNJ problematic.[188] The CBD, although providing a possible framework for such a comprehensive approach, was not given a clear mandate to deal with this matter, and as a matter of fact accepts the jurisdictional framework set out in the LOSC,[189] and as the discussion in chapter 7 of this volume details, the international community preferred to further address this issue in the framework of the law of the sea and the United Nations General Assembly, while the CBD in relation to MPAs made a more limited contribution through its practice in relation to EBSAs. Whether the BBNJ Agreement will be successful in addressing the absence of a competence to holistically manage MPAs remains to be seen, but the requirement of consistency with the LOSC and the apparent deferral to existing bodies and instruments through the 'not-undermining' requirement does not bode well. As discussed above, different options to deal with the relationship between MPAs and ABMTs have been tabled and the final choice in that respect may impact on the urgency that will be accorded to working towards a coherent network of MPAs. Similar considerations apply to the other provisions of the Revised Draft Agreement, which were discussed above, that will be relevant to defining the process for designating and managing MPAs.

As the practice of the ISA indicates, although the existence of a broad mandate allows the adoption of ABMTs, making use of this mandate in practice is not a given, suggesting the need for more detailed regulation at the outset. The ISA adopted a first REMP, for the CCZ in 2012, well after the initial phase of mining operations in this area. Mining interests impacted on the initial selection of APEIs in the CCZ, while their location was further adjusted to avoid any overlap with mining areas and reserved areas. The further development of REMPs continues lagging behind the development of mining activities.

187 That approach would obviously have required curtailing the competence of sectoral bodies to act independently, something which could not have been achieved through the LOSC for bodies whose mandate is not defined by the Convention, but by their separate constitutive instruments. At the same, the LOSC could have contained more detailed obligations for its States Parties as regards cooperation and coordination between these bodies.

188 See also Ardron and others (n 15) 105–06 for a discussion on how to achieve a balance between sectoral and conservation interest and the problems involved.

189 CBD art 22.

Further initiatives for developing additional REMPs originally got underway beyond the ISA. The limited involvement of the ISA in part may have been due to insufficient funding. The ISA seemingly has gotten more directly involved at the time that the BBNJ process moved to the phase of the negotiation of the BBNJ Agreement at the IGC. This allowed the ISA to stake out a more convincing claim that it is successfully fulfilling its mandate under Article 145 of the LOSC.

The discussion of the OSPAR and CAMLR Conventions as well as their respective Commissions also vividly illustrates the impact of specific (user) interests on the process of establishing MPAs. In the context of the OSPAR Convention, this concerns, among others, the interest of coastal States over their maritime zones, including the continental shelf beyond 200 nautical miles, which is subjacent to the high seas water column. The discussion of the Arctic Ice High Seas MPA in the OSPAR Commission also highlights how individual (coastal) States may block an MPA designation due to political considerations. A similar consideration applies to CCAMLR, in which case a limited number of States with fishing interests have been able to drag out the consideration of MPA proposals for years. These examples also suggest that having a more specific regime for the identification, establishment and management of MPAs in ABNJ may not necessarily speed up the process. In that connection, it should be realized that rejecting the idea of working towards a network of MPAs as such is difficult to justify, both in terms of existing political commitments and the law.[190] However, raising objections in relation to, eg, the need for the designation of specific areas may even be supported by reference to the law. For instance, opponents may commit to cooperation on MPAs in the abstract, but at the same time argue that, in a given case, an MPA designation is not justified due to a lack of a sufficient scientific basis, or may reject specific management measures because they do not properly balance conservation and use. Even if such arguments on the law may not be altogether convincing, it is much easier to put public pressure on a State that rejects the idea of protecting the ocean as a matter of principle, than to 'name and shame' a State that avows to be committed to international cooperation, and only questions the appropriateness of specific measures.

The above discussion might suggest that meeting Aichi Target 11, or the more ambitious target of the IUCN of 30% no-take MPAs,[191] would be best served by

---

190 However, it may be noted that certain member States of the CCAMLR seemingly are backtracking on the commitments they assumed in this respect and a similar observation arguably is applicable to the OSPAR Commission.

191 It should be noted that this goal does not necessarily require that 30% of ABNJ are designated as no-take MPAs. A recent study finds that 'we could achieve 90% of the maximum

identifying and establishing such MPAs pro-actively, ie, before the interests of specific activities will have built up to such an extent that States representing these interests will be able to credibly block such a development. In itself, this might seemingly be part of a potentially successful strategy. At the same time, the experience in the OSPAR Commission and CCAMLR indicates that user States and coastal States – which most States in regional sea programs are – will also be following such developments with keen interest. The current framework – and the discussion of the Revised Draft Agreement indicates that the same will be the case under the BBNJ Agreement – offers these States ample room to impact on the process of establishing MPAs (and ABMTs).

In the end, whether the glass is half empty or half full as concerns the protection of the marine environment in ABNJ through MPAs and ABMTs remains to be seen. Agreement on specific ABMTs may be more easily secured than agreement on (no-take) MPAs, but may be tailored to user interests to a too large extent. At the level of principle, it will be critical how the international community and individual States will develop their perspectives on justice, knowledge, space and power. What weight will be given to serving justice to different interests, how will knowledge be gathered, shared and weighed in decision making, how much space are we prepared to set aside for nature and wilderness values and how will decision making be set up to contribute to realizing these goals?

---

potential biodiversity benefits from MPAs by strategically protecting 21% of the ocean (43% of EEZs and 6% of the high seas)' in Enric Sala and others, 'Protecting the global ocean for biodiversity, food and climate' (2021) 592 Nature 397, 398. This finding underlines the importance of also effectively managing AWNJ. As regards, ABNJ, the 6% figure may be put in proper perspective by realizing that currently less that 2% of the oceans are covered by no-take MPAs, while most of these MPAs are located in AWNJ (see above text at n 182). And as Sala and others (ibid 398) further observe:

> We also find many priority areas in the high seas around seamount clusters, offshore plateaus and biogeographically unique areas such as the Antarctic Peninsula, the Mid-Atlantic Ridge, the Mascarene Plateau, the Nazca Ridge and the Southwest Indian Ridge.

CHAPTER 9

# The Relevance of the Human Right to Science for the Conservation and Sustainable Use of Marine Biodiversity of Areas beyond National Jurisdiction

## *A New Legally Binding Instrument to Support Co-production of Ocean Knowledge across Scales*

*Elisa Morgera*

## 1 Introduction

This chapter will put forward the argument that the priority in the ongoing negotiations of a new international legally binding instrument on marine biodiversity of areas beyond national jurisdiction (BBNJ Agreement) should be framing clear international cooperation obligations on the co-production of ocean knowledge,[1] in order to support transformative conservation and sustainable use of BBNJ.[2] Co-production is understood here as 'social partnership and joint governance', that relies on the development of 'shared concepts of

1 As opposed to more open-ended obligations or hortatory treaty language on cooperation: See, for instance, the proposed obligation to 'promote' international cooperation in marine scientific research and in the development and transfer of marine technology under art 6 of the Revised Draft text of an agreement under the United Nations Convention on the Law of the Sea on the conservation and sustainable use of marine biological diversity of areas beyond national jurisdiction (2020) UN Doc A/CONF.232/2020/3, Annex (Revised Draft Agreement). See also the objective to '[promote the generation of knowledge and technological innovations, including by promoting and facilitating the development and conduct of marine scientific research in areas beyond national jurisdiction, in accordance with the Convention;]' in Revised Draft Agreement art 1.c (ibid).

2 Transformation is 'a fundamental, system-wide change that includes consideration of technological, economic and social factors, including in terms of paradigms, goals or values' and to '[o]bstacles to achieving transformative change, including unequal power relations, lack of transparency, vested interests, unequal distribution of the costs and benefits of actions, tendencies for short-term decision-making, the psychology of losses and gains, the logic of market-driven processes, the lack of policy coherence and inertia'. See IPBES, Initial scoping report for Deliverable 1 (c): A thematic assessment of the underlying causes of biodiversity loss and the determinants of transformative change and options for achieving the 2050 Vision for Biodiversity (2021) available at <https://ipbes.net/sites/default/files/Initial_scoping_transformative_change_assessment_EN.pdf> accessed 23 July 2021.

 | DOI:10.1163/9789004506367_010

collaboration'.[3] These shared concepts could build upon the principles and requirements for resilience of socio-ecological systems, such as continuous learning, adaptive systems thinking, openness, and long-term monitoring and data sharing.[4]

Marine areas beyond national jurisdiction (ABNJ) (the high seas and the Area)[5] represent '4 billion years of evolution'[6] and 'contain 90% of the total biomass of the global ocean', encompassing a 'wide range of ecological processes and dynamics, from large-scale migrations by hundreds of species to low-productivity, highly stable deep-sea benthic ecosystems rich in biodiversity'.[7] But we have incomplete understanding of these dynamics, and of ecological impacts of human activities on them, which in itself undermines current conservation and sustainable use efforts.[8]

After revealing the science-related underpinnings of the topics under negotiation, the chapter will explore how and to what extent the different dimensions of the human right to science can help address power dynamics in ocean knowledge production with a view to clarifying legal and policy questions around the multilateral governance of BBNJ. The chapter will then apply international human rights obligations across all topics under negotiation (marine genetic resources (MGRS); area-based management tools (ABMTS); environmental impact assessments (EIAS); and capacity building and technological transfer), emphasizing their inter-linkages. This also will shed new light on the institutional architecture needed for more coherent, sustainable and equitable approaches to international cooperation for the conservation and sustainable use of BBNJ, through inclusive co-production of ocean science across scales.[9]

---

3 Brigitte Nerlich, 'The Co-production Confusion' University of Nottingham blog post (20 March 2015) available at <https://blogs.nottingham.ac.uk/makingsciencepublic/2015/03/20/the-co-production-confusion/> accessed 23 July 2021, indicating that this understanding is mainly used in public policy but overlaps in part with Science and Technology Studies.

4 Siddharth Yadav and Kristina Gjerde, 'The Ocean, Climate Change and Resilience: Making Ocean Areas beyond National Jurisdiction More Resilient to Climate Change and Other Anthropogenic Activities' (2020) 122 Marine Policy 104184, 6.

5 United Nations Convention on the Law of the Sea (opened for signature 10 December 1982, entered into force 16 November 1994) 1833 UNTS 3 (LOSC), Parts VII and XI.

6 Alex Rogers and others, 'Marine Genetic Resources in Areas Beyond National Jurisdiction: Promoting Marine Scientific Research and Enabling Equitable Benefit-sharing' (2021) 8 Frontiers in Marine Science 667274.

7 Guillermo Crespo and others, 'Beyond Static Spatial Management: Scientific and Legal Considerations for Dynamic Management in the High Seas' (2020) 122 Marine Policy 104102, 1–2.

8 ibid.

9 In this context, 'scale' is understood as different levels of social organization, from local to global, with a view to understanding how knowledge on the effectiveness of natural

## 2 Why is Ocean Knowledge Co-production Central to the BBNJ Agreement?

The most contentious topic in the BBNJ negotiations is certainly benefit-sharing from MGRs, to the point that it is often seen as an obstacle to the conservation elements of the package. It is here suggested, instead, to consider MGRs as the most prominent exemplar of common equity challenges across marine scientific research (MSR): MGRs are the tip of the iceberg due to the evidence of inequalities that arise from intellectual property applications, whereby only ten countries in the world appear to be benefitting from deep-sea research.[10] But other aspects of deep-sea research are equally in the hands of a handful of States. There is only a restricted number of countries that can afford the costs and risks of deep-sea research vessels and therefore can control who has access to that source of knowledge. The vast majority of developing countries are not part of bioprospecting efforts and are also greatly underrepresented in marine taxonomic research.[11] In effect, 'field capacity at the most basic level of technical and scientific knowledge [of the ocean] is lacking' in most regions of the world[12] and 'despite centuries of hydrographic survey effort, we have more and better data to describe the surface of the Moon or Mars than for most of the Earth's seas'.[13] This gap is particularly felt in the Caribbean, Africa and Oceania where nautical charts need to be urgently modernized and made compatible with satellite-based positioning systems, but capacity to

resource management approaches can scale up/down: Oran Young, *Governing Complex Systems: Social Capital for the Anthropocene* (MIT Press 2017) 37. The term scales also serves to allude to separate, but inter-related questions of knowledge and management of different levels of socio-ecological systems, from cells, microbiomes to ecoregions.

10 Only 10 countries account for 90% of patents related to MGR (the US, Japan, certain EU countries, Switzerland and Norway): Sophie Arnaud-Haond, Jesús Arrieta and Carlos Duarte, 'Marine Biodiversity and Gene Patents' (2011) 331 Science 1521.

11 Arianna Broggiato and others, '*Mare Geneticum*: Balancing Governance of Marine Genetic Resources in International Waters' (2018) 33 International Journal of Marine and Coastal Law 3, 15–16, referring to Kim Juniper, 'Use of Marine Genetic Resources' in Michael Banks, Caroline Bissada and Peyman Eghtesadi Araghi (eds), *The First Global Integrated Marine Assessment World Ocean Assessment I* (UN 2016) 7–8, and Iris E Hendriks and Carlos M Duarte, 'Allocation of Effort and Imbalances in Biodiversity Research' (2008) 360 Journal of Experimental Marine Biology and Ecology 15, 17.

12 Montserrat Gorina-Ysern, 'Marine Scientific Research: Overview of Major Issues, Programmes and their Objectives' in Hance D Smith, Juan Luis Suarez de Vivero and Tundi Agardy (eds), *Routledge Handbook of Ocean Resources and Management* (Routledge 2015) 127, 128.

13 Robert Wilson, 'Surveying the Sea' in Smith and others (n 12) 462.

plan and implement a prioritized survey programme is lacking.[14] Meanwhile, nations with modern charts 'actively prevent the release of data',[15] and restrict marine scientists' mobility and access because of 'the link between obtaining improved knowledge of the ocean and [States'] growing interest in exploring offshore natural resources and technological advances that might be relevant to naval security'.[16]

In addition, growing Global North-South scientific collaborations are 'characterized by pharmaceutical or biotech companies working with established centres of excellence located in high-income countries'.[17] As a result of these, as well as the increasing reliance on sequencing technologies and bioinformatics, 'the capacity to undertake genomic research … is inequitably distributed among countries'.[18] Thus a call has been made to urgently 'promote inclusive and responsible research and innovation that addresses equity differentials and fosters capacity and access to technology, while facilitating the realization of commitments to conserve and sustainably use the ocean's genetic diversity'.[19]

Deep-sea knowledge is what allows for enhanced understanding of the need for, and effectiveness of, conservation and sustainable use approaches in areas beyond national jurisdiction (ABNJ), as well as in areas within national jurisdiction (AWNJ) due to the ecological connectivity of the ocean that relies on currents and the movement of migratory species.[20] Understanding the 'ocean genome' (the whole of the genetic material present in all marine biodiversity, including both the genes and the information they encode) is essential for 'determining the abundance and resilience of biological resources', 'increas[ing] awareness of the pressures facing marine biodiversity' and 'informing the designation of [marine protected areas (MPAs)] as well as innovative approaches to conservation'.[21] But while our knowledge is making

14 ibid 470.

15 ibid 475.

16 Anna-Maria Hubert, 'Marine Scientific Research and the Protection of the Seas and Oceans' in Rosemary Rayfuse (ed), *Research Handbook on Marine Environmental Law* (Edward Elgar 2015) 313, 314.

17 Robert Blasiak and others, *The Ocean Genome: Conservation and the Fair, Equitable and Sustainable Use of Marine Genetic Resources* (World Resources Institute 2020) 26.

18 ibid 3.

19 ibid.

20 Ekaterina Popova and others, 'So far, yet so close: ecological connectivity between ABNJ and territorial waters' (2019) IIED Policy Brief available at <https://pubs.iied.org/17500iied> accessed 26 July 2021; Yadav and Gjerde (n 4) 4–5.

21 Blasiak and others (n 17) 3.

strides into the ocean genome, what we continue not to know is still vast. For instance, the 'functions of some 90 percent of genetic sequences collected from viruses remain unknown'.[22] In that connection, it is also underscored that '[a]cknowledging the potential commercial value of biodiversity' – which tends to dominate the BBNJ negotiations, as opposed to the benefits of MGRs for knowledge for conservation – 'may lead to better funding for biodiversity surveys that access a broad range of marine life and assess these for bioactivity, which may lead to improved biodiversity conservation measures'.[23]

So, States with limited ocean knowledge are going to be necessarily less able to participate in decisions on EIAs, MPAs and other ABMTs in ABNJ,[24] as well as less able to manage sustainably marine spaces within national jurisdiction if they are among those with strongest connectivity to ABNJ and the shortest timeframes of connectivity.[25] In turn, it is down to these decisions on the creation of area-based and other management tools in ABNJ to 'safeguard genetic diversity at the ecosystem level'.[26] This underscores underlying epistemic justice and recognition issues below the surface of the negotiations on ABMT.

In addition, there are fundamental equity questions related to competing uses that may be impacted upon by ABMTs and that may benefit and disadvantage different sectors and groups: Being able to influence the evidence base upon which these decisions will be taken is a significant power that rests on the ability to produce the best available science. The role of science is also crucial to support the assessments of cumulative and transboundary impacts on marine biodiversity, which is expected to be a much-needed innovation of the BBNJ Agreement. Which sectors of scientific knowledge will be relevant to that end remains to be clarified, as it remains open to negotiations if explicit references to climate change, ocean acidification, and deoxygenation will be included in the BBNJ Agreement.[27] On the whole, the equity and capacity gap

---

22 ibid 8.

23 ibid 14.

24 This is to a certain extent recognized in the Draft BBNJ text where capacity-building refers specifically to the capacity to develop, implement, monitor and manage, including to enforce, any ABMTs, including MPAs; and 'the capacity to conduct and evaluate environmental impact assessments [and strategic environmental assessments]' in Revised Draft Agreement art 42.

25 Popova and others (n 20). For a discussion on ecological connectivity and references to 'adjacency' in the BBNJ Revised Draft Agreement, see Joanna Mossop and Clive Schofield, 'Adjacency and Due Regard: The Role of Coastal States in the BBNJ Treaty' (2020) 122 Marine Policy 103877.

26 Blasiak and others (n 17).

27 Revised Draft Agreement arts 1(6) and 14(e); Annex I (f) and Annex II, (a)(iv). Although see unbracketed text under General Approaches: 'approach that builds ecosystem

in deep-sea knowledge production affects the opportunities of countries in the Global South to influence the further development of the law of the sea. The link between ocean knowledge and law development is already recognized under the law of the sea.[28]

Scientific cooperation provides not only the means to improve the quality of MSR, but also spreads opportunities for deep-sea research, including technology sharing and co-development across different countries which enhances capacity for ocean management. The capacity gap for integrated ocean science and holistic ocean governance is particularly felt vis-à-vis the need to bring together environmental, social and economic dimensions of different human activities, and all ecosystem components, both within and beyond national jurisdictions.[29] It is therefore to be welcomed that during the BBNJ negotiations, MGRs have been increasingly linked to the negotiations on capacity building and technology transfer,[30] showing that the topic of MGRs can have a constructive influence on the negotiations of other elements of the package (as opposed to being widely seen as a problematic element that hinders progress in other areas of the BBNJ Agreement). Focusing on the fundamental contribution of the study of MGRs of ABNJ to 'increasing humankind's knowledge about nature'[31] serves to understand that scientific research and cooperation on MGRs can underpin all elements of the package.

Along similar lines, the negotiations on MGRs have also opened the door for integrating the recognition and consideration for traditional knowledge (TK) across the different elements of the package.[32] TK has been increasingly recognized as relevant for the BBNJ Agreement in relation to: connectivity of species and marine processes across areas within and beyond national jurisdiction; management practices that can provide models for ABNJ; and (revived) traditional instrument-free navigation in areas within and beyond national

---

resilience to the adverse effects of climate change and ocean acidification and restores ecosystem integrity' Revised Draft Agreement art 5(h).

28 LOSC art 238; see also Nele Matz-Lück, 'Article 238' in Alexander Proelss (ed), *United Nations Convention on the Law of the Sea: A Commentary* (Hart 2017) 1609.

29 Marjo Vierros and Harriet Harden-Davies, 'Capacity Building and Technology Transfer for Improving Governance of Marine Areas both Beyond and Within National Jurisdiction' (2020) 122 Marine Policy 104158, 1.

30 Revised Draft Agreement art 42(f).

31 Rüdiger Wolfrum, 'Concluding Remarks' (2009) 24 The International Journal of Marine and Coastal Law 343, 346.

32 See unbracketed text under Consultation and assessment of ABMT proposals at Revised Draft Agreement art 18(2)(c); under Impact Assessment and evaluation at Revised Draft Agreement art 31(1).

jurisdiction, which may provide leads for bio-prospecting.[33] But equity questions concerning epistemic justice and recognition have emerged about the inclusion of TK in the notion of 'best scientific knowledge' and the degree of participation of TK holders with regard to EIAS and MPAS.[34]

Advancing basic knowledge about MGRS of ABNJ more equitably, by genuinely partnering with scientist from the Global South and TK holders, can support the co-production of knowledge on the interconnectivity of the ocean and its relevance for life and well-being on Earth, which is relevant to the realization of multiple Sustainable Development Goals (SDGS) across all the elements of the BBNJ Agreement.

### 2.1 *Relevant Obligations under the Law of the Sea*

To that end, it is helpful to recall relevant LOSC obligations that should inform the BBNJ negotiations.[35] First of all, even if LOSC Part XII does not say so explicitly, scientific expertise, methods and information are necessary to implement the obligations on the protection of the marine environment, notably in light of the precautionary principle. This can be seen as an integral part of due diligence obligations[36] to continuously predict, monitor and respond to risks to the marine environment through exchange of information and establishing appropriate scientific criteria for rules on marine pollution.[37] Relying on the results of EIAS, that are to be published or distributed through competent international organizations, can also be considered part of this due diligence requirement,[38] and the deliberate withholding of monitoring results could amount to a material breach of LOSC.[39]

---

33 Marjo Vierros and others, 'Considering Indigenous Peoples and Local Communities in Governance of the Global Ocean Commons' (2018) 119 Marine Policy 104039; Clement Yow Mulalap and others, 'Traditional Knowledge and the BBNJ Instrument' (2020) 122 Marine Policy 104103, 1 and 6.

34 Revised Draft Agreement arts 5(i), 10bis, 16(1), 21(4), 31(2), 34(2), 35(3), 49(2), 51(3)(b) and (4)(b), 52(5)(e), and Annex II (b)(iii). However, see unbracketed text under Consultation and assessment of ABMT proposals at Revised Draft Agreement art 18(2)(c); under Impact assessment and evaluation at Revised Draft Agreement art 31(1).

35 Revised Draft Agreement art 4(1).

36 Hubert, 'Marine Scientific Research' (n 16) 318, referring to *Advisory Opinion, Responsibilities and Obligations of States sponsoring persons and entities with respect to activities in the Area* (February 1, 2011) ITLOS, Seabed Disputes Chamber, para 113.

37 LOSC arts 200, 201 and 204(1); James Harrison, *Saving the Oceans through Law* (Oxford University Press 2017) 35; Tim Stephens, 'Article 201' in Proelss (n 28) 1345; Eike Blitza, 'Article 204' in Proelss (n 28) 1363. See also the Revised Draft Agreement under capacity building: Revised Draft Agreement arts 43(2) and 46(1).

38 LOSC art 194; Harrison (n 37) 34; Detlef Czybulka, 'Article 194' in Proelss (n 28) 1303.

39 LOSC art 205; Eike Blitza, 'Article 205' in Proelss (n 28) 1367.

In addition, due diligence includes the duty to cooperate, and as part of that an obligation to integrate the efforts of scientists and remove obstacles to MSR for mutual benefit,[40] so obligations to support MSR are 'for the benefit of all'.[41] This is necessary to create opportunities for all to contribute to the establishment of scientific criteria to keep pace with scientific understanding of threats to the marine environment in light of precaution,[42] with a view to identifying emerging threats such as ocean acidification.[43] The role of the BBNJ instrument, therefore, in supporting the creation of favorable conditions for MSR, as required under LOSC, can be to further develop the obligation to cooperate through the conclusion of international agreements to '*integrate the efforts of scientists* in studying the essence of phenomena and processes occurring in the marine environment and the interrelations between them'.[44]

This would entail supporting 'dialogue and inter[action] among scientists' with a view to integrating their findings both for intra- and inter-disciplinarity for better understanding 'the role of the ocean in the life of the planet'.[45] While LOSC obligations of scientific cooperation, extending both to the conduct of MSR, and the analysis of information for ocean management, may appear quite open-ended, it has been argued that absolute inaction would be a violation of LOSC.[46] In effect, it can be further argued that the duty to cooperate would be violated also in the absence of active attempts to bring parties to the negotiating table, refusing invitations to negotiate, or not negotiating in good faith with a view to advancing cooperation.[47] In particular, good faith entails the need to show other countries individually and the international community as a whole respect by taking into account the reasonable interests and legitimate expectations of other States[48] in a predictable manner,[49] so as to show trustworthiness and predictability. This can be demonstrated by relying on multilateral institutions to support the effective, objective and even-handed promotion and

40 LOSC arts 242 and 243.
41 Hubert, 'Marine Scientific Research' (n 16) 320–21.
42 LOSC art 201.
43 Tim Stephens, 'Article 200' in Proelss (n 28) 1342.
44 LOSC art 243 (emphasis added).
45 LOSC art 243; see Irini Papanicolopulu, 'Article 243' in Proelss (n 28) 1637.
46 LOSC art 242; see Irini Papanicolopulu, 'Article 242' in Proelss (n 28) 1631 and 1634.
47 *Guyana v Suriname*, (Award, 17 September 2007) PCA 2004-04, paras 476–77.
48 Michel Virally, 'Review Essay: Good Faith in Public International Law' (1983) 77 American Journal of International Law 130.
49 Saul Litvinoff, 'Good Faith', (1997) 71 Tulane Law Review 1645, 1664.

protection of the international community's interests.[50] A 'genuine intention to achieve a positive result',[51] in this context, would also require treaty interpretation in good faith, that is avoiding unreasonably strict literal interpretations when they would allow a Party to obtain an unfair advantage, or exercise rights in a way that would be damaging to another Party,[52] to the detriment of the effectiveness of a treaty.[53]

These rules therefore provide the legal basis for elaborating further regulation to clarify the margin of discretion of States in this connection.[54] The BBNJ negotiations could thus be understood as the multilateral process that LOSC Parties are currently using to engage in, to create common platforms and adequate financing for scientific research cooperation.[55] Equally, the negotiations should be understood as a process to expand on LOSC obligations to 'actively promote … the *strengthening of the autonomous [MSR] capabilities of developing States*',[56] to ensure that scientific cooperation effectively gives scientists from the Global South and TK holders the opportunity to participate and benefit.[57]

These considerations have a bearing on LOSC obligations related to technology transfer. The 'key criterion' in LOSC technology transfer regime is enabling all parties concerned to benefit on an equitable basis from developments in MSR, particularly those aimed at stimulating the social and economic development of developing countries with due regard to their capacity in marine sciences.[58] Obligations of scientific and technical assistance towards developing states are mandatary, but do not clarify the extent of States' discretion. This reflects broader reluctance by developed States to agree to stricter rules, even if this affects overall effectiveness of LOSC obligations to protect the marine environment.[59] These obligations, however, entail strengthening

---

50 Bruno Simma, 'From Bilateralism to Community Interests in International Law' (1994) IV (250) Recueil des Cours 217, 319.

51 *Delimitation of the Maritime Boundary in the Gulf of Maine Area (Canada v United States)* [1984] ICJ Reports 246, para 87; Alexander Orakhelashvili, 'Treaty Interpretation: Effectiveness and Presumptions' in Alexander Orakhelashvili, *The Interpretation of Acts and Rules in Public International Law* (Oxford University Press 2008) 415; Robert Kolb, *Good Faith in International Law* (Hart Publishing 2017) 43.

52 Orakhelashvili (n 51) 415.

53 Malgosia Fitzmaurice, 'The Law of Treaties' in Malcolm N Shaw (ed), *International Law* (6th edn, Oxford University Press 2008) 810, 832–38.

54 Papanicolopulu, 'Article 242' (n 46) 1631 and 1634.

55 ibid 1639.

56 LOSC art 244(2) (emphasis added).

57 Irini Papanicolopulu, 'Article 244' in Proelss (n 28) 1641.

58 Yoshifumi Tanaka, *The International Law of the Sea* (Cambridge University Press 2012) 350.

59 LOSC art 202; James Harrison, 'Article 202' in Proelss (n 28) 1349.

the autonomous scientific capacity in developing states,[60] to reduce reliance on external assistance in the long term, including to conduct EIAs.[61]

Overall, the LOSC regime provides some elements for supporting ocean knowledge co-production, which is also called for by marine scientists,[62] but these elements are not fully developed and connected effectively with one another. In effect, there has been limited international law research on the LOSC regime on MSR and capacity building,[63] and LOSC rules on technology are seen as 'weak' and 'unclear'.[64] In addition, LOSC rules on capacity building are largely not implemented, due to the '(still prevailing) lack of political will on the part of developed states',[65] and generally 'fall short … [of ensuring] continuous cooperation'.[66] The following sections will explore whether the interpretation of LOSC provisions in the light of other relevant areas of international law can help developed deeper international cooperation obligations on MSR, capacity building, technology transfer and environmental protection.

### 2.2 *The Potential of a Broader Notion of Fair and Equitable Benefit-sharing*

Against this background, the argument advanced here is that the BBNJ negotiations should clarify the scope, and limit the discretion of developed states in implementing, international obligations on marine scientific cooperation, capacity building and technology transfer because of the inter-dependence of LOSC obligations to protect the marine environment. This argument is reinforced by the consideration of the human rights dimensions of ocean knowledge co-production, as well as the human rights implications of failed or limited efforts in advancing ocean knowledge production, and of the resulting ineffective conversation and unsustainable use of the ocean.

To develop this argument, the international law concept of fair and equitable benefit-sharing[67] can support the consideration of effectiveness, human rights, and equity in MSR across the BBNJ negotiations.[68] Equity, as a general

60 LOSC art 244(2).
61 LOSC art 202; Harrison, 'Article 202' (n 59) 1351.
62 Rogers and others (n 6) 15.
63 Gorina-Ysern (n 12) 129; Kristin Bartenstein, 'Article 266' in Proelss (n 28) 1766.
64 Irini Papanicolopulu, 'Article 278' in Proelss (n 28) 1811.
65 Bartenstein, 'Article 266' (n 63)1765.
66 Kristin Bartenstein, 'Article 269' in Proelss (n 28) 1788.
67 Elisa Morgera, 'The Need for an International Legal Concept of Fair and Equitable Benefit-sharing' (2016) 27 European Journal of International Law 353.
68 This chapter makes the case that fairness, equity and efficiency are interlinked. On equity and efficiency as included in LOSC preamble, as opposed to fairness and equity under the Convention on Biological Diversity (signed 5 June 1992, entered in force 29

principle of international law, can support an evolutive interpretation of LOSC.[69] Rather than necessarily focusing on the notion of benefit-sharing enshrined in the common heritage regime,[70] which remains controversial in the BBNJ negotiations, it has already been suggested to build upon fair and equitable benefit-sharing as enshrined in the ecosystem approach under the CBD as recognition and reward for ecosystem stewards, particularly developing countries and TK holders.[71] Reference to the ecosystem approach does not seem controversial in the BBNJ negotiations, even if equity – which is considered part and parcel of it under the CBD – is.[72]

Based on a combined reading of interpretative materials, 'sharing' principally conveys the idea of agency, as opposed to the passive enjoyment of benefits,[73] and therefore a shift away from unidirectional (likely, top-down) or one-off flows of benefits. This interpretation thus focuses on the agency and active participation of developing countries and TK holders in the identification of benefits. In addition, benefit-sharing usually relies on a menu of benefits, the nature of which can be economic and non-economic. This arguably allows taking into account beneficiaries' needs, values, and priorities through a contextual selection of the combination of benefits that may best serve to lay the foundation for partnership.[74] This, in turn, is considered essential to build lasting capacity[75] and enhance access to ocean science and advance scientific cooperation through long-term mentoring and networking.[76] The expression 'fair and equitable', which is generally left to subsequent negotiations,

---

December 1993) 1760 UNTS 79 (CBD), see Fran Humphries and others, 'A Tiered Approach to the Marine Genetic Resources Governance Framework under the Proposed UNCLOS Agreement for Biodiversity beyond National Jurisdiction (BBNJ)' (2020) 122 Marine Policy 103910.

69 Elisa Morgera, 'Fair and Equitable Benefit-sharing in a New International Instrument on Marine Biodiversity: A Principled Approach towards Partnership Building?' (2018–19) 5 Maritime Safety and Security Law Journal 48.

70 LOSC art 140.

71 As *recognition* and *reward* for the use of TK and for the customary sustainable management and conservation of biological resources: Principles of the Ecosystem Approach, CBD Decision V/6 (2000), para 9 and Principle 8; Refinement and elaboration of the ecosystem approach, CBD Decision VII/11 (2004), annex, rationale to Principle 4. As discussed in Morgera, 'International Legal Concept' (n 67).

72 eg Revised Draft Agreement art 5.

73 Mikel Mancisidor, 'Is There such a Thing as a Human Right to Science in International Law?' (2015) 4 European Society of International Law 1.

74 Morgera, 'New International Instrument' (n 69).

75 Vierros and Harden-Davies (n 29) 2.

76 Rogers and others (n 6) 18.

expresses the rationale of balancing competing rights and interests,[77] with a view to integrating both procedural and substantive dimensions of justice[78] into a relationship that is regulated by international law and is characterized by power imbalances.[79] The recourse to the twin expression 'fair and equitable' thus serves to make explicit both procedural dimensions of justice (fairness) that determine the legitimacy of certain courses of action, as well as substantive dimensions of justice (equity).[80] In practice, they entail an iterative, concerted and good-faith dialogue (procedural dimension) to develop a common understanding of what different States may see as benefits (substantive dimension) arising from the conservation and sustainable use of BBNJ. This approach can support mutual learning, adaptive governance,[81] and explicit engagement with power imbalances, which have been underscored by scholars advocating for centering BBNJ governance on resilience of socio-ecological systems[82] and the inclusion of TK.[83]

In the BBNJ context, this dialogue can serve to develop a common understanding across the different views of equity and of benefits that have already been voiced in the negotiations. For instance, the US and other developed States affirmed that research and development on MGRs of ABNJ is a highly costly and time-consuming endeavor with uncertain results, that, when successful, would benefit humanity in the form of scientific advancements contributing to global public health, food security and environmental protection. These countries have indicated openness to some form of benefit-sharing, that would leave a wide margin of discretion through codes of conduct or the *ad hoc* sharing of data and research results, capacity building and scientific collaboration, but they have opposed monetary benefit-sharing.[84] On the other hand, developing countries have argued that monetary benefit-sharing should be included, together with non-monetary ones, so that both sharing the

77 Ciarán Burke, *An Equitable Framework for Humanitarian Intervention* (Hart 2014) 197–98 and 250–51.

78 By analogy with the standard of fair and equitable treatment in international investment law, see Roland Kläger, *Fair and Equitable Treatment' in International Investment Law* (Cambridge University Press 2011) 130.

79 ibid.

80 ibid 141.

81 Morgera, 'New International Instrument' (n 69).

82 Yadav and Gjerde (n 4) 5–6.

83 Vierros and others (n 33) 7.

84 Elisa Morgera, 'Benefit-sharing in marine areas beyond national jurisdiction: where are we at? (Part 1)' BeneLex Blog (2014) <https://benelexblog.wordpress.com/2014/05/23/benefit-sharing-in-marine-areas-beyond-national-jurisdiction-where-are-we-at-part-i/> accessed 26 July 2021.

revenues arising from the commercial exploitation of MGRS, as well as sharing opportunities to participate in scientific expeditions, follow-up research, relevant technology and research results, could contribute in predictable ways to increasing developing countries' capacities to conduct MSR and contribute to the protection of the marine environment and its sustainable use.[85]

Applied at the multilateral level, the proposed interpretation of benefit-sharing opens the door for developing countries to co-identify the benefits and needs for transformative ocean governance through the integrated implementation of capacity-building, technology transfer, scientific cooperation and information-sharing obligations, even if these obligations are all dependent on resources in donor countries, who for that reason tend to 'call the shots'.[86] Co-identification of benefits, however, can support more effective delivery through multilateral facilitative and brokering arrangements to operationalize relevant duties of cooperation with a view to ensuring equitable distribution across different regions, monitoring of effectiveness, and learning from experience. The need for such an approach has already been demonstrated in other international processes, such as the International Seabed Authority, and the International Maritime Organization.[87] In addition, the proposed interpretation of benefit-sharing can support the engagement with another question about equity and benefits that has not yet emerged in the BBNJ negotiations. Climate change and its 'impacts on both ocean circulation and the global distribution of species indicat[ing] that today's patterns of ecological connectivity will not remain static in time'.[88]

On a separate but related note, fair and equitable benefit-sharing is, together with free, prior and informed consent (FPIC), necessary to recognize and respectfully integrate indigenous peoples and local communities for their global contributions to the conservation and sustainable use of biodiversity, as well as their knowledge systems,[89] in ocean science-policy interfaces at different levels. Integrating TK in the BBNJ Agreement, building upon other global environmental scientific processes such as the Intergovernmental Science-Policy Panel on Biodiversity and Ecosystem Services,[90] fair and equitable

---

85 ibid.

86 Earth Negotiations Bulletin (ENB), *Summary and analysis of the third session of the BBNJ Preparatory Committee* (vol 25 2017) (121 and 124).

87 Elisa Morgera and Mara Ntona, 'Linking Small-Scale Fisheries to International Obligations on Marine Technology Transfer' (2018) 93 Marine Policy 214.

88 Popova and others (n 20).

89 CBD art 8(j); Morgera, 'International Legal Concept' (n 67) 370.

90 Annex II to decision IPBES-5/1: Approach to recognizing and working with indigenous and local knowledge in the Intergovernmental Science-Policy Platform on Biodiversity and Ecosystem Services (2017). This is currently reflected in bracketed text referring to

benefit-sharing would need to apply to all relevant BBNJ Agreement elements, thereby allowing for the co-identification of benefits beyond the current State-centric model, and enhancing both transdisciplinary and inclusive ocean governance.[91] Transdisciplinarity ('the recognition of different knowledge systems, and the inclusion of underrepresented types of knowledge'[92]) is increasingly seen as an essential element for transformative governance ('an approach to environmental governance that has the capacity to respond to, manage, and trigger regime shifts in coupled socio-ecological systems at multiple scales … [having the] capacity to shape non-linear change'[93]). Transdisciplinary governance can complement and contribute to *integrative* and *inclusive* governance, which respectively aim to ensure that solutions have sustainable impacts at other scales and in other sectors, and to integrate those whose interests are currently not being taken into consideration, and those who represent values that contribute to sustainable development.[94] All these dimensions are seen as inter-related elements of transformative governance,[95] and can encompass the notion of 'inclusive innovation' that has been advocated for the stewardship of the ocean genome[96] through proposals supporting ocean knowledge co-production.

The following sections will thus explore whether this broader notion of fair and equitable benefit-sharing as part of the ecosystem approach can serve to address equity concerns in the production of ocean science as a condition for more inclusive and effective conservation and sustainable use of BBNJ. This question will be answered by reflecting on the interplay of international human rights law and international biodiversity law, as fair and equitable

prior and informed consent or approval and involvement of these indigenous peoples and local communities. The clearing-house mechanism may act as an intermediary to facilitate access to such traditional knowledge. Access to such traditional knowledge shall be on mutually agreed terms (Revised Draft Agreement art 10bis; in references to 'best available scientific information and knowledge, including relevant traditional knowledge of indigenous peoples and local communities' (Revised Draft Agreement arts 5(a) and 10bis). See also Yow Mulalap and others (n 33) 7.

91 See the proposal for including indigenous and local knowledge as a dynamic and living system of knowledge under the BBNJ Agreement in Humphries and others (n 68) 11–12.

92 Ingrid Visseren-Hamakers and Marcel Kok, 'Introduction' in Ingrid Visseren-Hamakers and Marcel Kok (eds), *Transforming Biodiversity Governance* (Cambridge University Press forthcoming 2021).

93 ibid. See also Yadav and Gjerde (n 4) 6.

94 Elisa Morgera and others, 'Integrative and Inclusive Governance for Ocean Biodiversity' in Visseren-Hamakers and Kok (n 92).

95 Visseren-Hamakers and Kok (n 92).

96 Blasiak and others (n 17) 37.

benefit-sharing is also part and parcel of the human right to science (the right of everyone to benefit from scientific advancements).[97] Notably, it will be investigated how a broad notion of fair and equitable benefit-sharing fits both the ecosystem approach and the human right to science, helping to clarify the content of the duty to cooperate under LOSC by recognizing power and capacity imbalances in current MSR in ABNJ and the need for genuine partnerships as opposed to one-off forms of collaboration.

## 3 The Relevance of the Human Right to Science

The focus on the human right to science, as will be discussed below, helps to reveal that LOSC obligations related to scientific cooperation, capacity-building and technology transfer, which are often seen in purely inter-State terms, have human rights implications. Thus, while developed countries interpreted these obligation in terms of almost unfettered discretion, the degree of discretion is limited by the need to implement also relevant international human rights law.[98] In the particular context of the BBNJ negotiations, human rights implications should be connected to vulnerable communities in countries with strongest connectivity to ABNJ.[99] As our scientific understanding of other inter-connections between ecosystem services in ABNJ and human well-being on Earth progresses, we can also expect to be able to point to human rights implications for other societies or vulnerable groups in different States.

The human right to science is seen as an autonomous right that is worthy of protection for its contribution to the continuous raising of the material and spiritual standards of living of all members of society, both for individual emancipation and collective economic and social progress.[100] As such, it contributes to the enjoyment of other human rights such as the rights to food and health,[101] and is therefore significant for the realization of SDGS 2 (hunger)

97 Universal Declaration of Human Rights (1948) UN Doc A/810 at 71, art 27.

98 For an initial discussion, Elisa Morgera, 'Fair and Equitable Benefit-sharing at the Crossroads of the Human Right to Science and International Biodiversity Law' (2015) 4 Laws 803.

99 Popova and others (n 20).

100 Aurora Plomer, *Patents, Human Rights and Access to Science* (Edward Elgar 2015).

101 William A Schabas, 'Study of the Right to Enjoy the Benefits of Scientific and Technological Progress and its Applications' in Yvonne Donders and Vladimir Volodin (eds.), *Human Rights in Education, Science and Culture: Legal Developments and Challenges* (Ashgate Publishing 2007); Mancisidor (n 73); Audrey R Chapman, 'Towards an Understanding of the Right to Enjoy the Benefits of Scientific Progress and its Applications' (2009) 8 Journal of Human Rights 1.

and 3 (health and well-being). In addition, the right to science contributes to '[protecting] and [enabling] each person to develop his or her capacities for education and learning, to form enduring relationships with others, to take equal part in political, social and cultural life and to work without fear of discrimination',[102] therefore playing a part in the implementation of SDGs 4 (education), 8 (decent work) and 10 (inequality).[103]

In that sense, the human right to science supports reflecting on how the BBNJ instrument can contribute to the realization of inter-connected SDGs, as aptly summarized by SDG target 14a 'Increase scientific knowledge, develop research capacity and transfer marine technology ... in order to improve ocean health and to enhance the contribution of marine biodiversity to the development of developing countries'.[104] While these are not objectives that have been spelt out in the BBNJ negotiations, they underscore the opportunity (and in actual fact the obligation for States parties to relevant treaties) to develop the BBNJ Agreement in a mutually supportive way[105] with other international agreements, notably international human rights treaties, as recommended in 2020 by the UN Special Rapporteur on Human Rights and the Environment.[106]

### 3.1 *The Content of the Human Right to Science*

The human right to science is not a new right. It was proclaimed in the Universal Declaration of Human Rights[107] and has been enshrined in several treaties, including the International Covenant on Economic, Social and Cultural Rights,[108] so its legally binding force is not under discussion. Admittedly,

---

102 Plomer (n 100).

103 See also Morgera and Ntona (n 87).

104 Mara Ntona and Elisa Morgera, 'Connecting SDG 14 with the other Sustainable Development Goals through Marine Spatial Planning' (2018) 93 Marine Policy 295.

105 Riccardo Pavoni, 'Mutual Supportiveness as a Principle of Interpretation and Law-Making: A Watershed for the WTO-and-Competing-Regimes Debate?' (2010) 21 European Journal of International Law 649.

106 David Boyd, Report of the Special Rapporteur on the Issue of Human Rights Obligations Relating to the Enjoyment of a Safe, Clean, Healthy and Sustainable Environment, (2020) UN Doc A/75/161, para 88(j).

107 See Schabas (n 101) on the broad consensus regarding the inclusion of the human right to science in the Universal Declaration of Human Rights.

108 International Covenant on Economic, Social and Cultural Rights (opened for signature 16 December 1966, entered into force 3 January 1976) 6 ILM 360 (ICESCR) art 15. See also Charter of the Organization of American States (opened for signature 30 April 1948, entered into force December 13, 1951) 119 UNTS 3, art 38; American Declaration on the Rights and Duties of Man (adopted 2 May 1948) O.A.S. Res XXX, art XIII; Additional Protocol to the American Convention on Human Rights in the Area of Economic, Social and Cultural Rights (opened for signature 17 November 1988, entered into force 16

however, the scope, normative content and obligations of States with regard to the human right to science had remained underdeveloped until recently. For this reason, there have been virtually no efforts to implement the obligations to promote, protect and fulfil this right. Nonetheless, current efforts to clarify the content of the right to science provide useful insights for present purposes and indicate that international human rights bodies will devote increasing attention to States' conduct in this area.

In 2011, the UN Special Rapporteur in the field of cultural rights, Farida Shaheed, suggested that the right to science encompasses four distinct elements: the right to access the benefits of science by everyone without discrimination; the opportunity for all to contribute to scientific research; the obligation to protect all persons against negative consequences of scientific research or its applications on their food, health, security and environment; and the obligation to ensure that priorities for scientific research focus on key issues for the most vulnerable.[109] It is clear, therefore, that these normative elements chime with the notion of 'inclusive innovation' advocated with regard to the ocean genome, namely 'explicitly includ[ing] those who have been excluded from the development mainstream ... and produc[ing] and deliver[ing] innovative solutions to the problems of the poorest and most marginalised communities'.[110]

All the dimensions of the human right to science are relevant to the BBNJ negotiations on MGRs. Legal scholarship on the right to science has put forward arguments that 'sharing' benefits is a key conceptual element that emphasizes agency.[111] Even if not everyone may play an active part in scientific advancements, all persons should indisputably be able to participate in the benefits derived from it.[112] This interpretation chimes with the argument outlined above that benefit-sharing conveys the idea of the active participation in the

November 1999) 28 ILM 156, art 14; Arab Charter on Human Rights (adopted 23 May 2004), reprinted in International Human Rights Reports 893 (2005), art 42.

109 UNGA, Report of the Special Rapporteur in the field of cultural rights Shaheed: the right to enjoy the benefits of scientific progress and its applications (UN Doc A/HRC/20/26, 14 May 2012) paras 1, 25 and 30–43.

110 Blasiak and others (n 17) 37.

111 Mancisidor (n 73).

112 Chapman (n 101) 5–6. Note that not all versions of the right to science in different international human rights materials refer to benefit-sharing. For instance, whereas the Universal Declaration of Human Rights refers to sharing in the benefits of scientific advancement, the International Covenant on Economic, Social and Cultural Rights refers to the 'right to enjoy benefits'. However, Mancisidor (n 73) has argued that the understanding of the wording used in the Declaration should contribute to the interpretation of the different wording in the Covenant in full.

identification of benefits and sharing modalities among those actors that are directly involved in deep-sea science and those that are not, and across different worldviews.[113] The added value of benefit-sharing is thus to foster deeper international cooperation, based on the recognition of power and capacity imbalances and of the need for a relationship as opposed to a one-off form of collaboration related to matters of common concern of humankind.[114]

The other dimensions of the right, as spelt out by Rapporteur Shaheed, serve to address power dynamics that are affected or engendered by science and technology and are not explicitly addressed under international biodiversity law or the law of the sea. The benefit-sharing process could thus serve to critically assess whether information-sharing, capacity building and marine technology transfer lead to non-discriminatory results, prioritize the needs of the vulnerable, and factor in the need to protect against negative consequences of scientific research. In that way, the benefit-sharing process can prevent dependency on external, ready-made solutions that may not fit particular circumstances, or may allow for the exertion of undue influence by donor countries.[115] The human right to science, therefore, emphasizes key substantive considerations (non-discrimination, priority benefitting the vulnerable, the prevention of environmental harm) that should inform the BBNJ negotiations on topics underpinned by scientific cooperation, as well as capacity building and technology transfer related to MGRs, with a view to grounding ocean science co-production.

In 2020, the Committee on Economic, Social and Cultural Rights elaborated a General Comment to further clarify the content of the human right to science, emphasizing that 'the development of science in the service of peace and human rights should be prioritized by States over other uses'.[116] The Committee elucidated that the human right to science applies to natural as well as social sciences, and to pure as well as applied research.[117] Core obligations include ensuring access to those applications of scientific progress that are critical to the enjoyment of the right to health and other economic, social

113 Morgera, 'Crossroads' (n 98) 803–31.

114 Morgera, 'International Legal Concept' (n 67) 365.

115 Elisa Morgera, Elsa Tsioumani and Matthias Buck, *Unraveling the Nagoya Protocol: A Commentary on the Nagoya Protocol on Access and Benefit-sharing to the Convention on Biological Diversity* (Brill 2014) 313 and 331.

116 Committee on Economic, Social and Cultural Rights, General Comment No 25 (2020) on science and economic, social and cultural rights (arts 15(1)(b), (2), (3) and (4) of the International Covenant on Economic, Social and Cultural Rights (2020) UN Doc E/C.12/GC/25, para 6).

117 ibid.

and cultural rights; and prioritizing allocation of public resources to research in areas where there is the greatest need for scientific progress in health, food and other basic needs related to economic, social and cultural rights, and the wellbeing of the population, especially with regard to vulnerable and marginalized groups.[118] In light of these obligations, it appears a priority for States to first of all identify collectively the greatest need for progress in ocean science to support basic economic, social and cultural rights, taking into account ecological connectivity between areas within and beyond national jurisdiction, as well as our evolving understanding of the ecosystem services provided by BBNJ. This is the first essential step as to maximize opportunities (and in fact ensure compliance with underlying international obligations) for States to ensure that BBNJ Agreement serves to realize multiple SDGs and the premise for ocean knowledge co-production.

In addition, the General Comment explicitly indicated that the human right to science also applies to inter-State relations, so that the 'collective benefits of knowledge should be shared globally'.[119] The duty to cooperate internationally towards the fulfilment of all economic, social and cultural rights,[120] results in States' obligation to recognize the benefits from international scientific cooperation and to take steps through diplomatic and foreign relations, to promote an enabling global environment for the advancement of science and the enjoyment of the benefits of its applications,[121] so as to take into account 'deep international disparities among countries in science and technology'.[122] So States engaged in international law-making processes, are to promote collaboration between scientific communities of developed and developing countries to meet the needs of all countries and facilitating their progress, while respecting national regulations.[123] From the perspective of international human rights law, multilateral agreements should enable developing countries to build their capacity to participate in generating and sharing scientific knowledge and

118 ibid, para 52.

119 Anna-Maria Hubert, 'The Human Right to Science and Its Relationship to International Environmental Law' (2020) 31 European Journal of International Law 625. See also Jacqueline Peel, 'The "Rights" Way to Democratize the Science–Policy Interface in International Environmental Law? A Reply to Anna-Maria Hubert' (2020) 31 European Journal of International Law 657.

120 ICESCR art 2 and arts 55 and 56 of the Charter of the United Nations, (1945) 1 UNTS XVI.

121 ICESCR art 15(4).

122 UN Doc E/C.12/GC/25, para 79.

123 UN Doc E/C.12/GC/25, para 79.

benefiting from its applications, as States acting on the international stage 'cannot ignore their human rights obligations'.[124]

Furthermore, the human right to science has implications for the recognition and respect of TK under the BBNJ Agreement, and the underlying human rights of indigenous peoples and other knowledge holders. The Committee on Economic, Social and Cultural Rights clearly indicated that when negotiating international agreements, States should ensure that TK is protected through an obligation to obtain FPIC when State or non-State actors conduct research, take decisions or create policies related to science that have an impact on indigenous peoples or when using their knowledge.[125] While these are critical but succinct indications, Parties to the Convention on Biological Diversity (CBD) that are negotiating the BBNJ Agreement can also rely on the 2016 CBD Mo'otz Kuxtal Guidelines on consent and benefit-sharing from the use of TK. These Guidelines have been intergovernmentally negotiated with significant inputs from indigenous peoples' representatives, and were adopted by consensus.[126] The Guidelines contain several elements that serve to explain what 'free' prior and informed consent means, which remains controversial in international biodiversity[127] and human rights law.[128] Fundamentally, the Guidelines emphasize that FPIC is a '*continual* process of building mutually beneficial, *ongoing* arrangements between users and holders of TK, in order

124 UN Doc E/C.12/GC/25, para 79, citing E/C.12/2016/1.

125 UN Doc E/C.12/GC/25, para 40.

126 Elisa Morgera, *Towards International Guidelines on Prior Informed Consent and Fair and Equitable Benefit-sharing from the Use of Traditional Knowledge*, BeneLex Blog (9 December 2015) <https://benelexblog.wordpress.com/2015/12/09/towards-international-guidelines-on-prior-informed-consent-and-fair-and-equitable-benefit-sharing-from-the-use-of-traditional-knowledge/> accessed 26 July 2021.

127 It may be noted that CBD Parties' have divergent views on adopting the terminology FPIC in the title of The Mo'otz Kuxtal Voluntary Guidelines for the development of mechanisms, legislation or other appropriate initiatives to ensure the 'prior and informed consent', 'free, prior and informed consent', or 'approval and involvement', depending on national circumstances, of indigenous peoples and local communities for accessing their knowledge, innovations and practices, for fair and equitable sharing of benefits arising from the use of their knowledge, innovations and practices relevant for the conservation and sustainable use of biological diversity, and for reporting and preventing unlawful appropriation of traditional knowledge (CBD Dec. XIII/18, 2016) (hereinafter Mo'otz Kuxtal Voluntary Guidelines).

128 eg Mattias Åhrén, *Indigenous Peoples in the International Legal System* (Oxford University Press 2016) 217–18; José Carolos Morales (Expert Mechanism on the Rights of Indigenous Peoples), *Follow-up Report on Indigenous Peoples and the Right to Participate in Decision-making, with a Focus on Extractive Industries* (2012) UN Doc A/HRC/21/55, paras 38(b), 39(h) and 43.

to build trust, good relations, mutual understanding, intercultural spaces, knowledge exchanges, and to create new knowledge and reconciliation'.[129] This is a key clarification that consent or approval is an iterative process, not a one-time exercise, which 'should underpin and be an integral part of developing a relationship between users and providers of [TK]'.[130] In line with this understanding, the Mo'otz Kuxtal Guidelines emphasize that benefit-sharing is also about iterative partnership building, rather than a top-down, one-time or unilateral flow of benefits where indigenous peoples are passive beneficiaries.[131] Furthermore, the Mo'otz Kuxtal Guidelines draw attention to the role of benefit-sharing in supporting cultural reproduction, by stating that 'benefit-sharing could include a way of recognizing and strengthening the contribution of indigenous peoples and local communities to the conservation and sustainable use of biological diversity, including by supporting the intergenerational transmission of [TK]'.[132] All these elements can inform substantive and institutional modalities of international cooperation in the BBNJ context, feeding into a clearer and more integrated approach to ocean knowledge co-production.

On the whole, compared to other human rights that are also relevant for the BBNJ negotiations, the human right to science focuses on the agency for developing countries, as well as TK holders, in co-identifying benefits and more equitable modalities for international scientific cooperation for the protection and full realization of other human rights (and multiple SDGs), with an emphasis on the vulnerable. Thus, the human right to science can be used to support the progressive development of the international law in relation to the marine environment to support 'effective, equitable, democratically legitimate and accountable processes and outcomes in relation to the application of science and technology'.[133] Along these lines, the BBNJ Agreement should contribute to enhancing the capacity of developing countries (particularly those that are most connected to ABNJ) and of TK holders to contribute to ocean science and participate in more integrated, inclusive and transdisciplinary decision making on BBNJ, by fostering co-production of ocean knowledge and transformative governance. This in turn would require inter- and trans-disciplinary research to develop new, or adapt existing, scientific methods and tools, such as modelling, to the respectful and constructive integration of TK, although

129 Mo'otz Kuxtal Guidelines, para 8 (internal citations omitted) (emphasis added).
130 ibid.
131 ibid para 23(a). The need for partnership with indigenous and local knowledge is also underscored by Yow Mulalap and others (n 33) 7.
132 Mo'otz Kuxtal Guidelines, para 13.
133 Hubert, 'Human Right to Science' (n 119) 625.

some international experience on the integration of indigenous and local knowledge in global scientific assessments is being accrued.[134]

It must be acknowledged, however, that there continues to be skepticism and criticism that recourse to human rights is inherently anthropocentric and detracts from focusing on ecosystem integrity, which could be considered at the core of the BBNJ Agreement objectives of conservation and sustainable use of biodiversity. It is argued here, however, that growing scientific understanding of the inter-dependencies of human well-being and biodiversity reveals a potentially undue concern about anthropocentricity: humans are part and parcel of ecosystems, as deeply as at the level of microbiota, for instance.[135] So, as long as human rights are used to the benefit of that inter-dependency, ecosystems stand to benefit as much as humans. The consideration of these inter-dependencies opens sites for a more informed political debate that move away from an expert-driven and technocratic approach focused on minimizing damage that is 'prevalent in international environmental law',[136] and speaks to the concerns about anthropocentrism. Instead, a broader understanding of the risks and benefits for both humans and nature can be supported by the consideration of the different dimensions of the right to science.[137]

Ultimately, the human right to science helps to bring into the BBNJ deliberations more serious and systematic consideration of the power issues that characterize MSR and that prevent transformative governance. After all, for the BBNJ Agreement to make a real difference in the implementation of LOSC provisions on MSR that can contribute to effective conservation and sustainable use of BBNJ, real-life challenges need to be understood and addressed.[138] As social scientists have amply demonstrated, notwithstanding a culture of peer review and sharing among scientists, in practice (natural and social) sciences may be marked by competitiveness, secrecy and vested interests, and the need for interdisciplinarity may prevent the application of the checks of established disciplinary standards.[139] Exogenous power dynamics at play in science have

134 Vierros and others (n 33) 7.

135 World Health Organization and Secretariat of the Convention on Biological Diversity (WHO/CBD), *State of Knowledge Review on Biodiversity and Health, Connecting Global Priorities: Biodiversity Human Health,* 2016, Summary and Key messages <https://www.cbd.int/health/doc/Summary-SOK-Final.pdf> accessed 26 July 2021.

136 Hubert, 'Human Right to Science' (n 119) 655.

137 ibid 652.

138 Venice Statement on the Right to Enjoy the Benefits of Scientific Progress and its Applications (2009) paras 13(c) and 16.

139 Sheila Jasanoff, 'Serviceable Truths: Science for Action in Law and Policy' (2015) 93 Texas Law Review 1723, 1738–40.

also been increasingly revealed.[140] The impacts of neoliberalism on scientific research practices include the diminution of public funding, the narrowing of scientific agendas on the needs of commercial actors, and the intensification of intellectual property rights impeding the production and dissemination of scientific findings.[141]

These and other evolving features of scientific endeavors have critical, but often overlooked, implications for legal distinctions between commercial and non-commercial research, for instance. Besides pure taxonomic activity, empirical analysis of scientific practices has found it extremely difficult to predict if and when genetic resources will be used for research and/or for R&D purposes so the lines between non-commercial/commercial, basic/applied research are increasingly blurred and even the existence of intellectual property rights may not be a sufficient basis for determining whether research is commercial or non-commercial.[142] As a result, the selection and framing of research questions, and the selection and use of evidence,[143] have implications for other public policy objectives down the line such as inclusiveness, responsiveness to societal needs,[144] and fit into social practices and local meaning.[145]

## 4 What Difference Could the Human Right to Science Make for the BBNJ Negotiations?

Applying the lens of international human rights law, and in particular the human right to science, to the governance of BBNJ is necessary, first, to clarify that international scientific cooperation is not just a matter of the law of the

140 Nico Stehr, 'The Social and Political Control of Knowledge in Modern Society' (2003) 55 Science Journal 643; Saskia Vermeylen, Georges Martin, and Roland Clift, 'Intellectual Property, Rights Systems and the Assemblage of Local Knowledge Systems' (2008) 15 International Journal of Cultural Property 201, 210.

141 Special Issue on Science and Technology Studies and Neoliberal Science of (2010) 40 Social Studies of Science.

142 Elisa Morgera and Miranda Geelhoed, 'The notion of "Utilisation" in the Nagoya Protocol and the EU ABS regulation for the upstream actors' (2016) Report to the European Commission available at <https://ec.europa.eu/environment/nature/biodiversity/international/abs/pdf/ABS%20Final%20Report%20upstream%20users.pdf> accessed 26 July 2021.

ENB PrepCom4 (n 86).

143 Jasanoff, 'Serviceable Truths' (n 139) 1742–43.

144 Sheila Jasanoff, 'Technologies of Humility: Citizen Participation in Governing Science' (2003) 41 Minerva 223.

145 Sheila Jasanoff, 'A New Climate for Society' (2010) 27 Theory, Culture & Society 233.

sea and of international biodiversity law. This should not come as a complete surprise, as LOSC itself indicates that MSR is to be conducted in compliance with all relevant regulations,[146] which 'opens the door for the right to science to influence the interpretation of [this] regime'.[147] Clarifying that international obligations on marine scientific cooperation provide a vehicle for implementing human rights, in turn, serves to underscore their legally binding nature,[148] as questions have been raised in the BBNJ negotiations about whether or not the BBNJ Agreement should include mandatory provisions on benefit-sharing, technology transfer and capacity building.[149]

In addition, interpreting the obligations that are framed in general terms under LOSC and the CBD in a mutually supportive way also in the light of international human rights law, serves to clarify the limits to States' discretion and the content of their due diligence obligations. For instance, States have minimum standards to meet in negotiating treaty provisions on benefit-sharing, capacity building and technology transfer, including intellectual property, in the light of application of the human right to science to inter-State relations. This is quite a remarkable departure from the LOSC deference to intellectual property rights seen as the 'promise of profit secured by exclusive commercialization rights'.[150] Rather than allowing States to choose between 'legislative, administrative or policy measures' on benefit-sharing,[151] legislative guarantees should be specifically required to ensure protection of relevant human rights.[152] In addition, obligations on ABMTs and EIAs need to clarify due diligence standards in preventing negative impacts on the human rights of individuals and communities that are exposed to the impacts of activities in ABNJ because of ecological connectivity.[153] Furthermore, human rights standards need to be applied to the notion of consultation and participation[154] across

146 LOSC art 240(d).
147 Hubert, 'Human Right to Science' (n 119) 647.
148 ibid 628.
149 eg Revised Draft Agreement art 44.
150 Kristin Bartenstein, 'Article 267' in Proelss (n 28) 1774.
151 Revised Draft Agreement art 10.
152 With regard, for instance, to protecting the rights of TK holders, see Inter-American Court of Human Rights, *Case of the Saramaka People v. Suriname*, Judgment (Preliminary Objections, Merits, Reparations and Costs) 28 November 2007, para 194.d; *Case of Kaliña and Lokono Peoples v Suriname*, Judgment (Merits, Reparations and Costs) 25 November 2015, para 305(d); *Kichwa Indigenous Communitiy of Sarayaku v Ecuador* Judgement (Merits and reparations) 27 June 2012, paras 299–300.
153 Popova and others (n 20).
154 See Yadav and Gjerde (n 4) 6, on the importance of participation for resilience.

the BBNJ instrument, moving beyond an unqualified notion of public participation or stakeholder engagement.

### 4.1 *MGRs, Capacity Building and Technology Transfer*

As I have argued elsewhere,[155] the human right to science can support a principled and integrated approach to multilateral benefit-sharing from MGRs, fostering deeper cooperation on the basis of existing LOSC obligations on scientific research, capacity building, technology transfer and environmental protection. This could allow for the BBNJ Agreement to contribute to responsible and inclusive research and innovation as 'the low chance of commercial success from biodiscovery, combined with the long timeframe for potential financial returns, means that some of the most significant benefits are non-monetary, emerging from the research process itself rather than from commercial products'.[156]

So far in the BBNJ negotiations, proposals have generally focused on types and triggers of benefits. Benefit-sharing was then linked to access, based on the idea that different pre-conditions could be set for access for different actors or thresholds, including requirements to provide capacity building and technology transfer for the analysis and use of MGRs.[157] Among the possible conditions, one was identified as an upfront monetary contribution by upstream researchers into a global benefit-sharing fund as a mandatory advance payment, or as a voluntary payment to ensure exclusive access to certain MGRs.[158] Another (additional or alternative) option was for upstream researchers (collections and academic research institutions[159]) to ensure facilitated access to MGRs samples and research findings, on the basis of existing LOSC obligations on MSR. The sharing of pre-cruise information, samples and the publication of cruise reports, have the potential to minimize the need for re-sampling,[160] thereby contributing to preventing environmental harm, while expediting access to MGRs and generally supporting MSR cooperation 'through transparency and coordination at regional and global scales'.[161] As the

155 Morgera 'International Legal Concept' (n 67). This proposal was supported by Blasiak and others (n 17) 38–39.
156 Blasiak and others (n 17) 38.
157 ENB (n 68).
158 Broggiato and others (n 11) 28–29.
159 *Morgera and Geelhoed (n 142).*
160 Thomas Greiber, 'Common Pools for Marine Genetic Resources: A Possible Instrument for a Future Multilateral Agreement addressing Marine Biodiversity in Areas beyond National Jurisdiction' in Evanson C Kamau and Gerdg Winter (eds), *Common Pools of Genetic Resources: Equity and Innovation in International Biodiversity Law* (Routledge 2013) 399, 409; Rogers and others (n 6) 8 and 12.
161 Rogers and others (n 6) 5 and 17.

value of genetic resources is not clear at the time of access, payments by operators further down the research-and-development chain were also considered upon commercialization of products derived from MGRs.[162] Options for benefit-sharing decoupled from access have also been put forward in the literature.[163] Fundamentally, however, divergent views persist in the negotiations on whether and how benefit-sharing should be equitable, whether monetary benefit-sharing should be required, and whether an international benefit-sharing mechanism would be needed.[164]

Against this background, the argument developed here is to assess various technical proposals for the BBNJ Agreement [165] based on a broad understanding of fair and equitable benefit-sharing as part of the human right to science and the ecosystem approach. In other words, shifting from the argument often voiced during the BBNJ negotiations that new benefit-sharing obligations could negatively impact on MSR and its contribution to conservation and sustainable use of BBNJ,[166] to a logic of ocean knowledge co-production. Thus, the merits of different technical proposals should be assessed on the basis of whether they support a more concerted, institutionalized multilateral approach to ensure responsiveness to the needs of beneficiaries, provide oversight of the distribution of benefits across different regions and scales, and contribute to a more systematic encouragement of virtuous cycles through capacity building and technology transfer. Such an assessment should focus on the co-identification of real-world opportunities to increase the capacities in the Global South and among TK holders to actively participate in transformative ocean conservation and management, in the light of a shared understanding of power imbalances. To that end, an appropriate multilateral institutional structure would identify collectively the greatest need for progress in ocean science to support basic economic, social and cultural rights, taking into account ecological connectivity between areas within and beyond national jurisdiction, as well as our evolving understanding of the ecosystem services provided by BBNJ.

This would require engaging directly with developed States in their capacity as ocean research funders and discussing funding priorities and coordinated approaches, with a view to increasing the 'rigor, efficiency and effectiveness in

162 Broggiato and others (n 11); Morten Tvedt and Ane Jorem, 'Bioprospecting in the High Seas: Regulatory Options for Benefit Sharing' (2013) 16 Journal of World Intellectual Property 150, 154.
163 Humphries and others (n 68).
164 Revised Draft Agreement art 11.
165 Broggiato and others (n 13); Humphries and others (n 69); Tvedt and Jorem (n 161).
166 ENB (n 86).

a number of aspects of MSR including on MGRs of ABNJ',[167] with a view to supporting long-term capacity-building and technology transfer and skills development (particularly for early-career researchers) across disciplines through knowledge co-production, including to contribute to EIAs.[168] Funders should also reflect on supporting new collaborative approaches and learning across scales,[169] as a way to support ocean knowledge co-production and transformative governance.

The human right to science can also support negotiations on digital sequence information under the BBNJ process, focusing on existing information-sharing obligations, promoting transparency and the gradual development of multilateral governance of genetic resource-related information.[170] This institutionalized approach could further respond to the considerations made under the human right to science on technology transfer.[171] Shaheed pointed to an

> implied obligation for developing countries [to prioritize] the development, import and dissemination of simple and inexpensive technologies that can improve the life of marginalized populations rather than innovations that disproportionately favour educated and economically affluent individuals and regions.[172]

She then underscored a

> corresponding obligation for industrialized countries to comply with their international legal obligations through provisions of direct aid, as well as development of international collaborative models of research and development for the benefit of developing countries and their populations.[173]

---

167 Rogers and others (n 6) 18 and 20.

168 ibid 15 and 18.

169 Morgera and Ntona (n 87).

170 For a summary of how this issue was discussed in the BBNJ negotiations, Charles Lawson and Michelle Rourke, 'Digital Sequence Information as a Marine Genetic Resource under the Proposed UNCLOS Legally Binding Instrument' (2020) 122 Marine Policy 103878. See also the proposal for including digital sequence information in Humphries and others (n 68) 9–11.

171 Morgera 'International Legal Concept' (n 67). For a different view, see Rumiana Yotova and Bartha Knoppers, 'The Right to Benefit from Science and Its Implications for Genomic Data Sharing' (2020) 31 European Journal of International Law 665.

172 Shaheed (n 109) para 68.

173 ibid.

These recommendations should be read in conjunction with the need to take into account the preferences of intended beneficiaries and local contextual elements in assessing which technologies may be usefully and equitably shared, as was cautioned by former UN Special Rapporteur on the Right to Food, De Schutter.[174] A global institutionalized approach to benefit-sharing could thus support States' compliance with their international human rights obligations in the joint setting of priorities and understanding of 'legitimate interests'[175] and 'needs of developing States'[176] in terms of basic economic, social and cultural rights, taking into account ecological connectivity between areas within and beyond national jurisdiction, as well as our evolving understanding of the ecosystem services provided by BBNJ in the context of capacity building and technology transfer.

Such an institutionalized approach could take the form of a multilateral platform for dialogue, learning, oversight and priority-setting to integrate expertise from the bottom up and support the agency of beneficiaries (TK holders and scientists from the Global South), as well as database managers. This would be with a view to ensuring transparency, continuous learning and genuine partnership-building to identify and assess obstacles, and to propose enhancements, to the interoperability of existing systems and the distribution of benefits across regions and scales.[177]

### 4.2 *EIAs and ABMTs*

The four dimensions of the human right to science can also be linked to the underlying obligations of scientific cooperation underpinning environmental impact assessments and area-based management tools in the BBNJ negotiations, with a view to supporting ocean knowledge co-production. The BBNJ Agreement could approach existing inequity by providing multilateral institutional approaches and rules that can help to ensure that all States: can equally share in the benefits from scientific advances that can support ABMTs and EIAs without discrimination; can have an opportunity to contribute to scientific research; can

---

174 Olivier De Schutter, 'The Right of Everyone to Enjoy the Benefits of Scientific Progress and the Right to Food: From Conflict to Complementarity' (2011) 33 Human Rights Quarterly 304, 348.

175 Revised Draft Agreement art 7.d.

176 Revised Draft Agreement art 9.4.

177 Elisa Morgera, Stephanie Switzer and Miranda Geelhoed, 'Study for the European Commission on 'Possible Ways to Address Digital Sequence Information – Legal and Policy Aspects' (December 2019) available at <https://ec.europa.eu/environment/nature/biodiversity/international/abs/pdf/Final_study_legal_and_policy_aspects.pdf> accessed 25 October 2021.

contribute to protect against negative consequences of scientific research or its applications on food, health, security and the environment; and set priorities for scientific research that focus on key issues for the most vulnerable.

Notably, there is a need to include provisions in the BBNJ Agreement on 'strategic environmental assessments', which remain controversial[178] even if CBD Parties have an obligation to carry out SEAs.[179] Strategic assessments would need to consider potential impacts on human rights, as well as opportunities to contribute to the different dimensions of the right to science. This would respond to the need to ensure that networks of MPAs support sustainable use for key services such as harvesting genes for product development by industry, or wilderness areas to protect pristine habitats that provide key ecosystem services for those actors.[180]

In addition, support should be provided for advancing research to test the potential outcomes of protecting genetic diversity in multiple, connected MPAs.[181] More specific international obligations and standards[182] on environmental impact assessments and strategic environmental assessments, in turn, could support the integration of genetic biodiversity into the planning and decision-making of multiple sectors that may impact and benefit from the ocean genome.[183] Equally, EIAs should refer to relevant human rights considerations, while currently there are controversial references to more generic 'interrelated socioeconomic [social and economic], cultural and human health impacts'.[184]

### 4.3 *Institutions*

The institutional structure to support the implementation of the BBNJ Agreement needs thus to be conceived also in human rights terms.[185] The reference to 'needs assessment' in the current BBNJ Agreement draft, for instance,[186] should be expanded to an obligation to identify collectively the greatest need for progress in ocean science to support basic economic, social and cultural rights,

178 Revised Draft Agreement arts 1(13), 21bis(c), and partial brackets in art 28.
179 Harrison (n 37) 46; CBD art 14(b).
180 Blasiak and others (n 17) 29.
181 ibid 31.
182 Revised Draft Agreement art 23(3) alt1.
183 Blasiak and others (n 17) 30.
184 Revised Draft Agreement.
185 For an overview of the institutional options explored so far in the BBNJ negotiations, see Nichola Clark, 'Institutional Arrangements for the New BBNJ Agreement: Moving beyond Global, Regional, and Hybrid' (2020) 122 Marine Policy 104143.
186 eg Revised Draft Agreement art 44(4).

taking into account ecological connectivity between areas within and beyond national jurisdiction, as well as our evolving understanding of the ecosystem services provided by BBNJ. Thus, the governing body of the BBNJ Agreement should have the powers necessary to promote an enabling global environment for the inclusive advancement of ocean science and the enjoyment of the benefits of its applications,[187] in the face of the current deep international disparities among countries in science and technology. It should further support States in ensuring access to those applications of scientific progress that are critical to the enjoyment of the right to health and other economic, social and cultural rights; prioritizing allocation of public resources to research in areas where there is the greatest need for scientific progress in health, food and other basic needs related to economic, social and cultural rights, and the wellbeing of the population, especially with regard to vulnerable and marginalized groups.[188] In respectfully integrating TK, it should also ensure respect for the human rights of indigenous peoples and local communities, with a view to sharing equitably the benefits of BBNJ conservation and sustainable use.[189]

The proposed scientific and technical body composed of experts from different disciplines (notably integrating social sciences, as underscored by the UN Decade of Ocean Science, for 'transformative ocean science'),[190] including TK holders,[191] could then provide a platform for learning about the actual barriers to the realization of equity and fairness in participating in ocean knowledge production and sharing benefits from ocean science with a view to identifying solutions across scales. The scientific and technical body would then facilitate dialogue with expected beneficiaries, with a view to co-developing integrated responses across a range of actors and different communities of practices involved in the use of MGRs and digital sequence information in different sectors. This would be based on shared understanding of changing scientific practices, and foster understanding of the different economics underpinning particular sectors and their contributions to BBNJ conservation and sustainable use.[192]

The proposed clearinghouse could also be created in more ambitious terms under the BBNJ Agreement: not just as an online repository of information,

187 ICESCR art 15(4).

188 UN Doc E/C.12/GC/25, para 52.

189 Vierros and others (n 33).

190 Summary of the Implementation Plan of the UN Decade for Ocean Science for Sustainable Development 2021–2030 (2021), 11 and 13.

191 Revised Draft Agreement art 49. This is also supported in the Implementation Plan of the UN Decade for Ocean Science (ibid). Along similar lines, Humphries and others (n 68) 11–12.

192 Morgera, Switzer and Geelhoed (n 177).

but as an interactive platform to support concerted and iterative dialogue to map and match to the priorities of beneficiaries in effectively making use of, and contributing to the production of, ocean science for the conservation and sustainable use of BBNJ. This could serve to implement the right to science in terms of setting priorities for the vulnerable, by supporting a focus on 'high-priority material' for instance,[193] and assessing issues leading to discriminatory results in the sharing of information, by monitoring effectiveness through feedback and periodic consultations. In addition, it could serve to provide institutional support for brokering of scientific cooperation, capacity-building and technology-transfer opportunities.[194] This is particularly necessary as 'a full inventory of national marine science capacity is lacking, as is an inventory of ocean-related [capacity building and technology transfer] efforts'.[195] It could focus initially on non-monetary benefits, with a view to exploring in the interim technological solutions to move towards monetary benefit-sharing, by tackling systematically inter-operability of databases and other online tools, facilitating the sharing of effective capacities and technologies to make use of them, and enhancing opportunities for collaboration that can help ensure that all participate in relevant research efforts.[196]

## 5 Conclusions

The BBNJ negotiations present an opportunity to spell out in more detail the duty to cooperate in the conservation and sustainable use of BBNJ in a mutually supportive manner, not only with international biodiversity law, but also international human rights law. Such a policy and legal coherence can also enhance the chances of a new international treaty to contribute synergistically to the realization of several SDGs.[197] To that end, the BBNJ negotiations should prioritize the development of obligations that can contribute to ocean

193 International Treaty on Plant Genetic Resources for Food and Agriculture (ITPGR) Res 3/2015.

194 Morgera 'International Legal Concept' (n 67); Humphries and others (n 68) 4; Rogers and others (n 6) 18.

195 Vierros and Harden-Davies (n 29) 2.

196 Morgera, Switzer and Geelhoed (n 177).

197 Human Rights Council Res 37/24 and 37/25 (2018). Also note the proposal to showcase contributions to the SDGs through the benefit-sharing mechanism of the BBNJ Agreement in Humphries and others (n 68) 9, and the importance of capacity building for the realization of multiple SDGs in Vierros and Harden-Davies (n 29) 4.

knowledge co-production as an essential path towards transformative ocean governance.

In particular, the BBNJ Agreement could build on a broad notion of fair and equitable benefit-sharing, which draws both from the ecosystem approach and from the human right to science, to devise more detailed forms of international scientific cooperation across all elements of the package with a view to maximizing its contributions to ocean health and its multiple impacts on human wellbeing. Fundamentally, this will support the agency of countries in the Global South and TK holders in the co-identification of benefits and modalities for advancing ocean science and ocean governance. The BBNJ Agreement can thus provide detailed processes, criteria and structures for multilateral dialogue and oversight on the multiple equity issues underlying all elements of the BBNJ package with a view to building stronger partnerships for the advancement of knowledge, conservation and sustainable use of marine biodiversity across current capacity disparities.

The human right to science can help to identify and address injustices and power imbalances in the production and use of ocean knowledge, that in turn prevent more effective efforts to conserve and sustainably use BBNJ. The human right to science further serves to clarify that these injustices are considered a matter of international human rights law so States have specific obligations to prevent negative impacts on human rights arising from these power asymmetries in developing the BBNJ Agreement. This normative understanding provides the rationale and the content for enhanced international cooperation and more defined due diligence obligations to co-develop effective solutions for the conservation and sustainable use of BBNJ through inclusive ocean science. A broadly conceived benefit-sharing process could thus serve to develop clearer rules and an institutionalized approach to critically assess whether information-sharing, capacity building and marine technology transfer lead to non-discriminatory results, prioritize the needs of the vulnerable, and factor in the need to protect against negative consequences of scientific research.

Furthermore, the BBNJ Agreement should include obligations that support the co-production of ocean science as a basis for truly joint governance based on shared concepts of scientific collaboration and increased capacities in the Global South and among TK holders to actively participate in transformative ocean conservation and management across scales. To that end, it is necessary to develop an appropriate multilateral institutional structure to identify collectively the greatest need for progress in ocean science to support basic economic, social and cultural rights, taking into account ecological connectivity between areas within and beyond national jurisdiction, as well as our evolving understanding of the ecosystem services provided by BBNJ. These are essential steps to ensure compliance with existing international obligations on the protection of the marine environment, on biodiversity and on human rights, so as to ensure that BBNJ Agreement serves to realize multiple SDGs.

CHAPTER 10

# The Construction of Ocean Space in Areas beyond National Jurisdiction

*A Fisheries Perspective*

*Richard Barnes*

## 1 Introduction

This chapter examines the development of fisheries regulation in areas beyond national jurisdiction (ABNJ) from a constructivist approach. In doing so, it provides important insights into how the construction of space is influenced by law making and institutional constraints, some of which reflect bias or imbalance in powers structures in international law. Many have defended law as a discreet and coherent discourse, but few have argued that it operates in isolation from material, social, or political discourse.[1] Recognizing this wider context, constructivist approaches to international law show how social interaction and practice can create and give effect to law.[2] In this tradition, law is viewed as a continuous communicative process wherein interactions between various actors, conditioned through institutional structures and practices, make law and generate compliance with it.[3] As constructivism focuses

1 Whilst the terms social and political are more commonly used, 'material' is less familiar. Here, and in the rest of this chapter, it refers to physical objects, resources and spaces (as well as their physical attributes) that frame social relations.

2 See for example, Jutta Brunnée and Stephen J Toope, 'Constructivism and international Law' in Jeffrey L Dunoff and Mark A Pollack (eds), *Interdisciplinary Perspectives on International Law and International Relations: The State of the Art* (Cambridge University Press 2012). This approach specifically underpins Myres S McDougal and William T Burke, *The Public Order of the Oceans* (Yale University Press 1982).

3 See for example Abram Chayes and Antonia H Chayes, *The New Sovereignty: Compliance with International Regulatory Agreements* (Harvard University Press 1995); Harold H Koh, 'Why Do Nations Obey International Law? Review of *The New Sovereignty: Compliance with International Regulatory Agreements* by A Chayes and A Handler Chayes, and of *Fairness in International Law and Institutions* by TM Franck' (1997) 106 Yale Law Journal 2599; Moshe Hirsch, 'The Sociology of International Law' (2005) 55 University of Toronto Law Journal 891; Ian Johnstone, *The Power of Deliberation: International Law, Politics and Organizations* (Oxford University Press 2005); Jutta Brunnée and Stephen J Toope, *Legitimacy and Legality in International Law: An Interactional Account* (Cambridge University Press 2010).

 | DOI:10.1163/9789004506367_011

on discursive, interactional practices, it is well-suited to bridging between law and other social science discourse[4] and to engaging with discourse about materiality.[5] Materiality here refers not simply to things as the mere object of legal relations (ie artifacts and their attributes), it also includes the meaning vested in such things, which in turn can constitute social and cultural practices and identities in respect of those things.[6] This is important, because we need to understand how law influences and is influenced by the material world. Constructivism offers a more complete account of how and why law is created than approaches which focus simply on law as a system of rules flowing from formal sources. This makes constructivism a valuable tool to examine how the current regime for the governance of ABNJ is developing, how different factors influence law-making for ABNJ, and how it could develop. In ABNJ, the development of a legal regime is closely bound up with wider material, social or political concerns, so it is important that we are sensitive to these.[7]

Using fisheries in ABNJ as an exemplar, I argue that international law plays a critical role in constructing ocean space, but that an insensitive use of international law can limit the possibilities for the more effective governance of oceans space and limit the opportunities for certain interests to feed into debates and decisions about how to regulate activities in ABNJ. By way of clarification, space here is used not merely to describe the physical domain; I am making an ontological commitment to the oceans as a material space characterized by dynamic and fluid qualities, as a social space where meaning is constructed, and as a common space beyond the exclusive domain of individual States.[8] The material, legal and social conditions that are at play in ABNJ demand a holistic, integrated approach to oceans governance and the accommodation of fisheries within an international legally binding instrument on ABNJ (BBNJ Agreement). To do otherwise draws an artificial boundary between fishing and other activities in ABNJ; it ignores the fact that fishing has the largest impact

4 Friedrich Kratochwil, *Rules, Norms, and Decisions: On the Conditions of Practical and Legal Reasoning in International Relations and Domestic Affairs* (Cambridge University Press 1989).

5 Alexander Wendt, 'Anarchy is what states make of it: the social construction of power politics' (1992) 46 International Organization 391.

6 Ian Woodward, *Understanding Material Culture* (Sage 2007).

7 UNGA Res 48/263 (17 August 1994) states that 'political and economic changes, including in particular a growing reliance on market principles, have necessitated the re-evaluation of some aspects of the regime for the Area and its resources'.

8 Henri Lefebvre, *Production of Space* (1974) (Donald Nicholson Smith tr, Oxford University Press 1991). More recently, see Kimberley Peters and Philip Steinberg, 'The ocean in excess: Towards a more-than-wet ontology' (2019) 9 Dialogues in Human Geography 293.

on the health of marine biodiversity.[9] More profoundly, it impedes the opportunities for the interactions that are a necessary part of the law creation process; it limits the opportunities to remedy the situation.

The construction of ocean space is an interactional process. Accordingly, the absence of, or limitations upon, interactional mechanisms deny law a proper function in constructing social space. For Brunnée and Toope, social norms emerge from social interaction and social learning, which, in turn, generate shared understandings.[10] This ensures law is congruent with external norms. When combined with a theory and practice of legality this generates legitimacy and compliance. Yet this is not without its challenges. As Brunnée and Toope point out:

> One of the major theoretical controversies within constructivism today relates to the power of shared understandings to shape the perceptions and decisions of social actors. How does one understand the balance between the explanatory power of structure, including structures of ideas and discourse, and of agency? Do people retain significant agency over their own behavior, or do they tend to replicate intersubjective habits, discursive patterns, or pre-existing practices?[11]

This chapter contributes to this debate by making explicit how law structures the interactions where these considerations are at play in the development of a regime for ABNJ. If we deny or limit the possibilities for interaction, then we risk embedding structural weaknesses within the governance regime for ABNJ. If fisheries are not exposed to regular and critical insights from other ocean perspectives such as environmental concerns, then this will limit the influence of such concerns on the management of fish stocks. And if this is a deliberate strategy, then it is one that not only perpetuates unstainable or harmful fishing practices,[12] it undermines the effectiveness and legitimacy of the wider regime for ABNJ.

---

9 Richard Barnes, 'Fisheries and Biodiversity' in Malgosia Fitzmaurice, David M Ong and Panos Merkouris (eds), *Research Handbook on International Environmental Law* (Edward Elgar 2010) 542.

10 Brunnée and Toope, *Legitimacy and Legality* (n 3).

11 Brunnée and Toope, 'Constructivism' (n 2) 123.

12 One can point the failure of CITES to deal with Atlantic Bluefin Tuna as an example of this type of 'closed' thinking. Renée Martin-Nagle, 'Unsuccessful Attempt to List Atlantic Bluefin Tuna in CITES Appendix I' (2010) 25(4) International Journal of Marine and Coastal Law 609.

Although the emerging regime for ABNJ is potentially inclusive, some rules or processes advanced in the BBNJ Agreement could exclude particular interests. For example, the 'not undermine' principle has been used to limit regulatory possibilities and to excise fisheries management from the scope of the BBNJ Agreement.[13] Although it is acknowledged that fisheries are a central element of oceans governance, they have been largely excluded from the process of developing a BBNJ Agreement.[14] This is despite the impact fishing has on marine biodiversity and the indirect impact area-based management tools (ABMTs) and environmental impact assessments (EIAs) may have upon fishing in ABNJ. States have taken the position that the BBNJ Agreement 'should not undermine existing relevant legal instruments and frameworks and relevant global, regional and sectoral bodies'.[15] And since existing frameworks and bodies are already dealing with fisheries, the BBNJ Agreement should not interfere with those existing mandates. If we adopt a wide construction of the duty to 'not undermine', then despite well-noted failings in the management of some international fisheries,[16] the opportunity to extend a degree of oversight or control – even through institutionalized engagement – will be missed. As a result, this will consolidate the exclusive mandate of regional fisheries management organisations (RFMOs) and renders them less susceptible to influences from [within] wider ocean governance processes.[17] At best, necessary

---

13 Zoe Scanlon, 'The art of "not undermining": possibilities within existing architecture to improve environmental protection in areas beyond national jurisdiction' (2018) 75 ICES Journal of Marine Science 405; Andrew Friedman, 'Beyond "not undermining": possibilities for global cooperation to improve environmental protection in areas beyond national jurisdiction' (2019) 76 ICES Journal of Marine Science 452.

14 Richard Barnes, 'Fisheries and ABNJ: Enhancing and Advancing Cooperation' in Tomas Heidar (ed), *New Knowledge and Changing Circumstances in the Law of the Sea* (Brill 2020) 124–53.

15 UN Doc A/RES/72/249, 19 January 2018 [7].

16 See for example, the failure of the IATTC to agree conservation and management measures for 2021. See <www.globaltunaalliance.com/general/gta-expresses-profound-disappointment-at-lack-of-tropical-tuna-management-in-eastern-pacific/> accessed 20 April 2021.

17 On the governance gaps and limits of RFMOs, see Daniela Diz Pereira Pinto, *Fisheries Management in Areas beyond National Jurisdiction: The Impact of Ecosystem Based Law-Making* (Martinus Nijhoff 2013); Brian Pentz and Nicole Kenk, 'The 'responsiveness gap' in RFMOs: The critical role of decision-making policies in the fisheries management response to climate change' (2017) 145 Ocean & Coastal Management 44; Erik J Molenaar, 'Participation in Regional Fisheries management Organizations' in Richard Caddell and Erik J Molenaar (eds), *Strengthening International Fisheries Law in an Era of Changing Oceans* (Hart 2019); James Harrison, 'Key Regional Fisheries Governance Challenges' in Caddell and Molenaar, ibid; Richard Caddell in 'International Fisheries Law and Interactions with Global Regimes and process', in Caddell and Molenaar (ibid).

interactions between fisheries and environmental bodies will be left to ad hoc measures, such as the North-East Atlantic Fisheries Commission and OSPAR Memorandum of Understanding in 2008.[18] However, ad hoc cooperation is well-short of the strong, system-wide cooperation that is required to effectively govern ABNJ.[19]

This chapter makes three specific contributions to the debates about the governance of ABNJ. The first is to demonstrate the critical importance of law in structuring the construction of social space. The second is to demonstrate the need for law to be sensitive to the material and social conditions at play in ABNJ – something that seems to be lacking at present. There is much debate in the literature about the meaning of 'not' undermine' and about how the BBNJ Agreement can and should relate to existing laws and institutional mandates. For this reason, I focus specifically on the need for integrated and holistic governance. My third contribution is situated in the debate about the meaning of not undermine, and shows the importance not only of enabling constructive interactions in the BBNJ Agreement, but for the Agreement to positively orchestrating these interactions through strong institutional processes and directive use of general principles of law.

The chapter proceeds as follows. Part 2 shows that the construction of ocean space is a contextual, interactional process. Drawing upon Steinberg, Allott and Ranganathan, I demonstrate the importance of power and values (or their exclusion) in the construction of ocean space. In Part 3, I advance how we think about constructivism by grounding the construction of ocean space in three core conditions (material connectivity, legal integration and social sensitivity). This serves to reinforce a more holistic interactional approach by foregrounding the necessary physical and social conditions that underpin law-making. It also shows how law can include/exclude or prioritise/marginalise certain interests at a structural level. In Part 4, the development of the BBNJ Agreement is examined in light of the requirements for interaction and cooperation that constructivism requires. Here I argue that we need stronger provisions for institutional cooperation and substantive provisions that can facilitate the interaction between fisheries and other activities in ABNJ. The chapter concludes with

18 OSPAR has adopted MOUs with the International Seabed Authority (2011) and the North Atlantic Salmon Conservation Organization (2013). A collaborative arrangement was also agreed between OSPAR and the Sargasso Sea Alliance in 2012. These are available at <www.ospar.org/about/international-cooperation/memoranda-of-understanding> accessed 20 April 2021.

19 James Harrison, *Saving the Oceans Through Law* (Oxford University Press 2017) 277–81 and 308–09. This is discussed further below in Part 4.

a call for the BBNJ Agreement to embody strong institutional mechanisms for cooperation that will enable it to orchestrate interactions between all the relevant interests at play in ABNJ.

## 2 Three Perspectives on the Construction of Ocean Space

The oceans might be viewed as a mere object of human regulation. In this narrow view, law simply applies to this space and rules are designed to serve human needs. However, this view of the oceans and law fails to account for the complexity of material and social conditions within which law operates. In reality, the shape and content of law is influenced by the physical world and vice versa. Law may define how we interact with the world and, in that sense, it is constitutive of our relationship with it. At the same time, through our legally constituted interactions with the world we can change the world. For example, by drawing maritime boundaries, we commit ourselves to a 'category' of shared or straddling fish stocks since fish move across human-made legal boundaries. In turn, how we regulate fisheries as a shared resource impacts upon the material condition of those fish stocks. The physical condition of those stocks may be in a better or worse condition as a consequence of that (more or less effective) way of regulating them. In this sense, law helps constitute the form the material world takes. The point here is that the 'legal world' and the 'material world' are mutually constituted; they are not separate from each other.

The view that the oceans and their resources are merely something used by society, and not mutually constitutive of society, has been challenged by Steinberg and others.[20] Steinberg argues that the history of the law of the sea shows the oceans to be a social space where meaning and values are constituted and reconstituted.[21] As I argue below, this process is dynamic and potentially unstable. Drawing on the work of Steinberg, Allot and Ranganathan, I show how the law of the sea is structurally flawed, and if we ignore and fail to respond to these flaws, then we will undermine the holistic and inclusive regulation of ocean space, and adversely impact on the state of our oceans.

---

20 Philip E Steinberg, *The Social Construction of the Ocean* (Cambridge University Press 2001). See also Carolyn Trist, 'Recreating Ocean Space: Recreational Consumption and Representation of the Caribbean Marine Environment' (1999) 51 The Professional Geographer 376; Marie Ntona and Mika Schröder, 'Regulating oceanic imaginaries: the legal construction of space, identities, relations and epistemological hierarchies within marine spatial planning' (2020) Maritime Studies 241.

21 Steinberg, ibid 21–22.

### 2.1 *Steinberg: 'Social Construction of the Oceans'*

As a political geographer, Steinberg is well-placed to explore the relationships between the material and the social. Steinberg's review of the literature in political economy, political geography, resource management and international relations theory shows that most research in these fields has been applied or empirical in method, focusing on specific sectoral activities, rather than an inclusive, integrated whole;[22] and that this literature generally treats the oceans as a passive object of human activity.[23] More specifically, the focus has been on the oceans as a provider of resources, as means of transport, and as a battleground between States.[24] Steinberg considers these approaches to be limited because they treat the oceans as something external to society, either a constraint on action or a thing to be used, but otherwise not connected to or influencing wider social structures and processes.[25] To address the limitations of such perspectives, Steinberg advances a more nuanced account of nature-society interactions, one that is sensitive to socio-economic power structures. This is done using a territorial political economy basis to explain the dynamic way in which the oceans are constructed as a social space:

> ... elements of a space's social construction may be tied to the material organization of society, which itself is a function of the natural material base and the technologies and systems of social organization developed for transforming nature so as to sustain social life. The political-economic logic and structures of a given society lead social actors to implement a series of uses, regulations, and representations in specific places, including ocean space. Once implemented in a particular space, each aspect of the social construction (each use, regulation, and representation) impacts the others, effectively creating a new "nature" of that space. This "second nature" is constructed both materially and discursively, and it is maintained through regulatory institutions. Finally, the social construction of space impacts the material organization of society, both directly and indirectly through its reconstruction of the nature that provides the foundation for social organization.[26]

---

22 ibid ch 1.

23 ibid 10.

24 ibid 11.

25 ibid 20.

26 ibid 21–22.

This recursive pattern of mutually constituting natural and social processes is the foundation of social organisation. It is achieved through use (economic activities such as trade or fishing), regulation (process of control – territoriality) and representation (discourse of development, geopolitics and law).[27] Law is but one part of this pattern, albeit an important one.[28]

How this applies to fisheries in ABNJ can be illustrated briefly.[29] For much of its history, the high seas have been viewed as a non-exclusive space beyond national jurisdiction where fishing and navigation occurred. This nature of space was originally constructed as a sort of *res communis* (*regulation*), a space where States exercise freedom of the seas to navigate and to fish – subject to legal obligations of due regard and non-harmful use (*discourse*). This status reflected the common pool nature of the space, but was also predicated upon an assumption that limited activities did not disturb the material nature of the oceans (ie impede navigation routes or deplete finite yet renewable fish stocks). Society, organized around broadly capitalist structures, perpetuated this status ensuring our capacity to transform the ocean to value. Over time, human activities (*use*) increased to the point where use conflicts arose, and resources became depleted. This was not a singular event; it is something manifest in a series of events over time.[30] These adverse changes to the material basis of the oceans were the product of both the way ocean space was constructed and regulated (open access), but also a product of institutional organisation, technology, market forces and consumptive demand that enabled and demanded more intensive fishing. This demanded greater exclusivity to ensure the value

27 Somewhat confusing for lawyers is Steinberg's use of the term 'regulation' – this refers not to regulation in a technical legal sense. Rather it refers to the process by which individuals/societies exert territoriality, ie define, bind, reify and control space toward some social end (Steinberg, ibid 29). It is control in the broader sense or whether something is excludable, sharable or subject to stewardship (ie *res nullius*/*res communis*). A lawyer would use regulation to describe a technical process of rulemaking. For Steinberg, this legal process is described as a discourse through which specific social meaning is constructed (along with development and geopolitics), ibid 32–38. The distinction between regulatory and representative elements is perhaps blurred by the fact that regulation (ie territorial control) and representation (ie rule-making) combine to construct meaning and the this coming together occurs within the process of law-making and manifest in legal texts.

28 ibid 34–36.

29 A range of examples is provided by Steinberg. A pertinent example is the story of the deep seabed and the move from freedom of the seas to common heritage of mankind, ibid 180–88.

30 For an overview, see Olav S Stokke, *Governing High Seas Fisheries: The Interplay of Global and Regional Regimes* (Oxford University Press 2001).

capture from the oceans (eg the regime of the exclusive economic zone (EEZ), and to an extent the LOSC/Fish Stocks Agreement approach to the high seas). In turn, the 'new' nature of ocean space (ie the EEZ, and to a lesser extent the high seas) changed the way the oceans were socially constructed, moving from freedom of the seas to a regime where stewardship and management responsibility take priority (*regulation*). This is then 'normalized' through the development of detailed legal rules, eg restrictions on access and fishing in some areas being conditional upon adherence to the rules of regional management bodies (*legal discourse*).[31] This recursive process continues to its next stage where the capitalist pressure to secure exploitation of marine biological resources in ABNJ competes with countervailing tendencies to secure the integrity of natural systems.[32] This is considered in more detail in Part 4 below.

Steinberg's approach is compelling. It is grounded in a grand sweep of qualitative evidence using examples from non-modern and capitalist societies.[33] And it charts the progress of these ideas and the resultant regulatory regimes produced for the ocean.[34] Most importantly, Steinberg captures the idea of the oceans as a contested space, and hence a site for social transformation.[35] But there are limits to his approach. First: how do we reconcile different constructions of the sea; and second: how do we account for the significant structural influence that law may have in shaping the transformative potential of ocean space. On the first point, Steinberg accepts that each construction may obscure the material reality of those who earn a living from the sea.[36] This may hide the influence different groups have in the construction of social space. He specifically refers to those who earn a living from the sea (seafarers, fishers and dockworkers). Yet, implicit in his approach is the recognition of a wider category of 'knowledge creators' through which society constructs social meaning and order. Presumably, this includes, inter alia, scientists, artists, lawyers, diplomats, journalists and teachers. On the second point, Steinberg's analysis is not fine-grained enough to show how these voices come together to construct social reality at particular regulatory moments, such as the negotiation of a treaty.[37] These different actors can feed into the construction of social space,

31 Steinberg (n 20) 125–35, 176–80.
32 ibid 187–88. See also Part 3.
33 ibid chs 2–5.
34 ibid.
35 Steinberg (n 20) 190–91, 206–09.
36 ibid.
37 See for example Steinberg's short discussion of the three United Nations Conferences on the Law of the Sea. ibid 143–49.

but they do not all have the same influence on transforming their construction of the oceans into its legal framing (or indeed geopolitical or cultural framing for that matter). This legal framing is significant because it fundamentally structures subsequent interactions between those persons who live and work at sea or use it in other ways.

Given the importance that different actors have in the construction of legal rules and, ultimately, social space, the challenge then is to examine within particular spaces or times, how the process of social construction works. The ongoing negotiation of the BBNJ Agreement is a valuable testing site. It is a pivotal moment in the construction of ocean space; it is a deliberative, plenary moment of regulatory agenda setting.[38] I return to this in Part 4, but must first show how law influences the construction of social space.

Steinberg shows the importance of an inclusive and integrated understanding of discourse in constructing social space, and he acknowledges that law has a key role to play in constituting social reality, that it operationalizes, legitimizes social relations; it 'naturalizes' material reality.[39] This is correct, but law operates in particular ways and mediates how different actors can influence the construction of space. At sea, law may determine who can do things, where and how. It may control the opportunities for interaction that help construct space in an immediate sense by the people who use the sea. Law carries a particular history and structure and with it a latent set of values that can influence the outcomes of legal process. For example, some persons have legal standing to raise a claim, but others do not. Some legal persons have accredited status to participate in negotiations, but others do not. The construction of social space is influenced by the inter-State rules. International law plays a central role in the construction of ocean space, but its structure and mode of operation may influence outcomes by privileging or excluding certain voices or by marginalizing certain types of interest.[40] If we look at the work of Phillip Allott, the means by which some material or social interests are marginalized in the international law creation process becomes obvious.

### 2.2 *Allott: 'International Law and Its Aggregative Effects'*

Allott has written widely on the structure of international law in the idealist tradition, and many of his core arguments concern the construction of social reality through ideas and wordsso are relevant to the present

38 Barnes, 'Fisheries and ABNJ' (n 14) 133–34.

39 Steinberg (n 20) 35.

40 Nico Krisch, 'International Law in Times of Hegemony: Unequal Power and the Shaping of the International Legal Order' (2005) 16(3) European Journal of International Law 369.

discussion.[41] Here I draw upon Allott's theory of the aggregation of interests in 'Mare Nostrum'[42] to reinforce two key arguments that I make about law as a constructive social process. First, since the oceans are an international space, a space beyond the exclusive authority of individual States, the primary regulation of activities occurs at the inter-State level. Accordingly, the State-centric method of interaction may result in certain (non-State) views or interests being marginalised. Second, law plays a foundational role in constructing space (eg through constitutive treaties), and so structures later opportunities for the reconstruction of social space. Accordingly, if we are to ensure participation and encompass within the construction of social space interactions between interested or affected actors, the law creation process must be structured so as to ensure there is space for wider public interests to emerge. Failure to be inclusive entrenches existing power structures and may detach the regulation of ocean space from its material condition.

Allott observes that in international law, our primary social reality is one based upon sovereignty of the State.[43] All persons and land territory are linked to one State or another through the respective principles of nationality and sovereignty. Within this construction of the international social order, relationships operate as follows. First there is an aggregation of national interests, that is to say, the interests of individuals and groups within a State, through some form of domestic legal-political process of government and this is fed into the international system. International interests are then formed through the interactions of States (and other international actors) in international fora, eg treaty negotiations. In this way, the creation of important social norms is the product of the double aggregation of domestic and then State interests, and one where the international social reality takes on a life of its own, with State interests being the 'original interests' (international law is 'law for States and by States' with other interests being of indirect concern). This marginalizes the interests of subnational groups. The cycle is completed when international law feeds back into domestic social systems according to the relational principles

41 Philip Allott, *The Health of Nations. Society and Law beyond the State* (Cambridge University Press 1998); *Eunomia: New Order for a New World* (2nd edn, Oxford University Press 2001).

42 Philip Allott, '*Mare Nostrum*: A New International Law of the Sea' (1992) 86 American Journal of International Law 764. Allott's arguments about integration, participation and accountability reinforce the general approach made in this chapter. However, the main specific point I am making relates to how law structures interests, hence the focus on aggregation and public interests.

43 ibid 774–76.

which determine the interface between the two social systems. Individuals then conduct themselves according to these 're-aggregated rules'.

Clearly, this process can distort the creation of social norms. First, it may fail to take into account sub-national interests that are not adequately represented by governments (or other international actors). Indeed, when States act in particular fora, such as an RFMO, delegates are often experts, who think and act as, for example, the 'fisheries arm' of the State. Such diplomatic silos may marginalise other concerns in sectoral fora. Second, the process does not take into account transnational interests that are not exclusive to the aggregating process within a single State, for example, the interests of multinational corporations or transnational NGOs. Even transnational actors speak to their constituents, so it is arguable that a similar aggregating logic applies to transnational actors too. For example, when civil society groups channel individual interests, they aggregate such interests according to their own organisational logic or values.[44] It may be argued that the lobbying power of such actors enables them to advance their interests more directly, and that this could be a 'corrective' avenue to ensuring 'other' interests feed into the process. However, the point is that process is distorting of interests because it operates without formal checks and balances on such influences.[45] At the very least, the influence of these practices on legal outcomes is poorly understood.[46] Third, it may exclude the common interests of all humanity, that is interests which are not merely attained through the aggregation of State system interests. In order to avoid such consequences, it is essential for law to create space for participation and the development of other interests in order to allow wider social objectives to form.[47] For Allott, the United Nations Convention on the Law of the Sea (LOSC)[48] is important because it recognises a range of actors and interests that is more widely representative of an international society and accords them space to participate

44 Karin Bäckstrand and Jonathan W Kuyper, 'The democratic legitimacy of orchestration: the UNFCC, non-state actors, and transnational climate governance' (2017) Environmental Politics 764.

45 Jonathan I Charney, 'Transnational Corporations and Developing Public International Law' (1983) Duke Law Journal 748.

46 Michele M Betsill and Elisabeth Corell (eds), *NGO diplomacy: The influence of nongovernmental organizations in international environmental negotiations* (MIT Press 2008). On the BBNJ process specifically, see Robert Blasiak and others, 'The role of NGOs in negotiating the use of biodiversity in marine areas beyond national jurisdiction' (2017) 81 Marine Policy 1.

47 Allott, *Mare Nostrum* (n 42) 777.

48 United Nations Convention on the Law of the Sea (signed 10 December 1982, entered into force 16 November 1994) 1833 UNTS 396 (LOSC).

in the law creation process.[49] By articulating participatory rights and public interests the Convention (in a truly constitutional sense) is able to shift away from the false dialectic of mere inter-State interests. What is important here is not whether this process is 'perfect', but that it exists and so maintains the possibility of change and process in the way social reality is created.

If we apply this thinking to the BBNJ process, then it becomes critical to retain the possibility of change through inclusive processes and through the grounding of values/social objectives into the text of the BBNJ Agreement. Inclusivity is advanced through institutional processes, and values/social objectives are set through the use of carefully designed treaty objectives and general principles. These two approaches are vital because the BBNJ Agreement should enhance the constitutive reach of the 1982 Convention to ABNJ. The BBNJ Agreement is not a mere sectoral regulatory tool; it will be a foundational instrument for ABNJ that structures future social interactions. In varying degrees, the interests of States and other actors in ABNJ include: the protection of the marine environment, fishing, navigation, mineral extraction and the exploitation of genetic materials. These interests are not singular, nor do they exist in isolation. ABNJ are a shared space of shared interests, and the legal process should enable those interests to come to together to constitute social norms and practices that fully reflect the material nature of that space and the actors' interests. If the opportunities for such interests to come together within institutional process are limited, then this will impede the way in which social order is constructed.

If we look at a recent analysis of the development of an ocean space regime (the seabed) by Ranganathan, we can see how the construction of social spaces is vulnerable to 'regulatory capture', and how this has structural consequences for the ongoing development of the regime for the Area.

### 2.3 *Ranganathan: 'The Constitutive Consequences of Law'*

Ranganathan describes the enclosure of the ocean floor as a 'grab'.[50] This echoes Steinberg, not only describing how exclusive claims to the ocean floor objectify the ocean and deny it as a site of value creation, but also showing that the end product of this process was to secure resource use benefits for a few States and corporations. Here law and lawyers played a critical role in driving these outcomes. Although her main focus is the seabed beyond national jurisdiction, her analysis necessarily includes the historical development of the

49 Allott, *Mare Nostrum* (n 42) 778–79.

50 Surabhi Ranganathan, 'Ocean Floor Grab: International Law and the making of an Extractive Imaginary' (2019) 30(2) European Journal of International Law 573, 576.

continental shelf that was a precursor to the regime of the Area. Ranganathan argues that this resource grab was underpinned by two factors: ocean floor geography (material conditions) and economics (use).[51] Both were treated as 'given' facts. Yet both were constructs reified through law and bearing but a tenuous link to material reality. Law was used to reify an extractive imaginary about the seabed – 'reconstituting ocean space into a distinctive legal imaginary'.[52] Here, the geography of the continental shelf as a natural prolongation of the landmass was less a fact and more a device used to explain and underpin legal claims despite anomalies inherent in the approach. Ranganathan reinforces the point that legal entitlements to maritime zones and their delimitation did not accord with the natural geography that was used to justify them.[53] Similarly, she highlights that the divide between water column/seabed or living/non-living drew artificially separated natural systems.[54] Ultimately, the corresponding legal constructs (eg natural prolongation) facilitated acquisitive processes. In order to secure exclusive control of resources and economic benefit, legal arguments were developed to separate the seabed from the superjacent waters (and the freedom of the seas).[55] The imagined potential of the seabed following the Truman Proclamation (and later the deep seabed by Pardo) hypostasized the seabed as a commercial mining space even before this was a reality. The end product of this was the 1994 Agreement on the Implementation of Part XI of the LOSC being based mainly on commercial rather than redistributive principles.[56]

> [T]his configuration has relied on – and continues to draw legitimacy from – a construction of the seabed as socio-culturally, economically and ecologically disembedded – that is, as remote, insulated and lacking local constituencies or pre-existing 'systems of meaning and practice' that

51 ibid 586–96.

52 ibid 586.

53 ibid 591.

54 ibid 590.

55 Ranganathan is keen to show that the process was influenced by a range of acts or representations and narrative created by non-State actors. It was fed by economic and non-economic interests, political solidarity, suspicion, parochial and cosmopolitan urges. But critically, it was heavily influenced by international lawyers. Here she cites the influential work of Hersch Lauterpacht ('Sovereignty over Submerged Areas' (1950) 27 British Yearbook of International Law 376): it was 'unlikely that any purely doctrinal opposition of lawyers – even if otherwise well founded – would be able to stem the hitherto uniform progress of claims and developments, which are not intrinsically unreasonable, in the matter of the "continental shelf" '. Ranganathan ibid 592–93.

56 ibid 596.

> would be ousted by the 'narrow predication of "universal interest" ' on its mining potential.[57]

This was very much a pragmatic approach by lawyers desirous of developing a common-sense, order-based system of international law.[58] Their approach required law to adapt to new circumstance rather than to adhere to doctrinal truth. In this sense, neither material nor legal coherence was essential – what mattered most was whether the rules could secure respect. Whilst this pursuit of order might be admired, it did so at the expense of important distributive concerns. Ultimately, law played a critical role in constructing the social space of the seabed around an idea of commercial mining in a way that resulted in unequal distributions of material reality and constrained possible solutions to problems of inequality and environmental harm.

Whatever the rights and wrongs of this process, the legal imaginary became part of the legal actual and this in turn influenced later constitutive practices. As Ranganathan observes, 'we have a story of reification; the seabed, undeniably, contains both oil and minerals, but their importance, and value, was consolidated through law'.[59] Lawyers played a critical role in framing the emergent social reality. States may have made claims to the continental shelf, but 'lawyers did much of the work of normalizing this model – exclusive national jurisdiction for the sake of effective exploitation – which has characterized the law'.[60] Lawyers drafted the texts and presented States with the options for how to achieve their interests. Arguably, the development of the general regime for ABNJ as framed in the Draft text of an Agreement under the United Nations Convention on the Law of the Sea on the Conservation and Sustainable Use of Marine Biological Diversity of Areas Beyond National Jurisdiction (Draft Agreement) is repeating the mistakes of history. Just as the legal text of the continental shelf regime constrained future possibilities for its governance, the Draft Agreement includes legal text (ie a notion of 'not undermine' that could be construed in wider terms) which risks detaching and reifying the differences between materially connected interests (fish/wider marine biodiversity), and it denies any institutions established under the BBNJ Agreement any power to change legal relationships in existing regional or sectoral bodies, including fisheries management bodies.

Hindsight gives us the opportunity to learn lessons: the first is to see how law can fundamentally structure how we engage with the material world. This may

57 ibid 577.
58 ibid 593.
59 ibid 591.
60 ibid 594.

be subtle, but with profound effects on access to and use of critical resources. Second, once values are fixed in law, they become difficult to shift. For example, the common heritage of mankind (CHM) principle applicable to the Area may entail measures for the protection of the marine environment, and the International Seabed Authority (ISA) has sought to adopt regulations and recommendations in mining codes in response to this. However, Ranganathan views these as ameliorative efforts (an ecological fix) that work towards 'better mining'.[61] Ecological principles are subverted to the overarching mining logic of the regime and so forestall questions about whether it should be mined at all. The key point is to recognise how law can reify certain values and how law exerts significant influence over how ocean space is subsequently constituted. Law is instrumental and it serves to frame the constructive process – influencing how certain actors or interests are represented in international interactions. As such law subtly, but fundamentally influences how those voices are heard. More than this it structures the power to create or change legal (and other) relationships.

If the oceans are a site of value creation, then the absence of explicit provisions that control the adverse impact of fishing on ABNJ, and the lack of strong institutional engagement between fisheries interests and wider environmental concerns could serve to further insulate fisheries from wider environmental and ecological imperatives.

### 2.4 *The Influence of Law on the Construction of Social Space in ABNJ*

A critical and common thread to constructivist approaches is their dependence upon some form of interactive process (claim/counter-claim; argument; justificatory discourse).[62] This is the process through which normative expectations are produced and sustained, whether this is through the internalisation of new values by actors,[63] or the practice of legality.[64] A consequence of this is that international law should ensure that these interactions are not prevented or limited through the structural isolation of materially relevant actors or interests.

International law plays a pivotal role in constructing ocean space – especially for ABNJ. Indeed, the negotiation of the BBNJ Agreement is construction

61 ibid 596–97.

62 Myres S McDougal and W Michael Reisman, 'The Prescribing Function in World Constitutive Process: How International Law is Made' (1980) 6 Yale Studies in World Public Order 249; Harold H Koh, 'Transnational Legal Process' (1996) 75(1) Nebraska Law Review 181, 184; Chayes and Chayes (n 3) 25–26; MacDougal and Burke (n 2); Johnstone (n 3) 3; Hirsch (n 3) 902.

63 Ryan Goodman and Derek Jinks, 'How to Influence States: Socialization and International Human Rights Law' (2004) 54 Duke Law Journal 621–703.

64 Brunnée and Toope, *Legitimacy and Legality* (n 3) 20–33.

in action. A wide range of interests and voices can and should play a role in constructing ocean space. Since this is a shared space where many activities overlap or impact on each other, the process of construction should be inclusive of interests and voices that speak to them (ie shipping, fishing, resource extraction, environmental goods and services, and those that engage in them). However, unless international law includes and integrates such interests, then the construction of ocean space will be hampered.[65] I accept that I make the assumption here that inclusivity will lead to a (more) satisfactory construction of ocean space, and that this assumption is open to challenge. However, what is more difficult to deny is that an inclusive approach (and hence the possibility of both more, and more varied, interactions) carries with it the greater possibility that a better construction of space will emerge through an iterative process. Indeed, the institutionalisation of exclusion can do structural violence to the construction of ocean space by distorting the recursive process through which space and society reconstitute themselves. As Allott shows, the participatory and aggregating structure of international law is already predisposed to exclusion of certain interests, so this further exclusion of interests in ABNJ is something we must be on guard against. For Ranganathan, the regime for the Area has already proven vulnerable to the exclusion of some interests through the entrenchment of commercial mining interests. This privileging of interests in the construction of social space could happen again if the development of the BBNJ Agreement fails to properly accommodate interests and effective participatory processes. To avoid that outcome, the legal needs cooperative mechanisms that accommodate a wide range of material and social interests. Material interests should include all material aspects of ocean use in ABNJ – otherwise law risks becoming detached from its material basis. Social interests should reflect the wider interests of society as far as practicable, and not merely sectors interested in the exploitation of marine genetic resources. The process ought to be deliberative and structured, rather than passive because ad hoc interactions may simply default to engagement by limited groups of powerful, self-interested actors. Finally, the process needs to be explicit and transparent in how it makes use of higher order principles. Otherwise, it is susceptible to capture by powerful or competing interest groups.[66]

65 There are risks arising from integration, particularly if this is seen to run counter to individual State interests. See further Karen N Scott, 'Environmental Governance: Managing Fragmentation through Institutional Connection' (2011) 12 Melbourne Journal of International Law 177, 211–15.

66 Vito De Lucia, 'Competing Narratives and Complex Genealogies: The Ecosystem Approach in International Environmental Law' (2015) 27 Journal of Environmental Law 91.

## 3 A More Holistic and Inclusive Construction of Ocean Space

The purpose of this Part is to show that the regulation of ocean space in ABNJ should be an inclusive, interconnected process.[67] To achieve this, we need to be sensitive to the structural influence law has on the opportunities for the construction of space. We also need to maintain structures and processes in law that enable interactions between activities that are materially, legally, and socially connected. Each of these three points is addressed in turn.

Although the construction of social space is a function of recursive social processes, it operates in respect of material conditions that influence both the possible and probable outcomes of social interactions.[68] Material conditions are those physical and socially constructed attributes of things that shape our relationship with them. As the story of Canute and his stand against the tide shows,[69] it is impossible to ignore the material qualities of the oceans when we regulate them. The material qualities of the oceans are, for example, their fluid and tidal nature.[70] Thus law cannot command the tide, but it can manage how we interact with it. The material turn is central in other disciplines like archaeology, anthropology and history, and important to Actor Network Theory or Science and Technology Studies.[71] However, the need for law to be sensitive to the material qualities of its regulatory focus is often assumed or marginalized in legal discourse.[72] This marginalisation of the material occurs because law foregrounds its subjects – the recipients of legal rights and duties, and backgrounds law's objects – the things that are the objects of rights and duties. Yet,

67 Although the focus is specifically on ABNJ, it is clear that integrated approaches also should encompass areas within national jurisdiction.

68 See for example, Oran R Young, *The Institutional Dimensions of Environmental Change: Fit, Interplay, and Scale* (MIT Press 2002).

69 Colin Hay, 'King Canute and the 'Problem' of Structure and Agency: On Times, Tides and Heresthetics' (2009) 57(2) Political Studies 260.

70 The material attributes of the oceans extend to its wider physical attributes. This is partially recognised in LOSC art 1(4).

71 Sheila Jasanoff (ed), *States of Knowledge: The Co-production of Science and Social Order* (Routledge 2004); Bruno Latour, *Reassembling the Social. An Introduction to Actor Network Theory* (Oxford University Press 2005).

72 This is only recently explored in Jessie Hohmann and Daniel Joyce (eds), *International Law's Objects* (Oxford University Press 2018). Arguably an extreme extension of this is the idea that objects should have legal standing because this is the best way of protecting them vis-à-vis anthropocentric concerns. Thus, in New Zealand and India, rivers have been granted the status of legal persons. Erin L O'Donnell and Julia Talbot-Jones, 'Creating legal rights for rivers: lessons from Australia, New Zealand, and India' (2018) 23 Ecology and Society (article 7).

the influence of material things on law and social order is inescapable. It is most profound in respect of property law (law between people in respect of things),[73] but it is critical too in the regulation of natural resources and the environment.[74] And in the law *of the sea*. In the context of natural resources (including fisheries), materiality is important for two reasons. First natural resources may be regarded as more fundamentally connected with questions of human existence *per se*.[75] That is to say that ensuring the existence of and access to (clean) water, air, food supplies and the means of shelter are common to all persons and pre-requisites for the existence of life and society. This ought to elevate their regulatory significance above other considerations. Second, the material qualities of things determine how they may be regulated. Land, air, water, fish, forests, minerals and so on possess different material qualities. Each has different functions within natural systems that must be accounted for in the design of legal rules. We cannot treat the oceans as but fluid. The common pool nature of the oceans should shape our regulatory options. We cannot ignore the way food chains operate or how fish are part of wider ecosystems. In each case, the construction of meaning occurs between the human and non-human thing. In a legal sense, the nature of a thing influences how we can use or regulate it. The history of the law of the sea is littered with examples of how the nature of the seas or the attributes of things has influenced their regulation: unboundable waters or mobile fish stocks.[76] The material nature of the thing influences how the legal regime develops, and law in turn shapes how we perceive and use that material thing. In summary, law cannot ignore the material nature of its object and in ABNJ this includes fish stocks.

Turning to the second pillar (legal process), if the construction of ocean space works through law, then law will subject the process of construction to the logic and function of law as a system of rules. Law operates by reference to existing rules and institutions.[77] This claim need not depend upon an

73 Stephen R Munzer, *A Theory of Property* (Cambridge University Press 1990) 74; Gregory S Alexander, 'Constitutionalising Property: Two Experiences, Two Dilemmas' in Janet McLean (ed), *Property and the Constitution* (Hart 1999) 95.

74 Richard Barnes, *Property Rights and Natural Resources* (Hart 2009) 37–39 and 54.

75 ibid.

76 More recently ecosystem-based approaches take the complex interaction between nature and society to another level. Seemingly grounded in nature, ecosystems are also social constructs – the product of still contested scientific knowledge and values. See Cécile Barnaud and Martine Antona, 'Deconstructing ecosystem services: Uncertainties and controversies around a socially constructed concept' (2014) 56 Geoforum 113.

77 Aspects of this rule are found in the prohibition of a non liquet, Herch Lauterpacht, 'Some Observations on the Prohibition of "Non Liquet" and the Completeness of the Law' in *Symbolae Verzijl* (Martinus Nijhoff 1958) 199 and Julius Stone, '*Non Liquet* and

exhaustive survey of legal institutions and rules, it can be substantiated by reference to the general method of law.[78] Law as both a general institution and branch of practical reason operates according to certain 'ground rules', for example, reasoning by analogy or precedent.[79] It is desirable that law is systematic and ordered – so that conduct can be planned. Yet law must also be flexible so that rules can be developed to accommodate new circumstances. If we are to mediate between competing legal claims or reconcile the tension between stability and change (something at the heart of discussions about the BBNJ Agreement mandate to not undermine existing instruments and bodies), then we need to give reasons. Law is an interactive process, and its capacity to advance depends upon the capacity of legal actors to use reason to persuade both a legal audience (eg judges, diplomats, legislators) and a plenary legal community (members of the constituent society to which law applies ie States or individuals). The contingency of law upon reason means that the progress of law is fundamentally shaped by the process of legal reasoning.

In this respect, MacCormick presents a convincing account of what makes (legal) reasons compelling. Reasons are compelling because they are universalizable, consequence sensitive, reasonable and coherent.[80] Universalisation requires that we commit to the consequences of our decisions in similar situations (ie we treat like cases alike). Consequentialism requires us to act consistently with pre-existing rules or principles so that we do not undermine the institutional authority of law.[81] It also requires us to consider the wider social consequences of a rule (for example rejecting a rule that might engender too much liberty to cause harm – such as an absolute freedom of the seas). Reasonableness requires legal authority to be exercised with due regards to 'relevant considerations'.[82] What is relevant will depend upon how the scope of legal authority is delimited – such as the proper scope of jurisdiction, or having

the Function of Law in the International Community' (1959) 35 British Yearbook of International Law 124. In defence of non liquet, Daniel Bodansky, 'Non Liquet *and the Incompleteness of International Law*' in Laurence Boisson de Chazournes and Philippe Sands (eds) *International Law, the International Court of Justice and Nuclear Weapons* (Cambridge University Press 1999) 153–70.

78 A similar argument is made by Brunnée and Toope, who draw upon the work of Fuller to construct their ground rules of legal obligation. Brunnée and Toope, *Legitimacy and Legality* (n 9) 20–33

79 See generally, Neil MacCormick, *Legal Reasoning and Legal Theory* (Oxford University Press 1978) 153, 187–88; Cass Sunstein, 'On Analogical Reasoning' (1993) 106 Harvard Law Review 741, 778–79.

80 MacCormick ibid 100.

81 ibid 101ff.

82 ibid 181ff.

regard to certain criteria when exercising discretion (this is illustrated in Part 4). Coherence requires that a rule fit or make sense within the structure of an accepted set of higher order rules or principles (eg duty not to cause harm, sustainable development).[83] Coherence reinforces the importance of law as order, but also as a purposive social enterprise, whereby law guides conduct towards a view of a good or satisfactory way of life. To the extent that these factors are used to explain why rules are adopted or decisions are made, then law exerts a capacity to compel. MacCormick's approach is consistent with constructivist approaches to law in that it applies to specific legal transactions or law-making instance. Critically, it is sensitive to both the legal and extra-legal context and consequences. MacCormick foregrounds the systemic context within which law operates and shows the contingency of legal reasoning and existing legal and social institutions. If we apply MacCormick's account of legal reasoning to how rules for ABNJ are developing, we can show that the requirements of both the consequence sensitivity of reasoning and the systemic nature of legal reasoning demand that legal rules reflect both the material objects of law and the power structuring effects of law. This strengthens the argument for inclusion of fisheries (or strong cooperative mechanisms) within the BBNJ Agreement because fish and fishing are very important material aspects of ABNJ and the Agreement will have impacts on the structuring of legal relationships in ABNJ.[84]

Although I have sought to emphasise the influence of law on the construction of ocean space, it is important to remember that law does not occur in a vacuum. As demonstrated by Steinberg and others, it is set against wider economic, political and social conditions.[85] A function of law is to regulate social co-existence in the pursuit of values that are partially independent of law.[86] Law is a social practice and as such it is not immune to wider social expectations and values – it must respond to such concerns.[87] These are the concerns of those who are ultimately affected by the operation of legal rules. The point here is not to argue in favour of any particular social rules or values.

83 ibid 193–230.

84 Part 4, below.

85 Steinberg (n 20). On the general construction of knowledge, see Paul Boghossian, *Fear of Knowledge: Against Relativism and Constructivism* (Oxford University Press 2007). On the causal and epistemic dependence of law, see Janina Dill, *Legitimate Targets? International Law Social Construction, and US Bombings* (Cambridge University Press 2015).

86 David Lyons, 'Normal Law, Nearly Just Societies, and Other Myths of Legal Theory' in Roger Brownsword (ed), *Law and the Public Interest* (F Steiner 1993).

87 This is not to deny a wider debate about what it means to say law is a social practice. See Matthew N Smith, 'Law as a Social Practice: Are shared activities at the foundations of law?' (2006) 12 Legal Theory 265.

Nor is it to engage in a wider and more controversial debate about the relationship between law and other forms of social order. Rather, it is to point out that as a matter of practice, law cannot operate as an abstract, acontextual discipline. This in turn favours a context sensitivity to wider social practices and institutions in the development of legal rules. This can be illustrated with an example: Article 27 of the International Covenant on Civil and Political Rights (ICCPR) provides that minorities 'shall not be denied the right … to enjoy their own culture …'. General Comment 23 of the Human Rights Committee has further explained that:

> … culture manifests itself in many forms, including a particular way of life associated with the use of land resources, especially in the case of indigenous peoples. That right may include such traditional activities as fishing or hunting and the right to live in reserves protected by law. The enjoyment of those rights may require positive legal measures of protection and measures to ensure the effective participation of members of minority communities in decisions which affect them.[88]

Indigenous peoples are not to be denied access to the *material* basis of their culture. Just as law must mediate material concerns, it must accommodate wider social conditions.[89] As the ICCPR example shows, material, legal and social factors elements do not operate in isolation. These three elements interact in the construction and operation of legal regimes. In the case of fisheries, we are concerned with socio-ecological systems whereby the interaction of human and natural systems changes the systems and so demand adaptive responses.[90] Thus overfishing of coastal waters caused the collapse of some fish stocks. Recognition of the economic drivers of this pressure gave rise to access limitations in order to reduce pressure on stocks to help them recover. However, it also pushed surplus fishing capacity onto the high seas – since the economic drivers of overfishing remained. This generated pressure to restrict access to high seas stocks or risk their collapse. These interactions form part

88 Human Rights Committee, General Comment 23, art 27 (Fiftieth session, 1994), Compilation of General Comments and General Recommendations Adopted by Human Rights Treaty Bodies, UN Doc HRI/GEN/1/Rev.1 38 (1994), para 7.

89 Stephen Allen, Nigel Bankes and Øyvind Ravna (eds), *The Rights of Indigenous Peoples in Marine Spaces* (Hart 2019).

90 Elinor Ostrom, 'A diagnostic approach for going beyond panaceas' (2007) 104 Proceedings of the National Academy of Sciences 15181.

of a dynamic system, and individual components cannot be understood in isolation.[91]

To summarise, the material and social contingency of law, and the nature of law as a systemic, reason-based discipline commits us to an inclusive, pluralistic, coherent and integrated approach. Despite this, some of law's ground rules may operate so as to influence the construction of ocean space to the exclusion of some of these considerations. This is shown in more detail next in the analysis of the BBNJ process and Draft Agreement.

## 4 The BBNJ Negotiations: The Construction of Ocean Space in Action

As demonstrated in Parts 2 and 3 of this chapter, the construction of social space is an interactional process. And as a legal process, it needs to be holistic and inclusive. In this light, we can view the BBNJ process as both constructing social space in action and a process of patterning or structuring future interactions. During the negotiations, the acts of perceiving, speaking, reasoning, claiming, contesting, categorizing, debating, negotiating, and producing a treaty text, are part of the process of construction, a process helping generate shared understandings. Yet we can also see, according to Allott's notion of aggregation, how this process captures a limited range of inter-State interests. According to our 'model' of construction in Part 3, the recursive process must respond to the material reality of ABNJ. It must also be sensitive to the way in which law shapes the ongoing construction of social reality. This is critical since the BBNJ Agreement will fundamentally structure the way in which future interactions occur.

In this part, I argue that the capacity of the BBNJ Agreement to structure present and future interactions is specifically shaped: first, by the way it enables different actors (and hence interests) to participate in the process of law development; second, by the way the BBNJ Agreeement structures intersections between such actors, namely by defining its relationship with other legal instruments and institutions; and third, by the way the BBNJ Agreement's aims and objectives guide cooperation through such procedures.

91 There is a burgeoning literature on systems-based approaches: James A Wilson, 'Matching social and ecological systems in complex ocean fisheries' (2006) 11 Ecology and Society (article 9) available at <www.ecologyandsociety.org/vol11/iss1/art9/main.html> accessed 20 April 2021; Serge M Garcia and Anthony T Charles, 'Fishery systems and linkages: from clockworks to soft watches' (2007) 64 ICES Journal of Marine Science 580.

The second argument is focused on two sets of provisions in the Draft Agreement that may come into tension: those requiring the BBNJ Agreement not to undermine existing regimes; and those setting out its institutional process for cooperation. I argue that in order to allow for a more inclusive constructive process, and to advance coherence and integration, we should give priority to strong, proactive cooperative mechanisms rather than a sweeping requirement not to undermine. This approach not only enables more interactions; it is consistent with the wider integrating forces that permeate the law of the sea and that connect the law with the material condition of the oceans. As De Lucia argues, we should think like the ocean and elaborate an oceanic 'lawscape' better aligned with ecological realities.[92] To privilege an expansive concept of 'not undermining' would be to constrain the interactional possibilities that enable wider material and legal interests to feed into the construction of social space in ABNJ. It is true that there are opportunities for interaction and construction of ocean space to occur in other fora, both material (through actual use of the seas) and through discourse (ie law-making in other fora such as regional organisations). However, this decentralised approach risks fragmenting the construction of social space. As stated before, the multi-lateral scope of the BBNJ Agreement means that it will play a pivotal role in setting future agendas. This failure to accommodate possibilities for fisheries interests to interact with other interests in ABNJ in such a constitutional text risks structurally limiting the possibilities for the construction of ocean space.

The third argument is that we need to underpin the agreement with strong general principles and substantive duties to have due regard to wider interests, including fishing. A principled approach, as advocated by Oude Elferink,[93] could ameliorate the exclusion of fisheries by guiding the substantive focus for how different sectoral processes can interface. Although the Draft Agreement provides some options for cooperation and coordination,[94] it remains unclear how the BBNJ Agreement can orchestrate interactions and integrate thinking towards a holistic regime for ABNJ. I argue that the articulation of general principles alongside standards and mechanisms for reviewing the development of such principles will provide a powerful means of enabling shared understandings to emerge in future interactions.

---

92 Vito De Lucia, 'The BBNJ negotiations and ecosystem governance in the Arctic' (2019) Marine Policy 103756, section 4.3.

93 Alex G Oude Elferink, 'Governance Principle for Areas Beyond National Jurisdiction' (2012) 27 International Journal of Marine and Coastal Law 205.

94 See further Part 4.2 below.

### 4.1 *Participation in the Process of Constructing Social Space in ABNJ*

Participants involved in interactions or law creation moments play critical roles in both the construction of social space and in constructivist approaches to international law-making. So, who are these actors? And does their participation influence the BBNJ process?

We can readily identify the actors participating in the BBNJ process from official records. The United Nations General Assembly (UNGA) established an Ad Hoc Open-ended Informal Working Group in 2004 to study issues relating to the conservation and sustainable use of marine biological diversity beyond areas of national jurisdiction.[95] Predominantly comprised of members of foreign ministries, a small number of States included representatives from fisheries departments.[96] Expertise and capacity varied considerably between States. Working Group sessions were also attended by a number of bodies including: inter-governmental organisations (ie the Asian-African Consultative Organization, the Caribbean Community, the EU, the IUCN, and the Pacific Islands Forum); UN Specialised Agencies (ie Food and Agriculture Organization, Intergovernmental Oceanographic Commission, World Intellectual Property Organization, and the International Seabed Authority) and bodies (eg Convention on Biological Diversity (CBD) Secretariat and UNEP); other IGOs (South East Atlantic Fisheries Commission (SEAFC), North East Atlantic Fisheries Commission (NEAFC), and Oslo and Paris Convention for the Protection of the Marine Environment in the Northeast Atlantic (OSPAR)); and a range of NGOs (Fridtjof Nansen Institute, Greenpeace, the International Chamber of Commerce, the International Coastal and Ocean Organization, the Natural Resources Defence Council, the Pew Environment Group, Sylvia Earle Alliance, and the WWF). One may also note that behind many such bodies is a hidden range of actors, with some officially registered observers acting as proxies for participants from other organisations that do not have official accreditation.

Arguably, the wider range of participants involved and interests at play in Working Group discussions, contributed towards a widely drawn mandate to develop an agreement on the conservation and sustainable use of marine biodiversity in ABNJ. UNGA Resolution 69/292 of 19 June 2015 put in motion the process for formally developing an implementation agreement.[97] The

95 UNGA Res 59/24, 17 December 2004, UN Doc A/Res/59/24, 4 February 2005.

96 eg, the EU, Canada, Indonesia, Japan, Namibia, Norway, Philippines, Republic of Korea, and the Russian Federation, see for example <www.un.org/depts/los/biodiversityworkinggroup/documents/participants_wg9.pdf> accessed 20 April 2021.

97 UNGA Res 69/292, UN Doc A/Res/69.292, 6 July 2015.

Resolution was, in principle, open to including fisheries, although the detail of this remained to be worked out. A preparatory committee (PrepCom) open to all Member States of the UN, its specialized agencies and Parties to the LOSC was established and tasked with making recommendations to the UNGA on the elements of a draft text of a binding agreement.[98] Although States have again driven this process, there was considerable input from both IGOs and NGOs.[99] It was attended by 91 States Parties to the LOSC, 10 Non-States Parties, seven IGOs, five UN specialised agencies, five UN funded programmes and agencies, 17 NGOs and two private commercial groups. All RFMOs were invited to attend PrepCom, but only a few attended: the North Pacific Fisheries Commission, the Northwest Atlantic Fisheries Organization (NAFO), and the SEAFC, and, even then, the RFMOs possessed only a limited role as observers.[100] In short, the process is broadly inclusive, but by no means exhaustive of interest groups, and RFMOs appear to have been marginally involved.

A similar spread of participation is evident in the intergovernmental conference charged with drafting the BBNJ Agreement. Crucially, formal participation is limited to members of the UN, members of the specialized agencies and parties to the LOSC.[101] However, observer status has been granted to representatives from a wide range of organisations, including UNGA observers (eg the International Council for the Exploration of the Sea), specialized agencies of the UN and related organizations, interested global and regional organisations, accredited NGOs, and associate members of regional commissions.[102] The records of participants indicate a wide range of attendance, particularly from research institutions and environmental organisations.[103] Given the present focus on the position of fisheries, it is notable that there has been engagement from fisheries organisations. The FAO, NEAFC, NAFO and NPFC have attended all sessions of the Intergovernmental Conference (IGC) to date, the South East Atlantic Fisheries Organization attended the second and third sessions, and the

98 ibid para [1(a)].

99 Robin Warner, 'Conserving marine biodiversity in areas beyond national jurisdiction: co-evolution and interaction with the law of the sea' in Donald R Rothwell and others (eds), *The Oxford Handbook of the Law of the Sea* (Oxford University Press 2015).

100 Formal participation was limited to State Members of the United Nations, members of the specialized agencies and parties to the Convention. UNGA Res 69/292, [1(a)].

101 UNGA Res 72/249, 19 January 2018, [8].

102 ibid [12–15].

103 UN Doc A/CONF.232/2018/INF.3, 28 September 2018; UN Doc A/CONF.232/2019/INF.3/Rev.2, 26 April 2019; UN Doc A/CONF.232/2019/INF/5/Rev.1, 23 October 2019.

Inter-American Tropical Tuna Commission and the International Commission for the Conservation of Atlantic Tuna attended the third session.[104]

Having identified the range of actors involved, we can turn to considering their influence on the BBNJ process. Unfortunately, there is only limited qualitative research on the BBNJ process to draw upon, and this does not cover the full duration of the negotiations, which are still ongoing.[105] What we do know is that despite initial recognition that fishing should fall within the scope of the agreement, States moved towards excluding fisheries management from the scope of the BBNJ Agreement.[106] The exclusion of any direct provision on fisheries has happened despite the recognized importance of a holistic, inclusive regime for the governance of ABNJ, and despite the presence of some States and non-State actors pushing for the inclusion of fisheries within the BBNJ Agreement.[107] In the absence of more fine-grained data on the negotiations, only some general observations on the extent of participation and influence of different interest groups and actors can be offered.

First, there may simply be a lack of interest in participating in ABNJ issues. Arguably, ABNJ are quite removed from the reality of everyday life of most people, so they tend to attract the engagement only from dedicated interest groups. In other words, the material connection wider society has with the oceans is weak or distant and this places ocean issues out of sight and out of mind. As I have argued previously, this is rooted in a more fundamental structural dislocation of ocean issues from the social and legal interests of society.[108] So far,

104 ibid.

105 Robert Blasiak and others conducted a frequency analysis of statements made by delegates during PrepCom1, showing OECD member were more likely to mention the dangers of undermining existing fisheries mandates, but there is no other data on the later or qualitative influence of delegates on outcomes of the negotiating process. Robert Blasiak and others, 'Negotiating the Use of Biodiversity in Marine Areas beyond National Jurisdiction' (2016) 3 Frontiers in Marine Science 224. More generally, see Christian Downie, 'Towards an Understanding of State behavior in Prolonged International Negotiation' (2012) 17 International Negotiation 295.

106 Richard Barnes, 'The Proposed LOSC Implementation Agreement on Areas Beyond National Jurisdiction and its Impact on International Fisheries Law' (2016) 31 *International Journal of Marine and Coastal Law* 583. The exclusion extends into the acute debates about how to treat fish in the context of MGR, and the difference between fish as a commodity or repository of genetic material. David Leary, 'Agreeing to disagree on what we have or have not agreed on: The current state of play of the BBNJ negotiations on the status of marine genetic resources in areas beyond national jurisdiction' (2019) 99 Marine Policy 21, 26.

107 Barnes ibid 594–95.

108 Richard Barnes, 'Environmental Rights in Marine Spaces' in Sanja Bogojević and Rosemary Rayfuse (eds), *Environmental Rights in Europe and Beyond* (Hart, 2018) 49–85.

the BBNJ process has never really reached 'the mainstream' and been able to attract wider engagement in the process, even though there is an increasing awareness of the deep-sea riches, the blue economy and high seas biodiversity. When we compare the BBNJ negotiations with other fora, such as the CBD or the Paris Climate talks and the resulting agreement, the differences seem stark. During the Paris Climate talks, NGOs, companies and sub-national public bodies have become 'essential agents' of treaty implementation in climate fora.[109] This may be through capacity support, advocacy, or private initiatives, such as business pledges. This agency can result in the inclusion of their interests being formalized in the resultant agreement. The Paris Agreement clarifies in its Preamble that it is essential to engage 'all levels of government and *various actors*', and the Clean Development Mechanism makes explicit reference to involvement by public and private entities. When the text was adopted, the Conference of Parties (COP) recognized the interests of a wide range of interests and the need to 'mobilize stronger and more ambitious climate action by all Parties and non-Party stakeholders, including civil society, the private sector, financial institutions, cities and other subnational authorities, local communities and indigenous peoples'.[110] This is important recognition of the material interests at stake. Similarly, there is research showing that non-States delegates are playing an influential role in the outcomes of the CBD COP.[111] These examples may cast light on the wider culture and value of participation in international law-making, although there remains a degree of resistance to empowering non-State actors.

States remain resistant to conceding authority to non-State actors in the formal law-making process. Without detouring too much into questions of legal personality and authority under international law, we can point to a body of research that shows the cautious approach of States to empowering other actors.[112] Negotiation of the BBNJ BBNJ Agreement is principally conducted by

---

109 Karin Bäckstrand, Jonathan W Kuyer, Björn-Ola Linnér and Eva Lövbrand, 'Non-state actors in global climate governance: from Copenhagen to Paris and beyond' (2017) 26(4) Environmental Politics 561.

110 Report of the Conference of the Parties on its twenty-first session, held in Paris from 30 November to 13 December 2015, FCCC/CP/2015/10/Add.1, 2.

111 Rebecca Witter and others, 'Moments of influence in global environmental governance' (2015) Environmental Politics available at <http://dx.doi.org/10.1080/09644016.2015.1060036> accessed 20 April 2021.

112 Andrew Guzman, 'International Organizations and the Frankenstein Problem' (2013) 24(4) European Journal of International Law 999; Cedric Ryngaert, 'Non-State Actors: Carving Out a Space in a State-Centred International Legal System' (2016) 63 Netherlands International Law Review 183.

States, with administrative barriers set to entry to the negotiations for other actors, even as observers.[113] Indeed, President Lee and others have repeatedly characterized the BBNJ negotiations as a State-led process. Even if other actors can inform the discussions, they have no direct role to play in the decision-making process. Of course, the formal and informal records of the negotiations do not capture the full extent of the interactions between the different participants.[114] For example, the records of the side events show active engagement by groups like the Nippon Foundation, the High Seas Alliance, and Pew Charitable Foundation.[115] There are also informal events organized by civil society and research institutions that engage formal delegates. However, we are left to speculate as to whether or not such events, formal and informal, make a difference.

Finally, and most importantly, there is a lack of interest from some States to include fisheries in the BBNJ Agreement because this would weaken the authority of those same States to pursue their interests in existing regional fisheries arrangements. As Benvenisti and Downs argue, powerful States seek to maintain fragmentation because it enables them to maintain their dominance by reducing opportunities for weaker actors to create coalitions across institutions. Fragmentation increases the transaction costs of change because change must occur in multiple fora. Thus fragmentation frees powerful States of accountability for problems of their own making that are presented as the result of systemic deficiencies rather than as flowing from their inaction.[116] Broude argues that the integration of substantive norms produces pressure to integrate authority.[117] This means that even general or indirect references to fisheries in the BBNJ Agreement may challenge the authority that limited groups of States enjoy within RFMOs. It could also expose RFMOs to greater scrutiny over the extent to which fishing activities are compatible with the potentially more far-reaching provisions on environmental protection. The bottom line here is that there is a resistance from States to the inclusion of fisheries in the BBNJ

113 Personal correspondence with De Lucia. NGO participation requires registration through ECOSOC. See <www.un.org/bbnj/content/participation> accessed 20 April 2021.

114 Some formal records are available at <www.un.org/bbnj/> accessed 21 April 2021. Informal reporting of proceedings is provided by, for example, the IISD available at <https://enb.iisd.org/process/water_wetlands_coasts.htm> accessed 21 April 2021.

115 United Nations, BBNJ, Side Events, Fourth Substantive Session available at <www.un.org/bbnj/content/side-events> accessed 21 April 2021.

116 Eyal Benvenisti and George W Downs, 'The Empire's New Clothes: Political Economy and the Fragmentation of International Law' (2007) 60 Stanford Law Review 595.

117 Tomer Broude, 'Principles of Normative Integration and the Allocation of International Authority: The WTO, the Vienna Convention on the Law of Treaties, and the Rio Declaration' (2008) 6 Loyola University Chicago International Law Review 173.

Agreement. However, the implications of this are that it will hamper an inclusive construction of ocean space in ABNJ by reducing or limiting the potential for some material interests to feed into the law-making process, both during the negotiations and through the operation of a future agreement. If we look at the Draft Agreement, we can see how this is happening through the limitation of opportunities to the recursive construction of interests in ABNJ.[118]

### 4.2 *Orchestrating Procedural Interactions through the BBNJ Agreement*

The BBNJ Agreement is broadly concerned with the conservation and sustainable use of BBNJ, but the main focus of its text is on four thematic issues: marine genetic resources (MGRs), including benefit sharing; ABMTs; EIAs; and capacity-building, including technology transfer.[119] Despite the material reality of the oceans as an integrated, socio-ecological system, the Draft Agreement reflects only part of that reality. Although the BBNJ Agreement will form part of a wider system of rules that can be drawn upon to regulate matters outside of its scope, this does not mean that it can or should operate separate to such matters. As I argue elsewhere, this is problematic for practical reasons, since fishing is the main cause of biodiversity loss.[120] The development of EIAs or ABMTs necessarily depends upon input (eg data) from fisheries, and when

118 On adaption within the BBNJ Agreement, see Catherine Blanchard, Carole Durussel and Ben Boteler, 'Socio-ecological resilience and the law: Exploring the adaptive capacity of the BBNJ agreement' (2019) 108 Marine Policy 103612.

119 There is a growing literature on these topics, and I do not intend covering this in any detail. See generally Robin Warner, 'Strengthening Governance Frameworks for Conservation and Sustainable Use of Marine Biodiversity in Areas beyond National Jurisdiction: Southern Hemisphere Perspectives' (2017) 32 International Journal of Marine and Coastal Law 607; Cymie Payne, 'Biodiversity in High Seas Areas: An Integrated Legal Approach' (2017) 21 ASIL Insights. On EIA, see Alex G Oude Elferink, 'Environmental Impact Assessment in Areas Beyond National Jurisdiction' (2012) 27 International Journal of Marine and Coastal Law 449; Meinhard Doelle and Gunnar Sander, 'Next Generation Environmental Assessment in the Emerging High Seas regime: An Evaluation of the State of the Negotiations' (2020) 35 International Journal of Marine and Coastal Law 498. On MGR and benefit sharing, see Leary (n 106); Fran Humphries and others, 'A tiered approach to the marine genetic resource governance framework under the proposed UNCLOS agreement for biodiversity beyond national jurisdiction (BBNJ)' (2020) Marine Policy (article 103910). On capacity-building, see Harriet R Harden-Davies and Kristina Gjerde, 'Building Scientific and Technological Capacity: a Role for Benefit-sharing in the Conservation and Sustainable Use of Marine Biodiversity beyond National Jurisdiction' (2019) 33 Ocean Yearbook 377; Marjo K Vierros and Harriet R Harden-Davies, 'Capacity building and technology transfer for improving governance of marine areas both beyond and within national jurisdiction (2020) Marine Policy (article 104158).

120 Barnes, 'International Fisheries Law' (n 106).

EIAS or ABMTS are implemented, they will impact upon the conduct of fishing activities in areas subject to protective measures. If the BBNJ Agreement lacks mechanisms for engaging with other material interests, then it denies space not just for those issues now, but also into the future because the BBNJ Agreement determines the pattern of future interactions in the construction of social space.

If we look beyond the four thematic issues, there are three general provisions that could enable interactions with wider actors and interests:[121] Article 4 on the relationship with the LOSC and other relevant global and regional instruments; Article 6 on international cooperation; and Article 48 establishing a COP.[122]

The relationship between the BBNJ Agreement and existing legal instrument is set out in Article 4. Arguably, the sum effect of Article 4 is to prioritise respect for existing institutional structures above the need for integrated and holistic approaches to regulating ABNJ. Article 4 provides that nothing in the agreement shall prejudice the rights, jurisdiction and duties of States under the LOSC, and that it shall also be interpreted and applied in manner consistent with the LOSC.[123] Such a provision is not unusual. It is designed to ensure consistency between different but related treaties (see eg Article 4 of the UN Fish Stocks Agreement (UNFSA)[124]). However, the cumulative effect of the rest of Article 4 is to strengthen the influence of pre-existing arrangements. Article 4(3) of the Draft Agreement states that the rights and jurisdiction of coastal States in areas within national jurisdiction (AWNJ) *shall be respected* in accordance with the LOSC. This can be contrasted with Article 7 of the UNFSA, which requires *compatibility* between conservation and management measures between the high seas and AWNJ. Compatibility neither restricts types of conservation measures *per se*, nor does it establish any normative hierarchy; rather it encourages constructive engagement to secure compatibility and so incentivises new ways of

121 Arguably, this should include dispute settlement. See further Mossop (ch 13) in this volume.

122 Revised draft text of an agreement under the United Nations Convention on the Law of the Sea on the conservation and sustainable use of marine biological diversity of areas beyond national jurisdiction, A/CONF.232/2020/3, 18 November 2019 (Revised Draft Agreement). Cooperation is also supported in specific provisions, such as arts 14-5 (area-based management tools), art 28 (conducting strategic environmental assessment), art 43(capacity-building).

123 ibid art 4(1).

124 United Nations Agreement for the Implementation of the Provisions of the United Nations Convention on the Law of the Sea of 10 December 1982 relating to the Conservation and Management of Straddling Fish Stocks and Highly Migratory Fish Stocks (opened for signature 4 August 1995, entered into force 11 December 2001) 2167 UNTS 3 (UNFSA).

structuring relationships. Use of the term 'respect' in Article 4 suggests some degree of priority for existing jurisdictional rights, and so could act as a potential constraint on regulatory possibilities. It could be argued that the reference back to the LOSC is unproblematic because the LOSC contains the possibilities for new types of interactions between different interests, such as fishing and biodiversity. Perhaps this is the case, but without wanting to rehearse more complex arguments about the evolutive nature of the LOSC, the fact remains that this channels arguments about regime interaction through the lens of the LOSC. Thus, it favours the established LOSC balance of interests, rather than new opportunities of interaction under the BBNJ Agreement. De Lucia argues that compatibility is advanced in BBNJ Agreement, noting that this could be read into provisions requiring cooperation, such as Article 15(5).[125] However, there is no explicit reference to compatibility in the Draft Agreement and it is not clear that the term 'not undermining' means the same as compatibility. He correctly observes that compatibility would need to be transformed into a key principle and involve a positive duty to adopt compatible conservation measures.[126]

Of all the provisions addressing the relationship of the Draft Agreement to other agreements, Article 4(3) is significant because it most clearly constrains the scope of the BBNJ Agreement:

> This Agreement shall be interpreted and applied in a manner that [respects the competences of and] does not undermine relevant legal instruments and frameworks and relevant global, regional, subregional and sectoral bodies.[127]

The term 'undermine' is ambiguous, but it risks having a chilling effect on legal developments.[128] This is evident from the negotiations where some States have used it as a device to limit the scope of the agreement.[129] The logic here is that because the UNFSA and RFMOs regulate fisheries, the BBNJ Agreement should leave these matters alone. This could be viewed as favouring the status

125 De Lucia (n 92) section 4.2.

126 ibid.

127 The text in brackets indicates a provision which has alternatives or where some States have expressed a view for its omission. This does not imply that non-bracketed text is agreed.

128 Although the UNFSA uses a similar term (eg arts 7(2)(a), 17(4), 18(1) and 20(7)), these provisions seek to constrain flag States from undermining conservation and management measures. These provisions do not seek to preserve the mandates of other bodies.

129 Namely, Iceland, Japan and Russia. See *Earth Negotiations Bulletin* (2016) 25(97) 1–2; *Earth Negotiations Bulletin* (2016) 25(98) 2.

quo and protecting existing interests.[130] In response, one could argue that the requirement to 'not undermine' gives fisheries bodies a strong voice in the ABNJ process in the sense that it reinforces their authority, and it indirectly connects the BBNJ Agreement to existing regimes. It might be viewed as a manifestation of legal coherence. However, I would challenge such a view. First it ignores the fact that existing mandates seek to advance integration between sectors and institutions. Second, the requirement to 'not undermine' is a negative provision. It allows a space for interactions, but it does not establish a constructive institutional process for different interests to be 'worked out'. There is also a real risk that this could result in a status quo bias and one that constrains new approaches, depending upon who is in control of the process to determine the meaning of 'not undermine'. This could operate as a veto or build into the structure of the BBNJ Agreement a prioritisation of commercial fishing practices. As I have argued elsewhere, a restrictive approach to 'not undermine' should be rejected.[131] Alternative constructions of the concept should be used to enable the BBNJ Agreement to adopt measures that fill gaps or enhance the mandates of other institutions to regulate new matters. Such a reading would at least be consistent with a desirable capacity for the ABNJ regime to adapt to changed circumstances. Interestingly, the present draft of Article 4(3) contains an alternative textual option 'to respect' existing mandates. If adopted, this textual optioncould drive positive, constructive engagement, rather than potentially freeze interactions between regimes.[132] It could prompt better communication and coordination between the different sectoral institutions.

Article 6 exhorts States to

> cooperate under this Agreement for the conservation and sustainable use of marine biological diversity of areas beyond national jurisdiction, including through strengthening and enhancing cooperation with and among relevant legal instruments and frameworks and relevant global, regional, subregional and sectoral bodies and members thereof in the achievement of the objective of this Agreement.

---

130 Benvenisti and Downs (n 116).

131 Barnes, 'Fisheries and ABNJ' (n 14).

132 On cooperation between regimes from an international relations perspective, see Xinyuan Dai, Duncan Snidal and Michael Sampson, 'International Cooperation Theory and International Institutions' Oxford Research Encyclopedia of International Studies available at <https://doi.org/10.1093/acrefore/9780190846626.013.93> accessed 20 April 2021.

It is potentially critical to the future development of ocean space in ABNJ because it establishes the principal treaty mechanism for the recursive construction of material and social interests. At present, the text is drawn in terms of a basic commitment to cooperate. Beyond this it does little to structure or facilitate interactions. Ideally, specific forms of cooperation need to be mandated and structured. For example, Iceland submitted a proposal for a regional consultative process.[133] This is not a holistic solution, but at least a step in the right direction by having a structured cooperative process. There also need for checks and balances on how cooperation operates, as well as oversight. If cooperation is be left to ad hoc, self-interest driven actions by a limited group of State actors, then this could negatively influence the construction of ocean space by excluding actors or allowing particular accounts of ocean space (eg pro-exploitation or sectorally divided visions) to prevail.

These shortcomings could be ameliorated through an institutional process, such as a COP. In the Draft Agreement, this is provided for in Article 48, which contains proposals for periodic meetings of a COP. The COP would have authority to establish rules and procedures for itself and any subsidiary body it may wish to establish, as well as the remit to review the implementation of the BBNJ Agreement, exchange information, promote cooperation, set budgets, review the effectiveness of the BBNJ Agreement and, if necessary, propose measures to strengthen or reform it. As it stands in the Draft Agreement, the COP is mainly focused on oversight of internal processes. Thus, it will '[monitor and] and keep under review the implementation' of the agreement.[134] Of course, the adoption of decisions and recommendation by the COP will only have effect inter se on States parties.[135] This means that its influence on other regional and sectoral activities will occur only indirectly through the influence of States in those other fora. Article 48(4)(c) is a potentially critical provision because if could enable more inclusive holistic interactions on issues of oceans governance. The draft provision provides that the COP shall:

> Promote cooperation and coordination with and among relevant legal instruments and frameworks and relevant global, regional, subregional and sectoral bodies, with a view to promoting coherence among efforts towards, and the harmonisation of relevant policies and measures for,

133 Textual proposals submitted by the delegation by 20 February 2020, 52–54 available at <www.un.org/bbnj/sites/www.un.org.bbnj/files/textual_proposals_compilation_article-by-article_-_15_april_2020.pdf> accessed 20 April 2021.

134 Revised Draft Agreement art 48(4).

135 ibid art 48(4)(a).

> the conservation and sustainable use of marine biological diversity of areas beyond national jurisdiction [, including by establishing processes for cooperation and coordination with and among relevant global, regional, subregional and sectoral bodies] [, including by inviting other global, regional, subregional and sectoral bodies to establish processes for cooperation].

Presently this is drafted in weak terms – it refers only to 'promotion' with a 'view to promoting coherence'. Critically, the options for establishing processes of cooperation and coordination with sectoral bodies (such as RFMOs) are in square brackets and so only negotiating options at present. A COP with a limited remit could perpetuate the structural weaknesses inherent in ABNJ governance and limit inclusive and holistic governance opportunities.

### 4.3 *Orchestrating Substantive Interactions through the BBNJ Agreement*

General principles serve a number of integrative functions – something that is critical to effective governance of ABNJ. For present purposes, two are relevant. First, they can provoke the creation of new rules in a structured way; they establish general frameworks for action that can be advanced through more detailed rules.[136] In doing so they contribute to the advancement of the values inherent in such principles.[137] This is important because the meaning and content of principles contained within the BBNJ Agreement are not exclusive to the Agreement; the principles cut across the wider law of the sea and international law and their meaning may be shaped by practices in these other legal regimes. As such, this can help create opportunities for a wider set of values to feed into ABNJ discourse and, in turn, the practices of bodies operating in ABNJ.

The second integrating function of general principles is to assist in the process of interpreting and applying rules as they apply to novel situations.[138] This can be achieved through an interstitial, gap-filling function as described by Lowe,[139] or as a supplementary means of clarifying ambiguous or uncertain language. Principles are value orientated and so can be used to explain why

---

136 M Cherif Bassiouni, A Functional Approach to "General Principles of International Law' (1990) 11 Michigan Journal of International Law 768, 777ff; Robert Kolb, 'Principles as Sources of International Law (with special reference to good faith)' (2006) Netherland International Law Review 1, 7. See also the point about non-liquet (n 77).

137 Kolb describes them as value catalysers, ibid 29.

138 Bassiouni (n 136) 776.

139 Vaughan Lowe 'Sustainable development and unsustainable arguments' in Alan Boyle and David Freestone (eds) *International law and sustainable development: past achievements and future challenges* (Oxford University Press 2005) 21.

sets of rules exist. Thus, the reasons underpinning a principle can be used to inform the interpretation or application of a rule.[140] This echoes the reasons-contingent nature of law discussed in Part 3.

Article 5 of the Draft Agreement sets out ten principles/approaches potentially applicable to ABNJ: the principle of non-regression; the polluter pays principle; the CHM principle; the principle of equity; the precautionary principle; an ecosystem approach; an integrated approach; an ecosystem resilience and integrity approach; and the non-transfer of harm principle. The content of this provision has been contentious. For example, a much-reduced set of principle presented to the third session of the IGC drew strong reactions from the room and led to the reintroduction of a longer list of principles in the current Draft Agreement, including both the precautionary and the CHM principles. These debates over which principles to include arguably reflects the power of principles to shape the future regime of ABNJ. Still, this list of principles has been reduced from the longer list of 22 principles in the President's Aid to Negotiations for the second session of the IGC.[141] Notable omissions to the current draft are the principles of transparent and open-decision-making, public availability of information and stewardship.[142] To these we could add a missing principle of compatibility and a requirement of having due regard to the rights and interests of other States (although this is arguably carried over from the LOSC). These omissions from the list of generally applicable principles are important because the principles facilitate interactions and enable opportunities for new social and material interests to emerge. Transparent/open decision-making and public availability of information can help ensure accountability of actors in a system prone to marginalise non-dominant interests. Compatibility and due regard can direct users to develop mutually beneficial solutions to potential conflict of use/interest situations. And stewardship, which conditions use of things according to overriding duties of conservation and preservation, ensures a necessary focus on the material conditions of ABNJ.[143] It offers an alternative value structure to the CHM, which is both contested and skewed towards exploitative ideals.[144]

---

140 Kolb (n 136) 32–33.

141 A/CONF.232/2019/1, 3 December 2018.

142 Advocates of a principle-based approach include David Freestone, 'Principles Applicable to Modern Ocean Governance' (2008) 23 International Journal of Marine and Coastal Law 385. See also Oude Elferink (n 93).

143 This definition of stewardship is taken from Barnes (n 74) 157.

144 Ranganathan (n 50).

The principles indicate the core values underpinning the treaty and can thus influence the direction of policy and practice under the BBNJ Agreement.[145] They could imbue a BBNJ agreement with the adaptive qualities necessary for responding to change in a dynamic physical environment. Principles framed in open-ended terms enhance the capacity of the treaty to adapt to new circumstances and may provide opportunities for cross-fertilisation of practices between different activities. The inclusion of common sets of principles in different treaty texts creates linguistic and legal connections between different instruments – connections that can enable the development of practices in different fields in a constructive way. This function of general principles can be particularly important in the event of any disputes arising under the BBNJ Agreement.[146] Principles can be used to internalise (ie make subject to inter-se treaty practice) the external (ie wider meanings or practices of a general principle) and so establishes an epistemic link between the subject matter of the treaty at hand and external subject matter.[147] Here general principles can be a starting point for the development of generally accepted international rules and standards for ABNJ.[148] At the very least, the inclusion of general principles in the BBNJ Agreement creates points of common interest and so sets the tone and direction for such interactions. And any technical body or COP can be a forum for reporting and discussing progress on the implementation of such principles. Given the risk that institutional process can reify a limited set of values and interests, it is important that the BBNJ Agreement structures cooperation in pursuit of a wider, value inclusive set of principles. The BBNJ Agreement must include principles of transparency, integration and due regard since these principles engender inclusive and constructive interaction between different interest groups. And the text must ensure that the principles cut across all substantive matters within the BBNJ Agreement, rather than being separated into discrete sections on different activities (eg EIAS or ABMTS).[149]

145 Katherine Houghton, 'Identifying new pathways for ocean governance: The role of legal principles in areas beyond national jurisdiction' (2014) 49 Marine Policy 118.

146 This type of reasoning features in the *Responsibilities and obligations of States with respect to activities in the Area* (Advisory Opinion, 1 February 2011) ITLOS Reports 2011 [125–35].

147 Of course, much depends upon the modalities for 'operationalizing' the principles in practice. See Vito De Lucia, 'The Ecosystem Approach and the negotiations towards a new Agreement on Marine Biodiversity in Areas beyond National Jurisdiction' (2019) 2 Nordisk miljörättslig tidskrift/Nordic Environmental Law Journal 7.

148 Catherine Redgwell, 'Mind the Gap in the GAIRS: The Role of Other Instruments in LOSC Regime Implementation in the offshore Sector' in Nigel Bankes and Seline Trevisanut (eds), *Energy from the Sea. An International Law Perspective on Ocean Energy* (Brill 2015) 40, 57–58.

149 See for example, Revised Draft Agreement (n 122) arts 7, 14 and 42.

### 4.4 *Strengthening the BBNJ Agreement and the Opportunities for Constructing Social Space*

Drawing together the arguments presented in Parts 2 and 3, it is important that any institutional mechanism possesses three qualities to ensure that inclusive interactions take place and that the law is able to develop constructively. First, cooperation must enable opportunities for a wide range of material and social interests to be articulated in the law-creation process for ABNJ. In practice, this means providing an opportunity for a range of actors (eg industry/civil society/scientific community) who have a material interest in the activities in ABNJ to participate in the activities of decision-making fora. A key challenge here is the limited remit of the Draft Agreement and the fact that as currently framed, the BBNJ Agreement will be unable to influence the mandates of existing bodies (such as RFMOs) that are so critical to decision-making in and constructing space in their respective sectors. Participation of different actors within the BBNJ agreement alone may not be sufficient to fully integrate governance of ABNJ. This requires opportunities for influence to be made both within the institutional structures of the BBNJ Agreement and in related forums. The institutional mechanisms established in an BBNJ Agreement need to be active, deliberative and structured. This could be through formal consultative processes, or by directly mandating States Parties to establish cross-sectoral regional cooperative arrangements, as pioneered by OSPAR and NEAFC. Third, any institutional process should be explicitly subject to a requirement to respect the BBNJ Agreement's general principles. This should be accompanied by standards or procedures for evaluating the implementation of principles. This can help harmonise the institutional and substantive development of the regime for ABNJ. By requiring that existing institutional practices align with the BBNJ Agreement, States (and institutional bodies) will be pressured to frame their conduct in terms of common values.

## 5 Future Fisheries: The Importance of Interactions and Inclusive Institutional Arrangements

The lessons from this chapter are not merely practical ones for the future regulation of ocean space. This chapter contributes to a wider understanding of the relationship between the law creation process and power. By showing how law structures interactions in respect of ocean spaces and risks marginalising certain interests, I caution against conservative thinking (referring to both State-centric and narrowly legalistic thinking) and highlight the importance of designing inclusive processes into our legal institutions. If we do this carefully, then these processes can orchestrate in a constructive way a more inclusive and holistic regime for ABNJ.

Although many activities are brought together within the framework of LOSC and related instruments, the mundane regulation of such activities is often pursued through discrete sectoral regimes for fisheries, shipping, pollution control, deep seabed mining and marine scientific research. The fact that these activities are connected in a material way renders a diffuse and atomised system of control (eg flag State jurisdiction, sectoral regulation) flawed.[150] We need to recognise and respond to the material connectivity of space and activities in ABNJ. As Molenaar and Oude Elferink have stated, '[c]ooperation will always be essential to effectively manage specific activities in the high seas or to protect the marine environment of the high seas'.[151] Cooperation is particularly important for fisheries, given the wider impact it may have on other activities and that cooperation is fundamental to the effectiveness of fisheries governance on the high seas.

An inclusive, cooperative framework, with interactional opportunities for States may be part of the basic structure of the law of the sea. However, such a cooperative approach is a work in progress. As this chapter shows, when space is institutionalized in a sectoral way this may consolidate and constrain interactional opportunities. Despite efforts to ensure that the scope of fisheries management is more geographically complete and integrated into wider environmental concerns, the current legal system remains flawed. The LOSC and related instruments have so far failed to ensure that resources in ABNJ are properly protected against the adverse impacts of fishing. The UNFSA does not address discrete high seas stocks, and whilst it provides a framework for the development of RFMOs, it does not require RFMOs to act in conformity with its provisions.[152] This can be done voluntarily, but it lacks systematic implementation.[153] Some RFMOs have the competence to regulate the activities of

150 Robin M Warner, 'Conserving marine biodiversity in areas beyond national jurisdiction: co-evolution and interaction with the law of the sea' (2014) Frontiers in Marine Science, 20 May 2014 available at <www.frontiersin.org/articles/10.3389/fmars.2014.00006/full#B44> accessed 20 April 2021.

151 Erik J Molenaar and Alex G Oude Elferink, 'Marine protected areas in areas beyond national jurisdiction: The pioneering efforts under the OSPAR Convention' (2009) 5(1) Utrecht Law Review 5.

152 Kristina Gjerde and others, *Regulatory and Governance Gaps in the International Regime for the Conservation and Sustainable Use of Marine Biodiversity in Areas beyond National Jurisdiction* (IUCN 2008) 9.

153 Margaret A Young and Andrew Friedman, 'Biodiversity Beyond National Jurisdiction: Regimes and their Interaction' (2018) 112 AJIL Unbound 123, 128.

members in parts of the high seas, but the extent of their regulatory coverage is limited both geographically and materially.[154] In these respects there are significant gaps in the scope and extent of international fisheries law.[155]

This chapter has shown that development of a legal regime for ABNJ is closely bound up with wider social, political and economic concerns. It must also reflect the material nature of ocean space in ABNJ. A constructivist perspective allows us to better understand how these wider social and material interactions are shaped through the process of law creation and application. Lawyers and diplomats do not enjoy exclusive domain over the material underpinnings of social practice or domain over those wider social practices. However, in ABNJ, law appears to occupy a privileged position. As areas between, but common to States, ABNJ are truly international spaces. They sit outside the territorial space of the State and beyond many of the usual social institutions that can influence the ongoing construction of space. Here, international law in general, and the future BBNJ Agreement in particular, will play an influential role in how space is constructed in the future. The creation of a treaty and its entry into force can have significant impacts on the future possibilities for constituting social space. This is because treaties can be difficult to amend or change. Law is not immutable, but how it develops and adapts is heavily constrained by the institutional structure of law and the practices of legal reasoning. Witness the widely accepted narrative of the LOSC as a 'constitution for the sea'. The legal relationships and power structures that international law creates ripple out and influence wider social economic and political practices, which in turn create or limit the opportunities for future change.

The current debate about the scope of the BBNJ Agreement, and how it relates to wider management of fisheries illustrates the way in which law may embed structural limitations on the possibilities for creation of social space. The current legal regime for ABNJ is not structured in a way that drives a holistic, integrated construction of social space in ABNJ. And the BBNJ Agreement risks further exacerbating this. Whilst there are broad provisions within the LOSC and other instruments that exhort inclusive, integrated approaches, there are noted gaps in both the institutional and substantive reach of the law of the

154 Erik J Molenaar, 'Current legal and institutional Issues Relating to the Conservation and Management of High-Seas Deep-Sea Fisheries' in FAO, *Report and documentation of the Expert Consultation on Deep-sea Fisheries in the High Seas. Bangkok, Thailand, 21–23 November 2006. FAO Fisheries Report No 838* (FAO 2007).

155 David Freestone and Gerald Mangone, 'The Law of the Sea Convention: Unfinished Agendas and Future Challenges' (1995) 10 International Journal of Marine and Coastal Law 151.

sea which remains too focused on a sectoral approach. The Draft Agreement is insufficiently concerned with correcting some of the structural weakness in the existing regime. By implication, this limits the way in which States (and other actors) can engage in issues of oceans governance. It institutionalises who has a voice, what can be said, and where. The BBNJ Agreement will structure the constitution of space. It will fundamentally structure and influence the interests and values that are at play in the future construction of ocean space. If we are not to stymie the construction of ocean space, then the BBNJ Agreement needs to ensure that it is inclusive of the material and social values inherent in ocean spaces beyond national jurisdiction. This argument should apply to any concern (energy generation or navigation), but it is particularly acute with regards to fishing given its material impact on marine biodiversity. This means creating opportunities for a wider range of actors to engage in the governance of ABNJ and ensuring that the requirement to 'not undermine' does not undermine an integrated approach to governance. It also means having active, deliberative and structured procedures for institutional cooperation between different regional and sectoral regimes. It means drawing the work of RFMOs into the wider governance arrangements that are developing for ABJN in a way that exposes them to greater accountability and to thinking about the oceans in a more integrated way. It also means ensuring that general principles permeate the whole interactional structure of the BBNJ Agreement, and in turn ripple out to other regional arrangements, and that these principles include not just the precautionary approach, ecosystem-based approaches, non-harmful use, and best use of science, but extend to transparency, public availability of information, due regard and stewardship. Such procedural and substantive changes could enhance the potential of the BBNJ Agreement to positively influence the future governance of ABNJ both within its own institutional structures and through those of other bodies, such as RFMOs, that are critical to the governance of ABNJ.

CHAPTER 11

# Ships in ABNJ – Broadening Jurisdictional Opportunities for Non-flag States

*Henrik Ringbom*

## 1 Introduction*

As far as shipping is concerned, the term 'areas beyond national jurisdiction' (ABNJ) is somewhat misleading. It is an age-old principle of international law that ships on the high seas are always subject to the jurisdiction of their flag State. Since almost any activity in ABNJ, including scientific research, seabed mining and the laying of cables and pipelines, involves ships, the jurisdictional regime for shipping is of particular relevance for understanding the overall balance of rights and duties in ABNJ.[1]

Traditionally only the flag State has jurisdiction over ships on the high seas, unless specifically provided otherwise. Regulatory control over activities in ABNJ is thus dependent on the role and interest taken by the ship's flag State. This approach is largely cemented in the undisputed legal authority for any question relating to the jurisdiction of States over maritime activities, the 1982 United Nations Convention on the Law of the Sea (LOSC).[2] The main rule, as set out in Article 92(1) of the LOSC, is that ships, 'save in exceptional cases expressly provided for in international treaties or in this Convention, shall be subject to its [flag State's] exclusive jurisdiction on the high seas'.[3]

---

* I am greatly indebted to Erik Molenaar and Arron Honniball for their inspiring research in this field and their very helpful comments on an earlier draft. Any errors and misconceptions are entirely my own.

1 Whilst this chapter addresses shipping broadly, encompassing not only commercial shipping but also research, fishing and sea-based mining activities, the analysis does not extend to fixed or semi-fixed objects in the oceans, such as fish farms and ocean-based energy installations.

2 LOSC and its provisions on the high seas are commonly considered to be representative of customary international law. See eg Douglas Guilfoyle, 'The High Seas' in Donal Rothwell and others (eds), *The Oxford Handbook of the Law of the Sea* (Oxford University Press 2015) 209.

3 Curiously, LOSC art 92(1) does not make exception for rules that exist under international customary law. As is observed by Rosemary Gail Rayfuse, *Non-Flag State Enforcement in High Seas Fisheries* (Martinus Nijhoff Publishers 2004) 22, however, this omission can hardly preclude the development of exceptions based on customary law. She therefore prefers to refer to

 | DOI:10.1163/9789004506367_012

Despite the clear position of LOSC on this matter, and the convention's general status as a 'Constitution for the Oceans', a strong emphasis on the exclusivity of flag States' jurisdiction arguably fails to provide the complete picture on the nature and extent of States' jurisdiction over ships on the high seas as of today.[4] Strictly relying on LOSC and its Article 92 also fails to explain why certain exercises of jurisdiction by non-flag States related to activities on the high seas appear to be more acceptable than others, in theory as well as in practice.

Numerous examples from State practice illustrate that flag States' jurisdiction is far from exclusive, even in the absence of specific treaty exceptions.[5] The exclusivity is being challenged from many directions. States acting – individually or collectively – in their capacity of port States increasingly claim competences and functions that used to belong to the domain of flag States alone. Legal developments in specific fields, such as criminal law, also tend to strengthen the role of non-flag States in dealing with matters on board ships,[6] while jurisdictional avenues outside the law of the sea, notably links on the basis of the nationality of natural persons or corporation, are increasingly being sought to complement flag State jurisdiction.[7] Developments in international private law similarly tend to de-emphasize the exclusivity of flag States, eg in relation to the applicable law of shipping employment contracts.[8]

---

the 'primacy' of flag State jurisdiction. See also Arron N Honniball, 'The Exclusive Jurisdiction of Flag States: A Limitation on Pro-active Port States?' (2016) 31(3) The International Journal of Marine and Coastal Law 519–20.

4 A review of a gradually changing academic opinion on this rigidness of exclusive flag State jurisdiction is undertaken in Honniball (n 3) 504–09 and 519–25.

5 Several examples will be discussed in section 2 and 3 below. See also Yaodong Yu, Yue Zhao and Yen-Chiang Chang, 'Challenges to the Primary Jurisdiction of Flag States Over Ships' (2018) 49 Ocean Development & International Law 85.

6 See eg Kate Lewins, 'Jurisdiction over Prosecution of Criminal Acts on Cruise Ships and Regulation of the Cruise Ships Industry' (2018) Background paper submitted to Australian Parliamentary Inquiry, on behalf of the Maritime Law Association of Australia and New Zealand available at <www.aph.gov.au/Parliamentary_Business/Committees/House_of_Representatives_Committees?url=spla/crimes%20at%20sea/subs/sub001.pdf> accessed 26 April 2021.

7 See eg Richard Caddell, George Leloudas and Bariş Soyer, 'Emerging Regulatory Responses to IUU Fishing' in Richard Caddell and Erik J Molenaar (eds), *Strengthening International Fisheries Law in an Era of Changing Oceans* (Hart 2019).

8 See eg the review of EU case law on this matter in Bevan Marten, *Port State Jurisdiction and the Regulation of International Merchant Shipping* (Springer 2014) 202–210. See also Laura Carballo Piñero, 'Port State Jurisdiction over Labour Conditions: A Private International Law Perspective on Extra-territoriality' (2016) 31 International Journal of Marine and Coastal Law 531; Thor Falkanger, 'Ship registration and choice of law in relation to contracts of employment' (2017) 502 MarIus: Scandinavian Institute of Maritime Law Yearbook 7.

These developments indicate that other States' trust in flag States' capacity and will to address and resolve problems related to activities on the high seas has not improved over time. At the same time, new technologies provide increasing opportunities for non-flag States to monitor and control activities on the high seas even without physical presence at the scene.[9]

All these elements contribute to a changing nature of non-flag State jurisdiction over activities on the high seas. In particular, the shift from physical *at-sea* enforcement measures on the high seas towards *ex-post* enforcement measures relying on other jurisdictional bases than those specifically provided for in LOSC. This, it is argued, fundamentally changes the jurisdictional setup for the high seas and should be reflected, or at least acknowledged, in the ongoing negotiations of an international legally binding agreement (BBNJ Agreement) which is currently under preparation to enhance the conservation of biodiversity within areas beyond national jurisdiction (BBNJ).[10]

The current State of play on the precise nature and scope of flag State jurisdiction is however far from straightforward. This is illustrated by the recent *Norstar* judgment by the International Tribunal for the Law of the Sea (ITLOS), in which the majority of judges took a very limited view on the possibilities of non-flag States to regulate foreign ships on the high seas,[11] while a seven-judge strong minority adopted a very different stance, emphasizing that the exclusivity of flag State jurisdiction applies to enforcement jurisdiction, but not

9 This is also acknowledged in the preamble to the 2009 Agreement on Port State Measures to Prevent, Deter and Eliminate Illegal, Unreported and Unregulated Fishing (PSMA), acknowledging 'the rapidly developing communications technology, databases, networks and global records that support port State measures'. For some examples in the domain of high seas fisheries, see eg Natalie Klein, 'Strengthening Flag State Performance in Compliance and Enforcement' in Caddell and Molenaar (n 7).

10 The reference text used here is the (heavily bracketed) revised draft text of 18 November 2019, UN Doc A/CONF.232/2020/3, 'Revised draft text of an agreement under the United Nations Convention on the Law of the Sea on the conservation and sustainable use of marine biological diversity of areas beyond national jurisdiction' (Revised Draft Agreement) available at <https://undocs.org/en/a/conf.232/2020/3> accessed 26 April 2021.

11 *M/V 'Norstar' (Panama v. Italy)*) (Judgment, 10 April 2019) ITLOS 25, in particular at para 225, where the Tribunal found that 'the principle of exclusive flag State jurisdiction is an inherent component of the freedom of navigation … [which] … prohibits not only the exercise of enforcement jurisdiction on the high seas by States other than the flag State but also the extension of their prescriptive jurisdiction to lawful activities conducted by foreign ships on the high seas'. This passage has since been reiterated and endorsed in para 527 of the *Enrica Lexie* (*Italy v. India*) (2 July 2020) PCA 2015-28 available at <https://pcacases.com/web/sendAttach/16500> accessed 26 April 2021.

to prescriptive jurisdiction.[12] The result is a confused message on the nature of flag State jurisdiction, which emphasizes the need for further research in the field.

Against this background, the present chapter seeks to analyze the scope of jurisdiction over ships in ABNJ in further detail. What exactly is referred to by the exclusivity of flag State jurisdiction? Are there different types of jurisdiction involved? Is this matter only regulated by the law of the sea, or are other jurisdictional principles under international law of relevance as well? What are the rules and principles left to guide us if we accept that in certain cases other States (non-flag States) may also have jurisdiction over ship activities on the high seas? What implications does this have for the ongoing deliberations on the BBNJ Agreement?

The chapter adopts a bird's eye perspective to the different aspects of jurisdiction and their mutual relationship, which necessarily affects the possibility to undertake a detailed discussion on any of the issues raised. It is divided into three main parts. Section 2 looks at the nature of non-flag State jurisdiction in some more detail, both in the law of the sea and in light of other international legal developments since the conclusion of LOSC. On that basis, section 3 discusses the available 'jurisdictional space' for non-flag States to assume a role in exercising jurisdiction over activities in ABNJ in more detail. Section 4 concludes by placing the findings in the context of to the ongoing BBNJ negotiations.

## 2 LOSC and Jurisdiction over Ships on the High Seas

### 2.1 *General*

Despite uncertainties with respect to its theoretical foundation,[13] flag State jurisdiction has always represented the core form of jurisdiction over ships. Flag States have jurisdiction over their ships irrespective of the ship's location: when in coastal waters of another State, jurisdiction may be shared with the coastal State, while ships on the high seas are in principle subject to the

12 See n 34.

13 Daniel Bodansky, 'Protecting the Marine Environment from Vessel-Source Pollution: UNCLOS III and Beyond' (1991) 18(4) Ecology Law Quarterly 719, 736, with further references, notes that the juridical basis of flag State jurisdiction 'has always been somewhat murky'.

exclusive jurisdiction of the flag State. This applies since the very birth of international law,[14] and is essentially founded in pragmatism.[15]

LOSC is the obvious starting point for any question relating to the jurisdiction of States over maritime activities.[16] It was already noted that the main rule set out in LOSC, and indeed its predecessor from 1958, is that of exclusive jurisdiction by a flag State over its ship, subject to express exceptions.[17] The question that is becoming increasingly relevant to resolve is what this exclusivity refers to. The core of the difference between the majority and minority opinion in the *Norstar* judgment, is whether exclusivity is limited to *enforcement* jurisdiction or if it also extends to the right to regulate ships on the high seas (*prescriptive* jurisdiction). This question will be addressed in section 2.2, while the – arguably more relevant – distinction between two different types of enforcement jurisdiction is highlighted in section 2.3.

As an introductory remark, it is relevant to highlight that lawful enforcement, whatever the jurisdictional basis, presupposes that the enforcing State has both enforcement jurisdiction (the power to take measures to ensure compliance)[18] and prescriptive jurisdiction (the authority to adopt rules that make the violation unlawful in the first place[19]) over the violation in question.[20]

---

14 Hugo Grotius, *Mare Liberum* (1609); Hugo Grotius, *Mare liberum 1609–2009* (rev, ed, tr Robert Feenstra, Brill 2009).

15 The traditional justification was based on the flag State's jurisdiction over the ship-owning company and the circumstance that the flag State was the only State that was capable of exercising effective enforcement jurisdiction over its ships. As for the high seas, exclusivity is also justified by the absence of any other suitable authority for exercising jurisdiction over ships in ABNJ. See eg *Le Louis* [1817] EWHC 165 (Admlty) 1464, 1475.

16 See n 2.

17 LOSC art 92(1), quoted above in section 1.

18 For a more detailed definition of prescriptive, enforcement and adjudicative jurisdiction, see eg para 101 of the American Law Institute's, Restatement (Fourth) Foreign Relations Law of the United States, published in 2018. See also William S Dodge, 'Jurisdiction in the Fourth Restatement of Foreign Relations Law' (2017) 18 Yearbook of Private International Law, 143, 145–46.

19 § 101(a) of the Restatement (Fourth) (n 18) defines prescriptive jurisdiction as 'the authority of a state to make law applicable to persons, property, or conduct'.

20 As is noted by Oscar Schachter, *International Law in Theory and Practice* (Martinus Nijhoff Publishers 1991) 257, 'enforcement activity within a State requires that the law being enforced is internationally valid within the jurisdiction to prescribe'. See also Frederick Alexander Mann, 'The Doctrine of International Jurisdiction Revisited after Twenty Years' (1984) 186 Recueil des Cours, Collected Courses of the Hague Academy of International Law, 34–35; Cedric Ryngaert, 'The concept of jurisdiction in international law' in Alexander Orakhelashvili (ed), *Research Handbook on Jurisdiction and Immunities in International Law* (Edward Elgar Publishing 2015) 57–58.

Where enforcement jurisdiction on the high seas is specifically provided for in LOSC or other agreements, prescriptive jurisdiction may be presumed, even if not explicitly provided. However, the reverse is not necessarily true. Prescriptive jurisdiction is thus necessarily larger than enforcement jurisdiction, as is also evidenced by several examples in LOSC where the jurisdiction to prohibit a certain conduct is not matched with a jurisdiction to take enforcement measure against a ship that engages in such conduct.[21]

### 2.2 *Distinguishing Prescriptive and Enforcement Jurisdiction*

LOSC does not provide any explicit jurisdiction for other States to regulate foreign ships on the high seas. This is a natural consequence of the absence of sovereignty of any State on the high seas. The independence of flag States is further emphasized by their liberty to set their own conditions for registering ships under their flag.[22] Yet it does not mean that flag States would not have obligations with respect to ships on the high seas. On the contrary, a number of provisions require flag States to ensure that their ships, wherever they operate, comply with a minimum set of 'generally accepted' international rules and practices,[23] even if the flag State has not formally signed up to those rules.[24] However, other States' right to take measures against flag States that fail to meet their obligations is limited indeed.[25]

Non-flag States' possibilities to take action against individual *ships*, which is the focus here, is somewhat more complex, but similarly inclined towards flag State jurisdiction. LOSC does not include a general enforcement jurisdiction for non-flag States on the high seas, but provides for exceptional jurisdiction to take measures in case the ship is: engaged in piracy; engaged in slave trade; without nationality; or engaged in unauthorized broadcasting.[26]

---

21 Numerous discrepancies exist, eg, in Part XII of the Convention between the right of States to regulate ship-source pollution in different maritime zones and their right to take enforcement measures against ships violating those rules.

22 LOSC art 91(1). See also M/V *'Virginia G'* (*Panama v. Guinea-Bissau*) (Judgment, 14 April 2014) ITLOS 19, paras 112–13.

23 Notably LOSC arts 94(3), (4) and 217.

24 LOSC arts 94(5) and 211(2). See also International Law Association, London Conference (2000), Committee on Coastal State Jurisdiction Relating to Marine Pollution, Final Report, 479–80; The discussion on the extent of these duties in the Award by the Arbitral Tribunal in the *South China Sea Arbitration* (*Philippines v China*) (Award, 12 July 2016) PCA Case 2013–19, para 1082.

25 LOSC art 94(6). Maria Gavouneli, *Functional Jurisdiction in the Law of the Sea* (Martinus Nijhoff Publishers 2007) 18 refers to 'the complete and total uselessness' of the reporting possibility for non-flag States which is provided for in that paragraph.

26 LOSC arts 99–110, the first two follow directly from art 22 the 1958 Convention on the High Seas; the latter two were added into LOSC.

The extent of the jurisdiction varies. With respect to piracy and unauthorized broadcasting, the jurisdiction includes a right of seizure, ie a right to arrest the ship engaged in the activity in question. For others, jurisdiction is limited to a right of approach and, if needed, visit (to verify the facts on board the suspected ship) and even that only if there is 'reasonable grounds for suspecting' that the ship is engaged in any of the listed activities.[27] In all cases, at-sea enforcement has to be undertaken by warship or military aircraft or other ships or aircraft clearly marked and identifiable as being on government service.[28]

In addition, LOSC includes two cases of enforcement jurisdiction on the high seas for a specific coastal State: in the case of hot pursuit,[29] and to avoid pollution or a threat of pollution of its coastline or related interests from a maritime casualty or acts related to such a casualty 'which may reasonably be expected to result in major harmful consequences'.[30]

No corresponding express exceptions exist with respect to prescription.[31] Every express exception from exclusive flag State jurisdiction in LOSC, in other words, relates only to enforcement. Since Article 92(1) specifically refers to 'exceptional cases expressly provided for in international treaties or in this Convention', it is not far-fetched to conclude that the exclusivity of flag State jurisdiction referred to in that article is similarly aimed at enforcement jurisdiction (and the limited prescriptive jurisdiction that inherently goes along with such specific enforcement jurisdiction).

Indeed, it is difficult to find any support for the assertion that Article 92 constitutes a universal limitation of non-flag States right to regulate activities of foreign ships on the high seas, the most obvious example being on regulation on the basis of its jurisdiction over its nationals.[32] Furthermore, there is nothing in the drafting history of Article 92(1) that suggests that the exclusivity of flag State jurisdiction goes beyond enforcement measures on the high seas

27 LOSC art 110(1).

28 LOSC arts 107, 109(4), and 110(1) and (5).

29 LOSC art 111.

30 LOSC art 221, which is based on the 1969 International Convention Relating to Intervention on the High Seas in Cases of Oil Pollution Damage.

31 As was noted above (n 20 and 21). However, expressing enforcement jurisdiction implicitly presumes prescriptive jurisdiction over the matter.

32 James Crawford, *Brownlie's Principles of Public International Law* (9th edn, Oxford University Press 2019) 285, observes that enforcement jurisdiction is 'to be distinguished from a state's jurisdiction to prescribe, which is not regulated by UNCLOS but by the general law'.

against a particular ship.[33] On this basis, it seems justified to conclude, as the minority in the *Norstar* judgment did,[34] and the majority of academic writers,[35] that the exclusivity referred to in Article 92(1) is limited to enforcement jurisdiction.

## 2.3 *Distinguishing at-sea Enforcement from* 'Ex-Post' *Enforcement*

### 2.3.1 General

Enforcement may however be carried out in different ways, which will also affect the jurisdictional framework. The enforcement rules discussed above concern physical enforcement measures against ships while on the high seas. Such at-sea enforcement measures need to be distinguished from *ex-post* enforcement measures.[36] The latter term refers to enforcement measures against ships for matters that concern ships' activities on the high seas, but that are taken at a later stage, when the ship is no longer on the high seas. Such *ex-post* enforcement can for example take the form of enforcement measures by a (port) State where the ship subsequently makes a call, or in the form of adjudicative jurisdiction by courts in a State that has jurisdiction over the events under its national laws. *Ex-post* enforcement measures thus represent a sub-group of enforcement measures, encompassing both measures targeting the ship itself, such as detention, arrest or refusal to enter the port, and punitive (adjudicative) measures, such as prosecution of key persons involved in its operation or penalties imposed on crew, owners or others associated with the ship. The category accordingly includes both administrative and judicial enforcement measures and may be directed at the ship itself or at natural or legal persons.

---

33 See eg Myron H. Nordquist (ed-in-chief), *United Nations Convention on the Law of the Sea 1982 A Commentary* (vol III, Martinus Nijhoff Publishers 1995) 123–27; Douglas Guilfoyle, in Alexander Proelss (ed), *United Nations Convention on the Law of the Sea, A Commentary* (CH Beck 2017) 701–03.

34 See in particular para 19 of the Joint Dissenting opinion of Judges Cot, Pawlak, Yanai, Hoffmann, Kolodkin and Lijnzaad and Judge ad hoc Treves in *Norstar* (n 11): 'nothing in the text of the Convention, in its *travaux préparatoires*, in other international treaties, in customary international law, or in the practice of States suggests that art. 87 and its corollary art. 92 altogether excludes the right of non-flag States to exercise their prescriptive criminal jurisdiction with respect to activities on the high seas'.

35 See notably Douglas Guilfoyle, *Shipping Interdiction and the Law of the Sea* (Cambridge University Press 2009) 276–77; Guilfoyle (n 34) 702–03. See also the overview of academic views provided in Honniball (n 3).

36 For a somewhat similar differentiation, see Rayfuse (n 3) 328ff, distinguishing non-flag States' 'control' measures from 'sanctions'.

In jurisdictional terms, the difference is that the actual enforcement takes place within the territory of the enforcing State, which ensures a clear link between the State and the ship as far as the enforcement is concerned. Instead, the key matter here is whether the State has a right to exercise its enforcement jurisdiction with respect to matters that previously have taken place on the high seas, (or possibly will take place on the high seas, after the departure of the ship).[37] This relates to how far, in terms of geography and subject matter, the *prescriptive* jurisdiction of the enforcing State extends.

This distinction between different types of enforcement measures was not addressed in any amount of detail in *Norstar*, including in the minority opinion, but was recognized and emphasized by the Permanent Court of International Justice in 1927 in the *Lotus* judgment,[38] which appears to be the basis for the conclusion in *Norstar*.[39] While subsequent provisions included in various law of the sea treaties have had the effect of 'correcting', or limiting the scope of the *Lotus* judgment, those measures have not affected its fundamental distinction between the two types of enforcement measures discussed here.

### 2.3.2 LOSC

The distinction is maintained in LOSC too, albeit somewhat more discretely. Three articles specifically refer to the availability of enforcement of violations on the high seas by other means than at-sea enforcement. Each of these articles adopts a different approach to the prescriptive basis of the jurisdiction.

Article 97 addresses penal or disciplinary jurisdiction following collisions or other incidents of navigation on the high seas. Paragraph 3 preserves the exclusivity of flag State jurisdiction when it comes to at-sea enforcement measures against the ship itself,[40] while the first paragraph, which specifically refers to *ex-post* enforcement, includes another limitation:

> In the event of a collision or any other incident of navigation concerning a ship on the high seas, involving the penal or disciplinary responsibility of the master or of any other person in the service of the ship, no penal or disciplinary proceedings may be instituted against such person except

---

37 This variant of port State jurisdiction is sometimes labelled 'departure State jurisdiction'. See eg Erik J Molenaar, 'Port State Jurisdiction' in *Max Planck Encyclopedia of Public International Law* (Oxford University Press 2014) para 15.

38 *S.S. Lotus* [1927] Permanent Court of International Justice A 10, 18–19.

39 *Norstar* (n 11) para 216.

40 LOSC art 97(3) reads 'No arrest or detention of the ship, even as a measure of investigation, shall be ordered by any authorities other than those of the flag State'.

> before the judicial or administrative authorities either of the flag State or of the State of which such person is a national.

The provision was originally included in the 1958 Convention on the High Seas to limit the jurisdiction of non-flag States, not to extend it, as a response to – and 'correction' of – the broad range of jurisdictional bases accepted in the *Lotus* judgment, including the State of the nationality of the victim of the collision.[41] Its inclusion and history thus suggest that for high seas activities that are not covered by the article, similar limitations do not exist, if a basis for the jurisdiction can be found under general international law.[42]

Second, Article 109 on unauthorized broadcasting from the high seas also separates physical at-sea enforcement (paragraph 4) from *ex-post* adjudication jurisdiction (paragraph 3). As to the latter, the list of available jurisdictional bases is exhaustive, but it covers a very wide spectrum, representing all main bases for extra-territorial jurisdiction.[43]

Third, Article 218(1) authorizes port States to institute proceedings against foreign ships' violations of international discharge standards for ships on the high seas regardless of whether or not they have been affected by such discharges. The novelty of the article is that it establishes enforcement jurisdiction for high seas activities without requiring any other jurisdictional link to the enforcing State than the temporary presence of the ship in its port. The significance of the provision thereby lies in that it creates the prescriptive extra-territorial jurisdiction of non-flag States in the defined cases.[44] This, in turn, suggests that a corresponding extra-territorial extension of adjudicative jurisdiction cannot be done by analogy to other high seas activities.

Apart from such more or less express references to *ex-post* jurisdiction, some LOSC articles implicitly suggest that (port) States may use their territorial sovereignty for placing requirements on foreign ships, including where those requirements relate to matters that have taken place beyond the State's coastal

41 See also Donald R Rothwell and Tim Stephens, *The International Law of the Sea* (2nd edn, Hart Publishing 2016) 159.

42 To this effect Honniball (n 3) 512.

43 LOSC art 109(3) grants adjudicative jurisdiction to: the flag state; the state of registry of the installation; the state of which the person is a national; any state where the transmissions can be received; or 'any State where authorized radio communication is suffering interference'.

44 Brian D Smith, *State Responsibility and the Marine Environment, the Rules of Decision* (Clarendon Press 1988) 232, observed that LOSC art 218 'is not an expansion of enforcement authority. States always possess authority to enforce prescriptions within territory. The expansion is in the reach of prescriptions'.

jurisdiction.[45] In these cases, jurisdiction is based on the temporary subsequent presence of the ship in the territory of the enforcing State, but no guidance is provided regarding the foundation for the prescriptive jurisdiction or on what limitations for the exercise of port State jurisdiction apply. Advice on those issues accordingly has to be sought in other areas of international law.[46]

The main inference of the above for the matter under discussion is that different jurisdictional principles govern at-sea and *ex-post* jurisdiction over activities on the high seas. The absence of an explicit prescriptive basis for non-flag States to exercise *ex-post* jurisdiction in LOSC does not necessarily mean that such exercise is prohibited or limited to express exceptions laid down in other agreements. The examples illustrate that, while the situation differs between subject matters, LOSC is not a closed jurisdictional system, and the system often implicitly or explicitly relies on other principles of jurisdiction under international law.[47] The availability of such jurisdictional principles for justifying *ex-post* enforcement measures on the high seas eventually depends on their status more generally under international law.[48]

### 2.3.3 Subsequent Practice

Finally, it should be noted that the distinction between at-sea enforcement and *ex-post* enforcement relating to the high seas seems to be maintained in post-LOSC treaty-making practice. Existing agreements granting jurisdiction for non-flag States over activities on the high seas are principally concerned with at-sea enforcement jurisdiction, ie physical enforcement measures against an individual suspected ship on the high seas. The main examples in this field relate to drug trafficking, terrorism-related crimes, and migrant smuggling. All cases indicate a significant reluctance to challenge the exclusivity of flag State jurisdiction on the high seas.

Subsequent efforts to strengthen drug trafficking enforcement in treaties on the basis of Article 108 of the LOSC have not significantly confronted the exclusivity of flag State jurisdiction on the high seas,[49] at the multilateral level at least.[50]

---

45 Notably LOSC arts 25(2), 211(3) and 255.

46 See also LOSC art 27(5) extending criminal jurisdiction over foreign to acts committed before the ship's arrival to the territory of the non-flag state, hence including acts committed on the high seas.

47 Section 3.3.1 below.

48 Section 3.3 below.

49 Art 17 of the 1988 UN Convention Against Illicit Traffic in Narcotic Drugs and Psychotropic Substances remains solidly based on *ex-ante* consent by the flag State to any degree of enforcement by other States, and the 1995 Council of Europe Agreement on Illicit Traffic at Sea is only insignificantly more far-reaching in this respect.

50 A number of bilateral treaties have been concluded on the illicit trade with drugs at sea, some of which provide for significant limitations of the exclusive flag State enforcement

Threats relating to terrorism and the proliferation of weapons of mass destruction have been dealt with in several different fora. The 2005 Protocol to the 1988 Suppression of Unlawful Acts (SUA) Convention includes a boarding regime with respect to suspicious vessels, but one which is based on various forms of flag State consent.[51] It has been complemented by bilateral agreements that have curtailed the exclusivity of flag State jurisdiction to some extent[52] and, occasionally, by more targeted resolutions by the UN Security Council (UNSC).[53]

The international agreements of relevance to migrant smuggling do not include any limitations to the exclusive jurisdiction of flag States on the high seas either.[54] However, in view of the European migration crisis in 2015, the UNSC stepped in to provide a role to non-flag States.[55] This development,

jurisdiction. See eg Robin Geiss and Christian J Tams, 'Non-Flags as Guardians of the Maritime Order: Creeping Jurisdiction of a Different Kind?' in Henrik Ringbom (ed), *Jurisdiction over Ships – Post-UNCLOS Developments in the Law of the Sea* (Brill 2015) 35–38.

51 Art 8bis of the Protocol, which includes opt-in solutions in the form of a presumed consent by the flag State in the absence of a response within four hours, or as an *ex-ante* acceptance of flag State consent to board and search suspicious ships. See eg Guilfoyle (n 35) 257; Geiss and Tams (n 50) 43–46.

52 A large number of bilateral agreements have been initiated by certain States, notably the US, with a broad number of States, including all major flag States in the world, through the Proliferation Security Initiative (PSI). The main trend in those agreements, too, is a general respect for the flag State jurisdiction, though some of them provide for presumed consent by the flag State in time limits of two to four hours, but only if the request remains unanswered, not if it is turned down. On these, see the analysis by Henning Jessen, 'United States' Bilateral Shipboarding Agreements – Upholding Law of the Sea Principles while Updating State Practice' in Ringbom (n 50) 50–81.

53 The UNSC has not adopted any Resolution under chapter VII of the UN Charter that would directly challenge the exclusivity of flag State jurisdiction, though UNSC Resolution No 1874 (2009) on the security situation in North Korea comes close, in that it establishes that, in case a flag State refuses to consent to inspection, the Security Council 'decides that the flag State shall direct the vessel to proceed to an appropriate and convenient port for the required inspection' and authorizes and requires the port State to seize and dispose of any relevant items found on board (paras 10–14).

54 See notably arts 8 and 9 of the 2000 Protocol against the Smuggling of Migrants by Land, Sea and Air, Supplementing the United Nations Convention Against Transnational Organized Crime.

55 In particular, a series of resolutions have been adopted on the use enforcement powers against migrant smuggling vessels on the high seas off the coast of Libya. Resolution 2240 (2015), adopted under ch VII of the UN Charter, declares an exceptional one-year period, which has since been renewed and remains in force, during which States are exceptionally authorized to inspect and even seize the ship, provided they 'make good faith efforts

closely intertwining the law of the sea with refugee law and human rights law, illustrates an increased preparedness to make use of binding UNSC resolutions to deal with emergencies at the high seas where the exclusivity of flag State jurisdiction may otherwise impede effective enforcement measures.[56]

With respect to at-sea enforcement relating to high seas fisheries of straddling and highly migratory fish stocks, the development has been a combination of the provisions of the UN Fish Stocks Agreement (UNFSA) and subsequent rules by regional fisheries management organizations or arrangements.[57]

In brief, this practice indicates that even limited departures from the exclusivity of flag State jurisdiction on the high seas in the form of at-sea enforcement are dealt with by means of treaties or other binding mechanisms, thereby reflecting the formal requirements of exceptions to exclusivity as provided for in Article 92(1) of the LOSC. In this sense, the agreements and UNSC resolutions referred to above not only confirm, but effectively strengthen the flag State's exclusivity with regard to at-sea enforcement on the high seas.[58] The examples are still based on some form of consent by the flag State, either at the individual at-sea enforcement situation or by *ex-ante* consent by becoming a party to the agreement in question. Interestingly, the most recent UNSC resolutions on migrant smuggling in the Mediterranean indicate a small shift in this regard.[59]

Conversely, there are few international agreements seeking to establish a right of non-flag states to take *ex-post* enforcement measures relating to high seas violations, ie to extend the *prescriptive* jurisdiction of non-flag States to

---

to obtain the consent of the vessel's flag State prior to using the authority outlined in this paragraph' (paras 7–10).

56 See also Martin Ratcovich, *International Law and the Rescue of Refugees at Sea* (Stockholm University 2019).

57 UNFSA art 21 provides a possibility for flag States parties to consent to at-sea enforcement by other parties on the high seas, which has not been used in practice. See Erik J Molenaar, 'Regional Fisheries Management Organizations' in Marta Chantal Ribeiro and others (eds), *Global Challenges and the Law of the Sea* (Springer 2020) 100. However, a less direct form of *ex-ante* flag State consent is foreseen in arts 8 and 17. In practice it has been noted that there is a growing expectation that flag States, both members and non-member in RFMOs, will grant the necessary consent to RFMOs. See eg Rayfuse (n 3) 327; the more recent review of the practice of RFMOs, undertaken in Arron Nicholas Honniball, *Extraterritorial Port State Measures: The basis and limits of unilateral port state jurisdiction to combat illegal, unreported and unregulated fishing* (PhD thesis, Utrecht University 2019) ch 5.

58 Natalie Klein, *Maritime Security and the Law of the Sea* (Oxford University Press 2011) 134.

59 See n 55.

the high seas. In this field, the development has been less coordinated, taking place through unilateral legislations or actions by individual States or regions, without a basis in treaties established for the purpose or, in some cases, included on a case-by-case basis in UNSC Resolutions.[60] Instead, jurisdiction over foreign ships has generally been founded on the presence of the ships in question in the ports or internal waters of the enforcing State.[61]

Apart from the serious maritime crimes covered by the SUA Convention regime,[62] the main exception in this regard is found in the field of high seas fisheries, where both the UNFSA and the Agreement on Port State Measures to Prevent, Deter and Eliminate Illegal, Unreported and Unregulated Fishing (PSMA) include provisions on *ex-post* enforcement measures against violations of fishing standards on the high seas.[63] The listed measures focus on port access and trade measures, which as far as the law of the sea is concerned, implies withholding of benefits for the vessel in question rather than constraining its rights.[64] Both agreements highlight that they are not to be construed as limiting the range of (additional) enforcement options for port States to exercise their territorial sovereignty over ships in their ports under international law.[65]

Looking at ongoing treaty-making projects, the Revised Draft Agreement[66] does not include any express exception to flag States' exclusive jurisdiction

---

60 See eg the very broad range of measures imposed on UN member States to enforce the sanctions against ships trading with North Korea under SC Resolution 1718 (2006) and subsequent resolutions available at <www.un.org/securitycouncil/sanctions/1718> accessed 26 April 2021.

61 Some key examples are referred to in section 3.2.3 below.

62 See n 51. Art 6(1)(c) of the 1988 Convention specifically calls for States to establish their jurisdiction over the offences covered by the Convention (ie serious offences involving threats to the safety of navigation of the ship and a series of terrorism-related offences that were added through the 2005 Protocol) if committed by their nationals. Optional jurisdiction for those can be established under art 6(3) if 'a national of that State is seized, threatened, injured or killed'.

63 In particular the references to prohibition of landings and transshipments in art 23(3) of the UNFSA and the, further-going, arts 8 and 18(1) of the PSMA.

64 On this distinction, see in particular Erik J Molenaar, 'Port State Jurisdiction toward Comprehensive, Mandatory and Global Coverage' (2007) 38 Ocean Development and International Law 225; Molenaar (n 57) 101, also notes that the question of benefits and rights may be quite different if viewed from an international trade law perspective, and that many of the denied benefits therefore may involve important trade law implications.

65 UNFSA art 23(4). Art 4(1)(b) of the PSMA specifically adds, 'including their right to deny entry thereto as well as to adopt more stringent port State measures than those provided for in this Agreement'.

66 See n 10.

over at-sea enforcement. This contrasts with the UNFSA – another LOSC implementing agreement which, in many respects, provides the relevant precedent for the BBNJ process. As to *ex-post* enforcement, the Revised Draft Agreement essentially leaves the implementation and enforcement to be governed by general international law.[67] Apart from a single general provision on implementation,[68] Part II of the text, dealing with area-based management tools (ABMTs), includes a more specific article on implementation. Article 20 accepts that international law may provide a basis for further-going implementation measures, including for non-flag States, provided the activity is under their jurisdiction or control.[69] Further implementation measures through global, regional, subregional and sectoral bodies is specifically promoted.[70] The chosen formulations, which are modelled on Articles 8 and 17 of the UNFSA, open up for future regional and sectoral enforcement measures and policies.

### 2.4 *Conclusion*

It follows from the above that the exclusivity of flag State jurisdiction referred to in Article 92(1) falls short of providing a general exclusivity of jurisdiction over ships on the high seas. Not only does the provision refer to enforcement jurisdiction, as was correctly noted by the minority in the *Norstar* judgment, but it is also limited to at-sea enforcement measures taken physically against ships while on the high seas. The other main category of enforcement jurisdiction, labelled here *ex-post* enforcement, represents a lighter and more indirect interference with ships' navigational rights and the freedom of the high seas. It may not even be directed against the ship at all, but against other persons and entities linked to its operation, and is thereby even further distanced from such traditional principles of the law of the sea.

Different types of enforcement jurisdiction accordingly need to be separated in view of their differences in terms of jurisdictional foundation. A schematic view of the main categories is provided in Figure 11.1.

---

67 Revised Draft Agreement art 4(1).

68 Revised Draft Agreement art 53(1) obliges the parties to 'take the necessary legislative, administrative or policy measures, as appropriate, to ensure the implementation of this Agreement'.

69 Revised Draft Agreement art 20(2).

70 Revised Draft Agreement art 20(4). See also Revised Draft Agreement para 6 relating to non-parties to the BBNJ Agreement.

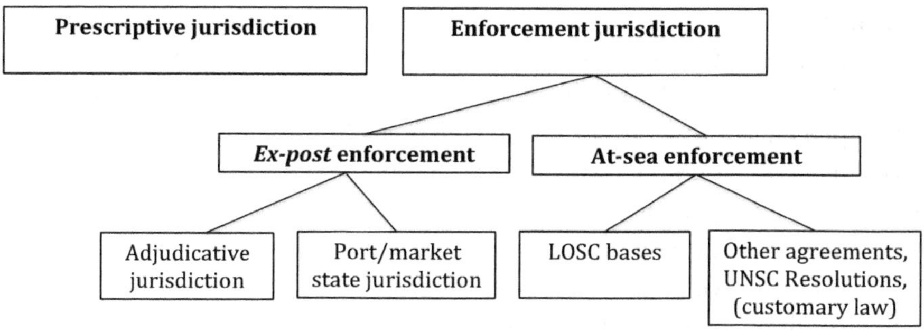


FIGURE 11.1 Bases of non-flag State jurisdiction over ships on the high seas

Those distinctions, however, represent only a first, rather basic, observation on the nature of jurisdiction on the high seas. A fuller understanding of the available 'jurisdictional space' of non-flag States relating to foreign ships' activities on the high seas calls for a closer study of the nature and extent of both prescriptive and *ex-post* enforcement jurisdiction.

## 3 Available Jurisdictional Space for Dealing with Matters on the High Seas

### 3.1 *General*

The review of LOSC and subsequent practice above suggest that it is in the field of *ex-post* enforcement measures that the jurisdictional opportunities for non-flag States lie. The regulatory possibilities and limitations linked to exercising this jurisdiction with respect to activities on the high seas are addressed below. Section 3.2 assesses the jurisdictional opportunities under the law of the sea framework, which centers on the extent to which States may exercise such jurisdiction in their capacity as port or market States. Section 3.3 then explores whether and to what extent other bases of jurisdiction in international law could provide a basis for such jurisdiction by non-flag States.

### 3.2 *Port State Jurisdiction*

#### 3.2.1 General

In contrast to the rigid limitations of coastal State jurisdiction over foreign ships, port States are largely left outside the jurisdictional scheme of LOSC. Instead, the jurisdiction of port States originates in the sovereignty of States over their territory and the voluntary presence of a ship in that territory.[71] It is well-established that internal waters, for jurisdictional purposes, may be assimilated to the land territory of the State and that ships, through their voluntary presence in the port or internal waters of another State, subject themselves to the territorial jurisdiction of that State.[72] As a starting point, a port State is hence free to impose its national rules on foreign ships and to enforce those rules by reasonable means of its choice, at least as far as they do not relate to matters which are completely internal to the ship.[73]

It is similarly widely accepted in international law that there is no general right of access of ships to foreign ports and that port States, *a fortiori*, have the right to place conditions on such access.[74] LOSC itself employs a wording in a number of provisions that confirms the existence of that right of port States.[75]

Those rights, however, do not provide unlimited jurisdiction to regulate foreign ships. As was already noted, the physical presence of a ship in the territory does not in itself justify enforcement of any type of requirements; a valid prescriptive basis is still required.[76] Apart from potential treaty restraints and the general enforcement safeguards and other reasonableness requirements,[77] the available jurisdiction for port States to undertake *ex-post* enforcement measures with respect to foreign ships relating to their activities beyond the port State's national waters essentially depends on three separate issues to be discussed further below: the type of requirement imposed; the type of

---

71 The reference in arts 218 and 220 to vessels that have *voluntarily* entered the port, excludes ships which have been forced to the port, but is commonly also understood as excluding the application of these articles to ships which have arrived following *force majeure* or distress.

72 LOSC art 2.

73 See eg Robin Rolf Churchill and Alan Vaughan Lowe, *The Law of the Sea* (3rd edn, Manchester University Press 1999) 65–69.

74 Alan Vaughan Lowe, 'The Right of Entry into Maritime Ports in International Law' (1977) 14 San Diego Law Review 597; Louise de la Fayette, 'Access to Ports in International Law' (1996) 11(1) International Journal of Marine and Coastal Law 1. This right was confirmed in *Nicaragua v. United States of America* [1986] ICJ Reports 1986, para 213.

75 See n 45.

76 See n 20. See also Geert De Baere and Cedric Ryngaert, 'The ECJ's Judgment in Air Transport Association of America and the International Legal Context of the EU's Climate Change Policy' (2013) 18 European Foreign Affairs Review 402. 'Just as in criminal jurisdiction, the presence of ships in territory is not constitutive for the *existence* of the jurisdiction but merely conditions its *exercise*'; Sophia Kopela, 'Port-State Jurisdiction, Extraterritoriality, and the Protection of Global Commons' (2016) 47 Ocean Development & International Law 93–95, 105.

77 See n 133.

enforcement measures taken; and the availability of a jurisdictional basis to justify the extra-territorial reach.

### 3.2.2 Type of Requirement

For many types of unilateral requirements imposed by a port State there is no need to specify the geographical extent of the requirement. If the subject of regulation is a 'static' or 'continuous' condition of the ship (such as typically a requirement relating to the construction, design, equipment or manning (CDEM) of the ship), the violation 'follows' the ship. In this case the violation also takes place in the port itself where the State's prescriptive jurisdiction is undisputed. For example, a requirement that fishing vessels entering ports of the regulating State shall have a functioning device on board for recording their fisheries activities on the high seas would fall under the category of static measures and hence would be subject to territorial jurisdiction, while the actual use of the device on the high seas would be a matter of conduct which needs to be described in geographical terms, hence needing an extra-territorial jurisdictional basis for the high seas.

Static port State requirements are thus, despite their impact on navigational freedoms, easier to justify in a jurisdictional sense than requirements prescribing a certain conduct by the ship or its crew on the high seas.[78] Quite a few existing port State requirements relate to static requirements and thus effectively apply in all areas where the ships in question operate.[79] There are no international judgments on the validity of such requirements and national case law on the matter is scarce and inconclusive.[80]

---

78 Molenaar (n 37) para 20; Cedric Ryngaert and Henrik Ringbom, 'Introduction: Port State Jurisdiction: Challenges and Potential' (2016) 31(3) International Journal of Marine and Coastal Law 379; Robin Churchill, 'Port State Jurisdiction Relating to the Safety of Shipping and Pollution from Ships – What Degree of Extra-territoriality?' (2016) 31(3) International Journal of Marine and Coastal Law 442, 454–58. See also the discussion of the distinction between CDEM and other measures in Henrik Ringbom, *The EU Maritime Safety Policy and International Law* (Brill 2008) 337–41 and 433–35; Sophia Kopela, 'Making Ships Cleaner: Reducing Air Pollution from International Shipping' (2017) 26 Review of European, Comparative & International Environmental Law 231, 239–40.

79 Well known examples include unilateral requirements on oil tanker constructions imposed by the United States (1990 Oil Pollution Act (Pub. L. 101-380)) and the European Union (Regulation 417/2002 on the accelerated phasing-in of double hull or equivalent design requirements for single hull oil tankers).

80 *William Rodman Sellers v. Maritime Safety Inspector* [1998] Court of Appeal in New Zealand, CA 104/98 which ruled out the imposition of CDEM measures, has been widely criticized in legal literature. CDEM requirements by port States were specifically accepted in the Swedish judgment *Miljönämnden i Helsingborgs kommun v. HH Ferries and Sundbusserne* [2006] Svea Court of Appeal, Environmental Court of Appeal (Miljööverdomstolen) M

The jurisdictional distinction between different types of requirement and the location at which they are breached opens up for jurisdictional 'constructions' by the port State. Even where the targeted issue concerns in fact a certain conduct on the high seas, there may be regulatory techniques available to 'territorialize' the conduct. By defining the offence in terms that ensure that the violation only takes place in the port,[81] transforming the operational requirement into a CDEM requirement,[82] or focusing on secondary conduct that is related to the violation but takes place in the port,[83] some of the jurisdictional hurdles relating to the extra-territorial impact could be overcome. The real target of such violations may relate to conduct that has occurred well before the ship entered the waters of the enforcing port State. Yet the labelling of the offence means that the violation has occurred within the territorial jurisdiction of the port State. Even if widely practiced,[84] such techniques may seem questionable from a jurisdictional point of view. Proposals to use port States' territorial jurisdiction in this way have rightly been held to 'work a strain on the logic of the principles [of jurisdiction]'.[85] Yet, they correspond in a technical sense to the principles of territorial jurisdiction.[86]

---

8471-03. A very extensive understanding of the reach of port State jurisdiction in an aviation context was expressed by the Court of Justice of the EU, in the IAATA Case 366/10, ECLI:EU:C:2011:864, para 125.

81 See eg Section 59C of the Australian Great Barrier Reef Marine Park Act 1975, under which the punishable offence is 'to enter an Australian port after navigating without a pilot if … a regulated ship navigates without a pilot in the compulsory pilotage area'. See also Vaughan Lowe and Christopher Staker, 'Jurisdiction' in Malcolm D Evans (ed), *International Law* (3rd edn, Oxford University Press 2010) 332.

82 For example by focusing on the availability on board of 'magic pipes', by-passing the required installations measuring the amount of oil in discharged wash-waters, instead of targeting actual illegal discharges.

83 eg failure by the crew to provide adequate records of fuel consumption or ballast water management for the entire duration of the ship's voyage or failure to co-operate with port State enforcement officials.

84 See eg Lowe and Staker (n 82) 332; Richard A Udell, 'United States Criminal Enforcement of Deliberate Vessel Pollution: A Document-Based Approach to MARPOL' in Davor Vidas (ed), *Law, Technology and Science for Oceans in Globalisation – IUU Fishing, Oil Pollution, Bioprospecting, Outer Continental Shelf* (Martinus Nijhoff Publishers 2010) 269.

85 Smith (n 44) 176.

86 ibid. See also Lowe and Staker (n 81) who take the view that the legal acceptability of this kind of jurisdictional claims will have to depend on the way in which they are received and reacted upon by other States in practice.

### 3.2.3 Type of Enforcement Measure

The absence of a right of access to ports, and the consequent right of port States to place conditions on such access, suggests that the legality of the port State's requirements also depends on what type of enforcement measures it takes against non-complying ships.[87] If the enforcement measure in question is the denial of a benefit to which the ship has no right, the availability of prescriptive jurisdiction for the measure is not relevant. This includes a series of potentially powerful measures, including the prohibition of landing catches caught on the high seas in violation of the port or market State's unilateral requirements, limitations with respect to the denial of current or future port access altogether. In so far as it is not otherwise bound by other international treaties, such as trade agreements,[88] a State that refuses port access for ships that have engaged in certain conduct on the high seas, may, in other words, do it on the basis of its right to refuse access independently of whether or not it has explicit prescriptive jurisdiction to regulate the conduct in question.

The denial of market-related benefits as a vehicle for exercising jurisdiction over events taking place on the high seas has been used in fisheries regulation for decades. A well-established example is the prohibition to land catches that have been unlawfully caught on the high seas.[89] In commercial shipping, State practice is less widespread, but in particular since the turn of the Millennium, there have been examples of port States conditioning access to their ports of vessels based on their conduct beyond the State's own coastal waters.[90]

---

87 See notably Molenaar (n 64).

88 While such legal restraints may be very important, not least in a fisheries context, they cannot be discussed here. On the role of international trade law in limiting port State jurisdiction, see eg Molenaar (n 37) Part C; Andrew Serdy, 'The Shaky Foundations of the FAO Port State Measures Agreement: How Watertight Is the Legal Seal against Access for Foreign Fishing Vessels' (2016) 31(3) International Journal of Marine and Coastal Law 422; Erik Romée van der Marel, 'Evaluating Market Conditionality in Fisheries – International Law and Global Administration' (PhD thesis, UiT The Arctic University of Norway 2019) ch 7.

89 To some extent this practice, as was noted in n 63 has been codified in international fisheries agreements. For an overview of national and regional practice in this regard, see Honniball (n 57) chs 6 and 7.

90 Available examples range from measures with relatively mild impact on navigational freedoms, such as notification and reporting obligations prior to port entry (see eg Bevan Marten, 'Port State Jurisdiction over Vessel Information: Territoriality, Extra Territoriality and the Future of Shipping Regulation' (2016) 31 International Journal of Marine and Coastal Law 470; Kopela (n 76) 96–97), to more intrusive requirements, such as obligations to perform certain environmental operations prior to entering the port (eg the 2001 Australian ballast water management requirements, which were modified in 2015 and aligned with the 2004 International Convention for the Control and Management of

In certain international treaties that have been developed since the turn of the Millennium, the right of port States to place conditions for access to their ports has explicitly been confirmed.[91] Some recent IMO conventions have also included a provision stating that they are not intended to limit the residual jurisdiction of port States to apply further-going measures in accordance with international law.[92]

### 3.2.4 Availability of Extraterritorial Jurisdictional Basis

For enforcement measures that cannot be justified under any of the above considerations, an express basis for the extra-territorial jurisdiction is required. This would typically apply to adjudicative measures, such as penalties or other punitive measures, including confiscation of property. This type of jurisdiction is not limited to port States but may be invoked by any State that has a sufficient jurisdictional link to the extra-territorial conduct in question.

It was already noted in Section 2.2 above that LOSC contains few explicit references to such jurisdiction for non-flag States relating to the high seas. In practice too it seems that punitive measures have been sparingly applied for violations on the high seas.[93] Yet, that is not necessarily the end of the matter, as several provisions implicitly require going beyond LOSC to clarify the reach of non-flag States' prescriptive jurisdiction. The spatial jurisdictional scheme as laid down in the law of the sea is therefore not the only jurisdictional system of relevance for governing the reach of adjudicative jurisdiction in respect of high seas violations. The availability of other international jurisdictional bases is considered separately in section 3.3 below.

Ships' Ballast Water and Sediments, BWMC), and to keep a record of the port-based ships' overall $CO_2$ emissions (EU Reg 2015/757 on the monitoring, reporting and verification of carbon dioxide emissions from maritime transport) or to have a pilot on board during prior passage in an international strait (see eg Australian requirements with respect to the Torres Strait referred to in Molenaar (n 37) para 21. See also Kopela (n 76) 101–02).

91 eg SOLAS reg XI-2/9 (2.2 and 2.5).

92 See eg art 1(3) of the 2001 International Convention on the Control of Harmful Anti-fouling Systems on Ships and art 2(3) of the BWMC.

93 The main legislative examples relate to pollution violations, which have a basis under LOSC art 218. Such penalties are required under EU Dir 2005/35 on ship-source pollution and on the introduction of penalties for infringements, but do not appear to have led to convictions for pollution incidents on the high seas. A review of penalties in the fisheries sector is undertaken by Honniball (n 57) section 5.3.5, also concludes that available examples are limited and tend to relate to exceptional circumstances. See also Molenaar (n57) 102.

### 3.3 *Bases for Extra-territorial Jurisdiction under General International Law*

#### 3.3.1 General

Extra-territorial jurisdiction of States to legislate in respect of activities occurring beyond their own territory has to be based on a specific principle of jurisdiction that is recognized under international law.[94] The most widely recognized principles are: active personality principle; the passive personality principle; the protective principle and the universality principle.[95] A detailed examination of those uncodified principles is beyond the scope of this chapter. For present purposes it suffices to note that the principles enjoy varying degrees of international acceptance and that the one which is most relevant here is the one that is subject to least controversy, which is the active personality principle, providing jurisdiction on the basis of nationality. For this reason, the latter principle is discussed separately in Section 3.3.2 below, while some other principles are only briefly mentioned in Section 3.3.3.

Whether an alternative jurisdictional basis for *ex-post* enforcement measures against foreign ships' activities on the high seas is available through these principles essentially depends on the relationship between LOSC and general international law. This relationship is not entirely straightforward. While the general principles of jurisdiction do not feature in LOSC, it is clear that the jurisdiction allocated to flag, coastal and port States in different sea areas in LOSC have their inspiration in – and may be traced to – those principles.[96] The key question for present purposes is whether the LOSC regime entails the exclusion of other jurisdictional principles under general international law or whether those principles could be applied concurrently.

The absence of any reference to the general jurisdictional principles could be taken as indicating that LOSC represents a *lex specialis* regime that overrides any other bases of jurisdiction for matters taking place on the high seas.[97]

---

94 Michael Akehurst, 'Jurisdiction in International Law' (1972–1973) XLVI British Yearbook of International Law 167; Lowe (n 86) 340–42; Ryngaert (n 21) with further references.

95 Cedric Ryngaert, *Jurisdiction in International Law* (2nd edn, Oxford University Press 2015) ch 4.

96 Gavouneli (n 25) 7, 33–34.

97 See eg Geiss and Tams (n 49) 21, considering that the exclusive flag state jurisdiction of LOSC art 92(1) 'supersedes other [jurisdictional] links, including traditional categories such as ownership and nationality of seafarers, or more recent grounds justifying assertions of jurisdiction in other fields such effects or impact'. (Footnote omitted). Similarly, Doris König, 'Flag of Ships' in Rüdiger Wolfrum (ed), *Max Planck Encyclopaedia of Public International Law* (Oxford University Press 2009) para 25: 'As a rule, other States have no right to exercise prescriptive, enforcement, and adjudicative jurisdiction over foreign ships on the high seas'.

However, the text of the LOSC does not purport to exclude other jurisdictional bases where the Convention itself does not provide guidance. The eighth paragraph of its Preamble specifically affirms that 'matters not regulated by this Convention continue to be governed by the rules and principles of general international law'.

Indeed, the horizontal nature of international law would not permit a convention, however constitutional it may be, to rule out the application of other jurisdictional bases, to the extent they are based in customary international law, which is arguably the case for at least some of the bases for extra-territorial jurisdiction.[98] Rather, as is recognized in LOSC itself, the law of the sea does not exist in isolation from other legal branches of international law, but is an integrated part of it and should be understood in relation to developments in general international law.[99]

In view of such considerations, and the observations made in Section 2.3 above, it seems justified to conclude that the LOSC does not constitute an exhaustive source for apportioning jurisdiction over activities on the high seas. While the Convention represents a manifestation and in most cases a clarification of the application of the principles of jurisdiction under general international law to the subject matters regulated therein, it does not replace them in the sense that alternative jurisdictional principles would necessarily be excluded.

### 3.3.2 Nationality (Active Personality)

The connection between the State and its nationals is one of the oldest legal links in international law, and a State's jurisdiction over its nationals for activities carried out beyond a State's territory is not in doubt. It was already noted above that LOSC includes a few explicit examples of non-flag State jurisdiction over matters taking place on the high seas, such as notably jurisdiction over collision cases and 'other incidents of navigation' as regulated in Article 97 and in respect of unauthorized radio broadcast in Article 109(3)(c).[100] By contrast

98 Ryngaert (n 95).

99 Apart from the eighth preambular paragraph quoted, above, this follows explicitly from eg LOSC arts 87(1), 237 and, with some qualifications, art 311. The need to interpret LOSC in light of subsequent developments of agreements and principles has also been established by international case law, eg in the Order of the *Southern Bluefin Tuna* Cases (provisional measures) (*New Zealand v. Japan; Australia v. Japan*) (27 August 1999) ITLOS 3 and 4, para 70; *Request for an advisory opinion by Sub-regional fisheries Commission* (2 April 2015) ITLOS 21, para 120; *Chagos Marine Protected Area Arbitration* (*Mauritius v United Kingdom*) (Award, 18 March 2015) PCA Case 2011–03, para 538; *South China Sea Abritration* (n 24) paras 942 and 945.

100 Section 2.3 above.

the reference to 'nationals' in respect of high seas fisheries in Articles 116 and 117 is of lesser relevance for the present context, due to that term's historic context.[101]

Despite the absence of any international treaty specifically authorizing criminal jurisdiction for the State of nationality for 'ordinary' crimes on the high seas,[102] it seems clear that cases like assault, manslaughter or murder on board ships on the high seas are not subject to the exclusive jurisdiction of the flag State. The jurisdiction of the State of nationality of the perpetrator over such acts, wherever they occur, is one of the key principles of international criminal law, which is widely present in States' legislation and appears to be entirely uncontested.[103]

The principle applies to national criminal law in general and is not necessarily limited to particularly violent crimes. Within the realm of marine biodiversity protection, nationality as a basis for jurisdiction is explicitly acknowledged in earlier instruments, including notably in the International Convention for the Regulation of Whaling,[104] but also in various EU measures aimed at IUU fisheries.[105]

---

101 The term dates back to the 1958 Convention and essentially replaces the term 'vessel'. Based on preparatory work for that convention 'the term "nationals" denotes fishing boats having the nationality of the States concerned, irrespective of the nationality of the members of their crews'. See Report of the International Law Commission covering the work of the eighth session (A/3159), art 49, Commentary, para 2. II *Yearbook of International Law Commission* (1956) 287. See also Myron H Nordquist (ed), *United Nations Convention on the Law of the Sea: A Commentary* (vol 2, Brill Nijhoff 1993) 282. The term is 'nationals' in this meaning is no longer used in the FSA.

102 In n 62 it was noted that the main international convention covering crimes at sea, the SUA Convention does include active personality as a mandatory basis of jurisdiction in art 6(1)(c), but is limited to serious crimes as listed in its art 3. See, however art 5(1)(c) of the 1998 Convention on the Protection of the Environment through Criminal Law (European Treaty Series No. 172; not in force), which not only permits, but requires its parties to establish jurisdiction if the offence is committed 'by one of its nationals if the offence is punishable under criminal law … if the place where it was committed does not fall under any territorial jurisdiction'.

103 See eg Alla Pozdnakova, *Criminal Jurisdiction over Perpetrators of Ship-Source Pollution, International Law, State Practice and EU Harmonization* (Martinus Nijhoff 2013) 72–76.

104 Art IX(1) of the 1946 International Convention for the Regulation of Whaling specifically requires its parties to ensure 'the punishment of infractions against the said provisions in operations carried out *by persons or* by vessels under its jurisdiction' (emphasis added).

105 See eg the EU's IUU Regulation (Council Regulation 1005/2008 establishing a Community system to prevent, deter and eliminate illegal, unreported and unregulated fishing) arts 39(1) and 40(2).

An element which is not often raised in a shipping context is that jurisdiction based on nationality also extends to corporations that are registered in the enforcing state.[106] This represents a significant avenue to jurisdiction, given that ship-owning companies, fisheries, mining and other corporations will commonly be heavily involved in activities on the high seas undertaken under another State's flag. The potential relevance of jurisdiction over the shipowner has increased with the development of open registers, through the separation of the nationality of the ship from that of its owners,[107] but other associated corporations within the jurisdiction of the enforcing State, including insurance companies, charterers and various domestic service providers, may be equally relevant to target for an effective enforcement regime.[108]

Accordingly, international law does not prevent a State, or a group of States, from adopting their own standards for high seas activities and to enforce those measures by means of subsequent enforcement action against companies registered in those States, independently of the flag State involved. This arguably extends to collisions and other incidents of navigation regulated in Article 97 of the LOSC.[109] A potential concern is that States with a strict enforcement policy with respect to their corporations are exposed to a competitiveness risk, in view of the ease by which corporations, just like ships, can be re-registered in another jurisdiction to avoid enforcement actions. This risk could be partially mitigated through a multilateral approach to jurisdiction over corporations.

A potential limitation to the use of nationality as a jurisdictional basis could be placed by the 'ship as a unit'-doctrine, under which '[t]he ship, everything on it, and every person involved or interested in its operations are treated as an entity linked to the flag State' and that '[t]he nationalities of these persons are not relevant'.[110] The recent confirmation of this doctrine by courts

106 The relevance of nationality as a basis for jurisdiction over corporations was emphasized by the ICJ in *Barcelona Traction Barcelona Traction, Light and Power Company, Limited* (*Belgium v. Spain*) [1970] ICJ Reports 1970.

107 See also art 9 (on corporations) of the ILC draft Articles on diplomatic protection UN Doc A/61/10 and *Yearbook of the International Law Commission, 2006*, vol II, Part Two.

108 See eg the range of players associated with targeted ships targeted by the UNSC sanctions against North Korea under SC Resolution 1718 (2006) available at <www.un.org/securitycouncil/sanctions/1718> accessed 26 April 2021. As to the role of various forms of marine insurance. See also Caddell and others (n 7) 395–408.

109 The wording of LOSC art 97 specifically concerns cases where physical persons, ie the master or 'any other person in the service of ship' have been charged in relation to the incident on the high seas. It does not rule out that a State where the company is registered takes judicial action against that company or its officials. See also Pozdnakova (n 103) 76.

110 *M/V 'Saiga'* (No.2) (*Saint Vincent and the Grenadines v. Guinea*) (1 July 1999) ITLOS 2 para 106. The doctrine was taken a step further in the *Arctic Sunrise Arbitration* (*Kingdom of*

and tribunals[111] has led some to question whether legal action on the basis of nationality of persons or companies is available, or whether it means, in combination with exclusive flag State jurisdiction on the high seas, that only the flag State has jurisdiction over persons linked to the ship.[112]

However, the context in which the 'ship as a unit'-doctrine has been used to date needs to be distinguished from the present setting. In all cases referred to above, where the doctrine has been applied, the matter has related to whether the flag State is entitled to seek redress on behalf of, and in protection of, shipowners, crew members, cargo interests etc., irrespective of their nationality, or whether its right in this regard is limited to claims relating to the ship itself.[113] That is a different matter, aimed at facilitating at a practical level the flag State's possibility to protect the interests of crew members and others linked to the ship. It does not limit the rights of the State of nationality of the crew or corporations to exercise jurisdiction over their nationals, possibly concurrently with the flag State.[114] Indeed, any limitation of other States' jurisdiction in this regard would effectively amount to immunity against trial for unlawful acts on the high seas by any other entity than the flag State.[115] Accordingly, the 'ship as a unit'-doctrine was rightly not raised in the *Norstar* case, which specifically concerned the jurisdiction of a non-flag State to take action against violations taking place on the high seas.[116]

---

*the Netherlands v. Russian Federation*) (Award on the Merits, 14 August 2015) PCA 2014-2, para 172, by including the flag State's right to make claims on behalf of enforcing State's (Russia's) own citizens. See also Nelson F Coelho, *Unilateral Port State Jurisdiction – The Quest for Universality in the Prevention, Reduction and Control of Ship-Source Pollution* (PhD thesis, University of Utrecht, School of Law 2019) 306–07.

111 Apart from the cases referred to in the previous footnote, the doctrine has also been confirmed in *Virginia G* (n 22) paras 126 and 127. See also P Chandrasekhara Rao and Philippe Gautier, *The International Tribunal for the Law of the Sea – Law, Practice and Procedure* (Edward Elgar Publishing 2018) 319–20.

112 Tams and Geiss (n 57). See also Yoshifumi Tanaka, 'Jurisdiction of states and the law of the sea' in Orakhelashvili (n 20) 139.

113 It was specifically noted in *Saiga* (n 110) para 106, that 'the Convention considers a ship as a unit, as regards the obligations of the flag State with respect to the ship and the right of a flag State to seek reparation for loss or damage caused to the ship by acts of other States and to institute proceedings under Article 292 of the Convention'.

114 To this effect, see art 18 of the ILC Draft Articles on Diplomatic Protection. For a historic review, see also Arthur D Watts, 'The protection of alien seamen' (1958) 7(4) International and Comparative Law Journal Quarterly 691, 701–02.

115 Moreover, as was noted in section 2.3 above, the need for jurisdictional limitations imposed by LOSC art 97(1) indicates that general legal situation is that active personality jurisdiction applies with respect to crimes committed by crew members on the high seas.

116 The doctrine was not mentioned in the main judgment in *Norstar* (n 11). In the preliminary objections judgment, though, Italy as the non-flag state unsuccessfully sought rely

### 3.3.3 Other Jurisdictional Bases

Having concluded that the nationality of persons and corporations may represent a perfectly justifiable basis for jurisdiction for subsequent enforcement measures with respect to foreign ships' activities on the high seas, it is a small step to conclude that the same applies to any other basis of extra-territorial jurisdiction, to the extent that those bases are accepted under general international law.

The challenge in this respect lies in establishing the level of acceptance of the jurisdiction principle. International law on extra-territorial jurisdiction is quite unsettled. While the existence of certain principles to this effect is widely acknowledged, their respective status, scope of applicability and mutual relationship remain uncertain, due to a notable lack of authoritative judgments at international level, and a multitude of national judgments which point in diverse directions.[117] The State of flux in this area of international law has led certain legal scholars to settle for a rather more generic single jurisdictional principle 'of genuine connection between the subject matter of jurisdiction and the territorial base or reasonable interests of the State in question'.[118]

All jurisdictional bases for extra-territoriality mentioned above may have some relevance to ships' activities on the high seas. The passive personality principle bases the jurisdiction on the basis of the nationality of the victim. This is a somewhat less established variant of the nationality principle, which could be relevant for the high seas by providing for jurisdiction for the State whose nationals where victims of the event on the high seas, such as murder, rape, assault etc. The principle is acknowledged in a series of anti-terrorist conventions, including as an option in Article 6 of the SUA Convention.[119] Yet, the principle is probably also available for high seas crimes that are not covered by that convention, and is increasingly being used in national legislation, at least

---

on the doctrine when objecting to the flag state's right to bring the claim in the absence of damage caused to any of its nationals. See paras 230–32 of the preliminary objections judgment of 4 November 2016.

117 See eg the Final Report of the ILA's Committee on Extra-territorial Jurisdiction, International Law Association, Report of the Sixty-Seventh Conference, Helsinki, Finland, International Law Association, London, 1996) 521–22 and 525. See also Ryngaert (n 95) ch 4.

118 Crawford (n 32) 441. See also Mann (n 20) 43–51; Andreas F Lowenfeld, *International Litigation and the Quest for Reasonableness, Essays in Private International Law* (Clarendon Press, 1996) 228–32; Robert Jennings and Arthur Watts (eds), *Oppenheim's International Law Ninth Edition, Volume I Peace, Introduction and Part 1* (Longman 1992) 457–58, 468. See also §211 of the US Restatement (Fourth) on Foreign Relations Law published in 2018 discussed in Dodge (n 18) 153.

119 Art 6(3) referred to in n 62.

for more severe crimes.[120] This is a logical development flowing from the gradual separation between the flag State and the ship that has taken place over the past decades, as well as from the increasing multiplicity of nationalities on board a ship (notably with respect to passenger ships).[121] However, in collision and incidents of navigation, this type of jurisdiction is specifically ruled out by Article 97 of the LOSC.

The universality principle is accepted in principle as a basis for jurisdiction, but is of limited relevance here, given that only very serious crimes, such as genocide, crimes against humanity or war crimes are commonly considered to give rise to this type of jurisdiction. The prime example of universal jurisdiction in the law of the sea is piracy, as defined and regulated in Articles 100–109 of the LOSC. Apart from that, there are few activities on the high seas that could give rise to this type of jurisdiction.[122]

The protective or security principle refers to the right of a State to enforce a limited category of offences which threaten the security of the State or the integrity of its government, even if the offence is committed outside its territory. The more detailed scope of this principle – notably with respect to the types of offences which are covered – is subject to debate, but in general the threshold of 'threat' for the State concerned which it seeks to cover is set quite high, involving vital interests of the State.[123] The examples tend to focus on enforcement rather than prescriptive jurisdiction, which is also true for the main example found in the law of the sea, ie the right of intervention in the case major pollution threats.[124] Another example which can be traced back to this principle is the jurisdictional regime relating to unauthorized broadcasting (in Article 109 of the LOSC), which in a somewhat more modern format could be understood to include activities such as disturbance of GPS or other

120 See eg Gavouneli (n 25) 30; Lewins (n 6); Ryngaert (n 95) 112, assesses that 'the lack of international protests against jurisdictional assertions based on passive personality may surely boost its legality'.

121 For examples of practical issues that arise when the flag State does not exercise its enforcement jurisdiction over crimes at sea and other States have insufficient jurisdictional bases in their national laws, see eg IMO Docs LEG 88/7/2 (Japan, 2004) and LEG 93/12/3 (India, 2007).

122 For an overview of universality as a basis of jurisdiction in the law of the sea, see eg Gavouneli (n 25) 19–29.

123 The protective principle is traditionally considered to involve crimes against the security or political stability of the State. See eg Ryngaert (n 95) 114–19.

124 LOSC art 221. The rules on suppression of drug trafficking also find their basis in this principle.

vital communication signals on the high seas or possibly interferences with submarine cables in the Area.

In parallel with those bases, an argument is increasingly made for including another basis for extra-territorial jurisdiction, based on States taking unilateral enforcement action in the interest of protecting common concerns that do not easily fit into the traditional jurisdictional principles and are insufficiently protected by other international solutions.[125] Protecting global commons, such as the high seas, would be an obvious candidate for benefiting from such a principle.[126] Oceans are inter-linked, the world community as a whole benefit from the well-being of the high seas and all States suffer from the drawbacks of their unsustainable exploitation. Yet in jurisdictional terms they are beyond the reach of any State. 'Free-riders' benefit from the absence of control of exploitation giving rise to concerns linked to the 'tragedy of commons'. Indeed, the need for protecting and ensuring the sustainable use of the high seas is well established in LOSC and a range of other treaties.[127]

In the specific context of port State jurisdiction, Kopela has suggested, that '(t)he concept of common concern and the collective nature and objective of the protection of global commons may legitimize the exercise of extraterritorial jurisdiction'.[128] By referring to other academic authors, she puts forward the argument that 'the encroachment upon the interests of the flag State is outweighed by the protection and regulation of common interests that include the interests of the flag State itself. Sovereignty in this sense is not sidelined but exercised for the protection of global interests'.[129] It is accordingly the global harmful effect of the activity which constitutes the jurisdictional link, irrespective of where the activity took place.[130]

Ultimately, the validity of any jurisdictional claim under customary law will depend on how they are received by other States when exercised, which will place significant weight on whether other States will protest against such

---

125 Kopela (n 76) 108–10. See also Thomas Cottier and others, 'The Principle of Common Concern and Climate Change' (2014) 52 Archiv des Völkerrechts 296; De Baere and Ryngaert (n 76) 401.

126 See also Thea Coventry, 'Appropriate Measures at Sea: Extraterritorial Enforcement Jurisdiction over Stateless Migrant Smuggling Vessels' (2019–20) 7 Maritime Safety and Security Law Journal, 13.

127 Kopela (n 76) 109; Jutta Brunee, 'Common areas, common heritage and common concern' in Daniel Bodansky and others (eds), *Oxford Handbook of International Environmental Law* (Oxford University Press 2007).

128 Kopela (n 76) 109.

129 ibid.

130 cf De Baere and Ryngaert (n 76) 402.

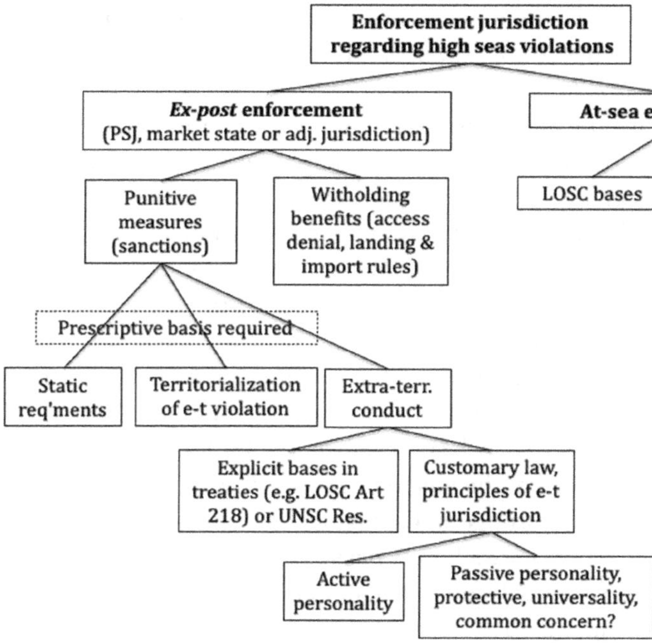


FIGURE 11.2 Available opportunities for non-flag States to exercise jurisdiction over ships' activities on the high seas

assertions of jurisdiction.[131] On the basis of practice so far, it seems that the few available instances of subsequent enforcement by non-flag States has not given rise to much protest by flag States or other States.[132]

### 3.4 *Conclusion*

The elements discussed in this section call for a further refinement of Figure 11.1. An effort to complete the original figure with the various enforcement options and their relationship to prescriptive jurisdiction is made in Figure 11.2.

The figure indicates that a broad variety of jurisdictional avenues may be available to States seeking to enforce their rules relating to foreign ships on the

131 ibid. See also Akehurst (n 94) 176; Lowe (n 86).

132 On that basis, Marten (n 8) 104, maintains that a growing body of State practice on extra-territorial port State requirements is likely to result 'provided laws governing extraterritorial operations are carefully tailored, meaning enforcement on a day-to-day basis is unobtrusive enough to compel compliance without giving rise to international protest'. See also ibid 114 and 233–35. A similar conclusion with respect to port State measures in fisheries is drawn by Honniball (n 57) 346.

high seas. Any of the boxes without a downward connecting line represents a potential jurisdictional opportunity for such enforcement. The extent of the *ex-post* jurisdiction depends on the choice of enforcement measure (loss of entitlement/benefit or punitive measures). Punitive measures, which would normally be the most powerful and precise category of enforcement measures, cannot be based on the territorial presence of the ship alone, but need a solid prescriptive jurisdictional basis for the requirement. Whether or not the requirement is extra-territorial, in turn, follows from the type of requirement at issue (eg whether it relates to conduct or static features). Yet, even rules relating to extra-territorial conduct may be justified, despite the limited bases for them in LOSC. Other bases of jurisdiction under international law do exist and may be relied on for the purpose, not least in the field of jurisdiction based on nationality, for natural as well as legal persons. In addition, developments point at increasing acceptance of the idea that special jurisdiction is available to deal with threats to common concern that would otherwise not be enforced, and the case for that kind of jurisdiction is particularly strong if the relevant requirements are based in a global agreement aiming at protection of common spaces for the benefit of mankind as a whole.

It should be highlighted, however, that even if a basis for jurisdiction is available, it does not necessarily mean that the exercise of that jurisdiction by non-flag States is lawful. In particular where enforcement targets the ship itself and its freedom to navigate and exercise commerce, a fair share of limitations follows from the safeguards' clauses of LOSC Part XII section 7.[133] Limitations may also follow from other treaty commitments, whether imposed by bilateral or multilateral, maritime, commercial, trade or other treaties, and from principles of general international law, such as the prohibition of discrimination or of abuse of rights. Proportionality requirements may also place limitations on the enforcement measures which may reasonably be taken against ships that fail to comply with the port State's requirements.

This type of limitations, which may be grouped together under the general heading of 'reasonableness criteria', inherently lack in specificity and depend on the circumstances of the individual case. In the end, they all center on the nature and proximity of interest of the enforcing State and the proportionality and reasonableness of the measures taken in relation to the objective pursued. Clearly enforcing requirements that are laid down in a global convention, negotiated by the global community as a whole, aimed at protection of global

133 LOSC arts 223–32. This includes the rules of art 230 that only monetary penalties shall be used as a penalty for violations beyond the territorial sea and that the recognized rights of the accused shall be observed.

commons represent a very strong case for tipping the balance in favor of parallel jurisdiction of non-flag States over activities on the high seas.[134]

## 4 Conclusions, with Particular Reference to the Ongoing BBNJ Treaty Negotiations

The direction of the development in this field of international law is clear. The exclusivity of flag States' jurisdiction over ships is being challenged from many directions and this includes jurisdiction over activities on the high seas. While the exclusivity of at-sea enforcement measures remains more or less intact, and has progressed mainly through treaty-making, the main legal advances lie in the field of *ex-post* enforcement. The development is in part to be noted in some international agreements specifically recognizing a 'residual' jurisdiction of port States to take unilateral measures that exceed the agreed requirements, but the main development has taken place in State practice relating to non-flag State jurisdiction, usually without support in treaties.

The main vehicle for a development away from the exclusive flag State jurisdiction has been the imprecise (and hence also dynamic) principles on territorial and extraterritorial jurisdiction in international law, which have permitted States and regional organizations to develop their practice without much objection by other States. The jurisdictional potential for the development has accordingly been latently available for port States to use for decades, but has also evolved over time, through a gradual development of the principles governing *ex-post* enforcement jurisdiction over extra-territorial activities. Yet, the underlying reason for the development lies in factual and scientific developments. Increasing awareness of the ecological state of the oceans and increasing concerns and evidence that flag State jurisdiction alone is not sufficient to address the threats facing the oceans today are particularly relevant elements in this respect, but the development is also driven by the availability of new technological tools to monitor activities on the high seas.

This development of the jurisdictional setting of the high seas does not appear to be caught up by recent case law at the international level, leading to an emerging discrepancy between views among academics and developments in State practice, on the one hand, and international courts and tribunals on

134 See eg Alan Vaughan Lowe, 'The Problems of Extraterritorial Jurisdiction: Economic Sovereignty and the Search for a Solution' (1985) 34 The International and Comparative Law Quarterly 724, 734: 'extraterritorial claims are more likely to be acceptable when used in service of legislation upholding generally held values'.

the other hand. The discrepancy is particularly fueled by the recent *Norstar* judgment which bluntly rules out a role for non-flag States without making a proper differentiation between the various type of jurisdictional principles and elements involved. The even more recent *Enrica Lexie* award is even less explicit on the reasons for endorsing *Norstar* on this point, which contributes to a rather confused message conveyed by the award on jurisdiction.[135]

The ongoing BBNJ process provides a regulatory opportunity for the community of States to clarify and advance the development of the jurisdictional principles governing the high seas. However, the indications are that major ground will not be broken in this area, as issues linked to jurisdiction over ships on the high seas have been largely avoided so far in the negotiations. Yet, as this chapter has sought to demonstrate, even a complete absence of a role for non-flag States in the forthcoming BBNJ Agreement does not signify the end of opportunities for those States to take enforcement measures against ships engaged in illicit or undesirable actions in relation to BBNJ.

As far as physical at-sea enforcement measures on the high seas are concerned, the rule remains that of exclusive flag State jurisdiction, subject to explicit treaty exceptions. The availability of exemptions based on customary international law is less certain, partly because of the omission of any reference to such exemptions in Article 92(1) of the LOSC, and partly due to the uncertain availability of any such customary norms in the field of at-sea enforcement. The absence of provision on at-sea enforcement in the Revised Draft Agreement is not entirely surprising, given that exemptions to flag State exclusivity with regard to such measures on the high seas generally tend to focus on crimes with a more immediate societal impact, for which *ex-post* enforcement may not even be available as an effective option, such as terrorism, drug dealing and migrant smuggling.[136]

The jurisdictional opportunities for non-flag States wishing to enforce future measures protecting BBNJ therefore lie in the domain of *ex-post* enforcement measures. This type of enforcement involves less intrusion with navigation and may be expected to grow with technological advances, such as satellite-based monitoring tools, that permit authorities to be up to date with activities on the high seas without physical presence in the area.

---

135 Arron Honniball, 'The '*Enrica Lexie*' Incident Award and Exclusive Flag State Jurisdiction' (2020) Blog post at the Centre for International Law, National University of Singapore available at <https://cil.nus.edu.sg/the-enrica-lexie-incident-award-and-exclusive-flag-state-jurisdiction-by-arron-n-honniball/> accessed 26 April 2021.

136 See n 49–57.

A number of *ex-post* enforcement measures are available under international law, which is implicitly even acknowledged in the Revised Draft Agreement.[137] Requirements relating to technical standards or other static measures could be imposed by port States, on the basis of territorial jurisdiction, subject to respecting the appropriate safeguards for such measures. While representing a very powerful tool for exercising jurisdiction over foreign ships generally, in particularly when used in concert in larger geographic areas, this option is of more limited use in the BBNJ context, given that the key issues addressed in the instrument relate to the activities and conduct of ships on the high seas, rather than features such as the construction, design or manning of ships. Yet it is not ruled out that conduct could in some cases be effectively translated into static requirements or otherwise be 'territorialized' to secure the prescriptive jurisdiction.[138]

Available enforcement measures under international law also include the denial of access to markets and other benefits in the port to which the ship has no legal right, and even access to the port itself. The Revised Draft Agreement accepts, at least as far as ABMTs are concerned, that global, regional or sectoral bodies could develop further conservation and management measures,[139] which may provide a basis for the further development of such enforcement measures.

A missing link from the point of view of non-flag States is the jurisdiction to impose sanctions and other punitive measures against foreign ships that fail to meet the required standards of conduct on the high seas. This covers adjudication jurisdiction exercised by courts, but also administrative measures of a punitive nature, such as administrative fines or arguably even the 'punitive' detention of a ship, to the extent such measures specifically relate to ships' activities on the high seas. The legal challenge here relates to securing the required prescriptive jurisdictional basis for the extra-territorial measure. LOSC includes little express support in this regard outside violations of international discharge standards, while the Revised Draft Agreement establishes general obligations for the parties to collaborate but, at least as far as ABMTs are concerned, postpones the matter by ultimately leaving the prescriptive

137 Apart from the general implementation obligation in Revised Draft Agreement art 53(1) (n 68), art 20(2) (quoted in n 69) authorizes parties to adopt more stringent measures to implement area-based conservation and management measures in conformity with international law.

138 See n 81–83.

139 See n 70.

powers in the hands of the body in charge of adopting conservation and management measures.[140]

However, the required basis can be found in jurisdictional principles outside the law of the sea, to the extent they are generally recognized. The principle of active personality is strong enough under international law to provide for jurisdiction against persons holding the nationality of the enforcing State, irrespectively of where the violation has physically occurred. This principle applies not only to physical persons but also to companies registered in that country, which is also recognized in the Revised Draft Agreement with regard to sharing benefits of MGRs.[141]

Other jurisdictional bases are not quite as accepted, but may nevertheless provide a jurisdictional basis, depending on the case at hand. The passive personality and universality principles are less likely to be relevant in the BBNJ context, but there could be scope for application of the protective principle, not least in a collective manner, as is suggested by the discussions on jurisdiction based on 'common concern'. While the status of common concern as a basis for jurisdiction is still unclear, it is difficult to find a better context for advancing its relevance than through an agreement that is specifically designed for protecting the global commons. In support of such a common approach, the Preamble of the draft BBNJ Agreement specifically refers to the desire of the parties to 'act as stewards of the ocean in areas beyond national jurisdiction on behalf of present and future generations'.[142]

The bases for extra-territorial jurisdiction represent an unsettled field of international law, and their acceptance and applicability eventually depend on how the instances of their application are received by other States. From this perspective, too, it is obvious that any provisions in the Revised Draft Agreement highlighting the collective high seas governance responsibilities of all States serve to strengthen the case for jurisdiction by non-flag States.

Strengthening the possibility of non-flag States to contribute in the enforcement of the new agreement would seem particularly justified in view of the purpose of the BBNJ Agreement.[143] A provision that would confirm other

140 Revised Draft Agreement art 19 includes two alternatives, distinguished mainly by the role of regional bodies in the decision-making process relating to the adoption of ABMTs. Revised Draft Agreement art 10 on MGRs employs somewhat stronger wording by obliging the parties to take 'the necessary legislative, administrative or policy measures, as appropriate' to ensure that the various obligations set out in the article are met.

141 The reference to 'natural or juridical persons under their jurisdiction' in Revised Draft Agreement art 11(5) indicates an intention to extend the jurisdictional focus beyond the classical law of the sea bases.

142 Revised Draft Agreement Preamble, para 4.

143 As provided in Revised Draft Agreement art 2.

States' right to take *ex-post* enforcement measures with respect to violations would be helpful in this regard,[144] and would neither challenge ships' right to navigate freely on the high seas nor 'undermine existing regimes'.[145] On the contrary, acknowledgment of the right of non-flag States to take specific and targeted enforcement measures, including penalties, against violations in defined conditions would more likely serve to streamline the enforcement regime of the high seas, by reducing pressure for more broad-brushed enforcement measures with potentially even larger effects on ships' navigational freedoms, such as denial of port entry and market access.

Potential concerns by flag States about their jurisdictional rights could be alleviated by specifically introducing a priority of jurisdictions: several precedents exist where non-flag State jurisdiction only sets in if the flag State fails to address the matter in a given period of time.[146] This type of jurisdictional prioritization, or 'subsidiarity', would serve to reconcile the interests of the flag State with those of other States, while at the same time enclosing potential enforcement gaps linked to flag State exclusivity.

The basic premise of the BBNJ negotiations is that ABNJ represent a shared concern which is not sufficiently protected by international law. This should be reflected, not only in clear obligations for ships while on the high seas, but also in effective opportunities to enforce that regime. The policy concern, in other words, should be matched by jurisdictional opportunities. A number of such opportunities are available on the basis of general international law, but the ongoing negotiations represent a unique opportunity to strengthen and clarify the role of non-flag States. Leaving the matter unaddressed in the future BBNJ Agreement may be a convenient way of avoiding the issue, and postponing the

144 An example of how this could be achieved is the third paragraph of the preamble of the PSMA, in which the parties recognize

> [t]hat measures to combat illegal, unreported and unregulated fishing should build on the primary responsibility of flag States and use all available jurisdiction in accordance with international law, including port State measures, coastal State measures, market related measures and measures to ensure that nationals do not support or engage in illegal, unreported and unregulated fishing.

145 A guiding principle for the negotiations has been that 'the process and its result should not undermine existing relevant legal instruments and frameworks and relevant global, regional and sectoral bodies' (UNGA Resolution 72/249, paras 6 and 7). Art 4(3) of the Revised Draft Agreement accordingly provides that the agreement 'shall be interpreted and applied in a manner that [respects the competences of and] does not undermine relevant legal instruments and frameworks and relevant global, regional, subregional and sectoral bodies'. (Brackets in original).

146 Examples are available in LOSC arts 218(4) and 228 and UNFSA art 21.

matter to be dealt with by other institutions and authorities in the future may be a political way out. However, neither solution contributes to clarity or uniformity of practice, nor indeed to improved protection of the global commons, which represents the very purpose of the exercise.

CHAPTER 12

# Imagining a Polycentric Approach to Institutional Governance for Marine Areas beyond National Jurisdiction

*Kristine Elfrida Dalaker**

## 1 Introduction**

Marine areas beyond national jurisdiction (ABNJ) cover nearly two-thirds of the world's ocean.[1] These vast areas contain some of the world's unique marine ecosystems, including seamounts, hydrothermal vents, deep-sea trenches, deep-sea coral reefs, cold seeps, and pockmarks.[2] The ecosystems within these areas contain genetic resources that are attracting growing interest for use in a variety of commercial applications, including pharmaceuticals and cosmetics.[3] In addition, ABNJ provide a wealth of resources and services, including seafood and raw materials, genetic and medicinal resources, air purification, climate regulation, and habitat and cultural services.[4]

* PhD Research Fellow, Norwegian Centre for the Law of the Sea, Faculty of Law, UiT The Arctic University of Norway.

** This author is greatly appreciative to the editors, as well as to Nele Matz-Lück and Alexander Proelss for their helpful feedback on this chapter. This author also wishes to thank the Fram Centre for funding this author's participation at the BBNJ intergovernmental conference, which informs the research that underlies this chapter through the project entitled, 'Assessing the Implications of a Global Treaty on Marine Biodiversity in Areas Beyond National Jurisdiction for Ecosystem-based Governance in the Arctic Ocean (ARCTIC_BBNJ II)', Norsk Polarinstitutt Grant nr 66005.

1 IUCN, 'Governing Areas Beyond National Jurisdiction' available at <www.iucn.org/resources/issues-briefs/governing-areas-beyond-national-jurisdiction> accessed 1 November 2020. See generally Glen Wright and Julien Rochette, 'Regional Ocean Governance of Areas Beyond National Jurisdiction: Lessons Learnt and Ways Forward' (2019) STRONG High Seas Project 5 available at <www.prog-ocean.org/wp-content/uploads/2019/03/STRONG-HS_Lessons-Learnt-Report.pdf> accessed 1 November 2020.

2 Food and Agriculture Organization of the United Nations, 'Deep Sea Ecosystems' available at <www.fao.org/fishery/topic/166310/en> accessed 1 November 2020.

3 David Leary and others, 'Marine Genetic Resources: A Review of Scientific and Commercial Interest' (2009) 33 Marine Policy 183, 189.

4 IUCN (n 1).

 | DOI:10.1163/9789004506367_013

ABNJ are global commons where no State sovereignty exists under the United Nations Convention for the Law of the Sea (LOSC).[5] The governance of these areas is the subject of a new ocean treaty that is being negotiated in the United Nations. The mandate of the negotiations is to conclude an international legally binding instrument (BBNJ Agreement)[6] under LOSC for the conservation and sustainable use of marine biodiversity in areas beyond national jurisdiction (BBNJ) in an intergovernmental conference (IGC).[7] The IGC negotiations are organized around the four elements of the 'package deal': (i) marine genetic resources (MGRs), including questions on sharing of benefits (ii) area based management tools (ABMTs), including marine protected areas (MPAs); (iii) environmental impact assessments (EIAs); and (iv) capacity building and the transfer of marine technology.[8]

ABNJ comprise the Area and the high seas.[9] While the Area and its mineral resources are treated as the 'common heritage of mankind' (CHM), the high seas are grounded in the freedom of navigation and the freedom to fish, among others.[10] The treatment of these maritime zones as ABNJ under the LOSC underlies the tension in the BBNJ process.[11] While developing States have generally aligned themselves with the view that all living marine resources (including MGRs) in ABNJ should be treated as the CHM,[12] developed States tend to hold the view that these marine resources should be subject to high seas freedoms.[13] These deeply entrenched views about the legal status of these

5 United Nations Convention on the Law of the Sea (opened for signature 10 December 1982, entered into force 16 November 1994) 1833 UNTS 3 (LOSC) arts 86 and 89.

6 In this chapter, 'BBNJ Agreement' and 'treaty' are used interchangeably.

7 UNGA A/Res/72/249, 'International legally binding instrument under the United Nations Convention on the Law of the Sea on the conservation and sustainable use of marine biological diversity of areas beyond national jurisdiction' available at <www.undocs.org/A/RES/72/249> accessed 1 November 2020. Individual sessions of the IGC are referred to numerically. For example, the first session is referred to as IGC-1.

8 ibid.

9 LOSC art 1(1) and part VII.

10 ibid part VII.

11 See LOSC; UNGA Res 72/249 (n 7). See Lan Nguyen (ch 5) in this volume.

12 With regard to fish and other biological resources in ABNJ, there is convergence around the view at the IGC that the BBNJ Agreement will not apply to those marine living resources used as a commodity. See Revised draft text of an agreement under the United Nations Convention on the Law of the Sea on the conservation and sustainable use of marine biological diversity of areas beyond national jurisdiction (Revised Draft Agreement) available at <https://undocs.org/en/a/conf.232/2020/3> accessed 1 November 2020, art 8. See also Richard Barnes (ch 10) in this volume for a discussion on how the BBNJ Agreement should relate to fisheries management in ABNJ.

13 Summary of the Third Session of the Intergovernmental Conference on an International Legally Binding Instrument under the UN Convention on the Law of the Sea on the

resources have persisted throughout the nearly twenty years of BBNJ process discussions, echoing the ideological issues that complicated the negotiation of the deep seabed mining provisions of the LOSC during the Third United Nations Conference on the Law of the Sea.[14]

The existing ocean governance framework for ABNJ has been described as chaotic and fragmented, as well as inadequate to provide for the conservation and sustainable use of BBNJ.[15] Several commentators have suggested that polycentric governance may provide an effective model for the long-term health and sustainable use of these areas. Polycentric governance is 'a mode of *hybrid* problem-solving governance in which sovereign states and non-state parties actively collaborate, roughly as equal partners, to address certain kinds of highly complex problems that appear to be beyond the capacity of sovereign states alone to solve'.[16] Given the fragmented nature of this regulatory space and the number and diversity of stakeholders operating within this space,[17] it is timely to explore whether and how a polycentric approach may provide an effective model for the governance of ABNJ.

Elinor Ostrom, a renowned political scientist, studied the governance of the commons and is the academic who propounded the theory of polycentric governance for which she was awarded the 1990 Nobel Prize for Economics. Ostrom's theory has gained traction in emerging and evolving theories of post-sovereign governance and climate change governance, for although polycentric systems may appear chaotic and fragmented, they may be more ordered and successful in achieving sustainable outcomes than they actually appear.[18] Given the relevance of these theories to the management of common-pool resources (CPRs) – such as the world's oceans[19] – this author believes that

Conservation and Sustainable Use of Marine Biodiversity of Areas Beyond National Jurisdiction: 19-30 August 2019' 25(218) Earth Negotiations Bulletin (IISD Reporting Services, 2 September 2019) (ENB IGC-3 Summary); see this author's notes from IGC-3 (on file with author) (Author's IGC-3 Notes).

14 Satya N Nandan, Michael W Lodge and Shabtai Rosenne (eds), *United Nations Convention on the Law of the Sea 1982: A Commentary* (vol 6, Martinus Nijhoff Publishers 2002) 35–54.

15 IUCN (n 1).

16 Bradley C Karkkainen, 'Post-Sovereign Environmental Governance' (February 2004) 4(1) Global Environmental Politics 74.

17 For a discussion of existing ocean governance of ABNJ, see Section 2.

18 Robin Mahon and Lucia Fanning, 'Regional Ocean Governance: Integrating and Coordinating Mechanisms for Polycentric Systems' (2019) 107 Marine Policy 3.

19 Nives Dolsak and Elinor Ostrom, 'The Challenges of the Commons' in Nives Dolsak and Elinor Ostrom (eds), *The Commons in the New Millennium: Challenges and Adaptations* (The MIT Press 2003) 3.

Ostrom's research may provide inspiration for solutions to ocean governance beyond the LOSC framework in ABNJ.

Ostrom's research examined the relationship between the sustainability of institutions and the sustainability of resources.[20] She concluded that robust institutions are integral to the sustainable management of CPRs.[21] Her work has resonated in the interventions made in the BBNJ process where several delegations have proposed the inclusion of *robust* institutional arrangements for the BBNJ Agreement.[22] However, they provided little indication of what robust may mean.[23] The Cambridge Dictionary provides some guidance as it defines 'robustness' as the quality of 'being strong, and healthy or unlikely to break or fail'.[24] Similarly, Ostrom ties the concept of robustness to the likelihood of success or failure of relevant institutional arrangements to achieve sustainable outcomes for common-pool resources. In addition, she found that the successfulness of the sustainability of a common-pool resource was tied to the sustainability of its institutions, thus allowing her to conclude that robust institutions are indeed integral to the sustainable management of common-pool resources.[25] This makes Ostrom's theory that much more appropriate for exploration within the context of ABNJ, specifically to the formulation of robust institutional arrangements for the BBNJ Agreement. To do so, this chapter uses the design principles that Ostrom posited to study the robustness of institutions.[26]

This chapter aims to explore whether the institutional framework of the anticipated BBNJ treaty lends itself to a polycentric approach, given that the negotiations are purely intergovernmental in nature and are taking place under the auspices of the LOSC regime, and if not, then what kind of polycentric governance could be imagined for the governance of marine ABNJ using an expanded regional seas program (RSP). The institutional arrangements that have been proposed throughout the IGC and its preparatory work serve as a starting point for analysis, using the Revised Draft Agreement text prepared by the IGC President Rena Lee (Revised Draft Agreement),[27] together with the

20 See Section 4 for citations and further elaboration.

21 ibid.

22 ibid.

23 ibid.

24 Cambridge Dictionary available at <https://dictionary.cambridge.org/dictionary/english/robustness> accessed 1 November 2020.

25 Elinor Ostrom, 'Beyond Markets and States: Polycentric Governance of Complex Economic Systems' (June 2010) 100(3) The American Economic Review 652–53.

26 See Section 4.

27 Revised Draft Agreement (n 12).

textual proposals submitted by the participating delegations up to and including 20 February 2020.[28] In those instances where the Revised Draft Agreement is not instructive on institutional arrangements, the analysis is supplemented by using the interventions and proposals put forward by participating delegations at the IGC and in its preparatory work (PrepCom).[29] If the BBNJ process loses momentum, is significantly delayed and/or fails, inspiration for a polycentric approach for the governance of these areas can be found in the interventions delivered in the BBNJ process, specifically to the expanded UN Environmental Program (UNEP) regional seas program proposed by Iceland[30] and Norway[31] at IGC-1 (Expanded RSP), which serves as the basis for this chapter's principle-by-principle analysis using Ostrom's design principles.[32]

This chapter is organized as follows: first, it introduces key elements of existing ocean governance of ABNJ, which includes emphasis and detail on regional frameworks that could be employed in applying a polycentric approach. Second, it gives an overview and status of the BBNJ process, particularly the participating delegations and their proposed approaches to institutional arrangements. Third, it provides the background and context to the polycentric approach by examining Elinor Ostrom's theory of polycentric governance of CPRs and the design principles that Ostrom distilled from her research. It

28 Textual proposals submitted by delegations by 20 February 2020, for consideration at the fourth session of the Intergovernmental conference on an international legally binding instrument under the United Nations Convention on the Law of the Sea on the conservation and sustainable use of marine biological diversity of areas beyond national jurisdiction (the Conference), in response to the invitation by the President of the Conference in her Note of 18 November 2019 (UN Doc A/CONF.232/2020/3) available at <www.un.org/bbnj/sites/www.un.org.bbnj/files/textual_proposals_compilation_-_28_feb_2020.pdf> accessed 1 November 2020.

29 Development of an international legally-binding instrument under the United Nations Convention on the Law of the Sea on the conservation and sustainable use of marine biological diversity of areas beyond national jurisdiction (UNGA A/Res/69/292) available at <https://documents-dds-ny.un.org/doc/UNDOC/GEN/N15/187/55/PDF/N1518755.pdf?OpenElement> accessed 1 November 2020.

30 Iceland, 'General Exchange of Views (Item 6)' available at <http://statements.unmeetings.org/media2/19407974/iceland-bbnj-igc-general-statement-item-6.pdf> accessed 1 November 2020; Iceland, 'Measures such as Area Based Management Tools, including Marine Protected Areas (item 7)' available at <http://statements.unmeetings.org/media2/19408198/iceland-bbnj-igc-abmt-statement-10-september.pdf> accessed 1 November 2020.

31 Norway, 'General Exchange of Views (Item 6)' available at <http://statements.unmeetings.org/media2/19407965/norway.pdf> accessed 1 November 2020; Norway, 'Measures such as Area Based Management Tools, including Marine Protected Areas (item 7)' available at <http://statements.unmeetings.org/media2/19408185/norway-item-7.pdf> accessed 1 November 2020.

32 See this author's notes from IGC-1 (on file with author) (Author's IGC-1 Notes) 66, 80, 82.

then provides a brief analysis of the institutional arrangements proposed at the IGC using Ostrom's design principles, followed by a principle-by-principle analysis of the existing institutional arrangements in order to explore what could be imagined for the conservation and sustainable use of BBNJ using an Expanded RSP. The chapter closes with its findings and concluding remarks.

## 2 Existing Ocean Governance of ABNJ

The governance of ABNJ is comprised of a patchwork of global, sectoral and regional agreements, arrangements, targets and other initiatives that are described in more detail in this Section 2. Particular emphasis is given to those aspects of regional governance that could be used in an Expanded RSP.

### 2.1 *Global Governance*

The point of departure for the governance of ABNJ is the legal framework set out in the LOSC. The LOSC takes a functional approach, providing for the rights and obligations of States for each of the maritime zones.[33] The environmental duties and obligations of States are set out in the LOSC and its implementing agreements for each of the maritime zones, including those that comprise ABNJ.[34] Deriving and further implementing these environmental duties and obligations is one of the aims of the BBNJ treaty negotiations.[35]

Another legal regime that is closely related to the BBNJ process, but is situated outside the LOSC framework, is the Convention on Biological Diversity (CBD),[36] whose objectives include the conservation of biological diversity,[37] the sustainable use of its components, and the fair and equitable sharing of

---

33 See LOSC.

34 LOSC arts 116–119, 194–197, 209; Agreement relating to the implementation of Part XI of the United Nations Convention on the Law of the Sea of 10 December 1982 (signed 18 July 1994, entered in force 16 November 1994) 1836 UNTS 3; United Nations Agreement for the Implementation of the Provisions of the United Nations Convention on the Law of the Sea of 10 December 1982 relating to the Conservation and Management of Straddling Fish Stocks and Highly Migratory Fish Stocks (opened for signature 4 August 1995, entered into force 11 December 2001) 2167 UNTS 3 (UNFSA).

35 Revised Draft Agreement art 2.

36 Convention on Biological Diversity (signed 5 June 1992, entered in force 29 December 1993) 1760 UNTS 79 (CBD).

37 CBD art 2 defines biological diversity as 'the variability among living organisms from all sources including, inter alia, terrestrial, marine and other aquatic ecosystems and the ecological complexes of which they are part: this includes diversity within species, between species and ecosystems'.

the benefits arising out of the utilization of genetic resources.[38] However, Article 4 of the CBD limits the Convention's application beyond national jurisdiction to jurisdiction over processes and activities concerning the components of biological diversity.[39] This limitation has curtailed the influence of the CBD on the BBNJ process, where the IGC negotiations are situated under the LOSC.

Despite the CBD's jurisdictional limitation in ABNJ, the CBD has inspired and informed the BBNJ process in various ways,[40] but especially in relation to the criteria for designating MPAs and the use of terms and definitions relating to MGRs.[41] There has, however, been some resistance to the wholesale import of particular provisions and definitions used in the CBD into the negotiations of a treaty under the LOSC framework.[42]

Additional targets and commitments are provided by other initiatives. In 2010, objectives relevant to BBNJ were adopted within the CBD, which are known as the 'Aichi Targets'.[43] The Rio+20 outcome document, *The Future We Want*, reaffirmed many of these objectives.[44] At the Rio+20 Conference, States also agreed to develop the Sustainable Development Goals (SDGs)[45] to bring together the Millennium Development Goals and environmental concerns into one comprehensive global development agenda. The SDGs were adopted in 2015, with an Ocean SDG (SDG 14), which includes targets related to the conservation of marine ecosystems and effective regulation of fishing.[46] The CBD has called for collaboration from the UNEP Regional Seas Programme (see below) in reaching these targets through regional workshops and learning

38 ibid art 1.

39 ibid art 4.

40 See also Oude Elferink and Kerr (ch 7) in this volume.

41 'Summary of the Second Session of the Intergovernmental Conference on Marine Biodiversity of Areas Beyond National Jurisdiction: 25 March–5 April 2019' 25(195) Earth Negotiations Bulletin (IISD Reporting Services, 8 April 2019) (ENB IGC-2 Summary).

42 For a telling example of the tension between the BBNJ process and the CBD that may explain this resistance, see Alice Vadrot, 'Why Negotiations on Marine Biodiversity "Came Close to Collapsing"' (15 February 2019) available at <www.maripoldata.eu/why-negotiations-on-marine-biodiversity-came-close-to-collapsing/> accessed 1 November 2020.

43 Strategic Plan for Biodiversity 2011–2020 and Aichi Targets available at <www.cbd.int/decision/cop/?id=12268> accessed 1 November 2020.

44 *The Future We Want*, Outcome Document of the United Nations Conference on Sustainable Development Rio de Janeiro, Brazil, 20–22 June 2012 (UNGA A/Res/66/288).

45 Transforming our world: the 2030 Agenda for Sustainable Development (UNGA A/Res/70/1).

46 ibid.

exchange programs under the Sustainable Ocean Initiative Action Plan (2015–2020) and similar initiatives.[47]

### 2.2 *Sectoral Governance*

There are several international organizations with sectoral mandates in ABNJ. Fishing is covered by the mandate of the Food and Agriculture Organization of the United Nations (FAO), which is complemented on the regional level by regional fisheries management organizations (RFMOs) and other regional and sub-regional fisheries management arrangements. Straddling and highly migratory fish stocks in areas beyond national jurisdiction are governed by the UN Fish Stocks Agreement.[48] The exploration and exploitation of mineral resources in the Area is governed by the International Seabed Authority (ISA).[49] Shipping and dumping fall under the governance of the International Maritime Organization (IMO). Marine science is dealt with under the auspices of the Intergovernmental Oceanographic Commission (IOC) of the United Nations Educational, Scientific and Cultural Organization (UNESCO). Trade and intellectual property relating to BBNJ are considered in the context of the World Trade Organization (WTO) and the World Intellectual Property Organization (WIPO). Other sectoral instruments relevant to BBNJ include the International Convention on the Regulation of Whaling[50] and the Convention on the Conservation of Migratory Species of Wild Animals.[51]

### 2.3 *Regional Governance*

The United Nations Environmental Programme (UNEP) is of particular importance to regional governance. UNEP was created in 1972 to serve as a focal point for environmental action and coordination within the United Nations system.[52] Eighteen regional initiatives, involving more than 143 States,[53] are

---

47 David Joseph Attard, Malgosia Fitzmaurice and Alexandros Ntovas (eds), *The IMLI Treatise on Global Ocean Governance, vol II: Specialized Agencies and Global Ocean Governance* (Oxford University Press 2018) 169–70.

48 See UNFSA.

49 LOSC art 1(1).

50 International Convention on the Regulation of Whaling (adopted 2 December 1946, entered into force 10 November 1948) 364 UNTS 1953.

51 Convention on the Conservation of Migratory Species of Wild Animals (signed 23 June 1979, entered into force 11 January 1983) 1651 UNTS 333.

52 United Nations Environmental Programme (UNEP) available at <www.unenvironment.org> accessed 1 November 2020.

53 UNEP Regional Seas Programme, 'Participating Countries' available at <www.unenvironment.org/explore-topics/oceans-seas/what-we-do/working-regional-seas/why-does-working-regional-seas-matter-2> accessed 1 November 2020.

taken through UNEP's Regional Seas Programme for the protection and sustainable use of marine environments on the regional level through a 'shared seas' approach (these regional initiatives are collectively referred to herein as RSOs).[54] While UNEP provides overall coordination for the RSP, six of these RSOs are administered directly by UNEP, seven fall outside of UNEP administration (where the RSOs were established under the auspices of UNEP but secretariat and other administrative functions are provided by another body), and four are administered independently. (but attend the UNEP meetings and cooperate with other RSOs within the RSP).[55] The RSOs under the RSP comprise both conventions and action plans, which are tailored to each region's unique environmental, socio-economic and political requirements, but generally include five common elements: (i) economic assessment, (ii) economic management, (iii) economic legislation, (iv) institutional arrangements, and (v) financial arrangements.[56]

For this chapter's analysis in Section 4, it is important to understand how the work of the RSP is implemented; therefore, an examination of the RSOs' institutional structures is warranted. The coordination of activities within each RSO takes place within Secretariats or through regional coordinating units (RCUs) and regional activity centers (RACs).[57] The RCUs (or their equivalents) serve as the 'nerve center' for the action plans that are taken on a regional basis to meet the objectives of each RSO.[58] The RCUs have overall responsibility for the implementation of the action plans, together with the implementation of policies and other strategies that are adopted and/or agreed to by the member

54 UNEP Regional Seas Programme, available at <https://www.unep.org/explore-topics/oceans-seas/what-we-do/regional-seas-programme> accessed 1 November 2020. By a 'shared seas approach', UNEP – through the RSP – attempts to engage neighboring countries in measures and actions plans to protect their common marine environment.

55 ibid. The different types of institutional arrangements utilized amongst the RSOs would be relevant to the implementation of the anticipated BBNJ treaty using the Expanded RSP approach discussed in Section 4 herein.

56 UNEP Regional Seas Programme, 'Action Plans and Conventions' available at <http://web.unep.org/regionalseas/who-we-are/regional-seas-action-plans> accessed 1 November 2020. For more detail, see <www.unenvironment.org/explore-topics/oceans-seas/what-we-do/working-regional-seas/regional-seas-action-plans> accessed 1 November 2020.

57 UNEP Regional Seas Programme, 'Why Does Working with Regional Seas Matter?' available at <www.unenvironment.org/explore-topics/oceans-seas/what-we-do/working-regional-seas/why-does-working-regional-seas-matter> accessed 1 November 2020.

58 ibid. OSPAR organizes its work across work areas, such as 'Biological Diversity and Ecosystems', which are then organized into committees, together with their corresponding subsidiary Intersessional Correspondence Groups (ICGs).

States.[59] The RCUs coordinate external cooperation with UN agencies, other international organizations, and non-governmental organizations (NGOs), and also facilitate capacity building within their own RACs and with member States.[60]

The RACs (or their equivalents) report directly to the RCUs and serve a key role in the implementation of the action plans at the regional, sub-regional, and national levels.[61] The function of the RACs is to carry out all activities related to the action plan as adopted and agreed by the member States of each RSO.[62] Funding support for the RACs is generally provided by the member States through funding mechanisms set out in the action plans.[63]

Regions that include ABNJ in their geographic coverage are:[64] (i) the Mediterranean through the Mediterranean Action Plan under the Barcelona Convention;[65] (ii) the North-East Atlantic through the OSPAR Convention;[66] (iii) the Southern Ocean through the Convention for the Conservation of Antarctic Marine Living Resources (CCAMLR);[67] the South-East Pacific through the Lima Convention;[68] and (iv) the South Pacific through the Nouméa Convention.[69] The first three RSOs listed above have taken action in ABNJ

59 ibid.

60 ibid.

61 ibid; see eg Barcelona Convention, Mediterranean Action Plan, Regional Activity Centre for Specially Protected Areas available at <www.rac-spa.org> accessed 1 November 2020.

62 ibid.

63 ibid.

64 Attard, Fitzmaurice and Ntovas (n 47) 176. UNEP contributed a study to PrepCom4 on the regional seas programmes covering areas beyond national jurisdiction, see <www.un.org/Depts/los/biodiversityworkinggroup/Regional_seas_programmes_ABNJ.pdf> accessed 1 November 2020.

65 Convention for the Protection of the Marine Environment and the Coastal Region of the Mediterranean (adopted 16 February 1976 and amended 10 June 1995; entered into force 12 February 1978 and 9 July 2004, respectively) 1102 UNTS 45 (Barcelona Convention).

66 Convention for the Protection of the Marine Environment of the North-East Atlantic (opened for signatures 22 September 1992, entered into force 25 March 1998) 23 LOSB 32 (OSPAR).

67 Convention on the Conservation of Antarctic Marine Living Resources (opened for signature 20 May 1980, entered into force 7 April 1982) 1329 UNTS 48 (CCAMLR).

68 Convention for the Protection of the Marine Environment and Coastal Area of the South-East Pacific (entered into force 12 May 1986) 1648 UNTS 3.

69 Convention for the Protection of the Natural Resources and Environment of the South Pacific Region (entered into force 22 August 1990) available at <https://www.ecolex.org/details/treaty/convention-for-the-protection-of-the-natural-resources-and-environment-of-the-south-pacific-region-tre-000892//> accessed 1 November 2020.

through the creation of MPAs and serve as relevant sources for analysis in this chapter's Section 4.[70]

Outside of the regional seas framework, other regional initiatives that may impact BBNJ have been undertaken through various actors who share common goals and interests in marine environmental protection. For instance, Large Marine Ecosystems (LMEs) are used to implement ecosystem-based management measures.[71] Other regional initiatives have been undertaken through political and economic organizations, such as the European Union (EU), the African Union (AU), the Association of Southeast Asian Nations (ASEAN), and the Caribbean Community (CARICOM) and *ad hoc* groups, such as the Sargasso Sea Commission, and must also be taken into consideration in any polycentric approach.[72]

## 3 Overview and Status of the BBNJ Process

To imagine a polycentric approach for institutional governance for ABNJ, it is necessary to begin with an overview and status of the BBNJ process. This Section 3 provides a brief summary of the development of the BBNJ process, describes who is participating in the IGC and in what capacity, and sets out the approaches to the institutional arrangements proposed in the negotiations.

### 3.1 *Development of the BBNJ Process*[73]

Both the importance of, and the threats to, BBNJ were formally addressed by the United Nations in 2003.[74] Questions were raised regarding the lack of

---

70 Attard, Fitzmaurice and Ntovas (n 47) 176–78; UNEP Regional Seas Application of Area-based Management Tools, including Marine Protected Areas – Case Studies (UN Environment Regional Seas Reports and Studies No. 214: 2019) available at <https://wedocs.unep.org/bitstream/handle/20.500.11822/28392/Ocean_SDG1.pdf?sequence=1&isAllowed=y> accessed 1 November 2020.

71 Large Marine Ecosystems Hub, see <www.lmehub.net> accessed 1 November 2020. Although LMEs are used primarily in areas within national jurisdiction, there are a number of Arctic LMEs that have been adopted by the Arctic Council, underscoring their value as a regional tool.

72 Glen Wright and others 'Partnering for a Sustainable Ocean: The Role of Regional Ocean Governance in Implementing SDG14' (2017) IDDRI available at <www.iddri.org/en/publications-and-events/report/partnering-sustainable-ocean-role-regional-ocean-governance> accessed 1 November 2020.

73 See also Henriksen (ch 4) in this volume.

74 Report on the Work of the United Nations Open-ended Informal Consultative Process on Oceans and the Law of the Sea, Letter dated 9 June 2003 from the Co-Chairperson of the

effective legal and institutional mechanisms for protecting vulnerable marine ecosystems in ABNJ.[75] Discussions on these issues led to a recommendation to form the *Ad Hoc* Open-Ended Informal Working Group on Marine Biodiversity in Areas Beyond National Jurisdiction (BBNJ Working Group).[76] It was not until 2011 that the BBNJ Working Group recommended that a process be initiated to consider the four elements of the 'package deal' described above.[77] The package deal gained momentum and political support during the 2012 Rio Conference, eventually leading to the establishment and convening of the PrepCom.[78] The PrepCom ran for four two-week sessions in 2016 and 2017, at the conclusion of which the PrepCom fulfilled its mandate and adopted its report.[79]

On 24 December 2017, the UN General Assembly decided to convene the IGC to elaborate the text of a BBNJ Agreement for the conservation and sustainable use of BBNJ to be held over the course of four two-week sessions from 2018 to 2020.[80] The language of the IGC mandate set out in UNGA Resolution 72/249 follows that of the PrepCom mandate requiring consideration of the four elements of the package deal, with the additional requirement that the work and results of the IGC be fully consistent with the LOSC.[81] At the time of writing, three of four sessions of the IGC have been concluded, with the fourth session having been postponed to a later date by resolution of the UN General Assembly due to the coronavirus disease 2019.[82]

Consultative Process addressed to the President of the General Assembly (UNGA Doc A/58/95) available at <http://undocs.org/A/58/95> accessed 1 November 2020.

75 ibid.

76 ibid.

77 Letter dated 30 June 2011 from the Co-Chairs of the Ad Hoc Open-ended Informal Working Group to the President of the General Assembly (UNGA Doc A/66/119) Annex, para 1(b).

78 Report of the Preparatory Committee established by General Assembly resolution 69/292: Development of an international legally binding instrument under the United Nations Convention on the Law of the Sea on the conservation and sustainable use of marine biological diversity of areas beyond national jurisdiction (UN Doc A/AC.287/2017/PC.4/2 dated 31 July 2017) available at <www.un.org/ga/search/view_doc.asp?symbol=A/AC.287/2017/PC.4/2> accessed 1 November 2020.

79 ibid.

80 UNGA Res 72/249 (n 7).

81 ibid para 7. The mandate includes the following proviso: 'that this process and its result should not undermine existing relevant legal instruments and frameworks and relevant global, regional and sectoral bodies'.

82 UNGA Decision 74/543 to Postpone the Fourth Session of the Conference (provisionally available as A/74/L.41) available at <https://undocs.org/en/a/74/l.41> accessed 1 November 2020.

### 3.2 *Participating Delegations*

With regard to participation in the IGC, the UN General Assembly invited: (i) UN Member States; (ii) conference representatives of organizations and other entities that have received a standing invitation from the General Assembly; (iii) representatives of interested global and regional intergovernmental organizations and other interested international bodies that were invited to such conferences and summits; (iv) relevant NGOs with ECOSOC status and those that were accredited to relevant conferences and summits to participate as observers, *where participation means attending formal meetings, unless otherwise decided by the conference in specific situations;* (v) associate members of regional commissions to participate as observers; and (vi) representatives of relevant specialized agencies, as well as other organs, organizations, funds and programs of the UN system as observers.[83] Over 120 member delegations, nearly 20 intergovernmental organizations (IGOs) and over 40 NGOs participated in the first three substantive sessions of the IGC at the UN Headquarters in New York.[84]

### 3.3 *Proposed Approaches to Institutional Arrangements for the BBNJ Treaty*

Thus far, the delegations have proposed three approaches to the institutional arrangements for the BBNJ treaty: (i) a global approach; (ii) a regional and/or sectoral approach; and (iii) a hybrid approach.[85] Those delegations that support a global approach call for a global mechanism to employ a centralized, comprehensive approach over activities in ABNJ.[86] Those delegations

83 UNGA Res 72/249 (n 7) paras 8, 12 (emphasis added), 13–15.

84 See Intergovernmental Conference of Marine Biodiversity in Areas Beyond National Jurisdiction, 'Participants' available at <www.un.org/bbnj/content/first-substantive-session> and <https://undocs.org/a/conf.232/2019/inf.3/rev.2> accessed 1 November 2020.

85 For the formalization of these approaches in the BBNJ process, see 'Chair's Overview of the Third Session of the Preparatory Committee', Preparatory Committee Established by General Assembly Resolution 69/292: Development of an International Legally Binding Instrument under the United Nations Convention on the Law of the Sea on the Conservation and Sustainable Use of Marine Biological Diversity of Areas Beyond National Jurisdiction available at <www.un.org/depts/los/biodiversity/prepcom_files/Chair_Overview.pdf> accessed 1 November 2020.

86 'Chair's Overview of the Second Session of the Preparatory Committee' available at <www.un.org/depts/los/biodiversity/prepcom_files/Prep_Com_II_Chair_overview_to_MS.pdf> accessed 1 November 2020. See also 'Summary of the First Session of the Preparatory Committee on Marine Biodiversity of Areas Beyond National Jurisdiction: 28 March – 8 April 2016' 25(106) Earth Negotiations Bulletin (IISD Reporting Services, 11 April 2016) (ENB PrepCom1 Summary); 'Summary of the Second Session of the Preparatory Committee on Marine Biodiversity of Areas Beyond National Jurisdiction: 26 August – 9 September 2016'

that support traditional high seas freedoms have called for a decentralized, regional and/or sectoral approach, favoring reliance on existing regional and sectoral bodies for implementation.[87] Those delegations that support a hybrid approach propose that the BBNJ Agreement set out internationally agreed standards and obligations at the global level, which could be implemented by States at the regional and sectoral levels.[88]

Several delegations elaborated on aspects of the approaches in the negotiations, suggesting that the institutional arrangements include a Conference of the Parties (COP),[89] a scientific and technical body,[90] a secretariat (possibly through an expanded mandate of the UN Division for Ocean Affairs and the Law of the Sea (DOALOS)),[91] and a clearing house mechanism,[92] all of which have been included in the Revised Draft Agreement.[93] With regard to the establishment of subsidiary bodies, there is growing convergence among the delegations for an evolutionary approach.[94] Several interventions emphasized that if there is a demonstrated need for the establishment of a subsidiary body, it should be done so in a manner that is cost-effective and avoids duplicating the mandates of existing bodies.[95]

In discussing the approaches, the delegations expounded on the criteria for the institutional arrangements, proposing that the resulting arrangements: (i) be 'fit-to-purpose', cost-effective and efficient;[96] (ii) promote transparency and accountability;[97] and (iii) foster participation and inclusiveness.[98] Additionally,

25(118) Earth Negotiations Bulletin (IISD Reporting Services, 12 September 2016) (ENB PrepCom2 Summary).

87 ENB PrepCom1 Summary (ibid) 5–6; ENB Prepcom2 Summary (ibid) 4.

88 'Preparatory Committee on Conservation and Sustainable Use of Marine Biological Diversity of Areas Beyond National Jurisdiction' New Zealand Submission (December 2016) 1.

89 Revised Draft Agreement art 48.

90 ibid art 49.

91 ibid art 50.

92 ibid art 51.

93 ibid part VI (Institutional Arrangements).

94 ibid art 48(4)(d); ENB IGC-2 Summary (n 41) 13; see this author's notes from IGC-2 (on file with author) (Author's IGC-2 Notes).

95 China is an example of a delegation that supported this view.

96 'Chair's non-paper on elements of a draft text of an international legally-binding instrument under the United Nations Convention on the Law of the Sea on the conservation and sustainable use of marine biological diversity of areas beyond national jurisdiction' 28 February 2017, 93–95, 94 (n 690).

97 ibid 93 (n 680), (n 682) and (n 684).

98 Kristine Dalaker Kraabel, 'The BBNJ PrepCom and Institutional Arrangements: The Hype about the Hybrid Approach' in Myron H Nordquist, John Norton Moore and Ronan Long

there was support for the BBNJ Agreement to include a 'robust, but cost-effective institutional structure'.[99] There was also support for the view that representatives from relevant organizations, both governmental and non-governmental, concerned with BBNJ should be afforded the opportunity to take part in meetings of sub-regional and regional organizations and arrangements as observers or otherwise, to account for the region-specific issues and the different environments, stakeholders, and activities.[100]

Several delegations have noted the significance of institutional arrangements,[101] suggesting that 'form follows function' and preferring to negotiate institutional arrangements after the four substantive elements of the package have been agreed.[102] Therefore, there has been little development of the three approaches to institutional arrangements at the IGC.[103] In the discussions that have been held on institutional arrangements, the hybrid approach has enjoyed strong support with several delegations calling for elaboration in upcoming negotiations.[104] The regional approach has also been the subject of discussions, with some delegations proposing a strict regional approach and others offering an Expanded RSP (which is discussed in more detail below).[105] Some delegations, in supporting a regional approach, stated that the BBNJ Agreement should provide the floor for any regulation rather than a ceiling, thereby allowing regional bodies and frameworks with the choice of implementing stronger, more restrictive measures for the conservation and sustainable use of BBNJ.[106]

(eds), *The Marine Environment and United Nations Sustainable Development Goal 14 (Life Below Water)* (Brill/Nijhoff Publishing 2018) 158–60. See Chair's Non-Paper (n 96) 93–103; ENB PrepCom1 Summary (n 86) 16, 19; ENB PrepCom2 Summary (n 86) 16, 17, 20.

99 Chair's Non-Paper (n 96) 94 (n 690).

100 ibid 93.

101 See this author's notes from PrepCom4 (on file with author) (Author's PrepCom4 Notes) 106.

102 ENB IGC-2 Summary (n 41) 13; Author's IGC-2 Notes (n 94) 152, 160–61.

103 'Summary of the Fourth Session of the Preparatory Committee on Marine Biodiversity of Areas Beyond National Jurisdiction: 10-21 July 2017' (IISD Reporting Services, 24 July 2017) 25(141) Earth Negotiations Bulletin (ENB PrepCom4 Summary) 16. See Author's PrepCom4 Notes (n 101) 77, 101. See ENB IGC-2 Summary (n 41) and ENB IGC-3 Summary (n 13).

104 'Summary of the First Session of the Intergovernmental Conference on an International Legally Binding Instrument under the UN Convention on the Law of the Sea on the Conservation and Sustainable Use of Marine Biodiversity of Areas Beyond National Jurisdiction: 4-17 September 2018' 25(179) Earth Negotiations Bulletin (IISD Reporting Services, 20 September 2018) 8, 15 available at <http://enb.iisd.org/download/pdf/enb25179e.pdf> accessed 1 November 2020.

105 ibid 7–9; Author's IGC-1 Notes (n 32).

106 ibid. See also OSPAR (n 66) preamble, para 11 (more stringent measures at regional level are permitted).

Given the convergence around the view that 'form follows function', without substantive agreement on the elements of the package deal or on the ambitiousness of the treaty, no one can predict the resulting institutional architecture of the treaty. Assuming that the IGC eventually concludes with the adoption of a treaty, it is the view of this author that a hybrid approach to the institutional arrangements should be used. The key component of a hybrid approach is the incorporation of a global process to serve as a forum to set international guidelines and standards and conduct overall coordination (perhaps through a clearing house mechanism), amongst other functions to be enumerated.[107] If the BBNJ process loses momentum, is significantly delayed and/or fails – whether by failing to conclude a treaty or because the resulting treaty does not include a global forum – the key component will fail to come into being.[108] The burden and responsibility for the conservation and sustainable use of BBNJ would therefore fall to existing regional, sub-regional, national and sectoral bodies and frameworks. Such an outcome would do little more than maintain the status quo, calling into question the very purpose and need for the BBNJ negotiations.

This does not mean that proposals made in the BBNJ process should be disregarded, but rather they can be used to spawn innovative and creative solutions. For this chapter, inspiration can be found in the Expanded RSP proposed by Iceland[109] and Norway.[110] Iceland proposed the expansion of the roles of both RSOs and RFMOs to provide for as much global coverage as possible, suggesting that the BBNJ Agreement could include provisions that mandate that these regional organizations 'work together to complement rather than undermine each other'.[111] The RSOs would serve as coordinators through the use of existing mechanisms, where the RSOs are the institutional bodies that bring together all international organizations that have legal competence under international law to manage activities in that particular region (ie, relevant RSOs, RFMOs, FAO, IMO, ISA, etc.).[112] Iceland's approach foresees that the regular review of

107 New Zealand Submission (n 88); Chair's Non-Paper (n 96).

108 In the negotiations, the UNFSA has been raised as a cautionary tale of a global treaty that does not include a COP or a global forum, but merely provides for a review conference four years after the entry into force of the Agreement. See UNFSA art 36. The fear of this author is that a weak version of hybrid approach will be used, especially one that does not include a COP or other global forum. See Dalaker Kraabel (n 98).

109 Iceland, 'General Exchange' (n 30); Iceland, 'ABMTS' (n 30).

110 Norway, 'General Exchange' (n 31); Norway, 'ABMTS' (n 31).

111 Iceland 'ABMTS' (n 30) 2–3.

112 ibid 2–3. Iceland suggests that a model cooperation agreement would be annexed to the treaty.

the implementation of the treaty would take place through a review conference (similar to the UN Fish Stocks Agreement), which would be organized by DOALOS.[113] Norway echoed these sentiments, putting forth an example of how an MPA could be adopted using the RSP mechanism.[114] More generally, Norway suggested that an integrated approach to the management of the resources in ABNJ is needed, where 'both conservation and use are assessed together'.[115] Norway also stated that clearer obligations need to be established with regard to cross-sectoral cooperation, the sharing of information and experience, and the standardization and harmonization of procedures for ABMTs and EIAs.[116]

The views of Iceland and Norway were informed in large part by their experience with regional bodies, particularly the North East Atlantic Fisheries Commission (NEAFC) and OSPAR. NEAFC, for instance, noted in its intervention at IGC-2 that it had amended and expanded its mandate to include the management of biodiversity – not just fish stocks.[117] For its part, OSPAR emphasized in its intervention, the collective arrangement it entered into with NEAFC (among others), and noted further that cross-sectoral and cross-regional coordination is essential to ecosystem-based management.[118]

Given this brief overview and status of the BBNJ process, the participants, and the approaches to the governance of these vast marine areas, this chapter next explores how polycentric governance theory may provide inspiration for the institutional governance of these areas.

## 4 A Polycentric Approach to Institutional Arrangements for BBNJ

Ostrom stated, 'Instead of presuming that optimal institutional solutions can be designed easily and imposed at low cost by external authorities, I argue that "getting the institutions right" is a difficult, time-consuming, conflict-invoking process'.[119] In an attempt to imagine how to 'get the institutions right' for the governance of marine ABNJ, this Section 4 introduces Ostrom's polycentric governance theory, providing elaboration on the eight design principles she

113 ibid. Furthermore, Iceland stated that its approach may enable delegations to agree to a treaty that did not undermine the mandates of existing organizations.

114 Norway 'ABMTs' (n 31).

115 Norway 'General Exchange' (n 31) 2.

116 ibid.

117 Author's IGC-2 Notes (n 94) 14.

118 ibid 165. See OSPAR 'Collective Arrangement' available at <https://www.ospar.org/about/international-cooperation/collective-arrangement> accessed 1 November 2020.

119 Elinor Ostrom, *Governing the Commons* (Cambridge University Press 1990) 14–15.

articulated to assess the robustness of institutional arrangements used to govern the management of CPRs. This Section then provides a brief analysis of the institutional arrangements proposed at the IGC using Ostrom's design principles, before delving into a principle-by-principle analysis of the institutional arrangements that could be imagined for the conservation and sustainable use of BBNJ using the Expanded RSP.

### 4.1 *Background and Context to Polycentric Governance*

Elinor Ostrom's theory of polycentricity serves as the starting point for the discussion of a polycentric approach to institutional arrangements for marine ABNJ. For the purpose of creating a common vocabulary for this chapter, 'polycentricity' is governance that is characterized by multi-scale governing authorities, institutions, and bodies rather than a centralized governing body,[120] 'institutions' are the formal and informal mechanisms that shape social and individual expectations, interactions, and behavior,[121] and a 'CPR' refers to a natural or man-made resource system from which potential beneficiaries cannot be efficiently excluded from obtaining benefits from its use.[122] Ostrom described a resource system as consisting of stock variables that produce a maximum quantity of a flow variable (ie, resource units) without harming the stock or the resource system itself.[123]

Ostrom and others determined that the oceans, the gene pool, and the atmosphere are all resource systems suitable for study and exploration using a polycentric approach.[124] They did, however, note the challenges that are inherent in managing the resource units within these CPRs in that they can be 'fugitive' and often cannot be stored.[125] Regardless of these challenges, it follows that marine ABNJ is a CPR for which a polycentric approach is appropriate for consideration, where ABNJ is the resource system and the resource unit is marine biodiversity.

The focus of Ostrom's research arose in part out of a direct challenge to Hardin's 1968 *Tragedy of the Commons*, where Hardin provided only two choices for the successful sustainable management of resources: either the

120 Ostrom, 'Beyond Markets and States' (n 25).

121 Margaret M Polski and Elinor Ostrom, 'An Institutional Framework for Policy Analysis and Design' in Daniel H Cole and Michael D McGinnis (eds), *Elinor Ostrom and the Bloomington School of Political Economy: A Framework for Policy Analysis* (Lexington Books 2017) 14.

122 Ostrom, *Governing the Commons* (n 119) 30.

123 ibid.

124 Dolsak and Ostrom (n 19) 3.

125 ibid 5.

resources were managed through private enterprises or through a centralized top-down governmental institution.[126] In contrast, Ostrom and others found that communities that had achieved some level of 'success' in sustaining these resources had relied on institutions that could not be characterized as either public or private.[127] Ostrom explained that '[b]y "successful" [CPR] institutions, [she meant] institutions that enable individuals to achieve productive outcomes in situations where temptations to free-ride and shirk are ever present'.[128] Most importantly, she also found that the successfulness of the sustainability of a CPR was tied to the sustainability of its institutions.[129]

Ostrom's seminal research on the governance of CPRs, *Governing of the Commons*, comprises a meta-analysis of multiple cases where resource users had organized themselves to protect a CPR from overuse, examples of which included the management of CPRs primarily within small- and medium-scale systems, such as irrigation systems, forests, fisheries, and pastures.[130] To answer the question of what types of rules appear to be most successful in sustaining the productive use of CPRs, Ostrom collected and analyzed the meta-data across these cases.[131] From that analysis, Ostrom distilled the institutional elements that were present within *robust*, successful institutions and governance systems, describing these elements as 'design principles',[132] which she defined individually as a 'conception used either consciously or unconsciously by those constituting and reconstituting a continuing association of individuals about a general organizing principle'.[133] Each of these principles is a function of either power or knowledge, where power is manifested as autonomy, participation, decision-making, and judicial and administrative processes, and where knowledge is manifested through the compilation, collection, access and availability of data, scientific knowledge, and ecological conditions.

Since the publication of *Governing of the Commons*, Cox and others improved Ostrom's design principles,[134] which improvements Ostrom also

126 Garrett Hardin, 'The Tragedy of the Commons' (1986) 162(3859) Science, New Series 1243.

127 Ostrom, 'Beyond Markets and States' (n 25).

128 Ostrom, *Governing the Commons* (n 119) 15.

129 Ostrom, 'Beyond Markets and States' (n 25) 652–53.

130 Ostrom, *Governing the Commons* (n 119); Ostrom (n 25) 649–50.

131 Ostrom, 'Beyond Markets and States' (n 25) 649.

132 Ostrom, *Governing the Commons* (n 119) 60–61. 'However, I was really undertaking a study of robustness of systems that already existed'. Elinor Ostrom, *The Future of the Commons: Beyond Market Failure and Government Regulations* (The Institute of Economic Affairs 2012) 77.

133 Ostrom, *Future of the Commons* (n 132) 31–32.

134 Michael Cox, Gwen Arnold and Sergio Villamayor Tomas, 'A Review of Design Principles for Community-based Natural Resource Management' (2010) 15(4), Ecology and Society.

adopted.[135] The 'improved' design principles include: (1A and 1B) clearly defined user and resource boundaries; (2A and 2B) congruence with local conditions, both ecological conditions and local rules on appropriation and provision;[136] (3) collective-choice arrangements; (4A and 4B) monitoring the resource and users; (5) graduated sanctions; (6) conflict resolution mechanisms; (7) minimal recognition of rights to organize; and (8) for 'nested enterprises' (groups that are part of large-scale systems), appropriate coordination among relevant groups.[137]

To understand how the design principles may be applied to marine ABNJ, one example in Ostrom's research that is helpful to this analysis is her work on the CPR of forestries. Her research began as a research program and was later established as the International Forestry Resources and Institutions (IFRI) network for the purpose of investigating how institutional arrangements impact forests and the communities that rely on them in Africa, Asia, Latin America, and the United States.[138] IFRI recognizes the relationship between sustainable natural resources and sustainable institutional arrangements and has organized its work around the following themes: biodiversity, livelihoods, institutions, and forest carbon (focused on climate change).[139] IFRI's research design includes a network of Coordination Research Centres (CRCs) that are located in regions around the world and utilize a common research methodology and database, both of which are taken from environmental and social sciences.[140] The organization of the CRC network allows for standardization of processes and data-entry forms, yet also allows for flexibility to fit the local ecology of the geographical scope of each CRC.[141]

135 Ostrom, 'Beyond Markets and States' (n 25) 653.

136 In *Governing the Commons*, Ostrom's research focused primarily on 'local' commons, 'local' conditions and 'local' rules. How her design principles can be applied to large-scale systems is discussed in Section 4.3.4.

137 Ostrom, 'Beyond Markets and States' (n 25) 653.

138 Daniel H Cole and Elinor Ostrom, 'The Variety of Property Systems and Rights in Natural Resources, in Daniel H Cole and Michael D McGinnis (eds), *Elinor Ostrom and the Bloomington School of Political Economy: Resource Governance* (Lexington Books 2015) 123, 139.

139 IFRI, 'Themes' available at <http://ifri.forgov.org/research/themes/> accessed 1 November 2020.

140 IFRI uses the Institutional Analysis and Development (IAD) framework, which was developed at the Workshop in Political Theory and Policy Analysis at Indiana University where Ostrom served as a Professor of Political Science. See the IFRI website on 'Research Design' available at <http://ifri.forgov.org/about-us/what-is-ifri-2/> accessed 1 November 2020.

141 ibid.

IFRI's network of CRCs allows for data about forests and communities that rely on them to be collected, stored, and analyzed over time.[142] The data can be used to: (i) conduct baseline studies; (ii) measure change over time in forest conditions and in local governance structures; and (iii) share information with relevant stakeholders.[143] From this data, conclusions can be drawn about the sustainability of these CPRs by determining how the institutional arrangements affect the local ecology, how the rules of governance have developed and been maintained over time, and whether the CPR users consider the governance system to be legitimate and equitable.[144]

Ostrom's design principles, together with the collaborative network of CRCs and its findings, provide ample inspiration for the consideration of a polycentric approach to institutional governance of marine ABNJ, as is discussed in more detail below.

### 4.2 *Brief Analysis of the Institutional Arrangements Proposed at the IGC Using Ostrom's Design Principles*

At the request of State delegations, President Rena Lee produced on 27 November 2019 the Revised Draft Agreement for consideration of the delegations at what was to be IGC-4 in March and April of 2020, which has since been postponed until a later date.[145] In President Lee's closing remarks at IGC-3, she said that the Revised Draft Agreement would not reflect all views of the delegations but would be representative of those areas on which she determined there had been a convergence of views.[146]

The Revised Draft Agreement reflects that there is no agreement on institutional arrangements, nor any agreement on many provisions that fall within Ostrom's design principles, including access and distribution of benefits, decision making, monitoring, enforcement, dispute resolution, rulemaking, or on a clearing house or other coordinating mechanism.[147] These areas of non-agreement do not mean that a preliminary analysis cannot be undertaken at this juncture of the negotiations, particularly when it comes to the first design principle.

142 IFRI, 'About Us' available at <http://ifri.forgov.org/about-us/what-is-ifri-2/> accessed 1 November 2020.

143 IFRI (n 140).

144 Cole and Ostrom (n 138) 141–42; Amy R Poteete, Marco Janssen, and Elinor Ostrom, *Working Together: Collective Action, the Commons, and Multiple Methods in Practice.* Princeton, NJ: Princeton University Press, 2010.

145 Revised Draft Agreement; UNGA Dec 74/543 (n 82).

146 Revised Draft Agreement, 'Note by the President'.

147 Revised Draft Agreement.

Ostrom's first design principle, as further developed by Cox and others, requires clearly defined boundaries, both of the resource users and the resource itself.[148] The resource and the boundary rules regarding its use can be defined in a myriad of ways – what it is, how and when it can be accessed, used, or extracted, and where it can be found, among others.[149] For instance, unlike the UN Fish Stocks Agreement that includes a definition of 'fish' that are the subject of the Agreement,[150] the Revised Draft Agreement does not include a definition of the CPR that is the subject of the treaty, namely: 'marine biological diversity'.[151] In addition, there is no agreement on the definition of 'marine genetic resources' or access to them,[152] nor has any agreement been reached on the objectives and scope of application of the treaty.[153] This lack of clearly defined boundaries is emblematic of the BBNJ process as a whole where the negotiations have arguably lost some focus and ambition since the inaugural session of the IGC. This is a view that has been openly expressed at the negotiations, the best example of which was made by Japan in its intervention at IGC-3, where the head of its delegation stated that there was no common understanding of what the IGC was trying to achieve, noting further that without consensus on the objectives of the treaty, other issues would not progress without agreement on the main issues.[154] By casting Japan's intervention (and other delegations who have voiced similar views) in the light of Ostrom's analytical framework, it can be argued that if the IGC is to result in robust institutional arrangements for the conservation and sustainable use of BBNJ, clarity must first be reached on defining the CPRs that are the subject of the treaty, together with agreeing to clear statements on the objectives and scope of application of the treaty. Therefore, within the context of the BBNJ process, the first design principle acts as a prerequisite to further analysis using Ostrom's remaining seven design principles.[155]

148 Cox and others (n 134).

149 ibid.

150 UNFSA art 1(c).

151 Revised Draft Agreement art 1. The Revised Draft Agreement does not even include a definition based on the CBD's definition of 'biological diversity'. See n 36. If the Revised Draft Agreement remains unchanged, this issue could be resolved as a matter of treaty interpretation.

152 ibid arts 1, 9 Alt 1, 9 Alt 2, 10.

153 ibid arts 2, 3, 7, 8, 14, 21bis, 42.

154 Author's IGC-3 Notes (n 13) 6.

155 Ostrom was of the view that the design principles serve as a good beginning for the generation of questions regarding the robustness of a CPR system. Elinor Ostrom, *Understanding Institutional Diversity* (Princeton University Press 2005) 270–71. McGinnis expounded on Ostrom's statement, 'I leave it as an exercise for the reader to translate these

Not only must the resource be clearly defined under Ostrom's first design principle, this principle has been interpreted to require that the common group of members or stakeholders be clearly defined.[156] In the BBNJ process, the membership is determined by the UN General Assembly in convening the IGC under the LOSC.[157] The rights and responsibilities under the LOSC, however apportioned, begin and end with States.[158] Several delegations have emphasized this fact throughout the PrepCom, and now in the IGC, that the BBNJ process is a 'member-driven process', meaning that the Conference leadership should not exert or impose its will over the work or its results but should instead be guided by the will of the participating States.[159]

However, the UN General Assembly has recognized the importance of including other stakeholders and therefore invited IGOs and NGOs to participate in the process, in most cases as observers.[160] Although the BBNJ process has encouraged broad participation, there are barriers to participation, such as the imposition of certain requirements, including ECOSOC credentialing and registration, which can complicate and discourage participation.[161] For instance, this author understood anecdotally that some RFMOs encountered issues in the registration process and were unable to participate in IGC-3.[162] In addition, several participants have commented on the limited participation by the private sector.[163] Such participation as in the case of shipping, fishing, deep seabed mining, and submarine cable industries, is through membership organizations – including the IMO, the ISA, and the International Cable Protection Committee, respectively.[164] Other private sector industries are represented through their membership in the World Ocean Council, which has

questions into forms best suited for application to the factors they deem most important for understanding the research puzzle or policy concern that serves as the focus of their work'. Michael D McGinnis, 'The IAD Framework in Action: Understanding the Source of the Design Principles in Elinor Ostrom's *Governing the Commons*' in Daniel H Cole and Michael D McGinnis (eds), *Elinor Ostrom and the Bloomington School of Political Economy: A Framework for Policy Analysis* (Lexington Books 2017) 106–07.

156 Cox and others (n 134).

157 UNGA Res 72/249 (n 7).

158 ibid.

159 ENB IGC-3 Summary (n 13); Author's IGC-3 Notes (n 13).

160 UNGA Res 72/249 (n 7).

161 ibid.

162 Author's IGC-3 Notes (n 13).

163 ibid.

164 BBNJ, 'Participants' (n 84).

kept a relatively low profile in the negotiations but seems to be making recent efforts to publicize its attendance, having held a side event at IGC-3.[165]

Moreover, as the organization of the work of the IGC has changed – from large, formal proceedings to smaller, less formal meetings – so has the ability of some stakeholders, such as NGOs, to fully participate in the negotiations.[166] As UNGA Resolution 72/249 states, the ability of observers may be restricted as decided by the Conference leadership.[167] For the NGOs attending IGC-3, this meant that although they enjoyed full participation in the formal meetings, their participation in the several informal informals scheduled during the session was limited to five seats to be shared amongst the 40 participating NGO delegations.[168] Even though there was recognition that the commencement of informal informals was essential to the progress of the negotiations, it came at the price of broad participation by all invited and credentialed stakeholders in all aspects of the BBNJ process.[169]

The reality is that the BBNJ process will continue as a 'member-driven process' under the LOSC framework.[170] Although it is arguable that the BBNJ process does not capture or include all resource users in the negotiation process, in the view of this author it does not necessarily mean that the lack of complete inclusiveness in the process forecloses the possibility of robust polycentric solutions. This is evident by the existence of such solutions within the present LOSC framework, an example of which includes the international cooperation mechanism of sub-regional and regional fisheries management organizations and arrangements under the UN Fish Stocks Agreement to sustainably manage highly migratory and straddling fish stocks in the high seas.[171]

### 4.3 *Principle-by-principle Analysis of the Institutional Arrangements for the Conservation and Sustainable Use of BBNJ Using an Expanded RSP*

If the BBNJ process is significantly delayed and/or fails, rather than acceding to the status quo as many delegations have warned against, users of this CPR may want to consider an alternative to the ongoing process.[172] For that purpose,

165 Author's IGC-3 Notes (n 13).
166 ibid.
167 UNGA Res 72/249 (n 7).
168 Author's IGC-3 Notes (n 13).
169 ibid.
170 ENB IGC-3 Summary (n 13); Author's IGC-3 Notes (n 13).
171 UNFSA part III.
172 Maintaining the status quo is something that several delegations have advocated against. ENB IGC-3 Summary (n 13).

this chapter examines the robustness and feasibility of an Expanded RSP using Ostrom's design principles. This is accomplished by examining provisions of the existing institutional architecture of the three RSOs that have taken action in ABNJ through the establishment of MPAs by reviewing their legal instruments through the lens of Ostrom's design principles. Where relevant, examples are included of recent actions that these RSOs have taken that may impact the protection of BBNJ. Following that examination, this Section 4.3 concludes with recommendations for legal actions that would need to be taken to implement a robust system of institutional governance for an Expanded RSP for the conservation and sustainable use of BBNJ.

This author's analysis does not follow Ostrom's eight design principles numerically but has been tailored to the management of this particular CPR.[173] The analysis thus begins with the first principle, followed by a discussion of 'nested enterprises' in large-scale governance systems under the eighth design principle, and concludes with a grouped discussion of the second to seventh design principles.

#### 4.3.1 First Design Principle as a Prerequisite: Clearly Defined User and Resource Boundaries

As discussed in Section 4.2 above, the satisfaction of the first design principle, clearly defined user and resource boundaries, serves as a prerequisite in the analysis. In the context of an Expanded RSP, each regional body would need to ensure that the identity of the shared group and those with rights over the CPRs have boundaries that are clearly delineated. In this regard, Ostrom recognized the importance of transparency to this design principle, 'Being able to get a good idea of where is the boundary, who is involved, [and] what rules are involved is essential'.[174]

Where the BBNJ process – being a global process – has failed (as yet) to articulate with specificity the resource and its users, regional bodies – such as RSOs – appear to have been better able to identify the resource, rules regarding its use and its users. For example, the Barcelona, CCAMLR, and OSPAR Conventions all define the geographic scope of the instrument.[175]

173 See n 155.

174 Ostrom, *Future of the Commons* (n 132) 88. See the 'Transparency' proposal in the textual proposals to the Revised Draft Agreement 'Proposal for a New Article 50bis' submitted by New Zealand (also on behalf of Australia, Canada, Norway, and the Pacific Small Island Developing States) 348.

175 Barcelona Convention art 1 (Geographical Coverage); CCAMLR arts 1, 1(4), which sets out the scope of geographic application of the Convention; OSPAR arts 1(a), 1(b), which defines 'maritime area' and 'internal waters'.

CCAMLR provides further definition and scope of the instrument by defining the Antarctic marine ecosystem as the 'complex of relationships of Antarctic marine living resources with each other and with their physical environment'.[176] Furthermore, CCAMLR defines the CPRs that are the subject of the instrument, by setting out the meaning of 'Antarctic marine living resources' as the 'populations of fin fish, molluscs, crustaceans and all other species of living organisms, including birds, found south of the Antarctic Convergence'.[177]

An example of an RSO that has taken further steps to define the CPR within the context of biological diversity and its users is OSPAR. In 1998, the first Ministerial Meeting of the OSPAR Commission adopted Annex V on the Protection and Conservation of the Ecosystems and Biological Diversity of the Maritime Area, where it specifically uses the definitions of 'biological diversity', 'ecosystem', and 'habitat' set out in the CBD.[178] The inclusion of these definitions, together with the inclusion of other obligations that refer to the CBD, not only provides clarity of the resource, it promotes harmonization across other relevant legal frameworks.[179] The Annex also provides clarity of the users of this resource by reaffirming that no program or measure shall be undertaken relating to the management of fisheries, and if such an action is indicated, that it should be referred to the attention of a competent authority who has competence to take such action.[180] Similarly, if an action is desirable with respect to marine transport, then that proposed action should be referred to the IMO for its consideration and attention.[181]

This review suggests that these three RSOs are further along than the BBNJ process in satisfying the prerequisite of defining the resources, rules regarding their use and their users under the relevant legal instruments. When this perquisite is met, it allows for a relatively straightforward ordering and analysis of the rules that apply to the conservation and sustainable use of CPRs.

176 CCAMLR art 1(3).

177 ibid art 1(2).

178 OSPAR, Annex V, art 1; See OSPAR Ministerial Meeting, Sinatra, Portugal (1998), adopting Annex V; see preamble, paras 1, 5–7.

179 OSPAR, Annex V, art 2. The Barcelona Convention also promotes the protection and preservation of marine biodiversity, see eg Barcelona Convention art 10 (Conservation of Biological Diversity).

180 OSPAR, Annex V, art 4(1).

181 ibid Annex V, art 4(2).

### 4.3.2 Eighth Design Principle for the Overall Coordination amongst Nested Enterprises

In combating commons problems that require collective action at differing levels and scales (such as climate change, or by implication in this case, to the conservation and sustainable use of BBNJ), Ostrom asserted that polycentric approaches can complement overarching global agreements.[182] Her view has given rise to the contention that polycentric governance arrangements are preferable to monocentric governance arrangements in managing and protecting CPRs.[183] Although polycentric systems often appear to be overly 'complex, chaotic and fragmented', they may be more ordered than they appear, allowing for mutual monitoring and adaptation.[184]

To govern CPRs in large-scale systems, small-scale organizations tend to be 'nested' within a large-scale organization, allowing for systems to exist at multiple levels, with some autonomy at each level.[185] For that reason, Ostrom maintained in accordance with her eighth design principle that for 'nested enterprises' (groups that are part of large-scale systems), there must be appropriate *coordination* amongst the relevant groups.[186] For CPRs that are part of a large-scale system, Ostrom's eighth design principle encompasses aspects of the second to seventh design principles in that appropriation, provision, monitoring, enforcement, conflict resolution, and governance activities are often organized at multiple levels within such nested enterprises.[187]

Nested enterprises within large-scale systems may be advantageous because 'local knowledge can [be used to] inform the design of diverse, context-specific rules at the small-scale organizational level', while large-scale organizations within these systems can support and enhance the ability of local users to deal with issues of local significance.[188] Nested enterprises may also facilitate subsidiarity in which problems can be addressed at the most relevant and capable scale.[189] In a nested polycentric system, rules at the level of the large-scale

---

182 Elinor Ostrom, 'Polycentric Systems for Coping with Collective Action and Global Environmental Change' (2010) 20(4) Global Environmental Change. A recent example: Andrew J Jordan and others, 'Emergence of Polycentric Climate Governance and its Future Prospects' (2015) 5 Nature Climate Change.

183 David Sloan Wilson, Elinor Ostrom and Michael E Cox, 'Generalizing the Core Designs Principles for the Efficacy of Groups' (2013) 90S Journal of Economic Behavior & Organization S21.

184 Mahon and Fanning (n 18) 3.

185 Ostrom, *Future of the Commons* (n 132) 82.

186 Ostrom, *Governing the Commons* (n 119) 101–02 (emphasis added).

187 ibid 90.

188 Mahon and Fanning (n 18) 3 (quoting Gruby and Basurto).

189 ibid 3; Cox and others (n 134).

organization can be written in a general form that can then be tailored to local circumstances at the level of the small-scale organizations.[190]

Ostrom noted the importance of large-scale organizations in nested enterprises.[191] In a polycentric system where a large-scale organization is responsible for the management of a CPR across a large region, a large-scale organization can add overall competence to help monitor performance, impose sanctions, obtain reliable information, and provide conflict resolution mechanisms to manage the resource.[192] Accessing reliable information is essential to long-term sustainability of CPRs, yet few local communities have the resources to access such information.[193] Large-scale organizations within nested enterprises are often better placed in terms of resources to provide scientific information and technical assistance to local users, which Ostrom and later Cox and others found was important in the promotion of local partnerships, both vertically and horizontally within nested enterprises.[194]

Within the context of regional ocean governance, Mahon and Fanning found that among 20 ocean regions they studied 'most regions had 10 or more arrangements at regional and sub-regional levels, reflecting what appears to be a high degree of multilevel polycentricity'.[195] In accord with Ostrom's research findings, they found that local communities had developed a high number of 'indigenous' arrangements, rather than following the guidance that had been promoted by external and global bodies.[196] Mahon and Fanning noted that this indicated 'there is potentially much more to regional governance than FAO Regional Fisheries Bodies and the UN Environment Regional Seas bodies, which have been the primary focus for decades'.[197] They also noted that many of the indigenous arrangements had the potential to promote further integration and coordination for ocean sustainability at various levels of governance.[198]

---

190 Elinor Ostrom, 'Crossing the Great Divide: Coproduction, Synergy, and Development' (1996) 224(6) World Development 1073, 1082.

191 Ostrom, *Understanding* (n 155) 278.

192 Ostrom, *Future of the Commons* (n 132) 81–82.

193 Ostrom, *Understanding* (n 155) 278.

194 ibid; Cox and others (n 134).

195 Mahon and Fanning (n 18) 1.

196 ibid. Here, indigenous means those arrangements that developed within the region and not those promoted either externally or globally.

197 ibid 1, citing the findings of Robin Mahon and Lucia Fanning, 'Regional Ocean Governance: Polycentric Arrangements and Their Role in Global Ocean Governance' (2019) 107 Marine Policy.

198 Mahon and Fanning (n 18) 1.

In the absence of a treaty, let alone an ambitious one with a global forum, UNEP's large-scale system of governance of the RSP serves as an example of a nested set of enterprises described by Ostrom and elaborated on by Mahon and Fanning, where the participating member States of an RSO adopt an action plan, where the RCU oversees the overall implementation and coordination of the action plan, and where the RAC serves as the 'nerve center' to carry out all activities related to the implementation of the action plan.[199] The large-scale organization within each RSO provides overall decision making, conflict resolution, monitoring, and implementation, while the RACs serve as smaller units of governance where more locally-based actions take place.[200] In this way, the RSO governance instruments also provide subsidiarity to UNEP's large-scale governance system.[201]

The RSO governance instruments often recognize the value of nested enterprises and the coordinating function they provide. For example, the Preamble to the OSPAR Convention recognizes that concerted action at the national, regional and global levels is essential for sustainable management, and that the common interests of the contracting state parties should induce cooperation at the regional and sub-regional levels.[202] The Barcelona Convention is similar in that the contracting state parties recognize that close cooperation is imperative for those States and international organizations concerned with the implementation of a coordinated and comprehensive regional approach to the protection and enhancement of the Mediterranean marine environment.[203] CCAMLR also emphasizes the need to cooperate with others both vertically and horizontally.[204]

What is not clear from a review of the legal instruments referred to in this sub-section 2 is whether, despite the recognition and promotion of the importance of coordination, there is sufficient vertical and horizontal coordination within the existing RSOs. This suggests that the mere obligation to promote cooperation amongst the nested enterprises may not be sufficient in the

199 UNEP website.

200 See eg OSPAR art 10 (Commission), art 12 (Secretariat), art 13 (Decisions and Recommendations), 20 (Right to Vote), art 22 (Reporting to the Commission), art 23 (Compliance), art 24 (Regionalisation), art 32 (Settlement of Disputes).

201 Mahon and Fanning (n 18) 3.

202 OSPAR preamble, paras 3 and 8.

203 Barcelona Convention Preamble; UNEP, 'Coordinating Unit for the Mediterranean Action Plan, Secretariat to the Barcelona Convention and its Protocols' available at <https://www.unep.org/unepmap/> accessed 1 November 2020.

204 CCAMLR 'Cooperation with Others' available at <www.ccamlr.org/en/organisation/cooperation-others> accessed 1 November 2020.

absence of a global coordinating mechanism, which could be provided by the BBNJ Agreement.

### 4.3.3 Grouped Discussion of Second to Seventh Design Principles amongst Nested Enterprises

Nested enterprises for the management of CPRs provide vertical and horizontal functions in large-scale governance systems.[205] The functions that Ostrom identified in successful large-scale governance systems fall within the second to seventh of Ostrom's design principles (see Section 4.1 above).[206]

With regard to the first part of the second design principle, congruence with local environmental conditions is required in order to ensure that the ecological costs and benefits are both clear and harmonized.[207] In Ostrom's research, she and her colleagues found that within the context of community forests that are managed within nested enterprises, local communities have both the knowledge and the vested interest in the long-term sustainable use of the forests.[208] Therefore, rules that are informed by local knowledge and enforced by these community groups often result in successful management outcomes.[209] Ostrom's findings were reaffirmed in Mahon and Fanning's research on regional ocean governance where indigenous arrangements were found to have contributed to the conservation and sustainable use of marine resources on a regional basis.[210]

In line with the principle relating to the value of local knowledge to the management of the CPR, Article 24 of the OSPAR Convention provides that the Commission may decide to alter any decision or recommendation (whether the timetable or all or part of the applicable area to which the decision or recommendation applies) in order to accommodate the ecological and economic conditions of the regions or sub-regions to which the Convention applies.[211]

205 Cox and others (n 134).

206 ibid.

207 Harmonization is given further support as referred to in a recital to Annex V of OSPAR that recalls 'the importance of coordination and harmonization of work in different forums for the protection of marine species and their habitats'. Other instruments also promote cooperation and harmonization in different forums for the protection of marine species and habitats. See eg Barcelona Convention art 3(2), art 4(3)(d), art 13; CCAMLR Preamble, art XV, XXIII, OSPAR Resolution Preamble.

208 Harini Nagendra and Elinor Ostrom, 'Polycentric Governance of Multifunctional Forested Landscapes' (2012) 6(2) International Journal of the Commons.

209 ibid.

210 Mahon and Fanning (n 18).

211 OSPAR art 24.

In addition, Annex V to the OSPAR Convention requires that the Commission 'consider aspects of national strategies and guidelines for the conservation and sustainable use of biodiversity as they affect the regions and subregions of the affected area', and 'take into account the programs and measures undertaken by the Contracting Parties in waters under their sovereignty or jurisdiction'.[212] The Barcelona Convention permits participating member States to enter into bilateral and multilateral agreements, including regional and sub-regional agreements, for the 'promotion of sustainable development, the protection of the environment, [and] the conservation and preservation of natural resources', provided that such agreements are consistent with the Convention and are made available to the other parties through the Convention's secretariat.[213]

The second design principle also requires that there must be adequate rules of appropriation and provision amongst the users, which are congruent with local conditions.[214] Such rules include: (i) rules of appropriation restricting time, place, technology and/or quantity of the resource, and (ii) rules of provision regarding money, labor, and/or materials.[215] Ostrom found that well-tailored rules of appropriation and provision at the local level accounted for the sustainability of CPRs.[216] Congruence with local conditions allowed for local users to adopt different sets of rules to deal with distinctively local problems.[217] Conversely, Ostrom found that unequitable access and benefits undermined collective efforts, resulting in unsuccessful outcomes in the management of the CPR.[218]

Within the context of the three RSOs, rules regarding the harvesting of Antarctic marine resources are set out in the CAMLR Convention and its supporting instruments.[219] While the Barcelona Convention does not ensure equitable access and benefits, it serves as an example of an RSO that requires participating member states to take into account the social, economic and technological conditions in the context of access to and transfer of environmentally sound technology.[220] Specifically with regard to the provision of technical assistance relating to marine pollution, participating member states

212 ibid Annex V, art 3. The duty is subject to Article 4 which requires that no program or measure that be adopted that relates to fisheries.

213 Barcelona Convention art 3(2).

214 Ostrom, *Governing the Commons* (n 119) 92. See Revised Draft Agreement Part II.

215 ibid.

216 ibid.

217 ibid.

218 Ostrom, *Governing the Commons* (n 119).

219 See CCAMLR.

220 Barcelona Convention art 4(4)(b).

to the Barcelona Convention are also required to give priority to the special needs of developing countries in the Mediterranean region.[221]

Ostrom found that 'localization' is not only an essential element of the second design principle, but it is an essential element of the remaining design principles. For example, the third design principle, collective-choice arrangements, requires that users be able to make and modify their own rules by consensus.[222] Ostrom found that in systems that were sustainable, local users had developed high levels of trust and reciprocity and usually had the autonomy to determine some of their own rules.[223] Local users who trusted each other were more likely to limit their use of the CPR and comply with the rules regarding its use.[224] The local users had worked together over time; they shared a common understanding of the resource and were guided by local leadership.[225] Further, local users who were connected by multiple issues over a long period of time were able to leverage those linkages to induce cooperation.[226] She concluded that one of the reasons the design principles enhance robustness in nested enterprises was that those who were most knowledgeable about the rules' effects on the resource were the local users who had a part in making the rules.[227]

Ostrom identified monitoring of the resource as the fourth design principle, which she found is critical to assessing the effectiveness of the measures that have been put in place to manageably sustain and protect the resource.[228] In studying the management of forestries, Ostrom found that one of the most likely indicators of sustainability was the inclusion of a robust monitoring mechanism.[229] Specifically, Ostrom found in her large-scale studies that one of the most important factors affecting the success of resource management systems of CPRs was the inclusion of *local* monitoring in the monitoring mechanism.[230] She found that local users pay attention to what is happening if they

221 ibid art 13(3).
222 Ostrom, *Governing the Commons* (n 119).
223 Ostrom, *Future of the Commons* (n 132) 80.
224 Ostrom, 'Beyond Markets and States' (n 25) 661.
225 Ostrom, *Future of the Commons* (n 132) 80.
226 Dolsak and Ostrom (n 19) 17.
227 Ostrom, *Future of the Commons* (n 132) 79.
228 Klaudija Cremers, Glen Wright and Julien Rochette, 'Strengthening, Monitoring, Control and Surveillance of Human Activities in Marine Areas Beyond National Jurisdiction: Challenges and Opportunities for an International Legally Binding Instrument' (2020) 122 Marine Policy.
229 Ostrom, *Future of the Commons* (n 132) 82–83.
230 ibid.

are invested in the outcome and have rights to both collect and protect.[231] In addition, monitoring at the small-scale organizational level is often less expensive than at a higher organizational level.[232]

Likewise, because managing a CPR is inherently vulnerable to free riders and exploitation,[233] monitoring users for non-compliance (second part of the fourth design principle) is just as critical as protecting the resource from overuse.[234] Detecting non-compliance must be done at relatively low cost, which can be achieved through local monitoring.[235] Ostrom found that participants in a system that is characterized by the design principles perceive the system as legitimate, often because they have been involved in the rule making process, and know that compliance with the rules is being monitored.[236]

Closely related to monitoring is the fifth design principle, which deals with non-compliance with the rules.[237] In those instances where non-compliance is found, a set of graduated sanctions should be available.[238] Ostrom found that severe sanctions at the large-scale organizational level were often not needed.[239] Rather, gossip or a reminder at the local level was sufficient in most cases, but Ostrom found that more severe sanctions must also be available.[240]

With regard to the sixth design principle requiring conflict resolution mechanisms, Ostrom found that robust institutional arrangements include mechanisms that ensure it is possible to resolve conflicts quickly and at a low cost in ways that are perceived as fair by the users.[241] Systems that met this design principle enhanced robustness because it was possible to resolve conflicts before they escalated.[242] Within nested enterprises, this was often accomplished at the local level.[243]

The seventh design principle recognizes that there must be minimal recognition of rights to organize, meaning that groups of users must have flexibility to make their own rules.[244] Ostrom concluded that externally imposed rules

---

231 ibid.
232 ibid.
233 Ostrom, *Governing the Commons* (n 119) 6.
234 ibid 94–100.
235 ibid.
236 Ostrom, *Future of the Commons* (n 132) 79.
237 Ostrom, *Governing the Commons* (n 119) 94–100.
238 ibid.
239 ibid.
240 ibid.
241 Ostrom, *Understanding* (n 155) 278–79. See also Mossop (ch 13) in this volume.
242 Ostrom, *Future of the Commons* (n 132) 79.
243 ibid 81-82; Ostrom, *Governing the Commons* (n 119) 100–01.
244 ibid 101.

were unlikely to be adapted to local conditions and would therefore fail to satisfy the third design principle.[245] Moreover, the diversity of solutions amongst the large systems stimulated learning and increased performance over time.[246] The local users tended to rely on unique aspects of the local resource and culture when developing their approach to managing the resource.[247] A local approach often resulted in solutions that differed from the remedies promoted at the higher organizational levels.[248]

Having considered Ostrom's views and findings under the third to seventh design principles, it is then necessary to examine how and to what extent the three RSOs meet the third to seventh design principles. With regard to the third design principle of consensus-based decision making, all three RSO conventions provide rules for the making of decisions at the large-scale organizational level. The CAMLR Convention provides that '[d]ecisions of the Commission on matters of substance shall be taken by consensus', while matters other than those of substance shall be taken by a simple majority of the members of the Commission present and voting.[249] OSPAR similarly sets out the decision making rules in its Convention, providing that all decisions and recommendations shall be adopted by unanimous vote, and if such unanimity cannot be achieved, then all such decisions or recommendations shall be adopted by a three-quarters majority vote of the Contracting Parties.[250] The Barcelona Convention, instead of including the decision making rules in the instrument itself, sets out the functions of the Bureau and its terms of reference in Rules of Procedure adopted by the meetings of the Contracting Parties.[251] What is not clear from a review of the RSO legal instruments is whether the RACs (or their equivalents) have flexibility to tailor measures at a small-scale organizational level.[252]

245 ibid; Ostrom, *Future of the Commons* (n 132) 80.

246 Ostrom, *Future of the Commons* (n 132) 80.

247 ibid.

248 Ostrom, *Understanding* (n 155) 278–79. For a further discussion of what may encompass a 'local' approach, see Section 4.3.4 below.

249 CCAMLR art XII.

250 OSPAR art 13(1).

251 Barcelona Convention art 19.

252 A sample of documents for RACs (and their equivalents) were reviewed, which include: Barcelona Convention, Mediterranean Action Plan, Regional Activity Centre for Specially Protected Areas available at <www.rac-spa.org> accessed 1 November 2020; OSPAR 'Biological Diversity & Ecosystems' available at <www.ospar.org/work-areas/bdc> accessed 1 November 2020; CCAMLR 'Basic Documents' available at <www.ccamlr.org/en/document/publications/basic-documents-december-2011> accessed 1 November 2020.

The same questions arise with regard to the fourth to seventh design principles as to whether the existing RSO arrangements meet the design principles at the lower organizational levels. Although each of the three RSO Conventions provides for monitoring,[253] compliance,[254] dispute resolution,[255] and some flexibility in the adaptation of measures to local conditions at the large-scale organizational level,[256] it is not clear from a review of the legal instruments that these design principles have been sufficiently 'localized' at the lower organizational levels.[257] The possibility, however, exists that informal and/or 'indigenous' arrangements (as referred to by Mahon and Fanning) are used at lower levels within the system but are not necessarily reflected in the legal instruments.[258] If an Expanded RSP would be considered for marine ABNJ, it would be imperative to conduct a stock take to determine the existence and characteristics of, and participants in, such arrangements.

In considering how a polycentric approach for the governance of these vast marine areas could work within an Expanded RSP, it is helpful to examine Ostrom's findings regarding the characteristics of those systems that meet the fourth to seventh design principles, particularly how these systems 'localize' the principles at lower organizational levels. An examination of her relevant findings is set out below beginning with the fourth design principle of monitoring.

From this review of a sample of RSO legal instruments, although it is unclear whether local considerations have been incorporated at the various levels of these three RSOs, it does not prohibit the conclusion that the existing RSP as a whole could serve as a foundation for the establishment of robust institutional arrangements using an Expanded RSP with significant amendments and adjustments as described more particularly below.

---

253 Barcelona Convention art 12 (Monitoring) (limits monitoring to pollution by competent authorities), art 17 (UNEP to regularly report to Contracting Parties on implementation of the Convention and Protocols), art 26 (Reports by Contracting Parties); CCAMLR art XV (Scientific Committee assesses the effects on the Antarctic marine living resources), art XXIV (System of observation and inspection); OSPAR art 10 Commission (Review condition of maritime area) 22 (Reporting to the Commission by Contracting Parties).

254 Barcelona Convention art 27 (Compliance Control); CCAMLR art XXI (Compliance and sanctions); OSPAR art 23 (Compliance).

255 Barcelona Convention; CCAMLR art XXV; OSPAR art 32.

256 See eg Barcelona Convention Preamble, art 3(2); OSPAR art 24.

257 See n 255.

258 Mahon and Fanning (n 18).

#### 4.3.4 Recommendations to Achieve Robust Institutional Governance for an Expanded RSP for the Conservation and Sustainable Use of BBNJ

From the above principle-by-principle analysis, the following questions can be posed: (i) to what extent do the existing institutional arrangements of the RSP (using the three RSOs samples) meet Ostrom's design principles; (ii) and if so, what measures could be taken to build upon the existing institutional arrangements to expand the RSP so that it meets the design principles.

To answer the first question, the broad conclusion that can be drawn from the above principle-by-principle analysis of the three RSOs is that the RSP's existing institutional architecture is largely in line with Ostrom's eight design principles at the large-scale organizational level. Where the RSP appears to be lacking is in the sufficient localization of the design principles at lower organizational levels in the RSP. This observation underscores the inherent difficulty that vexes those dealing with ocean governance issues: how to make the use and care of vast marine areas a local concern?

Perhaps the solution may come in part from the use of the word 'local', which connotes a local fisherman in a small village – with no apparent connection to the distant high seas. Ostrom uses great care in her use of language and the 'crafting' of definitions, so there is some hesitation in departing from her word choice, but the continued use of the word 'local' may hinder imagining a polycentric solution to the governance of ABNJ. One commentator uses the word 'community' when referring to local users of a CPR.[259] In that way, identifying a 'community of users' or a 'community of stakeholders' in accordance with the first design principle becomes a more straightforward exercise, following which, provided that the resource and rules regarding its use are also clearly defined, the institutional arrangements would need to be tailored to the 'community' in order to meet the remaining design principles.[260] Identifying members of the community of stakeholders of ABNJ is beyond the scope of this chapter, but one could imagine that this community could include: adjacent States, sectoral governance bodies, other regional governance bodies, indigenous peoples, members of the private sector, NGOs, etc.[261]

---

259 Cox and others (n 134).

260 This author wishes to distinguish a 'community of stakeholders', which is a term that has been coined for the narrow purposes of this chapter, from the larger study of community interests in international law.

261 See Section 2 of this chapter on existing governance of areas of beyond national jurisdiction for possible members of the community of stakeholders.

To answer the second question, given the obvious limitations of regional ocean governance arrangements to support the governance of ABNJ, institutional changes would need to be made to implement an Expanded RSP. The necessary changes would likely include the expansion of the membership, geographical scope, and mandate of each of the RSO conventions. In those RSOs where the resource and its users are not already clearly defined, definitive actions would need to be taken to do so.

Given that the existing UNEP Regional Seas Programme is a set of nested enterprises as described by Ostrom's research, for an Expanded RSP to meet the eighth design principle, appropriate coordination of the second to seventh design principles is essential. Within the context of the conservation and sustainable use of BBNJ, vertical coordination would include access and benefit sharing, monitoring, enforcement, dispute resolution, and governance activities, while horizontal coordination would include strengthening collaborative arrangements (and/or creating new ones) with other global (eg, CBD), sectoral, regional, sub-regional and national bodies. Both vertical and horizontal coordination could be accomplished through making appropriate adjustments to UNEP's existing governance structures. Vertical coordination, in particular, would require that the institutional arrangements be sufficiently tailored (or 'communitized') to allow for the flexibility and autonomy at the lower organizational levels to meet the design principles.

Imperative to the ability of an Expanded RSP to meet all eight of Ostrom's design principles is the availability of reliable information and 'FAIR data'.[262] To achieve this, Ostrom's collaborative network of CRCs that she established for forestries under IFRI could be used as a model, where the functions of the CRCs could be housed within each of the RSOs. Like IFRI's CRCs, the work of CRCs organized within an Expanded RSP could include work that focused on the following themes: marine biodiversity, livelihoods, institutions, and climate change (which could include global warming, sea level rise, ocean acidification, and their associated effects and remedies). As with IFRI's collaborative CRC network, the methodology and processes could be standardized across the network, while allowing each RSO-CRC sufficient flexibility to adapt its work to the unique ecology and ecosystems encompassed within the geographic scope of each RSO. Where appropriate, the data collected within the RSO could be linked to OBIS or other relevant data and information clearing

262 FAIR data is data and/or meta-data that is findable, accessible, interoperable, and reusable.

houses.[263] A collaborative CRC network housed within an Expanded RSP could provide data that could be collected, stored, and analyzed over time. Such data could be used to conduct baseline studies and monitor both the resources and the institutional arrangements over time, which could then be made readily available to the community of stakeholders.

To conclude, recommendations for the use of an Expanded RSP for the conservation and sustainable use of BBNJ include institutional changes to the existing institutional arrangements of the RSOs, the strengthening and/or creation of arrangements for vertical and horizontal coordination, and the establishment of a CRC network to be housed within the RSOs' existing institutional framework.

## 5 Conclusion

In this author's view, neither the LOSC nor law in and of itself can provide solutions for the conservation and sustainable use of BBNJ. In seeking other disciplines and theories for inspiration for the management of these vast marine areas, Ostrom's theory of polycentric governance of CPRs emerged as a likely candidate for exploration, for it seeks to determine the optimal distribution of power and knowledge across levels of governance that will result in sustainable institutions, and in turn, sustainable CPRs.

This chapter's imagination of a polycentric approach to the governance of marine ABNJ concludes the following. One, the BBNJ process, as evidenced by the Revised Draft Agreement, has yet to define the resource that will be subject to the treaty, the rules regarding its use, or the users of the resource. In addition, the scope and objectives of the treaty have yet to be agreed. The present inability of the process to meet Ostrom's first design principle bodes ill for the probability of the BBNJ process meeting the remaining design principles and resulting in a robust set of institutional arrangements.

Two, the principle-by-principle analysis of the existing arrangements suggests that the existing RSP is likely to meet the design principles at the large-scale organizational level. However, it appears that the design principles have not been sufficiently tailored to allow for the flexibility and autonomy at the lower organizational levels to meet the design principles. It also appears that

263 OBIS, the Ocean Biodiversity Information System, is an open-access data and information clearing house on marine biodiversity for science, conservation and sustainable use, which is maintained by IOC-UNESCO.

inadequate vertical and horizontal coordination exists within the nested enterprises to satisfy the eighth design principle.

However, the principle-by-principle analysis does not foreclose the possibility of finding a polycentric solution to the conservation and sustainable use of BBNJ using an Expanded RSP.

Three, an Expanded RSP that was conceived in line with this chapter's recommendations would allow for the 'communitization' of Ostrom's design principles to the lower organizational levels, vertical and horizontal coordination, and the availability of reliable information and FAIR data.

Ostrom said that 'getting the institutions right' is key to successful management of CPRs. It is a difficult process that tests the patience, time, and skill of the best of diplomats, lawyers, scientists, and policy makers. Ultimately, an Expanded RSP that follows this chapter's recommendations is worthy of consideration as it would likely meet Ostrom's design principles, resulting in a robust set of institutional arrangements for the conservation and sustainable use of BBNJ.

CHAPTER 13

# Dispute Settlement in Areas beyond National Jurisdiction

*Joanna Mossop*

## 1 Introduction*

The dispute settlement provisions in Part XV of the 1982 United Nations Convention on the Law of the Sea (LOSC)[1] have been heralded as an incredible achievement that was an indispensable part of the complex package deal negotiated by States in the 1970s.[2] In providing for compulsory dispute settlement for most disputes arising under the Convention, it was an unprecedented extension of third-party dispute settlement in international law. Since then, Part XV has been incorporated into a number of other agreements, most notably the United Nations Fish Stocks Agreement (UNFSA).[3] The purpose of this chapter is to examine the relevance of dispute settlement to issues arising in areas beyond national jurisdiction (ABNJ) and the negotiations of a new international legally binding instrument (ILBI) for the conservation and sustainable use of marine biodiversity in areas beyond national jurisdiction (BBNJ). Because the focus of the ILBI is on the conservation and sustainable use of marine biodiversity, this chapter explores the suitability of traditional dispute settlement processes for resolving violations of environmental law in ABNJ and considers options for dispute settlement in the ILBI.

Dispute settlement provisions raise questions of power, justice and legitimacy. Classical international law theorists have often framed international law

* The author thanks the editors, James Harrison and Donald Rothwell for their comments on earlier versions of this chapter. The research for this chapter was commenced while the author was a MacCormick Fellow at Edinburgh Law School.

1 United Nations Convention on the Law of the Sea (opened for signature 10 December 1982, entered into force 16 November 1994) 1833 UNTS 3 (LOSC).

2 John E Noyes, 'Compulsory Third-Party Adjudication and the 1982 United Nations Convention on the Law of the Sea' (1989) 4 Connecticut Journal of International Law 675, 676.

3 United Nations Agreement for the Implementation of the Provisions of the United Nations Convention on the Law of the Sea of 10 December 1982 relating to the Conservation and Management of Straddling Fish Stocks and Highly Migratory Fish Stocks (opened for signature 4 August 1995, entered into force 11 December 2001) 2167 UNTS 3 (UNFSA).

 | DOI:10.1163/9789004506367_014

as the antithesis to international relations based on power and coercion.[4] In this vein, international law and dispute settlement processes are often seen as a counter to the power of States, particularly the more powerful nations.[5] While there are many issues and problems with the way that dispute settlement works in international law, most would consider judicial settlement of international disputes as offering an alternative to resolution of disputes in violent or coercive ways. Some have argued that dispute settlement processes offer a sense of justice for States whose rights have been breached and to reassure that international law was complied with.[6] Others have argued that power remains an important factor in the success of dispute settlement. For example, Morgenthau argued that dispute settlement processes could only work in situations where there is no underlying tension, as States are reluctant to submit disputes about key interests to a third-party process.[7] In Krisch's analysis of hegemonic states, he argues that, while powerful states are drawn to international law as a tool for stabilization and pacification, methods of enforcement such as dispute settlement impose considerable constraints on those states.[8] ABNJ are, by their nature, outside the territorial sovereignty of any State and therefore all States have an interest in ensuring that the rules of international law are complied with. In the oceans, the existence of the principle of the common heritage of mankind (CHM) arguably heightens the interest of the international community in the observance of international law.[9] As will be discussed below, there are limits to the ability of the dispute settlement process in the LOSC to deal adequately with disputes arising in respect of protection of the environment in ABNJ.

4 Richard H Steinberg and Jonathan M Zasloff, 'Power and International Law' (2006) 100 American Journal of International Law 64, 65. See also Nico Krisch, 'International Law in Times of Hegemony: Unequal Power and the Shaping of the International Legal Order' (2005) 16 European Journal of International Law 369, 370.

5 Robin Churchill, 'The General Dispute Settlement System of the UN Convention on the Law of the Sea: Overview, Context, and Use' (2017) 48 Ocean Development and International Law 216, 218.

6 Eric De Brabandere, 'International Dispute Settlement – from Practice to Legal Discipline' (2018) 31 Leiden Journal of International Law 459, 460.

7 Hans J Morgenthau, Albert A Michelson and Leonard Davis, *Politics Among Nations: The Struggle for Power and Peace* (5th edn, Alfred A Knopf 1973) 422.

8 Krisch (n 4) 379.

9 The Seabed Disputes Chamber referred to the 'common interest of all States in the proper application of the principle of [CHM] which requires faithful compliance with the obligations set out in Part XI'. *Responsibilities and Obligations of States with respect to Activities in the Area, Advisory Opinion,* [2011] ITLOS Reports 10, [76].

This chapter first explores the purpose behind Part XV and the reasons why compulsory dispute settlement was included in the LOSC. Second, the chapter evaluates whether subsequent developments have met original expectations. Third, the chapter critically examines the ability of traditional international dispute settlement to resolve disputes involving collective interests including harm to ABNJ. Next, the chapter makes some observations about the draft articles and proposals in relation to dispute settlement that were made during sessions of the Intergovernmental Conference (IGC) on an ILBI under the LOSC on the conservation and sustainable use of BBNJ. It assesses two possible additions to the ILBI: advisory opinions and non-compliance procedures (NCP). It will be seen that the process established in Part XV may not be suitable to apply unamended to the ILBI. Rather, lessons can be learned from Part XV's weaknesses in applying to violation of environmental norms in order to strengthen the process in the ILBI. The chapter concludes with a discussion of the role that power, legitimacy and justice has played in the dispute settlement provisions of the LOSC and might play in negotiations for the ILBI.

## 2 Dispute Settlement in the LOSC

### 2.1 *Part XV of the LOSC*

The dispute settlement provisions in Part XV of the LOSC are comprised of three main sections. First, there is an obligation to settle disputes peacefully, and States are empowered to choose any peaceful means to resolve disputes, which might include agreeing to opt out of compulsory procedures.[10]

Second, the Convention establishes a process for compulsory settlement of disputes arising from the interpretation and application of the LOSC, by which it is meant that recourse to third-party dispute settlement is available at the request of one party to a dispute.[11] States may choose in advance their preferred forum for such disputes from four options: the International Court of Justice (ICJ); the International Tribunal for the Law of the Sea (ITLOS); an arbitral tribunal; or a special arbitral tribunal comprised of scientific or technical experts.[12] In the event that parties have not accepted the same procedure, the default forum is an arbitral tribunal constituted under Annex VII.[13] The court

10 LOSC art 281.
11 ibid art 286.
12 ibid art 287(1).
13 ibid art 287(5).

or tribunal can prescribe provisional measures, and if an arbitral tribunal has not yet been constituted, ITLOS may provide such provisional measures.[14]

The third feature of Part XV involves exclusions from compulsory procedures. These exclusions were necessary to get agreement on including compulsory dispute settlement in the Convention.[15] Automatic exclusions focus on exercises of coastal State jurisdiction in areas under their jurisdiction including the exclusive economic zone (EEZ) and the continental shelf, especially decisions about fisheries and consent to marine scientific research.[16] Although such decisions can be required to proceed to conciliation, the results of that process do not bind the coastal State. States also have the option to exclude further categories of disputes including maritime boundary delimitation, historic bays or titles, military activities or law enforcement related to fishing and marine scientific research.[17] The fact that some subject matters were considered too sensitive reinforces Morgenthau's theory that states will be reluctant to relinquish control, or power, over matters that are core to a state's interest.[18]

The negotiation of such comprehensive provisions, including compulsory dispute settlement for many categories of disputes, was unprecedented in international law at the time. Churchill has pointed out that at the time, communist and some developing States were ideologically opposed to using international courts to settle disputes.[19] Why then, was it possible to reach agreement on its inclusion in the LOSC? A number of explanations have been identified, with the main reason being the need to ensure the stability of the regime.[20] The history of the law of the sea prior to the LOSC was one of a proliferation of unilateral claims and 'creeping coastal State jurisdiction' underpinned by deep disagreements about the respective rights of States in the ocean. While agreement on the extent of maritime zones and the rights therein meant that many of these disagreements were resolved, it was recognized that the constructive

14 ibid art 290.

15 Churchill (n 5) 219.

16 LOSC art 297. The operation of art 297 is complex, and as has been pointed out, the characterisation of the dispute is crucial in determining whether a dispute is excluded from compulsory jurisdiction. See Alan E Boyle, 'Dispute Settlement and the Law of the Sea: Problems of Fragmentation and Jurisdiction' (1997) 46 International & Comparative Law Quarterly, 37, 42.

17 LOSC art 298.

18 Morgenthau (n 7) 422. See also Natalie Klein, *Dispute Settlement in the UN Convention on the Law of the Sea* (Cambridge University Press 2005) 256, referring to maritime delimitation disputes as lying 'at the very heart of sovereignty'.

19 Churchill (n 5) 233.

20 Klein (n 18) 25.

ambiguity of many parts of the LOSC might lead to a need for judicial interpretation. The LOSC was a package deal comprised of a system of compromises, and a strong dispute settlement system was considered necessary to maintain the integrity of that deal.[21]

Protecting the stability of the deal was a significant goal for powerful countries such as the United States, which needed to protect freedom of navigation in order to ensure their navies could have free movement throughout the world.[22] The Soviet Union as well as the United States saw a benefit in compulsory dispute settlement to deal with States that attempted to interfere with navigational rights.[23] In this case, the advantage for major States was that they would not have to resort to power-based tactics to enforce the Convention, tactics which may back-fire diplomatically.

Another factor that may have influenced States to agree to compulsory dispute settlement was the levelling nature of third-party dispute settlement. For countries that lack military or political power, especially developing States, the ability to hold more powerful States to account in a court or tribunal is a valuable option.[24] The concerns expressed by some small States during the negotiations of the Geneva Conventions in 1958, that powerful States might use compulsory dispute settlement to bring unnecessary legal action as a means of exerting pressure, appear to have largely disappeared.[25] It certainly helped that compulsory dispute settlement had featured in some treaties by the time the dispute settlement provisions were negotiated.[26]

### 2.2 *Compulsory Dispute Settlement Post-1994*

Following the entry into force of the Convention, dispute settlement procedures in Section 2, Part XV of the LOSC have been perhaps less frequently used

---

21 John E Noyes 'Compulsory Third-Party Adjudication and the 1982 United Nations Convention on the Law of the Sea' (1989) 4 Connecticut Journal of International Law 675, 682.

22 Alan E Boyle, 'UNCLOS Dispute Settlement and the Uses and Abuses of Part XV' (2014) 47 Revue Belge de Droit International 182, 185. This is consistent with Krisch's view of hegemonic States and international law, which argues that international rules (including dispute settlement) lower the costs of enforcement which is an advantage for powerful States. See also Krisch (n 4) 373.

23 Elliot L Richardson, 'Power, Mobility and the Law of the Sea' (1980) 58 Foreign Affairs 902, 911.

24 Noyes (n 21) 68; Klein (n 18) 21.

25 Klein (n 4) 15–16.

26 Churchill (n 5) 217.

than the negotiators may have anticipated.[27] In early years, many of the disputes were focused on prompt release applications. The ICJ heard a number of maritime boundary delimitation cases, although they were not brought under Part XV. In recent years, the number of substantive issues considered by third-party settlement has increased,[28] possibly reflecting more familiarity, and hence comfort, with the LOSC processes. However, several key factors have limited the ability of the dispute settlement process to fulfil the role anticipated by the framers of the Convention. First, the limitations imposed under Article 297 in practice have narrowed the scope of disputes subject to compulsory procedures.[29] Second, the exclusion of disputes arising under more than one treaty where the other treaty has a voluntary dispute settlement clause, based on the *Southern Bluefin Tuna* case, has had a major impact.[30] Third, States are generally reluctant to submit their disputes to international courts and tribunal, primarily because they prefer to retain control over the dispute.[31]

A further obstacle has been that some powerful States – the Russian Federation and China – have each objected to the use of Part XV where they contest jurisdiction.[32] In each case, the respondent State refused to participate in the hearings on jurisdiction or merits.[33] The Russian Federation and China issued a joint statement in 2016 that 'it is crucial for the maintenance of international legal order that all dispute settlement means and mechanisms are based on consent and used in good faith and in the spirit of cooperation, and their purposes shall not be undermined by abusive practices'.[34] Of course, the argument that a State has not consented to proceedings under Section 2 of Part

27 Rosemary Rayfuse, 'The Future of Compulsory Dispute Settlement under the Law of the Sea Convention' (2005) 36 Victoria University of Wellington Law Review 683, 710.

28 Churchill (n 5) 226.

29 eg The UK argument in the Chagos Arbitration: *Chagos Marine Protected Area Arbitration* (*Mauritius v United Kingdom*) (Award, 18 March 2015) PCA Case 2011–03 [245]–[248].

30 See discussion below at 4.1.

31 Churchill (n 5) 225.

32 *The 'Arctic Sunrise' Case* (*Kingdom of the Netherlands v Russian Federation*) (Provisional Measures, 22 November 2013) ITLOS; *South China Sea Arbitration* (*Philippines v China*) (Award, 12 July 2016) PCA Case 2013–19. See also Churchill (n 5) 230. Churchill calls the refusal of China and Russia to participate in cases 'a major blow to the integrity, authority and legitimacy of the LOSC dispute settlement process'.

33 Kate Parlett, 'Jurisdiction of the Arbitral Tribunal in *Philippines v China* Under UNCLOS and in the Absence of China' (2016) 110 AJIL Unbound 266, 267.

34 The Declaration of the Russian Federation and the People's Republic of China on the Promotion of International Law (25 June 2016) available at <www.mid.ru/en/foreign_policy/position_word_order/-/asset_publisher/6S4RuXfeYlKr/content/id/2331698> accessed 11 November 2020.

XV ignores the fact that, by ratifying the LOSC, all State Parties have essentially agreed in advance to the submission of disputes to third party resolution.

Some efforts have been made to expand the use of the LOSC dispute settlement provisions.[35] For example, Part XV processes were directly incorporated into the UNFSA[36] and the Convention on the Protection of Underwater Cultural Heritage 2001.[37] Other treaties have conferred jurisdiction on the ITLOS in certain circumstances, including the 1993 Compliance Agreement[38] and the 1996 Protocol to the London Convention.[39] However, these provisions are rarely, if ever, used.

In addition, the vast majority of tribunals and courts that have had to consider whether jurisdiction exists over a particular dispute have found in favour of the existence of jurisdiction. This 'expansive approach' to jurisdiction arguably increases the number of cases that have been decided by dispute settlement procedures.[40]

## 3 Part XV LOSC and Areas beyond National Jurisdiction

This section of the chapter evaluates the role of Part XV in resolving disputes in relation to ABNJ. In particular, it explores the ability of Part XV to support obligations aimed at environmental protection. These disputes often do not easily fit into the usual mould of disputes resolved by third-party dispute settlement processes. It concludes with a brief analysis of cases brought under Part XV with application to ABNJ.

---

35 For a list of all conventions conferring jurisdiction on ITLOS, see <www.itlos.org/jurisdiction/international-agreements-conferring-jurisdiction-on-the-tribunal/> accessed 12 May 2021.

36 UNFSA art 30.

37 Convention on the Protection of Underwater Cultural Heritage (opened for signature 2 November 2001, entered into force 2 January 2009) 2562 UNTS 3, art 25.

38 Agreement to Promote Compliance with International Conservation and Management Measures by Fishing Vessels on the High Seas (opened for signature 29 November 1993, entered into force 24 April 2003) 2221 UNTS 91, art IX.

39 1996 Protocol to the Convention on the Prevention of Marine Pollution by Dumping of Wastes and Other Matter (opened for signature 7 November 1996, entered into force 24 March 2006) 36 ILM 1, art 16.

40 Alan Boyle and James Harrison, 'Judicial Settlement of International Environmental Disputes: Current Problems' (2013) 4 Journal of International Dispute Settlement 245, 255.

### 3.1 *The Nature of Disputes in ABNJ and* Erga Omnes *Obligations*

Disputes in international law are typically bilateral, involving an injured State seeking redress against a State it alleges has violated international law. Such disputes can arise out of activities in any place, including on the high seas. For example, a complaint that one State has interfered with another State's rights in relation to its flagged vessels would essentially be a bilateral dispute no matter where the interference occurred. In such cases, the injured State has standing before international tribunals to bring a claim for reparations, provided the tribunal has jurisdiction.

A number of the provisions in the LOSC are for the protection of the marine environment. In some cases, harm to the environment will involve harm to the interests of a State, such as when a coastal State is complaining that areas under its jurisdiction have been harmed by pollution. In these circumstances, the bilateral model of dispute settlement is appropriate for resolving the dispute, so long as a court or tribunal has jurisdiction over the matter.

However, it is entirely possible that harm can be done to the marine environment, in violation of the LOSC provisions, but the harm is to ABNJ. In this case, harm to an area in which all States have an interest (the high seas or the Area) is in effect a harm that is suffered by all States. Alternatively, the harm may involve the violation of treaties or general international law norms owed to a group of States. This may or may not result in physical harm to commons areas.

International law obligations that are owed to all States are known as *erga omnes* norms.[41] Commentators often distinguish between norms that arise as a matter of general international law (*erga omnes*), and obligations under multilateral treaties that State parties to the treaty owe to the other parties (*erga omnes partes*).[42] The common factor between these versions of *erga omnes* norms is that they are owed to the international community in view of its common values.

---

41 *Barcelona Traction, Light and Power Company, Limited (Belgium v Spain)* (Judgment) [1970] ICJ Reports 3, 32.

42 Art 1, Institut de droit international, Resolution: Obligation Erga Omnes in International Law, Krakow Session 2005, available at <www.idi-il.org/app/uploads/2017/06/2005_kra_01_en.pdf> accessed 12 May 2021. The resolution classifies both as *erga omnes* norms, while others distinguish between them. See eg Christian J Tams, *Enforcing Obligations Erga Omnes in International Law* (Cambridge University Press 2004) 123; Yoshifumi Tanaka, 'Reflections on Locus Standi in Response to a Breach of Obligations Erga Omnes Partes: A Comparative Analysis of the Whaling in the Antarctic and South China Sea Cases' (2018) 17 Law and Practice of International Courts and Tribunals 527, 528.

Identifying which norms are *erga omnes* can be difficult, and there can be temptation to include almost too many norms in that category.[43] However legal obligations which are intended to benefit the international community, including the CHM, have been suggested to fit into these categories.[44] Some commentators have suggested that all obligations intended to protect the global environment are owed *erga omnes*.[45] Harrison has argued that most of the rules in the LOSC, and particularly those aimed at protecting the environment, are *erga omnes*.[46] In the Advisory Opinion issued by the Seabed Disputes Chamber of ITLOS, the Chamber described the obligations relating to the preservation of the environment of the high seas and the Area as *erga omnes* in character.[47] Craik has referred to the enforcement of *erga omnes* norms as the 'public function' of dispute settlement, in which the goal is to maintain and secure the values and objectives of the wider community.[48]

As a result, the provisions of the LOSC pertaining to protection of the environment, at least, can be classified as *erga omnes* norms. In relation to the ILBI, it is likely that the provisions designed to protect the marine environment will, by extension, also be *erga omnes* norms.

A key question is whether any member of the international community can enforce violations of the norms against the violator on behalf of the community, even if that State has not itself suffered injury (often referred to as *actio popularis*). This is often referred to as a question whether a State has standing to bring a case in such circumstances.

---

43 See the Separate Opinion of Judge Higgins in the Construction of a Wall advisory opinion, when she suggested that the Barcelona Traction case is 'frequently invoked for more than it can bear'. *Legal Consequences of the Construction of a Wall in the Occupied Palestinian Territory* (Advisory Opinion) [2004] ICJ Reports 136, 216.

44 Malgosia Fitzmaurice, 'Liability for Environmental Damage Caused to the Global Commons' (1996) 5 Review of European Comparative & International Environmental Law 305, 309; Duncan French, 'Common concern, common heritage and other global(-ising) concepts: rhetorical devices, legal principles or a fundamental challenge?' in Michael Bowman, Peter Davies and Edward Goodwin (eds), *Research Handbook on Biodiversity Law* (Edward Elgar 2016) 334, 352.

45 Tams (n 42) 119. See also James Crawford, 'Responsibility for Breaches of Communitarian Norms: An Appraisal of art 48 of the ILC Articles on Responsibility of States for Internationally Wrongful Acts' in Ulrich Fastenrath and others (eds), *From Bilateralism to Community Interest: Essays in Honour of Bruno Simma* (Oxford University Press 2011) 224, 226; Boyle and Harrison (n 39) 259.

46 James Harrison, *Saving the Oceans through Law* (Oxford University Press 2017) 25, 39.

47 *Seabed Advisory Opinion* (n 9) [180].

48 A Neil Craik, 'Recalcitrant Reality and Chosen Ideals: The Public Function of Dispute Settlement in International Environmental Law' (1998) 10 Georgetown International Environmental Law Review 551, 563.

Although some have argued that it is not settled that *actio popularis* is available to non-injured States,[49] the general view is that it is possible for a non-injured State to bring a dispute against a State that has violated an *erga omnes* norm. Article 48 of the ILC Draft Articles on State Responsibility[50] provides for the invocation of responsibility against a State by any other State in two circumstances.[51] First, the obligation that has been breached must be owed to a group of States including that State and the obligation is established for the protection of a collective interest of the group. Alternatively, the obligation breached may be owed to the international community as a whole. Crawford has described Article 48 as providing a balance between the collective interest in compliance with basic community values and the countervailing interest in not encouraging the proliferation of disputes.[52]

Courts have not always been consistent about giving standing to non-injured States to bring disputes. The International Court of Justice has refused States permission to bring cases in some situations.[53] However, in the case between Belgium and Senegal on the obligation to prosecute or extradite for crimes of torture, the ICJ recognized that common interests in compliance with the Convention against Torture entitled any State party to make a claim about a breach by another State party.[54] In the case between the Gambia and Myanmar, the ICJ confirmed that the shared values of the parties to the Genocide Convention meant that a party did not need to be specially affected to invoke the responsibility of another party under the Convention.[55] In each of the Conventions against Torture and Genocide, the treaty itself makes it clear that disputes can be brought by any party to the Treaty.[56]

---

49 See, eg Fitzmaurice, (n 44) 309; Rüdiger Wolfrum, 'Enforcing Community Interests Through International Dispute Settlement: Reality or Utopia?' in Ulrich Fastenrath and others (eds), *From Bilateralism to Community Interest: Essays in Honour of Bruno Simma* (Oxford University Press 2011) 1132, 1137. Although Judge Wolfrum does conclude that dispute settlement for the purpose of protecting community interests is possible in international law (at 1139).

50 Draft arts on Responsibility of States for Internationally Wrongful Acts with commentaries (2001).

51 Draft art 48(1).

52 Crawford (n 45) 227.

53 *South West Africa (Liberia v. South Africa) (Ethiopia v. South Africa), Second Phase* (Judgment) [1966] ICJ Reports 47. See also Tanaka (n 42) 541.

54 *Questions relating to the Obligation to Prosecute or Extradite (Belgium v. Senegal)* (Judgment) [2012] ICJ Reports 422, 69.

55 *Application of the Convention on the Prevention and Punishment of the Crime of Genocide (The Gambia v Myanmar)* (Provisional Measures, 23 January 2020) ICJ.

56 Convention on the Prevention and Punishment of the Crime of Genocide (opened for signature 9 December 1948, entered into force 12 January 1951) 78 UNTS 277, art IX;

Standing was not directly addressed by the ICJ in the *Whaling in the Antarctic* case, in which Australia brought a case against Japan alleging a violation of the International Convention for the Regulation of Whaling.[57] Although Australia was not directly injured by Japan's whaling activities, the Court did not question its right to bring the case and appeared to treat the application as an *erga omnes partes* question.[58]

Recent practice from the ICJ, therefore, indicates that it is willing to allow standing on the basis of 'shared values' and a 'common interest' in preventing a violation of the relevant treaty. The fact that the ICJ did not question standing in the *Whaling in the Antarctic* case lends support to the use of *erga omnes* environmental norms as a basis of standing in such cases.

### 3.2 *Limitations of Traditional Dispute Settlement for Enforcing Environmental Obligations*

Despite the recognition of *erga omnes* norms, the actual use of dispute settlement to enforce them is still rare.[59] This is particularly true for environmental law obligations. Traditional bilateral dispute settlement in international law is less than ideal for enforcing *erga omnes* environmental norms for a number of reasons. First, even if the legal obligation at issue is owed *erga omnes* and a State may have standing to bring a dispute, it is still necessary to establish that a court or tribunal has jurisdiction over the dispute, which is not easy to do in many cases.[60] In addition, harm caused to common areas rather than areas under national jurisdiction provides less incentive for States to bring an expensive and politically sensitive case.[61] Disputes involving environmental problems are complex and polycentric,[62] frequently involving a variety

---

Convention Against Torture and other Cruel, Inhuman or Degrading Treatment or Punishment (opened for signature 10 December 1984, entered into force 26 June 1987) 1465 UNTS 85, art 30.

57 *Whaling in the Antarctic* (*Australia v. Japan: New Zealand intervening*) (Judgment) [2014] ICJ Reports 2014, 226.

58 See Tanaka (n 42) 536.

59 André Nollkaemper, 'International Adjudication of Global Public Goods: The Intersection of Substance and Procedure' (2012) 23 European Journal of International Law 769, 777.

60 Margaret Young, 'International Adjudication and the Commons' (2019) 41 University of Hawai'i Law Review 353, 372; Giorgio Gaja, 'Claims Concerning Obligations *Erga Omnes* in the Jurisprudence of the International Court of Justice' in Riccardo Pisillo Mzzeschi and Pasquale De Sena (eds), *Global Justice, Human Rights and the Modernization of International Law* (Springer Nature 2018) 39, 42.

61 ibid 45.

62 Tim Stephens, 'The Limits of International Adjudication in International Environmental Law: Another Perspective on the Southern Bluefin Tuna Case' (2004) 19 International Journal of Marine and Coastal Law 177, 194.

of treaties and customary norms,[63] making them difficult to resolve in an international court or tribunal. The difficulty of establishing a link between the harm suffered and a breach of a particular State's obligations can be problematic.[64]

Even if a State does bring a case to enforce a norm owed to the international community, the process may not allow for all interested States to participate, and will bind only the parties to the dispute.[65] Although New Zealand applied, and was given permission, to intervene in the *Whaling in the Antarctic* case, Japan opposed the intervention, demonstrating that parties to disputes may not appreciate third States becoming involved. It has been noted that, although the ICJ and ITLOS have provisions in their statutes for interventions from other States, no such provision is made in the case of arbitration under the LOSC.[66] However, when a dispute involves the interpretation of a common treaty provision, or indeed an interest held by the international community as a whole, the potential exclusion of other interested States from the dispute is a matter for concern. Craik has suggested that the exclusion of other interested parties from arbitral proceedings makes them unfit for pursuing community interests.[67] Bruno Simma stated his concern thus:[68]

> the observer is frequently torn between feelings of satisfaction because international law is finally being invested with some of the social accountability long developed in domestic law, and fears that the still primitive, still essentially bilateralist infrastructure upon which the new, more progressive edifices rest will turn out to be too weak to come to terms with the implications of such community interest.

---

63 Boyle and Harrison (n 40) 250.

64 Karen Scott, 'Non-compliance Procedures and Dispute Resolution Mechanisms under International Environmental Agreements' in Nigel White, Duncan French and Matthew Saul (eds), *International Law and Dispute Settlement: New Problems and Techniques* (Hart 2010) 225, 227; Martti Koskenniemi, 'Breach of Treaty or Non-compliance? Reflections on the Enforcement of the Montreal Protocol' (1992) 3 Yearbook of International Environmental Law 123, 126.

65 Stephens (n 62) 194; Nollkaemper (n 59) 778. Of course, requests for advisory opinions permit a much broader range of States (and potentially non-State entities) to participate in the argument, although they are not binding. See further 4.2.1.

66 Boyle and Harrison (n 40) 264.

67 Craik (n 48) 567.

68 Bruno Simma, 'From Bilateralism to Community Interest in International Law' (1994) 250 Recueil des cours 217, 295.

### 3.3 *Previous Disputes*

As can be expected, given the challenges in using traditional dispute settlement to resolve environmental disputes, the nature of disputes arising under Part XV of the LOSC have primarily been bilateral in nature, focusing on the alleged violation of one State's rights by another. For example, disputes include the arrest of a vessel for violating coastal State regulations in their maritime zones,[69] prompt release applications,[70] maritime boundary delimitation between two States,[71] or a failure to consult affected States.[72] Of course a bilateral dispute can involve a range of issues, as illustrated by the *South China Sea* case, which involved, among other concerns, the interpretation of Article 121 of the LOSC and environmental provisions in Part XII.[73]

Very few of the cases initiated under the LOSC have focused on issues affecting ABNJ. The key exception is the advisory opinion of the Seabed Disputes Chamber of ITLOS on the Responsibilities and Obligations of States Sponsoring Persons and Entities with Respect to Activities in the Area.[74] That advisory opinion, issued at the request of the International Seabed Authority (ISA), addressed a range of issues including the responsibility of States under the LOSC, ISA regulations and customary international law. Many commentators have noted that the advisory opinion not only made a significant contribution to the clarification of international law and international environmental principles generally, but also gave considerable guidance as to how States were to implement their obligations under Part XI of the LOSC.[75] Importantly, the Chamber concluded that, in the case of harm to the environment due to a

69 eg *M/V 'Norstar' (Panama v Italy)* (Judgment, 10 April 2019) ITLOS; *Arctic Sunrise* case (n 32); *M/V 'Virginia G' (Panama v Guinea-Bissau)* (Judgment, 14 April 2014) ITLOS 4.

70 eg *Tominmaru (Japan v Russian Federation)* (Prompt Release, Judgment) ITLOS Reports 2005–07, 74; *The Grand Prince Case (Belize v France)* (Prompt Release, Judgment) ITLOS Reports 2001, 17; *M/V 'Saiga' (Saint Vincent and the Grenadines v Guinea)* (Prompt Release, Judgment) ITLOS Reports 1997, 16.

71 *Delimitation of the Maritime Boundary between Bangladesh and Myanmar in the Bay of Bengal (Bangladesh v Myanmar)* (Judgment, 14 March 2012) ITLOS Reports 2012, 4; *Barbados v Trinidad and Tobago* (Award, 11 April 2006) PCA 2004–02.

72 *MOX Plant (Ireland v United Kingdom)* (Provisional Measures) ITLOS Reports 2001, 95; *Chagos Marine Protected Area Arbitration* (n 29).

73 *South China Sea* (n 32).

74 *Seabed Advisory Opinion* (n 9).

75 See, eg David Freestone, 'Responsibilities and Obligations of States Sponsoring Persons and Entities With Respect to Activities in the Area' (2011) 105 American Journal Of International Law 755; Duncan French, 'From the Depths: Rich Pickings of Principles of Sustainable Development and General International Law on the Ocean Floor – The Seabed Disputes Chamber's 2011 Advisory Opinion' (2011) 26 International Journal of Marine and Coastal Law 525; Rosemary Rayfuse, 'Differentiating the Common: The

breach of obligations by a Sponsoring State, any State could bring an action to recover damages. This is due to the '*erga omnes* character of the obligations to protect the marine environment on the high seas and in the Area'.[76] This conclusion on the part of the Chamber was seen by some as ground-breaking, and 'potentially radical'.[77] In light of the status of the Area as the CHM, the finding that obligations are *erga omnes* may not really be that radical. What is interesting to consider is whether a tribunal would come to the same conclusion in relation to obligations in the high seas, which is governed by the freedom of the seas rather than CHM. It seems that, in addition to the Chamber, other commentators consider that the *erga omnes* appellation can be applied there as well.[78]

Another case that had the potential to interpret obligations relating to ABNJ was the *Southern Bluefin Tuna* case.[79] This case arose when Australia, Japan and New Zealand failed to reach agreement on total allowable catch (TAC) in the Commission for the Conservation of Southern Bluefin Tuna.[80] Australia and New Zealand initiated an arbitration under Part XV, arguing that Japan, which had begun an experimental fishing program that exceeded the previously agreed TAC, had breached obligations under the LOSC.[81] Australia and New Zealand had a direct interest in ensuring Japan stayed within the TAC as this may have affected the status of the fish stock that they both targeted. At a preliminary stage, ITLOS granted provisional measures designed to ensure the parties continued to cooperate to ensure the stock was not endangered prior to the constitution of the arbitral tribunal.[82] This has been noted by some as adopting a precautionary approach.[83] Had this case reached the merits stage, then the decision could have provided important guidance on States' obligations in ABNJ. However, the arbitral tribunal held that it did not have

Responsibilities and Obligations of States Sponsoring Deep Seabed Mining Activities in the Area' (2011) 54 German Yearbook of International Law 459.

76 *Seabed Advisory Opinion* (n 9) para 180. The Chamber referred to art 48 of the ILC Articles on State Responsibility to support this view.

77 French (n 75) 546.

78 eg Harrison (n 46). See also discussion at 3.1.

79 *Southern Bluefin Tuna* (*New Zealand v Japan, Australia v Japan*) Award on Jurisdiction and Admissibility (2000) XXIII RIAA 1.

80 ibid [24].

81 ibid [30].

82 ibid [90].

83 eg Adriana Fabra, 'The LOSC and the Implementation of the Precautionary Principle' (2000) 10 Yearbook of International Environmental Law 15, 17.

jurisdiction due to a voluntary dispute settlement provision in the regional fisheries management organization (RFMO) convention.[84]

Despite the existence of obligations in the LOSC relating to the protection and preservation of the marine environment in ABNJ, no State has successfully brought a dispute against another on the basis of *erga omnes* norms under Part XV. Judge Wolfrum has argued that it is entirely consistent with Part XV of the LOSC for States to bring a case involving a violation of an *erga omnes partes* obligation under the Convention. In his view, Article 288, giving jurisdiction to a court or tribunal over 'any dispute concerning the interpretation or application of this Convention', can be read to allow a case to be filed that is not based on an injury to the individual interests of the applicant State.[85] The obstacles to such cases discussed above may have played a role in dissuading States from bringing such cases, although it is difficult to find evidence that this was the case.

It is also interesting that no compulsory dispute settlement has been initiated under the UNFSA dispute settlement provisions. Article 30 of that Agreement applies Part XV of the LOSC *mutatis mutandis* to disputes concerning the interpretation or application of the Agreement as well as RFMOs. A number of factors could contribute to this. It is possible that the *Southern Bluefin Tuna* decision refusing jurisdiction may have had a depressing effect as States may not have thought that jurisdiction would exist where RFMO conventions had different dispute settlement procedures.[86] It is also possible that the lack of cases reflects the obstacles to bringing cases relating to ABNJ already discussed. Another factor is that the existence of a compulsory dispute settlement process may encourage States to negotiate or compromise when issues arise that could be subject to such a process.[87] There is also a range of ways in which action can be taken against non-compliant States and their vessels without resorting to dispute settlement provisions, such as using RFMO

84 *Southern Bluefin Tuna* (n 79). The jurisdictional aspects of the arbitral decision are discussed below.

85 Wolfrum (n 49) 1144. This is supported by similarly broad wording in art 279 to the effect that 'State Parties shall settle *any dispute* between them concerning the interpretation or application' of the LOSC by peaceful means.

86 See further below at 4.1. See also the *Chagos Arbitration* (n 29) which indicated that disputes involving straddling stocks would be excluded from jurisdiction unless they related to activities beyond the EEZ [300].

87 Peter Örebech, Ketill Sigurjonsson and Ted McDorman, 'The 1995 United Nations Straddling and Highly Migratory Fish Stocks Agreement: Management, Enforcement and Dispute Settlement' (1998) 13 International Journal of Marine and Coastal Law 119, 138.

compliance committees, port State inspections and sanctions against non-cooperating non-parties to the RMO.[88]

Overall, while the LOSC contains obligations in relation to State conduct in ABNJ that could be classified as *erga omnes*, very few disputes have been brought or raised under the dispute settlement procedures. Only one contentious case can really be counted as relating to ABNJ, and even then, it was brought by States with a real interest in ensuring compliance with RFMO obligations. The other is an advisory opinion. This paucity of examples arguably reinforces the problems with using dispute settlement processes for enforcement of ABNJ obligations, particularly environmental duties. If a State violates its obligations and there is no directly affected State, the chances are high that the dispute settlement procedures may not be used, despite the affirmation in the Seabed Advisory Opinion that any State could enforce *erga omnes* norms.

## 4 Dispute Settlement and the ILBI

The ILBI, should it be concluded, will impose a variety of obligations on States, some of which will involve measures for the conservation and sustainable use of biodiversity, including obligations relating to the marine environment in ABNJ. Others will relate to the utilization of marine genetic resources (MGRS) and transfer of technology and capacity building. Although some aspects of the ILBI will create bilateral obligations (owed between particular States),[89] many of the obligations will be owed to the international community and there will be a general interest in ensuring the conservation and sustainable use of marine biodiversity.[90] This raises questions about the form of possible dispute settlement clauses in the ILBI.

The negotiations for an ILBI were authorized by General Assembly Resolution 72/249 in December 2017.[91] Four sessions of the IGC were approved,

88 eg Dorota Englender and others, 'Cooperation and compliance control in areas beyond national jurisdiction' (2014) 49 Marine Policy 186.

89 One example would be an obligation on a State undertaking an environmental impact assessment to consult a particularly affected State during its preparation. A failure to consult may give rise to a bilateral dispute between those States.

90 A more in-depth exploration of the types of disputes that may arise under the ILBI is found in Liesbeth Lijnzaad, 'Dispute Settlement for Marine Biodiversity beyond National Jurisdiction: Not an Afterthought' in Helene Ruiz Fabri and others (eds), *A Bridge Over Troubled Waters: Dispute Resolution in the Law of International Watercourses and the Law of the Sea* (Brill Nijhoff 2020) 147, 159.

91 Discussions that led to this authorization began in 2006 with the first meeting of the Ad Hoc Open-ended Informal Working Group established by the General Assembly available

and at the time of writing three sessions have been completed and two draft texts issued. To date, the dispute settlement provisions have received relatively little attention in the IGC, with approximately an hour of discussion during IGC3.[92] The first and second draft texts proposed identical dispute settlement provisions.[93] Draft Article 54 (common to both drafts) imposes an obligation to settle their disputes by peaceful means, while draft Article 55 applies Part XV of the LOSC *mutatis mutandis* to disputes about the interpretation or application of the ILBI. A State's acceptance of a forum under Article 287 of the LOSC applies to the ILBI, unless that State chooses another forum for disputes under the ILBI, and non-Parties to the LOSC may also choose a forum for disputes under the ILBI.

The draft provisions follow a similar format to some articles in the UNFSA dispute settlement process. The formula of Part XV applying *mutatis mutandis*[94] to issues of interpretation of the ILBI is the same as Article 30(1) of UNFSA, although the draft ILBI provisions are less extensive overall than the UNFSA Articles on dispute settlement.[95]

Whether it is sufficient to simply follow the UNFSA approach is questionable. Indeed, the application of Part XV *mutatis mutandis* may be very difficult in a treaty that will relate to legal instruments well beyond the law of the sea, including intellectual property and international environmental law.[96] Negotiators would be well-advised to consider the dispute settlement provisions more closely prior to the conclusion of negotiations.

---

at <www.un.org/Depts/los/biodiversityworkinggroup/marine_biodiversity.htm> accessed 12 May 2021.

92 The history of discussions in the PrepCom and IGC is discussed in Lijnzaad (n 90) 157.

93 Draft text of an agreement under the United Nations Convention on the Law of the Sea on the conservation and sustainable use of marine biological diversity of areas beyond national jurisdiction A/Conf.232/2019/6 (Draft Agreement); Revised draft text of an agreement under the LOSC on the conservation and sustainable use of marine biological diversity of areas beyond national jurisdiction, 27 November 2019 available at <www.un.org/bbnj/sites/www.un.org.bbnj/files/revised_draft_text_a.conf_.232.2020.11_advance_unedited_version.pdf> accessed 28 November 2019 (Revised Draft Agreement).

94 Meaning 'with the necessary changes'.

95 A comparison between the ILBI and UNFSA dispute settlement provisions is explored in Joanna Mossop, 'Dispute Settlement in the New Treaty on Marine Biodiversity in Areas beyond National Jurisdiction' (23 December 2019) NCLOS Blog available at <http://site.uit.no/jclos/files/2019/12/J-Mossop-Dispute-Settlement-in-the-BBNJ-Treaty-NCLOS.pdf> accessed 12 May 2021.

96 Lijnzaad (n 90) 161.

The following section discusses some options and issues that could be addressed in the ILBI,[97] including the parallel dispute settlement problem created by the *Southern Bluefin Tuna* case and proposals for using advisory opinions and compliance mechanisms.

### 4.1 *Parallel Dispute Settlement Problem*[98]

One reason that no disputes have been brought under Article 30 of UNFSA may be due to the *Southern Bluefin Tuna* award, which was the first substantive dispute brought before an arbitral tribunal under Part XV of the LOSC. For reasons that will be explained, it is likely that potential disputes that have arisen under the LOSC and another treaty (such as an RFMO convention) have not been brought due to the existence of parallel dispute settlement clauses. However, the more recent decision in the *South China Sea* case has cast doubt on that aspect of the finding of the *Southern Bluefin Tuna* case.[99] This results in unfortunate uncertainty about the impact of a parallel dispute settlement provision in a related treaty.

The reason that this could pose a problem for the ILBI is that the treaty is likely to overlap with other treaties establishing global, regional or sectoral bodies (GRSBs). These may include treaties such as the LOSC and UNFSA, to which Part XV already applies. However, other treaties will have different dispute settlement clauses. In such cases there may be uncertainty about whether compulsory dispute settlement is available due to the parallel jurisdiction problem.

The tribunal in the *Southern Bluefin Tuna* award considered whether it had jurisdiction over a dispute that arose under the LOSC and an RFMO convention.[100] It concluded that, where a dispute arose under the LOSC and another treaty, Article 281 of the LOSC meant that the existence of a voluntary dispute settlement procedure in the other treaty amounted to an agreement between the parties to exclude the compulsory dispute settlement procedures of the LOSC.[101] In that case, the fact that Article 16 of the Convention for the

97 For an overview of all proposals made during the PrepCom and IGCs, see Yubing Shi, 'Settlement of disputes in a BBNJ agreement: Options and analysis' (2020) Marine Policy available at <https://doi.org/10.1016/j.marpol.2020.104156> accessed 12 May 2021.

98 This section develops ideas first articulated in Mossop, 'Dispute Settlement' (n 95).

99 *South China Sea* (*Philippines v China*) (Award on Jurisdiction and Admissibility, 29 October 2015) [223] available at <https://pca-cpa.org/en/cases/7/> accessed 12 May 2021.

100 *Southern Bluefin Tuna* (n 79). At issue was the Convention for the Conservation of Southern Bluefin Tuna (opened for signature 10 May 1993, entered into force 20 May 1994), art 16 available at <www.ccsbt.org/en/content/basic-documents-commission> accessed 12 May 2021.

101 *Southern Bluefin Tuna* (n 79) 43–44.

Conservation of Southern Bluefin Tuna stated that parties could choose to submit their dispute to third party settlement was considered to rule out the application of the compulsory processes. In a dissenting opinion, Sir Kenneth Keith argued that Article 281 required an explicit statement ruling out recourse to the compulsory procedures under the LOSC.[102]

The *Southern Bluefin Tuna* award has been criticised by some commentators. They argued that the effect of the award was to severely limit the cases in which the compulsory dispute settlement procedures can apply where a dispute arises under more than one treaty.[103] This is particularly a problem since the majority of treaties have a dispute settlement clause similar to that in the Convention for the Conservation of Southern Bluefin Tuna.

The *Southern Bluefin Tuna* arbitration arose prior to UNFSA's entry into force. The arbitral tribunal suggested at the end of its decision that the UNFSA might avoid the procedural problems encountered in that case.[104] At first glance it is hard to see how this might be, given that the importation of Part XV into the UNFSA also brings in Article 281, which would consequently apply to the dispute settlement clause in the other treaty. However, it has been suggested that the crucial element was the inclusion of Article 30(2) of UNFSA, which applied Part XV to disputes arising under RFMO treaties. The effect of Article 30(2) would be to ensure that the dispute settlement provision in the RFMO treaty would be essentially overridden by Part XV, thus allowing the compulsory dispute settlement procedures to apply.[105] This interpretation has not been tested yet by any court or tribunal, but appears sound.

Boyle has suggested that the approach taken by the tribunal in *Southern Bluefin Tuna* was not followed in two cases.[106] The first was in the *Mox Plant*

102 *Southern Bluefin Tuna* (n 79) 54 (Separate Opinion of Justice Sir Kenneth Keith).

103 eg Bernard H Oxman, 'Complementary Agreements and Compulsory Jurisdiction' (2001) 95 American Journal of International Law 277; Alan Boyle, 'The *Southern Bluefin Tuna* Arbitration' (2001) 50 International and Comparative Law Quarterly 447; David A Colson and Peggy Hoyle, 'Satisfying the Procedural Prerequisites to the Compulsory Dispute Settlement: Did the Southern Bluefin Tuna Tribunal Get it Right?' (2003) 34 Ocean Development and International Law 59. In support of the decision, see Barbara Kwiatkowska, 'The Australia and New Zealand v Japan Southern Bluefin Tuna (Jurisdiction and Admissibility) Award of the First Law of the Sea Convention Annex VII Arbitral Tribunal' (2001) 16 International Journal of Marine and Coastal Law 239; Klein, (n 24) 35–43.

104 *Southern Bluefin Tuna* (n 79) 48.

105 Jacqueline Peel, 'A Paper Umbrella Which Dissolves in the Rain: The Future for Resolving Fisheries Disputes under UNCLOS in the Aftermath of the Southern Bluefin Tuna Arbitration' (2002) 3 Melbourne Journal of International Law 53, 71.

106 Boyle (n 22) 201.

case in which the United Kingdom argued that the existence of a dispute settlement clause in the OSPAR Convention[107] meant that ITLOS did not have jurisdiction over the dispute.[108] The argument was based on Article 282 rather than 281, although it could be argued that similar approaches could be taken under both articles. However, the ITLOS decided that disputes arising under the OSPAR Convention did not involve the resolution of disputes under the LOSC and it would have jurisdiction.[109] The second case involved the same dispute, this time brought under the OSPAR Convention, in which the Arbitral Tribunal took a similar approach.[110] Because neither case involved the interpretation of Article 281, they are of limited assistance beyond the general approach taken by the tribunals.

The Arbitral Tribunal in the *South China Sea* award on jurisdiction returned to this issue in 2015.[111] The Tribunal dismissed the argument on Article 281 on the basis that the China-ASEAN Declaration on the Conduct of Parties in the South China Sea (DOC) was not binding.[112] Although it did not need to consider whether the DOC excluded other procedures, the Tribunal expressed its preference for the approach taken by Sir Kenneth Keith in the *Southern Bluefin Tuna* arbitration. The Tribunal concluded that a reference to voluntary dispute settlement under another instrument did not rule out the compulsory procedures under the LOSC. Rather, the decision to exclude the LOSC compulsory procedures required a clear statement opting out.[113]

Following this decision, there is a split between the holdings of the two cases. The conciliation commission in the dispute between Australia and Timor-Leste, while not deciding on the precise point at issue in the above two cases, interpreted a non-binding agreement between the two States not to seek settlement as consistent with compulsory dispute settlement.[114] Thus, it has been argued that the more recent application of Article 281 of the LOSC has

107 Convention for the Protection of the Marine Environment of the North-East Atlantic (OSPAR Convention) (opened for signatures 22 September 1992, entered into force 25 March 1998) available at <www.ospar.org/convention/text> accessed 12 May 2021.

108 *Mox Plant* (*Ireland v United Kingdom*) (Provisional Measures, Order of 3 December 2001) ITLOS Reports 2001, 95.

109 *Mox Plant* [48]–[53].

110 *Proceedings pursuant to the OSPAR Convention* (*Ireland – United Kingdom*) [2003] XXIII RIAA 59 [142].

111 *South China Sea* (n 99).

112 ibid [219].

113 ibid [224].

114 See *Timor-Leste v. Australia Conciliation*, Decision on Australia's Objections to Competence (19 September 2016) [56]–[57] available at <https://pcacases.com/web/view/132> accessed 20 June 2021.

both denuded dispute settlement provisions in other treaties of proper effect whilst allowing scope for more cases to be resolved under the LOSC compulsory processes.[115]

The result of this divergence in the jurisprudence is a lack of clarity about the effect of a dispute settlement clause in a treaty where a dispute might arise under two treaties including the LOSC or another treaty using its settlement provisions. On one reading, the mere existence of a standard, voluntary dispute settlement clause in the other treaty would rule out recourse to the compulsory procedures in Part XV. On another reading, the compulsory dispute settlement procedures are available unless the other treaty expressly rejects such a move.

It is not clear which approach future tribunals might take when disputes arising under more than one treaty will be submitted to them under Part XV. It should be noted that, since the *Southern Bluefin Tuna* arbitration, the trend for ITLOS and Annex VII tribunals has been to reject challenges to jurisdiction.[116] Therefore, it is likely that if a dispute arose, for example, under the ILBI and the Antarctic Treaty, the presence of a standard dispute settlement clause in the Antarctic Treaty may not prevent a Part XV tribunal finding it had jurisdiction over the dispute. If parties wish to add clarity to the dispute settlement provisions in the ILBI, it may be useful to include a clear direction on the implications of disputes arising under more than one treaty, or involving questions about priority between treaties.

### 4.2 *Further Options for Dispute Settlement under the ILBI*

#### 4.2.1 Advisory Opinion

One of the interesting developments during IGC3 was the proposal that the Conference of the Parties (COP) to be established under the ILBI be empowered to request an advisory opinion from ITLOS regarding the interpretation of the ILBI.[117] Not many delegations expressed a view about this proposal,[118] but it is an interesting option. As already discussed, in situations where disputes arise that affect common interests, a traditional bilateral dispute process

115 Natalie Klein, 'The Vicissitudes of Dispute Settlement under the Law of the Sea Convention' (2017) 32 International Journal of Marine and Coastal Law 332, 340.

116 ibid 342.

117 IISD, 'Summary of the Third Session of the Intergovernmental Conference (IGC) on the Conservation and Sustainable Use of Marine Biodiversity of Areas Beyond National Jurisdiction: 19–30 August 2019' (2019) 25/218 Earth Negotiations Bulletin, 19. This option had also been raised in the PrepCom: Lijnzaad (n 90) 157.

118 Based on the author's observations of Sessions 1-3 of the IGC.

may not produce ideal outcomes. States are less willing to commit to dispute settlement if they are not directly injured by the actions of another State and the process of third-party dispute settlement under international law tends to deny other States the opportunity to participate.[119] In this context the idea of authorizing the COP to request an advisory opinion is worth exploring.

Advisory opinions can contribute to the development of international law, such as when they identify a rule of customary international law or interpret a treaty provision.[120] Arguably, the two advisory opinions issued by ITLOS and its Seabed Disputes Chamber to date have been useful in expanding the understanding of the law.[121]

A key advantage of advisory opinions is that they allow a wider variety of States to participate and express their views.[122] In addition, some advisory processes allow international organizations to participate and make submissions.[123] For example, in the fisheries advisory opinion ITLOS received submissions from a range of international organizations including United Nations agencies, regional fisheries management organizations and the International Union for the Conservation of Nature. In addition, the Tribunal received two *amicus curiae* briefs from WWF.[124] This broad participation by non-State actors is a potentially positive aspect of advisory opinion jurisdiction.

So long as the decision to request an advisory opinion does not require a consensus of all parties, the possibility exists that the option could be used to balance the interests of power and justice. Examples illustrating this were the requests by the General Assembly for advisory opinions in relation to the construction of a wall by Israel in Palestinian occupied territory[125] and the question of the United Kingdom's decolonization process in Mauritius.[126] In both

---

119 Refer to the discussion above in section 3.2.

120 Karin Oellers-Frahm, 'Lawmaking through Advisory Opinions?' in Armin von Bogdandy and Ingo Venzke (eds), *International Judicial Lawmaking: On Public Authority and Democratic Legitimation in Global Governance* (Springer 2012) 69, 80.

121 *Seabed Advisory Opinion* (n 9); *Request for Advisory Opinion submitted by the Sub-Regional Fisheries Commission* (Advisory Opinion, 2 April 2015) ITLOS Reports 2015, 4.

122 Craik (n 48) 567.

123 Natalie Klein and Tim Stephens, 'Whaling in the Antarctic: Protecting Rights in Areas Beyond National Jurisdiction through International Litigation' in Clive H Schofield, Seokwoo Lee and Moon-Sang Kwon (eds), *The Limits of Maritime Jurisdiction* (Brill 2013) 525, 546.

124 See <www.itlos.org/en/main/cases/list-of-cases/case-no-21/> accessed 12 May 2021.

125 *Construction of a Wall* (n 43).

126 *Legal Consequences of the Separation of the Chagos Archipelago from Mauritius in 1965* (Advisory Opinion, 25 February 2019) ICJ available at <https://www.icj-cij.org/en/case/169/advisory-opinions> accessed 12 May 2021.

cases the request for an advisory opinion was able to by-pass the limitations imposed by the veto power in the Security Council.

However, advisory opinions can attract criticism. Some have argued that the use of advisory opinions in the *Wall* and *Chagos* cases were an abuse of the process, because advisory opinions should not be used to substitute for contentious cases.[127] The ICJ has never declined to exercise its discretion to deliver advisory opinions, attracting criticism for becoming involved in highly political issues.[128] Therefore, it can be expected that there will be delegations at the IGC who are not in favour of including options for advisory opinions.

Advisory opinions are not a panacea to the limitations of traditional dispute settlement. They cannot be a mechanism for law enforcement as they are not binding on States.[129] Their findings are necessarily general and may themselves be difficult to interpret or apply in particular factual circumstances. Nevertheless, the few advisory opinions that have been issued in the law of the sea have had significant impact on the understanding of legal obligations under the LOSC.

There is, of course, the question whether ITLOS is able to consider a request for an advisory opinion, even if it is authorized by an international instrument such as a BBNJ ILBI. In the fisheries advisory opinion, the ITLOS was asked to provide an advisory opinion on the request of the Sub-Regional Fisheries Commission, pursuant to a power conferred by the constituent treaty.[130] Ten States made submissions to ITLOS arguing that it did not have jurisdiction to provide an advisory opinion in that case as it is not authorised by the LOSC.[131] The key objection was that the LOSC does not establish a general advisory jurisdiction, and the option was included in the rules of procedure that were established by the Tribunal itself.[132] Nevertheless, ITLOS decided in that case that it did have such jurisdiction when provided for by a treaty.[133] Although

127 Karin Oellers-Frahm, 'Lawmaking through Advisory Opinions?' in Armin von Bogdandy and Ingo Venzke (eds), *International Judicial Lawmaking: On Public Authority and Democratic Legitimation in Global Governance* (Springer 2012) 69, 70.

128 Anthony Aust, 'Advisory Opinions' (2010) 1 Journal of International Dispute Settlement 123, 149.

129 Boyle and Harrison (n 40) 258.

130 Fisheries Advisory Opinion (n 121).

131 Submissions are available at <www.itlos.org/cases/list-of-cases/case-no-21/#c2272> accessed 12 May 2021.

132 See generally Tom Ruys and Anemoon Soete, '"Creeping" Advisory Jurisdiction of International Courts and Tribunals? The Case of the International Tribunal for the Law of the Sea' (2016) 29 Leiden Journal of International Law 155, 159.

133 Yoshifumi Tanaka, 'Reflections on the Advisory Jurisdiction of ITLOS as a Full Court: The ITLOS Advisory Opinion of 2015' (2015) 14 Law and Practice of International Courts and Tribunals 318.

not all States and commentators agree with the decision,[134] it could be argued that ITLOS' jurisdiction to provide advisory opinions when authorised under a treaty other than the LOSC is now a *fait accompli* and is unlikely to be reversed in the future.

#### 4.2.2 Non-compliance Procedures

In multilateral environmental agreements, the limitations of traditional dispute settlement have often led to the inclusion of other mechanisms to encourage and facilitate compliance with obligations that protect common interests.[135] The most common of these are non-compliance procedures (NCPs). Fitzmaurice and Redgwell argue that the primary objective in including any NCP in a multilateral treaty is to encourage States to comply with their treaty obligations and 'in the event of non-compliance, to provide a "softer" system to address non-compliance than that afforded by traditional dispute settlement procedures'.[136] Thus, NCPs can be considered to work alongside and complement traditional dispute settlement processes rather than replace them.[137]

Because such procedures do not rely on the legalistic aspects of bilateral dispute settlement, they are particularly appropriate for environmental issues.[138] It has been observed that in the context of environmental obligations it is preferable to seek to prevent breaches, and hence harm, rather than attempt to invoke State responsibility to 'cure' harm resulting from a breach.[139] NCPs are also likely to encourage just outcomes to the extent that the process provides support to States that are struggling to implement their obligations under the treaty due to incapacity, rather than wilful non-compliance. Such structural issues disproportionately affect developing States,[140] and are not

134 eg Ruys and Soete (n 132).

135 Boyle and Harrison (n 40) 256.

136 Malgosia A Fitzmaurice and Catherine Redgwell 'Environmental Non-Compliance Procedures and International Law' (2009) Netherlands Yearbook of International Law 35, 39.

137 Scott (n 64) 230. However, Stephens notes that, as a result of an increasing use of NCPs, '[i]nternational courts have … been sidelined within environmental regimes, with relatively few environmental agreements relying on their own adjudicative systems for managing compliance issues'. Tim Stephens, *International Courts and Environmental Protection* (Cambridge University Press 2009) 64.

138 Martti Koskenniemi, 'Peaceful Settlement of Environmental Disputes' (1991) 60 Nordic Journal of International Law 73, 80.

139 Scott (n 64) 228.

140 Nils Goeteyn and Frank Maes, 'Compliance Mechanisms in Multilateral Environmental Agreements: An Effective Way to Improve Compliance?' (2011) 10 Chinese Journal of International Law 791, 798.

addressed by a coercive enforcement approach represented by traditional dispute settlement.

NCPs are increasingly used in a range of environmental regimes to provide an administrative or political avenue to ensure that States comply with their obligations under the relevant treaties.[141] The features of NCPs vary considerably between treaties, but share some common elements. First, a body or committee is created within the institutions of the environmental regime with responsibility for examining alleged non-compliance. States at risk of non-compliance, or which are already non-compliant with their obligations may self-refer themselves to the body or be referred by (for example) the Secretariat or other party States. In a few cases, non-compliance can be reported or referred by individuals or NGOs. A key feature of almost all NCPs is the availability of assistance to help States become compliant with their obligations. This often takes the form of financial or technical assistance, and is a major reason why it is common for States to refer themselves to the body. In a few NCPs, more coercive options may be available to the bodies, such as issuing declarations of non-compliance or suspension of privileges under the treaty.

Although no NCP has been explicitly called for in the draft texts, it seems possible that one could be established for the ILBI. Draft Article 53 in the second draft text is titled 'Implementation and Compliance'. Paragraph 3 has bracketed text that provides that 'the Conference of the Parties shall consider and adopt cooperative procedures and institutional mechanisms to promote compliance with the provisions of this Agreement and to address cases of non-compliance'. This wording is consistent with the establishment of some form of NCPs.[142]

Is an NCP appropriate for the ILBI? It seems hard to argue that it is not. The key goal of the treaty is the conservation and sustainable use of BBNJ, and hence has strong environmental aspirations. For the reasons discussed above, environmental issues are not always easily suited for traditional, bilateral, forms of disputes settlement. This is particularly acute when addressing obligations owed in relation to ABNJ, when the likelihood of a specially affected State is much lower. Leaving issues to be resolved through enforcement of *erga omnes* norms through dispute settlement processes seems to leave an obvious gap in the potential opportunities to address non-compliance with the ILBI.

141 Scott (n 64).

142 Compare art 8 of the Montreal Protocol on Substances that Deplete the Ozone Layer, which states '[t]he Parties, at their first meeting, shall consider and approve procedures and institutional mechanisms for determining non-compliance with the provisions of this Protocol and for treatment of Parties found to be in non-compliance'.

Using NCPs in the ILBI also is consistent with the focus on capacity building and the transfer of marine technology (CBTMT) in the package deal. In echoes of the arguments raised when multilateral environmental agreements (MEAS) were being negotiated, developing countries have strongly emphasized that their ability to implement their obligations under the new treaty will depend on the availability of financial and technical assistance.[143] If the ILBI does establish a capacity building mechanism, then an NCP could facilitate access to assistance for those States that may lack capacity to fully implement their obligations. It should be acknowledged that not all of the obligations in the ILBI may be appropriate for resolution by an NCP. These might for example include obligations that relate to the utilization of MGRs. Therefore, an NCP in the ILBI might exclude some articles or sections of the instrument.

However, NCPs are not as familiar in law of the sea regimes as in MEAS, despite the fact that they arguably offer a more effective means of securing State compliance.[144] Some RFMOs have established compliance committees in recent years, although the focus of such committees is often in detecting non-compliance and imposing more coercive responses, such as the listing of vessels on blacklists. There is no reference to NCP in the LOSC, which may lead some delegations to rule out the possibility altogether, even though the ILBI will have many of the hallmarks of MEAS.

It remains to be seen whether States will agree to the inclusion of a reference to an NCP in the ILBI. If not, it might be that something could develop within the institution at a later stage if the COP considers it necessary.[145]

## 5 Conclusion: Power, Justice, and Legitimacy in LOSC Dispute Settlement Processes

The inclusion of dispute settlement provisions in a treaty, and the way those provisions are used, have connections to concepts of power, legitimacy and justice. As an alternative to using coercive means (based on military, economic, or political power) to settle conflict, dispute settlement provisions promise a just outcome based on the rule of law. For less powerful States, a strong dispute settlement process allows them to engage with more powerful States on an equal

143 Rachel Tiller and others, 'The once and future treaty: Towards a new regime for biodiversity in areas beyond national jurisdiction' (2019) 99 Marine Policy 239, 240.

144 Churchill (n 5) 232.

145 For comparison, see Christina Voigt, 'The Compliance and Implementation Mechanism of the Paris Agreement' (2016) 25 RECIEL 161.

footing and lessens the importance of the power dynamic between them. For powerful States, the attractiveness of dispute settlement provisions is more nuanced. The advantages of such a process include the ability to have a clear, relatively efficient, process for resolution of tension based on competing interpretation of legal rules. The disadvantages for such States include the possibility of being constrained to submit to third-party judgments which remove the control over the outcome that might normally favour a more powerful State.

In the LOSC, the development of a robust dispute settlement process, including compulsory third-party settlement of some matters, was possible because the interests of all States converged. Powerful States, particularly the United States and the USSR, had an interest in the ability to enforce rules that were considered essential to national interests, especially those around freedom of navigation. They saw the stability of the regime as important, following decades of different and expanding claims to jurisdiction by coastal States. Highly sensitive matters, or those considered close to the sovereignty of the State, were excluded from compulsory dispute settlement processes, which provided reassurance to both powerful and less powerful States that they would retain control over the outcome of vital issues.[146] For smaller States, the ability to hold more powerful States accountable to the rules reinforced an international system based on justice and the rule of law.

For one powerful State in particular, the United States, the dispute settlement provisions have been part of the argument used by those who oppose ratification of the LOSC. The concern for these opponents has been the idea that the United States would be compelled to submit to binding dispute settlement 'whenever another member State brings a lawsuit against it'.[147] Proponents of the ratification argue that the option to exclude military activities from the scope of compulsory dispute settlement makes the dispute settlement process acceptable.[148]

146 This is consistent with Morgenthau's observation that dispute settlement will be unsuccessful if it relates to sensitive issues for States. Morgenthau (n 7) 422.

147 Steven Groves, 'Accession to the UN Convention on the Law of the Sea Would Expose the US to Baseless Climate Change Lawsuits' (2012) 2660 Backgrounder. See also John Bolton and Dan Blumenthal, 'Time to Kill the Law of the Sea Treaty – Again' *Wall Street Journal* (29 September 2011) A15. This scepticism is not limited to the US. China has also attempted to minimise the possibility of appearing in Part XV procedures through claiming all exceptions. In general, China has expressed a strong preference to avoid third-party dispute settlement in favour of bilateral resolution of disputes.

148 For example, the exclusion of military activities from the scope of compulsory dispute settlement was a key requirement of the United States. See John F Turner, 'Accession to the 1982 Law of the Sea Convention and Ratification of the 1994 Agreement Amending Part XI of the Law of the Sea Convention' *Testimony before the Senate Environment and*

The use of the dispute settlement provisions under the LOSC has also been impacted by power dynamics. The refusal by China and Russia, two powerful States, to submit to arbitrations brought under Annex VII is a good example. It seems that the underlying reason for refusing to appear in most cases appears to be based on political rather than legal factors.[149] These include concerns about losing on the merits and wishing to signal an intention not to comply with the ultimate decision.[150]

One suggestion for the prominence of powerful States among those that do not appear in cases brought against them is that permanent members of the Security Council have some protection against non-compliance with ICJ decisions being taken up by that body.[151] Another possibility is that powerful States feel that the negative diplomatic consequences of non-appearance can be mitigated by their economic and military clout.

Another feature of China's refusal to appear in the *South China Sea* arbitration is its unprecedented attack on the legitimacy of the tribunal.[152] Chinese scholars are now emphasizing the importance of consent in international dispute settlement, arguing that 'the original consent of States Parties when they joined the treaty has often been violated by means of "evolutionary interpretation" '.[153] This is consistent with a view that China is acting consistently with international law only to the extent that it suits its national interest.[154] In the long term, this behaviour could cast doubt on the legitimacy of the dispute settlement process and the rules contained in the LOSC.

Despite these examples of non-appearance, the use of compulsory dispute settlement for many issues arising under the LOSC has underpinned a reasonably orderly approach to the interpretation of the Convention. Although power has played a role in individual disputes to some extent, the overall effect

---

*Public Works Committee* (23 March 2004) available at <https://2001-2009.state.gov/g/oes/rls/rm/2004/30723.htm> accessed 12 May 2021.

149 Bernard H Oxman, 'Nonparticipation and Perceptions of Legitimacy' (2019) 37 Berkeley Journal of International Law 235.

150 Stanimir A Alexandrov, 'Non-Appearance before the International Court of Justice' (1995) 33 Columbia Journal of Transnational Law 41, 64.

151 ibid 70.

152 Jiangyu Wang, 'Legitimacy, Jurisdiction and Merits in the South China Sea Arbitration: Chinese Perspectives and International Law' (2017) 22 Journal of Chinese Political Science 185, 193. Oxman (n 149) 24, considers one goal of non-appearance in cases may be to undermine the legitimacy of the proceedings.

153 Shi (n 97) 5.

154 Muthucumaraswamy Sornarajah and Jiangyu Wang, 'China, India, and International Law: A Justice Based Vision Between the Romantic and Realist Perceptions' (2019) 9 Asian Journal of International Law 217, 222.

of Part XV has been to support the stability of the LOSC. The decisions of courts and tribunals under Part XV have mostly been accepted by the participants. We are also seeing an emerging body of jurisprudence on the interpretation of the LOSC.

What does this mean for dispute settlement in the ILBI? In the preceding sections, a number of possible options for elaborating a dispute settlement process for the specific needs of the ILBI have been discussed. I have identified a number of obstacles in using traditional bilateral dispute settlement processes to resolve disputes that primarily impact on ABNJ or violate collective norms. The nature of the ILBI and its obligations may increase the focus on other approaches that could be included to increase the 'justice' available in cases where bilateral disputes are infeasible or impractical. Such approaches are common elsewhere and include the option of a COP requesting an advisory opinion or the establishment of NCPs.

The Seabed Advisory Opinion noted that obligations relating to the protection of the environment and the Area are *erga omnes* in nature. In part, this reflects the CHM that applies to the Area, but also the fact that the high seas are subject to no sovereignty claims. It is the interest of all of the international community that States observe their legal obligations, not only to each other, but in respect of the common good. Traditional dispute settlement has provided a route for justice in bilateral disputes, but has been less successful in relation to enforcing common interests. It is to be hoped that the ILBI will contain other mechanisms to encourage compliance by all States.

CHAPTER 14

# The Legal Regime of Areas beyond National Jurisdiction Viewed through the Lenses of Power, Knowledge, Justice and Space

*Lan Ngoc Nguyen, Alex Oude Elferink and Vito De Lucia*

## 1 Introduction

When we embarked on the journey that eventually brought us to this concluding chapter, we as editors had some general idea about what might be expected in terms of outcomes in relation to the four themes of the project that we had selected, ie power, knowledge, justice and space.[1] Having read and commented upon all of the chapters of our contributors on various occasions, we are fully convinced that this was a journey worth undertaking. All contributors, through the analysis of their individual topics, offer their own perspective on the themes. In doing so, the individual chapters both display commonalities and variations. In this concluding chapter we cannot possibly do justice to the rich harvest that our contributors have to offer, nor do we need to do that. The chapters are there to be read. What we do want to do in this concluding chapter is look at the broader picture. What are these main commonalities and variations in relation to the themes that we identified? Apart from revisiting the four themes, the current chapter also intends to reflect on a number of other issues that we consider deserve separate mention in the concluding chapter of a book dealing with the legal regime of areas beyond national jurisdiction (ABNJ). These issues are linked to the four themes of the book, but by also considering them separately we will be able to add more focus and detail. As a consequence, the remainder of this chapter is set up as follows. Section 2 revisits the themes of power, knowledge, justice and space. The themes are first discussed separately, while the final subsection looks at their interlinkages. The chapter finishes with two other issues that come up throughout the chapters of this volume. Section 3 looks at the relationship between ABNJ and areas within national jurisdiction (AWNJ), while section 4 considers the future

1 On the selection of these themes see Introduction, this volume, and especially section 4 therein.

 | DOI:10.1163/9789004506367_015

development of the regime for ABNJ, including the question what role a future agreement for the conservation and sustainable use of marine biodiversity in areas beyond national jurisdiction (BBNJ Agreement) might play in this respect.[2]

## 2 Revisiting the Themes of Power, Knowledge, Justice and Space

### 2.1 *Power*

As a social construct that is shaped by human action, law reflects in many and variable ways the distribution of power and interests in society. As was set out in the introductory chapter to this volume, we asked our contributors to reflect on the way power is distributed and how it affects decision-making in relation to ABNJ, and to consider how the distribution of rights and obligations, jurisdiction over ocean areas as well as activities, and participation in the relevant legal and governance processes play out in ABNJ. Individual chapters discuss how power operates during the negotiation of rules and after they have become the operational framework for ocean governance, as well as more broadly how power may determine the particular ways in which oceans are conceived, mapped, delineated, regulated and governed. The exercise of power is however often tempered by other considerations, such as ethical aspirations, political compromise or material limits. For example, the need to reach a broadly acceptable regime often requires addressing equity and fairness to a larger extent than powerful States might otherwise be willing to accept, while the need to reach a legitimate regime may lead to more inclusive decision-making procedures.[3] Yet power relations and the balance between conflicting interests remain ultimately contingent on political compromise. Material and ecological limits are not always taken sufficiently into consideration precisely in light of the politics of international law making.

2 There are two draft texts to date: Draft text of an agreement under the United Nations Convention on the Law of the Sea on the conservation and sustainable use of marine biological diversity of areas beyond national jurisdiction (17 May 2019) (UN Doc A/CONF.232/2019/6) (Draft Agreement) available at <https://digitallibrary.un.org/record/3811328?ln=en> accessed 27 July 2021; Revised draft text of an agreement under the United Nations Convention on the Law of the Sea on the conservation and sustainable use of marine biological diversity of areas beyond national jurisdiction (17 November 2019) (UN Doc A/CONF.232/2020/3) (Revised Draft Agreement) available at <https://undocs.org/en/a/conf.232/2020/3> accessed 27 July 2021.

3 On the issues of fairness and legitimacy in international law and decision making see eg, Thomas M Franck *Fairness in International Law and Institutions* (Clarendon Press 1995).

Once in existence, rules, while reflecting an existing power structure, may also be used by less powerful States as an additional tool to advance their interest.[4] As the discussion in various chapters demonstrates, the development of (principles of) environmental law and a greater awareness of the environmental degradation threatening ABNJ have been central contributing factors towards the initiation of the BBNJ process, which is seeking to curb the power of individual States to unilaterally exploit the ocean. At the same time, the slow pace of the BBNJ process and in particular the strong opposition to bring fisheries under the remit of the BBNJ Agreement, as discussed by Barnes in chapter 10, illustrate that the power of States with major maritime interests remains a key driver for developing, or stalling the development, of the regime for ABNJ.

De Lucia in chapter 2 explores the entangled relation between law, power and space and how (sovereign) power underpins a particular spatio-legal imagination that is crucial for the construction of ocean space, and for the delineation of ocean commons more particularly. The lasting impact of power on ocean law is detailed by Henriksen in chapter 4 of this volume. Mapping the debates that have emerged in the law of the sea, he shows that the power play has always had a clear bearing on the development of the law of the sea, specifically with regards to the regime for ABNJ. In particular, major maritime States strived to maintain the freedoms of the high seas for centuries, because they provided them with ample access to space and resources. The entry into the world community of new and mostly developing States who were proponents of community interests – or on a more cynical note, one might say, who used community interests and equity language to promote their own interests – provided the required support for the development of the common heritage of mankind (CHM) regime abrogating the regime of freedom of the high seas in relation to mineral resources. Nguyen in chapter 5 further observes that power continues to play a prominent role in the current negotiations on the BBNJ Agreement. As is detailed in various chapters, the interests of individual States or groups of States in using (the resources of) ABNJ continue to be the dominating driving force behind the discussions. As Nguyen further argues, the rift between, once again, developed and developing States regarding the principle to be applied in ABNJ, particularly with regards to marine genetic resources (MGRS), casts doubts over whether the BBNJ Agreement will eventually pursue

4 See further Shirley V Scott, 'International Law as Ideology: Theorizing the Relationship between International Law and International Politics' 1994 (5) European Journal of International Law 313.

the goal that it was set out to achieve, i.e., the conservation and sustainable use of BBNJ.

Chapter 13 by Mossop illustrates the above-mentioned nuanced impact of power in the operation of legal regimes. The chapter discusses the impact of power dynamics both on the inclusion of a compulsory dispute settlement system in the United Nations Convention on the Law of the Sea (LOSC)[5] and on individual disputes. Mossop argues that the development of a robust dispute settlement process was possible because the interests of all States converged to a large enough extent. The set-up of Part XV means that less powerful States can engage with more powerful States on an equal footing and be able to hold them accountable to the rules reinforced by an international system based on justice and the rule of law. At the same time, more powerful States are assured that there is a clear, relatively efficient, process for resolution of tensions. The fact that highly sensitive disputes were excluded from compulsory jurisdiction provided reassurance to both powerful and less powerful States that they would retain control over the outcome of vital issues.

In chapter 7, Oude Elferink and Kerr through a study of the relationship between the United Nations General Assembly (UNGA), the LOSC and the Convention on Biological Diversity (CBD),[6] illustrate the power of international institutions and their interactions on the framing of legal issues and the development of the legal regime for ABNJ. The central role that the UNGA has played in the BBNJ process resulted in a stronger focus on LOSC than the CBD, resulting in the development of the BBNJ Agreement under LOSC, and not the CBD. The appeal of the UNGA for elaborating the regime of BBNJ lies in its central role in international policy making in relation to oceans and law of the sea. At the same time, the relevance of the CBD and international environmental law more generally for the BBNJ Agreement, can be seen in the institutional arrangements of the Agreement, which are more akin to a multilateral environmental agreement than the LOSC. In chapter 8 Oude Elferink engages with the theme of power from the angle of decision-making power under LOSC in respect of MPAS and ABMTS. As he observes, the LOSC provides sectoral bodies with the competence to adopt ABMTS in relation to the specific activities they are competent to regulate, but it does not create a similar competence to identify, designate and manage marine protected areas (MPAS). In that sense, the division of decision-making power under the LOSC made the development

5 United Nations Convention on the Law of the Sea (opened for signature 10 December 1982, entered into force 16 November 1994) 1833 UNTS 3 (LOSC).

6 Convention on Biological Diversity (signed 5 June 1992, entered in force 29 December 1993) 1760 UNTS 79 (CBD).

of a comprehensive approach to the protection and the preservation of the marine environment in particular in ABNJ problematic.[7] Whether a future BBNJ Agreement will be successful in addressing the absence of a competence to holistically manage MPAs remains to be seen, but the requirement of consistency with the LOSC and the apparent deferral to existing bodies and instruments through the 'not-undermining' requirement does not bode well and may well further cement the existing power imbalance between user interests and non-user interests. That same imbalance is also teased out in other chapters of this volume. For instance, Barnes in chapter 10, after discussing Ranganathan's analysis of how the regime for the Area, focusing on mining interests, has muted other voices, discusses how a future BBNJ Agreement may or may not create similar imbalances. Poto in discussing decision-making power, in chapter 6 calls for a rebalancing of the division of power between decision-makers, arguing that procedural rights for nature and the rights of nature should be acknowledged and enshrined in a future BBNJ Agreement. She argues in particular that such a recognition should result in an alternative approach to Part IV of the current Revised Draft Agreement on environmental impact assessments (EIAS), which gives States the last word on the final decision, and thus the power to accept or dismiss the opinion of non-State actors on the environmental impacts of the activity under review. In a sense, chapter 6 draws attention to giving or returning power to the ocean, for it to be heard, to be represented and not merely be used as an object under the hands of humans.

### 2.2 *Knowledge*

Under the theme of knowledge, we invited our contributors to reflect upon the role knowledge in its various dimensions, eg, as expressed in the political epistemology embedded in law of the sea, marine scientific research and the right to science, the role that knowledge, or the lack thereof, plays in the construction of legal principles and regimes. As the preceding analysis indicates, the production of and access to knowledge or absence thereof has been critical to shaping the legal regime of ABNJ and its implementation. Knowledge about the mineral resources of the deep seabed provided an important impetus for the negotiations of what eventually became Part XI of the LOSC. The absence of knowledge about life in the deep sea, and its potential economic

7 This is less of an issue in AWNJ, because the coastal State has regulatory competence in relation to most activities and may unilaterally establish MPAs that allow regulating all of the activities concerned. At the same time, the division of competences between government agencies may lead to similar issues of coordination as those existing at the international level.

value, resulted in the LOSC not making any specific reference to the regime for the exploration and exploitation of those resources. Knowledge about these resources that became increasingly available in the 1990s led to the inclusion of the topic of access and benefit sharing of MGRs in the BBNJ process package. Knowledge will be essential to the implementation of all elements of that package as a part of a future BBNJ Agreement.

Knowledge as a tool for organizing our world view and assigning meaning has had a fundamental impact on our legal ordering of the ocean. As detailed by Henriksen in chapter 4, the conception of the ocean as a boundless space beyond the control of sovereign States provided an underpinning for the regime of freedom of the high seas as initially advocated by Grotius. As argued by De Lucia in chapter 2, the subsequent extension of coastal State jurisdiction through processes of territorialization, which found its culmination in the LOSC, and still casts a long shadow on the BBNJ negotiations, prevented a meaningful engagement with the materiality of the ocean. This approach, as he points out, is based on a western tradition of international law for ordering individual polities through territorial boundaries and sovereign legality. As a counterpoint to this position, Poto in chapter 6, discusses the key role played by indigenous knowledge in realizing ocean-centrism and ocean protection and using that knowledge as a building block for ocean-centered governance. To that end, the chapter proposes, among others, integrating a specific reference to the rights of nature and to the rights of the ocean in particular, tying rights of nature to duties and obligations of States and communities to protect and restore the marine environment. In addition, it is suggested that there is a need of revisiting the adoption of certain terms that reflect Western ideological hegemony of the human domination over nature.

Bankes in chapter 3 demonstrates, through the application of Hohfeld's idea of fundamental legal concepts to the LOSC and the current Revised Draft Agreement, how legal science may offer a clearer understanding and constructing legal relationships. The chapter views the LOSC as a power-conferring instrument, but considers that it uses terms that are not precise enough to convey the different types of relationships between different actors and observes that the Revised Draft Agreement is built upon this imprecision. Bankes calls attention to the need to use more precise language to avoid future controversy about the implications of treaty language. Similar lessons may be drawn from chapter 10, in which Barnes submits the legal regime of ABNJ to a constructivist analysis. As he argues:

> international law plays a critical role in constructing ocean space, but that an insensitive use of international law can limit the possibilities for

> the more effective governance of oceans space and limit the opportunities for certain interests to feed into debates and decisions about how to regulate activities in ABNJ.

A third example of the relevance of producing knowledge about possible formats for governance of ABNJ is offered by Dalaker's use of Ostrom's model of polycentric governance to investigate the role of regional environmental management regimes in chapter 12.

Several chapters acknowledge that the ever-changing nature of knowledge and increased knowledge provide the impetus for the development of the legal regime for ABNJ. For example, Ringbom in chapter 11 argues that future measures that may be taken by non-flag States to protect BBNJ will be mainly in the domain of ex-post enforcement measures, which may be made possible and develop due to technological advances leading to the availability of information to a broader circle of actors than previous was the case. Oude Elferink and Kerr for their part in chapter 7 detail that increased knowledge about resources in the Area, as well as ecologically or biologically significant areas (EBSAS), for example, helped garner support for the creation of a specific regime for ABNJ. Similarly, Henriksen in chapter 4 argues that increased understanding of the existence and the condition of the resources in ABNJ, such as of ocean biodiversity and ecosystems, and new knowledge concerning MGRS and their potential, drove the negotiations on and underlie the stalemate on the regime to exploit these resources. The question as to who is or should be the holder of knowledge is thus important in the governance of ABNJ. Chapter 8 by Oude Elferink indicates that knowledge is central to the identification, establishment and management of MPAS and areas-based management tools (ABMTS). Again, this makes it critical to establish what extensive a knowledge base is required, who holds that knowledge and/or is responsible for gathering it, and how it will be disseminated.

Morgera's chapter 9, linking the current development of the regime for BBNJ to human rights law and specifically the right to science, urgently illustrates the importance of an integrated approach to the production and sharing of knowledge. Framing ocean science and knowledge as a human rights issue, and not exclusively as a law of the sea issue, leads to a fundamentally different understanding of how the relevant legal framework for the sustainable use and conservation of BBNJ might and should be structured. It may be noted that there is a parallel with the interaction between the law of the sea and environmental law. For instance, as a number of chapters argue, the institutional architecture of that Agreement should not emulate that of the LOSC, but rather should take shape by borrowing from the knowledge base relating to the institutional architecture of multilateral environmental agreements.

As Morgera reiterates, deep-sea knowledge allows for enhanced understanding of the need for, and effectiveness of, conservation and sustainable use in ABNJ. However, in practice, there is only a restricted number of countries that can afford the costs and risks of deep-sea research vessels and therefore can control who has access to that source of knowledge. This situation is particularly detrimental for the ongoing BBNJ process. Morgera argues that all the topics under negotiation are underpinned by science and science plays a crucial role to support the assessments of cumulative and transboundary impacts on marine biodiversity, which makes the creation of broad access to knowledge a much-needed innovation of a future BBNJ Agreement.

### 2.3 *Justice*

The theme of justice for this project was specifically operationalized in terms of access to and utilization of marine resources, both in relation to the intra- and the intergenerational dimensions of justice. Framed in this way, this theme pervades the entire history of the law of the sea. Attributing access rights to specific actors implicitly denies those rights to others. This is done by the operation of specific rules of law, such as the attribution of sovereign rights over the resources of the exclusive economic zone to individual coastal States—to the exclusion of the international community, or is the result of how specific rules work out in practice. The freedoms of the high seas benefit those that have the capabilities to effectively make use of them, calling into question intragenerational equity. More recently, the law of the sea has come to grapple with the need to balance use of the ocean with its preservation, bringing the intergenerational dimension of justice to the fore.

The intra- and intergenerational dimensions of justice are considered in a number of chapters. In chapter 5, Nguyen argues that while high seas freedoms and CHM may be converging, justice – or the lack thereof – remains the core difference between the two principles. The need for equitable access to resources is not a major concern in the distribution of fisheries in the high seas, whereas the collective interests that CHM purports to protect are much more grounded in considerations of justice, manifested in the involvement of developing States in the administration of mining activities, equitable sharing of benefits amongst stakeholders, and the protection, conservation, and preservation of marine biological diversity for the interests of future generations. In relation to the BBNJ process, Nguyen submits that the current Revised Draft Agreement focusses to a much greater extent on intragenerational equity. The focus on benefit-sharing mechanisms, without incorporating the broader implications of CHM, moreover, moves the discussion back to interests of individual States.

Aspects of inter- and intragenerational equity are also discussed in chapters 7 and 8. Remarking on the relationship between the LOSC and the CBD, Oude Elferink and Kerr in chapter 7 argue that the two conventions are aligned as regards inter- and intra-generational and environmental justice by incorporating these concepts through the subsequent development of general international law. That obviously does not exclude the possibility that both conventions in their implementation of specific rights and obligations will yield different outcomes on these parameters. In this connection, it may be noted that the authors argue that the CBD represents a broader vision of ocean justice, implying a recognition that the freedom of the high seas needs to be regulated in line with this objective. In chapter 8 Oude Elferink addresses the need to safeguard and rebuild a heathy ocean for future generations through ABMTs and MPAs. In light of tensions between the future sustainability of the ocean and actual user interests, the chapter calls for a meaningful voice to be given to future generations, while also admitting that this is a difficult task, given the current power structure of international law. In addition to giving a voice to future generations, Poto in chapter 6 argues that in order to operationalize justice meaningfully, it would be important to give representation to nature in the form of participatory rights for nature, both in decision-making and in access to justice system on behalf of nature.

Morgera in chapter 9 deals head on with the theme of justice. After discussing the vital role that knowledge of the deep sea plays in the conservation of ABNJ, Morgera points out the existence of an equity gap in deep-sea knowledge production, which disproportionately affects the opportunities of countries in the Global South to influence the further development of the law of the sea. Against that background, Morgera proposes recourse to the notion of fair and equitable benefit-sharing as part of the ecosystem approach in order to address equity concerns in the production of ocean science. She argues that the twin expression 'fair and equitable' makes explicit both procedural dimensions of justice (fairness) that determine the legitimacy of certain courses of action, as well as substantive dimensions of justice (equity). The notion of fair and equitable benefit-sharing is reflected through the lens of the human right to science, which focuses on the agency for developing countries, as well as indigenous and local knowledge holders and seeks to co-identify more equitable modalities for international scientific cooperation for the protection and full realization of other human rights with an emphasis on the vulnerable.

In chapter 13, Mossop considers how compulsory dispute settlement mechanisms and reporting and compliance mechanism may contribute to delivering justice. Due to its (mostly) bilateral nature, compulsory dispute settlement is able to render justice in the individual case, but is less suitable for addressing issues of justice in a multilateral setting, including the protection of common interests. As, however, also is clear from Mossop's argument, bilateral dispute settlement under the LOSC in a number of instances has clarified the law in relation to the protection and preservation of the marine environment in a way that is conducive to contributing to furthering intra- and intergenerational justice. She further argues that approaches other than traditional dispute settlement could be included to increase the 'justice' available in cases where bilateral disputes are infeasible or impractical. Options that could be entertained are allowing a BBNJ Agreement Conference of the Parties (COP) requesting an advisory opinion or the establishment of NCPs. The experience with advisory opinions in the framework of the LOSC suggests that these might play a similar role under a future BBNJ Agreement. Depending on how they will be set up, reporting and compliance mechanisms may also have an important role to play in that respect.

### 2.4 *Space*[8]

ABNJ refers to a four-dimensional space that exists in physical reality. At the same time, ABNJ is a legal construct that poorly reflects that reality. Under current international law, ABNJ constitute those parts of the ocean that are not enclosed within the limits of national jurisdiction. The implications of that spatial fragmentation of the ocean are discussed in various chapters of this volume and will be further considered in section 3 below. Time, the fourth dimension of ocean space, also confronts the law, with its shortcomings. As was pointed out in the preceding section, the current law remains poorly equipped for dealing in a satisfactory manner with balancing current use with long-term sustainability.

Turning more specifically to ABNJ, they consist of commons areas underpinned by the concept of *res communis*. However, the legal regimes that regulate these commons areas differ, namely freedom of the high seas and CHM. These principles illustrate a different balance between individual freedom and collective interests that are struck in the high seas and the Area. However, as argued by Nguyen in chapter 5, the challenges posed to these two principles by the development of the law of the sea over the past decades have resulted in a narrowing gap between high seas freedom and CHM, and requires a shift in the regulatory approach which moves away from individual freedom to

8 The theme of space is also (implicitly) revisited in section 3 below.

ensuring collective interests. In addition to the law of the sea, as argued by Oude Elferink and Kerr in chapter 7, developments in international environmental law, particularly the CBD's emphasis on community interests further downplay the role of individual high seas freedoms, leading to a tendency to unify ocean space beyond national jurisdiction.

It is submitted that the larger emphasis on community interests would justify a new approach to ocean governance in ABNJ. Several chapters engage with this question from different perspectives. In chapter 11, Ringbom challenges the understanding that ABNJ is a space largely reserved for exclusive flag State jurisdiction, and discusses different legal bases for the exercise of non-flag State jurisdiction in ABNJ. Ringbom further argues that a future BBNJ Agreement would offer the opportunity to strengthen and clarify the role of non-flag States in order to ensure that ABNJ represent a shared concern, which currently is not protected sufficiently by international law. To what extent a future BBNJ Agreement will address this issue remains to be seen, and the likelihood exists that clarification and development of the law will mainly take place through State practice and the jurisprudence.

From a broader perspective, Dalaker in chapter 12 sees ABNJ as a space for testing a polycentric approach to governance, particularly Ostrom's theory of polycentric governance to help determine the optimal distribution of power and knowledge across levels of governance. As she argues, ABNJ are a space in which a patchwork of global, sectoral and regional agreements exists in a fragmented manner, both substantively and spatially. Thus, a polycentric governance model could be used for ensuring the long-term health and sustainable use of these areas. Also calling for a more inclusive model of governance, Poto in chapter 6 advocates for 'ocean-centered governance' which places the oceans in the center to replace the current State-centered system with its emphasis on the sovereign rights of States. The chapter develops ocean-centered governance within a participatory-constructed frame which recognizes the ocean as an inseparable part of life on Earth, a natural space that in itself needs to be respected for its intrinsic value, and not regarded merely as a host for resources that may be exploited for human consumption. Echoing the call to move from State-centric or sectoral approaches, Barnes in chapter 10 argues that the law has an important role to play in structuring social interactions in ABNJ. However, at the same time, law risks marginalizing certain interests and tends to ignore the material space of the ocean, ie, by ignoring the physical values of the ocean. Barnes sees a future BBNJ Agreement as a chance to newly define the frame for social interactions for ABNJ and to that end, calls for that Agreement to connect the law with the material condition of ocean space and for inclusive processes for governing ANBJ. At the same time, he cautions that a future BBNJ Agreement stands the risk of maintaining or further exacerbating the structural shortcomings of the ABNJ regime that is 'not structured in a way that drives a holistic, integrated construction of social space in ABNJ'.

Finally, space is the central dimension of chapter 2. Bringing together law, power and space, De Lucia discusses how international law is underpinned by a 'cartographic' understanding of space, which 'as a science of map-making and as a technology of power' has been crucial for how ocean spaces, and ocean commons, are understood and constructed by sovereign legality. A 'cartographic understanding of ocean commons', De Lucia suggests, 'reflects and refracts a fundamental spatio-legal ordering' that 'proceeds' from territorial thinking. 'Law of the sea', De Lucia continues,

> is permeated by such territorial thinking, and indeed has developed through increasing incursions and projections of territorial sovereignty into oceanic spaces. Thus, sovereignty has been all along the arbiter of the commons, it has been the crucial lens for deciding what the commons are (spaces outside of sovereignty) and where they are (beyond the limits of sovereign space).

Sovereign legality, observes De Lucia, 'has in other words *always* negatively defined the commons through its absence'. De Lucia however aims at problematizing such cartographic spatiality and sovereign legality, and at opening a 'conversation on other ways to think about ocean commons'.

### 2.5 *Interactions between Power, Knowledge, Justice and Space*

As the preceding discussion already should have made abundantly clear, the themes of power, knowledge, justice and space interact with each other in various ways. Without exhaustively unearthing these interactions, we briefly want to provide our readership with some pointers to assist them in reflecting upon the aspect of the individual chapters of this volume. Knowledge may empower the powerless, but may also be monopolized by knowledge holders to further cement existing power disparities. The legal ordering of the oceans is a social construct, whose specific spatial layering has been developed through interactions between power, knowledge and justice. As various chapters indicate, justice oftentimes is subordinated to considerations of power. This reflects one of the basic tensions of current international law. To make the law inclusive and universally applicable, a balance will have to be struck between accommodating the powerful and empowering the weak. As Henriksen argues in chapter 2, the law of the sea in general has opted for what he terms as a 'pragmatic' approach.

In the case of the LOSC, this led to far-reaching amendments to the regime for mining in Part XI through the 1994 Implementation Agreement to ensure universal participation in the Convention, including from the industrialized West.[9] Delegations at the intergovernmental conference (IGC) negotiating the future BBNJ Agreement eventually likely may have to face a similar choice between universal participation, including that of the powerful, and environmental and intra- and intergenerational justice.[10] De Lucia however draws out a general tendency towards the sovereign territorialization of the oceans and that such a tendency, while incomplete and subject to the contingencies of history, still remains operational in relation to how ocean space, including ocean commons, is legally ordered. Other examples of the interactions between the different themes are provided by Morgera's discussion of the linkages between knowledge and equity and Mossop's conclusion that the dispute settlement system of the LOSC promotes justice and 'lessens the power dynamic' between the parties to a dispute, although that promotion of justice at the same time is bound by the four corners of the law.

A recurring theme throughout this volume is the opposition between those involved in activities and those who are not. This is variously expressed as involving user States and non-user States or the interest of individual States engaged in activities in ABNJ and the community interest in preserving the sustainability of the ocean. All four themes are engaged in this dynamic. User states through their activities will have interests that are represented by a power-base in their government delegations during the BBNJ process and other intergovernmental governance structures more generally, while community interests may be much more diffuse. Knowledge about impacts of activities on the environment may also be unevenly spread between those engaged in activities and others. As various chapters argue, the spatial governance of the oceans is influenced by a push for allowing the continuation of existing activities or allowing the development of new activities. And although there may

9 Agreement relating to the implementation of Part XI of the United Nations Convention on the Law of the Sea of 10 December 1982 (signed 18 July 1994, entered in force 16 November 1994) 1836 UNTS 3 (1994 Implementation Agreement). It may of course be asked whether the developing States had a viable alternative to agreeing on a watering down of the common heritage regime through the 1994 Implementation Agreement. For a reflection of this question and an alternative history of the law of the sea and the LOSC see Alex G Oude Elferink, 'What if the United Nations Convention on the Law of the Sea had entered into force unamended; Business as usual or dystopia?' in Ingo Venzke and Kevin Jon Heller (eds), *Contingency in international law; On the possibility of different legal histories* (Oxford University Press 2021) 215–30.

10 See further section 4 below.

be a strong moral ring to ensuring intra- and intergenerational equity, their realization in the law of the sea has been proven to be difficult to the extent they are not aligned with current individual interests.

## 3 ABNJ and AWNJ

From a legal perspective, the regimes of ABNJ and AWNJ represent a fundamental divide.[11] That divide has obvious consequences for ocean governance and the future development of the law of the sea. As the introductory chapter to this volume observed:

> a future [BBNJ Agreement] will consolidate the existing division of the oceans in areas within and beyond national jurisdiction. The current negotiations on that agreement demonstrate the tenacity with which coastal States defend their interests in relation to their maritime zones. This remains a major obstacle against achieving an integrated ecosystem-based approach to ocean governance.

What does the current Revised Draft Agreement actually have to say about its scope of application and the relationship of ABNJ and AWNJ? Its Article 3(1) is straightforward, providing that '[t]his Agreement applies to areas beyond national jurisdiction'.[12] It may be noted that the Revised Draft Agreement in this respect differs from the Fish Stocks Agreement (UNFSA), which, although generally applicable to 'the conservation and management of straddling fish stocks and highly migratory fish stocks beyond national jurisdiction', provides that Articles 6 and 7 on the precautionary approach and compatibility of conservation measures within and beyond national jurisdiction are also

---

11 But see De Lucia (ch 2) in this volume, for a discussion of how both 'types' of ocean space remain subject to the same logic.

12 Art 1(4) of the Revised Draft Agreement indicates that the term '"Areas beyond national jurisdiction" means the high seas and the Area'. It may be noted that this definition implies a definitional inconsistency that is carried over from the LOSC. As art 1(1)(1) of the LOSC indicates, the Area comprises the seabed and subsoil 'beyond the limits of national jurisdiction', ie, the outer limits of the continental shelf at and beyond 200 nautical miles established in accordance with art 76 of the Convention. At the same time, Part VII of the LOSC on the regime of the high seas indicates that it is applicable to the part of the continental shelf beyond 200 nautical miles, as art 86 provides that its provisions 'apply to all parts of the sea that are not included in the exclusive economic zone, in the territorial sea or in the internal waters of a State, or in the archipelagic waters of an archipelagic State'.

applicable to 'the conservation and management of such stocks within areas under national jurisdiction', while coastal States are also required to apply the general principles contained in Article 5 of the UNFSA, *mutatis mutandis*.[13] It may be noted that the Revised Draft Agreement in its Article 5 contains a list of general principles that in general are no less relevant to AWNJ than the general principles contained in Article 5 of the UNFSA.

A comparison of the Revised Draft Agreement with the UNFSA is also not without interest as regards their relationship clauses. The UNFSA has a one-paragraph article—Article 4—on its relationship with the LOSC, providing that 'nothing in this Agreement shall prejudice the rights, jurisdiction and duties of States under the Convention. This Agreement shall be interpreted and applied in the context of and in a manner consistent with the Convention'. That relationship clause is repeated *verbatim* in Article 4(1) of the Revised Draft Agreement. However, the Revised Draft Agreement in its relationship clauses further provides that 'the rights and jurisdiction of coastal States in all areas under national jurisdiction, including the continental shelf within and beyond 200 nautical miles and the exclusive economic zone, shall be respected in accordance with the Convention'.[14] This paragraph is followed by two further relationship clauses, one of those being the so-called not undermine provision, which currently reads 'this Agreement shall be interpreted and applied in a manner that [respects the competences of and] does not undermine relevant legal instruments and frameworks and relevant global, regional, subregional and sectoral bodies'.[15] As is argued in a number of chapters, this provision may limit the potential of a future BBNJ Agreement for accomplishing a holistic approach to ocean governance. A comprehensive comparison of the relationship clauses of the Revised Draft Agreement and the UNFSA is beyond the scope of the present chapter,[16] but the Revised Draft Agreement seemingly is

---

13 United Nations Agreement for the Implementation of the Provisions of the United Nations Convention on the Law of the Sea of 10 December 1982 relating to the Conservation and Management of Straddling Fish Stocks and Highly Migratory Fish Stocks (opened for signature 4 August 1995, entered into force 11 December 2001) 2167 UNTS 3 (UNFSA) arts 3(1) and 3(2).

14 Revised Draft Agreement art 4(2).

15 ibid art 4(3).

16 For one thing, the setting of the negotiations of the two agreements is different. While in the case of the UNFSA the main goal was to develop a regime for transboundary resources, that is not the case for the BBNJ Agreement, with its focus on ABNJ. Or, as formulated by Henriksen in ch 4: 'In the BBNJ process, as the primary focus is on the ABNJ, the emphasis is on preventing negative effects of measures taken in the ABNJ on the rights and jurisdiction of adjacent coastal States'.

a step back as regards the conservation of and sustainable use of the ocean across jurisdictional boundaries.

Another issue concerning the relationship between ABNJ and AWNJ is future regulatory density. It might be seen as somewhat of an irony that the BBNJ process, which was initiated to address the governance gaps in the regime for ABNJ, likely is going to result in a situation where the obligations of States in relation to ABNJ are spelled out in more detail than for AWNJ, at least at the level of general law of the sea instruments.[17] For instance, while a future BBNJ Agreement will contain detailed provisions on ABMTs and MPAs, the LOSC hardly makes reference to these tools – neither for ABNJ nor for AWNJ. A similar observation applies to the EIAs regime of the Agreement as compared to the LOSC's assessment and monitoring requirements contained in its Part XII, section 4. At the same time, the picture may not be as bleak as it appears at first instance.[18] Take, for instance, the relationship clause contained in Article 4(2) of the Revised Draft Agreement on respect for the rights and jurisdiction of coastal States. As Article 4(2) indicates, such rights and jurisdiction 'shall be respected *in accordance with the Convention*'.[19] This implies that a coastal State in exercising its rights and jurisdiction also has to act in accordance with its obligations on the protection and preservation of the marine environment, including the duty to cooperate as defined in Article 197 of the LOSC. In relation to the not-undermine provision, it should be noted that its implications remain undefined in the Agreement and it is open to different interpretations, thus how it will play out in practice remains to be seen. Furthermore, if a future BBNJ Agreement were to live up to the promise of being a reflection of the state of the art as regards environmental protection, it has to potential to have a spill-over effect to AWNJ for various reasons. Practice under a future BBNJ Agreement may for instance be relevant to interpreting general principles of environmental law that not only are applicable to ABNJ, but also to AWNJ. In addition, it is to be expected that regional conventions on the protection and the preservation of the marine environment, most of which are currently only applicable to AWNJ, will extend their spatial scope of application to ABNJ.

17 See also Erik Molenaar, 'Multilateral Creeping Coastal State Jurisdiction and the BBNJ Negotiations' (2021) (36) International Journal of Marine and Coastal Law 5, 54–55; Tullio Treves, 'Principles and Objectives of the Legal Regime Governing Areas Beyond National Jurisdiction' in Erik J Molenaar and Alex G Oude Elferink (eds), *The International Legal Regime of Areas beyond National Jurisdiction: Current and Future Developments* (Martinus Nijhoff 2010) 7–25, 10.

18 For a discussion of the implications of the relationship clauses of the Revised Draft Agreement see also Molenaar (n 17) 32ff and 56–57.

19 Emphasis provided.

Implementation of obligations for the conservation and sustainable use of BBNJ may create a spill-over effect to AWNJ.

## 4 The Future of the Legal Regime of ABNJ and a Future BBNJ Agreement

The regimes of the high seas and the Area are part and parcel of the LOSC. That anchoring indicates that the high seas and the Area are here to stay as long as the LOSC continues to be accepted as the jurisdictional framework of the ocean. Although there have been challenges to that jurisdictional framework, these have been largely unsuccessful.[20] The stability that the LOSC has provided to the law of the sea in the last four decades is strikingly different from the instability of the law of the sea in the preceding four decades, notwithstanding attempts to codify the law of the sea through the four conventions adopted at the Geneva Conference on the law of the sea of 1958. In view of the vested interests in the current legal regime of the ocean, it is highly unlikely that it will be directly challenged in the foreseeable future. As developments after the adoption of the LOSC in 1982 indicate, that does not mean that the law has been set in stone. Piecemeal adaptation and development of the law has been taking place and will continue to do so. What does all of this mean for the regime of ABNJ? In this connection, a distinction may be made between the spatial extent of ABNJ and their substantive regime.

The LOSC defines the spatial extent of the high seas and the Area with reference to the outer limits of national jurisdiction.[21] Existing analyses of State practice indicate that the LOSC provisions on the limits of AWNJ demonstrate a large measure of compliance, notwithstanding challenges in individual cases.[22] Coastal States with a continental shelf beyond 200 nautical miles have invested significant resources in determining the outer limits of that continental shelf. Although the implementation of Article 76 is far from complete, this process will result in final and binding limits of the continental shelf around

20 For a further discussion see Donald R Rothwell and others (eds), 'Charting the Future for the Law of the Sea' in Donald R Rothwell and others (eds), *The Oxford Handbook for the Law of the Sea* (Oxford University Press 2015) 888–912, 889–92 and 904–12; Molenaar (n 17).

21 See above text at and n 12.

22 See eg Rothwell (n 20) 889–90; Robin R Churchill, 'The Impact of State Practice on the Jurisdictional Framework Contained in the LOS Convention, The Impact of State Practice on the Jurisdictional Framework contained in the LOS Convention' in Alex G Oude Elferink (ed), *Stability and Change in the Law of the Sea: The Role of the LOS Convention* (Martinus Nijhoff Publishers 2005) 91–143.

the globe, definitively setting the limits between the continental shelf and the Area. A similar process is lacking in relation to the outer limits of the EEZ, but the fact that in this case the outer limit is determined by a fixed distance-based limit makes any direct challenge easily detectable and open to credible protest by States interested in maintaining the jurisdictional limits set by the LOSC.[23]

The substantive regime of ABNJ has been continuously developing since the adoption of the LOSC, both through the practice of States and institutional frameworks. In that sense, the BBNJ process is not unique and, also if successfully concluded with the adoption of a BBNJ Agreement, will not put a stop to that development. The BBNJ process is unique as regards its scale and ambition as it could result in an effective overarching regime for the sustainable conservation and use of BBNJ and the marine environment of ABNJ more in general that is conspicuously lacking in the LOSC. To what extent that ambition will be realized remains to be seen. As is among others remarked by Henriksen (in chapter 4) and Oude Elferink and Kerr (in chapter 7), the BBNJ process in any case was never intended to remap the legal regime of ABNJ, and as the Revised Draft Agreement indicates, it is intended to operate within the jurisdictional limits set by the LOSC. But what impact may a BBNJ Agreement have while staying within those limits? As Bankes observes in chapter 3, the current negotiating text fails 'to be specific about the legal relationships as between ... States and as between the natural and juridical persons of those ... States exercising parallel and potentially competing freedoms'. A failure that may be explained by intention of a future BBNJ Agreement to not affect the jurisdictional framework of the LOSC. However, as Ringbom argues in chapter 11 in relation to the jurisdiction over the activities of vessels in ABNJ, although a future BBNJ Agreement will not clarify the extent of non-flag State jurisdiction, that development will continue to be driven by State practice and third-party dispute settlement procedures.

23 The main challenge in determining the validity of the outer limits of the EEZ is likely the use of baselines that are controversial. Although there are many examples of straight baselines that have been challenged, the impact of those baselines on the outer limits of the EEZ is in general limited. The use of insular features that may or may not fall under the scope of art 121(3) of the LOSC has a much larger impact on the extent of the high seas and the Area. However, the fact that States almost invariably claim an EEZ and continental shelf from such features excludes that disregard for art 121(3) will lead to further inroads on the extent of the high seas and the Area. Finally, it may be noted that the predicted rise of sea levels during the coming decades and beyond implies that the main issue in relation to the outer limits of AWNJ will be whether and if so how to prevent the landward shift of the outer limits of maritime zones or in the case of the submergence of islands, the complete loss of coastal State maritime entitlements.

Many of our authors express, albeit in different terms, that the question to what extent a future BBNJ agreement could be successful in fulfilling the ambition of providing an effective overarching regime for the sustainable conservation and use of BBNJ and the marine environment of ABNJ is up in the air. For instance, Henriksen in chapter 4 first submits that the BBNJ process 'does not seem to provide room for any fundamental rethinking or transformation of the law of the sea, but seems locked to the status quo and opening only for minor amendments or gradual evolution, consistent with the interests of the major States', but subsequently observes:

> [W]ith increasing negative effects of climate change on the oceans, marine species and ecosystems, the question is whether the debate will take another direction, giving environmental protection and justice a stronger voice and the recognition of the need for more coherent approaches that challenge the law of the sea.

In chapter 6, Poto expresses similar doubt about the capacity of the BBNJ process to deliver:

> Though the doubt remains as to whether the BBNJ negotiations are whitewashing history, and green/blue washing domination with many labels (protection, stewardship, and even nature's rights), the hope is still that the negotiations on a treaty on marine biodiversity in ABNJ will go in the direction of including elements of an ocean-centric model where the human communities responsibly protect the oceans.

Barnes, in chapter 10, submits that the 'current legal regime for ABNJ is not structured in a way that drives a holistic, integrated construction of social space in ABNJ. And the [BBNJ Agreement] risks further exacerbating this'. At the same time, he details how a future BBNJ might avoid doing so, among other pointing to the importance of the institutional design of the Agreement.[24]

It is however possible, and perhaps even urgent, as De Lucia suggests in chapter 2, to open new conversations that may open up new trajectories, new imagination, precisely at a time when a new global treaty is being negotiated.

---

24 On the importance of institutional design see also eg, Elizabeth M de Santo, 'Protecting biodiversity in areas beyond national jurisdiction: An earth system governance perspective' (2019) 2 Earth System Governance 1, 3–5; Alex G Oude Elferink, 'Exploring the future of the institutional landscape of the oceans beyond national jurisdiction' (2019) (28) RECIEL 236.

The question as to what level of ambition a future BBNJ Agreement should reach will also have to be considered by the delegations at the IGC. This both requires determining how much support there is for different options and how inclusive one wants a future BBNJ Agreement to be. Aiming for inclusiveness may result in a treaty text that does little to improve on the current status quo, while it is not a guarantee that those wanting to safeguard the status quo will actually become parties to the resulting Agreement.[25] Were it possible to agree on a higher level of ambition for a future BBNJ Agreement, its number of States parties may remain even more limited. However, if the number of parties would allow them to weigh in on decision-making in regional and sectoral bodies dealing with ABNJ, such an outcome might be preferable from an environmentalist perspective. The Agreement in that case might also be a point of reference for those advocating for the progressive development of the environmental regime for ABNJ.[26]

25 See also Shirley Scott, *International Law, US Power. The United States' Quest for Legal Security* (Cambridge University Press 2012) 239–42. As Scott (at 241) observes in relation to the US position on the LOSC:

> the United States has still not ratified it ... meaning that the treaty has bound the world at large to the provisions the United States wanted while the United States itself, preferring to rely on customary international law of the sea, has effectively reneged on the initial deal.

26 See also the chapter by Dalaker (ch 12) in this volume, who argues that a failure of the BBNJ process to come up with an effective global regime, will put:

> the burden and responsibility for the conservation and sustainable use of BBNJ would therefore fall to existing regional, sub-regional, national and sectoral bodies and frameworks. Such an outcome would do little more than maintain the status quo, calling into question the very purpose and need for the BBNJ negotiations.

# Index